CCSP Self-Study:
Cisco Secure Intrusion
Detection System (CSIDS)

Earl Carter

Cisco Press

800 East 96th Street
Indianapolis, IN 46240 USA

CCSP Self-Study:
Cisco Secure Intrusion Detection System (CSIDS)

Earl Carter

Copyright© 2004 Cisco Systems, Inc.

Published by:
Cisco Press
800 East 96th Street
Indianapolis, IN 46240 USA

Printed in the United States of America 1 2 3 4 5 6 7 8 9 0

First Printing February 2004

Library of Congress Cataloging-in-Publication Number: 2003104999

ISBN: 1-58705-144-3

Warning and Disclaimer

This book is designed to provide a reference on the Cisco Intrusion Protection System that can also be used to prepare for the Cisco Secure Intrusion Detection Systems exam, which is one of several exams required to achieve Cisco Certified Security Professional (CCSP) certification. Every effort has been made to make this book as complete and as accurate as possible, but no warranty or fitness is implied.

The information is provided on an "as is" basis. The authors, Cisco Press, and Cisco Systems, Inc. shall have neither liability nor responsibility to any person or entity with respect to any loss or damages arising from the information contained in this book or from the use of the discs or programs that may accompany it.

The opinions expressed in this book belong to the author and are not necessarily those of Cisco Systems, Inc.

Trademark Acknowledgments

All terms mentioned in this book that are known to be trademarks or service marks have been appropriately capitalized. Cisco Press or Cisco Systems, Inc. cannot attest to the accuracy of this information. Use of a term in this book should not be regarded as affecting the validity of any trademark or service mark.

Feedback Information

At Cisco Press, our goal is to create in-depth technical books of the highest quality and value. Each book is crafted with care and precision, undergoing rigorous development that involves the unique expertise of members from the professional technical community.

Readers' feedback is a natural continuation of this process. If you have any comments regarding how we could improve the quality of this book, or otherwise alter it to better suit your needs, you can contact us through email at feedback@ciscopress.com. Please make sure to include the book title and ISBN in your message.

We greatly appreciate your assistance.

Corporate and Government Sales

Cisco Press offers excellent discounts on this book when ordered in quantity for bulk purchases or special sales. For more information, please contact:

U.S. Corporate and Government Sales 1-800-382-3419 corpsales@pearsontechgroup.com

For sales outside of the U.S. please contact:

International Sales 1-317-581-3793 international@pearsontechgroup.com

Publisher	John Wait
Editor-in-Chief	John Kane
Executive Editor	Brett Bartow
Cisco Representative	Anthony Wolfenden
Cisco Press Program Manager	Nanette M. Noble
Acquisitions Editor	Michelle Grandin
Production Manager	Patrick Kanouse
Development Editor	Allison Beaumont Johnson
Project Editor	Ginny Bess Munroe
Copy Editor	Keith Cline
Technical Editors	Jerry Lathem
	Shawn Merdinger
	Danny Rodriguez
Team Coordinator	Tammi Barnett
Cover Designer	Louisa Adair
Composition	Mark Shirar
Indexer	Julie Bess

CISCO SYSTEMS

Corporate Headquarters
Cisco Systems, Inc.
170 West Tasman Drive
San Jose, CA 95134-1706
USA
www.cisco.com
Tel: 408 526-4000
      800 553-NETS (6387)
Fax: 408 526-4100

European Headquarters
Cisco Systems International BV
Haarlerbergpark
Haarlerbergweg 13-19
1101 CH Amsterdam
The Netherlands
www-europe.cisco.com
Tel: 31 0 20 357 1000
Fax: 31 0 20 357 1100

Americas Headquarters
Cisco Systems, Inc.
170 West Tasman Drive
San Jose, CA 95134-1706
USA
www.cisco.com
Tel: 408 526-7660
Fax: 408 527-0883

Asia Pacific Headquarters
Cisco Systems, Inc.
Capital Tower
168 Robinson Road
#22-01 to #29-01
Singapore 068912
www.cisco.com
Tel: +65 6317 7777
Fax: +65 6317 7799

Cisco Systems has more than 200 offices in the following countries and regions. Addresses, phone numbers, and fax numbers are listed on the
Cisco.com Web site at www.cisco.com/go/offices.

Argentina • Australia • Austria • Belgium • Brazil • Bulgaria • Canada • Chile • China PRC • Colombia • Costa Rica • Croatia • Czech Republic
Denmark • Dubai, UAE • Finland • France • Germany • Greece • Hong Kong SAR • Hungary • India • Indonesia • Ireland • Israel • Italy
Japan • Korea • Luxembourg • Malaysia • Mexico • The Netherlands • New Zealand • Norway • Peru • Philippines • Poland • Portugal
Puerto Rico • Romania • Russia • Saudi Arabia • Scotland • Singapore • Slovakia • Slovenia • South Africa • Spain • Sweden
Switzerland • Taiwan • Thailand • Turkey • Ukraine • United Kingdom • United States • Venezuela • Vietnam • Zimbabwe

About the Author

Earl Carter has been working in the field of computer security for approximately eight years. He first learned about computer security while working at the Air Force Information Warfare Center. Earl's primary responsibility was securing Air Force networks against cyberattacks. In 1998, he accepted a job with Cisco to perform IDS research for NetRanger (currently Cisco IDS) and NetSonar (Cisco Secure Scanner). Earl spent approximately one year writing signatures for NetRanger and developing software modules for NetSonar. Currently, he is a member of the Security Technologies Assessment Team (STAT) that is part of Consulting Engineering (CE). His duties involve performing security evaluations on numerous Cisco products as well as consulting with other teams within Cisco to help enhance the security of Cisco products. He has examined various products from the PIX firewall to the Cisco CallManager. Presently, Earl holds a CCNA certification and is working on earning his CCIE certification with a security emphasis.

About the Technical Reviewers

Jerry Lathem has been working with computers for 25 years and in the field of computer security for 15 years. He worked for 10 years with the Department of Defense as a research engineer, working on both information security and computer security. He joined the WheelGroup Corporation (later acquired by Cisco) early in its startup phase. He has a wide variety of experience including performing security assessments, developing both defensive and offensive software, and prototyping the first Cisco IDS module for the Catalyst switches. He is currently one of the lead developers for the sensing technology in the Cisco IDS product line.

Shawn Merdinger is a software engineer at Cisco Systems and has been in the computer network and security field for four years. He holds a master's degree in library and information science from the University of Texas at Austin.

Danny Rodriguez is currently a member of the Cisco Systems Security Consulting Services organization. As a network security engineer, Danny performs security posture assessments and security design reviews for Fortune 500 companies. The security posture assessments are in-depth external and internal network vulnerability assessments. He is also responsible for the training development of the security engineers on staff.

Also during his tenure with Cisco Systems, Danny was an education specialist with the Internet Learning and Solutions security training department. As an education specialist, he authored the Cisco Intrusion Detection courses and contributed lab exercises to the Cisco core security courses. Danny implemented a network design that enabled the use of remote lab equipment in Cisco security courses. He has also taught security courses to Cisco engineers, Cisco learning and channel partners, and end users of Cisco security equipment. Danny was also a key contributor to the CCSP certification.

Danny holds certifications as a CCDA and a Cisco Qualified Specialist (CQS) Cisco Security Specialist 1 (CSS1).

Dedications

Without my loving family, I would not be where I am today. They always support all the projects that I undertake. Therefore, I dedicate this book to my wife, Chris; my daughter, Ariel; and my son, Aidan. I would also like to dedicate this book to my parents, Tommy and Rosemary Carter, because if not for them, I would not be here today.

Acknowledgments

First, I want to say that many people helped me during the writing of this book (too many to list here). Everyone whom I have dealt with has been very supportive and cooperative. There are, however, several people who I think deserve special recognition.

I want to thank the Cisco IDS course developers (Jeanne Jackson, Danny Rodriquez, and everyone else who contributed to the course's development), whose course provided me with the foundation on which to develop this book. The technical editors—Danny Rodriguez, Shawn Merdinger, and Jerry Lathem—supplied me with their excellent insight and greatly improved the accuracy and clarity of the text. I also want to especially thank James Kasper who provided me with an excellent understanding of the various signature engines and how they operate and who was always willing to take the time to answer my various questions.

Finally, I want to thank Jesus Christ for gracing me with numerous gifts throughout my life, such as my understanding family who have helped me through the many long hours (and late nights) writing this book.

Contents at a Glance

Contents

Icons Used in This Book

Cisco Systems, Inc., uses a standardized set of icons to represent devices in network topology illustrations. The icon legend that follows shows the most commonly used icons that you might encounter throughout this book.

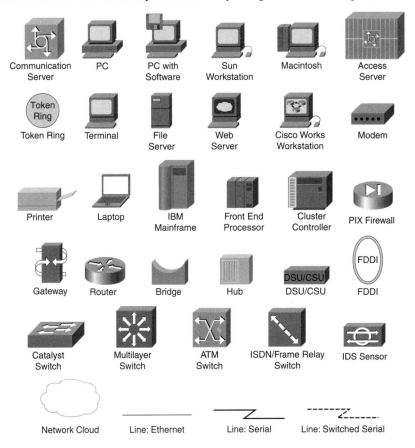

Command Syntax Conventions

The conventions used to present command syntax in this book are the same conventions used in the IOS Command Reference. The Command Reference describes these conventions as follows:

- **Boldface** indicates commands and keywords that are entered literally as shown. In actual configuration examples and output (not general command syntax), boldface indicates commands that are manually input by the user (such as a **show** command).

- *Italics* indicate arguments for which you supply actual values.

- Vertical bars (|) separate alternative, mutually exclusive elements.

- Square brackets [ ] indicate optional elements.

- Braces { } indicate a required choice.

- Braces within brackets [{ }] indicate a required choice within an optional element.

Foreword

CCSP Self-Study: Cisco Secure Intrusion Detection System (CSIDS) is a Cisco-authorized, self-paced learning tool that helps you understand foundation concepts covered on the Cisco Certified Security Professional (CCSP) exam. This book was developed in cooperation with the Cisco Internet Learning Solutions Group, the team within Cisco responsible for the development of the CCSP exam. As an early-stage exam preparation product, this book presents detailed and comprehensive coverage of the tasks that network engineers need to perform to build and support small- to medium-sized networks. Whether you are studying to become CCSP certified, or are just seeking to gain a better understanding of the products, services, and policies that enable you to build multirouter, multigroup internetworks, you will benefit from the information presented in this book.

Cisco Systems and Cisco Press present this material in text-based format to provide another learning vehicle for our customers and the broader user community in general. Although a publication does not duplicate the instructor-led or e-learning environment, we acknowledge that not everyone responds in the same way to the same delivery mechanism. It is our intent that presenting this material via a Cisco Press publication will enhance the transfer of knowledge to a broad audience of networking professionals.

Cisco Press will present other books in the Certification Self-Study series on existing and future exams to help achieve the Cisco Internet Learning Solutions Group's principal objectives: to educate the Cisco community of networking professionals and to enable that community to build and maintain reliable, scalable networks. The Cisco career certifications and classes that support these certifications are directed at meeting these objectives through a disciplined approach to progressive learning.

To succeed with Cisco career certifications and in your daily job as a Cisco-certified professional, we recommend a blended learning solution that combines instructor-led training with hands-on experience, e-learning, and self-study training. Cisco Systems has authorized Cisco Learning Partners worldwide, which can provide you with the most highly qualified instruction and invaluable hands-on experience in lab and simulation environments. To learn more about Cisco Learning Partner programs available in your area, go to www.cisco.com/go/authorizedtraining.

The books Cisco Press creates in partnership with Cisco Systems will meet the same standards for content quality demanded of our courses and certifications. It is our intent that you will find this and subsequent Cisco Press certification self-study publications of value as you build your networking knowledge base.

Thomas M. Kelly
Vice-President, Internet Learning Solutions Group
Cisco Systems, Inc.
December 2004

Introduction

This book explains every major aspect of the Cisco intrusion protection solution (IPS). This book uses the information provided by the Cisco IDS course as a foundation and expands on this information to provide a standalone source of information on the Cisco IPS suite of products. Besides serving as a useful reference on Cisco IPS, it also serves as a standalone study guide for the Cisco IDS exam. This exam represents one of the five major components of the Cisco Certified Security Professional (CCSP) certification.

Audience

This book is intended to provide a concise reference for Cisco IPS. It incorporates information on Cisco products from the endpoint products all the way up to the enterprise products. It can be used as a standalone reference to prepare for the Cisco IDS exam that is part of the CCSP certification. It also makes an excellent reference for someone who must maintain and operate Cisco IDS. Finally, it provides a useful supplement to the Cisco IDS course materials.

Before reading the book, you should have completed the CCNA certification or have equivalent-level knowledge. A strong user-level experience with the Windows 2000 operating system and a basic understanding of the Cisco IOS user interface are important, as well as having taken the Securing IOS Networks exam.

Organization

The book is organized into eight major parts. Each of these parts explains an aspect of Cisco IPS. Each section is divided into the chapters described here.

Part I, "Introduction to Network Security"

This section provides a good overview of network security. If you are unfamiliar with network security, this section is an excellent place to begin. It introduces the basic concepts that you need to understand as you read other sections in the book. If you are familiar with network security, you can probably skim through this section. The chapters in this section are as follows:

- Chapter 1: The Need for Network Security
- Chapter 2: Network Security and Cisco

Part II, "Intrusion Detection and the CIDS Environment"

This section introduces you to the concept of intrusion detection systems (IDSs) and introduces the concept of intrusion protection systems (IPSs). The philosophy behind various IDSs is examined along with their strengths and weaknesses. How Cisco fits into your overall IPS is explained, along with an explanation of the major components of the Cisco IPS. The chapters in this section are as follows:

- Chapter 3: Intrusion Detection Overview
- Chapter 4: Cisco Intrusion Protection
- Chapter 5: Cisco Intrusion Detection System (IDS) Architecture

Part III, "Cisco Network IDS Configuration"

This section forms the core explanation of the Cisco IDS. It explains how to configure the various types of IDS sensors and introduces the two tools (IDS Device Manager and IDS Event Viewer) that are supplied with your Cisco IDS sensors. Alarm management and signature configuration are explained in detail including configuring signature responses. The chapters in this section are as follows:

- Chapter 6: Capturing Network Traffic

- Chapter 7: Cisco IDS Network Sensor Installation

- Chapter 8: Cisco IDS Module Configuration

- Chapter 9: Cisco IDS Device Manager and Event Viewer

- Chapter 10: Sensor Configuration

- Chapter 11: Signature Configuration

- Chapter 12: Signature Response

- Chapter 13: Cisco IDS Alarms and Signatures

Part IV, "Cisco Endpoint Security"

Watching for attacks from the network perspective is only a part of your complete IPS. The Cisco IPS also includes protection for the endpoints (or hosts) on your network. Beginning with Cisco IDS version 4.x, the host-based solution is an agent solution based on the Okena StormWatch product. This section is comprised of only the following chapter, which explains the endpoint security solution in detail:

- Chapter 14: Host Intrusion Prevention

Part V, "CIDS Maintenance and Tuning"

Regularly updating your IPS and troubleshooting problems is vital to maintaining a high level of security on your network. This section is comprised of just the following chapter, which explains how to update your Cisco IDS software and highlights some common troubleshooting techniques:

- Chapter 15: Cisco IDS Maintenance and Troubleshooting

Part VI, "Cisco Enterprise IDS Management"

If you deploy a large number of sensors on your network, you will need to process a significant number of alerts. Managing these alerts effectively is crucial to using your Cisco IDS to protect your network from attack. This section introduces the enterprise tools that you can use to manage large deployments of IDS sensors. This section also includes a chapter on the Cisco Threat Response product. The chapters in this section are as follows:

- Chapter 16: Enterprise IDS Management

- Chapter 17: Enterprise IDS Monitoring and Reporting

- Chapter 18: Cisco Threat Response

Part VII, "Cisco Intrusion Protection System Upcoming Functionality"

The functionality provided by Cisco IPS is continually evolving. By the time that this book is published, many new features will have been introduced. Even during the writing of this book, the features available in Cisco IDS changed. This chapter attempts to explain some of the upcoming functionality that will probably be reality by the time the book is published. This section contains the following chapter:

- Chapter 19: Cisco Intrusion Protection System Upcoming Functionality

Part VIII, "Appendixes"

The appendixes provide information that does not fit easily into the major sections. The appendixes are as follows:

- Appendix A: Cisco Intrusion Protection Solution Tuning: Case Studies

- Appendix B: Answer to Chapter Review Questions

Conventions Used in This Book

This book is organized into eight major parts. If you are unfamiliar with Cisco IPS, you will probably gain the most benefit by reading each part beginning with Part I, "Introduction to Network Security." If you are already familiar with Cisco IPS, however, you can focus on the specific sections of interest. Furthermore, the layout of the parts enables you to quickly locate the needed information.

The text is sprinkled with notes and sidebars that highlight information that might be of particular importance to you. Some of these notes and sidebars point out potential problems, whereas others clarify terms used within the text.

Each chapter ends with a chapter summary and also contains a set of review questions. These questions are designed to highlight the major concepts in each chapter. The purpose of the review questions is to assist you in reviewing for the Cisco IDS exam. You can also use the questions to gauge your understanding of the material presented in each chapter. You can find the answers to the review questions in Appendix B.

Cisco Certified Security Professional

CCSP certification validates skills and knowledge in five key areas of network security:

- Firewalls

- Intrusion detection systems

- Virtual private networks (VPNs)

- Managing network security

- Cisco SAFE implementation

As organizations accelerate their interest in Internet business solutions, they will continue to seek qualified professionals who possess the skills necessary to ensure the security of all network-based transactions and to design secure business solutions. The expertise you develop when preparing for the CCSP designation adds to your skill set and helps you expand your professional options.

For more information on CCSP certification, refer to www.cisco.com/go/securitytrng.

Cisco Intrusion Detection Systems Course

The Cisco Secure Intrusion Detection Systems exam is one of several exams required to achieve CCSP, Cisco IDS Specialist, or Cisco Security Specialist 1 certifications. This course provides an explanation of the Cisco IPS through classroom instruction and lab exercises. Being based on the Cisco IDS course, this book also provides all the information necessary to prepare for this exam.

Cisco IDS Course Prerequisites

The prerequisites for the Cisco IDS course are as follows:

- Certification as a CCNA or the equivalent knowledge (optional)

- Strong user-level experience with Windows operating systems and a basic understanding of the Cisco IOS user interface

- Familiarity with the networking and security terms and concepts (learned via prerequisite training or by reading industry publications)

Upon completion of this chapter, you will be able to perform the following tasks:

- State the reasons for securing computer networks
- Identify the basic security concepts
- Define the four primary security threats
- Explain the phases of an attack
- Describe the approaches that attackers use to attack your network
- Identify the common network attack points
- Explain the common attack tools
- Identify common security weaknesses on your network

CHAPTER 1

The Need for Network Security

Studies estimate that the current size of the Internet includes approximately 171 million hosts[1], with more than 665 million unique users[2]. Many companies rely heavily on electronic commerce for their livelihood. Integrating the Internet into business operations is cost-effective and increases productivity. Telecommuters rely on remote access to get their work done. Home users frequently use cheap, high-speed Internet access to their homes through cable modems and digital subscriber lines (DSLs). The bottom line is that the Internet is carrying more traffic than ever before and still growing in size with no end in sight.

Along with this explosive growth comes an increased threat from Internet-related attacks. When someone mentions theft, you probably think of an intruder physically breaking into a facility and stealing valuable property. Traditional robberies require physical access to the target. The Internet, however, allows theft and break-ins to occur from anywhere in the world. Besides denying service to your computer resources, these attacks might attempt to steal your data (such as customer credit card numbers) or your intellectual property (such as the source code to your latest product).

NOTE   The only perfectly secure computer is one that is unplugged and in a locked vault. Unfortunately, this computer is also the most useless. This same principle applies to your network. All computer systems, network devices, and networks must be protected in some fashion while maintaining usability. More accessibility opens up more opportunities for an attacker, but if you secure your systems effectively, additional accessibility does not necessarily increase your security risk.

Implementing network security is crucial to maintaining an operational network, as well as to the continued success of your business. Numerous locations within your network are especially susceptible to electronic attacks.

Understanding what these areas are is the first step toward improving your security. Understanding the types of tools that attackers use against networks is vital. Attackers use various tools and techniques to gain unauthorized access to computer networks. All these tools exploit weaknesses in the network. These attacks represent a constant threat to your network and, more importantly, to your company's reputation. Security threats to networks fall into several distinct categories.

As you read through this chapter, you learn key facts in the following areas:

- Security threats
- Security concepts
- The phases of an attack
- Attack approaches
- Network entry points
- Hacking tools and techniques

Security Threats

Businesses use the Internet to reach out to millions of potential customers. Extranets enable efficient and effective communication with business partners. Employees rely on internal networks to perform operations such as filing trip reports and making travel reservations. E-mail enables everyone to communicate quickly and efficiently with people throughout the world. Remote access enables telecommuters to perform their work from home.

Disruption of your computer network is no longer just an inconvenience. An inoperable e-commerce website could potentially cost a company millions of dollars a day. Employee productivity comes to a standstill when the network fails. Networks must not only be operational, but also remain connected to other networks around the world to be useful.

This worldwide connectivity comes with a downside. Anyone with Internet connectivity represents a potential attacker. Hosts connected to the Internet are susceptible to attacks. Disgruntled employees motivated by revenge frequently attack internal networks. Furthermore, geography is no longer a barrier that limits attacks against your network.

Many threats impact the operation of your computer network. Natural threats, such as flood, fire, and tornadoes, cause unexpected disruptions. Although unexpected and infrequent, most companies have well-defined procedures to handle these natural, disaster-related threats. Security procedures designed to combat hacker attacks, however, are usually less thought out (if they exist at all). An unsecured network will definitely be attacked. The only question is when the attack will occur.

Intellectual curiosity drives many novice hackers to download attack tools and experiment with them on local and remote networks. Others get a thrill out of breaking into computers that are otherwise off-limits. Even if you think that your data is not interesting to an attacker, your network will be attacked. Attackers constantly search for systems that they can use as a launching platform for future attacks. By launching an attack from a compromised system, an attacker makes it difficult for anyone to identify that attacker because the traffic is not coming from the attacker's own host.

Hackers

Originally the term *hackers* referred to people who were curious and enjoyed learning everything that they could about a computer system (or anything else for that matter). Over time, some people started using this terminology to refer to people who break into computer systems. Then the term *cracker* appeared to refer to someone who attacked systems maliciously. Because different terms refer to different attackers with different motives, this book will try to consistently use the term *attacker* to refer to anyone who attacks your computer systems.

I installed a cable modem at my house to gain high-speed Internet access. When the cable modem installer arrived, I had not purchased the firewall that I planned to use. Because I did not yet have a firewall, I decided to attach my computer to a hub and watch for scans against my Windows system using a sniffer on a Linux computer. Within a day, I noticed some probing against my system. Along with attackers constantly searching for new victims, your computer is routinely attacked by viruses and worms (such as Code Red and Nimda) that automatically spread throughout the Internet.

Attacks on your network have two attributes. The first attribute (a continuum) is the level of expertise of the hacker. The level can be low, or *unstructured*, or it can be high, or *structured*. The second attribute is the physical location from which the attack is launched. It can be launched from an *external* network or from an *internal* location.

The following sections discuss each attribute.

Unstructured Threats

Hacking tools and scripts abound on numerous Internet sites. Some of these tools are explained later in this chapter, and others are covered in Chapter 2, "Network Security and Cisco." These explanations touch only the surface of the total number of tools available to an attacker.

Script Kiddies

Computer attackers range in skill from novice to highly advanced. Script kiddies fall at the bottom of this skill ladder. They have little or no programming skills, limited knowledge of what they are doing, and tend to use other people's scripts for mischief instead of learning how something works for themselves.

The majority of unstructured attacks against your network occur from *script kiddies* and moderately skilled attackers (many of whom already have limited access to your network, such as disgruntled employees). Most of the time, these attacks are driven by personal gratification. A small percentage of the time, these attacks are malicious in nature. In either case, the impact on your company's image can be significant.

Although the expertise of these attackers is usually minimal, unstructured threats still disrupt your network and represent a significant threat. Sometimes, just running a script against your network can break network functionality. For instance, running a Solaris exploit against other operating system (OS) types might have no effect or it might crash the system. A script kiddie might not realize this, and might blindly run a new attack script against all the hosts on your network (not just the Solaris systems). The only goal is to gain access to your network, but the script kiddie inadvertently crashes numerous systems on your network. Other times, a simple attempt to test someone's skill, without any malicious intent, can cause serious harm to your organization's reputation.

Suppose your network is set up as shown in Figure 1-1. The internal network is protected by a firewall. Your informational web server is located on a network, separate from the Internet and your internal network. The firewall restricts traffic to both the internal network and the publicly accessible servers. Externally originated traffic, however, is allowed from the Internet to your website (and other publicly accessible servers), but not to your internal network.

Now, assume that an attacker manages to break into your web server and stops some processes on the web server. Your web page is no longer accessible from the Internet. The first result is that customers lose their ability to communicate with your public presence on the Internet (your well-known website). After receiving complaints, you reboot your web server and your website is back up. In some situations, that is the end of the story. Other times, a news source learns of the attack and writes a news article about the attack on your network. Other news sources might join in by writing their own articles (especially Internet news sources). Quickly, news of the attack can spread in articles that might look like the following:

An unknown attacker broke into Company X's website yesterday. The web server remained inaccessible for more than 5 hours. The extent of the attack is unknown at this time.

Customers do not know your network topology. Their first reaction is that your entire network is insecure. They do not understand, or care, about the security separation between the website and the internal network. The incident places doubt on the security of your entire company in the eyes of your customers. Future customers might stay away for fear of having their credit card numbers compromised by an assumed lack of security.

Figure 1-1   *Basic Network Configuration*

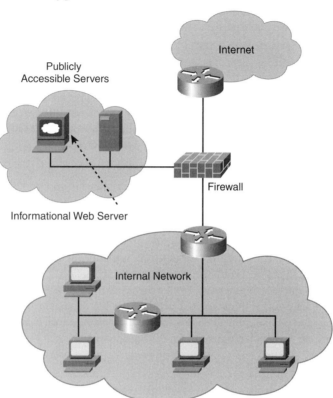

Structured Threats

Structured threats come from adversaries that are highly motivated and technically competent. Unlike script kiddies, these attackers have the technical proficiency to understand existing tools, adapt current attack tools, and create new custom tools. These attackers act alone or in small groups. They understand, develop, and use sophisticated hacking techniques to penetrate unsuspecting organizations.

The motivation behind structured threats is varied. Some common motivating factors include money, political activism, anger, and retribution for some hurt. Organized crime, industrial competitors, and state-sponsored groups hire technical experts to launch many structured attacks. These attacks almost always have a specific goal in mind, such as the acquisition of a competitor's source code. Major fraud and theft cases fall into the structured threat category.

Regardless of their motivation, these attackers can inflict serious damage on your network. A successful structured attack can destroy your entire business. Many times, the goal of a structured attack is to destroy a competitor.

External Threats

Attacks conducted without any privileged access to your network are known as *external threats*. Computer users across the world with Internet access are capable of launching external attacks against your network. This translates to a base of 665 million potential attackers with access to your network through the Internet.

You use your perimeter defenses as the first line of defense against external threats. By maintaining strong perimeter defenses, you minimize the impact of external threats against your network. Organizations usually spend most of their time protecting themselves against external threats.

When defending your perimeter, you must remember to consider traffic that you sometimes take for granted. E-mail traffic, for instance, is a universal form of communication that enables you to easily communicate with people across the world. But e-mail traffic also opens up your network to attack from many e-mail viruses. These viruses represent an unstructured external threat to your network. Protecting against this threat can require filtering your e-mail traffic at your network's perimeter as well as installing virus protection software on your individual systems.

NOTE   Sometimes, a network's security is labeled as having a hard shell with a chewy inside. This refers to devoting all your security resources to perimeter security. If an attacker breaks through your strong outer perimeter, he can easily compromise one machine after another inside your network. The more security layers that you create throughout your network, the stronger the security of your network will be. This requires securing both your network's perimeter as well as multiple locations within your internal network.

Internal Threats

According to numerous reports[3], the largest percentage of attacks against your network will be from the internal threat category. With *internal threats*, an attacker has some initial level of access to a computer system. The initial access can be an account on a server or physical access to the network. Furthermore, this access is not available to the general public. Disgruntled ex-employees, existing employees, and contractors usually have the access necessary to conduct internal attacks.

Sometimes, a structured attack against your network is conducted with the help of an insider. In this case, the attack becomes a structured internal threat. In this situation, the attackers can inflict severe harm against the network and easily steal valuable company information. A structured internal threat represents the most severe attack that can be launched against your network.

Security Concepts

Now that you have an understanding of the basic security threats that your network faces, it is time to examine the basic security concepts. Understanding these concepts is crucial to securing your network and defining a workable *security policy*. Furthermore, many attacks exploit weaknesses in one or more of these areas. Strengthening these areas of your network helps minimize the effectiveness of attacks against your network.

Security Policy

A *security policy* is a formal statement that outlines the rules by which access to your networks is controlled (see Chapter 2). All access to your information assets must abide by these rules. When installing security components on your network, these rules also establish a framework that defines what you need to check for and the restrictions that you need to impose on traffic in your network. An excellent reference to learn more about security policies is RFC 2196, "Site Security Handbook."

NOTE   You can find all RFCs online at http://www.isi.edu/in-notes/rfc*xxxx*.txt, where *xxxx* is the number of the RFC. If you do not know the number of the RFC, you can try searching by topic at http://www.rfc-editor.org/cgi-bin/rfcsearch.pl.

The following are key areas in which you need to direct your efforts for network security:

- **Authentication**—Authentication refers to the process of reliably determining the identity of an individual user or software process.

- **Authorization**—Authorization refers to the rules that determine who has permission to access the different resources on your network.

- **Confidentiality**—Confidentiality ensures that data is protected from being divulged to unauthorized parties. Specifically, confidentiality requires that information inside a computer system (in memory or on disk) and in transit (across a network) is accessible for reading only by authorized parties.

- **Integrity**—A system protects the integrity of data if it prevents unauthorized modification of the data. Modification includes creating, writing, changing, deleting, and replaying transmitted messages.

- **Auditing**—Auditing refers to the requirement that the use of computer system assets be logged. These auditing log files serve as a record of which users accessed which resources and at what time.
- **Availability**—Availability refers to the requirement that computer system assets are available to authorized parties when needed.

The Phases of an Attack

Attacks against your network are usually divided into three distinct phases. The first phase involves defining a goal for the attack. The second phase is reconnaissance, also known as *information gathering*. During this phase, the attacker attempts to gather information about your network to determine prime targets on your network. After collecting information about your network, the attacker proceeds to the third phase, the attacking phase.

The following sections discuss these stages.

Setting the Goals for the Attack

Before attacking a network or system, an attacker sets goals or objectives. When attacking your network, an attacker might have various goals:

- Data manipulation
- System access
- Elevated privileges
- Denying availability of network resources

An attacker might have a simple goal, such as looking for any systems running a specific OS to try out a new tool that the attacker found. An attacker might be trying to obtain well-protected trade secrets from a competitor.

Motivation also plays a significant factor. Some key motivations behind attacks include the following:

- Revenge
- Political activism
- Financial gain

Frequently, attackers attempt to disrupt your network to discredit your organization's image. Your organization's reputation is a prized asset that is difficult to build; yet it only takes potentially one denial-of-service (DoS) attack to irreparably damage that reputation.

Regardless of the complexity or motivation behind an attack, the goal dictates the approach that the attacker needs to use against your network.

Reconnaissance Before the Attack

Collecting information is the attacker's second step in launching an attack against your network. Successful reconnaissance is also the key to a successful attack. Attackers use two main mechanisms to collect information about your network:

- Public data sources
- Scanning and probing

Because scanning and probing is only collecting information about your network, some people do not consider this activity as an actual attack. Other people consider this activity as an actual attack, however, because in some situations it can sometimes cause a system to crash.

Public Data Sources

Sometimes an attacker begins the knowledge search by examining public information available on your company. Although this information is freely available, it can provide the attacker with a wealth of information on your network. An attacker can determine where your business is located, the business partners that you associate with, the value of your company's assets, and much more. An attacker might even collect usernames or product names to use in password-guessing attacks against your network. In many situations, network administrators pose security questions to common mailing lists (such as firewall configuration questions). This exchange of information might reveal how your security defenses are configured.

American Registry for Internet Numbers

The American Registry for Internet Numbers (ARIN) is a database that contains a wealth of information on systems connected to the Internet. By just entering an IP address, you can find information such as the company's address, the address of their DNS server, and the technical contact information. You can access the ARIN database at the following URL:

http://www.arin.net/index.html

Scanning and Probing

Whether starting with a public data search or electronic scanning, the attacker needs to locate vulnerable targets that can be attacked. Through scanning, the attacker uses reconnaissance to find specific resources on your network. Remote reconnaissance or information gathering is the unauthorized mapping of systems, services, or vulnerabilities on a network.

The goal of information gathering is to pinpoint weak points on the network where an attack is likely to succeed. By pinpointing specific weaknesses on the network, the attacker can launch an attack that generates minimal traffic or *noise* on the network. This greatly reduces the likelihood of detection during the actual attack.

An attacker has several avenues for remote reconnaissance. The attacker might attempt to gather information about your network through your Internet connection. Another potential path is to look for potential dialup lines by using a tool that dials a range of numbers looking for modem connections. The attacker might even attempt to locate targets on one of your business partner's network, hoping to find a back door into your network.

An attacker begins the reconnaissance by choosing a specific target network. The initial data mining usually provides the attacker with a list of networks that belong to your company. Domain Name System (DNS) records provide the attacker with a repository of information about networks registered to your company. Knowing that a network is registered, or belongs, to your company does not mean that the network is currently in use. Many companies have networks that are reserved for expansion and future growth. Therefore, the attacker must determine which IP addresses on the target network are associated with *live* computers.

DNS

DNS is a hierarchy of servers that provide an Internet-wide name to IP address mapping for the hosts on the Internet. This mapping enables users to enter an easy-to-remember host name to access a specific system. This host name (such as http://www.cisco.com) is then converted, using DNS, to an actual IP address (such as 198.133.219.25) that is necessary to communicate with the host across the network.

The intruder typically *ping sweeps* the target network to determine which IP addresses are associated with actual computers. After accomplishing this, the intruder determines which services or ports are active on the live IP addresses. From this information, the intruder queries all or common Internet ports on each system to determine which ones have active services, along with accessing their versions if possible. The intruder also attempts to discover the type and version of OS running on each target host. Basically, the attacker wants to learn as much information as possible about the systems on your network to increase the chances that the eventual attack will succeed.

Ping Sweep

IP provides basic control messages through the Internet Control Message Protocol (ICMP). One of these messages is an ICMP echo request, known as a *ping*. Its functionality is designed to determine whether a host can be reached electronically. When the host receives the ICMP echo request packet, it replies with an ICMP echo reply packet. Most systems include a program called ping that generates these ICMP echo request packets. An attacker sends ICMP echo request packets to all the IP addresses on the specific network. The actual hosts on the network respond with ICMP echo reply packets, indicating which IP addresses correspond to actual hosts.

Remote reconnaissance is somewhat analogous to a thief casing a neighborhood for vulnerable homes to break into. With houses, a thief looks for items such as unoccupied homes, open windows or doors, and easy-to-pick locks. The malicious hacker also looks for specific items when he cases your network. Some of these items include the following:

- Operating systems with known vulnerabilities
- Protocols with known weaknesses
- Services in use
- Network topology

By establishing a thorough picture of your network, the attacker can build a powerful toolkit. Then, at a later date, the attacker can conduct various attacks against your network, from a surgical strike to an all-out assault. The attacks against your network fall into three broad categories:

- Manipulating data
- Gaining access
- Denial-of-service

The Actual Attack

After mapping out your network, the attacker researches known vulnerabilities for the systems that were identified. Sometimes the attacker's current toolkit contains tools that already exploit vulnerabilities that exist on your network. The attacker's goal at this stage is to either manipulate data on your network, to gain access to resources on your network, or to deny access to resources on your network.

If system access to a host is achieved, a common goal is to attempt to escalate the attacker's privileges on the system, hoping to achieve administrator or root access. With privileged access, the attacker has unrestricted access to the host's services and data.

Root

On UNIX systems, the most privileged account is named *root*. This account has virtually unlimited powers on the system. Gaining *root* privileges on a system enables an attacker to totally control the system.

Gaining access to a host is commonly referred to as *compromising the host*. When a host is compromised, all the data and programs on the system can no longer be trusted, because the extent of the penetration is unknown. Any trust relationships the compromised host has with other resources on the network also become a threat to your network. After compromising a host, an attacker uses those trust relationships as a stepping stone to gain access to other hosts on the network. Often the compromises follow a domino effect, until the attacker has gained control of your entire network.

After compromising hosts on your network, an attacker frequently installs back doors that can be used to access the systems in the future without being detected. The attacker also can use these hosts to launch attacks against other networks. Tracing an attacker can be difficult if the attacker has bounced through several hosts. Furthermore, this can pose a liability risk to your site if the attacks through your host cause damage to someone else's network.

Attack Approaches

Regardless of the motivation or personal preferences, an attacker has several attack approaches from which to choose:

- Ad hoc
- Methodical
- Surgical strike
- Patient (slow)

Ad Hoc

An ad hoc attack approach is unstructured. An attacker using this approach is usually disorganized, launching various attack tools without any specific methodology. Many times, the ad hoc attacker launches an attack against a system just to see whether it will succeed (without even checking for the service being attacked), and the attacks frequently fail. With this approach, it is difficult to comprehensively locate targets on the network.

Methodical

The methodical approach provides a well-defined sequence of steps to attack a network. First, the attacker uses reconnaissance to locate targets. Next, the attacker locates exploits for known vulnerabilities on the targets that were identified during information gathering. Many times, a methodical attacker experiments with these exploits on practice systems, gaining insight into their effectiveness. Finally, when the attacker is satisfied with his toolkit, he starts attacking systems on the target network. This attack approach provides a high probability of success.

Surgical Strike

Often, an attacker uses an automated script against a network. The entire attack is completed in a few seconds, before system administrators or security analysts have time to react and make any decisions. This attack approach enables an attacker to conduct the attack efficiently and move to new targets quickly.

Patient (Slow)

With this final approach, the attacker uses either the ad hoc or methodical approach, but varies the speed at which the attack is executed. An attacker usually uses a patient (slow) approach to avoid detection. Many intrusion detection systems (IDSs) have difficulty detecting attacks that occur over long periods of time. A ping sweep performed in hours is likely to be detected, for example, whereas the same ping sweep occurring over a month is not.

Network Attack Points

Understanding the common attack points on your network is vital to establishing a sound security policy. These attack points also represent some of the items that you need to consider when you are deploying your Cisco IDS. The main attack points are as follows:

- Network resources
- Network protocols

Network Resources

Systems on a network represent a prime target for attack. Attacks against these resources generally fall into several broad categories:

- Data manipulation or access
- Account access

- Privilege escalation
- Exploiting trust relationships

Data Manipulation or Access

Many systems on your network have shared directories (either system or user created) that provide an entry point for an attacker. A common technique is for an attacker to look for shares that allow *anonymous* connections. An anonymous connection does not require authentication. Therefore, these shares provide an attacker with easy access to data.

Attackers love to take advantage of anonymous shares. Sometimes, these shares provide the attacker with the information needed to escalate the attack, such as account names and, potentially, passwords. At other times, an attacker uses anonymous shares to load a *Trojan horse program* onto the system. When a privileged user executes the Trojan horse program, that user unknowingly installs a back door for the attacker.

Trojan Horse Program

A Trojan horse program is a program that appears to perform some useful function. When the user runs the program, however, it also executes hidden functionality that attacks your system or opens up a back door for the attacker. For instance, a Trojan *Whack a Mole* game actually installs the NetBus Trojan on your system as you play the game.

Account Access

If an attacker can gain access to a valid account on your network, the attacker increases the chances tremendously of obtaining privileged access and eventually compromising your entire network. The first step in this process is to obtain valid account names. Account names are not hard to acquire. Many times, a person's e-mail account is equal to his logon account.

Besides obtaining account names, an attacker can also run password-guessing programs against your network. Many users choose passwords that can be easily obtained using a dictionary-based, password-guessing program. These programs repeatedly attempt to log on with an account using variations of words in their dictionary as the password. On most networks, password-guessing programs are effective at breaking weak user passwords.

NOTE   If your systems lock out an account after a specific number of login failures, attempts by an attacker to guess accounts on your network can actually result in a DoS attack against your network.

Privilege Escalation

Privilege-escalation attacks involve gaining elevated privileges from a nonprivileged account. These attacks are only useable if an attacker has an account on the target system.

Many nonprivileged accounts, such as anonymous access, provide widespread access to system resources. These accounts, however, can execute only a few commands and access specific files. Through privilege escalation, an attacker can convert an easily accessible account into an account with potentially unlimited capabilities.

After an attacker compromises your system, the attacker can install back doors and other hidden software (such as key loggers) on your system. Completely removing all of these hidden programs might require you to completely rebuild the OS, which is a time-consuming task.

Exploiting Trust Relationships

Trust relationships establish a privileged level of access between specific hosts on a network. This trust is usually based on an IP address or system name. An attacker can circumvent both of these mechanisms. Furthermore, if an attacker compromises one host in a trust relationship, the other members of the trust are soon to follow.

Network Protocols

Instead of attacking the resources on the network, an attacker sometimes attacks the integrity of the network protocols. The network protocols enable the resources on the network to communicate with each other. By manipulating the network protocols, an attacker hopes to achieve access to one of the resources on the network. Protocol attacks fall into two categories:

* Man-in-the-middle attacks
* Spoofing attacks

NOTE   It is also possible to deny access to a network protocol by launching a DoS attack against the protocol. In this situation, the attacker is not trying to gain access to your network resources, but just trying to prevent you from using a specific protocol.

Man-in-the-Middle Attacks

A man-in-the-middle attack refers to an attack that takes over a session between two hosts that are communicating through some protocol. The attack might either completely take over the session or might act as a relay in which it alters or passes only specific data from the valid hosts. For the attack to succeed, the attacker must be located on the network that lies between the two hosts (see Figure 1-2). The attacker can also manipulate conditions (such as routing tables) to direct traffic from the systems being attacked to the attacking system.

Figure 1-2 *Man-in-the-Middle Attack*

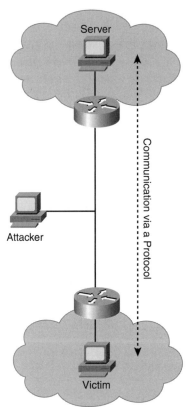

A common man-in-the-middle attack is *TCP hijacking*. TCP hijacking occurs when an attacker takes control of an existing TCP connection between two hosts. After taking control of the TCP session, the attacker can insert data and commands as the valid user who initiated the connection. By default, TCP provides minimal integrity checking and no confidentiality.

Spoofing Attacks

Many attacks rely on an attacker's ability to pretend to be someone he or she is not. Sending packets with another system's source IP address is known as *spoofing*. UDP-based protocols are especially vulnerable to this type of attack, as is the Address Resolution

Protocol (ARP). Unlike TCP-based protocols that use sequence numbers, UDP-based protocols use only the source IP address for authentication. Numerous attack tools enable an attacker to create packets from any source IP address that the attacker chooses.

Address Resolution Protocol

On Ethernet networks, data is sent between hosts using Ethernet frames. Hosts tend to send data based on IP addresses. Therefore, a mechanism is needed to translate IP addresses to physical Ethernet addresses. The Address Resolution Protocol (ARP) handles this conversion. ARP provides only the address for the next hop that the packet needs to go through. An IP packet might have to go through several hops before it reaches its final destination. The final destination is determined by the destination IP address of the packet. The designers of ARP did not even consider security during its development and it is highly susceptible to spoofing attacks. For more information on ARP, refer to RFC 826, "An Ethernet Address Resolution Protocol."

Hacking Tools and Techniques

Attackers and hackers use a variety of techniques in the attempt to gain access to your networks and computer resources. These techniques revolve around an initial data-collection phase, followed by an attack phase. Each of these phases requires tools. The tools and techniques used by attackers are as follows and are explained in the following sections:

- Using reconnaissance tools
- Compromising weakness in your network
- Implementing DoS techniques

Using Reconnaissance Tools

Before attacking a network, most attackers attempt to gather as much information as possible about potential targets on the network. Many tools are available to collect information about the computers on a network. Attackers use two types of tools in their reconnaissance attacks:

- Common administrative tools
- Common hacker scanning tools

Common Administrative Tools

Administrative tools enable the network administrator to debug day-to-day problems on the network. System administrators are responsible for troubleshooting problems on a computer network. To support this requirement, many troubleshooting tools are incorporated into existing operating systems. These tools include the commands **nslookup**, **ping**, **telnet**, **finger**, **rpcinfo**, and File Explorer. Unfortunately, an attacker can use these same tools to scan for information on your network.

Common Hacker Scanning Tools

Most common hacker scanning tools have been specifically designed to gather network information effectively. Many tools have been designed by hackers to collect information about hosts on a network. These tools are specifically designed to gather network information quickly and efficiently.

Sometimes, collecting information without being detected by IDSs is the primary design goal for tool creation. To that end, *stealth* tools are prized for their capability to avoid detection.

Some common scanning tools include the following:

- SATAN
- SAINT
- NMAP
- Strobe
- Firewalk
- NESSUS
- Ettercap

Compromising Weaknesses in Your Network

After mapping out potential targets, the attacker attempts to gain access on the target hosts using a variety of access techniques, including using specific exploitation tools. These tools are intended to compromise the following:

- Weak authentication
- Common services configured poorly
- Protocol weaknesses
- Trust relationships
- Application holes
- Back doors

Authentication Compromises

Determining usernames for a network is fairly easy. Many times, e-mail accounts are the same as logon accounts on internal networks. Gaining access to a logon account requires a username-password combination. Therefore, after gaining a list of account names, the attacker will probably attempt to discover valid passwords for these accounts. Sometimes, the attacker tries a few common passwords, such as a blank password or the password equal to the username. To achieve a more comprehensive coverage of possible passwords, the attacker usually uses a *password cracker* to brute-force guess passwords.

Password Crackers

A *password cracker* is a tool that tries multiple password combinations in an attempt to find an unknown password. Some tools use a dictionary of common words and phrases. Other tools check every possible character combination, which is known as performing a brute-force attack on the entire keyspace. Dictionary password crackers can potentially crack 25 to 60 percent of your users' passwords when run against your network[4].

The following are some common UNIX password crackers:

- Crack by Alec Muffett (UNIX)
- CrackerJack by Jackal (UNIX on DOS platform)
- QCrack by the Crypt Keeper
- John the Ripper by Solar Designer

The following are some common Windows 95/98/2000/NT password crackers:

- L0phtCrack 4.0
- ntPassword 4.0
- PWL-Key 1.06
- Pwlhack 4.10
- PWLVIEW 2.0
- John the Ripper by Solar Designer

Sometimes, a tool will attempt to determine a password by trying various password combinations against the actual system or application. This online password cracking can be detected by examining your log files. Other tools attempt to crack passwords offline by capturing password hashes and then attempting to determine the original passwords. This offline password cracking will not show up in system logs, because the attacker does not generate any login failures on the actual system.

In addition to using password crackers, attackers also use network sniffers to obtain passwords. Using a password cracker can be a time-consuming task. However, a password obtained using a network sniffer is usable immediately. Any protocol that fails to provide confidentiality is subject to having login credentials captured using a sniffer.

Authentication compromises also occur through shared directories and files on the network. Many shared directories require no authentication. If the share has write access, the attacker can place malicious executables on the system, hoping for a valid user to execute them, thus opening up the system.

Common Services Configured Poorly

Network services are located on well-known ports. The reconnaissance tools provide the attacker with a list of ports available to attack. These ports can be equated to services on well-known ports. A hacker knows these services and understands common configuration problems that can be exploited to gain access using these well-known services.

Network administrators frequently install operating systems using the basic installation from the distribution media. End users install software applications using the default configuration. Default installations are usually insecure. Some applications create default accounts with known default passwords.

Typical services configured poorly include the following:

- DNS servers
- Mail servers
- FTP servers
- Web servers
- Shared directories

Protocol Weaknesses

Many network protocols were developed when the Internet was in its infancy. At that time, the Internet represented a small group of researchers and security was not a significant concern. Therefore, protocol developers were not concerned with security during their design process. This resulted in protocols that are not suited to withstand the security threats present in the Internet today. Attackers use weaknesses in the original protocols to gain access to systems. The following are some common protocols with security weaknesses:

- ARP
- UDP
- TCP

- ICMP
- IP

ARP and UDP are susceptible to spoofing attacks, whereas TCP is subject to hijacking and sequence-number guessing attacks. Any IP-based protocol is subject to IP fragmentation attacks. Furthermore, all of these protocols are unencrypted, so an attacker can gain information by just sniffing the traffic stream.

Compromised Trust Relationships

An attacker can sometimes exploit trust relationships between hosts on the network. If an attacker sends information to one host in the relationship, which appears to originate from the other trusted host, the data might be accepted as valid. Depending on the nature of the trust, this spoofed data might be enough to gain access to the system.

Attackers assault trust relationships because they are frequently based on weak authentication mechanisms. The following are two common authentication mechanisms:

- IP-based authentication
- DNS-based authentication

IP addresses can easily be spoofed. Many IP protocols fail to provide an integrity mechanism to ensure that the data comes from a specific source. Therefore, IP addresses alone make a weak authentication token.

DNS-based authentication is a little stronger, but DNS servers are still subject to attack. One common DNS attack, called *DNS cache poisoning*, injects bad data into a DNS server's cache. Using bad DNS information results in failed DNS-based authentication.

Application Holes

Developers who write applications are driven by short timelines. Furthermore, additional user features drive new product releases. Security and protocol robustness are usually not a high development priority, unless the product is a security product, such as a firewall. When an application lacks robustness or is coded poorly, it is possible to disrupt the operation of the application by sending it malformed data. This malformed data may crash the application or enable the attacker to execute code via a buffer overflow.

Buffer Overflow

A buffer overflow occurs when an application fails to perform bounds checking on its input data. Frequently, by sending more data then the application is expecting, the attacker can cause information to be written onto the system's stack. If this information is carefully constructed, the attacker can cause specific instructions to execute on the system being attacked.

Sometimes development of security products, such as firewalls, is focused on how well the product processes data through it. This can leave these devices or software open to attack against the product itself.

Back Doors

Viruses and worms provide a vehicle for an attacker to wreak havoc on your network and potentially the Internet. However, the spread of viruses and worms is much harder to determine in advance. Viruses and worms usually lack an effective targeting capability to enable them to be used for attacking specific networks, but they can wreak havoc on a large scale.

Trojan horse programs enable an attacker to establish back doors on systems. However, Trojan horse programs require some type of transport vehicle. The transport vehicle usually performs something for the user while it installs the back door behind the scenes. A common transport vehicle is an e-mail message with a game or other attachment that the user is likely to open.

Whack a Mole

A popular transport mechanism for NetBus (a Windows backdoor program) is a game called *Whack a Mole*. The executable WHACKAMOLE.EXE is a self-extracting WinZip file. When a user runs the program, he gets to play an entertaining game. Behind the scenes, however, the program installs a back door. Beware of gifts in the form of free games.

Implementing Denial-of-Service Techniques

Many times, the goal of a cyber attacker is to disrupt the operation of a specific system or network. A large e-commerce corporation easily loses millions of dollars if the operation of its website is disrupted for even a short period of time. The losses because of missed sales can usually be calculated from historical sales figures. Customer confidence, which has a more devastating impact, is much harder to quantify.

The purpose of DoS attacks is to deny legitimate access to network resources. These attacks include everything from simple one-line commands to sophisticated programs written by knowledgeable hackers. Specifically, this chapter addresses the following types of DoS attacks:

- Network resource overload
- Host resource starvation
- Distributed attacks

Network Resource Overload (Bandwidth Consumption)

One common way to deny access to a network is by overloading a common resource necessary for network components to operate. The main common resource that can be attacked is network bandwidth. An attacker can fill the network bandwidth in several ways: generating lots of traffic, distributing the attack across numerous hosts, and using a protocol flaw that amplifies the attack by soliciting help from many different hosts on the target network.

For an attacker to fill up the network bandwidth, the attacker must generate more traffic than the target network can handle. As home users get faster and faster home network access, these attacks become more viable against wide-area network (WAN) connections that have relatively small bandwidth.

Network resource overload attacks sometimes use a technique called *amplification* to increase their effectiveness. A single 10 Mb network connection can generate, at most, 10 Mb worth of DoS traffic. This will not fill up a 100 Mb network. Suppose that an attacker has launched an attack from 11 different hosts. Now he has a maximum of 110 Mb (11 hosts * 10 Mb per host). Amplification attacks produce this effect on the target network by soliciting the help of other hosts on the target network. When an attacker sends a ping packet to the network address of the target, all hosts on that network receive it and many reply to it.

By sending packets that appear to originate from the target host, a target system is flooded with lots of packets. Appropriate access control list filtering can prevent external attackers from using amplification attacks against your internal networks. Common amplification attacks include the following:

- Smurf (amplification flood using ICMP ping packets)
- Fraggle (amplification flood using UDP protocol)

Figure 1-3 illustrates how an amplification attack works. The target of the attack is the host with the IP address 172.21.12.5. The attacker sends a forged ICMP packet into the target network. This packet has a source address of 172.21.12.5 and a destination of 172.21.255.255. Because the destination address is the network address, every host on the network responds to the ICMP request. All the replies are directed to the IP source address 172.21.12.5. In this example, a single spoofed packet generates five packets against the target machine. As the size of the network grows, the impact on the target host also grows.

NOTE   Worms, such as Code Red, can also spread quickly across your network, consuming your network bandwidth and crashing infrastructure components. These attacks, however, are more difficult to target against specific networks or systems.

Figure 1-3   *Amplification DoS Attack*

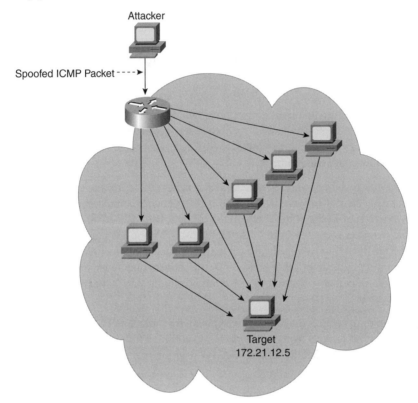

Host Resource Starvation

The resources available on a host are attack points as well. One such resource is the buffer that a host uses to track TCP connections. By filling up the buffer with invalid connection attempts, legitimate new connections are prevented. A common host resource starvation attack is SYN flood, which sends multiple SYN packets to a host. Some other TCP states that can be used in a resource starvation attack are ESTABLISHED, FIN_WAIT_1, FIN_WAIT_2, CLOSING, and LAST_ACK. Naptha is the tool commonly used to perform TCP resource starvation attacks.

Disk space is another commonly attacked resource on a device. If an attacker can fill up the disk space on a network device, the device usually crashes or reboots. Shared directories and files that are weakly protected can be a prime target for this type of attack. Another technique is to attack the host's system auditing functionality. By sending a flood of traffic that generates massive numbers of log file entries, an attacker can easily fill up the disk space on the host. Finding log entries for the real attack in the midst of these bogus log entries can be difficult.

Distributed Attacks

The latest trend in DoS attacks is for an attacker to compromise numerous hosts and then use all these compromised hosts to produce a massive attack against a specific target. This is known as a *distributed denial-of-service* (DDoS) attack. Malicious hackers have used various DDoS attacks to disrupt the websites for Yahoo, Inc., eBay, Inc., Amazon.com, Inc., and Buy.com, Inc. Each of these companies relies exclusively on its Internet connectivity, and more specifically its Internet website, to conduct multimillion-dollar business[5].

Generating enough traffic from a single host to disrupt the operation of a large web server can be difficult. However, using a large number of hosts simplifies the process greatly. Therefore, attackers have started using large numbers of compromised hosts to perform DDoS attacks. Figure 1-4 illustrates a basic DDoS attack.

Figure 1-4   *Distributed Denial-of-Service Attack*

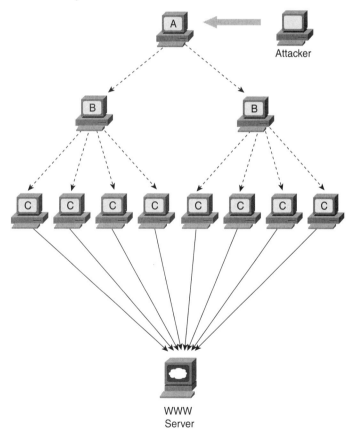

All the computers, except the WWW server and the Attacker, represent hosts that have been compromised by the attacker. Computer A represents the controlling host or client. The attacker connects to the client to launch his DDoS attack. Although the figure shows only one client, there can actually be multiple clients associated with a single DDoS attack. The computers in the next tier, labeled with a B, are known as *handlers*. A client can control multiple handlers. The computers at the final tier, labeled with a C, are called *agents*. Each handler can control many agents. As you can see from the diagram, the agents can easily flood the WWW server with more traffic than it can handle. For information on various DDoS attacks, refer to the following URL:

http://staff.washington.edu/dittrich/misc/ddos/

Home computer users are migrating toward high-speed Internet connections, such as cable modems and DSL. These connections are operational 24 hours a day. Attackers take advantage of this growing base of poorly protected hosts to establish agents for their DDoS attacks. Furthermore, it is difficult to track down the originator of the DDoS attack. Each tier obscures the path to the actual attacker who is launching the DDoS.

The targets of DDoS are multimillion-dollar, high-visibility websites. Most of these sites maintain customer bases in the millions. The following are some DDoS tools:

- Stacheldraht
- Trinoo (or trin00)
- Tribe Flood Network

Unknown Participation in DDoS

During a DDoS attack, an attacker uses numerous machines that have already been compromised. After compromising a system, the attacker installs a DDoS component (such as agents, handlers, and clients). A controlling program then launches a DDoS attack using these software components that are spread across numerous systems. The owners of these compromised machines usually do not even know that their machines have been compromised. Furthermore, when the attacker uses the compromised machines to conduct a DDoS, those owners of the machines are unwilling participants in the attack.

Summary

This chapter explained the need for network security. Your network is connected to the Internet along with 171 million other hosts and 665 million unique users. Protecting your resources is crucial to protecting your business. Attacks can be categorized as follows:

- Unstructured threats
- Structured threats

- External threats
- Internal threats

The following are key areas in which you need to direct your efforts for network security: authentication, authorization, confidentiality, integrity, auditing, and availability.

Network attacks result from a three-step process that involves defining the goals of the attack, collecting initial data, and then actually attacking the network. The attack itself can either be an attempt to gain access to your network or deny service to resources on your network. An increasingly popular DoS attack involves distributing the DoS over many machines, known as a distributed denial-of-service (DDoS) attack.

Regardless of the motivation or personal preferences, an attacker has several attack approaches from which to choose:

- Ad hoc
- Methodical
- Surgical strike
- Patient (slow)

Several points within your network are especially susceptible to attack, including the following:

- Network resources
- Network protocols

Attackers use numerous tools and techniques when attacking a network. These tools and techniques fall into the following categories:

- Reconnaissance tools
- Access tools and techniques
- Denial-of-service tools

The reconnaissance tools enable an attacker to collect information about your network. These tools might be generic system administrative tools or they might be highly customized scanners.

After collecting information on your network, the attacker attempts to gain access to your network using various tools and techniques. These tools focus on compromising weaknesses in your network. A prominent weakness on many networks is poor passwords. Therefore, password-cracking programs are usually effective at gaining access to your network.

Sometimes, an attacker is not interested in gaining access to your network. Instead, the attacker wants to prevent you from using your network resources. This is when the attacker uses his DoS tools. These tools disrupt your network resources in a variety of ways. One of the common DoS techniques is a distributed attack that uses the resources on many hosts to attack a single target system.

End Notes

[1] Internet Software Consortium; *Internet Domain Survey Number of Internet Hosts*:
http://www.isc.org/ds/host-count-history.html

[2] Computer Industry Almanac, Inc.; *USA Tops 160M Internet Users*:
http://www.c-i-a.com/pr1202.htm

[3] Computer Security Institute; *Cyber Crime Bleeds U.S. Corporations, Survey Shows;
Financial Losses from Attacks Climb for Third Year in a Row*: http://www.gocsi.com/
press/20020407.html

[4] Cisco Security Bytes; *Crack 5 Is Not the Only Cracker in Town*:
http://www.cisco.com/warp/public/779/largeent/issues/security/sbytes/
v02i05_0500.html

[5] Tech Web—The Business Technology Network; *Devastating DDoS Attacks Loom*:
http://www.techweb.com/wire/story/TWB20000927S0003

Review Questions

The following questions test your retention of the material presented in this chapter. The
answers to the review questions are in Appendix B, "Answers to Chapter Review
Questions."

1 What are the four types of network security threats?

2 What are the three main attack types?

3 What is the first line of defense against external attacks?

4 Why is network security needed?

5 Attacks against network resources fall into what categories?

6 What is a script kiddie?

7 What is reconnaissance?

8 What are some common motivations behind computer attacks?

9 What is a denial-of-service (DoS) attack?

10 What are the six security principles that define the security on your network?

11 What is the first step in a network attack?

12 What are the two common mechanisms that an attacker uses to collect information
about your network?

13 What are some of the weak areas on your network that attackers frequently attack?

14 What are some of the attack approaches commonly used by attackers?

15 What are some of common protocols with known vulnerabilities?

16 What are common network attack points?

17 When collecting information about your network, what are some of things that an attacker is looking for?

Upon completion of this chapter, you will be able to perform the following tasks:

- Explain the steps that you can take to secure your network
- Describe the ways in which you can monitor the security of your network
- Identify ways in which you can test the security posture of your network
- Explain the steps that you can take to improve the security on your network
- Describe the benefits of Cisco's Architecture for Voice, Video, and Integrated Data (AVVID)
- Explain Cisco SAFE

CHAPTER 2

Network Security and Cisco

Completely securing your network is impossible, but just securing your network to match your security policy can be a daunting task. Your network probably contains numerous security vulnerabilities. These security holes provide disgruntled employees and other attackers the openings necessary to gain unauthorized access to your network. Even well-secured networks require updating to address new vulnerabilities as they appear. Protecting your network is an ongoing process that involves securing, monitoring, testing, and improving your network's security posture.

Before you secure your network, you need to define what it means for your network to be secure. You accomplish this by establishing a thorough *security policy*. Your security policy represents the framework around which you construct all other security enhancements. From a high-level perspective, your security policy must do the following:

- Identify the organization's security objectives
- Document the resources to be protected
- Identify the network infrastructure with current network diagrams and inventories
- Identify the critical resources that need extra protection

More specifically, it is composed of at least the following procedures that define your security requirements:

- Login
- User accounts and groups
- Directory and file
- Data protection
- Secure transmission
- Remote and mobile user
- Virus control
- E-mail

The Security Wheel in Figure 2-1 illustrates the ongoing process needed to maintain the security of your network after you have established your security policy.

Figure 2-1 *Security Wheel*

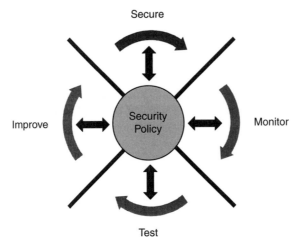

The Security Wheel breaks network security into four separate phases:

- Securing the network
- Monitoring network security
- Testing network security
- Improving network security

These phases are part of an ongoing cycle that continuously adjusts and strengthens the security of your network. Starting with a solid foundation is also a key factor in creating and maintaining a secure network. Today's business climate requires you to continually enhance your network to maintain a high level of productivity while adding new technologies. When adding functionality to your network, however, you want to make sure that it does not negatively impact your security posture. To address both of these concerns, Cisco has created the following frameworks that you can use as reference models when designing and enhancing your networks:

- Cisco Architecture for Voice, Video, and Integrated Data (AVVID)
- Cisco SAFE

Cisco AVVID outlines a flexible framework in which to deploy Internet business solutions, whereas Cisco SAFE details how to modularly secure your converged network. Both of these topics are explained in greater detail later in this chapter.

Securing the Network

To set the Security Wheel in motion on your network, you need to begin by securing your network. During this phase, you must protect the resources on the network from unauthorized access. Your security policy provides the framework outlining your security requirements, but trying to secure your entire network in one step is difficult. An easier approach is to break the task into smaller, more manageable pieces. You then can focus on hardening each of these pieces individually. Using this approach, securing your network can be broken down into the following workable categories:

- Tightening authentication
- Establishing security boundaries
- Providing confidentiality through virtual private networks
- Patching security vulnerabilities

Tightening Authentication

Attackers are constantly attempting to discover valid accounts on your network, along with their associated passwords. Therefore, limiting system access to only those users who need access is important. You can take specific steps to help facilitate stronger authentication:

- Define common privilege groups.
- Limit administrative access.
- Eliminate default passwords.
- Reduce anonymous access.
- Minimize trust relationships.
- Use one-time passwords.

Define Common Privilege Groups

Each resource on your network should have access restrictions. You must grant users who need access to these resources privileges. Defining the privileges needed on a per-user basis is a time-consuming task. A much more efficient method is to use common privilege groups.

Common privilege groups enable you to establish a set of privileges based on specific needs. Many times, these needs equate directly to specific jobs. Sample job categories include engineers, temporary employees, managers, and marketing personnel. Creating groups based on these categories enables you to easily define the privileges that each job requires. Instead of evaluating each new employee and determining the privileges on an individual basis (potentially having your singular decisions thwart your carefully defined authentication policies), you can instead add the employee to the correct group and the employee will have the privileges needed to perform his or her duties; that is, the employee will not have any privileges beyond what is needed to do the job. Furthermore, just tracking permissions on an individual basis can be a daunting task in itself.

Job classification also makes an adequate classification scheme with respect to user functionality. You must analyze your groups with respect to a generic hierarchy based on overall network privileges. With the hierarchical approach, you begin by defining the most privileged user account all the way down to the least privileged account that has access to your system. The following list shows a sample hierarchical classification based on privileges:

- Domain Administrators
- System Administrators
- Privileged Users
- Regular Users
- Anonymous and Guest Users

Using this hierarchical model, the most trusted account is the Domain Administrator. Anonymous and Guest Users receive the least amount of trust. If you apply this model correctly, the number of people in the most trusted categories (Domain and System Administrators, for example) is minimal. The user distribution forms a pyramid, with the least privileged users filling out the base and the administrators representing a small portion of the total number of users at the top.

Limit Administrative Access

If everyone has unlimited access to your facility (keys, alarm codes, and so on), it is difficult for you to enforce security procedures. Furthermore, when a security incident happens, you cannot easily determine who was involved in the incident.

The same principles apply to your computer network. You need to minimize the number of users who have privileged access, especially administrative access. This serves two important functions. First, it reduces the number of highly privileged accounts that an attacker can potentially compromise. Second, it enables you to enforce your security policy more effectively. Security and ease of use tend to constantly compete against each other. If too many users have administrative privileges, they usually override your security policy in favor of ease of use.

Eliminate Default Passwords

Many operating systems and applications create numerous accounts when they are installed. Some of these accounts have default names and default passwords. If these default passwords are not changed, they provide an ideal attack path, because they are available to attackers at numerous locations throughout the Internet. Like anonymous access, these default passwords can be used by anyone who knows the default password.

Furthermore, some of these default passwords enable an attacker to gain access to a privileged account. Table 2-1 shows some sample default passwords.

Table 2-1 *Sample Default Passwords*

Software	Username	Password
Windows NT	guest	<no password>
SQL Server	sa	<no password>
Oracle	internal	oracle
Netranger 2.2.1	root	attack
IRIX	lp	lp

Reduce Anonymous Access

You need to examine anonymous access closely. Because anonymous access does not require a password, anyone can use it to gain access to your network. Although conveniently allowing widespread access to system resources, anonymous access represents a prime initial target for attackers. Numerous attacks enable an attacker to elevate the privileges of anonymous access beyond the default allowed. Using these attacks, an attacker can quickly gain administrative privileges on your network (see Chapter 1, "The Need for Network Security").

Minimize Trust Relationships

Frequently, trust relationships provide access to data or resources based on a host's identity, normally without further authentication. Although these trust relationships simplify usability, they also come with significant security concerns. Many trust relationships are built on weakly authenticated credentials (such as DNS names and IP addresses), allowing an attacker an excellent entry point into your network. In other situations, by compromising one host, an attacker gains access to data and resources on other systems through the defined trust relationships. It is best to minimize the number of trust relationships within your network.

.rhosts Files

On UNIX systems, you can assign a trust relationship with another system by placing an .rhosts file in the home directory for an account. This file lists other hosts that are trusted. When others access your system using rsh from a trusted host, they are not required to enter a password (if they are logged in to the same account on their system). If you have the same account name on five different systems (all trusted using .rhosts files), when an attacker gains access to one of those systems, the attacker has access to all the systems (even if you have different passwords for your accounts on the different systems).

Use One-Time Passwords

To ensure that only authorized users access the network systems, the use of one-time passwords is recommended. (Authorized users are those users who have been granted permission to access network resources to perform a specific task or function.) By using one-time passwords, even an attacker who has determined a user's account name and password cannot log in to the network resource because the password is used only once.

One-Time Passwords

Logging in to a network requires a username and a password. If someone discovers another person's username and password, he can log in to the network using that person's account. With one-time passwords, however, the user enters a pass phrase into a device that generates a password that is valid only once and only for a limited time. Therefore, if an attacker views the username and password, he or she cannot use the password at a later time to gain access to the network.

Establishing Security Boundaries

Firewalls are designed to limit traffic flow on a network. Just as a physical firewall limits the spread of a fire, computer firewalls restrict network traffic flow to help enforce a predetermined security policy. Normally a company installs at least one firewall between the company's internal network and the Internet. When installing firewalls in your network, you have two tasks:

- Determine necessary traffic patterns.
- Define logical security zones.

Firewalls

A firewall is a security component that limits traffic flow to a protected network based on a predefined security policy. All traffic destined for the protected network must pass through the firewall. The firewall examines each packet traveling through it against the security rules that you have defined. Unauthorized traffic (for the protected network) is stopped at the firewall, and the firewall can generate security log entries to indicate security policy violations. Firewalls fall into several categories based on their operation, such as the following:

- Packet filtering
- Stateful packet inspection
- Application proxy

Determining Necessary Traffic Patterns

Your security policy needs to outline the specific network traffic that is allowed between segments in your network. Your Internet connection probably contains the most restrictions, but other segments in your network usually also have some traffic limitations. You can enforce these traffic restrictions by installing firewalls at key locations throughout your network.

You can think of these traffic restrictions like the locks (or card readers) on doors throughout your facility. Each employee has the ability to enter the building (but maybe only during business hours). A limited number of people have access to development labs. Only a couple of people have access to the electrical closet. Finally, visitors must check in with the receptionist before they can enter the facility. Each of these locks restricts the flow of people throughout your facility.

Typically, you restrict traffic into your network from the Internet using a firewall. You will probably not allow any Internet hosts to directly establish connections to a host on your protected network. You might install a mail server on a partially protected network, known as the *demilitarized zone* (DMZ), because Internet hosts need to connect to your mail server to deliver e-mail to your users. The mail server then can relay mail messages to your internal network. If you are concerned about viruses entering your network, you can block e-mail traffic with attachments. Some organizations even restrict the Internet websites that their employees are allowed to access.

Other traffic restrictions that you need to consider involve business partners and remote access. Many times, you have business partners who require access to your network resources to do their job. This access, however, needs to be controlled and limited to the least amount of resources and privileges as possible. Your employees also need to access your network from home and when they are traveling. Not allowing this access reduces productivity. Allowing it insecurely opens up your network to attack. You must examine each of these situations and establish traffic restrictions that enable your users to be productive while minimizing the risk to your network. Cisco SAFE architecture provides an excellent example for many of these restrictions and is explained in more detail later in this chapter.

Defining Logical Security Zones

Firewalls establish security zones and boundaries within your network. All traffic entering a specific zone must pass through a firewall. The firewall examines all the traffic going to a protected network. It passes only the traffic that is allowed by its security rules. Furthermore, these security zones, established by your firewalls, create choke points within your network at which your security policy can easily be enforced.

Security Stance

When establishing your security policy rules, you need to adopt a basic *security stance*. This security stance defines how you view restrictions to traffic on your network. The two stances that you can choose from are *inclusive* and *exclusive*. With the inclusive model, you allow everything that is not explicitly denied by your security policy. The exclusive model takes the opposite stance. It denies everything that is not specifically allowed by your security policy.

With the inclusive approach, you gradually narrow the allowed traffic as you determine which traffic is harmful to your network. This approach is commonly used in university environments where many students require varied access to system resources.

The exclusive approach, however, starts by denying everything. After you determine that specific traffic is safe and needed, you add it to the allowed traffic in your security policy. This approach is typically used in many business environments where the interest in protecting trade secrets overrides user convenience. Both approaches have their merits, and you need to carefully choose which approach best matches your organizational philosophy.

Providing Confidentiality Through Virtual Private Networks

Encryption provides confidentiality. Confidentiality and integrity are a must for sensitive traffic that needs to flow across an untrusted link, such as the Internet. You can use numerous approaches to incorporate confidentiality and integrity into your network traffic. One such approach is a *virtual private network* (VPN). VPNs provide an encrypted flow of traffic between two endpoints. An attacker who sniffs the network traffic between the endpoints of the VPN cannot gain significant reconnaissance because the traffic is encrypted. Furthermore, the added integrity prevents an attacker from inserting bogus traffic or replaying captured traffic.

Sniffing

Sniffing involves using a program that captures all the traffic that is visible to your network interface. Network administrators routinely use sniffers to monitor and analyze network traffic. Attackers, however, can also use these tools to capture network traffic. A common sniffer that you can use on both Windows and UNIX systems is called Ethereal. This program not only captures network traffic, it also decodes the packets for most of the common protocols.

Establishing a VPN within your network involves two tasks:

- Define the untrusted link.
- Define endpoints.

Virtual Private Network

A VPN provides confidentiality and integrity for network traffic between hosts or networks using encryption. Each endpoint of the VPN encrypts traffic destined for the other endpoint. The traffic between the endpoints can traverse untrusted networks without fear of revealing information to someone who can view the data stream on the untrusted network.

Define Untrusted Links

Any sensitive information needs to be protected if it travels across an untrusted link. The most obvious untrusted link is the Internet. The flow of sensitive traffic within your network, however, also needs to be examined. Many times, multiple departments need to access a common network (such as a server network). Using VPN tunnels, you can restrict unauthorized access to sensitive traffic that must leave security zones within your network.

Define Endpoints

When it comes to defining endpoints, you can do so in one of two ways:

- Host-to-host encryption
- Site-to-site encryption

With host-to-host encryption, the network traffic is encrypted at the source host and decrypted at the destination host (see Figure 2-2). This provides the highest degree of protection because the data never traverses the network in clear text. The encryption process, however, can use a significant amount of CPU processing.

Figure 2-2 *Host-to-Host Encryption*

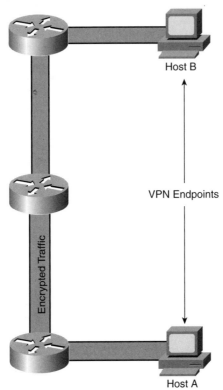

Site-to-site encryption uses VPN tunnels to encrypt all the traffic between two endpoints (see Figure 2-3). An endpoint, however, is usually a router or firewall (which can have specialized hardware to perform the encryption). Individual hosts do not incur a performance penalty due to encryption. The main drawback to site-to-site encryption is that the traffic is unprotected on the source and destination networks.

Figure 2-3   *Site-to-Site Encryption*

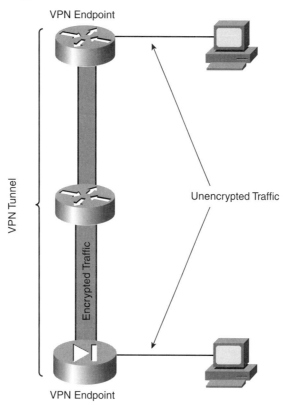

Patching Security Vulnerabilities

Vulnerability patching involves closing potential security holes that an attacker can use to gain access to systems on your network. Most operating systems turn on a default suite of services when they are first installed. Some of these services are needed, whereas others are not. For any services that are running, however, it is imperative that the latest security patches be applied to close security holes discovered with those services.

NOTE   To minimize the amount of vulnerability patching that you need to perform on your network, turn off any unneeded services. By removing the unused services, it is much more difficult for an attacker to find an entry point onto the system and, therefore, your network. An attacker frequently uses these unused services to execute denial-of-service (DoS) attacks against your network.

All reliable vendors maintain lists of security patches on their websites. You also can usually obtain security patches directly from vendor websites. Furthermore, many vendors have security mailing lists to which you can subscribe. These mailing lists send you e-mail notifications whenever a new security vulnerability is discovered. You can obtain operating system security patches from the following vendor websites, among others:

- http://www.cert.org/
- http://icat.nist.gov/icat.cfm
- Microsoft Windows at http://windowsupdate.microsoft.com
- Sun Microsystems at http://sunsolve.sun.com
- Mandrake at http://www.mandrakesecure.net/en/advisories/
- Various Linux at http://www.linux-sec.net/patches/
- Openbsd at http://www.openbsd.org/errata.html
- BSDI at ftp://ftp.bsdi.com/bsdi/patches
- SuSE at http://www.suse.com/us/private/download/updates/index.html

---

NOTE Due to time constraints, security patches are often created in a hurried timeframe. Sometimes security patches have caused more problems than the security hole the patches are designed to eliminate. Therefore, before blindly applying patches to your production system, apply the security patches to servers in a nonproduction environment. This can highlight problems before you apply the security patch to your production servers, thus preventing an accidental disruption of service.

Security Vulnerabilities: The Never-Ending Battle

Patching security vulnerabilities on your network is a never-ending battle. Attackers discover new security vulnerabilities continuously. Each of these new vulnerabilities opens a hole in your previously secure network. Monitoring security mailing lists will keep you informed of new security vulnerabilities, which you can download from your vendor's website.

Monitoring Network Security

After you have established a security policy and secured your systems as best as possible, the next step is to monitor the network to identify violations of the security policy.

Detecting violations in your security policy involves monitoring hosts and network traffic to determine when violations occur. Your security policy defines a group of rules representing acceptable access to network resources. It also might define acceptable network protocols. You need to establish a procedure to continuously check your network to verify that your security policy is followed. Your security policy might even mandate such checking to verify that your network is not being attacked.

Usually this involves monitoring your network. Monitoring falls into two categories:

- Manual
- Automatic

Manual Monitoring

Manual monitoring is usually accomplished by using the audit logging capabilities provided by the host operating system. These logs provide the system administrator with information, such as login failures, successful logins, and file access. To use these host-level audit facilities, the system administrator must first turn on the auditing and then, routinely examine the logs to check for activity that violates the security policy. This task can be very difficult due to large amounts of information (log file entries) and due to inefficient analytical tools.

Automatic Monitoring

Automatic monitoring involves watching network traffic to determine whether unauthorized activities occur on the network. This level of monitoring can be accomplished through the use of Cisco intrusion detection systems (IDSs) at both the network and host perspective. Cisco IDSs can automatically monitor network traffic by triggering alarms when specific intrusive activity is detected on your network traffic. Effective sensor deployment, however, is crucial to enabling successful monitoring. (For more detailed sensor deployment details, see Chapter 4, "Cisco Intrusion Protection.")

Testing Network Security

The third step in the Security Wheel involves proactively testing the network to confirm that the framework outlined in the security policy matches conditions implemented on your network. You also need to verify that known security vulnerabilities have been patched. This can be accomplished by running a network scanner against the hosts on the network to verify that all countermeasures have been installed correctly. You can test the current security posture of your network in two ways:

- Using network scanners
- Conducting professional security evaluations

Using Network Scanners

Attackers discover new security vulnerabilities daily. You need a mechanism to confirm whether specific vulnerabilities exist on your network. Manually checking each host is time-consuming and inefficient. Most system administrators use *network scanners* to facilitate checking for vulnerabilities on their networks. Although these tools provide you with useful information, they are not without problems. They sometimes identify vulnerabilities incorrectly, and other times they can miss vulnerabilities. Therefore, it is important to also monitor security mailing lists and other security news sources in conjunction with scanning your network with network scanners.

Network Scanners

Tools that examine hosts on a network to locate security vulnerabilities are known as *network scanners*. They provide an efficient mechanism to check the security posture of your network on a regular basis. Attackers use similar tools to locate potential entry points into your network. By running network scanners against your network, you gain a picture of your network from the eyes of an attacker.

Some common free network scanners include the following:

- NESSUS
- Cerebus Internet Scanner (CIS)
- SAINT
- SATAN

Some common commercial network scanners include the following:

- Internet Security Scanner
- Retina Network Security Scanner

Conducting Professional Security Evaluations

The preceding section described how to use security-scanning tools to perform an in-house assessment of the security of your network. You can think of that step as brushing and flossing your teeth on a regular basis. Just as you go to the dentist once or twice a year, you need to obtain a professional security evaluation of your network at least once a year.

Professional security assessments involve security professionals examining your network security from the eyes of an attacker. These professionals essentially attempt to break into your network using the same tools that an attacker uses. After their evaluation, they provide you a detailed report outlining the security weaknesses that they discovered, along with ways in which to minimize those weaknesses.

You can think of professional security assessments as a reality check on your network security. You might think that your security is sound; until you confirm this through a third party, however, you might be giving yourself a false sense of security. It is much better to hear about your security holes during a professional security evaluation that you control than through an actual attack on your network.

NOTE   Although professional security assessments give a reality check with respect to your network security, they do not perform an all-out assault on your network. A professional security assessment has rules and limitations, such as refraining from conducting DoS attacks. Therefore, these assessments might not highlight some of the attacks that a malicious attacker can launch against your network.

Improving Network Security

The last step in the Security Wheel is to take the information gathered through monitoring and testing and improve the security of the network. Only by continually cycling though the Security Wheel will the security of your network remain at its peak. Remember, new vulnerabilities and risks are discovered daily. You also must keep current on the latest security events. To do so, do the following:

- Monitor security news.
- Periodically review configuration files.
- Evaluate sensor placement.
- Verify the security configuration.

Monitoring Security News

Monitoring security news on a regular basis informs you about new tools and exploits that attackers are discovering.

Attackers locate security vulnerabilities daily. Some discoveries impact a larger audience than others. Vulnerabilities in BIND (the most popular DNS program) affect an extremely large audience. Other vulnerabilities impact only a few organizations. Any vulnerability that impacts your network is significant to the security of your network. You can locate security information in numerous places. Two excellent resources are:

- Security mailing lists
- Security websites

Security Mailing Lists

Several mailing lists provide a forum to disclose new security vulnerabilities and pose questions concerning security. By monitoring these mailing lists, you can learn about new exploits and harden you network against them. You also can learn workarounds to be used against new exploits until official patches come out. Some popular mailing lists and newsletters include the following:

- Bugtraq at http://www.securityfocus.com
- NTBugtraq at http://www.ntbugtraq.com/
- Security Focus newsletter at http://www.securityfocus.com
- Security Bytes newsletter at http://www.cisco.com/warp/public/779/largeent/issues/security/sbytes/

NOTE   The Security Focus website has numerous mailing lists that are focused on specific technologies, such as the following:

- Forensics
- Windows
- Linux
- Firewalls

Security Websites

Security websites, like security mailing lists, provide a collection point for security tools and information. Periodically reviewing these sites provides you with insight into the tools that attackers use against your network. You might want to use some of the tools to perform your own testing on your network. Some common security websites include the following:

- http://www.securityfocus.com
- http://www.freshmeat.net
- http://www.packetstormsecurity.org/
- http://www.cisco.com/pcgi-bin/front.x/csec/csecHome.pl
- http://www.debian.org/security/
- http://www.cve.mitre.org
- http://www.linuxsecurity.com/
- http://www.icat.nist.gov/icat.cfm
- http://www.securitytracker.com/

Periodically Review Configuration Files

The configuration files on your routers, firewalls, and other network devices enforce your security policy. Sometimes changes are made to these configurations that break your security policy. Other times, the configuration is entered incorrectly. As long as these inadequate configurations remain in effect, your network is more vulnerable to attack. Periodic configuration file reviews enable you to locate these breaks in your policy and correct them.

Evaluating Sensor Placement

Correctly placed sensors generate a wealth of information about traffic on your network. In many instances, correctly placed sensors can help you confirm that traffic restrictions imposed by your security policy are actually enforced on your network. As your network grows, you might need to reevaluate the placement of sensors to ensure that they are positioned to provide you with the best data possible. Another question that you need to consider is whether you have enough sensors deployed on your network to monitor it effectively. For a detailed analysis of Cisco IDS sensor deployment, see Chapter 4.

Verifying the Security Configuration

Along with detecting security policy violations, it also is important to verify that the security configuration outlined in your security policy is implemented correctly.

Designing an excellent security policy does not help secure your network unless you correctly translate that policy into usable device configurations that accurately implement the policy. One way to accomplish this is to review the configuration files on the network devices, such as firewalls, to verify that the security configuration is correct. You must also verify the security configuration for all of the other devices on your network. Because many of these devices do not have a single configuration file, analyzing their configuration is not as simple. Depending on the placement of the sensors for the Cisco IDS, you can use Cisco IDS to confirm that the security configuration is valid.

You can make a confirmation by placing an IDS sensor on the inside and outside of a firewall. If the security policy prohibits certain traffic from entering the network, the sensor inside the firewall can be configured to alarm if prohibited traffic is detected. Unlike periodic configuration file reviews, this technique provides immediate notification if the security configuration is invalid.

Besides continuously updating the security of your network via the Security Wheel, it helps to build your network on a proven foundation. To assist you in building your network on a strong foundation, Cisco has developed the following two frameworks to guide you in constructing your enterprise network:

- The Cisco Architecture for Voice, Video, and Integrated Data (AVVID)
- Cisco SAFE

Cisco Architecture for Voice, Video, and Integrated Data (AVVID)

The Internet is creating tremendous business opportunities. Internet business solutions such as e-commerce, supply chain management, e-learning, and customer care are dramatically increasing productivity and efficiency. Cisco AVVID outlines an enterprise architecture that provides an intelligent network infrastructure suited for today's Internet business solutions. Based on industry standards, Cisco AVVID provides a road map to combine a customer's business and technology strategies into one cohesive model. By following a proven architecture, you can rapidly and seamlessly deploy emerging technologies in your network with confidence.

NOTE   New components and capabilities are continually being incorporated into Cisco AVVID. For the latest information on the Internet business solutions supported by AVVID, go to the Cisco website at http://www.cisco.com/go/avvid.

To provide an open ecosystem, it is imperative to enable partners within the Cisco AVVID framework. Cisco realizes that to deliver complete Internet business solutions it is vital to team with integrators, strategic partners, and customers. Cisco AVVID offers a guide for these interactions by describing a consistent set of services and capabilities that form a basis for many types of partner relationships.

Cisco AVVID Architecture

Cisco AVVID is composed of following distinct layers:

- Clients
- Network platforms
- Intelligent network services
- Unified control plane
- Real-time communications
- Internet business solutions

Each of these layers serves as a building block to assist you in successfully and efficiently delivering Internet business solutions on your network.

Clients

Users will use a variety of devices to access the Internet through your network architecture. Because Cisco AVVID is based on standards, it enables your business solution to use a wide variety of devices, even some that are not yet being widely deployed. Instead of using proprietary access devices, you add functionality to your AVVID network through the intelligent network services provided in the infrastructure.

Network Platforms

Your network infrastructure provides both the physical and logical connection points for your users' devices. Network platforms are comprised of LAN switches, routers, gateways, and other equipment that interconnects users and servers. Although Cisco network platforms are competitive for features, performance, and price, their key capabilities are the integration and interaction with other elements of the Cisco AVVID framework. This layer of Cisco AVVID establishes a strong foundation for all the applications that you will integrate into your network to solve your business needs.

Intelligent Network Services

Intelligent network services represent software that operates on the network platforms to provide the end-to-end architecture for deploying your Internet business solutions throughout your network. The following list identifies some of the major intelligent network services provided through Cisco AVVID:

- Quality of service (QoS)
- Security
- Network availability

Having a consistent set of network services throughout your network enables you to roll out new Internet business applications and e-business initiatives very quickly without a major re-engineering of your network each time. On the other hand, networks built on "best-of-breed" strategies might claim higher performance for a specific device, but cannot be relied on to provide these sophisticated features end-to-end in a multivendor environment.

Best-of-Breed Solutions

A "best-of-breed" solution focuses on using devices or products that are the best at providing some specific type of functionality. By itself, a best-of-breed solution is (by definition) the best at what it does. When integrated into your network, however, a best-of-breed solution may not function optimally if it does not integrate well with your existing infrastructure. Whenever incorporating new features into your network framework, you must consider how the new functionality interacts throughout your entire network topology.

By supporting standards, Cisco AVVID provides for the migration and the incorporation of Internet business integrators. Furthermore, the added intelligent network services provided by an end-to-end Cisco AVVID solution far exceed what can be achieved through isolated best-of-breed solutions.

Unified Control Plane

A key part of any network architecture is a unified control plane, because it helps tailor the network infrastructure and customize the intelligent network services to meet the needs of your applications. This layer addresses features such as management, policies, content delivery, access, user privileges, scalability, and availability of web-based applications.

Real-Time Communications

A strong communication foundation enables the interaction between users and a variety of application platforms. Some of the key communication components include the following:

- Messaging
- Collaboration
- Video on demand
- Personal productivity
- Telephony processing
- Content routing
- Conferencing

Rapid deployment of Internet business solutions depends on consistent service control and communication services throughout your network. Cisco servers distributed throughout the network often provide this functionality. The service control and communication services represent the glue that joins the Internet technology layers of the Cisco AVVID framework with the actual business solutions, in effect tuning the network infrastructure and intelligent network services to the needs of your Internet business solutions. Furthermore, Internet business solutions are adapted for the best performance and availability on the network infrastructure by exploiting the end-to-end services available through the Cisco AVVID framework.

Internet Business Solutions

Enterprise customers deploy Internet business solutions to re-engineer their organizations and increase their productivity. Cisco does not necessarily provide the applications associated with each Internet business solution, but Cisco AVVID enables these applications (from various partners) to be enabled, in an accelerated fashion and delivered in a common framework. To compete effectively, companies need to migrate their traditional business models to Internet business models and deploy Internet business solutions. Cisco AVVID provides a framework upon which you can easily deploy and manage your e-business Internet business solutions.

Cisco AVVID Benefits

Cisco AVVID provides many ways to increase your company's productivity and build a competitive advantage. The benefits of using the Cisco AVVID framework fall into the following four categories:

- Integration
- Intelligence
- Innovation
- Interoperability

Integration

By leveraging Cisco AVVID, your network is built on a flexible framework. Applying the network intelligence inherent in IP in association with the Cisco AVVID framework, your company can easily develop and deploy a variety of tools that will improve the productivity of your network.

Intelligence

By prioritizing traffic and using intelligent network services, you can maximize network efficiency. Furthermore, this also enables you to optimize the performance of your network applications.

Innovation

Business needs continually change. Being able to react to these changes can be the difference between success and failure for your business. Using the Cisco AVVID framework enables you to easily and quickly implement new Internet business models. By adapting quickly to the changing business environment, you can strive to keep your business operating as efficiently and productively as possible.

Interoperability

The Cisco AVVID framework is built on proven standards. These standards, which apply to both protocols and application programming interfaces (APIs), enable open integration with numerous third-party developers. Therefore, you have more choices and flexibility when incorporating new technology into your network. This flexible robust architecture can become your enterprise's most strategic asset and powerful competitive advantage.

Cisco SAFE

Cisco AVVID provides an excellent framework with which to increase your company's productivity. Cisco SAFE builds on this framework by providing a secure migration path when you implement a converged voice, video, and data network. Deploying an Internet business solution without considering security is asking for trouble. Cisco SAFE provides you with a flexible framework that will empower your company to securely, reliably, and cost-effectively take advantage of the Internet economy.

Cisco SAFE is a collection of white papers and design guides that provide you with concrete examples of how to effectively incorporate security into your unique network environment.

SAFE Modular Blueprint

Cisco SAFE is a modular framework that provides a proven architecture with respect to security and reliability. The basic Cisco SAFE modular blueprint is outlined in the following white papers:

- SAFE: A Security Blueprint for Enterprise Networks
- SAFE: Blueprint for Small, Midsize, and Remote User Networks
- SAFE VPN: IPSec Virtual Private Networks in Depth
- SAFE: Wireless LAN Security in Depth
- SAFE: IP Telephony Security in Depth

NOTE   The basic Cisco SAFE white papers represent only a small portion of the total number of SAFE documents that have been created. The framework is continually being expanded as new technologies emerge (such as Voice over IP [VoIP] and wireless). You can find more information on Cisco SAFE by referencing Cisco's website at http://www.cisco.com/go/safe.

The Cisco SAFE blueprint provides a robust security blueprint that builds on the Cisco AVVID framework. By incorporating the following SAFE layers throughout your Cisco AVVID infrastructure, you ensure a comprehensive security solution:

- **Infrastructure layer**—Intelligent, scalable security services in Cisco platforms, such as routers, switches, firewalls, IDSs, and other devices
- **Appliances layer**—Incorporation of key security functionality in mobile handheld devices and remote PC clients

- **Service control layer**—Critical security protocols and APIs that enable security solutions to work together cohesively
- **Applications layer**—Host-based and network-based security elements that ensure the integrity of critical e-business applications

To facilitate rapidly deployable, consistent security throughout your enterprise, SAFE consists of modules that address the distinct security requirements for each area of your network. By adopting the SAFE blueprint, your security managers do not need to redesign the entire security architecture each time you add a new service to your network. The modular structure makes it easy and cost-effective to secure each new service as needed. Furthermore, these new modules can be easily integrated into your overall security architecture.

One of the unique characteristics of the SAFE blueprint is that it is the first industry blueprint that recommends exactly which security solutions should be deployed in which sections of the network, as well as why the solutions should be deployed. Each module in the SAFE blueprint is designed to specifically provide maximum performance for e-business, while at the same time enabling enterprises to maintain security and integrity.

SAFE Benefits

Besides establishing a secure e-business environment, implementing the SAFE blueprint provides the following benefits:

- Foundation for migrating to converged networks
- Modular security deployment
- Integrated network security protection

By implementing a converged network, you can efficiently deploy voice, video, and data on the same infrastructure. Implementing SAFE provides the foundation to migrate to a converged network securely and affordably. Being modular in nature, the SAFE blueprint enables you to deploy security in a cost-effective phased approach based on your network environment, resources, and needs. Finally, the SAFE blueprint integrates network protection via high-level security products and services.

Summary

To secure your network, you must construct a security framework. This framework is defined by a security policy. Your security policy must do the following:

- Identify the organization's security objectives
- Document the resources to be protected
- Identify the network infrastructure with current maps and inventories
- Identify the critical resources that need extra protection

Using your security policy as a baseline, you need to secure your network. The Security Wheel outlines a process to continuously secure your network. The Security Wheel consists of four major phases:

- Securing your network
- Monitoring your network
- Testing your network
- Improving your network's security

First, you secure your network by addressing the following four areas of network security:

- Tightening authentication
- Establishing security boundaries
- Providing confidentiality
- Patching security vulnerabilities

Monitoring your network is an important aspect of network security. Monitoring falls into two general categories:

- Manual
- Automatic

Testing the security of your network enables you to determine which vulnerabilities exist on your network. To locate security vulnerabilities on your network, you use a network scanner. A network scanner examines your network in much the same way that an attacker does when searching for weak points in your network. You can choose from numerous network scanners, both commercial and free.

Finally, you must take the information that you learned from monitoring and testing to improve the security of your network. You also need to monitor security news sources regularly. Securing your network is not something that you can do one time and forget. It is a continuous process that keeps evolving as attackers uncover new vulnerabilities, your network topology changes, and your security requirements change. Besides staying current on the latest security news, you also must evaluate and improve your existing security configurations and components to verify that they are protecting your network at the level you want.

Along with continually securing and monitoring your network, it is also important to initially build your network on a strong, flexible foundation. To maintain high productivity, your network must be able to take advantage of the numerous Internet business solutions. Cisco AVVID provides a flexible framework to build your converged network, but without security, this framework could still leave your network open to attack. Therefore, Cisco SAFE builds on the Cisco AVVID framework to establish a modular approach to securing your converged network.

Review Questions

The following questions test your retention of the material presented in this chapter. The answers to the review questions are in Appendix B, "Answers to Chapter Review Questions."

1 What are the four steps in the Cisco Security Wheel?

2 What is a security policy?

3 What two types of monitoring are commonly used to detect violations in your security policy?

4 What are some of the procedures that your security policy should cover?

5 What software tool do you use to test the security of your network?

6 How can IDS sensors be used to assist with implementing the Security Wheel?

7 What is an untrusted link?

8 What are the endpoints commonly used for the encryption boundaries on VPNs?

9 What are four areas that you need to examine to secure your network?

10 What is a firewall?

11 What basic security principle does a VPN provide?

12 What are the steps that you can take to tighten authentication on your network?

13 What is Cisco AVVID?

14 Where are two places that you can monitor security news on the web?

15 What is the difference between inclusive and exclusive security stances?

16 What are the two steps to establishing security boundaries on your network?

17 What is Cisco SAFE?

Upon completion of this chapter, you will be able to perform the following tasks:

- Define intrusion detection
- Explain the difference between false and true alarms
- Explain the different IDS triggering mechanisms
- Identify the different IDS monitoring locations
- Explain the basic signature responses
- Explain the basic IDS evasion techniques

CHAPTER 3

Intrusion Detection Concepts

Before deploying an intrusion detection system (IDS), you must understand the benefits that an IDS provides. An IDS is software and possibly hardware that detects attacks against your network. Besides detecting attacks, most IDSs also provide some type of active response to the attacks, such as resetting TCP connections and updating access control lists (ACLs) on your routers and firewalls. The general attacks against your network are explained in detail in Chapter 1, "The Need for Network Security," but the main attack categories are as follows:

- Reconnaissance attacks
- Access attacks
- Denial-of-service attacks

Detecting these attacks is the goal of intrusion detection. Intrusive activity can be detected in many different ways. Therefore, people have designed various types of IDSs to solve the intrusion detection problem. Although each type of IDS identifies various types of intrusive activity, they approach the problem from different perspectives. Each approach has its merits and drawbacks. By understanding how each type of IDS functions, you can make an informed decision as to which type of IDS is best suited for your business environment. Furthermore, you must also understand the common techniques that attackers will use to try to bypass detection by your IDS.

Intrusion Detection Definition

When you place a burglar alarm on the doors and windows of your home, you are installing an IDS for your house. The IDSs used to protect your computer network operate in a similar fashion. They detect intrusive activity that enters into your network. You can locate intrusive activity by examining network traffic, host logs, system calls, and other areas that signal an attack against your network. The specific traffic or events needed to trigger alarms depends on the type of IDS that you use. Each type of IDS has its strengths and weaknesses. Nevertheless, every IDS is defined by three common factors:

- IDS triggers
- IDS monitoring locations
- Intrusion detection response techniques

To understand these three factors, however, you need to understand the terminology used to describe the credibility of the alarms that an IDS generates. The alarm terminology is frequently used to describe an IDS, and understanding exactly what the specific terms mean is vital to determining the effectiveness of the IDS.

IDS Alarm Terminology

By definition, every IDS must generate some type of alarm to signal when intrusive activity has been detected on your network. No IDS, however, is 100 percent accurate. This inaccuracy means that your IDS will generate some alarms that do not correspond to actual intrusive activity, and potentially fail to alarm when an actual attack occurs. IDS alarms fall into two broad categories:

- False alarms
- True alarms

False Alarms

The first broad category of IDS alarms is known as *false alarms*. These alarms represent situations in which your IDS fails to accurately indicate what is happening on your network. "False" alarms fall into two major categories:

- False positives
- False negatives

False Positives

One of the most common terms associated with IDS alarms is a *false positive*. False positives occur when your IDS generates an alarm based on normal network activity. False positives force you to waste valuable time and resources analyzing phantom attacks. Over time, these false positives can also desensitize your security personnel so that when a real alarm comes in, it is ignored or slowly processed. A good analogy is a home burglar alarm that goes off accidentally. Each time it goes off, the police respond. If you have too many false alarms, the police will start charging you extra. Furthermore, after numerous false alarms, the police response time to your house diminishes significantly.

False Negatives

When your IDS fails to generate an alarm for known intrusive activity, it is called a *false negative*. False negatives represent actual attacks that the IDS missed even though it is programmed to detect the attack. Most IDS developers tend to design their systems to prevent false negatives. It is very difficult, however, to totally eliminate false negatives.

Nevertheless, false negatives represent a serious risk to your network security because they enable an attacker to launch an attack against your network undetected.

If you detect a situation in which a specific attack does not generate the appropriate alarm, this represents a software bug. Before you report this to the vendor using their reporting policy, however, you need to make sure that the false negative was not generated because the IDS is saturated with traffic and dropping packets.

True Alarms

The second broad category of IDS alarms is known as *true alarms*. These alarms represent situations in which your IDS accurately indicates what is happening on your network. "True" alarms also fall into two major categories:

- True positives
- True negatives

True Positives

The opposite of a false negative alarm is a true positive alarm. In the case of *true positives*, your IDS generates an alarm correctly in response to actually detecting the attack traffic that a signature is designed to detect. In an ideal world, 100 percent of the alarms generated by your IDS would be true positives, meaning that every alarm corresponds to an actual attack against your network. Because we do not live in an ideal world, we must settle for IDSs that generate true positives as well as missing some attacks (false negatives) and generating false positives in response to normal user traffic. To be effective, the number of attacks missed by your IDS should be extremely low. In most cases, it is preferable to have a signature generate a small number of false positives instead of letting any actual attacks get through undetected.

True Negatives

The last alarm classification is a true negative. Like false negatives, *true negatives* do not represent actual alarms that your IDS generates. Instead, a true negative represents a situation in which your IDS signature does not alarm when it is examining normal user traffic (the correct behavior). This makes a true negative the opposite of a false positive. When your IDS signatures are well written, they do not frequently generate alarms on normal user activity. On the other hand, poorly written or poorly tuned signatures can lead to numerous false positives. Again, in an ideal world, normal user traffic would not cause your IDS to generate an alarm, but false positives do occur. If your IDS generates too many false positives, its credibility begins to suffer.

IDS Triggers

The purpose of any IDS is to detect when an intruder attacks your network. Not every IDS, however, uses the same *triggering mechanisms* to generate intrusion alarms. There are three major triggering mechanisms used by current IDSs:

- Anomaly detection
- Misuse detection
- Protocol analysis

Triggering Mechanisms

Triggering mechanisms refer to the action that causes the IDS to generate an alarm. The triggering mechanism for a home burglar alarm could be a window breaking. A network IDS might alarm if it sees a packet sent to a certain port with specific data in it. A host-based IDS might generate an alarm if a certain system call is executed. Anything that can reliably signal an intrusion can be used as a triggering mechanism.

Anomaly Detection

Anomaly detection is also sometimes referred to as *profile-based detection*. With anomaly detection, you must build profiles for each *user group* on the system. This profile incorporates a typical user's habits, the services he normally uses, and so on. This profile defines the behavior characteristics for a user group, in essence establishing a baseline for the activities that a normal user routinely does to perform the job.

User Group

A *user group* represents a group of users that perform similar functions on the network. Sometimes you can build user groups based on job classification, such as engineers, clerks, and so on. Other times, you might want to assign groups based on departments. How you assign the groups is not important, as long as the users in the group perform similar activities on the network.

Building and updating these profiles represents a significant portion of the work required to deploy an anomaly-based IDS. The quality of your profiles directly relates to how successful your IDS will be at detecting attacks against your network. People have experimented with various techniques for constructing these user profiles. The most common approaches used to build user profiles include the following:

- Statistical sampling
- Rule-based approach
- Neural networks

Each user profile defines the normal pattern of activity for each user group on the system. Anytime a user deviates too far from the group's profile, the IDS generates an alarm. Providing the most flexibility to the user while detecting intrusive or unauthorized activity is a key challenge facing anomaly detection systems.

Benefits

Anomaly detection provides a couple of advantages:

- Enables tunable control over false positives
- Detects previously unpublished attacks

The user profiles form the heart of an anomaly-based IDS. An initial training period monitors the network for a predetermined period of time. This traffic is then used to create a user baseline. This baseline determines what normal traffic on the network looks like. If you use a statistical approach to profile creation, alarms are based on deviations from your defined normal state. In statistical terms, you measure deviation from normal by calculating the *standard deviation*. By varying the number of standard deviations required to generate an alarm, you can control the sensitivity of your IDS. This can also be used to roughly regulate the number of false positives that your IDS will generate, because small user deviations are less likely to generate false positives (although it will also widen the definition of normal user traffic).

Standard Deviation

Standard deviation measures the deviation from the median or average of a data set. When your data is based on a well-defined distribution, each standard deviation defines a percentage of data that should fall within it. For instance maybe 90 percent of all data falls within one standard deviation, 95 percent of the data falls within two standard deviations, and 98 percent of the data falls within three standard deviations. In this example, only two percent of the data should fall outside three standard deviations from the mean. Using this process, you can define statistically how abnormal specific data is.

The main advantage, however, of anomaly detection is that the alarms are not based on signatures for specific known attacks. Instead, they are based on a profile that defines normal user activity. Therefore, an anomaly-based IDS can generate alarms for previously unpublished attacks, as long as the new attack deviates from normal user activity. This results in the anomaly-based IDS being capable of detecting new attacks the first time that they are used.

Cisco Security Agent software is behavior- or profile-based. It routinely prevents attacks because the activity causes an application to perform an action that the application normally does not perform. An example of this might be a web application that suddenly attempts to change the information in the registry.

Drawbacks

On the downside, anomaly detection has several drawbacks, in that they:

- Usually require an initial training time.
- Do not protect the network during training.
- Require updating user profiles as habits change.
- Enable false negatives if traffic appears normal.
- Have difficultly correlating alarms to specific attacks.
- Can be complicated and hard to understand.

First, you must install your anomaly-based IDS and train it by having it monitor network activity for a specified period of time, which can be on the order of weeks. You use this training to observe traffic on the network and develop a definition of what traffic is considered normal. Defining what constitutes normal traffic is not a simple task. Furthermore, during this training time, the IDS is not protecting your network.

Avoiding Attacks During the Training Period

During the initial training period, it is vital that no attacks or back doors are present on the network. All the traffic occurring during training is establishing the patterns that represent normal user activity. If this includes intrusive activity, the intrusive activity will become part of the defined user profile, and thus become normal user activity.

Verifying that your network is free of attacks or back doors can be a daunting task. During the initial training period, however, you must make sure that you thoroughly analyze your network for any abnormal traffic that could be either attack traffic or traffic from an existing back door.

Another problem is that people tend to vary their activities. They do not always follow the same exact patterns repeatedly. If the initial training period is inadequate, or your definition of normal is old and inaccurate, false positives are inevitable. When users deviate from the normal routine, the IDS will generate an alarm if this activity falls to far away from normal. The IDS generates this alarm, even though no intrusive activity actually takes place.

The definition of normal will also change over the life of your network. As your network changes, the traffic that is considered normal can also change. If this happens, you will have to update your user profiles to reflect those changes. For a network that changes constantly, updating user profiles can become a major challenge.

Along with users generating false positives, a profile-based IDS will generate a false negative if the intrusive activity does not deviate from normal. Sometimes, intrusive activity can appear very similar to normal user traffic (especially if your definition of normal traffic is too broad). In these situations, it can be difficult or impossible for an anomaly-based IDS to distinguish this activity as intrusive and generate an alarm.

Unlike signature-based IDSs, anomaly-based IDSs do not have a direct correlation between alarms and potential attacks. When activity deviates from your established normal, your IDS will generate an alarm. It is then up to your security analyst to determine what the alarm actually means.

The final drawback for an anomaly-based IDS is its complexity. It is very difficult to explain how the system operates. With a signature-based IDS, if the system sees a specific sequence of data, it generates an alarm. With anomaly-based IDSs, however, you have complicated statistics or the information theory associated with neural networks. You must analyze each alarm to find out its root cause because there is usually not a direct correlation between alarms and specific attack signatures. Users are uncomfortable when they do not understand their IDS completely. Furthermore, this lack of understanding can reduce user confidence in the IDS.

Misuse Detection

Misuse detection, also known as *pattern matching*, looks for intrusive activity that matches specific activity. These systems are based on signatures that match typical patterns and exploits used by attackers to gain access to your network. Highly skilled network engineers research known attacks and vulnerabilities to develop the rules for each signature based on categories such as those outlined in the white paper titled "The Science of IDS Attack Identification" (http://www.cisco.com/en/US/products/sw/secursw/ps976/ products_white_paper09186a0080092334.shtml). Basically pattern-matching signatures fall into the following categories:

- Simple pattern matching
- Stateful pattern matching
- Protocol decode analysis
- Heuristic analysis

Building well-defined signatures reduces the chance of false positives, while minimizing the chance of false negatives. A well-configured misuse detection-based IDS should generate minimal false positives. If a misuse detection IDS continually generates false positives, its overall effectiveness is diminished.

Benefits

Misuse detection provides numerous benefits. Some of the key benefits include the following:

- Signatures based on known intrusive activity.
- Attacks detected are well defined.
- The system operation is easy to understand.
- The system detects attacks immediately after installation.

Each misuse-based IDS detects a defined set of attack signatures. By using a misuse-based IDS, you can be confident that these defined intrusive attacks will be detected.

With signature-based IDSs, each attack in the signature database has a signature name and identification. A user can display all the signatures in the database and determine exactly which attacks the IDS should alarm on. By knowing the specific attacks in the signature database, the users have confidence in their IDS's capacity to defend their networks. As new attacks come out, they can also verify that their IDS is updated to detect them.

Users understand the basic methodology behind a misuse-based IDS. Network engineers analyze real attacks and then develop signatures to detect this activity. A direct correspondence exists between alarms and attacks. A user can generate attack traffic and observe a specific alarm.

Finally, a signature-based IDS starts defending your network immediately upon installation. Unlike an anomaly-based IDS, an initial training period is not required for misuse-based IDSs.

Drawbacks

To detect intrusions, a misuse-based IDS examines information and then compares it to signatures in its database. Sometimes, however, this information is spread across multiple data packets. When a signature requires multiple pieces of data, the IDS must maintain state information about the signature, starting from when it sees the first piece of data. This state information must be maintained for the duration of the *event horizon.* To maintain state information, a misuse-based IDS requires storage or buffer space. This storage is normally RAM due to its quick retrieval speed. As the signature database grows, the amount of storage needed also increases. Furthermore, attackers might attempt to attack the IDS by filling up its storage with carefully crafted attacks.

Event Horizon

To detect an attack, a signature-based IDS examines the data presented to it. Sometimes many pieces of data are necessary to match an attack signature. The maximum amount of time over which an attack signature can be successfully detected (from initial data to complete attack signature) is known as the event horizon. The IDS must maintain state during this event horizon. The state information represents all the information observed for a specific attack signature. The length of the event horizon varies. For some attacks, the event horizon is from user logon to user logout, whereas for other attacks, such as a slow port scan, the event horizon can span weeks. Because most IDSs do no store state information for this length of time (a couple of weeks), these slow port scans are usually not detected by the IDS because the state information is deleted before the end of the event horizon.

Although they provide various benefits, misuse-based IDSs also have some drawbacks. The biggest disadvantages include the following:

- Managing state information efficiently (event horizon)
- Updating signature database as attacks are published
- Attacks that circumvent the IDS (false negatives)
- Unable to detect unpublished attacks

Because the misuse-based IDS compares network traffic against known signatures in its database, attackers will try to conceal their attacks. By making minor alterations to the attack data, they can sometimes slip the attack past the misuse-based IDS without generating an alarm, thus causing a false negative. (See "Intrusion Detection Evasion Techniques" later in this chapter for information on this topic.) The robustness of the signature definitions and the ability of the end user to tune the IDS signatures determine how successful a pattern-matching IDS is at preventing false positives.

As new attacks appear, the signature database used by the misuse-based IDS must be updated. Timely updating of the signature database is vital to a successful pattern-matching IDS. Keeping signature databases updated, however, is also very difficult.

The biggest drawback, however, to a misuse-based IDS is its inability to detect previously unpublished attacks. This does not mean that a pattern-matching IDS cannot detect *any* new attacks, however. When developers create new signatures, they try to make the signature as flexible as possible, while minimizing potential false positives. Using this technique, many signatures detect a class of attacks even though they are based on a specific exploit. For instance, the Fragment Overlap signature (ID 1201) checks for a situation in which your sensor detects overlapping fragmented traffic. An attacker can attempt to hide various attacks by sending overlapping fragments, but this signature will catch any attack that attempts to hide itself via overlapping fragmented traffic.

Protocol Analysis

The final triggering mechanism is a variation on misuse detection. Misuse detection looks for a specific attack signature in your network traffic. With protocol analysis, the IDS analyzes the data stream based on the normal operation of a specific protocol. Therefore, the IDS verifies the validity of the packets with respect to the protocol definition and then looks for specific patterns in the various fields of the protocol or a packet's payload. This in-depth analysis uses the RFC as a baseline and focuses on two major areas:

- Verifying validity of packets (based on protocol RFC)
- Checking the contents of payload

Using protocol analysis, not only must the attack traffic match a valid packet for the protocol in question, it must also then contain known attack traffic in the payload or protocol fields of the packet. For instance, Signature 4507 (subsignature ID 11) checks for SNMP traffic with an invalid request ID. This parameter is located in a different location depending on whether the traffic is SNMP version 1 or version 2. Because protocol analysis is performed on the SNMP traffic, the signature engine determines the type of SNMP traffic analyzed so that it knows where to look for the specific field being examined.

NOTE   Verifying packet validity can be difficult because many software implementations only partially implement the requirements outlined in the RFC. Furthermore, the specifications of many protocols are vague enough that the protocols can be misused without actually violating the protocol specification.

IDS Monitoring Locations

Now that you have a basic understanding of the intrusive activity that can generate alarms from your IDS, it is time to examine where your IDS watches for this intrusive traffic. The major IDS monitoring locations are:

- Host-based.
- Network-based.

Host-Based IDSS

Host-based IDSs check for intrusions by checking information at the host or operating system level. These IDSs examine many aspects of your host, such as system calls, audit logs, error messages, and so on. A typical host-based IDS deployment is illustrated in Figure 3-1.

Figure 3-1   *Host-Based IDS Deployment*

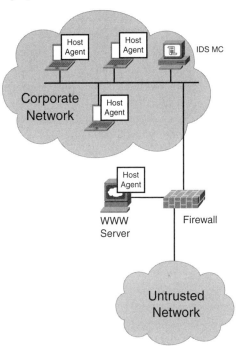

Benefits

Because a host-based IDS examines traffic after it reaches the target of the attack (assuming the host is the target), it has firsthand information on the success of the attack. With a network-based IDS, the alarms are generated on known intrusive activity, but only a host-based IDS can determine the actual success or failure of an attack.

Other items, such as fragment reassembly and variable Time-To-Live (TTL) attacks are difficult to detect using a network-based IDS (see "Intrusion Detection Evasion Techniques" later in this chapter). A host-based IDS, however, can use the host's own IP stack to easily deal with these issues. Because the host-based agent analyzes network traffic after it has been decrypted by the destination host, even data from encrypted protocols can be examined by the host-based agent.

Drawbacks

Host-based IDSs have a couple of drawbacks:

- Limited network view
- Must operate on every OS on the network

The first drawback to host-based IDSs is the limited network view with relation to attacks. It is difficult for host-based IDSs, for instance, to detect port scans across multiple hosts on a network. Therefore, it is almost impossible for a host-based IDS to effectively detect reconnaissance scans against your network. These scans represent a key indicator to more attacks against your network.

Another drawback to host-based IDSs is that the software must run on every device on the network. This represents a major development issue for heterogeneous networks comprised of numerous OSs. Sometimes a host-based IDS vendor will choose to support IDSs certain OSs because of these support issues. If not all the OSs on your network are supported by your host-based IDS software, your network is not fully protected against intrusions.

Network-Based IDSs

A network-based IDS examines packets traversing the network to locate attacks against the network. The IDS *sniffs* or captures the network packets and compares the traffic against signatures for known intrusive activity.

Sniff

To sniff network packets means to examine all the packets that are traveling across the network. Normally, a host only examines packets that are addressed to it specifically, along with packets that are broadcast to all the hosts on the network. To be capable of seeing all of the packets on the network, the IDS must place the network interface card (NIC) into promiscuous mode. While in promiscuous mode, the NIC examines all packets regardless of their destination address.

Cisco IDS enables you to construct a hybrid IDS that contains both network-based and host-based components. Using signatures, Cisco IDS uses network sensors to look at every packet going across the network and generates alarms when intrusions are discovered. You can easily configure Cisco IDS to exclude signatures and modify signature parameters to work optimally in your specific network environment. A typical Cisco IDS network-based deployment is shown in Figure 3-2.

A network-based IDS, however, does not have to be solely signature-based. It is possible to use other trigger mechanisms, such as anomaly detection in a network setting. The network-based label only refers to the location at which the IDS monitors the network traffic, not the triggering mechanism used to generate alarms.

Figure 3-2   *Network-Based Cisco IDS Deployment*

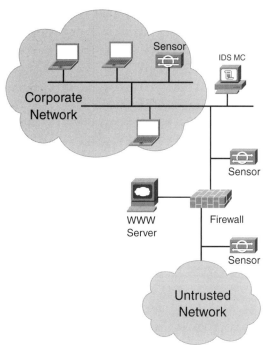

Benefits

A network-based IDS has a couple of benefits:

- It has an overall network perspective.
- It does not have to run on every OS on the network.
- New hosts can typically be protected without adding new IDS components.

By viewing traffic destined for multiple hosts, a sensor receives a network perspective in relation to the attacks against your network. If someone scans multiple hosts on your network, this information is readily apparent to the sensor.

Another advantage to a network-based IDS is that it does not have to run on every OS in the network. Instead, a network-based IDS relies on a limited number of sensor devices to capture network traffic. Managing these various sensor platforms is accomplished through a couple of management platforms. Based on specific performance requirements, you can choose different sensor platforms to provide complete coverage of your network. Furthermore, these sensing devices can easily be hardened to protect them from attack, because they serve a specific purpose on the network.

Drawbacks

A network-based IDS faces a couple of problems. The major problems are as follows:

- Bandwidth
- Fragment reassembly
- Encryption

The biggest drawback to network-based IDSs is bandwidth. As network pipes grow larger and larger, it is very difficult to successfully monitor all the traffic going across the network at a single point in real time, without missing packets. Instead, you normally need to install more sensors throughout the network at locations where the sensors can handle the traffic volume.

Network packets have a maximum size. If a connection needs to send data that exceeds this maximum bound, the data must be sent in multiple packets. This is known as *fragmentation*. When the receiving host gets the fragmented packets, it must reassemble the data. Maintaining these fragments on your sensor can potentially consume a large amount of memory on your sensor. Fragmentation is explained in more detail in the "Intrusion Detection Evasion Techniques" section later in the chapter.

Another drawback to network-based IDSs comes from users attempting to protect the privacy of their data connections. As more users and networks provide encryption for user sessions, the usable information available to a network-based IDS sensor diminishes. When the network traffic is encrypted, the network sensor is unable to match the encrypted data against its signature database (see "Intrusion Detection Evasion Techniques" later in this chapter).

Hybrid IDSs

Hybrid systems combine the functionality from several different IDS categories to create a system that provides more complete functionality than a traditional IDS. Some hybrid systems can incorporate multiple triggering mechanisms, such as protocol analysis and misuse detection. Others hybrid IDSs can combine multiple monitoring locations, such as host-based and network-based monitoring. The major hurtle to constructing a hybrid IDS is getting the various components to operate in harmony, and presenting the information to the end-user in a user-friendly manner.

NOTE   Cisco IDS provides components that enable you to construct a hybrid IDS that incorporates multiple IDS characteristics. With respect to monitoring locations, Cisco IDS supports both network-based and host-based monitoring along with utilizing misuse detection and protocol analysis to trigger alarms. The latest host-based component even incorporates an anomalous triggering mechanism.

Benefits

The benefits of a hybrid IDS depend mainly on the different IDS technologies that are combined together. A combined host-based and network-based system, for instance, provides the overall network visibility of a network-based IDS, as well as detailed host-level visibility. Combining anomaly detection with misuse detection can produce a signature-based IDS that is capable of detecting previously unpublished attacks. Each hybrid system needs to be analyzed on its unique strengths.

Drawbacks

Normally, hybrid systems attempt to merge multiple diverse intrusion detection technologies. Combining these technologies can produce a stronger IDS. Getting these different technologies to work together as a single IDS can be difficult. Presenting the information from these multiple technologies to the end user in a coordinated fashion can also be a challenge. Again, each hybrid system needs to be examined to understand its strengths and weaknesses.

Intrusion Detection Response Techniques

Many people consider intrusion detection to be a passive monitoring tool. Early IDSs just analyzed network traffic (looking for suspicious activity) or parsed system log files. To provide greater protection, the current IDSs incorporate more reactive responses and prevention measures to deal with malicious activity. These enhancements are migrating IDSs from a passive role to more of an active role in defending your network against attack. The major response techniques are as follows:

- TCP reset
- IP blocking
- Logging
- Access restriction

TCP Reset

One way to terminate a TCP connection is for one of the hosts involved in the connection to send a TCP packet with the RST flag set. Because the IDS is monitoring the traffic for the TCP connections on the network, it can also generate the appropriate TCP packet with the RST flag set to terminate an existing TCP connection.

When your IDS detects a known attack signature in a TCP session, it can send a TCP packet with the RST flag set to both the source and destination hosts involved in the connection.

These packets cause the hosts involved in the TCP connection to close the connection, thus temporarily halting the attack.

One of the drawbacks of the TCP reset response is that it does not prevent the attacker from launching further attacks against the network. Furthermore, the response action can only be used on TCP-based signatures.

IP Blocking

IP blocking provides a more comprehensive mechanism to prevent an attacker from continuing to attack your network after the attacker's initial activity is detected. Unlike TCP resets, IP blocking (once initiated) blocks all the traffic from the attacking host for a specified period of time. This prevents the attacker from launching any attack traffic from that host until the block has been removed.

To initiate IP blocking, your IDS communicates with a network device on your network and applies an access list entry that causes the source address of the attack to be denied. After a specified amount of time, this ACL entry is removed, thus allowing traffic from the previously blocked host to once again access your network. IP blocking and other signature responses are explained in detail in Chapter 12, "Signature Response."

Logging

Logging an attacker's actions on your network is very important. Cisco IDS provides an IP logging feature that captures the actual network packets associated with a specific attack. Analyzing this log information enables you to determine the extent of access that the attacker obtained. It also provides you with a documented history of the traffic generated by the attacker. This information can provide valuable support documentation in prosecuting the person or persons who attacked your network.

Access Restriction

A final IDS response is to restrict access to protected resources. Limiting access to system resources to specific realms or domains prevents an attacker from accessing these protected system resources. Without access, the attacker is unable to launch a successful attack against these resources. Host-based agents, for instance, can limit access to key system resources to prevent an attacker from compromising the system.

Intrusion Detection Evasion Techniques

With any security mechanism, attackers are continually trying to find ways to bypass these protection barriers. Bank robbers are constantly searching for ways to bypass traditional burglar alarms so that they can steal money without being detected. In the same way, attackers are continually trying to find ways to attack your network without being detected. Understanding the following common evasion techniques helps ensure that these avenues do not provide weaknesses in your overall security posture:

- Flooding
- Fragmentation
- Encryption
- Obfuscation
- TTL manipulation

Flooding

One way that attackers attempt to bypass your IDS is by flooding the network with intrusive activity. The goal of this flood is to generate thousands of alarms on your IDS console. Then in the middle of this overwhelming volume of alarm traffic, the attacker conducts a real attack. The attacker hopes that you will not be able to detect the real attack in the middle of all the bogus attack traffic, or respond to it in a timely manner. Unless you IDS has an efficient mechanism for consolidating this flood of alarm traffic, looking for the real intrusive activity can be similar to looking for a needle in a haystack.

Generating a flood of alarm traffic can also wreak havoc on your sensor's resources. Depending on the attack traffic being flooded, an attacker might attempt to consume all the memory or CPU processing power on your sensor. If an attacker can consume a large amount of the resources on your sensor with bogus attacks, the sensor might not have enough resources left to detect the attacker's actual attack against your network.

NOTE   Attackers are beginning to construct tools that generate thousands of alarms to confuse and overload an IDS. An example of such a tool is Stick (http://www.eurocompton.net/stick/projects8.html). This tool floods basic attacks at a network. Its goal is to try to overwhelm the IDS monitoring the network. Unless the IDS can determine that the attacks are invalid or otherwise manage the quantity of alarms generated, tools such as Stick can limit the effectiveness of an IDS.

Fragmentation

When network packets exceed the maximum size for the network, known as the *maximum transmission unit* (MTU), the packets must be chopped into multiple packets in a process known as *fragmentation*. When the receiving host gets the fragmented packets, it must reassemble the data. Not all hosts perform the reassembly process in the same order. Some

OSs start with the last fragment and work toward the first. Others start at the first fragment and work to the last. For normal network traffic, the reassembly order does not matter, because the fragments do not usually overlap, and if they do overlap, the overlapping data is identical. If the overlapping data is not the same, however, the results can differ for each reassembly process.

Attackers can send attacks inside of overlapping fragments to try to circumvent network-based IDSs. For example, assume that a packet is divided into the three fragments shown in Figure 3-3. If the fragments are reassembled from first to last, the assembly order is fragment A, fragment B, and fragment C. In this reassembled packet, the last 25 bytes of fragment B are overwritten by the first 25 bytes of fragment C. On the other hand, assembling the packet from last to first results in the last 25 bytes of fragment B overwriting the first 25 bytes of fragment C. In this area of overlap is where an attacker will attempt to hide his attack traffic. To completely analyze fragmented packets, a network sensor must also reassemble the fragments in both orders. Another way to handle this problem is to generate an alarm when fragments overlap (and the overlapping data differs), because this should not occur in normal traffic.

Figure 3-3   *Overlapping Fragments*

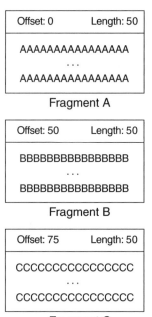

Offset: 0   Length: 50

AAAAAAAAAAAAAAAA
. . .
AAAAAAAAAAAAAAAA

Fragment A

Offset: 50   Length: 50

BBBBBBBBBBBBBBBB
. . .
BBBBBBBBBBBBBBBB

Fragment B

Offset: 75   Length: 50

CCCCCCCCCCCCCCCC
. . .
CCCCCCCCCCCCCCCC

Fragment C

Besides the ordering problem, reassembling fragmented traffic also requires your sensor to store all the individual fragments. This storage consumes memory resources on your IDS sensors. An attacker might flood incomplete fragmented traffic to cause your sensor to consume memory, hoping to launch a real attack after the sensor is low on system resources.

Encryption

One of the drawbacks with a network-based IDS is that it relies on traffic being sent across the network in clear text. If the data traversing the network is encrypted, your network-based IDS is not capable of examining that data. To protect user credentials and other sensitive information, users and network designers are relying on more and more encrypted sessions. Some common examples of encrypted sessions include the following:

- Secure Sockets Layer (SSL) connections to secure websites
- Secure Shell (SSH) connections to SSH servers
- Site-to-site VPN tunnels
- Client-to-LAN virtual private network (VPN) tunnels

If an attacker establishes an SSL connection to your web server, the attacker can then attempt to launch an attack against the website through the established secure connection. Because the traffic is encrypted, your network-based IDS will not be able to detect it. A host-based IDS, however, should still be able to detect this attack.

Obfuscation

Most attackers love to be able to attack your network without being detected. To get past your IDS undetected, many attackers attempt to disguise their attack traffic so that it does look like an attack. One way to accomplish this is through obfuscation. The following list shows some of the major obfuscation techniques:

- Using special characters
- Using hex representation
- Using Unicode representation

Using Special Characters

Control characters and other special characters have a special meaning when processed by the destination host. An example of this is the "../" when used in a URL. These characters, when translated by the destination server, will go back to the previous directory level in the URL. Suppose, for instance, that you specify the URL http://webserver/the/the/../attack/file.html. The web server will process this URL as if you had typed http://webserver/the/attack/file.html. Your IDS must be able to process these control characters to effectively locate attacks that have been obscured with various control characters. Processing the data stream without also processing the control characters will lead to missed attacks and false negatives.

Using Hex Representation

Most people are familiar with the normal ASCII representation for characters. Another way to represent these characters is to use the hexadecimal values. For example, the normal space character can also be represented by the hex value 0x20. Many text-based protocols understand either of these ways of representing characters. Your IDS must also understand these multiple representations. Otherwise, your IDS will not be able to effectively analyze data streams when looking for attack traffic.

Using Unicode Representation

Originally, computers used the ASCII character set to represent characters. This encoding scheme, however, only allows for 256 different characters (because each character is represented by a single byte). As computers became more prevalent, 256 characters were insufficient to provide a unique character for every character needed regardless of platform, program, or language. To overcome this limitation, another encoding mechanism was developed, known as *Unicode*.

Because Unicode uses multiple bytes to represent a single character, it enables a much larger character set than ASCII. This encoding scheme, however, also includes multiple representations for each normal ASCII character (potentially thousands of representations for common characters, such as the forward slash (/) character that is used in numerous attacks). Because the destination host interprets each of these representations as the same character, an attacker can send his attack using many different representations in an attempt to sneak the attack past your IDS. If your IDS does not check for these multiple character representations when performing pattern matching, the attacker's traffic can go across your network undetected.

Unicode

The Unicode encoding mechanism is documented by RFC 2279, "UTF-8, a Transformation Format of ISO 10646." This encoding mechanism basically uses multiple bytes to represent each character, whereas ASCII uses a single byte for each character. Different versions of Unicode use a different number of bytes to represent a single character. Across these multiple versions, you end up with potentially thousands of different representations for common characters (such as the /). Although each of the representations is different, the destination host will process them all as the /. Besides the RFC, you can also find more information on Unicode at http://www.unicode.org.

TTL Manipulation

When traffic traverses your network, each hop (routing device) decreases a packet's TTL value. If this value reaches 0 before the packet reaches its destination, the packet is discarded and an ICMP error message is sent to the sending host.

An attacker can launch an attack that includes bogus packets with smaller TTL values than the packets that make up the real attack. If your network-based sensor sees all of the packets, but the target host only sees the actual attack packets, the attacker has managed to distort the information that the sensor uses, causing the sensor to potentially miss the attack (because the bogus packets distort the information being processed by the sensor). Figure 3-4 illustrates this attack. The bogus packets start with a TTL of 3, whereas the real attack packets start with a TTL of 7. The sensor sees both sets of packets, whereas the target host only sees the real attack packets.

Figure 3-4   *Variable Time-To-Live Attack*

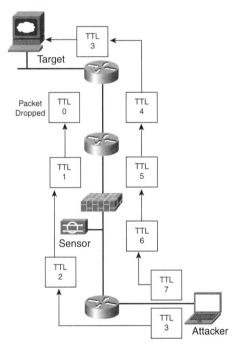

Although this attack is possible, it is very difficult to use in practice because it requires a detailed understanding of the network topology and location of IDS sensors.

Summary

Intrusion detection systems detect attacks against your network by generating alarms when they observe an intrusive activity. These alarms fall into the following categories:

- False positives
- False negatives
- True positives
- True negatives

Although many different IDSs exist, each supports one or more triggering mechanisms. The common triggering mechanisms are as follows:

- Anomaly detection
- Misuse detection
- Protocol analysis

Anomaly detection is more complex than misuse detection, but it provides the capability to detect previously unpublished attacks. The downside is that alarms are not correlated with specific known attacks. An alarm represents a deviation from normal user activity and must be investigated by your security analyst.

Misuse detection can only detect the attacks for which it has signatures. End users know exactly which attacks that a misuse-based IDS will alarm on by listing the signatures in the signature database. Providing updates to the signature database in response to new attacks, however, is a major challenge.

Protocol analysis involves adding another dimension to misuse detection. Besides looking for the normal attack traffic, protocol analysis also verifies that the traffic matches a valid packet for the protocol in question.

Besides IDS triggering, each IDS must also monitor you network at defined locations to obtain the data necessary for the triggering mechanisms to function. The two most common monitoring locations are:

- Host-based
- Network-based

Host-based IDSs check for intrusive activity on the actual hosts on your network. This may be error logs, system calls, or so on. The main benefit of a host-based IDS is that it can determine the success of the attack because the IDS is on the actual host that is being attacked. Host-based IDSs, however, have the drawback that their software must operate on every host on the network. This can be difficult for networks with numerous different OSs.

Network-based IDSs watch for intrusive activity at specific points in the network by observing the packets on the wire. One or more sensors watch the network and generate alarms whenever they observe intrusive activity. The benefit of a network-based IDS is that it does not have to run on every host in the network. Because the IDS is only examining network traffic, the developer is free to choose the best sensor platforms. The major drawbacks of a network-based IDS are:

- Bandwidth limitations
- Encryption

Sometimes a developer will combine multiple triggering mechanisms and monitoring locations into a single IDS. This new IDS is known as a hybrid. The main incentive behind developing hybrid systems is to increase the functionality of the IDS. A hybrid system can perform host-based and network-based monitoring. Another combination could be to combine anomaly detection with misuse detection. The hardest part in creating a successful hybrid system is making the different functions work together in a user-friendly manner.

Attackers are continually trying to find ways to bypass your IDS without being detected. Some of the common IDS evasion techniques are as follows:

- Flooding
- Fragmentation
- Encryption
- Obfuscation
- TTL manipulation

To provide greater protection for your network, IDSs are migrating from a passive role to a more active role in defending your network from attack. Some of the responses and actions that your IDS can perform in response to an attack include the following:

- TCP reset
- IP blocking
- Logging
- Access restriction

Review Questions

The following questions test your retention of the material presented in this chapter. The answers to the review questions are in Appendix B, "Answers to Chapter Review Questions."

1   What are the two major IDS monitoring locations?

2   What are the three types of IDS triggering mechanisms?

3   What is the purpose of an IDS?

4   What is anomaly detection?

5   What is the major drawback to host-based IDS monitoring?

6   What is misuse detection?

7   What is a major benefit of anomaly detection?

8   What is protocol analysis?

9   What are two major limitations of network-based IDSs?

10   What is obfuscation?

11   What is a hybrid IDS?

12   What are some common obfuscation techniques?

13   What are some benefits to misuse-based IDSs?

14   What are the drawbacks to pattern-matching detection?

15   What are some common IDS response techniques?

16   What are some drawbacks to anomaly detection?

17   What is the difference between a true positive and a true negative?

18   What are the common techniques used to evade detection by your IDS?

19   What is the difference between a false positive and a false negative?

Upon completion of this chapter, you will be able to perform the following tasks:

- Define the major features of Cisco intrusion protection solution
- Identify the different Cisco sensor platforms
- Explain Cisco Threat Response
- Identify the major sensor placement locations
- Explain the sensor deployment considerations

CHAPTER 4

Cisco Intrusion Protection

The Cisco intrusion protection system (IPS) is a comprehensive system that enables you to actively defend your network against network attacks, misuse, and unauthorized access. The system incorporates sensors and agents that perform real-time monitoring of traffic at locations throughout your network, from the network level all the way to the host level. Supporting a large base of sensor types enables you to easily and effectively integrate Cisco intrusion detection system (IDS) into almost any network topology.

Sensors monitor network traffic for alarms in real time through a monitoring interface. All alarms are then retrieved via the command and control interface by your management platform.

When your Cisco IDS analyzes network data, it looks for traffic patterns that represent attacks. Patterns can be as simple as an attempt to access a specific port on a specific host, or as complex as sequences of operations directed at multiple hosts over an arbitrary period of time. Besides relying solely on predefined attack patterns and protocol analysis, some Cisco IDS components are beginning to incorporate anomaly detection to enhance their attack detection capability. Furthermore, the Cisco Threat Response (CTR) product reduces your analysis task by performing intelligent threat investigation on the alarms generated by your Cisco IDS.

This chapter examines the Cisco intrusion protection solution by focusing on the following major topics:

- Cisco IDS solution overview
- Cisco IDS sensors
- Cisco Threat Response
- Cisco sensor management
- Cisco alarm monitoring and reporting
- Deploying Cisco IDS

Cisco Intrusion Detection System (IDS) Solution Overview

Cisco IDS enhances the security of your network by providing a comprehensive solution. Cisco IDS is comprised of various components that each enhance the security of your network. Combined into a single solution, these components secure your network by providing the following:

- Intrusion protection
- Active defense
- Defense in depth

Intrusion Protection

Incorporating intrusion protection into your network enables you to take an active role in defending your network against attack, misuse, and unauthorized access. Intrusion protection provides the following key capabilities:

- Enhanced security over classic solutions
- Advanced technology to meet changing threats
- Increased application attack resistance
- Effective attack mitigation
- Broad network visibility
- Greater protection against published and unpublished threats

Enhanced Security over Classic Solutions

Classic IDS solutions passively monitored the network. These systems generated alarms when intrusive activity was detected, but did not provide a comprehensive security solution. Many of these IDSs were not hybrid systems and focused only on specific aspects of your network as opposed to providing monitoring capabilities for every segment of your network. Cisco IDS provides the capability to easily monitor virtually every segment of your network topology. Along with monitoring every facet of your network, the Cisco IDS solution can respond to attacks by resetting TCP connections and blocking traffic from an offending host. Furthermore, the Cisco Security Agent software can actually prevent attacks against the individual hosts on your network.

Advanced Technology to Meet Changing Threats

The threats against your network are continually changing and evolving. Your IDS must evolve to meet these threats. By incorporating the latest IDS technology, Cisco IDS provides an advanced intrusion detection solution that is capable of addressing the changing threats that your network will face. The incorporation of the Intrusion Detection System Module (IDSM), host-based agents, and CTR are just a few examples of how Cisco is continually adding new technology to their IPS solution.

Increased Application Attack Resistance

Providing multiple layers of defense makes it more difficult for an attacker to gain access to the applications on your network without detection. Host-based agents can even prevent attacks from reaching the applications on your servers and desktop systems. These multiple security barriers increase the attack resistance of the applications on your network.

Effective Attack Mitigation

Cisco IDS provides a variety of signature responses to defend against attacks launched at your network. Combined with easily tunable signatures and multiple signature engines that facilitate the creation of custom signatures, Cisco IDS provides an environment to very effectively mitigate attacks against your network. The responses include the following:

- TCP reset
- Blocking
- IP logging

Broad Network Visibility

Supporting a wide range of sensors, you can deploy Cisco IDS throughout your entire network. These sensors enable you to achieve a very broad view of the activity on your network. By monitoring your network at numerous network segments, the chances of an attacker avoiding detection are greatly minimized.

Greater Protection Against Known and Unpublished Threats

With a signature database of approximately 1,000 signatures, Cisco IDS protects against a wide range of known security vulnerabilities at the network level. Combined with anomalous detection at the host level, Cisco IPS also provides protection against previously unpublished attacks. CTR enhances this protection capability by reducing your alarm analysis through intelligent threat investigation to identify valid attacks against vulnerable targets.

Active Defense

Traditionally, security administrators secured their networks by patching known vulnerabilities and defining security requirements such as password policies. This approach is similar to installing locks on the doors and windows of your house to keep burglars out. The problem with this approach is that it represents a passive approach to security.

Because networks are very dynamic entities, a passive approach to security does not provide enough protection in the constantly changing threat-ridden landscape. The Cisco IPS focuses on the following key components:

- Detection
- Prevention
- Reaction

Detection

Before you can do anything in response to an attack, you must detect that someone is attacking your network. Detection is a crucial component of your active defense because it forms the foundation to your security defenses. You can have a dozen different attack responses, but if an attacker can avoid detection, these responses will never be activated.

Another facet of detection is accurately determining the validity of the attacks being launched against your network. CTR performs intelligent threat investigation to help you determine which attacks are being launched at vulnerable targets along with the likelihood of the attack being successful. Combined with signature responses, you can efficiently protect your network while minimizing the impact on your normal network traffic.

Intelligent Threat Investigation

Many IDS systems generate alarms based solely on known attack traffic. The severity of these alarms is based on the damage that the attack can inflict on your network. Intelligent threat investigation goes beyond this by incorporating other factors into the equation, such as the target operating system, patches installed on the target, and target system analysis. By examining these additional factors, the severity of a specific alarm can be adjusted based on the likelihood of the attack being successful.

Prevention

Prevention comes into play after an attack is detected. Just detecting an attack informs you that someone is potentially attacking your network, but it does not necessarily prevent that attack from causing damage to your network. This is similar to an alarm going off because of a burglar breaking a window. Although the alarm is activated, the burglar might still be able to steal your property before the police arrive. By having an effective prevention capability, you actually prevent the attack from executing. Cisco host-based sensors can prevent intrusive traffic from gaining access to the applications on the servers and desktops throughout your network.

Reaction

The final component of an active defense is your ability to react to intrusive activity and halt future attacks from a malicious source. One way to protect your network is to continually watch for malicious traffic on your network and then prevent it from causing damage to your network after it has been detected. Using this approach, however, you keep letting the attacker try new attacks against your network until the attacker potentially finds one that succeeds. A more effective approach is to eliminate all traffic from a specific source address when you determine that the source is malicious. By blocking all traffic from the malicious source (the attacker's IP address), you can be confident that the attacker's traffic can't cause further damage to your network.

You can program your sensors to respond in various ways when different attacks are detected. This response is configurable per signature (usually based on the severity of the attack discovered). The possible responses are as follows:

- TCP reset
- Blocking
- IP logging

The Transmission Control Protocol (TCP) reset response essentially terminates the current TCP connection from the attacker by sending a *TCP reset packet* (see Figure 4-1). This response is effective only for TCP-based connections. UDP traffic, for example, is unaffected by TCP resets.

Figure 4-1   *TCP Reset Response*

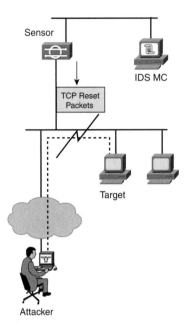

TCP Reset Packet

TCP provides a connection-oriented communication mechanism. The connection is established through a three-way handshake. To terminate a connection, each side of the connection can send a packet with the FIN bit set, signaling the end of the connection. It is also possible, however, for one side of the connection to abruptly terminate the connection by sending a reset packet (packet with the RST flag set) to the other side. The sensor uses this approach to terminate an attacker TCP connection. For a detailed explanation of TCP/IP protocols, refer to *The Protocols (TCP/IP Illustrated, Volume 1)*, by Richard Stevens (Addison-Wesley, 1994).

With the blocking option, the sensor updates the access control lists (ACLs) on one of your routers (or initiates a shun on one of your PIX firewalls) to deny all traffic from the offending IP address (see Figure 4-2). This response prevents the attacker from sending any further traffic into your protected network. (See Chapter 12, "Signature Response" for a detailed description of blocking.)

Figure 4-2   *IP Blocking Response*

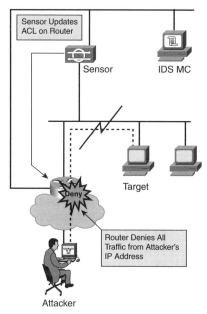

CAUTION   Blocking requires careful review before it is deployed, whether it is used as an automatic response or through operational guidelines for the operators. To implement blocking, the sensor dynamically reconfigures and reloads a Cisco IOS router's ACL (or initiates a shun on a PIX firewall). This type of automated response by the sensor should be configured only for attack signatures with a low probability of false positive detection (or in conjunction with CTR). It is also important not to enable automatic blocking on signatures in which an attacker can easily spoof the source address of the attack. In case of any suspicious activity that does not trigger automatic blocking, you can use the management platform to manually block the attacker. Cisco IDS can be configured to never block specific hosts or networks. This safety mechanism prevents denial-of-service attacks against the Cisco IDS and other critical components.

The third response, IP logging, only records what the attacker is doing (after triggering a signature with logging enabled) in a log file (see Figure 4-3). This option is passive and does not prevent the attacker from continuing the attack. With logging, the actual packets that the attacker is sending are captured on the sensor. You can then examine these packets to determine exactly what traffic the attacker was able to send against your network.

Figure 4-3 *IP Logging Response*

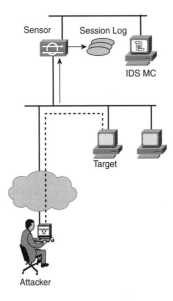

| NOTE | Do not confuse the traditional alarm logging with IP logging. Whenever a signature is triggered, an alarm event is generated and stored on the sensor. This is known as *alarm logging* and should not be confused with IP logging, which is a configurable alarm response. Alarm logging occurs for every signature that has not been disabled. |

Defense in Depth

Any comprehensive security solution needs to contain numerous layers. Breaking through multiple security barriers is definitely harder than having to break through only a single barrier. Cisco IDS protects a broad spectrum of security boundaries by supporting sensors from the host level up through the network level. Some of the major features include the following:

- Application-level encryption protection
- Security policy enforcement (resource control)
- Web application protection
- Buffer overflow detection
- Network attack detection
- Network reconnaissance detection
- Denial-of-service detection
- Multiple monitoring locations

Cisco IDS Sensors

Sensors form the workhorses of your Cisco IDS. They constantly monitor network traffic looking for potential attacks. Each network sensor checks network traffic looking for a match against one of the attack signatures in its signature database. The host-based agents use a behavior-based model to identify traffic that lies outside the traffic considered normal for a given user. The wide variety of sensors enables you to deploy your Cisco IDS to effectively create a robust defense and an in-depth solution to secure your network.

All Cisco IDS network sensors use two types of interfaces:

- Monitoring interface
- Command and control interface

Multiple Monitoring Interfaces

To monitor multiple network segments simultaneously, it is beneficial in some environments to have network sensors support multiple monitoring interfaces (multiple NIC cards). Beginning with Cisco IDS version 4.1, multiple monitoring interfaces are supported. Initially this functionality will be available on the IDS 4215 appliance sensor (the replacement for the 4120 sensor).

The Cisco IDS solution incorporates a wide variety of sensors. These sensors fall into the following categories:

- Network sensors
- Switch sensors
- Router sensors
- Firewall sensors
- Host agents

These different types of sensors also provide different levels of functionality. Table 4-1 outlines the basic capabilities provided by some of the various sensor platforms available for Cisco IDS versions 3.x and 4.x.

Table 4-1 *Sensor Capabilities*

Feature	Appliance Sensor	IDS Module	IDS Network Module
TCP reset	3.x/4.x	4.x	4.x
IP session logging	3.x/4.x	4.x	4.x
Shun/Blocking	3.x/4.x	3.x/4.x	4.x
Active updates	3.x/4.x	3.x/4.x	4.x
Signature language	3.x/4.x	3.x/4.x	4.x
Analysis support	3.x/4.x	3.x/4.x	4.x

Network Sensors

Each network sensor uses at least two network interfaces. One or more of these interfaces monitor network traffic while the other is a command and control interface. All communication with the management platform occurs over the command and control interface. For further information on basic sensor configuration, see Chapter 7, "Cisco IDS Network Sensor Installation."

When network data triggers a signature, the sensor logs the event. Your management platform regularly connects to the sensor to retrieve these events. This pull mechanism prevents the management system from being overwhelmed by a flood of alarm traffic.

NOTE Having the monitoring platform pull the alarm events from the sensor is new to Cisco IDS 4.0. In previous versions, the sensors pushed the alarm events to the monitoring platform. The push technique could lead to missed events if the monitoring platform was temporarily unreachable.

All network sensors are hardware appliances tuned for optimum performance. The hardware, including CPU and memory, for each appliance provides optimal IDS performance, while maintaining ease of maintenance. To protect the sensors, the appliance's host operating system is configured securely. Known security vulnerabilities are patched, and unneeded services are removed.

The 4200 series sensors come in six versions: IDS-4210 (being replaced by the 4215), IDS-4220, IDS-4230, IDS-4235, IDS-4250, and IDS-425-XL.

NOTE Although the IDS-4220 and IDS-4230 will operate with the Cisco IDS 4.0 software, these sensor models have reached end of sale (EOS). They are no longer sold and may no longer be supported.

Switch Sensors

The IDS Module (IDSM) for the Catalyst 6500 family of switches is designed specifically to address switched environments by integrating IDS functionality directly into a Catalyst 6500 series switch. The IDSM receives traffic right off the switch backplane, thus combining both switching and security functionality into the same chassis (see Figure 4-4).

Figure 4-4   *Catalyst 6500 IDS Module*

Some of the major features of IDSM include the following:

- Fully integrated line card
- Multi-VLAN visibility
- Full signature set
- Common configuration and monitoring
- No switching performance impact

There are two versions of IDSM. The original version is supported on Cisco IDS version 2.x and 3.x. A second-generation IDSM blade (IDSM-2) is the only version of IDSM that works with Cisco IDS 4.x.

Intrusion Detection System Module (IDSM)

The original IDSM placed a highly functional IDS sensor directly into the network switch, capturing data directly from the switch's backplane. IDSM can process 150 Mb worth of traffic. Similar to the 4200 series sensor, IDSM detects unauthorized activity on the network and sends alarms to your management platform. It does not, however, provide all of the functionality of the appliance sensor because it is based on a different code base.

IDSM is supported in both Cisco IDS versions 2.x and 3.x. It is not, however, supported by Cisco IDS 4.0 and greater.

Intrusion Detection System Module 2 (IDSM-2)

Unlike the original IDSM, IDSM-2 runs the same code that a Cisco IDS 4.x appliance sensor uses. This means that the IDSM-2 provides the identical functionality as the network sensors. The only differentiating factor is the bandwidth that the different network sensors can process. IDSM-2 can process 500 Mb worth of traffic.

For detailed information on configuration of IDSM-2, see Chapter 8, "Cisco IDS Module Configuration."

Router Sensors

Cisco IDS 4.x supports the following two types of router sensors:

- Cisco IOS IDS
- IDS network module

With Cisco IOS-based router sensors, the IDS functionality is incorporated into the actual Cisco IOS Software. This IDS functionality, however, is limited. The IDS Network Module is a card that you install on your router that has all the functionality of a Cisco IDS 4.0 appliance sensor.

Cisco Internetworking Operating System (IOS) IDS

The Cisco IOS-based router sensor integrates intrusion detection into Cisco IOS software. This Cisco IOS IDS can detect a limited subset of attacks compared to the network or switch sensors and is targeted for lower-risk environments. Some of the features of Cisco IOS IDS include the following:

- The latest software release includes 100 signatures.
- Alarms can be sent to a syslog server or PostOffice-aware device.
- Routers can drop packets and terminate TCP sessions in response to attacks.

If you want to use a Cisco IOS-based device to perform intrusion detection, your Cisco IOS device must meet the following software and hardware requirements:

- IOS Software Release 12.0(5)T or higher
- 1700, 2600, 3600, 3700, 7100, 7200, and 7500 series routers and the Catalyst 5000 series Route Switch Module (RSM)

NOTE   The original IDS functionality in Cisco IOS provided 59 signatures. With Cisco IOS Release 12.2(15)T, the number of signatures increases to 100.

IDS Network Module

The IDS Network Module incorporates the existing appliance sensor code base into a router's network module card. This provides a unique form factor to deploy Cisco IDS sensors on your existing infrastructure equipment. Because it runs the same code base as the appliance sensor, it offers the same management options, and provides a fully functional IDS sensor at a competitive price.

If you want to use an IDS Network Module to perform intrusion detection, your IOS device must have an available slot and be one of the following hardware platforms:

- 2600XM
- 2691
- 3660
- 3725
- 3745

Firewall Sensors

The firewall sensor integrates IDS functionality into the PIX firewall. Like the Cisco IOS-based IDS sensor, the PIX IDS functionality is limited compared to a network or switch sensor. The PIX IDS functionality is intended to add an extra measure of protection for lower-risk environments. Some of the features of the firewall sensor include the following:

- The latest software release includes 55 signatures.
- Alarms can be sent to syslog server.
- It can drop packets and terminate TCP sessions in response to attacks.

If you want to use a firewall sensor to perform intrusion detection, your firewall must meet the following software and hardware requirements:

- PIX firewall 5.2 or higher
- PIX firewall 506E, 515E, 525, and 535

Host Agents

To provide a comprehensive IDS solution, Cisco IDS provides sensors that you can deploy throughout your network. Agents at the host level provide a key component to this solution.

Originally, Cisco host-based agents used Entercept (based on a system call interception technique) provided through a partner agreement with Entercept Security Technologies. This capability has since been replaced by the acquisition of Okena and their Stormwatch product. The current host-based solution (Cisco Security Agent) uses a behavior-based approach to provide a valuable new addition to Cisco IDS functionality.

Cisco Threat Response

Common drawbacks to many IDS systems are the time and resources required to investigate the multitude of alarms representing possible attacks. Network-level sensors trigger alarms based on known attack signatures. These network sensors, however, can't determine whether the attack will succeed against its intended target. (For instance, the host might be patched against the given attack.) Analyzing *false alarms* wastes your valuable and limited security resources.

False Alarm

When an attack is launched against a system that is not vulnerable to the exploit being used, it is known as a false alarm. A common type of false alarm is running a Windows exploit against a Linux system. Many attacks are OS-specific because the vulnerabilities are related to unique OS characteristics. Running one of these attacks against another OS will not produce the same results as running it against the correct OS. Another type of false alarm is attacking the correct OS when the OS has been patched against the attack being used.

CTR enables you to identify false alarms. After eliminating false alarms through its analysis, CTR can vary the severity of alarms that represent actual attacks against valid targets. For instance, you might set the default severity of an alarm to low. Then, when CTR locates an instance of this alarm that is not a false alarm, it can increase the severity of the alarm generated to high to indicate that the attack is being launched against a vulnerable target.

NOTE   Currently, CTR and the sensor are not tightly integrated (meaning that the sensor generates an alarm, CTR modifies its severity, and then this modified alarm is retrieved by your monitoring software). Instead, your monitoring console and CTR both retrieve alarm information from your sensor. Then, CTR updates the severity of the alarms that it receives based on its analysis, but does not change the severity of the alarms retrieved directly from your sensor by your monitoring software.

Cisco Sensor Management

You may deploy multiple types of Cisco IDS sensors on your network to provide complete IDS coverage. Manually monitoring the alarms on each of these sensors is inefficient. The management and monitoring platforms provide the software interface necessary to configure, log, and display alarms (generated by your sensors) to effectively use your Cisco IDS to protect your network from attack. Furthermore, a single management system can consolidate all the alarms from multiple sensors into a single user-friendly interface. Cisco IDS provides the following management and monitoring options:

- Cisco Intrusion Detection Manager (IDM)
- Cisco IDS Event Viewer (IEV)
- Cisco IDS Management Center (IDS MC)
- Cisco IDS Security Monitor
- Cisco Secure Policy Manager (IDS version 3.x only)
- Cisco Intrusion Detection Director (IDS version 3.x only)

NOTE   This book does not provide information on Cisco Secure Policy Manager (CSPM) or Cisco Intrusion Detection Director (CIDD) because the focus here is mainly on Cisco IDS 4.x. These management platforms were described in detail in my previous book on Cisco IDS, *Cisco Secure Intrusion Detection System* (Cisco Press, 2001). These platforms are not supported with Cisco IDS version 4.x.

Cisco IDS 4.0 supports two graphical sensor management platforms:

- Cisco IDS Device Manager
- Cisco IDS Management Center

NOTE   Cisco IDS 4.x sensors also support a command-line interface that you can use to configure your Cisco IDS sensor. This command line is similar to the Cisco IOS command line that you use to configure Cisco routers. For more information on the command-line interface, see Chapter 7.

Cisco IDS Device Manager

Beginning with Cisco IDS version 3.1, you could manage your network sensors using a web-based interface. The Cisco IDS Device Manager (IDM) enables you to manage a single network sensor via an easy-to-use, graphical, web-based interface.

The following web browsers are compatible with IDM:

- Netscape (version 4.79 or later)
- Internet Explorer (version 5.5 Service Pack 2 or later)

NOTE	Although other web browsers can work with IDM, Cisco has only tested and verified two browsers (Netscape and Internet Explorer).

Cisco IDS Management Center

Managing your network sensors individually using IDM can be time-consuming if you have a large number of sensors deployed on your network. To manage larger numbers of network sensors, you can use Cisco IDS Management Center (IDS MC). This product enables you to manage up to 300 sensors across your network from a single management system (via a series of web-based screens).

IDS MC is a component of the CiscoWorks2000 VPN/Security Management Solution (VMS) product. You can deploy IDS MC in the following operating environments:

- Windows 2000 Server (Service Pack 3)
- Windows 2000 Professional (Service Pack 3)
- Solaris (version 2.8)

Cisco Alarm Monitoring and Reporting

Cisco IDS version 4.x supports two mechanisms to analyze the alarms generated by your network-based sensors:

- Cisco IDS Event Viewer
- Cisco IDS Security Monitor

Cisco IDS Event Viewer

Before Cisco IDS version 3.1, your only way to effectively analyze IDS alarms was through a director platform, such as CSPM or IDD. Cisco IDS version 3.1 introduced the Cisco IDS Event Viewer (IEV). IEV is a software application provided with your sensor that enables you to analyze the alarm traffic for up to five network sensors.

You can install IEV on the following two platforms:

- Windows NT 4 Service Pack 6
- Windows 2000 Service Pack 2

Cisco IDS Security Monitor

The Security Monitor is a component of the CiscoWorks2000 VMS product. Unlike IEV, Security Monitor enables you to consolidate events from up to 300 IDS devices.

Deploying Cisco IDS

One of the keys to successfully deploying Cisco IDS to protect your network involves understanding how to effectively deploy intrusion detection sensors throughout your network. The major factors impacting your placement of IDS sensors are as follows:

- Sensor selection
- Sensor placement
- Sensor deployment considerations
- Sensor deployment scenarios

Sensor Selection

Many factors will affect your decision on which Cisco IDS sensors to use throughout your network. Political, financial, and technical issues will impact your sensor selection. Political and financial issues are beyond the scope of this book so this section focuses on the technical factors that you need to consider when choosing Cisco IDS sensors to deploy on your network. You need to consider the following technical factors when choosing sensors:

- Network media
- Performance of intrusion detection analysis
- Network environment

Network Media

To capture network traffic on your network, your Cisco IDS appliance sensors use a NIC. This NIC must match the network media in use on your network. Cisco IDS supports the following common network media types:

- Ethernet
- Fast Ethernet
- Gigabit Ethernet

NOTE   The Gigabit Ethernet support is provided through both fiber (1000BASE-SX) as well as copper interfaces (10/100/1000BASE-TX).

Performance of Intrusion Detection Analysis

As your Cisco IDS sensor captures traffic, it must have enough processing power to analyze that traffic for intrusive activity. The performance of a sensor is rated by the amount of data per second that the sensor can capture and accurately analyze. Cisco provides sensors that have performance ratings from 45 Mbps to 1 Gbps. Cisco IDS provides the high-performance sensors, shown in Table 4-2.

Table 4-2   *Network Sensor Performance Ratings*

Sensor	Performance
IDS Network Module	45 Mbps
IDS 4215	80 Mbps
IDS 4235	250 Mbps
IDS 4250	500 Mbps
IDSM-2	600 Mbps
IDS 4250XL	1000 Mbps

Network Environment

The final factor impacting your sensor selection is your network environment. Different Cisco IDS sensors can handle various traffic loads. Cisco IDS sensors support the following network environments:

- Single T1/E1 environment
- Switched environment
- Multiple T3/E3 environment
- OC-12 environment
- Gigabit environment

Sensor Placement

Cisco IDS supports a variety of different sensor platforms. Each of these platforms has varying capabilities and is designed to operate in a specific network environment. You need to consider the following factors when deciding where to place sensors on your network:

- Internet boundaries
- Extranet boundaries
- Intranet boundaries
- Remote-access boundaries
- Servers and desktops

Figure 4-5 shows a sample network with IDS sensors monitoring key functional boundaries in the network.

Figure 4-5   *Deploying Sensors at Common Functional Boundaries*

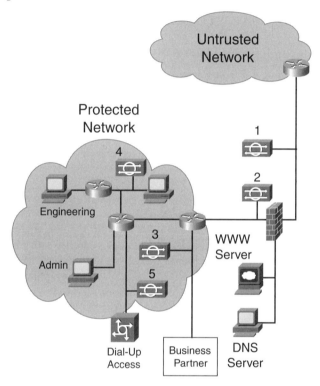

By carefully analyzing your network topology, you can identify the locations at which you want your Cisco IDS to monitor the traffic flow. Then you can determine which Cisco IDS sensor is appropriate for each monitoring location that you have identified.

Internet Boundaries

Sensor 1 in Figure 4-5 monitors the perimeter of the network. All traffic traveling to and from the untrusted network is visible to this sensor. In most networks, the perimeter protection refers to the link between your network and the Internet. Instead of monitoring the traffic outside the firewall, Sensor 2 examines only the traffic that actually passes through the firewall. This can reduce the amount of traffic that the sensor needs to process.

NOTE   Be sure to locate all Internet connections to your network. Many times, administrators forget that remote sites contain Internet connections. Sometimes, departments within your network have their own Internet connection (separate from the corporate Internet connection). Any connection to the Internet needs to be properly monitored.

Extranet Boundaries

Sensor 3 in Figure 4-5 is positioned so that it can monitor the traffic traversing the link between your network and your business partner's network. This extranet link is only as strong as the security applied to both of the networks that it connects. If either network has weak security, the other network becomes vulnerable as well. Therefore, extranet connections need to be monitored. Because the IDS sensor monitoring this boundary can detect attacks in either direction, you might consider sharing the expense of this sensor with your business partner.

Intranet Boundaries

Sensor 4 in Figure 4-5 monitors traffic between the engineering network and the finance network. This is an example of a sensor monitoring traffic between separate network segments within your network. Many times, you use intranets to divide your network into functional areas, such as engineering, research, finance, and human resources. At other times, organizations drive the boundary definitions. For instance, a company might be divided into several product or business units. Each of these business units can in turn also have functional boundaries such as engineering and research. Sometimes, both of these classifications define intranet boundaries.

In this example, the engineering network is separated from the finance network (and the router that separates the other networks) by its own router. For more protection, a firewall is also commonly used. In either situation, you can use a sensor to monitor the traffic between the networks and verify that the security configuration (for the firewall or router) is defined correctly. Traffic that violates the security configuration generates IDS alarms, which you can use as a signal to update the configuration of the firewall or router because it is enforcing the security policy.

Remote-Access Boundaries

Sensor 5 in Figure 4-5 monitors traffic coming from the dialup access server. Numerous war dialers are freely available on the Internet. Therefore, do not think that dialup lines are safe by assuming a hacker cannot determine the phone numbers of your dialup modems. Some common war dialers include the following:

- **Toneloc**—http://www.securityfocus.com/tools/48
- **Modem Finder**—http://packetstormsecurity.org/Win/mfsetup.zip

NOTE   Modems installed on desktop systems also represent a risk to your network. Attacks against these modems will not be detected by your network-based IDS.

Threats Posed by War Dialers

A *war dialer* is a tool that dials a specified range of phone numbers looking for modem connections. An attacker can start a war dialer on the computer and let it run for days, attempting to locate potential modem connections. Later, the attacker attempts to connect to the phone numbers that are listed as modems from the output of the war dialer program. If any of these modem connections has weak authentication mechanisms, the attacker easily infiltrates the network.

Many remote users also use home computers that are continuously connected to the Internet through high-speed Internet connections. If an attacker compromises one of these home systems, it can easily lead to an attack through your remote-access server.

Servers and Desktops

The current Cisco host-based agents enable you to deploy intrusion detection protection on your servers and desktop systems. Each host-based agent is actually a software application that runs on the individual systems on your network, serving as a security barrier around that individual host. These agents provide a final security blanket that can help protect your network from attack. These agents, like the network sensors, can report events to a centralized monitoring center.

Sensor Deployment Considerations

Deploying Cisco IDS on your network requires a well-thought-out design to maximize its effectiveness. Besides the basic sensor capabilities and placement, you must also consider the following important design issues when deploying Cisco IDS on your network:

- Sensor management
- Number of sensors
- Database management
- Software updates

NOTE   The use of encrypted protocols can also impact the deployment of your network sensors. If
you use virtual private networks (VPNs), for instance, you need to place your network
sensors after the VPN traffic is unencrypted. Otherwise, attacks can go unnoticed in the
encrypted data stream.

Sensor Management

Each of your Cisco IDS sensors is monitoring network traffic at a specific location in your
network. You must also, however, be able to communicate with your sensors using their
command and control interface. This communication path enables you to configure and
manage your sensors, as well as retrieve alarm events for monitoring and reporting. Cisco
IDS 4.0 uses a communication protocol that uses Transport Layer Security (TLS) / Secure
Sockets Layer (SSL) and Extensible Markup Language (XML) to provide a standardized
interface between devices. You have two options with respect to your sensor management:

- Out-of-band management network
- In-band management network

An out-of-band management network isolates the management traffic on a separate
network. This isolation minimizes the chances of an attacker attacking your management
systems, because the separate network contains only management traffic. With an in-band
management system, access to the management systems is performed through the normal
data network. In this situation, access to the management systems is usually limited to
specific hosts using access controls on the systems being managed. Although an in-band
management network is harder to secure, it is still commonly used.

Number of Sensors

The number of sensors that you plan to deploy on your network dictates how many
management consoles that you need to deploy to configure and manage your Cisco IDS
sensors. Each management solution is designed to effectively manage a specific number of
sensors. The current two management solutions for Cisco IDS 4.0 are as follows:

- IDS Device Manager (IDM)
- IDS Management Center (IDS MC)

IDM enables you to configure a single sensor. This software is provided with Cisco IDS
sensors that provide full IDS functionality. IDS MC, on the other hand, enables you to
configure up to a maximum of 300 sensors from one management and monitoring system.
The effective ratio depends on the number of alarms generated by your sensors. In normal
operation, a more realistic ratio is probably in the range of 20 to 30 sensors per monitoring
system.

Along with the actual management software, the number of sensors that you deploy on your network dictates the number of personnel that you need to employ to effectively manage your Cisco IDS devices.

Database Management

Your management system stores your sensor configuration information, along with event data from all of your sensors. You have a fixed amount of space on your management system database. Therefore, you need to determine how many days' worth of alarm data you can maintain on your management system without needing to archive the information out of your main system database. Periodically, you need to move these archive files to another system. When you know the frequency at which you need to back up your event data, you can then decide on an appropriate schedule to perform the data archival and backup.

Software Updates

New signatures are continually being added to Cisco IDS. It is vital that you have a well-defined plan on how to regularly update the software on your Cisco IDS devices. Some of the main questions that you need to consider include the following:

- How frequently are signature updates released?
- How frequently are software updates released?
- Where will the updates be stored locally?
- How will the updates be rolled out?

Sensor Deployment Scenarios

All the points where data enters your network represent potential locations at which an attacker can gain access to your network. You need to verify that each entry point is adequately monitored. Not monitoring an entry point into your network allows an attacker to penetrate your network undetected by your IDS. Common entry points into most networks that require protection include the following:

- Internet
- Extranet
- Intranet
- Remote access
- Server farm

Internet Protection

Your network's Internet connection makes your network visible to the entire Internet. Attackers worldwide can attempt to gain access to your network through this entry point. With many corporate networks, access to the Internet is directed through a single router. This device is known as a *perimeter router*. By placing a sensor behind this device, you can monitor all traffic (including attacks) destined for your corporate network. If your network contains multiple perimeter routers, you might need to use multiple sensors, one to watch each Internet entry point into your network.

NOTE   Current estimates project that 171 million hosts are connected to the Internet, with more than 665 million Internet users worldwide. Any of these users can potentially attack your network through your Internet connection. (Sources are "Internet Domain Survey Number of Hosts," by the Internet Software Consortium, http://www.isc.org/ds/host-count-history.html; and "USA Tops 160M Internet Users," by Computer Industry Almanac Inc., http://www.c-i-a.com/pr1202.htm.)

Extranet Protection

Many corporate networks have special connections to business partners' networks. Traffic from these business partners' networks does not always travel through your network's perimeter device; therefore, it is important to make sure that these entry points are also monitored effectively. These connections have an implied level of trust, but that trust can't be assured. By penetrating your business partners' networks, an attacker can use the extranet to infiltrate your network. You usually have little or no control over the security of your business partners' networks. Furthermore, if an attacker penetrates your network and then uses the extranet link to attack one of your business partners, you are faced with a potential liability issue.

Intranet Protection

Intranets represent internal divisions within your network. These divisions might be organizational or functional. Sometimes, different departments within your network require different security considerations, depending on the data and resources that they need to access or protect. Usually, these internal divisions are already separated by a firewall, signaling different security levels between the different networks. Other times, the network administrator uses ACLs on the router between network segments to enforce separate security zones. Placing a sensor between these networks (in front of the firewall or router) enables you to monitor the traffic between the separate security zones and verify compliance with your defined security policy.

Sometimes you also might want to install a sensor between network segments that have complete access to each other. In this situation, you want the sensor to monitor the types of traffic between the different networks, even though by default you have not established any physical barriers to traffic flow. However, any attacks between the two networks are quickly detected.

Remote-Access Protection

Most networks provide a means to access the network through a dialup phone line. This access allows corporate users to access network functionality, such as e-mail, when away from the office. Although this enhanced functionality is useful, it also opens up another avenue for an attacker to exploit. You probably need to use a sensor to monitor the network traffic from your remote-access server, just in case an attacker can defeat your remote-access authentication mechanism.

Many remote users use home systems that connect continuously through high-speed Internet connections, such as cable modems. Because these systems are usually minimally protected, attackers frequently target and compromise these home systems, which might also lead to a compromise of your remote-access mechanism. Other times, stolen laptops reveal a wealth of information on how to access your network. Therefore, even if you trust your users and remote-access mechanisms, it is beneficial to monitor your remote-access servers with IDS.

Desktop and Server Protection

Monitoring and protecting the various boundaries on your network is crucial to developing a strong security solution. The majority of the attacks currently available are written to exploit vulnerabilities in the common host operating systems, so the final security barrier is actually the hosts on your network. Cisco host-based agents enable you to monitor and protect traffic at the individual operating system level on all the hosts on your network.

Summary

Cisco IDS is a comprehensive IPS that uses signatures, protocol analysis, and anomaly detection to trigger intrusion alarms. It supports sensors from the network level all the way through the host level. Besides detecting intrusive traffic, Cisco IDS provides an active defense that focuses on the following three factors:

- Detection
- Prevention
- Reaction

Deploying sensors at multiple locations throughout your network enables you to develop a strong defense in depth solution. Besides detecting intrusive activity, sensors can also respond to attacks through the following three mechanisms:

- TCP reset
- Blocking
- IP logging

Cisco IDS sensors represent the eyes of your security solution. The more eyes that you have looking at your network, the less likely that it is that an attack will be able to sneak through your network undetected. You can deploy the following type of sensors throughout your network:

- Network sensors
- Switch sensors
- Router sensors
- Firewall sensors
- Host agents

Each sensor has a monitoring interface and a command and control interface. Using the monitoring interface, the sensor compares network traffic against the signatures in its signature database. If unauthorized activity is detected, your management system uses the sensor's command and control interface to communicate with the sensor and retrieve alarm events. Cisco IDS supports many different sensor platforms. The three sensors based on the Cisco IDS 4.0 appliance sensor code base are as follows:

- 4200 series appliance sensors
- IDSM-2
- IDS Network Module

The 4200 series sensors are PC appliances that can be placed at various locations throughout your network. The 4200 series sensors come in six varieties: IDS-4210 (to be replaced by the IDS 4125), IDS-4220, IDS-4230, IDS-4235, IDS-4250, and IDS-425-XL.

NOTE   The IDS-4220 and IDS-4230 have reached end of sale. They are no longer sold and may no longer be supported.

IDSM is an actual integrated line card that operates directly on the Catalyst switch. It receives packets directly from the switch's backplane. The switch's performance is not impacted, however, because the IDSM operates on copies of the network packets. With the second generation of IDSM (IDSM-2), this sensor runs the same code base as the appliance sensors. This makes both sensor platforms equal in functionality. Only IDSM-2 is supported by Cisco IDS 4.0 and greater.

The final Cisco IDS sensor based on the Cisco IDS 4.0 appliance sensor code base is the IDS Network Module. This sensor is a network module (card) that you insert into your router (similar to the IDSM being used in your Catalyst 6000 series switch).

To configure your sensors, you need to use some type of management platform. Cisco IDS 4.x supports the following two management platforms:

- IDS Device Manager (IDM)
- IDS Management Center (IDS MC)

IDM enables you to configure a single sensor. If you deploy many sensors on your network, IDM is not an effective solution. IDS MC enables you to manage up to 300 sensors from a single management system.

After configuring your Cisco IDS sensors, you also need a mechanism to view the alarms generated by your sensors. Cisco IDS 4.x supports the following two reporting and monitoring platforms:

- IDS Event Viewer (IEV)
- IDS Security Monitor

IEV enables you to monitor up to five sensors and is designed for small sensor deployments. If your Cisco IDS uses more sensors, you can use the Security Monitor product to monitor up to 300 sensors.

When deploying your Cisco IDS solution, you must consider the following major factors:

- Sensor selection
- Sensor placement

Some other considerations that you need to analyze include the following factors:

- Sensor management
- Number of sensors
- Database management
- Software updates

Finally, to be a true comprehensive security solution, your Cisco IDS needs to monitor the various boundaries on your network. Watching the multiple boundaries throughout your network reduces the risk of an attacker sneaking through your defenses undetected. Your Cisco IDS needs to provide protection at the following areas on your network:

- Internet protection
- Extranet protection
- Intranet protection
- Remote-access protection
- Desktop and server protection

Review Questions

The following questions test your retention of the material presented in this chapter. The answers to the review questions are in Appendix B, "Answers to Chapter Review Questions."

1 What are the two monitoring and reporting options available with Cisco IDS version 4.0?

2 What are the two programs that you can use to configure and manage your sensors with Cisco IDS version 4.0?

3 How many different types of sensor platforms are supported by Cisco IDS?

4 Which 4200 series sensors can process the most traffic?

5 What are the three types of responses that a sensor can perform in reply to an attack?

6 What is IDSM?

7 What is Cisco Threat Response?

8 What is a false alarm?

9 Where are the common network boundaries at which you need to deploy Cisco IDS sensors?

10 How many sensors can be managed by IDS MC?

11 You can use IEV to view the alarms from how many sensors?

12 If you are going to deploy 100 Cisco IDS sensors on your network, what management solution would you probably use?

13 If your Cisco IDS solution consists of two sensors, what monitoring and reporting tool would you probably use?

14 Cisco IDS provides an active defense for your network that focuses on what three factors?

15 What is IP logging?

16 How does the TCP reset response work?

Upon completion of this chapter, you will be able to perform the following tasks:

- Define the major components of the Cisco IDS 4.0 software architecture
- Explain the different user accounts and roles
- Explain the Cisco IDS 4.0 communication architecture

CHAPTER 5

Cisco IDS Architecture

By understanding the Cisco intrusion detection system (IDS) architecture, you can effectively and efficiently deploy Cisco IDS on your network and maximize its capabilities. Two important attributes are the software and communication architecture that Cisco uses. This chapter illustrates the major facets of the Cisco IDS 4.0 architecture and is divided into the following topics:

- Past software architecture
- Cisco IDS 4.0 software architecture
- Cisco IDS 4.0 communication architecture
- User accounts and roles

By understanding these various aspects of the Cisco IDS architecture, you will have a more complete understanding of how your Cisco IDS operates. Starting with Cisco IDS 4.0, the communication architecture was completely changed. To help illustrate these changes, it is helpful to first review the previous communication architecture.

Past Software Architecture

Prior to Cisco IDS 4.0, the communication architecture was based on the proprietary PostOffice protocol. With this communication architecture, your Cisco IDS sensors pushed alarm information to your director platform.

In the PostOffice environment, the sensor and director each had separate operational software components that were referred to as *services*. Because each major IDS function was accomplished by a separate service, the result was a security system that was fast, durable, and scalable. Figure 5-1 shows the architecture of a pre–version 4.0 sensor.

Figure 5-1 *Pre–Cisco IDS 4.0 Sensor Architecture*

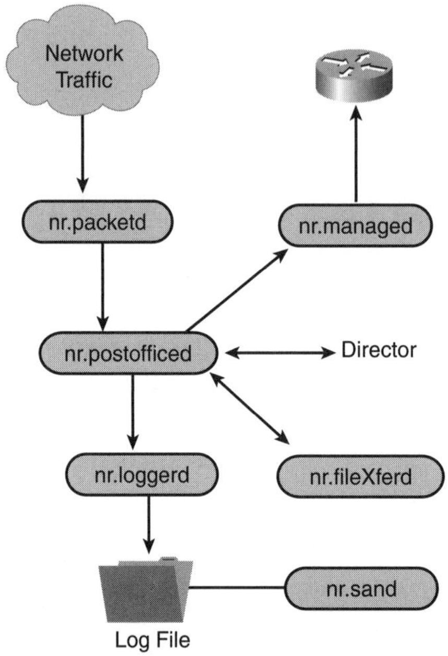

The sensor used nr.packetd to capture packets directly from your monitored network. nr.packetd then conducted an intrusion detection analysis on these packets to locate potential intrusive activity. Finally, nr.packetd forwarded any intrusion alarms to nr.postofficed for distribution.

nr.postofficed operated as a sort of traffic cop. It distributed messages based on your configured signature settings. For instance, if a signature was configured to block an attacking host, nr.postofficed routed the blocking message to nr.managed. nr.managed then created the appropriate access control list (ACL) and applied it to a specific interface on your Cisco IOS router. For a detailed explanation of the PostOffice architecture, refer to the first Cisco Press book on the Cisco IDS, *Cisco Secure Intrusion Detection System* (ISBN: 1-58705-034x).

Cisco IDS 4.0 Software Architecture

Beginning with Cisco IDS 4.0, the entire communication infrastructure on the sensors was rewritten. Therefore, the services running on the sensor were changed to match this new communication infrastructure. Figure 5-2 shows the Cisco 4.0 software architecture. By comparing this to the architecture illustrated in Figure 5-1, you can see how dramatically the sensor architecture has changed.

Figure 5-2   *Cisco IDS 4.0 Software Architecture*

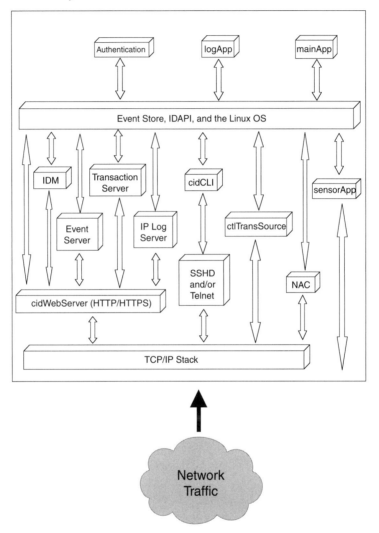

One of the main differences of the new architecture is that the sensor no longer pushes events to your monitoring system. Instead, with Cisco IDS 4.0, your monitoring system pulls the events from the sensor as it is ready to process the events. By pulling events from the sensors as it is ready to process them, the monitoring system no longer loses alarms, because the sensor is sending events when the monitoring system is not prepared to handle them.

The Cisco IDS 4.0 software architecture can be broken down into the following main interacting applications or processes:

- cidWebServer
- mainApp
- logApp
- Authentication
- NAC
- ctlTransSource
- sensorApp
- Event Store
- cidCLI

cidWebServer

The *cidWebServer* application is the sensor's web server interface that facilitates interaction between the sensor and other Cisco IDS components on your network. This web server is capable of both HTTP and HTTPS communication sessions. Instead of just providing static web pages, however, the web server provides functionality via several *servlets*. These servlets perform most of the real work accomplished via the cidWebServer application. One of the main functions provided by the web server is a front-end for the IDS Device Manager (IDM).

Servlets

A servlet is a shared library that is loaded into the cidWebServer process at run time.

The cidWebServer uses the following servlets to provide its functionality:

- IDM servlet
- Event Server servlet
- Transaction Server servlet
- IP Log Server servlet

NOTE   All of the cidWebServer application's servlets communicate with the Remote Data Exchange Protocol (RDEP). RDEP serves as the sensor's external communication protocol. For more information on RDEP, see the section "Cisco IDS 4.0 Communication Architecture" later in this chapter.

Intrusion Detection System Device Manager (IDM) Servlet

The IDM servlet provides the IDM web-based management interface. You can use this interface to configure your sensors one sensor at a time.

Event Server Servlet

The Event Server servlet is responsible for serving events to external management applications, such as IDS Event Viewer (IEV) and Security Monitor.

Transaction Server Servlet

Whenever an external management application needs to configure or control your sensor, it needs to initiate a control transaction with the sensor. The Transaction Server servlet manages these control transactions. For instance, IDS Management Center (IMC) uses control transactions to configure your sensors.

IP Log Server Servlet

The IP Log Server servlet enables external systems to assess IP log information from the sensor. Like alarm events, IP log information is stored on your sensor until retrieved by an external application (such as IEV).

mainApp

The *mainApp* process is the first application to be launched on the sensor. It is responsible for configuring the sensor's operating system configuration (such as the IP address). The mainApp also handles starting and stopping all the other Cisco IDS applications.

logApp

Your sensor logs various application messages to log files. The *logApp* application handles writing all of an application's log messages to the log files on the sensor. It is also responsible for writing an application's error messages to the Event Store.

Authentication

The *authentication* process configures and manages user authentication on the sensor. User access to the sensor is based on the following three factors:

- Username
- Password
- Assigned role

When accessing the sensor, a user must specify a valid username and password combination to gain authenticated access to the sensor. Then the authorization for the user is handled by the user role that is assigned to the specified username. User roles and accounts are explained in detail later in this chapter.

Network Access Controller (NAC)

Your sensors support the ability to block traffic from an attacking system. This blocking action is enabled by the sensor communicating with one of your network devices and updating an ACL to block the offending system (initiating a **shun** command on a PIX firewall). The sensor uses the *Network Access Controller* (NAC) process to initiate blocking.

ctlTransSource

Sometimes one of your sensors needs to initiate a control transaction with another one of your sensors. This functionality is performed by the *ctlTransSource* application. Currently, ctlTransSource is used to enable the master blocking sensor functionality. Master blocking functionality is explained in chapter 12, "Signature Response."

sensorApp

The *sensorApp* process performs the actual sensing functionality on the sensor. Initially, the sensorApp processes the signature and alarm channel configurations for the sensor. Then it generates alert events based on this configuration and the IP traffic that is traversing the sensor's monitoring interface. The sensorApp stores these events (like all other applications) in the Event Store. The sensorApp process is subdivided into the following two components:

- Virtual sensor
- Virtual alarm

Virtual Sensor

The virtual sensor component receives packets, processes them, and determines whether they constitute an alarm. It is comprised of the following functionality:

- Performs Layer 2 signature processing
- Compares fragmented traffic to signatures, looking for problems, such as excessive fragmentation, and performs fragment reassembly
- Provides persistent storage for captured traffic while it is analyzed

- Processes TCP traffic looking for stream-related signatures, such as a TCP hijack signature, and determines whether the traffic is part of a valid TCP stream
- Compares captured traffic to all of the various signatures

Virtual Alarm

The virtual alarm component is responsible for outputting alarms to the downstream Event Store, as well as for starting any configured event actions for the signature.

Event Store

The *Event Store* is a large, shared, memory-mapped file where all events are stored on your sensor. The Event Store holds the events on your sensor in a 4-GB circular queue until you retrieve those events using your monitoring software or the events get overwritten. By storing the events on the sensor, your alarms are not lost, even if your monitoring software losses network connectivity with your sensor for a short period of time. On the downside, if the circular queue fills up, your sensor will overwrite log information that you have not retrieved via your monitoring program. During normal operation, however, your sensor can log information for a couple of days without filling up the queue and overwriting any event data. The sensorApp is the only application that will write alert events into the Event Store, but all other applications might write log, status, and error events into the Event Store.

cidCLI

The *cidCLI* process is the process initiated when a user logs in to the sensor via either Telnet or Secure Shell (SSH). A separate cidCLI process is started for each command-line interfaced (CLI) user shell.

Cisco IDS 4.0 Communication Architecture

Beginning with Cisco IDS 4.0, the entire communication architecture was completely rewritten. The PostOffice protocol is no longer used. Instead, RDEP is now used for external Cisco IDS device communications. Internal sensor communication between applications has also been revised.

Communication Overview

Unlike previous versions of Cisco IDS (which relied on the PostOffice protocol), Cisco IDS version 4.0 is based on the following two communication protocols:

- Intrusion Detection Application Program Interface (IDAPI)
- Remote Data Exchange Protocol (RDEP)

IDAPI handles interaction between applications located on the same system, whereas RDEP is used for external communications that must traverse the network.

Intrusion Detection Application Program Interface

IDAPI handles intraprocess communication on your sensor. This interface provides a means to store and share data among the various IDS applications running on the same sensor.

Remote Data Exchange Protocol

Besides communicating between different applications or processes located on your sensor, your sensor must also communicate with other Cisco IDS components on your network, such as IEV. RDEP, which handles all sensor communications with external systems. It uses HTTP and Transport Layer Security / Secure Sockets Layer (TLS/SSL) to pass Extensible Markup Language (XML) documents (over an encrypted session) between the sensor and external systems. XML files on the sensor control the configuration and operation of your sensor.

RDEP operations begin with a client initiating an encrypted HTTP over a TLS/SSL connection with an RDEP server. This connection is authenticated to the RDEP server using valid login credentials. When the connection is established, the client sends an RDEP request to the RDEP server (see Figure 5-3).

Figure 5-3 *RDEP Requests and Responses*

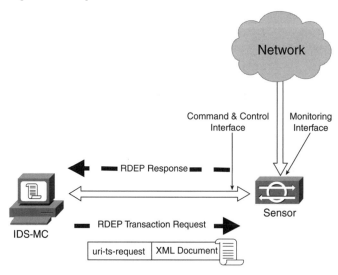

The RDEP server responds to the request with an RDEP response message. When the client initiates a request, it specifies one of the following keywords in the HTTP Uniform Resource Identifier (URI):

- **uri-es-request**   Event request
- **uri-ts-request**   Transaction request
- **uri-iplog-request**   IP log request

The client uses the **uri-es-request** keyword to specify an event request to the RDEP server. The client can issue one of the following two types of event requests:

- Queries
- Subscriptions

Queries are used to retrieve events from the sensor based on a specified query. These queries retrieve events from the events stored in the sensor's Event Store. These queries retrieve a snapshot of the events based on the query criteria.

Subscriptions enable a client to establish a live event feed with the sensor based on specific query criteria. Instead of performing a simple query against the Event Store, the subscription enables the client to retrieve events from the sensor over an extended period of time. After the client opens a subscription with the sensor, it can continuously retrieve new events by sending get requests for the subscription. Each get request will retrieve the events that have been received by the sensor since the last get request that was issued by the client.

Each RDEP message consists of an HTTP header section followed by an optional entity, or message body. Event and transaction message entity bodies consist of XML documents. Your sensor configuration is stored in XML documents on your sensor so processing XML information is built in to the Cisco IDS software architecture. The schema for the XML documents is based on the Intrusion Detection Interaction and Operations Messages (IDIOM) specification.

IDIOM

The Intrusion Detection Interaction and Operations Messages (IDIOM) specification defines the content of XML documents that are communicated between Cisco IDS devices using the RDEP protocol. By following the IDIOM and RDEP specifications, it is easy for third-party applications to interact with the Cisco IDS.

RDEP is an application-level communications protocol that is used to exchange IDS events, IP log information, and sensor configuration information between your sensor and an external system. RDEP communication is comprised of request and response messages. The following three classes of request messages are supported by RDEP:

- Event messages
- IP log messages
- Transaction messages

Event Messages

Event messages include IDS alarm, status, and error messages. Monitoring applications, such as IEV and the Security Monitor, use RDEP to retrieve these events from the sensor. Because the monitoring application is responsible for retrieving or pulling the events (such as alarms) from the sensor, it can request the events at a pace that it can handle.

Events on the sensor are stored in a 4-GB circular queue. Because this queue is large, your monitoring application can lose connectivity for a fairly long time without losing any alarms. Under normal conditions, the Event Store takes at least a couple of days to fill up. Nevertheless, your monitoring application must retrieve events from the sensor before the queue becomes full, otherwise the sensor will start overwriting the unread events. During normal operation, however, your sensor can log information for a couple of days without filling up the queue and overwriting any event data.

Circular Queue

The circular queue used by Cisco IDS is a 4-GB, fixed-length file. As events are added to the file, it gradually gets full. When the file is full, the sensor starts overwriting the events at the beginning of the file. This process is repeated indefinitely, enabling the sensor to maintain a fixed amount of storage for events.

IP Log Messages

You can configure signatures to log the packets coming from the attacking system after a signature fires. These packets are stored on your sensor and represent the actual packets coming from the attacking system. Through the IP log RDEP request messages, your external monitoring application can request copies of the IP log information stored on the sensor. This information can also be viewed via the sensor CLI interface.

Transaction Messages

The first two message types are used by external systems to retrieve information from your sensor. Your management software uses the transaction messages to configure and control the operation of your sensor. This is accomplished by sending XML information that the sensor uses to change the configuration on the sensor and alter its operational characteristics.

User Accounts and Roles

Access to your sensor is controlled through the establishment of user accounts. To authenticate each user who will be accessing your sensor, you assign them a username and a password. Then to limit the capabilities of each of these users, you assign their account a role that defines the operations that can be performed on the sensor. You can assign the following roles to user accounts on your sensor:

- Administrator
- Operator
- Viewer
- Service

The account roles enable users to configure the sensor as well as view or retrieve alarm information. Although the Viewer role does not have any configuration capabilities, it can retrieve sensor alarm events. This makes the Viewer role an excellent role to assign IEV, because it requires only the capability to retrieve information from the sensor.

Administrator

The *Administrator* role is the most privileged role that you can assign to a user who uses the sensor's CLI, IMC, or IDM program. Any accounts associated with the Administrator role can perform any available operations on the sensor as well as retrieve alarm events.

Operator

The *Operator* role is a cross between the Administrator role and the Viewer role. It enables a user to perform all viewing operations in association with some administrative functions.

Viewer

The *Viewer* role is the least privileged of all the user roles. It enables a user to access the sensor for viewing purposes only. It does not enable the user to change the configuration of the sensor.

Service

The *Service* role is a special account that enables users to log in to a native OS command shell rather than the sensor's normal CLI interface. The purpose of this account is not to support configuration of the sensor, but instead to provide an enhanced troubleshooting capability. By default, your sensor does not have a service account. You must create a service account to enable the Technical Assistance Center (TAC) to use this account during troubleshooting.

The sensor only enables you to assign the Service role to one account on the sensor. When the service account's password is set (or reset), the system's root account password is automatically synchronized to this new password. This enables the service account user to use the **su** command to access root privileges on the sensor.

CAUTION   Making modifications to your sensor using the Service account can make your sensor unsupported by the Cisco TAC. Cisco does not support adding services or programs to your sensor because it can impact the proper performance and functioning of the other IDS services.

Summary

Beginning with Cisco IDS version 4.0, Cisco reengineered the architecture on the Cisco IDS sensors. The PostOffice protocol is no longer used as the communication vehicle between Cisco IDS sensors and other Cisco IDS devices. Now the RDEP is used for all external sensor communication.

Your monitoring software pulls events from the sensor periodically. This replaced the previous push model in which the sensors sent their information to your monitoring software as they occurred.

The software changes incorporated into Cisco IDS fall into the following major categories:

* Cisco IDS version 4.0 software architecture
* Cisco IDS version 4.0 communication architecture
* User accounts and roles

The structure of the software on your version 4.0 Cisco IDS sensors breaks down the analysis process into the following three major functional components:

* Packet capture and decoding
* Virtual sensor processing
* Virtual alarm processing

Packets are captured off the network and decoded by Cisco IDS. This process involves performing the following operations:

* Capturing and buffering packets
* Parsing the Layer 3 and Layer 4 headers
* Checking the validity of the packet's checksums
* Checking the validity of the packet's length fields

Next Cisco IDS performs virtual sensor processing on the packets. This involves the following important operations:

* Layer 2 processing
* Fragment analysis and reassembly
* TCP stream analysis and reassembly
* Signature processing

Finally, when alerts are generated, they can trigger your sensor to react to the traffic via the following actions:

- Reset the TCP connection (reset action)
- Shun traffic from the attacking system (shun action)
- Log traffic from the attacking system (IP log action)

The communication between your sensors and other Cisco IDS devices is now based on RDEP. This protocol uses HTTP and TLS/SSL to pass XML documents between your Cisco IDS devices and your sensors. When an RDEP connection is established, the client issues an RDEP request and the RDEP server replies with a response message. The following three request message types are supported by RDEP:

- Event messages
- IP log messages
- Transaction messages
- Besides using a new communication protocol, Cisco IDS version 4.0 stores configuration information differently. In previous versions of Cisco IDS, configuration information was stored in various configuration files (such as packetd.conf and managed.conf). These configuration files contained tokens (such as RecordOfInternalAddress) to specify the sensor configuration. In version 4.0, much of the configuration information is consolidated into a few XML files.

User authentication has also changed dramatically with Cisco IDS version 4.0. Beginning in version 4.0, you no longer log in to an OS command line on your sensor. Instead, your users access the sensor through a Cisco IOS-like CLI. Furthermore, to restrict the operations that each user can perform on the sensor, you can assign one of the following roles to your users:

- Administrator
- Operator
- Viewer
- Service

The Administrator role is the most privileged, going down to the Viewer role, which is the least privileged. The Service role is a special role that enables you to gain system shell access. It is intended for troubleshooting purposes only and can only be assigned to one account on your sensor.

Review Questions

The following questions test your retention of the material presented in this chapter. The answers to the review questions are in Appendix B, "Answers to Chapter Review Questions."

1 How many different privilege roles can be assigned to a user account on your sensor?

2 What protocol is used between your sensor and other Cisco IDS devices?

3 What three major processing steps does your sensor use to analyze your network traffic?

4 Instead of using the tokens found in previous versions of Cisco IDS, in what format does Cisco IDS version 4.0 store its configuration data?

5 What is the most privileged role (that uses the sensor CLI) that you can assign to a user account?

6 What is the least privileged role that you can assign to a user account?

7 Is external sensor communication traffic via RDEP encrypted?

8 How large is the circular buffer where your sensor stores event information?

9 What are the three types of request messages supported by RDEP?

10 What are two types of RDEP event requests?

11 Can you assign the Service role to multiple accounts on your sensor?

12 What is the purpose of the service account?

13 Which protocol controls intraprocess communication?

Upon completion of this chapter, you will be able to perform the following tasks:

- Describe the basic types of devices used to capture traffic for your IDS sensors
- Explain the commands used to monitor network traffic using SPAN
- Explain the difference between using SPAN and RSPAN
- Explain the commands used to monitor network traffic using VACLs
- Identify the steps used to define a VACL

CHAPTER 6

Capturing Network Traffic

At the network level, your Cisco intrusion detection system (IDS) sensors are the eyes of your intrusion protection system (IPS). But to detect intrusive activity, your sensors must be able to view the traffic that is traversing your network. Through its monitoring interface, each of your sensors examines the network traffic that it sees. Unless the monitoring interface is plugged into a hub (and all traffic being monitored goes through that hub), you must configure your infrastructure devices to pass specified network traffic to your sensor's monitoring interface. Besides identifying the infrastructure devices that you can use to pass network traffic to your sensors, this chapter also examines the following three mechanisms that you can use to configure Cisco switches to mirror traffic to your sensor's monitoring interface:

- Switch Port Analyzer
- Remote Switch Port Analyzer
- VLAN access control lists

Traffic Capture Devices

For your Cisco IDS sensors to detect intrusive activity, they must be able to view the traffic that traverses your network. Your sensor's monitoring interface is directly connected to an infrastructure device that mirrors specified network traffic to your sensor for analysis. You can use the following three network devices to pass traffic to your sensors:

- Hubs
- Network taps
- Switches

Hubs

A hub is a very simple network device. Whenever a device connected to the hub generates network packets, the hub passes that traffic to all the other ports on the hub. Figure 6-1 shows how when Host A sends traffic to Host C, all the other devices connected to the hub also receive a copy of the traffic. The other devices connected to the hub just ignore the traffic that does not match their Ethernet Media Access Control (MAC) address.

Figure 6-1   *Hub Traffic Flow*

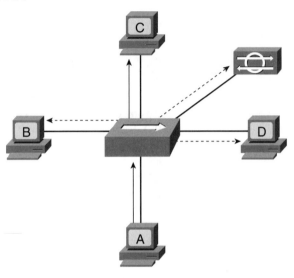

Ethernet MAC Address

Just like you can send traffic to a host based on its IP address at the IP layer, each host also has an address at the link layer known as the *Ethernet MAC address*. This address is a 48-bit (6-byte) value that indicates the link-layer address that other devices on the same network segment use to send traffic to it.

If the network segment that you want to monitor with your Cisco IDS sensor uses a hub, your sensor has access to the network traffic just by connecting its monitoring interface into a port on the hub. Unlike other devices that ignore the traffic that does not match their Ethernet MAC address, your sensor puts its interface in promiscuous mode so that it accepts all packets that its network interface card receives.

NOTE   Any system connected to a hub can place its interface card into promiscuous mode and view all the traffic traversing the network. That is one of the security risks associated with using a hub on a network.

Network Taps

Sometimes, you need to monitor a network segment between two infrastructure devices that are connected without an intervening switch or hub. In this situation, you can use a network tap to capture the traffic traversing the segment. A network tap is a device that enables you to split a full-duplex connection into two separate traffic flows (each flow representing the traffic originating from one of the two devices). The separate traffic flows can then be redirected to an aggregation switch and eventually to your sensor.

Aggregation Switch

An aggregation switch is just a switch that you use to combine the multiple traffic flows and pass the traffic to your sensor. When aggregating flows through the switch, however, you must be careful not to exceed the capacity of your sensor. If your sensor is an IDS 4215 appliance sensor, for instance, aggregating two 100-Mbps traffic flows can exceed the sensor's capabilities because it is not rated at 200 Mbps (the maximum capacity of the combined two flows). To handle higher traffic loads, you either need to deploy more sensors or use a sensor capable of monitoring higher traffic loads (such as the IDS 4250).

Figure 6-2 shows a situation in which you want to monitor the network traffic traversing between a Cisco router and a PIX firewall. Initially these devices are connected to each other directly. To enable you to monitor this traffic, you can install a network tap between these devices. The network tap then continues to pass the traffic between the router and the firewall, but also sends a copy of this traffic (via the two specific flows) to your aggregation switch.

Figure 6-2   *Network Tap Traffic Flow*

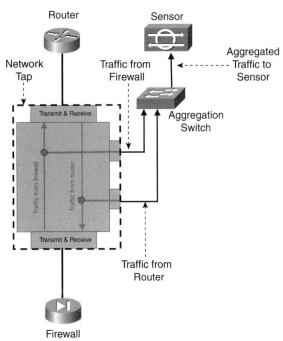

Switches

Probably the most common link-layer device on your network is a switch. Unlike a hub, a switch is more selective as to which ports it passes network traffic. The switch maintains a content addressable memory (CAM) table that maintains a mapping between Ethernet MAC addresses and the port on which that traffic was observed. When the switch receives traffic for an Ethernet MAC address that is not in its CAM table, it floods the packet out of all the ports (on the same VLAN) similar to a hub. But when the destination host replies, the CAM table is updated. Now when Host A sends traffic to Host C (see Figure 6-3), the traffic is only sent to Host C (instead of every device connected to the switch). In this scenario, your IDS sensor will not be able to monitor your network for intrusive activity, because the monitoring interface on your sensor does not receive all the traffic traversing your network.

Figure 6-3   *Switch Traffic Flow*

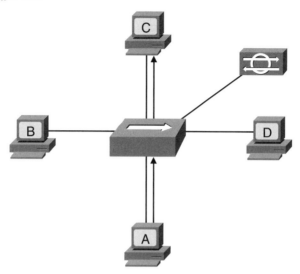

To overcome this problem, you need to configure your switch to mirror specific network traffic to your IDS sensor. With Cisco switches, you can use the following three features to enable your switch to mirror traffic to your IDS sensor's monitoring interface:

- Switch Port Analyzer
- Remote Switch Port Analyzer
- VLAN access control lists

NOTE   Not all the switch traffic capture features are available on every Cisco switch platform, but all Cisco switches support some form of the Switch Port Analyzer feature.

Switch Port Analyzer

The Switch Port Analyzer (SPAN) feature enables you to select traffic for analysis by a *network analyzer*. People refer to SPAN ports by various names, such as *port mirroring* or *port monitoring*. Regardless of the name used, the SPAN feature enables you to cause your Cisco switch to pass selected traffic to your IDS sensor's monitoring interface for analysis.

Network Analyzer

A network analyzer is a device that examines network traffic and provides you with statistics or information about your network traffic. Many network analyzers identify the different types of traffic and their frequency on your network. Using these statistics, you can tune your network to optimize its performance. Your IDS sensor also analyzes the traffic on your network when watching for intrusive activity.

Switched Port Analyzer (SPAN) Port Terminology

When configuring SPAN ports on your Cisco switch, you need to identify several characteristics about the SPAN ports. You will also hear several common terms and phrases used by people to describe the characteristics of SPAN ports. Understanding these terms is important in understanding the explanation of SPAN ports in configuration guides and other documentation. Table 6-1 outlines the major terms commonly used when discussing Cisco's SPAN feature.

Table 6-1   *SPAN Port Terminology*

Terminology	Description
Ingress traffic	Identifies traffic that enters the switch port.
Egress traffic	Identifies traffic that leaves the switch port.
Source port	Port on the switch that you want to monitor the traffic on.
Destination port	Port that receives the traffic (from the monitored ports). The network analyzer is normally connected to this port.
Monitor port	In Catalyst 2900XL/3500XL terminology, this refers to the destination port.
Local SPAN	Refers to a situation in which all of the monitored ports are located on the same switch.
Remote SPAN (RSPAN)	Refers to a situation in which the monitored ports are located on more than one switch. (This advanced monitoring feature is available only on some high-end Catalyst switches.)
Port-based SPAN (PSPAN)	Indicates that you are monitoring one or more source ports.
VLAN-based SPAN (VSPAN)	Indicates that you are monitoring all the ports that belong to one or more VLANs.
Administrative source	Refers to the list of ports or VLANs that are configured to be monitored.
Operational source	Refers to the list of ports or VLANs actually being monitored. This list can be different from the administrative source list in that it does not include ports that have been administratively shut down.

Transport Control Protocol (TCP) Reset Limitations

One of the actions that your sensor can take in response to detecting a TCP-based attack is to reset the TCP connection. The sensor resets the TCP connection by sending out TCP packets with the RST flag set to both the source and destination of the TCP connection via its monitoring interface.

Not all switches allow a port that is configured as the SPAN destination port to receive incoming traffic. Because the sensor's monitoring interface is usually a SPAN port on a Cisco switch, this presents a problem. If the switch does not enable the SPAN destination port to receive incoming traffic, the TCP RST packets will not be accepted, thus preventing the sensor from resetting the TCP connection. Therefore, if you use a SPAN port to capture your network traffic and plan to use the TCP reset capability, you need to verify that your switch supports the capability to receive incoming traffic on the SPAN destination port.

NOTE   Switches learn the Ethernet MAC addresses that they see coming from a specific port so that they can direct traffic to that port in the future (unless configured not to learn MAC addresses on a specific port). To prevent the sensor's Ethernet MAC address from being learned by the switch (enabling an attacker to potentially identify the location of the sensor and attack it), your Cisco IDS sensor uses a randomly generated Ethernet MAC address when it creates its TCP reset packets.

You will commonly use the SPAN feature on one of the following two types of switches:

- Catalyst 2900XL/3500XL switches
- Catalyst 4000 and 6500 switches

Configuring SPAN on these switch types varies so the configuration commands are explained separately for each type, beginning with the Catalyst 2900XL/3500XL.

Catalyst 2900XL/3500XL Switches

You can use a couple of commands to configure SPAN on the Catalyst 2900XL/3500XL platforms. The SPAN functionality on these devices, however, has several limitations that impact how you can capture network traffic. When configuring SPAN ports on the Catalyst 2900XL/3500XL platforms, use the following two commands:

- **port monitor**
- **monitor session**

NOTE	Both of the commands used on the 2900XL/3500XL switches to configure SPAN might not be available on every switch in this class of switches. For instance, some of the switches only support the **port monitor** command. Check the Cisco documentation on your specific switch to determine your switch's supported functionality.

port monitor Command

To monitor a specific port on your Catalyst 2900XL/3500XL switch, use the **port monitor** interface configuration command. You can also use this command to monitor all the ports assigned to a specific VLAN. The syntax for the **port monitor** interface command is as follows:

```
port monitor [interface mod/port | vlan vlan-id]
```

To remove the monitoring for a port or VLAN, use the **monitor port** command that initially established the monitoring with the **no** keyword. Table 6-2 describes the parameters for the **port monitor** interface configuration command.

Table 6-2   **port monitor** *Parameters*

Parameter	Description
interface	Type of interface being monitored, such as Fast Ethernet or Ethernet.
mod/port	The slot that the interface is in (usually 0) along with the specific port that you want to monitor.
vlan	Keyword indicating that you are specifying a VLAN to be monitored.
vlan-id	ID of the VLAN to be monitored. Valid IDs are in the range from 1 to 1005. You do not need to enter the leading 0s for the VLAN ID.

NOTE	When monitoring either a port or a VLAN on the Catalyst 2900XL/3500XL switches (using the **port monitor** command), your destination port must be a member of the same VLAN as the port or VLAN being monitored.

Assume that you have the following situation:

- You have a 3500XL switch.
- You want to monitor port FastEthernet 0/10.
- You want to monitor port FastEthernet 0/5.
- You sensor is connected to port FastEthernet 0/12.
- Both monitor ports are on VLAN 10.

To use SPAN to capture traffic for your sensor, you would use the following commands:

```
Switch# configure terminal
Switch(config)# interface fastethernet 0/12
Switch(config-if)# switchport access vlan 10
Switch(config-if)# port monitor fastethernet 0/10
Switch(config-if)# port monitor fastethernet 0/5
```

Using the **port monitor** command, do not directly specify the destination port on the command line. Instead, enter the configuration mode for the specific port (destination port), and then use the **port monitor** command to effectively turn it into a destination port.

NOTE   If you do not specify a port on the **port monitor** command, it causes the switch to monitor all ports that belong to the same VLAN as the port being configured. Also, if you enter the following command, this causes the switch to monitor all the traffic to and from the IP address configured on VLAN 1:

```
port monitor vlan 1
```

---

monitor session Command

Besides the **port monitor** command, you can also use the **monitor session** command to capture traffic on some Catalyst 2900XL/3500XL switches. This command enables you to specify whether you want to capture all the traffic to the monitored ports or just the received or sent traffic. The syntax for the **monitor session** command is as follows:

```
monitor session {session} {source {interface port(s)} [rx|tx|both]}
monitor session {session} {source vlan vlan_id [rx]}
monitor session {session} {destination {interface port}}
```

Unlike the **port monitor** command, when using the **monitor session** command you must explicitly specify the source and destination ports using two different forms of the command. Table 6-3 describes the parameters for the **monitor session** interface configuration command.

Table 6-3   **monitor session** *Parameters*

Parameter	Description
session	Number of the SPAN session. The only valid value is usually 1, but some switches support more than 1 SPAN session.
source	Keyword indicating that you are specifying a source port (port to be monitored).
source vlan	Keyword indicating that you are specifying a source VLAN (to be monitored).
destination	Keyword indicating that you are specifying a destination port for the SPAN session.
interface	Keyword indicating that you are specifying a port.

continues

Table 6-3   **monitor session** *Parameters (Continued)*

Parameter	Description
port(s)	The port to be configured as either a source or destination. The port includes the interface type, module, and port, such as FastEthernet 0/10. For source ports, you can specify a comma-delimited list or a range of ports (such as 10–20).
rx	Keyword indicating the you want to capture only the traffic received by the source ports (ingress traffic).
tx	Keyword indicating that you want to capture only the traffic transmitted by the source ports (egress traffic).
both	Keyword indicating that you want to capture all traffic on the source ports.
vlan	Keyword indicating that you are specifying a VLAN to be monitored.
vlan-id	ID of the VLAN to be monitored. Valid IDs are in the range from 1 to 1005. You do not need to enter the leading 0s for the VLAN ID.

Using the **monitor session** command, you need to define the source switch ports as well as the destination switch port, because this command is entered at the global configuration mode. Take the preceding example, which has the following characteristics:

- You have a 3500XL switch.
- You want to monitor port FastEthernet 0/10.
- You want to monitor port FastEthernet 0/5.
- You sensor is connected to port FastEthernet 0/12.
- Both monitor ports are on VLAN 10.

You can configure a SPAN port to capture network traffic for your sensor by using the following commands:

```
Switch# configure terminal
Switch(config)# monitor session 1 source interface fastethernet 0/5,10 both
Switch(config)# monitor session 1 destination interface fastethernet 0/12
```

NOTE   To remove a source port or destination port, you need to enter a **no** in front of your original **monitor session** command.

Some Catalyst 2900XL/3500XL switches only support one SPAN session. For this SPAN session, however, you can define as many source ports as you want. Furthermore, you can configure each of these source ports to capture incoming, outgoing, or incoming and outgoing traffic.

There can only be one destination port configured for the SPAN session. If you configure a second destination port, you will receive an error message. To change the destination port for your SPAN session, you must first remove the existing destination port (using the **no** form of the **monitor session** command). Then you can specify a new destination port for the SPAN session.

Catalyst 4000 and 6500 Switches

The SPAN functionality on Catalyst 4000 and 6500 switches provides more functionality than the SPAN functionality provided on the Catalyst 2900XL/3500Xl switches. On the Catalyst 4000 and 6500 switches, for example, you can typically configure four to six SPAN sessions, compared to one or two on the Catalyst 2900XL/3500XL. Plus your destination port can be configured to accept incoming traffic (which is useful for TCP reset functionality).

set span Command (for CatOS)

To capture traffic using the SPAN feature on a Catalyst 4000 or 6500, you need to use the **set span** switch command. This command enables you to designate the source ports and destination port for a SPAN association.

To remove an existing SPAN association, you need to use the **set span disable** switch command. The syntax for the **set span** command is as follows:

```
set span {src_mod/src_port...|src_vlans ...|sc0} {dest_mod/dest_port}
    [tx|rx|both] [inpkts{enable|disable}] [learning{enable|disable}]
    [multicast{enable|disable}] [filter vlans...] [create]

set span disable [dest_mod/dest_port | all]
```

Table 6-4 describes the parameters for the **set span** switch configuration command.

Table 6-4   set span *Parameters*

Parameter	Description
disable	Keyword to disable a SPAN association.
src_mod/src_ports	The module and the port numbers of the traffic to be monitored (source port).
src_vlan	Monitored VLANs.
sc0	Keyword to indicate the that inbound port is a valid source.
dest_mod/dest_port	The module and the port number assigned as the destination port for the monitored traffic.
tx	(Optional) Keyword to specify that egress traffic (information transmitted from the source port) should be captured.

continues

Table 6-4 set span *Parameters (Continued)*

Parameter	Description
rx	(Optional) Keyword to specify that ingress traffic (information received by source port) should be captured.
both	(Optional) Keyword to specify that ingress and egress traffic to source port should be captured.
inpkts enable	(Optional) Keywords that enable the receiving of normal traffic on the SPAN destination port.
inpkts disable	(Optional) Keywords that disable the receiving of normal traffic on the SPAN destination port.
learning enable	(Optional) Keywords that enable learning of Ethernet MAC addresses on the destination port.
learning disable	(Optional) Keywords that disable learning of Ethernet MAC addresses on the destination port.
multicast enable	(Optional) Keywords that enable capturing of multicast traffic on source ports (egress traffic only).
multicast disable	(Optional) Keywords that disable capturing of multicast traffic on source ports (egress traffic only).
filter *vlan(s)*	(Optional) Keyword and variable to identify which VLANs you want to monitor when monitoring trunk ports.
create	(Optional) If you do not specify the keyword **create** with the **set span** command and you have only one session, the session is overwritten. If a matching destination port exists, the particular session is overwritten (with or without specifying **create**). If you specify the keyword **create** and no matching destination port exists, the session is created.

If you want to configure SPAN so that traffic transmitted and received on port 3/9 and 3/12 (SPAN source ports) is mirrored on port 3/4 (SPAN destination), use the following command:

```
Console> (enable) set span 3/9,12 3/4 both create

Enabled monitoring of Ports 3/9,12 transmit/receive traffic by Port 3/4

Console> (enable)
```

Similarly, if you want to configure SPAN so that traffic received by VLAN 130 (SPAN source) is mirrored on port 3/4 (SPAN destination), use the following command:

```
Console> (enable) set span 130 3/4

Enabled monitoring of VLAN 130 transmit/receive traffic by Port 3/4

Console> (enable)
```

Remote Switch Port Analyzer

Sometimes you want to capture traffic from ports located on multiple switches. To accomplish this, you can use the Remote Switch Port Analyzer (RSPAN) feature available on certain Cisco switches.

RSPAN enables you to monitor source ports spread all over your switched network. This functionality works similarly to normal SPAN functionality, except that instead of traffic being mirrored to a specific destination port, the monitored traffic is flooded to a special RSPAN VLAN (see Figure 6-4). The destination ports can then be located on any switch that has access to this RSPAN VLAN.

Figure 6-4 *Remote SPAN Traffic Flow*

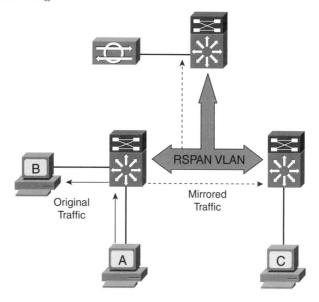

If you configure RSPAN to monitor traffic sent by Host A (see Figure 6-4), whenever Host A generates a packet to Host B, a copy of the packet is passed by an application-specific integrated circuit (ASIC) of the Catalyst 6000 Policy Feature Card (PFC) into the predefined RSPAN VLAN. From there, the packet is flooded to all the ports belonging to the RSPAN VLAN. All the interswitch links shown in Figure 6-4 are trunks. RSPAN uses these trunks to support the traversal of the RSPAN VLAN traffic. The only access points to the RSPAN-captured traffic are the defined destination ports (where you would locate your IDS sensors).

NOTE	The RSPAN feature is not available on all Cisco switches. Usually RSPAN is only available on the higher-end switches, such as the Catalyst 4000 and 6500. You also need to have a fairly new operating system version. Refer to the online Cisco documentation to determine whether your switch supports this feature.

set rspan Command

To use the RSPAN functionality (on the Catalyst 4000 and 6500 switches), use the **set rspan** switch command. You must also perform other configuration tasks, such as defining the trunks to carry the RSPAN VLAN traffic. For information on these other configuration tasks, refer to the "Configuring SPAN and RSPAN" documentation available at the Cisco website.

To remove an existing RSPAN association, you need to use the **set rspan disable** switch command. The syntax for the **set rspan** command is as follows:

```
set rspan source {mod/port...|vlans ...|sc0} {rspan_vlan} [tx|rx|both]
    [inpkts{enable|disable}] [learning{enable|disable}] [multicast{enable|disable}]
    [filter vlans...] [create]

set rspan disable source [mod/port | all]
set rspan destination {mod/port} {rspan_vlan} [inpkts{enable|disable}]
    [learning{enable|disable}]

    [multicast{enable|disable}] [filter vlans...] [create]

set rspan disable destination [mod/port | all]
```

Table 6-5 describes the parameters for the **set rspan** switch configuration command.

Table 6-5   set rspan *Parameters*

Parameter	Description
disable	Keyword to disable a SPAN association.
mod/port	The module and the port number for either the monitored or monitoring port.
vlans	Monitored VLANs.
sc0	Keyword to indicate the that inbound port is a valid source.
tx	(Optional) Keyword to specify that egress traffic (information transmitted from the source port) should be captured.
rx	(Optional) Keyword to specify that ingress traffic (information received by source port) should be captured.
both	(Optional) Keyword to specify that ingress and egress traffic to the source port should be captured.
inpkts enable	(Optional) Keywords that enable the receiving of normal traffic on the SPAN destination port.
inpkts disable	(Optional) Keywords that disable the receiving of normal traffic on the SPAN destination port.

Table 6-5   **set rspan** *Parameters (Continued)*

Parameter	Description
learning enable	(Optional) Keywords that enable learning of Ethernet MAC addresses on the destination port.
learning disable	(Optional) Keywords that disable learning of Ethernet MAC addresses on the destination port.
multicast enable	(Optional) Keywords that enable capturing of multicast traffic on source ports (egress traffic only).
multicast disable	(Optional) Keywords that disable capturing of multicast traffic on source ports (egress traffic only).
filter *vlan(s)*	(Optional) Keyword and variable to identify.
create	If you do not specify the keyword **create** with the **set rspan** command and you have only one session, the session is overwritten. If a matching RSPAN VLAN or destination port exists, the particular session is overwritten (with or without specifying **create**). If you specify the keyword **create** and no matching RSPAN VLAN or destination port exists, the session is created.

Virtual Local-Area Network (VLAN) Access Control List

VLAN access control list (VACL) access controls all packets on your Catalyst 6500 switch through the PFC. VACLs are strictly for security packet filtering and redirecting traffic to specific physical switch ports. Unlike Cisco IOS ACLs, VACLs are not defined by the direction of the traffic (inbound or outbound).

VACLs are mainly provided to filter traffic on the switch. The **capture** keyword enables you to use a VACL to mirror matched traffic to a designated capture port. This capture option specifies that packets that match the specified *flows* are switched normally, as well as being captured and transmitted to the configured capture port. Only permitted traffic is sent to the capture port. Using VACLs enables you to use a fine degree of granularity when specifying which traffic you want to capture. You can use VACLs to capture traffic for both IDS modules as well as appliance sensors.

Flows

A flow comprises a traffic stream between a source and destination IP address, a source port and destination port, or a combination of source IP address and source port in conjunction with a destination IP address and destination port. Your VACLs essentially define the flows that represent the interesting traffic on which you want your sensor to perform intrusion detection analysis. Furthermore, your Multilayer Switch Feature Card (MSFC) uses flows to effectively send packets between different VLANs by crossing the switch's backplane only once.

Defining Interesting Traffic

Intrusion detection analysis requires the examination of specific network traffic. VACLs provide you with granular control over the network traffic that you consider interesting. This interesting Ethernet traffic is captured by your VACL and passed to your sensor's monitoring interface. When defining your VACL, you have many options available to limit the traffic captured, such as the following:

- IP protocol
- Source or destination IP address
- Source or destination ports
- A combination of IP protocol, IP addresses, and ports

On a web farm, for example, port 80 (HTTP) and potentially port 21 (FTP) represent the services required for Internet users to access the web servers and retrieve data. Attackers launch software exploits against these ports. You can create a VACL that captures only traffic destined to these two ports, thereby reducing the amount of traffic sent to your sensor for intrusion detection analysis.

NOTE   In reality, you need to monitor more ports than 80 to watch for attacks against web server software. Several ports are commonly used for these services, such as 80, 8080, and 3128. To effectively examine traffic for web server exploits, you need to at least create VACLs to capture traffic destined for all ports on which you run web services. Capturing traffic for all the commonly used web server ports enables you to learn about misdirected attacks (attacks against ports on which you do not even run web servers).

To configure a VACL on your switch, you need to perform several steps. The steps that you need to perform vary, depending on which of the following two operating systems you are running on your Catalyst 6500 switch:

- CatOS
- IOS

Configuring Virtual Local-Area Network Access Control Lists (VACLs) Using CatOS

Configuring VACLs using CatOS is explained in the following section. For information on how to configure VACLs using IOS, refer to the documentation on the Cisco website. An example using CatIOS is also shown in Appendix A, "Cisco Secure IDS Tuning: Case Studies." When configuring a VACL on CatOS, you need to go through the following tasks:

Step 1   Define a security ACL.

Step 2   Commit the VACL to memory.

Step 3   Map the VACL to VLANs.

Step 4   Assign the capture port.

Define a Security Access Control List (ACL)

The first step in creating your VACL is to define the security ACL that will capture interesting traffic. You use the **set security acl ip** switch command to create a VACL. This command creates a VACL to capture IP traffic for intrusion detection analysis by specifying the **capture** keyword.

NOTE   To remove a VACL or VLAN mapping, use the **clear security acl map** switch command.

You build a VACL by defining the traffic that you want copied to your sensor's monitoring port. The system automatically appends an implicit **deny any any** statement to the end of your VACL. (This is analogous to regular ACLs.) Therefore, any traffic not explicitly permitted by your VACL is not allowed through your switch. Traffic flows with the capture option enabled are copied to the sensor's monitoring interface for analysis along with passing through the switch to their original destination.

The syntax for the **set security acl ip** command is shown using several different examples based on the type of traffic that you want to capture.

The syntax for capturing traffic for a single IP address is as follows:

```
set security acl ip acl_name permit src_ip_spec [capture]
```

The syntax for capturing IP traffic between a source IP address and a destination IP address is as follows:

```
set security acl ip acl_name permit [ip|0] src_ip_spec dest_ip_spec [capture]
```

The syntax for capturing ICMP traffic between a source IP address and a destination IP address is as follows:

```
set security acl ip acl_name permit [icmp|1] src_ip_spec dest_ip_spec
    [icmp_type] [icmp_code]|[icmp_message] [capture]
```

The syntax for capturing TCP traffic between a source IP address and a destination IP address is as follows:

```
set security acl ip acl_name permit [tcp|6] src_ip_spec [operator port [port]]
    dest_ip_spec [operator port [port]] [established] [capture]
```

The syntax for capturing UDP traffic between a source IP address and a destination IP address is as follows:

```
set security acl ip acl_name permit [udp|17] src_ip_spec [operator port [port]]
    dest_ip_spec [operator port [port]] [capture]
```

Table 6-6 describes the major parameters for the **set security acl ip** switch configuration command.

Table 6-6   **sec security acl ip** Parameters

Parameter	Description
acl_name	Unique name that identifies the lists to which the entry belongs.
permit	Keyword to allow traffic from the source IP address.
src_ip_spec	Source IP address and the source mask.
protocol	Keyword or number of an IP protocol.
dest_ip_spec	Destination IP address and the destination mask.
capture	Keyword to specify packets are switched normally and captured; permit must also be enabled.
ip | 0	(Optional) Keyword or number to match any IP packets.
icmp | 1	(Optional) Keyword or number to match ICMP packets.
icmp-type	(Optional) ICMP message type name or a number.
icmp-code	(Optional) ICMP message code name or a number.
icmp-message	ICMP message type name or ICMP message type and code name.
tcp | 6	(Optional) Keyword or number to match TCP packets.
operator	(Optional) Operands; valid values include **lt** (less than), **gt** (greater than), **eq** (equal), **neq** (not equal), and **range** (inclusive range).
port	(Optional) Number or name of a TCP or UDP port; valid port numbers are from 0 to 65,535.
established	(Optional) Keyword to specify an established connection; used only for TCP protocol.
udp | 17	(Optional) Keyword or number to match UDP packets.

To clarify the **set security acl ip** command, it is helpful to go through a couple of examples. The first example involves capturing traffic that matches the following requirements:

- The source network is the Class C address 172.21.166.0.
- The source ports are 1–1024.
- The destination network is the Class C address 172.21.168.0.
- The destination ports are 60–100.
- The traffic type is UDP.
- The security ACL name is UDPACL1.

The associated **set security acl** command is as follows:

```
Cat6 (enable) set security acl ip UDPACL1 permit udp 172.21.166.0 0.0.0.255
      range 1 1024 172.21.168.0 0.0.0.255 range 60 100 capture

UDPACL1 editbuffer modified. Use 'commit' to apply changes

Cat6k (enable)
```

The next example involves capturing traffic that matches the following requirements:

- The source address can be anything.

- The destination address can be anything.

- The traffic type is ICMP echo reply messages.

- The security ACL name is ICMPACL1.

The associated **set security acl** command is as follows:

```
Cat6 (enable) set security acl ip ICMPACL1 permit icmp any any
      echo-reply capture

ICMPACL1 editbuffer modified. Use 'commit' to apply changes

Cat6k (enable)
```

NOTE   When specifying either the *src_ip_spec* or the *dest_ip_spec*, you need to supply an IP address followed by a netmask. For the netmask, a 0 indicates a care bit (the value in the IP field specified in the ACL must match the value of the IP address in the packet being checked), and a 1 indicates bits that are not used when determining whether the IP address in the packet matches the address specified in the ACL (these "don't care" bits are automatically matched). The following keywords are also useful:

- Use the keyword **any** as an abbreviation for an IP address and netmask of 0.0.0.0 and 255.255.255.255, respectively.

- Use **host** *IP address* as an abbreviation for an IP address with a netmask of 0.0.0.0.

Commit the VACL to Memory

After defining the interesting traffic to be captured with the **set security acl ip** command, you need to commit the VACL to hardware. You use the **commit security acl** command. The syntax for this command is as follows:

```
commit security acl acl_name | all
```

You can either commit all the security ACLs by using the **all** keyword or you can specify the name of the specific security ACL to commit it to hardware. To commit the sample security ACLs that were shown previously in this chapter, use these commands:

```
Cat6 (enable) commit security acl UDPACL1

Hardware programming in progress...

ACL UDPACL1 is committed to hardware

Cat6 (enable) commit security acl ICMPACL1

Hardware programming in progress...

ACL ICMPACL1 is committed to hardware

Cat6 (enable)
```

Map the VACL to VLANs

Next you need to map your security ACLs to specific VLANs on your switch through the **set security acl map** command. The syntax for this command is as follows:

```
set security acl map acl_name vlan
```

You need to specify which security ACL (*acl_name*) that you want to map to which VLAN (*vlan*). If you want to map the previously described security ACL ICMPACL1 to VLANs 12 and 14, use the following commands:

```
Cat6 (enable) set security acl map ICMPACL1 12

ACL ICMPACL1 mapped to vlan 12

Cat6 (enable) set security acl map ICMPACL1 14

ACL ICMPACL1 mapped to vlan 14

Cat6 (enable)
```

Assign the Capture Port

Finally, you need to use the **set security acl capture-ports** command to define which ports on your switch receive the traffic captured by your security ACLs. The syntax for this command is as follows:

```
set security acl capture-ports {mod/ports...}
```

The only user parameter in this command is a list of ports on your switch to receive the traffic captured by your security ACLs. If your sensor's monitoring interface is connected to port 3 on slot 4, to define this port as the capture port for security ACLs, use the following command:

```
Cat6 (enable) set security acl capture-ports 4/3

Successfully set 4/3 to capture ACL traffic.

Cat6 (enable)
```

NOTE   To receive traffic from your VACL, your capture port must be trunking the VLAN from which the traffic originated. Your VACL might be capturing traffic from multiple VLANs and directing this traffic to multiple capture ports. By selectively enabling different VLANs on the different capture ports, you can limit the traffic actually sent to each individual capture port.

Configuring VACLs with the Cisco Internetworking Operating System (IOS) Firewall

When using the Cisco IOS firewall on your MSFC, you might be unable to directly configure VACLs to capture network traffic for your sensor. If you apply the **ip inspect** Cisco IOS firewall command on a specific VLAN interface, you can't create a VACL for that same VLAN at the switch level. These two features are incompatible. To overcome this limitation, however, you can use the **mls ip ids** MSFC router command to designate which packets will be captured by your security ACL.

With normal VACLs, the VACL establishes a security ACL that actually determines which traffic is allowed through the switch. With the **mls ip ids** command, however, you will be defining an extended ACL (on your MSFC) to designate which traffic will be captured. A copy of any traffic that is permitted by the extended ACL will be passed to your capture port, but the extended ACL will not prevent this traffic from reaching its intended destination.

When using the **mls ip ids** command, you need to go through the following steps to configure a VACL:

Step 1   Create the extended ACL.

Step 2   Apply the ACL to an interface or VLAN.

Step 3   Assign the capture port.

Create the Extended ACL

Just as in regular VACL configuration, the first step to creating an IOS firewall VACL is to define the interesting traffic. In this situation, the interesting traffic is determined by an extended ACL that you create on your MSFC. The command to create the extended ACL is **ip access-list** and its syntax is as follows:

```
ip access-list extended access-list-number {deny|permit} protocol source_IP
    source_wild-card destination_IP destination_wild-card [log|log-input]
```

Table 6-7 describes the major parameters for the **ip access-list** router configuration command.

Table 6-7   **ip access-list** Parameters

Parameter	Description
access-list-number	Number identifying the ACL being created. Valid values are between 100–199 and 2000–2699.
deny	Keyword indicating that the traffic being specified should be dropped by the ACL.
permit	Keyword indicating that the traffic should be allowed by the ACL.
protocol	Name or number of an IP protocol that defines the traffic that you are interested in. Some common keywords are **tcp**, **udp**, **icmp**, and **eigrp**.
source_IP	The source host or network IP address of packets that you are interested in.
source_wildcard	This mask indicates which bits in the source IP are used for comparison. Each 0 bit in the mask indicates bits in the source IP address that must match exactly to the address of the packet being checked. Bits set to a 1 are automatically matched.
destination_IP	The destination host or network IP address of packets that you are interested in.
destination_wildcard	This mask indicates which bits in the destination IP are used for comparison. Each 0 bit in the mask indicates bits in the destination IP address that must match exactly to the address of the packet being checked. Bits set to a 1 are automatically matched.
log	(Optional) Causes an informational logging message to be sent to the console when packets are matched to the ACL.
log_input	(Optional) Includes the input interface and source Ethernet MAC address in logging output.

The **ip access-list** command is executed on your MSFC, not your Catalyst switch console. Suppose you want to define an ACL (150) that permits UDP traffic from 10.20.30.1 to 10.30.30.1. To accomplish this, you enter the following commands on your router console:

```
MSFC# configure terminal
MSFC(config)# ip access-list extended 150 permit tcp 10.20.30.1 0.0.0.0
    10.30.30.1 0.0.0.0
MSFC(config)#
```

Apply the ACL to an Interface or VLAN

Next you need to apply the extended ACL to a VLAN interface on the MSFC. You use the **interface vlan** command to enter the configuration mode for a specific interface. Then you use the **mls ip ids** command to apply the extended ACL to that interface.

The syntax for the **interface vlan** command is as follows:

```
interface vlan <vlan_number>
```

The syntax for the **mls ip ids** command is as follows:

```
mls ip ids <acl_number>
```

To continue with this example, suppose that the traffic you want to monitor is on VLAN 40. You enter the following commands on your router to apply ACL 150 to VLAN 40:

```
MSFC# configure terminal
MSFC(config)# interface vlan 40
MSFC(config-if)# mls ip ids 150
```

Assign the Capture Port

Finally, you need to assign the capture port to receive the traffic that your extended ACL captured (permitted). You need to use the **set security acl** command to define your capture ports. This command is executed on your switch console.

NOTE   If your switch is running Cisco IOS rather than CatOS, use the **switchport capture** command to define your capture ports. For more information on this command, refer to the Cisco documentation.

The syntax for the **set security acl** command is as follows:

```
set security acl capture-ports <mod/ports>
```

Suppose that your sensor is connected to port 5 on the third card in your Catalyst 6500 switch. To enable this port to receive traffic from your VACL, enter the following command on your switch console to establish port 5 on module 3 as the capture port:

```
Cat6>(enable) set security acl capture-ports 3/5
```

Advanced Traffic Capturing

So far this examination has focused on the ways that you can use your Cisco switch to capture network traffic for analysis by your sensor. When using a Catalyst 6500 switch, the next step involves configuring the port on the switch through which your sensor receives its captured traffic.

By default, your appliance sensors are usually connected to your switch via a standard access port. Because this port is usually not configured as a trunk, your sensor will only receive traffic that belongs to the same VLAN as the VLAN assigned to the switch port.

The monitoring port on your IDS Module, however, is configured as a trunk port by default and accepts all the traffic that it receives. You might not want the IDS Module's monitoring port analyzing traffic from every VLAN on the switch. You can also configure the monitoring port for your appliance sensor as a trunk so that it receives traffic from multiple VLANs.

In both of these situations, you need to understand how to configure the trunking properties of the ports on your switch so that you can limit the desired traffic to only those VLANs that you consider interesting.

Trunk Configuration Tasks

When configuring a trunk port on your switch, you need to perform various tasks to change a specific port's characteristics. You use specific switch commands to change your port's properties, but you will essentially need to perform the following high-level tasks:

Step 1   Clear existing VLANs.

Step 2   Define VLANs to capture.

Step 3   Assign switch ports to a VLAN.

Step 4   Create a VACL.

Clear Existing VLANs

Some ports are configured as trunk ports by default, such as the monitoring ports on IDSM-2. These trunk ports are configured to trunk all the VLANs on the switch by default. Therefore, you need to remove the default configuration by clearing all the VLANs from your trunk port. The **clear trunk** switch command accomplishes this task and its syntax is as follows:

```
clear trunk <mod/port> [vlans]
```

Table 6-8 describes the parameters for the **clear trunk** switch configuration command.

Table 6-8   **clear trunk** Parameters

Parameter	Description
mod/port	Number of the module and the port on the module.
vlans	(Optional) Number of the VLAN to remove from the list of allowed VLANs. Valid ranges range from 2–1005 and 1025–4094.

To clear all the VLANs from the example destination port, enter the following command on your switch:

```
Cat6 (enable) clear trunk 3/5 2-1005,1025-4094
```

NOTE	Before removing VLANs from the allowed list of VLANs for a trunk, you normally need to know which VLANs are currently assigned to the trunk port. You can obtain this information by using the **show trunk** *mod/port* **detail** switch command.

Define VLANs to Capture

By default, trunk ports receive traffic from all the VLANs configured on the switch. Usually you need to limit the number of VLANs on a trunk port to prevent overloading the sensor with too much traffic. For each trunk port used to monitor traffic, you need to define the VLANs that you want the destination port to accept. The **set trunk** switch command enables you to add VLANs to an existing trunk port. The syntax for the **set trunk** command is as follows:

```
set trunk <mod/port> {on|off|desirable|auto|nonegotiate}[vlans]
     [isl|dot1q|negotiate]
```

Table 6-9 describes the parameters for the **set trunk** switch configuration command.

Table 6-9   **set trunk** *Parameters*

Parameter	Description
mod/port	Number of the module and the port on the module.
on	Forces the port to become a trunk port and persuades the neighboring port to become a trunk port. The port becomes a trunk port even if the neighboring port does not agree to become a trunk.
off	Forces the port to become a nontrunk port and persuades the neighboring port to become a nontrunk port. The port becomes a nontrunk port even if the neighboring port does not agree to become a nontrunk port.
desirable	Causes the port to negotiate actively with the neighboring port to become a trunk link.
auto	Causes the port to become a trunk port if the neighboring port tries to negotiate a trunk link.
nonnegotiate	Forces the port to become a trunk port but prevents it from sending DTP frames to its neighbor.
vlans	(Optional) Number of the VLAN to add to the list of allowed VLANs. Valid ranges range from 2–1005 and 1025–4094.
isl	(Optional) Specifies an Inter-Switch Link (ISL) trunk on a Fast or Gigabit Ethernet port.
dot1q	(Optional) Specifies an IEEE 802.1Q trunk on a Fast or Gigabit Ethernet port.
negotiate	(Optional) Specifies that the port become an ISL (preferred) or 802.1Q trunk, depending on the configuration and capabilities of the neighboring port.

Suppose you want to enable your destination port to accept traffic from VLANs 5 through 10. You enter the following command on your switch:

```
Cat6 (enable) set trunk 3/5 5-10 dot1q on
Adding vlans 5-10 to allowed list
Port(s) 3/5 allowed vlans modified to 5-10
Cat6 (enable)
```

Assign Switch Ports to VLANs

Besides configuring the VLANs that your destination port will accept, you also need to know how to assign ports on your switch to various VLANs. You do this with the **set vlan** switch command and its syntax is as follows:

```
set vlan <vlan_num> <src_mod/src_ports>
```

Table 6-10 describes the parameters for the **set vlan** switch configuration command.

Table 6-10   **set vlan** Parameters

Parameter	Description
vlan_num	The VLAN number to be assigned to the specified ports.
src_mod/src_ports	Number of the module and the ports on the module that you want to assign to the specified VLAN.

Suppose that you want to place ports 3 through 10 on module 2 into VLAN 10 and ports 4 through 8 on module 4 into VLAN 8. The switch commands to accomplish this are as follows:

```
Cat6 (enable) set vlan 10 2/3-10
VLAN 10 Modified
VLAN 1 Modified
VLAN  Mod/Ports
---- -----------------------
10   2/3-10
Cat6 (enable) set vlan 8 4/4-8
VLAN 10 Modified
VLAN 1 Modified
VLAN  Mod/Ports
---- -----------------------
10   2/3-10
     4/4-8
```

Create the VACL

You have now configured the characteristics of your trunk port that represents the connection to the monitoring interface on your sensor. You still need to go through the various tasks (explained earlier in this chapter) to create your VACL. Then you need to assign that VACL to the trunk port that you configured as its capture port.

Summary

Because your network sensors represent one of the significant ways that your Cisco IDS searches for intrusive activity on your network, it is vital that they observe the traffic traversing your network. Normally, you will use one of the following three devices to pass traffic to your sensors:

- Hubs
- Network taps
- Switches

When using switches to capture traffic for your sensor, you need to configure the switches to send traffic to your sensor's monitoring port using one of the following features:

- Switch Port Analyzer (SPAN)
- Remote SPAN
- VLAN access control lists (VACLs)

Lower-end switches (2900XL/3500XL) usually only support the SPAN feature, whereas the higher-end switches (Catalyst 4000 and 6500) tend to support all three options. Using VACLs provides the greatest granularity with respect to limiting the traffic that is sent to your sensor, but VACL configuration is also the most complex. When configuring a VACL, you need to go through the following steps:

Step 1   Define a security ACL.

Step 2   Commit the VACL to memory (NVRAM).

Step 3   Map the VACL to specific VLANs.

Step 4   Assign the capture ports.

Besides creating your VACL, you might also need to configure your destination port (capture port) as a trunk to enable it to receive traffic from multiple VLANs. To configure the trunk characteristics of your switch ports, use the following commands:

- **clear trunk**
- **set trunk**

Review Questions

The following questions test your retention of the material presented in this chapter. The answers to the review questions are in Appendix B, "Answers to Chapter Review Questions."

1   What are the three main mechanisms to capture traffic for network analysis on your Cisco infrastructure switches?

2   What are the three types of infrastructure devices that you use to capture network traffic for intrusion detection analysis?

3   When using SPAN to capture network traffic on a Catalyst 6500 switch, what traffic keyword do you use to capture only traffic leaving the switch from the specified ports?

4   What is local SPAN?

5   What traffic capture commands are available on the 2900XL/3500XL Cisco switches?

6   If you plan to use the TCP reset signature action in conjunction with SPAN, what functionality must the switch support?

7   What traffic capture options are available on the Catalyst 6500 switches?

8   What is RSPAN?

9   What is the first step in defining a VACL (when using CatOS)?

10 What keyword do you need to use when defining your security ACL to enable you to make a copy of the traffic for intrusion detection analysis?

11 What are some of the major ways that you can limit the traffic that your security ACL will capture?

12 Why does your sensor use random Ethernet MAC addresses when generating TCP reset packets?

13 What three traffic direction keywords can you use when defining a SPAN port on a Catalyst 6500 switch?

14 What command do you use to enable trunking on a specified port of your Catalyst 6500 switch?

15 What switch command do you use to remove VLANs from a trunk port?

16 What switch command do you use to add VLANs to a trunk port?

17 What Cisco IOS firewall command can interfere with your ability to use security ACLs?

18 What is the main difference between a switch and a hub?

Upon completion of this chapter, you will be able to perform the following tasks:

- Identify the various appliance sensor models
- Explain the different user roles available on the sensors
- Explain the various modes of the sensor's command-line interface (CLI)
- Explain how to use the sensor's CLI
- Explain the initial configuration tasks for a sensor

CHAPTER 7

Cisco IDS Network Sensor Installation

The Cisco IDS appliance is a critical component in your Cisco intrusion protection solution. Each Cisco IDS appliance is a high-performance IDS sensor. Cisco IDS version 4.0 supports the following appliance models:

- IDS 4210
- IDS 4215
- IDS 4220
- IDS 4230
- IDS 4235
- IDS 4250
- IDS 4250XL

NOTE   Both the IDS 4220 and IDS 4230 have reached end-of-sale (EOS) status. They can no longer be purchased.

Each of these sensors handles a different performance load, from 45 Mbps to 1000 Mbps. Depending on your network environment, you can choose the appropriate appliance to match your network bandwidth and traffic volume.

Installing your IDS appliances is the first step in integrating these important components into your Cisco intrusion protection solution. The explanation of the installation process focuses on the following areas:

- The IDS appliance
- IDS appliance CLI
- Installing the IDS appliance

The IDS Appliance

To watch your network for intrusive activity, you need to place IDS appliances at key locations throughout your network. Each of these sensors performs real-time analysis on your network traffic by looking for misuse and anomalies based on an extensive signature library. After detecting unauthorized activity, your IDS appliance can initiate various actions in response to the activity detected (see Chapter 4, "Cisco Intrusion Protection"). Your IDS appliances can even monitor syslog messages from your Cisco routers to detect violations of your network security policy.

Appliance Models

Understanding the features, connections, and interfaces of the different appliance models is vital when actually installing these devices on your network. Knowing the performance limitations assists in determining which appliance model matches your network environment. The following models are examined in detail in this chapter:

- IDS 4210
- IDS 4215
- IDS 4235
- IDS 4250
- IDS 4250XL

IDS 4210

The low-end sensor is the IDS 4210. Its capabilities are as follows:

- **Performance**—45 Mbps
- **Monitoring interface**—10/100BASE-T
- **Command and control interface**—10/100BASE-T
- **Optional interface**—No
- **Performance upgrade**—No
- **Form factor**—One rack unit

Rack Units

When installing equipment in a lab, space is a major concern. Normally, you use racks, which have numerous mounting holes, to efficiently install equipment in your lab. Because the width of the racks is fixed, rack-mountable equipment is usually measured by its height. The measurement used is known as rack units, where one rack unit equals approximately 1.75 inches.

Figure 7-1 shows the features located on the front of the IDS 4210 sensor.

Figure 7-1   *IDS 4210 Front Panel*

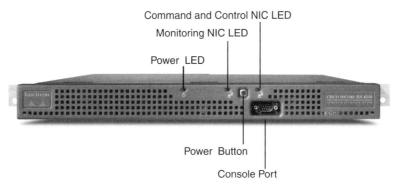

Most of the connections are located on the back of the IDS 4210, including the two Ethernet interfaces (see Figure 7-2). The command and control interface is located on the top, and the monitoring interface is the lower interface. The monitoring interface is int0 and the command and control interface is eth1.

Figure 7-2   *IDS 4210 Back Panel*

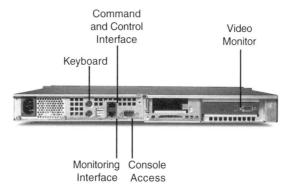

IDS 4215

The replacement for the IDS 4210 sensor is the IDS 4215. Its capabilities are as follows:

- **Performance**—80 Mbps
- **Monitoring interface**—10/100BASE-T
- **Command and control interface**—10/100BASE-T

- **Optional interface**—Four 10/100BASE-TX (4FE) monitoring interfaces (allowing a total of 5 monitoring interfaces)
- **Performance upgrade**—No
- **Form factor**—One rack unit

The front of the IDS 4215 sensor only has a couple of status indicators, as shown in Figure 7-3.

Figure 7-3 *IDS 4215 Front Panel*

The connections are located on the back of the IDS 4215 including the two default Ethernet interfaces and the optional four 10/100 monitoring interfaces (see Figure 7-4). The command and control interface is the built-in interface located on the right (labeled 10/100 Ethernet 1 on the chassis), and the monitoring interface is the built-in interface on the left (labeled 10/100 Ethernet 0 on the chassis). The four optional Ethernet interfaces are located in the upper-left corner of the chassis.

Figure 7-4 *IDS 4215 Rear Panel*

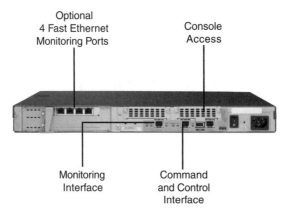

The built-in monitoring interface is int0, and the command and control interface is eth1. The four optional Ethernet interfaces are int2, int3, int4, and int5.

IDS 4235

The following are the technical specifications for the Cisco IDS 4235 sensor (shown in Figure 7-5):

- **Performance**—250 Mbps
- **Monitoring interface**—10/100/1000BASE-TX
- **Command and control interface**—10/100/1000BASE-TX
- **Optional interface**—Four 10/100BASE-TX (4FE) sniffing interfaces
- **Performance upgrade**—No
- **Form factor**—One rack unit

Figure 7-5   *IDS 4235*

The connections are located on the back of the IDS 4235 (see Figure 7-6). The command and control interface is located on the left (labeled on the chassis with a 2), and the monitoring interface is on the right interface (labeled on the chassis with a 1). The monitoring interface is int0, and the command and control interface is eth1.

Figure 7-6   *IDS 4235 Back Panel*

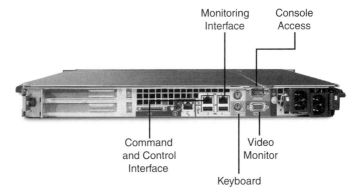

IDS 4250

The following are the technical specifications for the Cisco IDS 4250 sensor:

- **Performance**—500 Mbps
- **Monitoring interface**—10/100/1000BASE-TX
- **Command and control interface**—10/100/1000BASE-TX
- **Optional interface**—1000BASE-SX (fiber), four 10/100BaseTx (4FE) sniffing interfaces
- **Performance upgrade**—Yes
- **Form factor**—One rack unit

This sensor looks identical to the IDS 4235 (see Figure 7-5), except for the name plate. The connections located on the back of the IDS 4250 are identical to the IDS 4235 (see Figure 7-6). The command and control interface is located on the left (labeled on the chassis with a 2), and the monitoring interface is on the right interface (labeled on the chassis with a 1). The monitoring interface is int0, and the command and control interface is eth1.

IDS 4250XL

The following are the technical specifications for the Cisco IDS 4250XL sensor:

- **Performance**—1000 Mbps
- **Monitoring interface**—Dual 1000BASE-SX interface with MTRJ
- **Command and control interface**—10/100/1000BASE-TX
- **Optional interface**—No
- **Performance upgrade**—No
- **Form factor**—One rack unit

The sensor is an IDS 4250 appliance with the IDS Accelerator (XL) card installed in it. The connections located on the back of the IDS 4250XL are identical to the IDS 4235 and IDS 4250 with the exception of the IDS XL card (see Figure 7-7). The command and control interface is the leftmost of the two built-in interfaces and labeled on the chassis with a 2, and the monitoring interface is the IDS XL card ports. The monitoring interfaces are int2 and int3, and the command and control port is eth1.

Figure 7-7   *IDS 4250XL Back Panel*

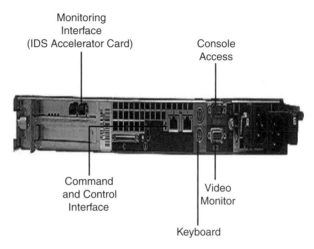

Appliance Restrictions

Hardware Considerations

Recommended Keyboards and Monitors

Appliance Restrictions

Although the version 4.0 IDS appliance is built on a general-purpose operating system, it is not a general-purpose workstation. Installing any applications other than the Cisco appliance software can impact the operation of the device and impair its performance. Therefore, Cisco prohibits installing software on your IDS appliance that is not part of the Cisco IDS software distribution. Using your Cisco IDS appliance for anything other than a Cisco IDS appliance is also prohibited.

Hardware Considerations

Successfully installing your IDS appliances requires you to consider several hardware factors that might impact your IDS appliance operation. These considerations fall into the following categories (some of which apply only to specific appliance models):

- Recommended keyboards and monitors
- Installing spare hard drives
- BIOS upgrades
- Swapping interface cards

Recommended Keyboards and Monitors

Based on experience and testing, Cisco has determined that not all keyboards and monitors are compatible with the IDS appliances. To assist you in installing your IDS appliance with minimal problems, Cisco has identified specific keyboards and monitors that have been tested and guaranteed to work with your IDS appliance.

Although other keyboards might operate fine with your sensor, Cisco recommends using one of the following keyboards with your IDS appliance for guaranteed compatibility:

- KeyTronic E03601QUS201-C
- KeyTronic LT DESIGNER

Although other monitors might operate fine with your sensor, Cisco also recommends using one of the following monitors with your IDS appliance for guaranteed compatibility:

- MaxTech XT-7800
- Dell D1025HT

Installing Spare Hard Drives

The spare hard drives are meant as replacements for your original hard drive should it fail. If your original hard drive becomes unusable, you can swap out the bad drive with your spare hard drive and then rebuild the Cisco IDS version 4.0 software following the installation instructions provided later in the chapter.

You might think that you can install the spare hard drives into your IDS 4235 and IDS 4250 appliances along with the original hard drive (giving you two drives on your appliance). If you install both hard drives into your appliance, the **recover** command might no longer be able to re-image the appliance. Furthermore, this is an unsupported configuration.

BIOS Upgrades

BIOS version A04 or later is required on the IDS 4235 and IDS 4250 appliances to run IDS 4.0 software. Without the correct BIOS, these appliances can hang during the boot process. Before upgrading your Cisco IDS software to version 4.0 on either an IDS 4235 or IDS 4250 appliance, you must ensure that your system is running the correct BIOS version. If your BIOS version is less than A04, you need to upgrade the BIOS.

NOTE   You must connect a keyboard and monitor to the appliance so that you can see the output on the monitor, because you can't upgrade the BIOS from a console connection.

CAUTION   Do not apply the BIOS upgrade on any Cisco IDS appliance other than either the IDS 4235 or IDS 4250 models.

Complete the following steps to create the BIOS upgrade disk:

Step 1   Copy the file BIOS_A04.exe to a Windows system.

NOTE   You can find this file in the /BIOS directory on the Cisco IDS 4.0 Upgrade/Recovery CD, or you can download it from the Cisco website.

Step 2   Insert a blank 1.44-MB floppy disk into the drive on the Windows system.

Step 3   To generate the BIOS update disk, double-click BIOS_A04.exe in the Windows file browser.

Complete the following steps to perform the actual BIOS upgrade on your sensor:

Step 4   Insert the newly created BIOS update disk into your IDS 4235 or IDS 4250 appliance.

Step 5   Boot the IDS appliance and follow the onscreen instructions.

CAUTION   Do not turn off the power during the actual BIOS upgrade process, otherwise the sensor may become unusable.

Step 6   Remove the BIOS update disk from the appliance while the appliance is rebooting, otherwise the BIOS upgrade will be started again.

Swapping Interface Cards

With Cisco IDS version 4.0, the command and control interface and the monitoring interface on the IDS 4220 and IDS 4230-FE appliances have been switched. Prior to version 4.0, the interfaces on these appliances were assigned as shown in Figure 7-8.

This change was made for a couple of reasons. The original monitoring interface did not support monitoring 802.1Q trunk packets or the tracking of dropped packets to support the 993 Dropped Packet alarm. The performance on the original monitoring interface is also lower than the built-in interface. For these reasons, version 4.0 uses the built-in interface as its monitoring interface.

Figure 7-8 *IDS 4220/4230 Interfaces Prior to 4.0*

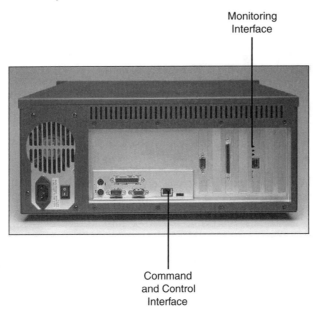

Monitoring
Interface

Command
and Control
Interface

CAUTION If you fail to swap your network connections, you will probably be unable to connect to
your sensor across the network.

IDS Accelerator Card

The performance of the IDS 4250 appliance is 500 Mbps. If you have higher performance
requirements, you can install the IDS XL card into your IDS 4250 appliance (see Figure 7-9).
With the IDS XL card installed in your sensor, its performance is increased to 1000 Mbps.
This card uses hardware acceleration to enhance the performance of your sensor.

Figure 7-9 *IDS Accelerator (XL) Card*

Installing the Accelerator Card

You will install the IDS XL card in the upper PCI slot on the IDS 4250 series appliance (see Figure 7-10).

Figure 7-10 *IDS 4250 Back Panel*

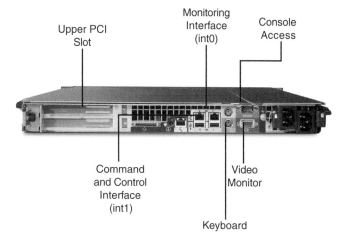

To install the XL card in your IDS 4250 appliance, you need to perform the following steps (refer to the documentation on the Cisco website for the most current installation procedure):

Step 1   Enter the **reset powerdown** command on the appliance CLI to power down the appliance.

Step 2   Remove the power cord and the other cables from the appliance.

Step 3   Unrack the appliance and move it to an electrostatic discharge (ESD)-controlled environment. Before opening the appliance, you need to use the appropriate ESD grounding equipment (such as an ESD wrist strap) to protect the appliance while you install the XL card.

Step 4   Remove the appliance cover by performing the following operations:

— Remove the single screw at the front of the chassis.

— Press the chassis release button on the left side of the appliance cover.

— Use the tabs at the rear of the system (one on the left and one on the right) to lift the appliance cover.

Step 5   Remove the PCI slot cover by performing the following tasks:

— Pull the chassis release button at the back of the chassis toward you to unlock the PCI slot covers.

— Remove the top PCI slot cover.

Step 6   Insert the XL card into the top PCI slot by using enough pressure to securely pop the card into place.

Step 7   Check the back of the chassis to ensure that the card is flush with the PCI slot, and release the PCI slot back to its original position to lock the PCI slot card in place.

Step 8   Close the appliance cover by performing the following tasks:

— Close the right side of the appliance cover.

— Close the left side of the appliance cover, pressing firmly along the edge to lock it in place.

— Replace the screw at the top of the chassis.

Step 9   Replace the power and other connections that you removed from the back of the chassis.

NOTE   The monitoring interface will now be the XL card. You will not be able to use the onboard monitoring interface in conjunction with the XL card. You can only use the onboard interface or the XL card, but not both at the same time.

Step 10   Reboot the appliance, but do not connect the fiber connections to the XL card.

CAUTION   A known problem can cause the appliance to fail to boot if the fiber connectors (on the XL card) are connected the first time that the appliance is booted. During the boot, the firmware is upgraded so the problem only occurs on the initial boot after installing the XL card. This problem only affects IDS 4250 appliances that you are upgrading, because the IDS 4250XL has been rebooted at the factory. Refer to the Release Notes for more information on this issue.

Step 11   After your appliance is completely booted (you see the login prompt), you can connect the fiber connections.

Step 12   Reconfigure the appliance.

IDS Appliance Command-Line Interface

Beginning with Cisco IDS version 4.0, the IDS appliance has a CLI similar to Cisco IOS Software that you can use to configure your sensor. When initially configuring you IDS appliance, you will use the CLI to perform many of the configuration steps.

NOTE	Although you can change most of the appliance's properties via the CLI, you will probably use the graphical user interfaces provided by IDS Device Manager or Management Center for Intrusion Detection System Sensors to perform most of the configuration changes to your appliance.

Using the CLI

You can configure essentially every property of your appliance via the CLI. Understanding the following CLI characteristics enables you to use the CLI more effectively:

- Prompts
- Help
- Tab completion
- Command recall
- Command case sensitivity
- Keywords

Prompts

The prompts displayed by the CLI are not user defined, but they do indicate the area of the CLI that you are currently operating in. For instance, the global configuration mode is indicated by the following prompt (with a sensor name of Sensor):

```
Sensor(config)#
```

For certain CLI commands, the system requires user input. When this happens, a prompt appears that displays an option enclosed in square brackets (such as [yes]). To accept this default value, all you need to do is press the Enter key. You can also override the default value by typing in another value.

When using the CLI, sometimes the information being displayed exceeds the number of lines available on the screen. When this occurs, the appliance presents you with the –more- interactive prompt (indicating that more information is available). To display more of the information, you have the following two options:

- Space key (displays the next screen)

- Enter key (displays the next line)

Sometimes you might want to abandon the current command line and start over with a blank command line. You can abort the current command line by using either the Ctrl+C or Ctrl+Q characters.

To return to a previous command level, use the **exit** command.

Help

To obtain help on a command, use the question mark (**?**) character. You can use the **?** character to obtain help in the following situations:

- After a complete command
- In the middle of a command

When using the help character after a complete command, enter the command, then a space, and then the help character (**?**). This displays the keywords or options that can be used with the partial command that you have already entered, such as the following:

```
Sensor# show ?
clock          Display system clock
events         Display local event log contents
history        Display commands entered in current menu
interfaces     Display statistics and information about system interfaces
privilege      Display current user access role
ssh            Display Secure Shell information
statistics     Display application statistics
tech-support   Generate report of current system status
tls            Display tls certificate information
users          Show all users currently logged into the system
version        Display product version information
sensor# show
Sensor#
```

NOTE   You can also use the help character (**?**) by itself to display all the commands currently available.

You can also enter an incomplete command or option and use the help character to display the commands or options that begin with the specified sequence of characters, such as the following:

```
Sensor# show c?
clock configuration
Sensor(config)# show c
```

Tab Completion

Sometimes you might be unsure of the complete command to enter. After you type the beginning of a command you can press the Tab key to have the system complete the command for you, as in the following command sequence:

```
Sensor# show co<Tab>
Sensor# show configuration
```

If multiple commands match the command segment that you typed, the system cannot fill in the command, but instead will just display your partial command again (indicating that multiple commands match the characters that you have already entered), as in the following command sequence:

```
Sensor# show c<Tab>
Sensor# show
```

The system will also redisplay the partially entered command if no valid command matches the character sequence that you entered, as in the following command sequence:

```
Sensor# show ca<Tab>
Sensor# show ca
```

Command Recall

To cycle through the commands that you have entered via the CLI session, you can use the Up Arrow and Down Arrow keys on your keyboard. When you reach the end of the list, you will see a blank prompt.

NOTE   Instead of the arrow keys, you can also use Ctrl+P for the Up Arrow and Ctrl+N for the Down Arrow.

Command Case Sensitivity

The CLI is not case sensitive. Both Configure and CONFigure represent the same command. When the system echoes the commands that you entered, however, it remembers the case that you typed in. Suppose that you type in the following at the command line:

```
Sensor# CONF
```

Now if you press the Tab key to invoke command completion, the system displays the following:

```
Sensor# CONFigure
```

Keywords

When using the CLI, you will enter various commands to change the configuration of your appliance. You can also use the following two keywords when entering commands via CLI:

- **no**
- **default**

If you want to reverse the effect of a command, just precede the command with the **no** keyword. The **shutdown** command disables an interface. Using the **no shutdown** command enables an interface.

Some commands have a default value. This is common with respect to signature tuning. To return certain commands to their default value, use the **default** keyword when entering these commands.

User Roles

Beginning with version 4.0, the IDS appliance incorporated multiple user roles. When you create an account, you must assign it a user role. This user role then determines the privileges of that account and consequently the operations that the user is capable of performing. Your IDS appliances support the following four user roles:

- Administrator
- Operator
- Viewer
- Service

Administrator

When you assign the Administrator role to an account, you enable the user of that account to perform every operation on the appliance that is available via the CLI. Some of the capabilities available to accounts with Administrator access are as follows:

- Add users and assign passwords
- Enable and disable interfaces
- Assign interfaces to an interface group
- Modify host allowed to access appliance
- Modify sensor address configuration
- Tune signatures
- Assign virtual sensor configuration
- Manage routers
- Full view access to events and configuration information

Operator

The second highest user role is the Operator role. Any accounts assigned the Operator role have unrestricted viewing capability to sensor information along with the following functions:

- Modify their own password
- Tune signatures
- Manage routers
- Full view access to events and configuration information

Viewer

The lowest privileged user role is the Viewer role. When you assign the Viewer role to an account, you enable the user to view the configuration and event data on your appliance, but the only information that the user can change on the appliance is the password. When creating accounts on the appliance, this is the default role for an account if one is not specified.

NOTE   Applications (such as the IDS Event Viewer) that you use to monitor the operation of your IDS appliance only require Viewer level access to the sensor to operate. You can create an account with Viewer access using the CLI, and then configure your monitoring applications to use this account when retrieving information from your IDS appliance.

Service

The Service role enables you to create a special account that has access to the native OS command shell rather than the sensor's normal CLI interface. The purpose of this account is not to support configuration of the sensor, but instead to provide an enhanced trouble-shooting capability. By default, your sensor does not have a service account. You must create a service account to enable the Cisco Technical Assistance Center (TAC) to use this account during troubleshooting.

The sensor only allows you to assign the Service role to one account on the sensor. When the service account's password is set (or reset), the root account's password is automatically synchronized to this new password. This enables the service account user to use the **su** command to access root privileges on the sensor.

Root Account

On UNIX based systems, the privileged super-user account is named root. This account is used for administration purposes and can perform all operations on the system.

CAUTION   Making modifications to your sensor using the Service account can make your sensor unsupported by the TAC. Cisco does not support adding any services or programs to your sensor because it can impact the proper performance and functioning of the other IDS services. Furthermore, access to the sensor through the Service account is logged.

CLI Command Modes

The CLI on your IDS appliance is organized into various modes. Each of these modes gives you access to a subset of the commands that are available on your IDS appliance. Numerous CLI modes are available on the IDS appliance, such as the following:

- Privileged EXEC
- Global configuration
- Interface command-control configuration
- Interface group configuration
- Interface sensing configuration
- Service
- Service alarm-channel-configuration
- Service host
- Service NetworkAccess
- Service virtual-sensor-configuration
- Tune micro engines
- Tune alarm channel

Privileged Exec

The *privileged EXEC* mode is the initial mode that you enter upon logging in to the IDS appliance. You can recognize this mode because it is comprised of just the sensor name followed by the pound sign (#) character, such as the following (assuming a sensor name of IDS4250):

```
IDS4250#
```

Some of tasks that you can perform at the privileged EXEC mode are as follows:

- Initialize the sensor
- Reboot the sensor
- Enter global configuration mode
- Terminate the current login session
- Display system settings

Global Configuration

Similar to the Cisco IOS Software, you need to enter the *global configuration* mode to change the configuration parameters on your IDS appliance. You access the global configuration mode by entering the **configure terminal** command from the privileged EXEC mode. When you enter this mode, the prompt changes to the following:

```
IDS4250(config)#
```

Some of tasks that you can perform at the global configuration mode are as follows:

- Change the sensor's host name
- Create user accounts
- Configure SSH, Telnet, and Transport Layer Security (TLS) settings
- Re-image the application partition
- Upgrade and downgrade system software and images
- Enter interface configuration modes
- Enter service configuration modes

Interface Command-Control Configuration

The *interface command-control configuration* mode is a third-level mode that enables you to perform the following tasks:

- Configure the IP interface information for the command and control interface
- Display current settings for command and control interface

You can recognize this mode because the prompt changes to the following:

```
IDS4250(config-if)#
```

Interface Group Configuration

The *interface group configuration* mode is a third-level mode that enables you to perform the following tasks:

- Add or remove a sensing interface to the interface group
- Disable the interface group
- Display current settings for the interface group

You can recognize this mode because the prompt changes to the following:

```
IDS4250(config-ifg)#
```

Interface Sensing Configuration

The *interface sensing configuration* mode is a third-level mode that enables you to perform the following tasks:

- Enable the sensing interface
- Disable the sensing interface
- Display current settings for the sensing interface

You can recognize this mode because the prompt changes to the following:

```
IDS4250(config-ifs)#
```

Service

The *service* mode is a generic third-level command mode. It enables you to enter the configuration mode for the following services:

- Alarm-channel-configuration
- Authentication
- Host
- Logger
- NetworkAccess
- SshKnownHosts
- TrustedCertificates
- Virtual-sensor-configuration
- WebServer

Service Alarm-Channel-Configuration

The *alarm-channel-configuration* mode is a third-level service mode that enables you to perform the following tasks:

- Display current alarm channel configuration
- Enter configuration mode for the alarm channel

You can recognize this mode because the prompt changes to the following:

```
IDS4250(config-acc)#
```

Through the alarm-channel-configuration mode, you can enter the *tune alarm channel* fourth-level mode, which enables you to tune the alarm channel parameters. You can recognize this mode because the prompt changes to the following:

```
IDS4250(config-acc-virtualAlarm)#
```

Service Host

The *host* mode is a third-level service mode that enables you to perform various host-related tasks such as the following:

- Enter the networkParams configuration mode
- Enter the timeParams configuration mode
- Display current settings

You can recognize this mode because the prompt changes to the following:

```
IDS4250(config-Host)#
```

The following two fourth-level configuration modes are accessible via the host mode:

- networkParams
- timeParams

The *networkParams* mode enables you to configure numerous host-related items, such as the following:

- Configure sensor IP address
- Define default gateway
- Define access lists
- Enable/disable the Telnet server

The networkParams mode is recognizable by the following command prompt:

```
IDS4250(config-Host-net)#
```

The *timeParams* mode enables you to configure time-related items, such as the following:

- Define Network Time Protocol (NTP) servers
- Configure the sensor's time zone
- Display current time configuration

You can recognize the timeParams mode because the prompt changes to the following:

```
IDS4250(config-Host-tim)#
```

Service NetworkAccess

The *NetworkAccess* mode is a third-level service mode that enables you to perform the following tasks:

- Configure settings for PIX firewalls controlled by the network access control (NAC) process
- Configure settings for routers controlled by the NAC process
- Display current NAC-related settings

You can recognize this mode because the prompt changes to the following:

```
IDS4250(config-NetworkAccess)#
```

You can also enter a general fourth-level mode that enables you to define many of the sensor's IP blocking (shun) settings, such as the following:

- Configure never-shun addresses
- Configure the master blocking sensor
- Enable access control list (ACL) logging
- Display current shun-related settings

You can recognize this fourth-level mode because the prompt changes to the following:

```
IDS4250(config-NetworkAccess-gen)#
```

Service Virtual-Sensor-Configuration

The *virtual-sensor-configuration* mode is a third-level mode service mode that enables you to perform the following tasks:

- Reset signature settings to the default configuration
- Display current virtual sensor configuration
- Enter micro-engine tuning mode

You can recognize this mode because the prompt changes to the following:

```
IDS4250(config-vsc)#
```

Through the virtual-sensor-configuration mode, you can access the *tune micro engines* mode (a fourth-level mode that enables you to tune the signature micro-engines). You can recognize this mode because the prompt changes to the following:

```
IDS4250(config-vsc-virtualSensor)#
```

Signature micro-engines are explained in Chapter 13, "Cisco IDS Alarms and Signatures."

Administrative Tasks

The sensor command line enables you to perform numerous administrative tasks, such as the following:

- Display the current configuration
- Back up the current configuration
- Restore the current configuration
- Display events
- Reboot the sensor
- Display tech support information

Some of these tasks are covered in Chapter 15, "Cisco IDS Maintenance and Tuning." For detailed information on how to configure these administrative tasks, refer to the CLI documentation on the Cisco website.

Configuration Tasks

The CLI provides you with a textual interface that enables you to configure essentially every facet of the sensor's configuration, such as the following:

- Configuring alarm channel system variables
- Configuring alarm channel event filters
- Viewing signature engines
- Configuring virtual sensor system variables
- Tuning signature engines
- Generating IP logs

Configuring these tasks through the CLI, however, is not a simple task. Most people prefer to use a graphical interface, such as Cisco IDS Device Manager, to configure these parameters. Numerous chapters in this book explain how to configure these characteristics of your sensor using both Cisco IDS Device Manager and Cisco IDS Management Center. For complete documentation on Cisco IDS version 4.0 CLI, refer to the documentation on the Cisco website at http://www.cisco.com/univercd/cc/td/doc/product/iaabu/csids/csids9/cmdref/index.htm.

Installing the IDS Appliance

When installing your sensor, the necessary steps vary depending on whether you are upgrading an appliance from version 3.1 or configuring a brand new appliance. In each situation, you must go through a series of initial configuration steps. If you are upgrading, however, you must also perform some initial tasks that are not required when installing a brand new version 4.0 appliance (because it comes with the 4.0 software already loaded on it).

Upgrading from 3.1 to 4.0

If you are upgrading an appliance from version 3.1 to version 4.0, you must install the version 4.0 software on your appliance using the Cisco IDS version 4.0 CD. Before installing this software on your appliance, however, you must save the current configuration on your appliance so that you can use the information when installing the version 4.0 software.

NOTE The 4.0 software is not an upgrade of the existing 3.1 software. When you install the 4.0 software, it removes your existing software (including all of your configuration information).

Obtaining 3.0 Appliance Configuration

You can obtain the current configuration on your 3.1 appliance by generating a diagnostic report through the IDS Device Manager. You can access the diagnostic report through the Administration, Diagnostics tabs (see Figure 7-11).

Figure 7-11   *IDS Device Manager Diagnostic Report in 3.1*

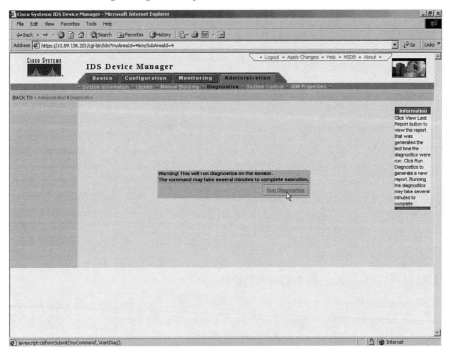

NOTE	The diagnostic report might take several minutes to complete.

When the report is complete, you can view the report by clicking the View Results icon displayed on the screen. The report displays in a new browser window on your system. You can then save this report to your system by using the File, Save As menu option.

At this point, you need to switch the command and control interfaces if you are upgrading either an IDS 4220-E or a 4230-FE appliance. Figure 7-12 shows the back panel for one of these sensors with the various connections labeled as they should be configured when using the 4.0 software.

Figure 7-12   *IDS 4220/4230 Back Panel in 4.0*

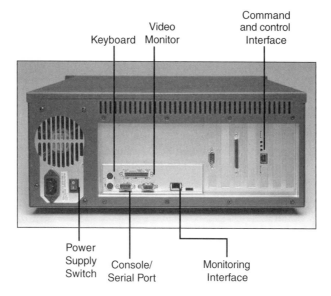

Installing 4.0 Software from CD

After powering on the appliance, insert the Cisco IDS Upgrade/Recovery CD into the CD-ROM drive located in the front of the appliance. A textual boot menu displays, explaining the two options that you can use to install the 4.0 software.

You can either install from a keyboard connected to the appliance or through a serial connection (via the console port). Your two options are as follows:

- **s** (for console port connection)
- **k** (for attached keyboard)

NOTE	While the software is loaded onto your appliance, you might see a blue screen (without any status messages). This occurs while files are being copied from the CD to your hard drive and is normal. Plus the default installation option is serial. So if you just press Return from the keyboard connected to the sensor (instead of entering **s** or **k**), the installation process will use the serial port rather than the connected monitor and keyboard.

When the installation is complete, you can continue with the sensor configuration. At this point, the steps are the same for both IDS appliances that are being upgraded as well as brand new appliances.

Initial Configuration Tasks

Whether you are installing a brand new appliance or upgrading an existing appliance, you need to complete the following initial configuration tasks:

- Access the CLI
- Run the **setup** command
- Configure trusted hosts
- Manually set the system clock

Some other tasks that you also might need to perform during initialization include the following:

- Change your password
- Add and remove users
- Add known SSH hosts

NOTE	Changing your password refers to using the **password** CLI command to modify the password for an existing account. You must change the password for the default cisco account to initially access the CLI.

Accessing the CLI

To begin you sensor initialization, you need to access the CLI using either an attached keyboard or a serial connection to the console port. The default account is *cisco* with a password of *cisco*. This account is assigned the role of Administrator, making it a privileged account on the system.

Immediately you are prompted to change this default password. Your new password must meet the following conditions to be accepted by your sensor software:

- At least eight characters long
- Not a dictionary word

Selecting Strong Passwords

Selecting strong passwords helps to ensure that an attacker cannot easily guess the passwords using commonly available password cracking tools. The sensor performs some basic checks to strengthen the passwords that you use, but you can also take steps to create strong passwords. Some things to keep in mind when selecting a password are as follows:

- Do not use only letters or only numbers.
- Do not use recognizable words.
- Do not use foreign words.
- Do not use personal information.
- Do not write your password down.

Some things that you can do to make your password selection better are as follows:

- Make the password at least eight characters long.
- Mix upper- and lowercase letters.
- Mix letters and numbers.
- Include nonalphanumeric characters, such as $ and &.
- Pick a password that you can remember.

Running the setup Command

When you access the CLI using the default cisco account, you will see the sensor# prompt. To configure the basic sensor parameters, run the **setup** command. This command enables you to configure the following sensor parameters:

- Host name
- IP address
- Netmask
- Default gateway

- Telnet server status (default disabled)
- Web server port (default 443)

NOTE If you are upgrading your appliance, you can obtain this information from the diagnostic report that you generated before installing the 4.0 software.

When you run the **setup** command, the sensor displays the currently configured options, such as in the following example:

```
sensor# setup
    --- System Configuration Dialog ---
At any point you may enter a question mark '?' for help.
Use ctrl-c to abort configuration dialog at any prompt.
Default settings are in square brackets '[]'.

Current Configuration:
service host
networkParams
hostname sensor
ipAddress 10.1.9.201
netmask 255.255.255.0
defaultGateway 10.1.9.1
telnetOption disabled
exit
exit
!
service webServer
general
ports 443
exit
exit

Current time: Tue Sep  9 05:19:42 2003
Setup Configuration last modified: Tue Sep  9 05:09:22 2003
Continue with configuration dialog?[yes]:
```

If you want to change the system configuration, you need to enter **yes** (or just press the Enter) at the following prompt:

```
Continue with configuration dialog?[yes]:
```

Then you will be prompted for the configuration parameters one by one. After you enter this information, the system will display the new values for the parameters and prompt you to accept the changes, as in the following:

```
The following configuration was entered.

service host
networkParams
hostname sensor
ipAddress 10.89.139.85
netmask 255.255.255.0
defaultGateway 10.89.139.1
telnetOption disabled
```

```
exit
exit
!
service webServer
general
ports 443
exit
exit
```

```
Use this configuration?[yes]:yes
```

Enter **yes** (or just press Enter) to save the configuration. You might also be prompted to reboot the sensor with the following command:

```
Continue with reboot? [yes]:
```

If you still need to configure a few more parameters, you can enter **no** at this prompt. You can make your additional changes, and then reboot the sensor to make all the changes take effect at the same time.

NOTE   To reboot the sensor later, use the **reset** command from the privileged EXEC mode.

Configuring Trusted Hosts

To access your sensor via the command and control interfaces, you need to configure the appropriate network access lists on your IDS appliance. The **accessList** command enables you to set any number of IP addresses (either host or network) that are allowed to establish connections (such as Telnet, FTP, SSH, and HTTP) to the sensor. The syntax for the **accessList** command is as follows:

```
accessList ipAddress IP Address¦Network Address netmask netmask
```

You configure network access lists via the host service. The following command sequence enables the network 172.21.16.0 to establish TCP connections with your sensor:

```
sensor# configure terminal
sensor(config)# service host
sensor(config-Host)# networkParams
sensor(config-Host-net)# accessList ipAddress 172.21.16.0 netmask 255.255.255.0
```

NOTE   When you set up access for a single host address, you do not need to specify the **netmask** parameter.

After configuring your trusted hosts, you will be able to access your sensor interactively across the network using either Telnet or SSH. SSH is the preferred method because the session with your sensor is encrypted. By default, the sensor is configured with an IP address of 10.1.9.201 and allows access to the sensor from any system connected to the 10.1.9.0 Class C subnet.

CAUTION   When changing the access restrictions on your sensor, you need to be careful. If you accidentally enter an incorrect value, you can easily prevent your own system from accessing the sensor. If this happens, you will need to restore connectivity by configuring the sensor from a directly connected keyboard and monitor or through the sensor's serial port.

Manually Setting the System Clock

In many network environments, you use automatic clock functionality, such as NTP. These configurations automatically adjust the time on your devices based on a known time source. If you do not have such a mechanism, you may need to set the time on your IDS appliance manually.

NOTE   The IDS Module obtains its time configuration from the Catalyst 6500 switch that it is housed in so you should not need to set the time using the **clock set** command.

To manually set the time on your IDS sensor, use the **clock set** privileged EXEC command. The syntax for this command is as follows:

```
clock set hh:mm:[ss] month day year
```

The parameters for the **clock set** command are described in Table 7-1.

Table 7-1   **clock set** *Parameters*

Parameter	Description
hh:mm:[ss]	Current time in 24-hour format. The seconds are optional.
day	Numeric value indicating the current day of the month (1–31).
month	Name of the current month (without any abbreviation), such as January or March.
year	The current 4-digit year value (such as 2003).

Suppose that you want to set the current time on your IDS appliance to 1 o'clock in the afternoon on January 1, 2004. To accomplish this, use the following command after logging in to your appliance:

```
sensor# clock set 13:00 January 1 2004
sensor#
```

Changing your Password

Each user on your IDS appliance is able to change his or her password. You can change your password via the CLI using the **password** global configuration mode command.

NOTE   You can also change your account password through the graphical management applications (such as IDS Device Manager).

The **password** command does not take any parameters. To change your password, you need to enter your old password, and then your new password twice (to verify that you entered it correctly, because it is not displayed on the screen). When entering a new password, you need to create strong passwords based on the guidelines listed earlier in this chapter. In addition, the passwords must match the basic checks performed by the sensor software, which are as follows:

- At least eight characters long
- Not a dictionary word

Adding and Removing Users

From the global configuration mode, you can add new users to your sensor, as well as remove existing users. The **username** global configuration mode command enables you to add new users. To remove an existing user, just insert the keyword **no** in front of the regular **username** command. The syntax for the **username** command is as follows:

```
username name [password password] [privilege Administrator¦Operator¦Viewer¦Service]
```

NOTE   Both the password and the privilege level are optional parameters of the **username** command. If you do not supply a password, the system prompts you for a password. And if you do not supply a privilege level, the system automatically assigns a role of Viewer to the new account.

The following sequence of commands illustrates the process of adding the user newuser to your sensor with a privilege level of Operator:

```
sensor# configure terminal
sensor(config)# username newuser privilege operator
Enter new login password: ******
Re-enter new login password: ******
sensor(config)# exit
sensor#
```

NOTE From the privileged EXEC mode, you can confirm your user configuration changes by running the **show users all** command. The following represents an example of the output from this command:

```
sensor# show users all
    CLI ID  User        Privilege
    16727   cisco       administrator
    27707   cisco       administrator
*   30599   operator1   operator
            viewer      viewer
sensor#
```

You will want to add accounts to support your network environment. At a minimum, you need to create an account with Viewer privileges that you can use to enable your monitoring application to access the sensor and retrieve alarm information.

Adding a Known SSH Host

Your sensor maintains a list of validated SSH known hosts so that the sensor can verify the identity of the servers that it communicates with when it is operating as an SSH client. Adding an entry to the known SSH hosts list also enables you to do the following:

- Automatically or manually upgrade the sensor via Secure Copy (SCP)
- Copy current configurations, backup configurations, and IP logs via SCP

The syntax for the **ssh host-key** command is as follows:

```
ssh host-key ip-address [key-modulus-length public-exponent public-modulus]
```

The parameters for the **ssh host-key** command are described in Table 7-2.

Table 7-2 ssh host-key *Parameters*

Parameter	Description
Ip-address	IP address of the SSH server
key-modulus-length	(Optional) ASCII decimal integer in the range [511–2048]
public-exponent	(Optional) ASCII decimal integer in the range [3–2^32]
public-modulus	(Optional) ASCII decimal integer, x, such that (2^key-modulus-length) < x < (2^[key-modulus-length + 1])

NOTE You normally specify only an IP address for the **ssh host-key** command. The sensor contacts the server and retrieves the other information. In addition, these keys are for SSH servers that the sensor needs to connect to. You do not have to define keys for the clients that connect to the sensor itself.

The following command sequence adds the SSH host key for 10.89.132.78 to the list of known SSH host keys:

```
sensor(config)# configure terminal
sensor(config)# ssh host-key 10.89.132.78
MD5 fingerprint is BE:70:50:15:2C:13:97:5C:72:53:06:9C:DC:4D:A3:20
Bubble Babble is xepof-tudek-vycal-cynud-tolok-holek-zygaf-kuzak-syfot-tubec-paxox
Would you like to add this to the known host table for this host?[yes]: yes
sensor(config)# exit
sensor#
```

Summary

Installing network sensors correctly is an important component in protecting your network using the Cisco intrusion protection solution. Cisco provides appliance sensors that support a wide range of bandwidths. The common appliance sensors and their associated performance ratings are as follows:

- **IDS 4210**—45 Mbps
- **IDS 4215**—80 Mbps
- **IDS 4235**—200 Mbps
- **IDS 4250**—500 Mbps
- **IDS 4250XL**—1000 Mbps

When installing these appliances, you need to understand specific hardware considerations that can impact your installation and the fact that these devices are designed specifically to perform intrusion detection analysis. Installing any other software on these systems can interfere with their analysis capabilities and reduce their overall performance.

Beginning with Cisco IDS version 4.0, the appliance sensors have an extensive CLI that enables you to configure every aspect of your sensor's operation. Although the commands differ, using the CLI is similar to Cisco IOS Software. The CLI is divided into the multiple configuration modes, each of which provides a subset of the commands available to the user, such as the following:

- Privileged EXEC
- Global configuration
- Interface command-control configuration
- Interface group configuration
- Interface sensing configuration
- Service
- Service alarm-channel-configuration
- Service host

- Service NetworkAccess
- Service virtual-sensor-configuration
- Tune micro engines
- Tune alarm channel

Although the CLI enables you to configure every aspect of the sensor, configuring certain aspects, such as signature tuning, is better suited to the graphical interfaces (such as Cisco IDS Device Manager). When troubleshooting, however, you can use this configuration capability to narrow down a specific problem or you can create custom configuration scripts that you use to adjust the operation of your sensor.

When installing the version 4.0 software, you need to perform some basic initialization steps to get the sensor running. The basic appliance initialization tasks are as follows:

- Run the **setup** command
- Configure trusted hosts
- Manually configure the time

The **setup** CLI command configures the following parameters:

- Sensor host name
- Sensor IP address
- Sensor netmask
- Default gateway
- Telnet server status
- Web server port

Some other tasks that you might need to perform during initialization include the following:

- Change your password
- Add and remove users
- Add known SSH hosts

Review Questions

The following questions test your retention of the material presented in this chapter. The answers to the review questions are in Appendix B, "Answers to Chapter Review Questions."

1 When you upgrade an IDS 4220 or IDS 4230-FE appliance, what must you do to ensure that you can monitor traffic correctly?

2 Which configuration mode enables you to define trusted hosts that are able to establish TCP connections with the sensor?

3 What character do you use to obtain help via the appliance CLI?

4 How can you recall a previous command that you entered when using the CLI?

5 What command enables you to allow a host or network to connect to the sensor?

6 What keyword do you use to reverse the effect of a CLI command?

7 How many different user roles are available to assign to accounts on your sensor?

8 What is the most privileged user role that you can assign to a user who uses the CLI?

9 Which user role only enables the user to examine the sensor's events and configuration but does not allow the user to change the configuration?

10 What parameters do you configure using the **setup** CLI command?

11 What is the purpose of the Service user role?

12 What command do you enter on the CLI to enter global configuration mode?

13 What command enables you to manually set the time via the CLI?

14 How many Service accounts can you have on your sensor?

15 What user role would you usually assign to the account that you use to enable your monitoring applications to retrieve information from your sensor?

16 What character do you use on the CLI to cause your sensor to automatically expand the rest of a command for you?

17 What extra step might you need to perform before upgrading the software on an IDS 4235 appliance to version 4.0?

18 What character do you enter to abort the current CLI command line and start over with an empty command line?

19 When a CLI command's output extends beyond a single screen, what character do you use to scroll the output up by a single line?

20 When a CLI command's output extends beyond a single screen, what character do you use to show the next screen of information?

Upon completion of this chapter, you will be able to perform the following tasks:

- Explain the features of the Intrusion Detection System Module (IDSM)
- Explain the differences between the first- and second-generation IDSMs
- Identify the ports available on the second-generation IDSM (IDSM-2)
- Identify the tasks required to initialize the IDSM-2
- Explain the basic troubleshooting tasks for the IDSM-2

CHAPTER 8

Cisco IDS Module Configuration

Besides the network appliance sensors, Cisco IDS also supports the Cisco IDS Module (IDSM), a switch-based sensor that resides in your Catalyst 6500 switch. Cisco IDS version 4.0 only supports the second-generation IDSM line card (IDSM-2). This chapter provides a detailed explanation of the IDSM-2 and the tasks required to configure it to operate as part of your overall Cisco intrusion protection system.

Cisco IDS Module (IDSM)

Cisco initially introduced the first-generation IDSM to enable you to integrate your Cisco IDS functionality directly into your Catalyst 6000 family switch and capture traffic directly off of the switch's backplane via a switch line card. With Cisco IDS version 4.0, Cisco introduced the second-generation IDSM, called the *IDSM-2*. This new module runs the same code base as the appliance sensor. Therefore, both platforms now support the same functionality.

Intrusion Detection System Module 2 (IDSM-2) Technical Specifications

If you are considering an IDSM-2 deployment throughout your network, you should understand its capabilities and requirements. The specifications for deploying IDSM-2 fall into the following two categories:

- Performance capabilities
- Catalyst 6500 requirements

Performance Capabilities

Like the original IDSM, the IDSM-2 is a single-slot switch card that provides the following enhanced capabilities:

- **Performance**—600 Mbps
- **Monitoring interface**—Gigabit

- **Command and control interface**—Gigabit
- **TCP reset interface**—Gigabit

Catalyst 6500 Requirements

Unlike the appliance sensor, the IDSM-2 is a switch card. Therefore, to deploy the IDSM-2 functionality, you must have a Catalyst 6500 family switch. Furthermore, to successfully use your IDSM-2 as another component in your overall Cisco IDS solution, your switch operating system must match one of the following requirements:

- Catalyst OS 7.5(1) or later (on Supervisor Engine)
- Cisco IOS Release 12.1(19)E or later

NOTE   Cisco IOS Software only supports Supervisor Engine 2 with Multilayer Switch Feature Card (MSFC).

Although meeting the operating system version on your Supervisor Engine enables you to install and use the IDSM-2 on your switch, there are also a couple of other requirements, depending on the features that you plan to use in conjunction with the IDSM-2.

You have several traffic-capture options on your Catalyst switch. The most common is probably the Switch Port Analyzer (SPAN) feature. If you plan to capture traffic using VLAN access control lists (VACLs), however, you also need to have a Policy Feature Card (PFC).

Your IDSM-2 also supports device management. This means that it can dynamically restrict network traffic by updating access controls on various network devices, such as the following:

- Cisco IOS routers
- Catalyst 6000 switches
- PIX firewalls

Key Features

The original IDSM incorporated IDS functionality directly into your switch infrastructure. This switch sensor provided the following capabilities:

- Merged switching and security into a single chassis
- Ability to monitor multiple VLANs
- Did not impact switch performance

This first-generation switch sensor, however, did not provide all the functionality of the appliance sensors. To enhance the capability of the switch sensor, the IDSM-2 provides more capabilities than the original IDSM. Besides increasing the performance capacity of the IDSM-2, it provides the following capabilities or features:

- Merged switching and security into a single chassis
- Ability to monitor multiple VLANs
- Does not impact switch performance
- Attacks and signatures equal to appliance sensor
- Uses the same code base of the appliance sensor
- Support for improved management techniques, such as the IDS Device Manager (IDM)

IDSM versus IDSM-2

The IDSM-2 incorporates many new capabilities that were previously unavailable with the original IDSM line card. Some of the enhanced functionality provided by IDSM-2 includes the following:

- TCP reset support
- IP logging support
- Command-line interface (CLI) support
- Full signature engine support
- Fabric-enabled
- Support for Remote Data Exchange Protocol (RDEP; pull method for event retrieval)
- Enhanced management support (IDM and CLI)

Fabric Enabled

Being fabric-enabled means that the module has a direct connection to the Catalyst 6500 forwarding bus.

Table 8-1 shows a comparison of the features supported by IDSM and IDSM-2.

Table 8-1   *IDSM versus IDSM-2*

Feature	IDSM	IDSM-2
SPAN/RSPAN	Yes	Yes
VACL capture	Yes	Yes

continues

Table 8-1   *IDSM versus IDSM-2 (Continued)*

Feature	IDSM	IDSM-2
Shunning	Yes	Yes
IEV	Yes	Yes
IDM	No	Yes
TCP resets	No	Yes
IP logging	No	Yes
CLI	No	Yes
Signature engines	No	Yes
Same code as appliance sensors	No	Yes
Fabric-enabled	No	Yes
Event retrieval method	PostOffice (push)	RDEP (pull)

IDSM-2 Configuration

Because the IDSM-2 shares the same code base as the appliance sensor, the initialization steps performed on the appliance sensor also apply to IDSM-2. The major difference between the appliance sensor and IDSM-2 is that you need to configure the capture ports on IDSM-2. These ports are internally connected to the switch's backplane, in contrast to the appliance sensor, where you physically connect the monitoring ports via Ethernet cables to your switch (or other network device).

IDSM-2 Initialization

To enable your IDSM-2 to become a functional component of your Cisco IDS, you need to perform the following basic initialization tasks:

- Verify IDSM-2 status
- Initialize the IDSM-2
- Configure the command and control port
- Configure the switch traffic capture settings

Verifying IDSM-2 Status

After installing the IDSM-2 into your Catalyst 6500 family switch, you can verify that the switch has recognized the IDSM-2 line card via the **show module** switch command (see "Catalyst 6500 Commands" later in the chapter). Executing this command provides detailed information about the line cards in your switch. You should see a line similar to the following for your IDSM-2 line card:

```
Mod Slot Ports Module-Type                 Model           Sub Status
 8   8    8    Intrusion Detection Syste WS-SVC-IDSM2      yes ok
```

The "ok" indicates that the card is working, and the correct name indicates that the switch correctly recognized the line card.

NOTE   It is also normal for the **show module** command to display a status of "other" rather than "ok" when the IDS Module is first installed. When the IDSM-2 completes its diagnostic routines and comes online, the status will change to "ok," but this may take up to 5 minutes.

Initializing the IDSM-2

The basic initialization tasks for the IDSM-2 are the same as the appliance sensor (see Chapter 7, "Cisco IDS Network Sensor Installation"). These tasks include the following:

- Access the CLI
- Run the **setup** command
- Configure trusted hosts

NOTE   Unlike the appliance sensor, the IDSM-2 receives its time from the Catalyst 6500 switch. To make sure that the time on the IDSM-2 is correct, however, you need to verify that the time zone on your supervisor card is correct. The IDSM-2 receives the Coordinated Universal Time (UTC) from the Catalyst 6500 switch and converts it to local time on the IDSM-2 using the time zone configured on the IDSM-2. This transfer occurs when the IDSM-2 is booted.

Some other tasks that you also might need to perform during initialization include the following:

- Change your password
- Add and remove users
- Add known Secure Shell (SSH) hosts

One of the benefits of having the same code base on both the appliance sensor and the IDSM-2 is that the configuration tasks then become very similar, which reduces the total amount of knowledge needed to install both types of sensors. Chapter 7 explains all of these initial configuration tasks in detail.

Configuring the Command and Control Port

To enable your monitoring applications and management software (such as IEV and IDM) to communicate with your IDSM-2, you need to configure the command and control port on IDSM-2. This includes assigning it an IP address and configuring the default gateway for the IDSM-2 command and control port.

Configuring the Switch Traffic Capture Settings

Besides establishing management access, you also need to configure the capture ports on your IDSM-2 so that your switch sensor can analyze your network traffic. Capturing important network traffic while not exceeding the IDSM-2's 600-Mbps capacity is the key to successfully deploying IDSM-2 on your network.

IDSM-2 Ports

To perform its operation, IDSM-2 includes several internal ports that fall into the following three functional categories:

- TCP reset port
- Command and control port
- Monitoring ports

NOTE   The ports on IDSM-2 are not physical ports that you can see. Instead, they are directly connected into the switch's backplane.

TCP Reset Port

The initial version of IDSM did not provide the capability to initiate TCP resets in response to attack traffic. This limitation has been overcome in IDSM-2 by the inclusion of a port specifically for generating TCP resets. The two monitoring ports on IDSM-2 cannot transmit the TCP resets packets. By providing a port specifically for the TCP reset traffic, the monitoring ports can focus strictly on capturing traffic.

Port 1 on the IDSM-2 is used for TCP reset traffic. You need to configure port 1 with the same settings (with respect to VLANs) as your monitoring ports. It will not be monitoring any traffic, but it needs to be able to generate a TCP reset for any connection that your IDSM-2 monitoring ports can analyze.

Command and Control Port

Your management application needs to be able to communicate with the IDSM-2 to change its configuration and operating characteristics. Your monitoring application also needs to access the IDSM-2 to retrieve alarms. Both of these operations are conducted through the command and control interface.

Port 2 on the IDSM-2 is the command and control interface. You will configure an IP address for this port (and assign the appropriate VLAN on your switch) to enable your IDSM-2 to be accessible from the network.

Monitoring Ports

The last two ports on the IDSM-2 are the monitoring ports. Your IDSM-2 receives all the network traffic that it analyzes through these two monitoring ports, ports 7 and 8. You can use either or both of these ports to monitor your network traffic. Due to processor limitations, the IDSM-2 is only capable of processing 600 Mbps of network traffic. The two monitoring interfaces are easily capable of exceeding the 600 Mbps limitation, so you must be careful to not overload your IDSM-2 with too much traffic. You can monitor for this situation by enabling Signature 993, Missed Packet Count, to determine whether your IDSM-2 is receiving more traffic than it can process.

NOTE	The reason that the IDSM-2 has two monitoring ports is that it uses the same accelerator card that is used by the IDS-4250 appliance sensor. This accelerator card provides two 1-gigabit interfaces.

Capturing Traffic

The IDSM-2 has the processing power to capture and analyze approximately 600 Mbps of network traffic. This traffic is captured directly off of the switch's backplane. You can use one of the following three mechanisms to capture network traffic for your IDSM-2 to analyze:

- RSPAN feature
- SPAN feature
- VACL capture feature

Each of these capture mechanisms has strengths and weaknesses. For a detailed description of these features refer to Chapter 6, "Capturing Network Traffic."

IDSM-2 Traffic Flow

Unlike the network appliance, the traffic flow to the IDSM-2 line card requires a little more explanation (see Figure 8-1). Furthermore, understanding this traffic flow is an important aspect of effectively using your IDSM-2 to capture and analyze network traffic. Although the IDSM-2 receives traffic directly from your switch's backplane, your Catalyst 6500 family switch must be configured to enable traffic to flow to and from the various ports on the IDSM-2 line card.

Figure 8-1 *IDSM-2 Traffic Flow*

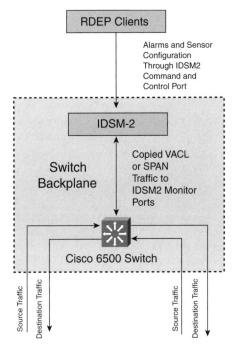

Traffic enters the Catalyst 6500 switch destined for a host or network. A copy of this traffic is then sent through the switch backplane to your IDSM-2 for intrusion detection analysis. Alarms are stored in the Event Store (just like the appliance sensors) until your monitoring application retrieves these alarms via the command and control interface.

Catalyst 6500 Switch Configuration

A significant portion of the initial setup of your IDSM-2 involves configuring the switch to send traffic to your IDSM-2 monitoring ports and enabling external applications to access the IDSM-2 via the command and control port. The following examples illustrate the commands that are used when the Catalyst 6500 is running CatOS. For an example of the commands used in a CatIOS environment, refer to Appendix A, "Cisco Secure IDS Tuning: Case Studies."

Configuring Command and Control Port

Your management and monitoring applications (such as IDM, IEV, IDS MC, and Security Monitor) access the IDSM-2 through the command and control interface. When initially configuring the IDSM-2 through its CLI, you assign the command and control interface an IP address and default gateway. To complete the configuration of the command and control port, however, you must also assign the correct VLAN to the command and control port on the Catalyst 6500 switch.

NOTE   The command and control port on your IDSM-2 is a prime target for attack. When configuring the command and control port on your IDSM-2, you need to minimize the ability of an attacker to access your IDSM-2 by constructing an out-of-band management network, such as a creating a specific management VLAN.

To define a VLAN for a port on your Catalyst 6500 switch, you use the **set vlan** command. This command groups one or more ports into a single VLAN. You can also use this command to set the private VLAN type or unmap VLANs. These extra features are explained in the Catalyst switch documentation. The syntax for the basic **set vlan** command is as follows:

```
set vlan vlan_num mod/ports
```

The parameters for the **set vlan** command are explained in Table 8-2.

Table 8-2   set vlan *Parameters*

Parameter	Description
vlan_num	Number identifying the VLAN
mod/ports	Number of the module and ports on the module that you want to add to the specifying VLAN

NOTE   The IDSM-2 command and control port (port 2) must be assigned to a VLAN that can communicate with your management and monitoring applications. Otherwise, you will not be able to configure the IDSM-2 or retrieve alarm information.

Suppose you place an IDSM-2 in slot 3 on your Catalyst 6500 switch and that your management VLAN is 120. To assign port 2 (the IDSM-2 command and control port) to VLAN 120, use the following command:

```
Console> (enable) set vlan 120 3/2
VLAN 120 modified.
VLAN  Mod/Ports
----  -----------------
120   3/2
Console> (enable)
```

Monitored Traffic

To analyze traffic, your IDSM-2 must receive traffic on its monitoring ports (port 7 and port 8). You need to configure your Catalyst switch to copy selected traffic to the monitoring ports on your IDSM-2 line card. You have the following three mechanisms to capture your network traffic:

- RSPAN feature
- SPAN feature
- VACL capture feature

Each of these options is explained in detail in Chapter 6. Therefore, the following sections focus on several different scenarios:

- Single IDSM-2 using SPAN
- Single IDSM-2 using VACLs
- Multiple IDSM-2s using VACLs

Single IDSM-2 Using Switch Port Analyzer (SPAN)

The first scenario is the simplest situation in which you want to monitor traffic from specific ports or VLANs using a single IDSM-2 line card and the SPAN feature. For this scenario, assume the following parameters:

- VLANs to be monitored are 136 through 138.
- Traffic is to be analyzed to and from the monitored VLANs.
- IDSM-2 is in slot 4.

To configure the SPAN feature, you use the **set span** switch command. The command to set up SPAN for this example is as follows:

```
cat6k> (enable) set span 136,137,138 4/7 both

Destination    : Port 4/7
Admin Source   : VLAN 136-138
Oper Source    : Port 4/3,8/1-2,9/1-2,15/1
```

```
Direction       : transmit/receive
Incoming Packets: disabled
Learning        : enabled
Multicast       : enabled
Filter          : -
Status          : active

cat6k> (enable)
```

This command causes copies of traffic from VLANs 136 through 138 to be sent to port 4/7 (the monitoring port on the IDSM-2). One of the drawbacks to this approach, however, is that for traffic between the monitored VLANs, the IDSM-2 receives duplicate packets (one when the packet leaves the source VLAN and another when the packet arrives at the destination VLAN). This can cause problems with certain signatures. To overcome this limitation, you can use VACLs to capture the same traffic without duplication (provided that you have a MSFC on your switch).

Single IDSM-2 Using VLAN Access Control Lists (VACLs)

This scenario examines how to do the preceding example using the VACL feature rather than the SPAN feature. Unlike the SPAN feature, which enables you to capture traffic from specific ports or VLANs, the VACL feature enables you to specify very granular traffic parameters such as the following:

- Source or destination IP addresses
- Source or destination ports
- IP protocol
- Combination of IP addresses, ports, and protocols

Another benefit of VACLs is that they can eliminate the capturing of duplicate packets (for packets going between two of the monitored VLANs) by taking advantage of *flows* in conjunction with the MSFC. Each packet in a flow is only sent to the capture port once.

Flows

A *flow* comprises a traffic stream between a source and destination IP address, a source port and a destination port, or a combination of source IP address and source port in conjunction with a destination IP address and destination port. Your VACLs essentially define the flows that represent interesting traffic on which you want your IDSM-2 to perform intrusion detection analysis. Furthermore, your MSFC uses flows to send packets between different VLANs by crossing the switch's backplane only once (thereby only sending one copy of the packet to the capture port).

For this scenario, use the following same parameters again:

* VLANs to be monitored are 136 through 138.
* Want traffic to and from the monitored VLANs.
* IDSM-2 is in slot 4.

To capture the specified traffic, you need to create a VACL to capture all IP traffic. (For an example of a security ACL that is not based on IP, refer to Appendix A.) You can define the VACL with the following commands:

```
cat6k> (enable) set security acl ip IPACL1 permit ip any any capture
IPACL1 editbuffer modified. Use 'commit' command to apply changes
cat6k> (enable)
```

Next you need to commit this VACL to memory using the **commit security acl** command. The example command to commit the security ACL is as follows:

```
cat6k> (enable) commit security acl IPACL1

Hardware programming in progress...

ACL IPACL1 is committed to hardware.

cat6k> (enable)
```

You must also map the VACLs that you create to the VLANs that you want them applied to. The **set security acl map** command performs this mapping. Using the specified VLANs, the commands to map our sample security ACL to the appropriate VLANs are as follows:

```
cat6k> (enable) set security acl map IPACL1 136

ACL IPACL1 mapped to vlan 136

cat6k> (enable) set security acl map IPACL1 137
ACL WEBACL1 mapped to vlan 137

cat6k> (enable) set security acl map IPACL2 138

ACL WEBACL2 mapped to vlan 138

cat6k> (enable)
```

Finally, you need to use the **set security acl capture-ports** command to define which ports on your switch receive the traffic captured by your security ACLs. Because the IDSM-2 in this example is in slot 4, the command is as follows:

```
cat6k> (enable) set security acl capture-ports 4/7
```

The capture port, however, will still not receive the captured traffic unless you configure the capture port to be a trunk that is trunking the VLANs that are being captured. You do this with the **set trunk** switch command. By default, the monitoring ports on the IDSM-2 are set to be trunk ports that trunk all the VLANs on the switch. So without any other configuration changes, the traffic captured will reach the IDSM-2's monitoring port and be processed by the IDSM-2.

NOTE	If you have a lot of VLANs configured on your switch, the monitoring port on the IDSM-2 will receive broadcast traffic for each of these VLANs. To eliminate this broadcast traffic (from VLANs that the IDSM-2 is not monitoring traffic on), you can use the **clear trunk** command to limit the monitoring port to only the VLANs that it is actually interested in (see "Trunk Configuration Tasks" later in the chapter). Remember to perform these operations on both monitoring ports.

Multiple IDSM-2s Using VACLs

With multiple IDSM-2 line cards in your switch, you need to decide how you want to divide you traffic between the two line cards (a maximum of 600 Mbps per IDSM-2).

This scenario examines the situation in which you have two IDSM-2 line cards over which you can distribute the captured traffic. Deciding which traffic to send to which IDSM-2 is your first major configuration task. You need to divide up the captured traffic so that neither IDSM-2 receives more the 600 Mbps. Suppose, for example, that you configure your IDSM-2s (located in slots 6 and 8) to analyze traffic from the following sources:

- IP traffic to and from 172.21.16.0 (VLAN 120)
- TCP traffic to and from 171.12.31.0 (VLAN 130)
- UDP traffic to and from 172.20.15.0 (VLAN 140)
- Web traffic (port 80) destined for 172.21.18.0 (VLAN 150)

After considering the traffic loads, you decide that one of your modules should only handle web traffic because you have a large collection of web servers. This leaves all the other traffic for the second module.

To capture the specified traffic, you need to create several VACLs and send the captured traffic to the monitoring ports on both of the IDSM-2s (using the port configuration to separate the traffic between the two modules). You can define the VACLs with the following commands:

```
cat6k> (enable) set security acl ip IPACL1 permit ip any any capture
IPACL1 editbuffer modified. Use 'commit' command to apply changes
cat6k> (enable) set security acl ip TCPACL1 permit tcp any any capture
IPACL1 editbuffer modified. Use 'commit' command to apply changes
cat6k> (enable) set security acl ip UDPACL1 permit udp any any capture
IPACL1 editbuffer modified. Use 'commit' command to apply changes
cat6k> (enable) set security acl ip WEBACL1 permit TCP any range 1 65535
     172.21.18.0 0.0.0.255 eq 80 capture

WEBACL1 editbuffer modified. Use 'commit' command to apply changes
cat6k> (enable) set security acl ip WEBACL2 permit TCP 172.21.18.0 0.0.0.255 eq 80
     any range 1 65535 capture
WEBACL2 editbuffer modified. Use 'commit' command to apply changes
cat6k (enable)
```

Next you need to commit these VACLs to memory using the **commit security acl** command. The commands to commit the example security ACLs are as follows:

```
cat6k> (enable) commit security acl IPACL1

Hardware programming in progress...

ACL IPACL1 is committed to hardware.

cat6k> (enable) commit security acl TCPACL1

Hardware programming in progress...

ACL TCPACL1 is committed to hardware.

cat6k> (enable) commit security acl UDPACL1

Hardware programming in progress...

ACL UDPACL1 is committed to hardware.

cat6k> (enable) commit security acl WEBACL1

Hardware programming in progress...

ACL WEBACL1 is committed to hardware.

cat6k> (enable) commit security acl WEBACL2

Hardware programming in progress...

ACL WEBACL2 is committed to hardware.

cat6k> (enable)
```

NOTE   Instead of using individual **commit security acl** commands, you can commit all the security ACLs by using the keyword **all** instead of using the individual ACL names.

You must map the VACLs that you created to the VLANs that you want them applied to. The **set security acl map** command performs this mapping. Using the VLANS specified in this example, the commands to map the sample security ACLs to the appropriate VLANs are as follows:

```
cat6k> (enable) set security acl map IPACL1 120

ACL IPACL1 mapped to vlan 120

cat6k> (enable) set security acl map TCPACL1 130

ACL TCPACL1 mapped to vlan 130

cat6k> (enable) set security acl map UDPACL1 140

ACL UDPACL1 mapped to vlan 140
```

```
cat6k> (enable) set security acl map WEBACL1 150

ACL WEBACL1 mapped to vlan 150

cat6k> (enable) set security acl map WEBACL2 150

ACL WEBACL2 mapped to vlan 150

cat6k> (enable)
```

Because you have configured your security ACL to send traffic to a capture port, you need to define what port or ports on the switch are considered capture ports. You use the **set security acl capture-ports** command to define the ports on your switch that will receive the traffic captured by your security ACLs. Because the IDSM-2s in this example are in slots 6 and 8, the command is as follows:

```
cat6k> (enable) set security acl capture-ports 6/7,8/7
Successfully set 6/7,8/7 to capture ACL traffic.
```

Finally, you need to make sure that the captured traffic is divided between the two modules by limiting the VLANs that each monitoring port receives. Because the monitoring ports are configured to trunk all VLANs by default, you first need to clear the existing VLANs, and then you can add the ones needed for monitoring. One IDSM-2 will monitor the web traffic on VLAN 150, whereas the other IDSM-2 will monitor all the other VLANs (VLANs 120, 130, and 140). The commands to accomplish this are as follows:

```
Cat6k (enable) clear trunk 6/7 1-1005,1025-4094
Removing Vlan(s) 1-1005,1025-4094 from allowed list.
Port  6/7 allowed vlans modified to .
cat6k> (enable) clear trunk 6/8 1-1005,1025-4094
Removing Vlan(s) 1-1005,1025-4094 from allowed list.
Port  6/8 allowed vlans modified to .
cat6k> (enable) clear trunk 8/7 1-1005,1025-4094
Removing Vlan(s) 1-1005,1025-4094 from allowed list.
Port  8/7 allowed vlans modified to .
cat6k> (enable) clear trunk 8/8 1-1005,1025-4094
Removing Vlan(s) 1-1005,1025-4094 from allowed list.
Port  8/8 allowed vlans modified to .
cat6k> (enable) set trunk 6/7 150
Adding vlans 150 to allowed list.
Port(s)  6/7 allowed vlans modified to 150.
cat6k> (enable) set trunk 8/7 120,130,140
Adding vlans 120,130,140 to allowed list.
Port(s)  8/7 allowed vlans modified to 120,130,140.
cat6k> (enable)
```

NOTE   Each IDSM-2 contains two monitoring ports. You need to use only one to capture and monitor your network traffic because each monitoring port is a gigabit and the IDSM-2's maximum processing capability is 600 Mbps. Therefore, it is beneficial to clear the VLANs on the second monitoring port (the one that you are not using) to make sure that it does not accidentally receive any traffic and reduce the performance of your IDSM-2. In this example, port 8 on each IDSM-2 is not used.

Trunk Configuration Tasks

Clearing unwanted VLAN traffic from your IDSM-2 monitoring ports prevents your IDSM-2 from wasting its processing time analyzing traffic that you might not want it to analyze. By default, the monitoring ports on your IDSM-2 (ports 7 and 8) are defined as trunking ports that trunk all the VLANs on your switch. Therefore, these ports will receive broadcast traffic for every VLAN on your switch. In addition, it will also receive traffic from every VLAN that you have mapped to your security ACLs.

CAUTION	When using multiple IDSM-2 cards in a single chassis, you must make sure that the monitoring port on each IDSM-2 line card receives only its specific VLANs to prevent overloading your IDSM-2s with too much traffic. The default port settings will send all the captured traffic to all of your IDSM-2 line cards.

Using the **set trunk** and **clear trunk** commands, you can configure which VLANs your monitoring ports trunk and thereby limit the amount of traffic that they will actually receive.

NOTE	Before removing VLANs from a trunk port, you need to know which VLANs are assigned to the trunk port. You can obtain this information by using the **show trunk** *mod/port* **detail** switch command.

Administrative Tasks

When using your IDSM-2, besides configuring the normal operational characteristics, you might also need to perform the following two administrative tasks:

- Enable a full memory test
- Stop the IDS Module

Enabling a Full Memory Test

By default, the IDSM-2 performs a partial memory test when it boots. In some troubleshooting situations, you might need to run a complete memory test. If your switch runs CatOS, you can configure your IDSM-2 to run a complete memory test by using the **set boot device** switch command. (Refer to the Cisco documentation for detailed information on this command.)

CAUTION   A full memory test takes significantly more time than a partial memory test (up to 12 minutes). This will considerably increase the time that it takes your IDSM-2 to come online.

Stopping the IDS Module

To prevent corruption of the IDSM-2, you must shut it down properly. To properly shut down the IDSM-2, you need to log in to the IDSM-2 and execute the **reset** command. The **reset** command on the IDSM-2 CLI enables you to reboot and power down the IDSM-2. The syntax for this command is as follows:

```
reset [powerdown]
```

The **reset** command without any options causes the IDSM-2 to perform an orderly reboot. If you add the **powerdown** option, the IDSM-2 will perform an orderly shutdown and place it in a state where it can be powered off.

NOTE   Do not remove the IDSM-2 line card from the switch until the module has shut down completely. Removing the module without going through the shutdown procedure can damage the module.

Troubleshooting

You might need to troubleshoot the operation of your IDSM-2. Besides running various commands on your Catalyst 6500 switch, you can also examine the status light-emitting diode (LED) on the IDSM-2 itself.

IDSM-2 Status Light-Emitting Diode (LED)

The front panel of the IDSM-2 contains a single LED. This LED provides you with a visual indication of the state of the IDSM-2 line card. This LED can be in one of the states listed in Table 8-3.

Table 8-3   *IDSM-2 Status LED*

Color	Description
Green	All diagnostics test passed; IDS Module is operational.
Red	A diagnostic other than an individual port test failed.

continues

Table 8-3   *IDSM-2 Status LED (Continued)*

Color	Description
Amber	The IDS module is running through its boot and self-test diagnostic sequence; or the IDS Module is disabled; or the IDS Module is in the shutdown state.
Off	The IDS Module power is off.

Catalyst 6500 Commands

Because the IDSM-2 is a line card in your Catalyst switch, you can use several switch commands to examine its operation. The following three commands provide detailed information on your IDSM-2 line card and its ports:

- **show module** command
- **show port** command
- **show trunk** command

show module Command

The **show module** switch command enables you to display information about the line cards that you have installed in your Catalyst 6500 switch. The syntax for **show module** command is as follows:

```
show module [mod]
```

The only parameter, *mod*, indicates the module number that the card is in. For instance on a 6509, you have 9 slots, so the module numbers are numbered from 1 to 9. If your IDSM-2 line card is in slot 8, you could view its information with the following **show module** command:

```
Cat6k> show module 8
Mod Slot Ports Module-Type              Model          Sub Status
--- ---- ----- ------------------------ -------------- --- --------
8   8    8     Intrusion Detection Syste WS-SVC-IDSM2   yes ok

Mod Module-Name          Serial-Num
--- -------------------- -----------
8                        SAD062004LV

Mod MAC-Address(es)                         Hw     Fw         Sw
--- --------------------------------------- ------ ---------- ----------------
8   00-e0-b0-ff-3b-80 to 00-e0-b0-ff-3b-87 0.102  7.2(0.67)  4.1(0.3)S42(0.3

Mod Sub-Type              Sub-Model           Sub-Serial Sub-Hw Sub-Sw
--- -------------------- -------------------- ---------- ------ ------
8   IDS 2 accelerator board WS-SVC-IDSUPG     .          2.0
Cat6k>
```

You can also specify the **show module** command without any parameters to obtain some basic information about the line cards in your switch, such as the following:

```
Cat6k> show module
Mod Slot Ports Module-Type              Model               Sub Status
--- ---- ----- ------------------------ ------------------- --- -------
 1   1    2    1000BaseX Supervisor     WS-X6K-SUP1A-2GE    yes ok
15   1    1    Multilayer Switch Feature WS-F6K-MSFC        no  ok
 3   3   48    10/100BaseTX Ethernet    WS-X6548-RJ-45      no  ok
 4   4    8    1000BaseX Ethernet       WS-X6408-GBIC       no  ok
 6   6    8    Intrusion Detection Syste WS-SVC-IDSM2       yes ok
 8   8    8    Intrusion Detection Syste WS-SVC-IDSM2       yes ok
 9   9   16    10/100/1000BaseT Ethernet WS-X6516-GE-TX     no  ok
Mod Module-Name          Serial-Num
--- -------------------- -----------
 1                       SAD04200CUH
15                       SAD04190BS5
 3                       SAD0612021X
 4                       JAB04040859
 6                       SAD0625018D
 8                       SAD062004LV
 9                       SAL06365QSP

Mod MAC-Address(es)                         Hw    Fw         Sw
--- --------------------------------------- ----- ---------- ----------------
 1  00-30-7b-95-26-86 to 00-30-7b-95-26-87 3.2   5.3(1)     7.6(1)
    00-30-7b-95-26-84 to 00-30-7b-95-26-85
    00-09-44-89-90-00 to 00-09-44-89-93-ff
15  00-30-7b-95-00-3c to 00-30-7b-95-00-7b 1.4   12.1(13)E3 12.1(13)E3
 3  00-01-63-d7-5a-ca to 00-01-63-d7-5a-f9 4.2   6.3(1)     7.6(1)
 4  00-30-a3-38-9a-30 to 00-30-a3-38-9a-37 2.3   4.2(0.24)V 7.6(1)
 6  00-10-7b-00-0e-e8 to 00-10-7b-00-0e-ef 0.102 7.2(1)     4.1(0.3)S42(0.3
 8  00-e0-b0-ff-3b-80 to 00-e0-b0-ff-3b-87 0.102 7.2(0.67)  4.1(0.3)S42(0.3
 9  00-09-11-e4-89-c4 to 00-09-11-e4-89-d3 2.2   6.3(1)     7.6(1)

Mod Sub-Type              Sub-Model           Sub-Serial  Sub-Hw Sub-Sw
--- -------------------- -------------------- ----------- ------ ------
 1  L3 Switching Engine   WS-F6K-PFC          SAD04200DP9 1.1
 6  IDS 2 accelerator board WS-SVC-IDSUPG     .           2.0
 8  IDS 2 accelerator board WS-SVC-IDSUPG     .           2.0
Cat6k>
```

show port Command

You can use the **show port** command to examine the different ports on your switch. While debugging, you might want to see the packet statistics and error information for the monitoring ports on your IDSM-2. If your IDSM-2 line card is in slot 8, you can examine the first monitoring port with the following **show port** command:

```
Cat6k> show port 8/7
* = Configured MAC Address

Port  Name                 Status     Vlan    Duplex Speed Type
----- -------------------- ---------- ------- ------ ----- ------------
 8/7                       connected  trunk     full 1000  Intrusion De


Port     Broadcast-Limit Multicast Unicast Total-Drop           Action
-------- --------------- --------- ------- -------------------- -----------
 8/7                 -         -        -                      0 drop-packets
```

```
Port  Status      ErrDisable Reason    Port ErrDisableTimeout  Action on Timeout
----  ----------  -------------------  ----------------------  -----------------
8/7   connected                     -  Enable                  No Change

Port  Align-Err  FCS-Err    Xmit-Err   Rcv-Err    UnderSize
----- ---------- ---------- ---------- ---------- ---------
8/7           0          0          0          0         0

Port  Single-Col Multi-Coll Late-Coll  Excess-Col Carri-Sen Runts     Giants
----- ---------- ---------- ---------- ---------- --------- --------- ---------
8/7           0          0          0          0         0         0         -

Port  Last-Time-Cleared
----- -------------------------
8/7   Fri May 16 2003, 16:50:42

Idle Detection
-------------
  --
Cat6k>
```

show trunk Command

The VLANs that the monitoring ports on your IDSM-2 are trunking determine what traffic is actually received by your IDSM-2. Initially, the monitoring ports are configured to trunk all the VLANs on your switch, but you might need to change this configuration to support multiple IDSM-2 line cards and limit broadcast traffic to the IDSM-2. To examine which trunks that a specific port trunks, you use the **show trunk** switch command. If your IDSM-2 line card is in slot 8, you can examine the trunks supported by the second monitoring port with the following **show trunk** command:

```
cat6k> (enable) show trunk 8/8
* - indicates vtp domain mismatch
Port       Mode        Encapsulation Status       Native vlan
--------   ----------  ------------- ------------ -----------
8/8        auto        negotiate     not-trunking 140

Port       Vlans allowed on trunk
--------   ----------------------------------------------------------------------
8/8        1-1005,1025-4094

Port       Vlans allowed and active in management domain
--------   ----------------------------------------------------------------------
8/8        140

Port       Vlans in spanning tree forwarding state and not pruned
--------   ----------------------------------------------------------------------
8/8
cat6k> (enable)
```

Summary

The second-generation Intrusion Detection System Module (IDSM-2) provides a fully functional sensor that is incorporated into your Catalyst 6500 switch. This module runs the same code base as the appliance sensor. Therefore, both of these platforms share the same functionality.

The specifications for the IDSM-2 are as follows:

- **Performance**—600 Mbps
- **Monitoring interface**—Gigabit
- **Command and control interface**—Gigabit

To perform its operations, the IDSM-2 provides four ports that are internally connected to the switch's backplane. These ports and their functionality are as follows:

- Command and control interface (port 2)
- Monitoring interface (ports 7 and 8)
- TCP reset interface (port 1)

You must configure your switch to enable external systems (such as IDM and IEV) to access your IDSM-2. Using the **set vlan** switch command, you can configure your command and control port (port 1) to the correct VLAN so that other systems can communicate with the IDSM-2 card.

You also have to configure the switch to pass information to one or both of the monitoring ports on your IDSM-2. The three mechanisms for capturing traffic are as follows:

- RSPAN feature
- SPAN feature
- VACL capture feature

The SPAN and RPSAN features are usually available on your Catalyst 6500 switch. To use the VACL capture feature, however, you must have Policy Feature Card (PFC) on your switch.

Besides using the CLI, you can troubleshoot the operation of your IDSM-2 by examining the status LED on the front of the IDSM-2 chassis. You can also use the following switch commands to examine characteristics of your IDSM-2:

- **show module**
- **show port**
- **show trunk**

Review Questions

The following questions test your retention of the material presented in this chapter. The answers to the review questions are in Appendix B, "Answers to Chapter Review Questions."

1 What ports on the IDSM-2 are used to monitor network traffic?

2 Which Catalyst switch command do you use to configure the correct VLAN on the command and control port when using CatOS?

3 What is the purpose of the TCP reset port on the IDSM-2?

4 Through which port do other devices (such as management and monitoring applications) communicate with the IDSM-2?

5 Which port on the IDSM-2 is used to send out the TCP reset packets for signature that after configured for TCP resets?

6 What options do you have to capture traffic for your IDSM-2 monitoring ports?

7 What command do you execute from the IDSM-2 CLI to reboot or power down the IDSM-2 line card?

8 What is the color of the IDSM-2 status LED when the module is operational?

9 What initial configuration command do you run from the IDSM-2 CLI to configure the basic IDSM-2 properties, such as host name and default gateway?

10 What switch command can you execute to verify that the Catalyst 6500 switch has recognized IDSM-2 line card?

11 To support VACLs to capture network traffic, your switch must have what type of hardware?

12 What switch commands do you use to limit the traffic from different VLANs that are actually sent to a monitoring port on your IDSM-2?

13 What switch command can you use to verify which VLANs the monitoring port on your IDSM-2 is currently trunking?

14 What three types of devices can your IDSM-2 perform device management on?

15 How many internal ports does the IDSM-2 have?

16 Which port on your IDSM-2 has an actual IP address?

Upon completion of this chapter, you will be able to perform the following tasks:

- Explain the basic structure of the IDS Device Manager (IDM) interface
- Identify the system requirements for IDM
- Explain how to configure views in IDS Event Viewer (IEV)
- Explain how to configure filters in IEV
- Explain how to view alarm information in IEV
- Identify the information contained in the Network Security Database (NSDB)
- Identify the basic database administration tasks for IEV

CHAPTER 9

Cisco IDS Device Manager and Event Viewer

For Cisco intrusion protection system deployments that use a small number of network sensors, you can take advantage of two graphical tools that enable you to configure and monitor the alarm events that your sensors generate. Maintaining, configuring, and monitoring your network sensors is vital to effectively using your Cisco intrusion protection system. The following tools are provided as part of your appliance software:

- Cisco IDS Device Manager
- Cisco IDS Event Viewer

This chapter provides a detailed examination of the IDS Device Manager interface as well as hands-on instructions on how to use IDS Event Viewer to view alarm information from your sensors.

Cisco IDS Device Manager

The Cisco IDS Device Manager (IDM) is a tool that enables you to configure and manage a single Cisco network sensor. This web-based tool provides you with a graphical interface to manipulate the operation of your sensor. Each IDS appliance running on your network has its own web server that provides access to the IDM application on the sensor.

System Requirements

Because the IDM is a web-based application, your only system requirement is using a supported web browser. Although any web browser may work with IDM, Cisco has verified that IDM works with the following web browsers:

- Netscape (version 4.79 or later)
- Internet Explorer (version 5.5 Service Pack 2 or later)

Installing Cisco IDS Device Manager

Because IDM is part of your sensor's software, you do not have any special installation instructions. After you initialize the sensor with the **setup** command-line interface (CLI) command (which configures the basic sensor operating characteristics, such as the IP address), IDM is automatically enabled and uses Secure Sockets Layer (SSL) by default. (For more information on the **setup** command, see Chapter 7, "Cisco IDS Network Sensor Installation.")

NOTE	You will need to modify the access list on the sensor to enable your host to access the sensor. By default, the sensor is configured to allow network connections only from the subnet that the sensor's command and control interface is on. By default, this is the 10.1.9.0 Class C subnet.

Cisco IDS Device Manager Interface Structure

Although the IDM user interface is graphical and easy to use, it is helpful to understand how the interface is structured. The IDM user interface is composed of the following major sections (see Figure 9-1):

- Configuration tabs
- Options bar
- TOC (table of contents)
- Path bar
- Tools bar
- Instructions box
- Activity bar
- Content Area

Figure 9-1   *IDM Interface*

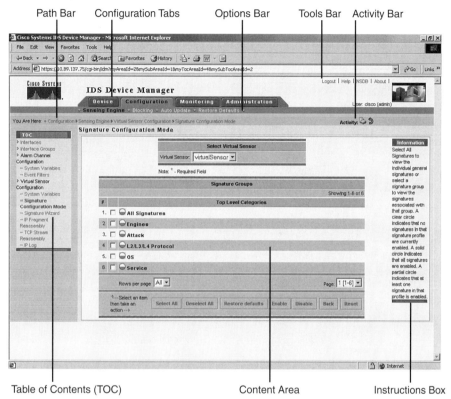

Configuration Tabs

The configuration of your sensor is broken down into the following four major categories:

- Device
- Configuration
- Monitoring
- Administration

To access one of the categories, click the tab labeled with the appropriate name. The tabs are located across the top of the IDM display.

Options Bar

After you click one of the major tabs, the options for that selection display in a list that is located on the screen just below the major tabs. Figure 9-1 shows a screen in which the user clicked the Configuration tab. The options associated with the Configuration tab are as follows:

- Sensing Engine
- Blocking
- Auto Update
- Restore Defaults

Clicking any of these options causes a menu of available choices to display on the left side of the IDM interface (known as the TOC).

IDS Device Manager Table of Contents (TOC)

The TOC is a menu of choices displayed down the left side of the IDM interface. It represents the list of suboptions that you can select (based on the option chosen). As you can see in Figure 9-1, the Sensing Engine option has 10 suboptions divided among the following four areas:

- Interfaces
- Interface Groups
- Alarm Channel Configuration
- Virtual Sensor Configuration

For Alarm Channel Configuration, you can choose from the following selections:

- System Variables
- Event Filters

For Virtual Sensor Configuration, you can choose from the following selections:

- System Variables
- Signature Configuration Mode
- Signature Wizard
- IP Fragment Reassembly
- TCP Stream Reassembly
- IP Log

Path Bar

The Path bar provides a visual road map indicating where you are with respect to the IDM interface. It is located above the TOC and below the Options bar and begins with the text "You Are Here."

Figure 9-1 shows a situation in which the Path bar's value is Configuration>Sensing> Virtual Sensor Configuration>Signature Configuration Mode. This indicates that you performed the following steps to reach the current screen:

Step 1   Clicked the Configuration tab

Step 2   Clicked the Sensing Engine option

Step 3   Clicked the Virtual Sensor Configuration>Signature Configuration Mode suboption

Tools Bar

Located at the upper-right portion of the IDM interface is the Tools bar. From the Tools bar, you can access the following items:

- Logout
- Help
- NSDB
- About

Clicking Logout logs out your current IDM user session. If you have made configuration changes that have not been saved, you are presented a pop-up that enables you to cancel the logout operation or continue with the logout, which will discard the unsaved changes.

Selecting Help opens up another browser window that displays context-specific help for the currently displayed page.

The Network Security Database (NSDB) option brings up the NSDB in a separate browser window.

Finally, the About option displays information about the version of IDM that you use.

Instructions Box

Some pages provide you with an Instructions box on the right side of the IDM display. This box (when displayed) provides you with a brief overview of the page that you have selected. This information is less than the amount of information provided through the Help option on the Tools bar.

Activity Bar

When you make changes to the sensor's configuration, they do not immediately become activated. You must still commit those changes or cancel them. The activity bar indicates when you have made configuration changes that have not been saved.

Content Area

The content area displays the information associated with the options that you select from the TOC menu.

Accessing IDS Device Manager (IDM)

Only one user can access IDM (on a single sensor) at a time. If another user is already accessing IDM, the system states that the user limit has been reached. At this point, you can either try to access the sensor later or forcibly log out the existing user so that you can log in.

To connect to the IDM, you need to enter the following URL into you web browser:

https://*<sensor ip address>*/

Next, you need to enter a valid username and password to gain access to the IDM web server on your sensor.

NOTE   Initially you must create an account on the sensor (using the sensor's CLI). You then use this account to log in to IDM and configure the sensor. To perform all possible configuration tasks, the account should have the Administrator role assigned to it.

Accessing Online IDM Help

IDM provides online documentation to assist in the configuration of the sensor. To access the online IDM, choose Help from the IDM Tools bar. The IDM Help contents display in a new web browser (see Figure 9-2).

Figure 9-2 *IDM Online Help*

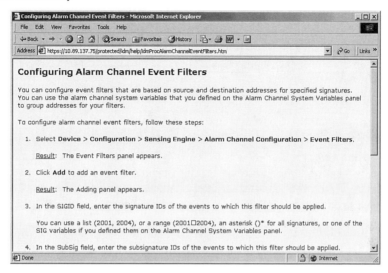

IDS Device Manager and Cookies

To track your user session, IDM uses temporary session cookies. These cookies are not stored on your system. If you have disabled cookies in your browser, IDM will not work properly, but you can perform one of the following tasks to enable IDM to operate correctly without opening up your browser to all cookies:

- Enable only session cookies (keep stored cookies disabled).
- Accept only cookies that originate from the IDM.

NOTE   No personal information is stored in the IDM cookie. It only contains a randomly generated value that is used by the IDM web server to bind your request to your existing session.

IDS Device Manager and Certificates

You access IDM through a web server that is running on your sensor. To provide an additional layer of security, default traffic to this web server is encrypted using the Transaction Layer Security (TLS) protocol (which is based on the Secure Sockets Layer [SSL] protocol).

TLS

Transport Layer Security is a protocol designed to manage the transmission of messages across an untrusted network. It operates between application layer (HTTP) processing and the transport layer (TCP) processing. For more information on the TLS protocol, refer to RFC 2246.

Transport Layer Security (TLS) Handshake

To begin an encrypted session, your browser must exchange information with the server in a process known as *handshaking*. During this process, you browser receives a certificate from the server. Your browser uses this certificate to validate the identity of the server. It must also perform the following checks on the validity of the certificate itself:

- Determine whether the issuer of the certificate is trusted.

- Verify the certificate has not expired.

- Verify that the common name of the subject identified in the certificate matches the URL host name of the server.

When you initially connect to your sensor, the initial certificate validity check will fail because the sensor issues its own certificate (self-signed certificate). This makes the sensor its own certificate authority (CA). This CA is not in the trusted list of CAs that your browser has, so your browser has no established trust relationship with the sensor's CA. Therefore, your browser presents you with the following three options:

- Accept the certificate for this session.

- Do not accept certificate and disconnect session.

- Accept this certificate forever.

The most convenient option is to accept the certificate forever so that you do not have to accept the certificate every time that you connect to the sensor. Before doing that, however, you need to validate the fingerprint of the certificate.

Validating Certificate Fingerprints

Before accepting the sensor's certificate, you need to use an *out-of-band* method to validate the certificate. This will prevent an attacker from masquerading as your sensor. Both fingerprints should match (the one from your browser and the one obtained out-of-band).

Out-of-Band

An out-of-band mechanism implies that you are not using the same network as your browser to obtain confirmation of the fingerprint for your sensor's certificate.

You need to obtain the fingerprint of the sensor's certificate from the sensor's CLI. To obtain this information, you need to log in to the sensor (preferably through a direct keyboard or console connection) and execute the **show tls fingerprint** command. The output of this command provides you with both the MD5 and SHA1 fingerprints for your sensor:

```
sensor#
sensor# show tls fingerprint
MD5: 6F:60:C5:75:17:59:A4:9C:F5:58:8B:78:90:08:1F:B9
SHA1: 6C:26:13:5E:B4:BF:0A:AA:42:DA:B0:A8:FD:29:39:F0:4F:F0:70:09
sensor#
```

You use these fingerprints to validate the certificate that your browser received from the web server. For Netscape, you use the MD5 fingerprint to validate your certificate. By clicking the More Info button, you will see a pop-up window that shows the MD5 fingerprint of the certificate (see Figure 9-3). This value should match the MD5 fingerprint displayed by the **show tls fingerprint** command.

Figure 9-3 *Netscape Certificate Fingerprint*

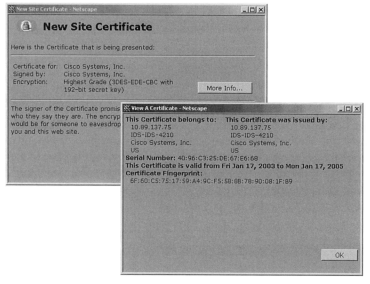

If you use Internet Explorer, you need to use the SHA1 fingerprint to validate the certificate. When Internet Explorer receives the certificate, it shows a pop-up window indicating you do not currently trust the CA that signed the certificate (but the other two certificate checks have passed). By clicking the View Certificate button, you will see a pop-up window that gives you more information concerning the certificate (see Figure 9-4). In the Certificate pop-up window, you need to click the Details tab and scroll down to the Thumbprint field. The value of the thumbprint should match the SHA1 fingerprint listed in the **show tls fingerprint** command.

Figure 9-4 *Internet Explorer Certificate Fingerprint*

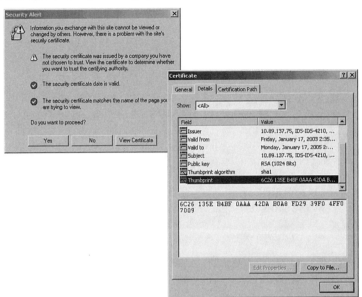

Cisco IDS Event Viewer

The Cisco IDS Event Viewer (IEV) is a Java-based application that enables you to monitor and manage alarms for up to five sensors. Filters and views enable you to more efficiently manage the events displayed by IEV. From IEV, you can also access the NSDB to obtain more background information on the alarms that you see. The NSDB provides detailed IDS signature and vulnerability information. You can use this information to assist in determining the threat posed to the network.

IEV is built on a relational database, MySQL, which allows for a scalable database. Data can easily be imported, exported, and deleted from the database, enabling you to control the size of the database.

System Requirements

IEV is designed to run on a system that meets several hardware and software requirements. The first requirement is that your system must run on one of the following operating systems:

- Windows NT, Service Pack 6
- Windows 2000, Service Pack 2

NOTE	Because these requirements change over time, you should visit the Cisco website (http://www.cisco.com) to find the latest supported versions.

During operation, IEV can consume significant resources on your system. Therefore, your system must meet or exceed the following hardware requirements:

- Pentium III 800 MÇz or greater
- 256 MB RAM
- 500 MB free disk space

When you install IEV on your system, it installs the following applications that it uses during its operation:

- Java 2 Runtime Environment version 1.3.1
- MySQL Server version 3.23

Installing Cisco IDS Event Viewer

Before you can install IEV on your system, you must download the IEV executable from the Cisco website. The Cisco software center is located at http://www.cisco.com/kobayashi/sw-center/. The name of this file will be similar to IEV-4.0-1-S37.exe.

CAUTION	If you are currently using IEV version 3.1, you cannot upgrade the existing version to 4.0. Instead, you must uninstall IEV version 3.1 before installing IEV version 4.0.

To successfully install IEV on your system, you need to be logged in to the system with an account that has administrative privileges. The actual installation process involves the following steps:

Step 1 Double-click the IEV executable to initiate the installation process. This will display the Welcome window.

Step 2 Click the Next button of the Welcome screen to proceed to the Select Destination Location window.

Step 3 Select the Destination Location by clicking the Browse button (if the default directory is not acceptable). When you have selected the directory you want, click the Next button to continue with the installation and display the Select Program Manager Group window.

Step 4 Select the program group to which you want to add the IDS Event Viewer icons. After selecting (or accepting the default group), click the Next button to continue and display the Start Installation window.

Step 5 Click the Next button to actually begin the installation of files onto your system.

Step 6 When the Installation Complete pop-up appears, click the Finish button to complete the installation process.

Step 7 When the Install pop-up appears, click the OK button to reboot the system or click the Cancel button to reboot later.

NOTE After you install IEV, the IDS services used by IEV are not started until the system is rebooted. So if you do not choose to reboot the system at the end of the installation process, remember that IEV is not usable until the system is rebooted.

Uninstalling Cisco IDS Event Viewer

If you are currently using IEV version 3.1, you will need to uninstall IEV before you can install IEV version 4.0. To successfully uninstall IEV on your system, you need to be logged in to the system with an account that has administrative privileges. The actual process involves the following steps:

Step 1 Choose Start>Program Files>Cisco Systems>Cisco IDS Event Viewer> Uninstall Cisco IDS Event Viewer to start the uninstall process.

Step 2 When the Select Uninstall Method window appears, select Automatic, and then click the Next button.

Step 3 When the Perform Uninstall window appears, click the Finish button to uninstall IEV.

NOTE If you are uninstalling IEV version 3.1, the uninstall program does not remove the paths that were created during installation. To complete the uninstall process, you need to remove paths that include \Cisco Systems\Cisco IDS Event Viewer\ from the PATH variable. Furthermore, because you are uninstalling the old version (as opposed to upgrading), your data is not saved.

Starting IDS Event Viewer

You have two ways to launch the Cisco IEV application. You can double-click the Cisco IEV icon located on your desktop, or you can launch the IEV application through the Windows Start menu. IEV is located at Program Files>Cisco Systems>Cisco IDS Event Viewer>Cisco IDS Event Viewer.

Specifying IDS Devices to Monitor

IEV can monitor alarm data from up to five different sensors. Before you can monitor alarm traffic, however, you must add the sensor to IEV. With IEV version 3.1, your sensor transmitted alarm information to specifically configured monitoring sources. In version 4.0, the monitoring application (such as IEV) retrieves the alarm data from the sensor. Therefore, you need to add the sensors or devices from which IEV needs to retrieve information.

Adding an IDS Device

After installing IEV on your monitoring host, you still need to add the IDS devices that you want IEV to monitor. When you add an IDS device, you need to specify the fields listed in Table 9-1.

Table 9-1   *IDS Device Fields*

Parameter	Description
Sensor IP Address	IP address of the IDS device that IEV will retrieve alarm data from.
Sensor Name	Name of the IDS device that IEV will retrieve information from.
Username	Username of a valid account on the IDS device.
Password	Password for the specified username.
Web Server Port	The port at which IEV will connect to on the IDS device to retrieve alarm data. (The default is 443.)
Communication Protocol	When retrieving information from the IDS device, IEV can use HTTPS (encrypted) or HTTP (not encrypted) to retrieve the alarm information.
Events to Retrieve	When retrieving events, IEV needs to know which events to retrieve. The default is to retrieve the latest events on the IDS device. You can also specify a beginning date and time for the events to be retrieved.
Excluded Severity Levels	You can also filter the alarms retrieved by IEV by excluding alarms with certain severity levels.

To add a new IDS device through IEV, you need to complete the following steps:

Step 1 If you have not started IEV, start the application by choosing Start> Programs, Cisco Systems>Cisco IDS Event Viewer>Cisco IDS Event Viewer to launch the IEV.

Step 2 When the IEV application starts, you need to select File>New>Device to bring up the Device Properties window (see Figure 9-5).

NOTE You can also add a new device by right-clicking the Devices folder located on the IEV main window.

Figure 9-5 *Device Properties Screen*

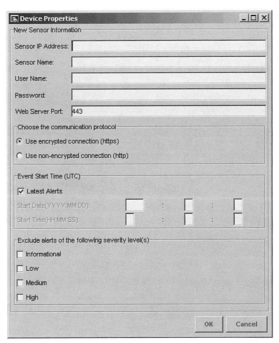

Step 3 Specify the IP address and name of your sensor. These should match the values you used when configuring your sensor.

Step 4 To retrieve information from the sensor, you must specify a valid account and its corresponding password.

Step 5   Specify the port on which your sensor's web server is listening. By
default, this is 443 for HTTPS.

Step 6   The default communication protocol is encrypted using HTTPS. If you
want to change this, you need to select Use Non-Encrypted Connection
(HTTP). You will also need to change the web server port.

NOTE   Using the nonencrypted communication option is not recommended because your login
credentials traverse the network in the clear.

Step 7   Specify which alerts you want IEV to retrieve from the sensor from the
following options:

—   Select the Latest Alerts check box to retrieve alerts starting with the
first alarm received after IEV connects with the sensor (the default).

—   By deselecting the Latest Alerts check box, you can specify a date
and time, causing IEV to retrieve all events from the sensor's Event
Store that match the specified criteria.

Step 8   Select which severity levels you want to exclude. When IEV retrieves
alarm data, it will not retrieve any alarms that match the severity levels
you have checked. To exclude any severity levels, choose one or more of
the following:

—   Informational

—   Low

—   Medium

—   High

Step 9   Click OK to save the device that you specified.

Step 10   If you use HTTPS, you need to validate the certificate on the sensor. The
Certificate Information shows you the certificate that IEV received from
the sensor (see Figure 9-6). You need to use an out-of-band mechanism
to validate this certificate (see the "Validating Certificate Fingerprints"
section earlier in this chapter). After validating the certificate, click Yes.

Figure 9-6 *Certificate Information Window*

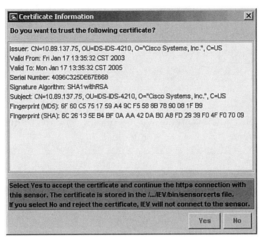

NOTE If your host cannot connect to the IDS device (or you have entered the sensor's IP address incorrectly), when you click OK you will receive an error message indicating that the sensor is unreachable and the certificate cannot be retrieved (see Figure 9-7).

Figure 9-7 *IOException Error*

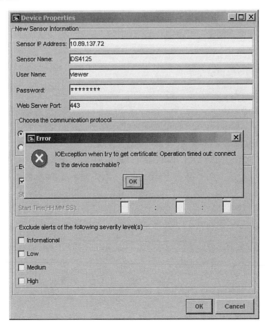

The new device will now show up under the Devices folder on the IEV main window. You can repeat this process for each of your sensors that IEV will be monitoring (up to the limit of five devices).

Editing IDS Device Properties

Sometimes you need to change the properties of one of the IDS devices that IEV monitors. Maybe you want to exclude informational alarms from being included in the alarms retrieved from one of your monitored IDS devices. To change the properties of an existing IDS device, you need to select Properties for that device. This option is found by right-clicking the sensor's name in the Devices list (see Figure 9-8).

Figure 9-8 *Device Management Options*

Deleting an IDS Device

If you decide that one of your IDS devices does not need to be monitored by IEV, you will need to delete it from the list of IDS devices. You can replace a couple of low-end sensors with a single, more powerful high-end sensor. No matter what the reason, you need to remove one of the IDS devices from IEV. To remove an IDS device from the device list, you need to select Delete Device. Like changing the properties of a device, the Delete Device option is available by right-clicking the IDS device name (see Figure 9-8). You are prompted for confirmation of the deletion (to prevent you from accidentally deleting an IDS device). After confirming the deletion, the device is removed, but this does not delete for this sensor alarm entries already stored in the IEV database.

Viewing IDS Device Status

To assist in troubleshooting and to analyze the statistics of your connection with a specific IDS device, you can view the status of any of the devices that IEV is monitoring. To view the status of an IDS device, right-click the device name and select Device Status (see Figure 9-8). This brings up the Device Status window, which displays the statistics of the connection with the device (see Figure 9-9).

Figure 9-9   *Device Status Window*

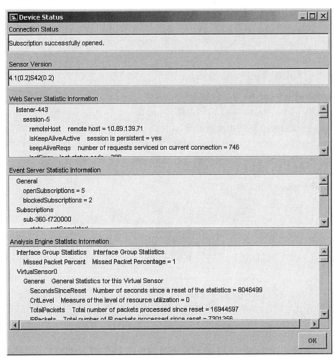

The Device Status window also displays the current status of the connection with the monitored device. This status can be one of the following:

- Subscription not yet open
- Subscription successfully opened

Accessing the Cisco IDS Device Manager

Besides viewing alarms from your monitored IDS devices, you can also quickly access IDM from the IEV user interface. If you want to examine the configuration of one of your IDS devices, just double-click the device name and it will launch your web browser and connect to the sensor's web server.

Configuring Filters

Managing the number of alarms that you need to manage with IEV is crucial to successfully monitoring the security posture of your network. Most organizations do not have an unlimited supply of manpower to examine every possible alarm that the sensors detect.

Some of these alarms are fairly innocuous (such as port sweeps) and do not always warrant investigation, especially with respect to some of the more severe alarms, such as someone attempting to gain system access on a server. In addition, some suspicious traffic detected from an external source might demand more attention than the same traffic between two internal hosts.

Using filters is one way to reduce the number of alarms that you need to analyze via the IEV interface. A filter is basically a set of restrictions that you can place on the alarms displayed by IEV when viewing alarms from your monitored IDS devices via a view. Any alarms matching the criteria that you specify are excluded from the view on which you apply the filter. You can create your filters based on the following filter functions (see Figure 9-10):

- By Severity
- By Source Address
- By Destination Address
- By Signature Name
- By Sensor Name
- By UTC Time
- By Status

Figure 9-10   *Filter Functions*

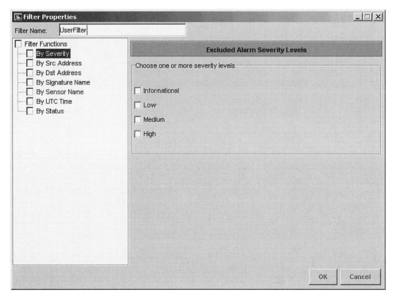

Each of these filter functions will be examined individually, but you can also combine multiple filter functions into a single complex filter. After you create a filter, you can then apply it to any of your default IEV views or any custom views that you have created.

NOTE	Filters do not remove alarm information from the IEV database. They just reduce the information displayed on the screen, thus enabling you to focus your analysis on a smaller set of data. You can always change your filters and view a different set of information. Each filter, however, is based on the actual alarm information in the IEV database.

Filtering on Source or Destination Address

When creating an address filter, you need to first decide what addresses the filter is going to apply to. You can apply different filter properties to both the source and destination addresses. Figure 9-11 shows the filter parameters for the source address. You can specify addresses in the following two ways:

- Single address
- Range of addresses

Figure 9-11   *Source Address Filter Parameters*

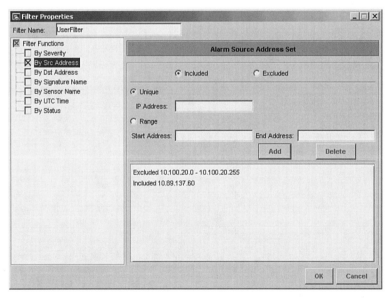

After specifying a unique address or range of addresses, you need to decide how the filter is going to use those addresses. You can choose one of the following two options:

- Included
- Excluded

If you choose Included, the filter causes IEV to display only the alarms that contain one of the specified IP addresses; if you choose Excluded, the filter removes alarms in which one of the IP addresses in the alarm matches one of the IP addresses that you specified.

You can specify multiple address inclusions and exclusions for a single filter (for either the source or the destination address). Figure 9-11 shows a source address filter that includes alarms from 10.89.137.60 and excludes alarms from the IP addresses in the range from 10.100.20.0 through 10.100.200.255.

Filtering on Alarm Severity

Besides filtering on the source or destination IP address, you can also filter on the severity of the alarm. When you decide to filter on alarm severity, you need to select one or more of the following severity levels to be filtered:

- Informational
- Low
- Medium
- High

Figure 9-12 shows an alarm severity filter that only displays alarms that have a High severity. Alarms with a severity of Informational, Low, or Medium are filtered out of the view.

Figure 9-12 *Alarm Severity Filter Parameters*

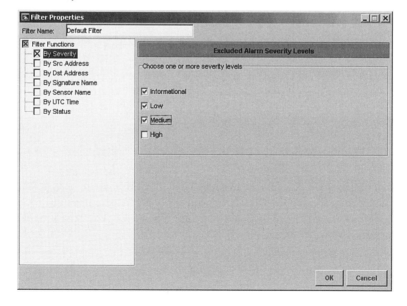

Filtering on Signature Name

Sometimes, you want to exclude specific signatures from your alarm view. Instead of specifying these exclusions by each individual signature ID, the signature filter enables you to efficiently specify the excluded signatures by name. Suppose your network does not include any UNIX systems. You might want to exclude all alarms based on attacks against UNIX systems because you do not have any of these systems on your network.

When specifying the signatures to be excluded, you can locate signatures by clicking one of the following signature tabs (see Figure 9-13):

- L2/L3/L4 Protocol
- Attack
- OS
- Service

Figure 9-13 *Signature Name Filter Parameters*

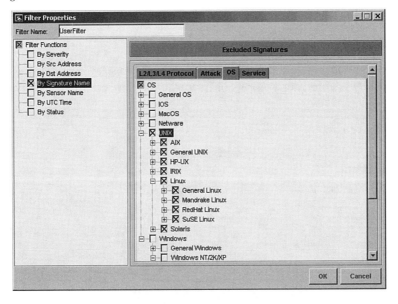

Each of these tabs presents the available signatures from a different perspective. For instance, by choosing the OS tab you can easily exclude all the signatures for a specific operating system. Figure 9-13 shows a filter that excludes all UNIX signatures from the associated view.

Filtering by IDS Device Name

If you have multiple sensors deployed in your network, you might want to create custom filters that exclude the alarm traffic from one or more of your IDS devices (see Figure 9-14).

Figure 9-14   *IDS Device Name Filter Parameters*

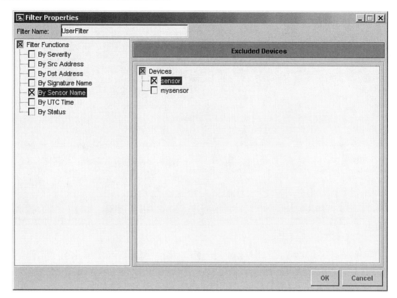

By clicking the box next to the sensor, you exclude events from that IDS device. This type of filter only makes sense if you have multiple sensors being monitored by IEV.

Filtering by Date and Time

Sometimes you want to filter the data source based on the time at which the events happened. When creating a date and time filter, you need to specify one or more date and time range that will be excluded from the data source when the events display on the screen (see Figure 9-15).

Figure 9-15 *Date and Time Filter Parameters*

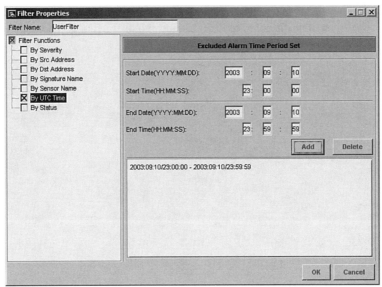

For each excluded time range, you specify the fields shown in Table 9-2.

Table 9-2 *Date and Time Filter Fields*

Field	Description
Start Date	The Start Date indicates the beginning time to start excluding events. You specify a 4-digit year, a 2-digit month, and a 2-digit day.
Start Time	The Start Time indicates the time on the Start Date that the event exclusion begins.
End Date	The End Date indicates the ending time to stop excluding events. You specify a 4-digit year, a 2-digit month, and a 2-digit day.
End Time	The End Time indicates the time on the End Date that the event exclusion stops.

For each time range, you click the Add button. If you want to remove any of the ranges defined for a date and time filter, click one of the existing ranges, and then click the Delete button.

Filtering by Status

Sometimes you want to filter the data source based on the status of the alarms. Each alarm can be in one of the following statuses:

- New
- Acknowledged
- Assigned
- Closed
- Deleted

These status values enable you to remove alarms from the display after they are no longer relevant. You might have someone who assigns new alarms to an engineer who will analyze them. By creating a view that excludes all alarm statuses except for New, you can easily identify new events as they happen. To create a filter that only shows new alarms, you would exclude all of the other alarm statuses (see Figure 9-16). When specifying the status values to be excluded, click the box next to that status name.

Figure 9-16 *Status Filter Parameters*

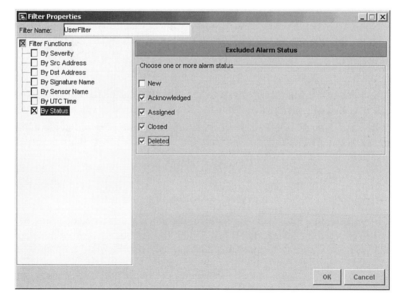

Creating a Filter

To create a filter, follow these steps:

Step 1   From the Cisco IDS Event Viewer main menu, choose File>New>Filter. This brings up the Filter Properties window (see Figure 9-16).

Step 2   Specify a name for your filter by entering an alphanumeric string (up to 64 characters). The default name of UserFilter is automatically provided.

Step 3   Click the name of the type of filter function that you want to define. This displays the appropriate parameters for that filter function.

Step 4   After defining the filter function parameters, the check box next to the name of that filter function (such as By Severity) should now be checked.

NOTE   Repeat Steps 3 and 4 for each filter function that you want to define for the current overall filter that you are creating.

Step 5   After you have defined all of your filter functions, click OK to save the filter definition.

NOTE   If the name of the filter that you specified already exists, you will have to confirm that you want to overwrite the existing filter (click Yes) before you can save the updated filter definition. If you do not want to overwrite the existing filter, click No and then rename the filter that you are creating.

Editing Filter Properties

After you create a filter, you might need to change the filter or examine the contents of the filter to confirm the events that it filters out. To change or examine the characteristics of an existing filter, right-click the filter name and select Properties. This brings up the Filter Properties window.

NOTE   The left side of the IEV display shows either the views that you have configured or the filters that you have created. You select which list is displayed by clicking either the Views or Filters tab at the lower left of the screen.

Deleting a Filter

Sometimes you want to remove a filter that you have created because it is no longer in use. To delete an existing filter, right-click the filter name and select Delete Filter. Then click Yes when prompted whether or not you really want to delete the specified filter.

NOTE   If you attempt to delete a filter currently applied to one or more views, you receive an error message indicating that the view could not be deleted, along with the views that currently use it (see Figure 9-17).

Figure 9-17   *Filter Deletion Error*

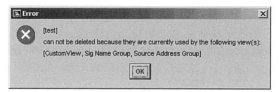

Configuring Views

IEV displays alarm data as views. These views aggregate alarm data and provide a high-level view of what is happening on your network. Through different views, you can group alarm data based on numerous factors, such as the following:

- Signature name
- Source address
- Destination address
- Sensor name
- Severity levels

IEV stores the information retrieved from your sensor into a relational database. Different sources of information are stored in different tables in the database. For instance, the real-time data from your sensor is stored in a table named *event_realtime_table*. If you import an IDS log file into IEV, it will be stored in a different table in the database. Then you can use the views that you have defined to group the data from any of these tables into a more manageable form.

Each view displays the alarm information in the form of an Alarm Aggregation table that consolidates the information based two or more of the following fields:

- Signature Name (mandatory)
- Source Address Count

- Destination Address Count
- Highest Severity
- Total Alarm Count (mandatory)

Then you can expand any of the rows in the Alarm Aggregation table to see an expanded view of the alarm data (Expanded Details Dialog window). Finally, you can expand any of these rows to see the actual individual alarm entries (Alarm Information Dialog window).

Because you can apply different views to the same data source, you can use different groupings to highlight different aspects of the alarm data. Furthermore, these groupings combined with filters enable you to reduce the number of alarms that you need to analyze. You can even specify the detail level of the alarms displayed to further consolidate your alarm view.

Sometimes it is helpful to examine individual alarms. At other times, however, a more consolidated view of the data proves more meaningful. Therefore, besides the default tabular alarm display, IEV also provides a graphical representation of the IDS alarm data that enables you to display alarm data in the following two formats:

- Area chart
- Bar graph

Default Views

Without creating any of your own custom views, you automatically have the following default views in IEV:

- Destination Address Group
- Source Address Group
- Severity Level Group
- Sig Name Group
- Sensor Name Group

Each of these views groups your alarm information based on a different alarm characteristic. The characteristic that you choose can dramatically impact the number of entries that appear on your screen. For instance, Figure 9-18 shows the alarms grouped with the Sig Name Group view.

Figure 9-18 *Sig Name Group View*

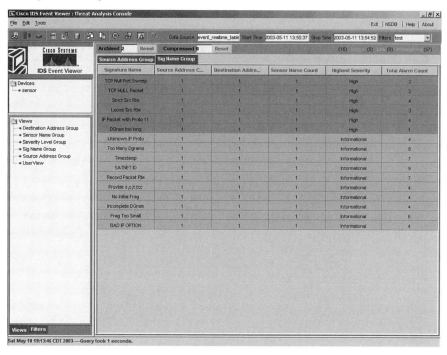

If you change the grouping to the Source Address Group, the number of entries changes dramatically (see Figure 9-19). This new grouping has only one entry, indicating that traffic from a single system has generated all of the 73 alarms.

Navigating Views

To access a defined view, click the View Name list in the Views folder. This displays the view in the panel to the right of the View folder. You can have multiple views open at one time (although only a single view is actually being displayed on the screen). You can change between these open views by clicking the tabs above the current view (see Figure 9-19). Each tab shows the name of an open view.

To close any of the views that you have open, you can right-click the View Name tab (see Figure 9-20). This brings up a drop-down menu that has the following options:

- Close "Sig Name Group"
- Close All Views
- Purge Table
- Delete All Rows from Database

Figure 9-19   *Destination Address Group*

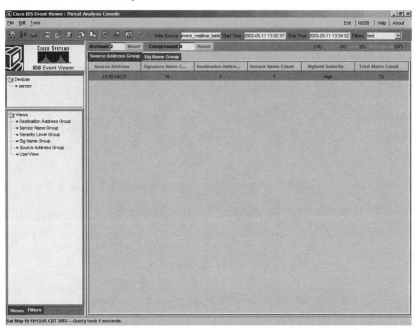

Figure 9-20   *Closing Views*

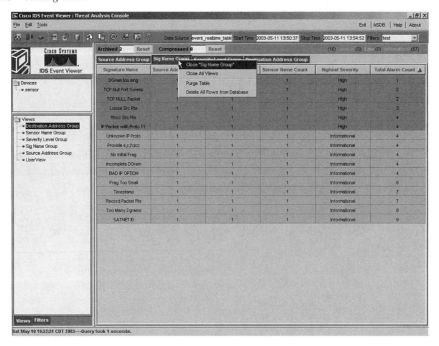

Creating a View

In conjunction with the default views, you may decide to create your own views to consolidate the alarm information from your sensor. To create your own custom view, follow these steps:

Step 1   Choose File>New>View from the main menu. The first screen of the View Wizard window opens (see Figure 9-21).

Figure 9-21   *View Wizard Screen 1*

Step 2   Assign a name to the view by entering the name in the View Name field.

Step 3   If desired, assign a filter to associate with the view using the Use Filter drop-down menu. Then you need to enable the filter by clicking the Use Filter check box.

Step 4   Select the grouping style for the view by selecting one of the check boxes within the Select the Grouping Style on Alarm Aggregation Table group box.

Step 5   Select the columns that you want displayed on the Alarm Aggregation table by selecting the check boxes within the Select the columns initially shown on alarm aggregation table group box.

Step 6   Choose the default secondary sort order criteria from the Column
Secondary Sort Order (Initially) drop-down menu.

Step 7   Click Next to continue. The second screen of the View Wizard opens (see
Figure 9-22).

NOTE   If you click Finished (rather than Next), the default values will be used for the data source
and the columns initially shown in the Alarm Detail table.

Figure 9-22   *View Wizard Screen 2*

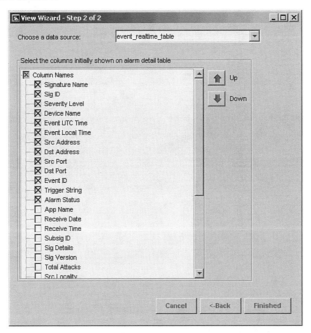

Step 8   Choose the default data source for the events from the Choose a Data
Source drop-down menu.

NOTE   Do not change the data source from event_realtime_table if you want to view IDS events
as they are retrieved from your sensor.

Step 9   Select the columns you want displayed in the Alarm Detail table by
selecting the check boxes within the Select the columns initially shown
on alarm detail table group box.

Step 10 To change the order of a specific field, first select the field name by clicking it. Then change the field's position by using the Up and Down buttons.

Step 11 Click Finished to save the settings to the view.

NOTE If the view name that you specified already exists, a prompt will ask whether you want to overwrite the existing view.

Editing View Properties

Besides creating your own views, you can change the properties of the existing views. To change the characteristics of an existing view, right-click the view name and select Properties (see Figure 9-23). This brings up the View Wizard and enables you to change the parameters for the existing view.

Figure 9-23 *Right-Click the View Name and Select Properties*

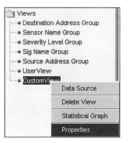

To quickly change the data source for a specific view, you can bypass the View Wizard update mechanism. To quickly change the data source for a view, follow these steps:

Step 1 Right-click the view name and choose Data Source. This brings up the Change Data Source window (see Figure 9-24).

Figure 9-24 *Change Data Source Window*

Step 2   Click the desired data source from the list of available data sources.

Step 3   Click OK to assign the new data source to the view.

Deleting a View

If you want to delete a view, just right-click the view name and select Delete View (see Figure 9-23). Before the view is deleted, you need to confirm the deletion by clicking Yes when the View Deletion Confirmation pop-up appears on the screen.

Viewing Event Data

Each view provides tables and graphs that organize the events for that view. The tables and graphs associated with views that use database tables (data sources) are explained in Table 9-3.

Table 9-3   *Tables and Graphs for Data Sources*

Parameter	Description
Alarm Aggregation table	The first table displayed for any view. You access the Alarm Aggregation table by double-clicking the view name.
Expanded Details Dialog table	Displays the details for a specific row listed in the Alarm Aggregation table. You access the Expanded Details Dialog table by right-clicking the row to be expanded and selecting Expand Whole Details.
Drill Down Dialog table	Displays the individual entries for a specific column in the Alarm Aggregation table (such as the individual source address related to a single signature). You access the Drill Down Dialog table by double-clicking a column (except the Signature Name or Total Alarm Count columns) in the Alarm Aggregation table.
Alarm Information Dialog table	Displays the individual alarms for a specific row in the Alarm Aggregation table. You access the Alarm Information Dialog table by double-clicking the Total Alarm Count field (on the row to be expanded) in the Alarm Aggregation table.
Statistical Graph	Displays the average number of alarms received by IEV based on the filter that is applied to the given data source. This may not be the true average number of alarms if a filter is applied. The time stamp represents the time at which IEV received the alarm (not when the sensor generated the alarm). You access the Statistical Graph by right-clicking the view name and choosing Statistical Graph.

Table 9-4 describes the tables and graphs associated with a continuously running (real-time) alarm feed.

Table 9-4   *Tables and Graphs for a Real-Time Thread*

Parameter	Description
Realtime Dashboard	Displays events as IEV receives them from the sensor(s). You can configure how often IEV retrieves the events and the maximum number of events to be displayed. You access the Realtime Dashboard by selecting Tools>Realtime Dashboard>Launch Dashboard.
Realtime Graph	Display the average number of alarms received by IEV. The time stamp represents the time at which IEV received the alarm (not when the sensor generated the alarm). You access the Realtime Graph by choosing Tools> Realtime Graph.

It is helpful to know how to manipulate the information displayed in the various tables and graphs used by the views.

Viewing All Columns

You can hide columns in the various tables by right-clicking the name of the column and selecting Hide Column. You can use this feature when working with the tables that contain many fields, such as the Alarm Information Dialog table and the Realtime Dashboard.

After hiding columns on a specific window, you can want to make those columns visible again. By right-clicking any column name in the table and choosing Show All Columns, you can unhide all hidden columns for the table.

Sorting Data in Columns

When you define a view, the initial sort order for the rows of the Alarm Aggregation table is based on the Highest Severity column and then on the field you specified in the Column Secondary Sort Order (Initially) when you defined the view.

You might want to change the sort order for various tables. To override the initial sort order, just double-click the column name of the field that you want to base the sort on. This sorts the rows based on that field in descending order. If you want to change to ascending order, double-click the same column name again. You can repeat this process on as many different columns as you want. Each time, the new sort will override the previous sort criteria.

Viewing Events in Realtime Dashboard

You can use the Realtime Dashboard to view a continuous stream of real-time events from the sensor. This enables you to view the actual stream of alarms that come from your sensor with the aggregation provided through the views. You can launch the Realtime Dashboard by selecting Tools>Realtime Dashboard>Launch Dashboard. This displays the Cisco IDS Event Viewer: Realtime Dashboard window (see Figure 9-25).

Figure 9-25 *Realtime Dashboard*

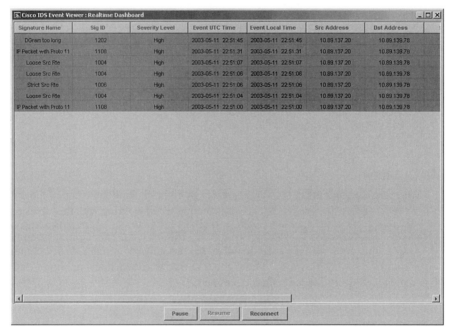

Viewing Events in a Graph

Instead of viewing events in tabular form, you can view them in a graph that displays the alarms per minute that the data source receives. You can obtain the following two types of graphs:

- Statistical Graph
- Realtime Graph

The Statistical Graph bases it information on the data source associated with a specific view. Because this view can have a filter applied to it, the alarm rate shown in the graph might not accurately represent the total number of alarms that the sensor receives. You can access the Statistical Graph for a specific view by right-clicking the view name and choosing Statistical Graph. Figure 9-26 shows a Statistical Graph using the bar format.

Figure 9-26 *Statistical Graph*

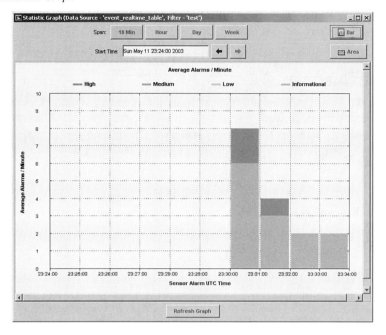

Figure 9-27 *Realtime Graph*

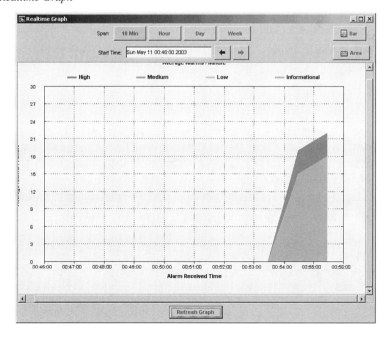

The Realtime Graph bases it information on a real-time data feed from your sensor. You can access the Realtime Graph by selecting Tools>Realtime Graph from the IEV main menu. Figure 9-27 shows a Realtime Graph using the area format.

Working with Alarms

The Alarm Aggregation table provides you with a consolidated view of the activity being detected on your network. From this high-level view, you can drill down or expand the information displayed to effectively analyze the alarms detected on your network. Besides viewing the information in the Alarm Aggregation table, you will also routinely perform the following tasks:

- View the Expanded Details Dialog table
- View individual alarms
- Set alarm status
- Add notes to an alarm
- Show alarm context
- Show attack details

Viewing Expanded Details Dialog Table

The Alarm Aggregation table contains several fields, including the following:

- Source Address Count
- Destination Address Count
- Sensor Name Count
- Total Alarm Count

The Expanded Details Dialog table expands these fields into their actual values rather than just a count. A single row in the Alarm Aggregation table will usually expand into multiple rows in the Expanded Details Dialog table. If the Alarm Aggregation table entry has a 4 in the Source Address Count field, for example, this will expand to four separate entries in the Expanded Details Dialog table (one for each IP address).

To access the Event Details Dialog table, you need to right-click the row in the Alarm Aggregation table that you want expanded and select Expand Whole Details (see Figure 9-28).

Figure 9-28 *Expand Whole Details Option*

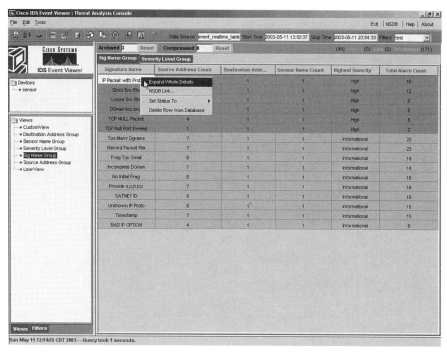

This brings up the Expanded Details Dialog table (see Figure 9-29).

The Expanded Details Dialog table contains a new entry for the items that were consolidated in the Alarm Aggregation entry using counts rather than actual values, using the following fields:

- Source Address
- Destination Address
- Sensor Name
- Severity Level
- Total Alarm Count

Figure 9-29 *Expanded Details Dialog Window*

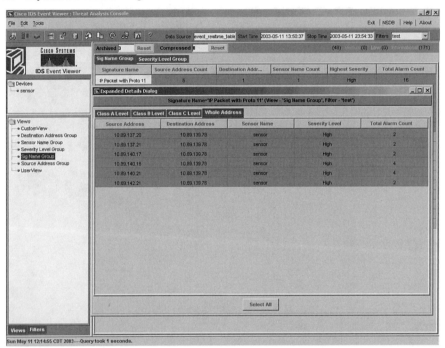

Viewing Individual Alarms

Sometimes you will want to examine the actual individual alarm entries. One way to accomplish this is to use the Realtime Dashboard described earlier in the chapter. But you can also examine the individual alarms for an entry in either the Alarm Aggregation table or the Expanded Details Dialog table. By double-clicking in the Total Alarm Count field for a specific row in the Alarm Aggregation table, you will see the Alarm Information Dialog window for that row (see Figure 9-30). This table displays all the individual alarms that were consolidated in the original row in the Alarm Aggregation table.

NOTE   You can also display an Alarm Information Dialog window for all the alarms consolidated in a single Expanded Details Dialog table row entry. Instead of double-clicking the Total Alarm Count field, you right-click the row to be expanded and choose View Alarms.

Figure 9-30 *Alarm Information Dialog Window*

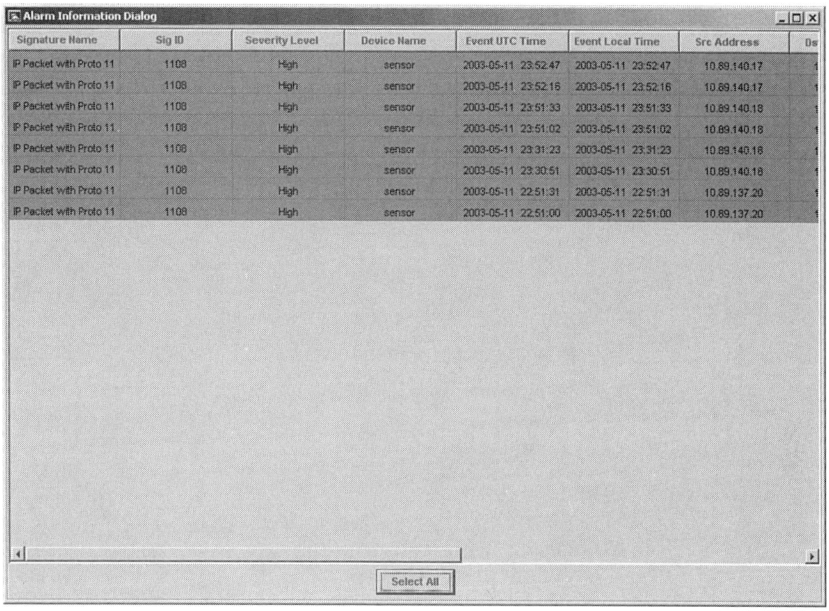

Setting Alarm Status

One of the properties that you can use to filter alarms is the alarm status. The alarm status is a user-configurable field to which you can assign one of the following values:

- New
- Acknowledged
- Assigned
- Closed
- Deleted

By default, the alarm entries have an alarm status of New. You might have an analyst watching the alarms on the sensor and changing their status to Acknowledged to indicate that he has observed the alarm and is working on getting the alarm assigned to someone to investigate it. When someone begins investigating the alarm, that person will change the alarm status to Assigned. After the alarm has been researched, it is changed to the Closed status.

By using the Alarm Status field to indicate that alarms are being analyzed, you can then create views (that filter all alarms with a status other than New). This view only displays new alarms. If the number of alarms in this view continues to grow, it quickly indicates that either the analyst is not acknowledging the new alarms or the alarms are coming in too quickly for your staff to process them.

To change the status of an alarm, right-click the alarm entry in the Alarm Information Dialog window and select Set Status To in conjunction with the next status that you want to assign to the alarm (see Figure 9-31).

Figure 9-31 *Changing an Alarm's Status*

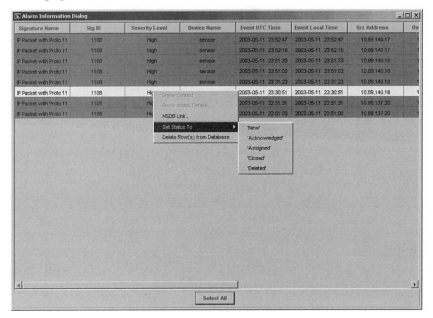

NOTE You can also select multiple alarms by holding the Ctrl key while clicking multiple alarms (or click the Select All button at the bottom of the Alarm Information Dialog window to select all the alarms). Then you can change the alarm status for all the selected alarms in a single operation.

Adding Notes to an Alarm

One of the fields that is part of an alarm entry is the Notes field. You can directly enter information into this field to store user information about the alarm. This information becomes part of the actual alarm entry in the alarm database. While viewing the Alarm Information Dialog window, you can add a note to an alarm by scrolling to the Notes field and double-clicking in this field on the entry that you need to enter a note.

NOTE   The Notes field might not be displayed because it is hidden. If you scroll through the Alarm Information Dialog window and do not find the Notes field, right-click one of the column names and select Show All Columns. This will unhide the Notes column.

Show Alarm Context

For TCP-based signatures that trigger on patterns in the TCP data stream, the sensor captures up to 256 characters of the TCP stream, which can be examined from the Event Viewer. These captured characters are called the *context data buffer*, and it contains keystrokes, data, or both in the connection stream around the string of characters that triggered the signature. You can use this feature to determine whether the triggered alarm was from a deliberate attack or whether it is an accidental set of keystrokes.

NOTE   Beginning with version 4.0, the context buffer actually includes the information that caused the signature to trigger.

To view the captured context data buffer, right-click the alarm you want to examine and choose Show Context from the drop-down menu (see Figure 9-32).

Figure 9-32   *Showing an Alarm's Context Buffer*

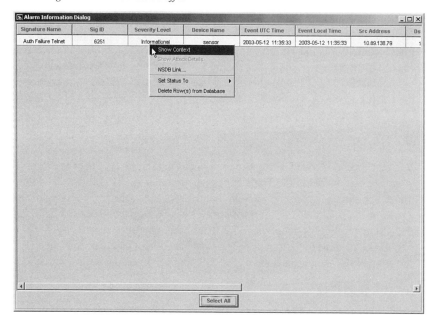

The Decode Alarm Context window displays the signature and context information (see Figure 9-33).

Figure 9-33 *Decode Alarm Context Window*

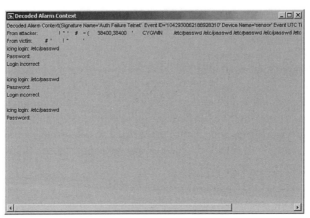

Network Security Database (NSDB)

The network security database (NSDB) is the Cisco HTML-based encyclopedia of network vulnerability information. You can examine the NSDB for a specific alarm. The Cisco Secure Encyclopedia (CSEC) is the online equivalent of the NSDB.

CSEC has been developed as a central warehouse of security knowledge to provide Cisco security professionals with an interactive database of security vulnerability information. CSEC contains detailed information about security vulnerabilities such as countermeasures, affected systems and software, and Cisco Secure products that can help you test for vulnerabilities or detect when malicious users attempt to exploit your systems. You can find the CSEC at http://www.cisco.com/go/csec.

Accessing the NSDB

You can access the NDSB from several places within the IEV user interface. At any time, you can click NSDB in the Tools bar (located at the upper-right corner of the IEV main menu). This displays the NSDB Main Index page (see Figure 9-34). You can also right-click a specific alarm in the Alarm Information Dialog window and select NSDB Link to access the NSDB Exploit Signature page for that alarm. One final way that you can access the NSDB is by right-clicking in the Signature Name field on a row in a specific view and selecting NSDB Link to access the NSDB Exploit Signature page for that alarm.

NOTE   The NSDB is provided with the IEV software. You do not need to access an external server. You update this database by applying signature updates to IEV similarly to how you update the signatures that you apply to your actual sensors.

Figure 9-34   *NSDB Main Index*

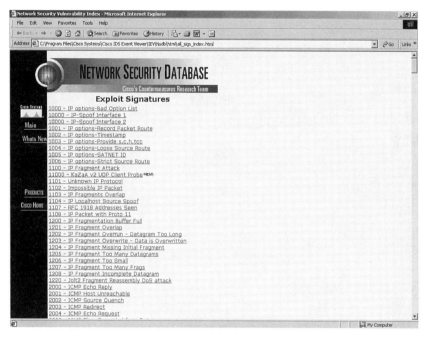

Signature Information

Each signature has an Exploit Signature page that describes the characteristics of the signature. A typical NSDB Exploit Signature page contains numerous fields that provide information about the signature that triggered the alarm. The following three fields provide you with very valuable information:

- Description
- Benign Trigger(s)
- Recommended Signature Filter

The Description field describes what type of traffic the signature is looking for in the network traffic. The Benign Trigger(s) field identifies situations in which the signature might trigger on normal user traffic, thus generating a false positive. The final field, Recommended Signature Filter, identifies a recommended filter that you can apply to your monitoring application to reduce the chances that the signature will generate false positives. Figure 9-35 shows an NSDB Exploit Signature page for the IP Packet with Proto 11 signature.

Figure 9-35 *NSDB Exploit Signature Page*

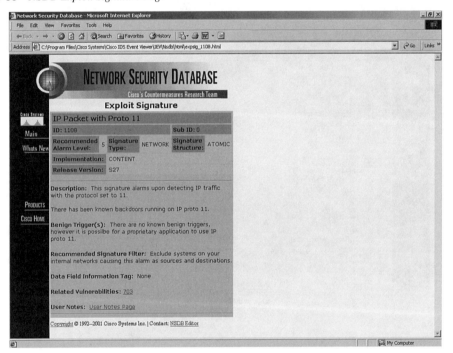

Related Vulnerability Information

Each exploit page provides a link to an NSDB Vulnerability page (the Related Vulnerabilities field) that provides information on the vulnerability associated with a given exploit. A typical NSDB Vulnerability page provides information about the vulnerability, such as the systems that are affected by it, known countermeasures, and the consequences of the vulnerability (see Figure 9-36).

Figure 9-36 *NSDB Vulnerability Page*

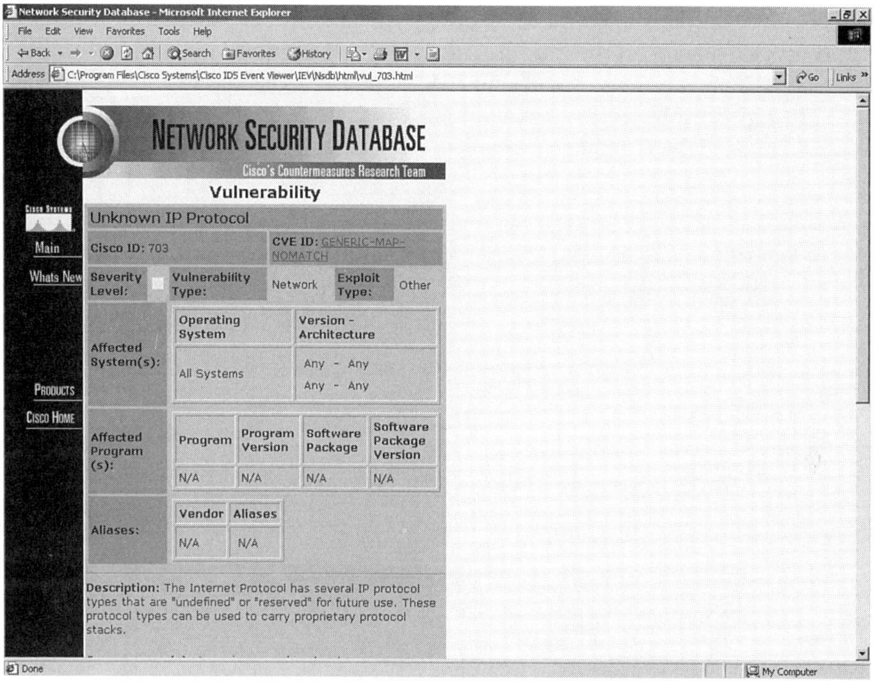

User Notes

To store your own information about specific signatures, the NSDB enables you to fill in a user notes HTML page for each specific signature. You can also store custom notes for every vulnerability in the NSDB. Initially, these notes pages are blank HTML pages. You need to update these files using an HTML document editor. The advantage of storing information in these notes pages is that these files are not overwritten when you update your IEV software.

Configuring Preferences

Most of the configuration changes that you perform when operating IEV involve manipulating views, filters, and data sources. You can also configure the frequency at which the views are updated (from the data sources), as well as the parameters that determine how events from the data sources are archived. The following sections explain how to configure these IEV preferences:

- Configuring Refresh Cycle
- Configuring Data Archival

Configuring Refresh Cycle

In Cisco IDS version 4.0, the monitoring applications "pull" information from your sensors at periodic intervals. The refresh cycle refers to the interval at which IEV retrieves information from your sensors and your IEV views are updated. Therefore, your views do not necessarily display events in real time. By default, IEV retrieves information from your sensors once every minute.

NOTE   To view the events from your sensors in real time, use the Realtime Dashboard.

To configure the refresh interval that IEV uses when retrieving alarm information, follow these steps:

Step 1   Choose Edit>Preferences from the main menu. The Preferences: Threat Analysis Console window opens (see Figure 9-37).

Figure 9-37   *Preferences: Threat Analysis Console Window*

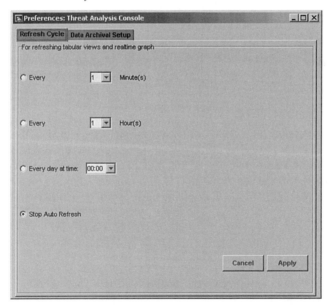

Step 2   If the refresh cycle parameters are not displayed, click the Refresh Cycle tab in the Preferences: Threat Analysis Console window.

Step 3   Select an option and choose a value for the refresh interval. Table 9-5 describes the interval options available.

Table 9-5   *Refresh Cycle Options*

Parameter	Description
Every *N* Minute(s)	Defines the number of minutes between refreshes. (Use the Minute(s) drop-down menu to choose the number of minutes.)
Every *N* Hour(s)	Defines the number of hours between refreshes. (Use the Hours(s) drop-down menu to choose the number of hours.)
Every Day at Time	Defines a specific time for the refresh to be performed each day. (Use the Every Day at Time drop-down menu to select a specific time.)
Stop Auto Refresh	Disables the automatic refresh feature.

Step 4   Click Apply to save the refresh cycle parameter settings.

Configuring Data Archival

Based on your policies, you can configure the following properties with respect to archiving the alarm events stored in your IEV database:

- Events to be archived
- Time at which events are archived
- Maximum number of events in real-time database
- Maximum number of archived files
- Maximum number of compressed archive files

These properties are controlled through the data archival settings. To configure these settings, follow these steps:

Step 1   Choose Edit>Preferences from the main menu. The Preferences: Threat Analysis Console window opens (see Figure 9-37).

Step 2   If the data archival parameters are not displayed, click the Data Archival Setup tab in the Preferences: Threat Analysis Console window. The Data Archival Setup parameters will display (see Figure 9-38).

Figure 9-38 *Data Archival Setup Window*

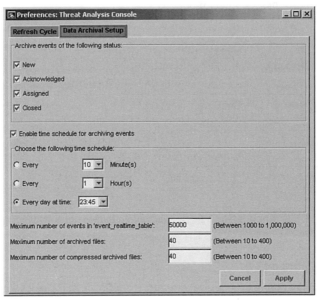

Step 3   Select one or more of the status values (for the events that you want to archive) by selecting the appropriate status check boxes from the Archive Events of the Following Status group box.

Step 4   Enable or disable the time schedule for the archiving events feature by selecting or deselecting the Enable Time Schedule for Archiving Events check box.

Step 5   Choose the time schedule for data archival. (The Enable Time Schedule for Archiving Events check box must be checked.) Table 9-6 describes the time schedule options.

Table 9-6   *Data Archival Time Schedule Options*

Parameter	Description
Every *N* Minute(s)	Defines the number of minutes between subsequent archives of the event data. (Use the Minute(s) drop-down menu to choose the number of minutes.)
Every *N* Hour(s)	Defines the number of hours between subsequent archives of the events. (Use the Hours(s) drop-down menu to choose the number of hours.)
Every Day at Time	Defines a specific time for the data archival to be performed each day. (Use the Every Day at Time drop-down menu to select a specific time.)

Step 6   In the Maximum Number of Events in event_realtime_table field, assign the maximum number of events to be recorded in the real-time database table.

Step 7   Assign the maximum number of files to be archived by entering a value in the Maximum Number of Archived Files field.

Step 8   Assign the maximum number of archived files to be compressed by entering a value in the Maximum Number of Compressed Archive Files field.

Step 9   Click Apply to save the data archival parameter settings.

Configuring Application Settings

To provide some of its functionality (such as connecting to IDM), IEV might need to interact with various applications. During the installation of IEV, default paths are assigned to these different applications. Depending on your system's configuration, these default values might not be correct. Complete the following steps to modify these settings:

Step 1   Choose Edit>Application Settings from the IEV main menu. The Application Settings window opens (see Figure 9-39).

Figure 9-39   *Configuring Application Paths*

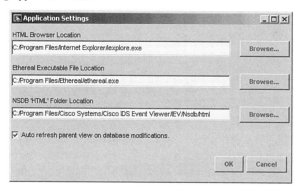

Step 2   Assign the location of the HTML browser. The default system web browser is identified during the installation. If you want to assign the location of a different HTML browser executable, use the Browse button to locate the HTML browser.

Step 3   Assign the location of the Ethereal application used to view IP log files by using the Browse button.

Ethereal

Ethereal is a free network protocol analyzer that runs on both UNIX and Windows systems. It enables you to analyze live data feeds or packets that have been captured to a disk file. You can obtain this software at http://www.ethereal.com/.

Step 4   Enable or disable the automatic refresh of a parent view on the database modifications feature by selecting or deselecting the Auto Refresh Parent View on Database Modifications check box.

Step 5   Click OK to save your settings.

Database Administration

IEV event information is stored in database tables. You use these tables as the data sources for the different views that you create. Besides the event_realtime_table (which is the table in which IEV stores all the events retrieved from your sensors), you can also import information into your own custom tables. Sometimes you might want to export information from a specific table and store it in a normal text file. Periodically, you will need to remove alarms from your database to prevent it from growing too large. This section focuses on the following three database administration operations:

- Importing log files
- Exporting tables
- Deleting alarms

Importing Log Files

IEV has an import function that enables you to import archived IDS log files. The files can be in either comma-separated (CSV) or tab-delimited format. By importing these archived files into the IEV database, you can then analyze their information by displaying them via your configured views.

Complete the following steps to import IDS log files into the IEV database:

Step 1   Choose File>Database Administration>Import Log Files from the IEV main menu. The Import Log Files window opens (see Figure 9-40).

Figure 9-40   *Import Log Files Window*

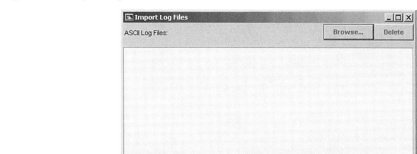

Step 2   Select the IDS log files to import into the database by using the Browse button to locate your files. You can specify IDS log files at one time. The log files that will be imported display in the Log Files field.

Step 3   Choose the field separator drop-down menu (either Comma [CSV] or Tab separated).

Step 4   Choose how to import the log files by completing either of the following:

— Select the Create New Table radio button, and enter a database table name in the corresponding field (not case sensitive).

— Select the Append to Existing Table radio button, and choose the name of an existing table to be appended.

Step 5   Click Import to import the IDS log files into the IEV database.

Exporting Tables

Besides importing alarm information into the IEV database, you can also export tables from the database (by using the export function). Complete the following steps to export IDS event tables:

Step 1   Choose File>Database Administration>Export Tables from the main menu. The Export Database Tables window opens (see Figure 9-41).

Figure 9-41   *Export Database Tables Window*

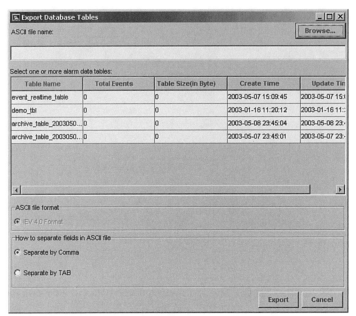

Step 2   Enter the destination filename where the data is to be exported or click the Browse button to locate the destination file.

Step 3   Select the database tables that you want to export by clicking the table name from the list of available tables.

NOTE   To select multiple tables, you need to hold down the Ctrl key while clicking the subsequent tables.

Step 4   Choose the delimiter character used when exporting the data, by selecting either Separate by Comma or Separate by Tab.

Deleting Alarms

The IEV database administration utility provides you with information about the IEV database. To view the database information, choose File>Database Administration>Data Source Information. The Data Source Information window opens (see Figure 9-42). This window provides the table names along with detailed information for each table. The Purge

Tables and Delete Tables buttons provide functions that enable you to delete events from a table or delete a table from the database. You must confirm the operation before IEV actually performs the purge or delete action.

NOTE When viewing alarms, you can delete individual alarm entries from the database. These entries are still in the database, but are just marked as deleted. When you purge a database table, the entries marked for deletion are actually removed from the database.

Figure 9-42 *Data Source Information Window*

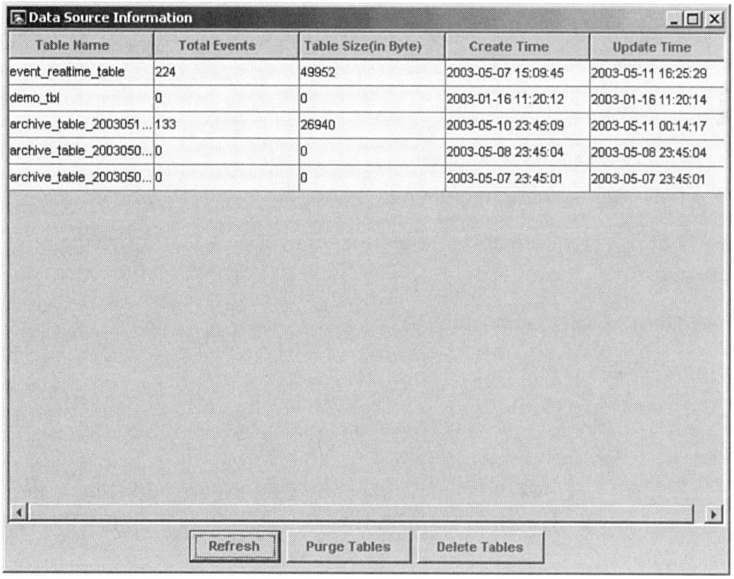
Data Source Information
Table Name | Total Events | Table Size(in Byte) | Create Time | Update Time
event_realtime_table | 224 | 49952 | 2003-05-07 15:09:45 | 2003-05-11 16:25:29
demo_tbl | 0 | 0 | 2003-01-16 11:20:12 | 2003-01-16 11:20:14
archive_table_2003051... | 133 | 26940 | 2003-05-10 23:45:09 | 2003-05-11 00:14:17
archive_table_2003050... | 0 | 0 | 2003-05-08 23:45:04 | 2003-05-08 23:45:04
archive_table_2003050... | 0 | 0 | 2003-05-07 23:45:01 | 2003-05-07 23:45:01
Refresh
Purge Tables
Delete Tables

Summary

To manage your IDS sensors on a small scale, Cisco IDS provides the Cisco IDS Device Manager (IDM). IDM enables you to easily manage sensors (one at a time) from a single web-based management console. Along with providing an online help facility, the IDM interface is divided into the following major areas:

- Path bar
- TOC (table of contents)
- Options bar

- Configuration tabs
- Tools bar
- Instructions box
- Activity bar
- Content area

By default, IDM encrypts its management communication via TLS.

Besides managing sensors, you also need to monitor the alarms that your sensors are generating. To monitor up to five sensors, Cisco provides the Cisco IDS Event Viewer (IEV). IEV provides a flexible Java-based application that retrieves events from your sensors and displays them in a very efficient manner.

IEV presents information to you in the form of a view. This view is comprised of the following tables:

- Alarm Aggregation table
- Expanded Details Dialog table
- Alarm Information Dialog table

The Alarm Aggregation table is a high-level overview that provides the following consolidated fields:

- Source Alarm Count
- Destination Alarm Count
- Sensor Name Count
- Total Alarm Count

The Expanded Details Dialog table expands these count fields into actual values. You can also gain access to the actual alarm entries by double-clicking the Total Alarm Count field in the Alarm Aggregation table.

To reduce the amount of traffic presented by your different views, you can associate a filter with each view. You can filter traffic based on the following functions:

- By severity
- By source address
- By destination address
- By signature name
- By sensor name
- By UTC time
- By status

When you install IEV, it comes with the following default views:

- Destination Address Group
- Source Address Group
- Severity Level Group
- Sig Name Group
- Sensor Name Group

Each of the views consolidates the information based on different fields. Each of these views is updated based on the parameters that you have configured for the frequency at which IEV retrieves information from your sensors (refresh cycle). You might also want to monitor the events from your sensor in real time. By accessing the Realtime Dashboard, you can watch the events from you sensor in real time.

Besides providing information in tabular form, IEV also enables you to display the following two graphical representations of alarm data:

- Statistical Graph
- Realtime Graph

Review Questions

The following questions test your retention of the material presented in this chapter. The answers to the review questions are in Appendix B, "Answers to Chapter Review Questions."

1 How many sensors can you manage with Cisco IDS Event Viewer?

2 What is Cisco IDS Event Viewer based on?

3 Where does IEV store the events it retrieves from your sensors?

4 After installing IEV, what do you need to add to the configuration to enable IEV to monitor a sensor on your network?

5 What are the functions that you can filter traffic on when using IEV?

6 What are the two ways that you can specify IP addresses when defining either a source or destination address filter?

7 What are the default views included with IEV?

8 How can you view the events coming from your sensor in real time?

9 What alarm statuses can you assign to alarm events?

10 How can you assign note information to a specific alarm?

11 What does the context buffer display?

12 How large is the context buffer?

13 What is the NSDB?

14 What determines how often IEV retrieves information from your sensor to update the database tables?

15 When using IEV what are the database administration functions that you will likely perform?

16 What is the default rate at which IEV retrieves information from your sensors?

17 What is the default alarm status?

18 What are the main types of NSDB pages?

19 When filtering on IP addresses, what are the two possible qualifiers that you can apply to the addresses to determine how they are used in the filter.

20 What authentication does IEV use to retrieve information from your sensor?

21 What are the three checks performed by your browser on a TLS certificate?

22 Which browser certificate check will the Cisco IDS sensor fail?

Upon completion of this chapter, you will be able to perform the following tasks:

- Identify the basic sensor configuration tasks
- Understand how to add users to your sensors
- Understand how to configure time on your sensors
- Identify the types of remote access to your sensors
- Understand how to configure remote access to your sensors
- Identify the basic Secure Shell (SSH) parameters
- Understand how to add sensors to Management Center for IDS Sensors (IDS MC)

CHAPTER 10

Sensor Configuration

When using Cisco IDS on your network, you need to perform various configuration tasks on your sensors. Although you can perform these operations via the sensor's command-line interface (CLI), you can also perform these tasks using your Cisco management applications after you have performed the basic initialization of the sensors (via the CLI). These operations fall into the following categories:

- Adding sensors in IDS MC
- Configuring network settings
- Configuring remote access
- Configuring time
- Adding users
- Viewing diagnostic information
- Viewing system information
- Rebooting the sensor

The two Cisco management applications (based on graphical user interfaces) that you can use to configure your sensors are as follows:

- IDS Device Manager (IDM)
- Management Center for IDS Sensors (IDS MC)

The IDS Device Manager is part of the sensor software. You can connect to a web interface on your sensor and use IDM to alter its configuration. Managing sensors individually through a web interface becomes inefficient as the number of sensors being managed starts to increase in number. To configure multiple sensors efficiently, you can use IDS MC. IDS MC is one of the following software packages that comprise the CiscoWorks VPN/Security Management Solution (VMS) bundle:

- Management Center for PIX Firewalls (PIX MC)
- Management Center for IDS Sensors (IDS MC)
- Monitoring Center for Security (Security Monitor)
- Management Center for VPN Routers (Router MC)

The IDS-specific components of the CiscoWorks VMS are described in greater detail in Chapter 16, "Enterprise IDS Management," and Chapter 17, "Enterprise IDS Monitoring and Reporting."

Adding Sensors in Management Center for IDS Sensors (IDS MC)

Before you can use IDS MC to manage your sensors, you need to add the sensors through the IDS MC interface. Because IDS MC is designed to manage up to 300 sensors, you have the option of adding individual sensors as well as creating groups of sensors.

NOTE   Because IDM resides on each individual sensor, there is no concept of adding sensors to IDM. You just connect to the sensor that you want to configure.

Sensor Groups

To facilitate management of your sensors through IDS MC, you can group your sensors into distinct groups. These groups enable you to categorize your sensors by functionality, location, or some other meaningful characteristics. With these sensor groups, you can then perform some configuration operations on the entire group as well as configure individual sensors within the group.

To add a sensor group to IDS MC, follow these steps:

Step 1   Click the Devices configuration tab from the main IDS MC screen.

Step 2   Select Sensor Group from the options bar. The Select Sensor Group window appears in the content area.

Step 3   Click the group that you want to place the subgroup under, and then select Create Subgroup. The Add Group window appears in the content area (see Figure 10-1).

Step 4   Enter a name for the new group in the Group Name field.

Step 5   Enter a description for the group in the Description field.

Step 6   Choose which group you want this group to inherit its values from. The default is to inherit parameters from the parent group. You can also click the pull-down menu to cause the new group to inherit its properties from any other existing group. Sensors in this group use the inherited values unless explicitly overwritten on a per-sensor basis.

Step 7   Click OK to save the group.

Figure 10-1 *Add Group Window*

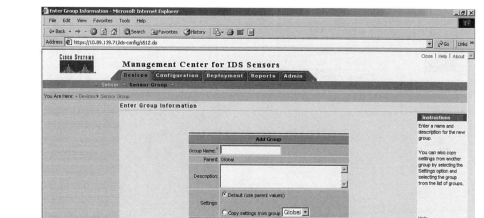

Individual Sensors

Besides defining the groups to place your sensors into, you also need to add the sensors that you will be managing through IDS MC. To add a sensor to IDS MC, follow these steps:

Step 1 Click the Devices configuration tab on the IDS MC main screen.

Step 2 Select Sensor from the options bar. The content area shows the hierarchical tree of sensors and sensor groups that you have already defined.

Step 3 Click the Add button. The Select Sensor Group window appears in the content area.

Step 4 Highlight the group in which you want to add the sensor by clicking the group name, and then click the Next button. The Identification window appears in the content area (see Figure 10-2).

Figure 10-2 *Identification Window in IDS MC*

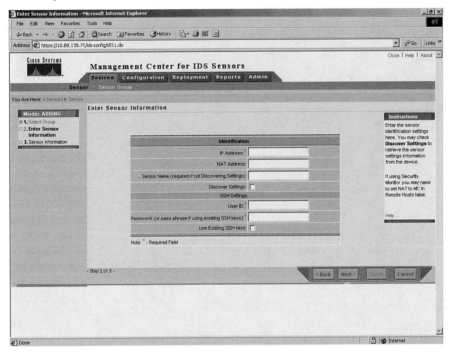

Step 5 Enter the IP address of the sensor to be added.

Step 6 Enter the user ID that IDS MC will use when connecting to the sensor. This must be a valid username that has been configured on the sensor.

Step 7 Enter the password (associated with the specified username) that IDS MC will use when connecting to the sensor. IDS MC will authenticate to the sensor using this password. You can also authenticate using SSH keys if you have already configured them for the account specified. In this case, you specify a passphrase instead of a password and check the Use Existing SSH Keys check box.

NOTE If you click the Discover Settings check box, you can skip Steps 8 and 10 because IDS MC will automatically retrieve this information by using the IP address that you specified (along with the username and password) to log in to the sensor via SSH and retrieve the sensor name and software version.

Step 8   Enter the sensor name (host name) of the sensor being added.

Step 9   Click Next.

Step 10 Specify the software version of the sensor being added.

Step 11 Click Finish to add the sensor. The new sensor will then be added to the hierarchal tree of sensors and sensor groups.

Configuring Network Settings

When you initially configured your sensor, you entered values for various network parameters, such as the following:

- Sensor IP address
- Web server port
- Sensor host name

You can also configure these values through IDM and IDS MC. To configure the network settings using IDM, select Device>Sensor Setup>Network. This screen enables you to configure the following network settings (see Figure 10-3):

- Sensor host name
- Sensor IP address
- Network mask
- Default gateway
- Enable Transport Layer Security (TLS)
- Web server port

TLS

Transport Layer Security is a protocol designed to manage the transmission of messages across an untrusted network. It operates between application layer (HTTP) processing and transport layer (TCP) processing. For more information on the TLS protocol, refer to RFC 2246.

Figure 10-3 *IDM Network Settings Window*

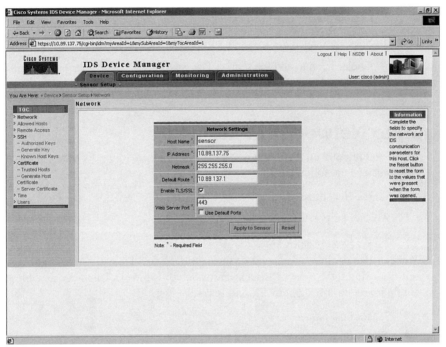

With IDS MC, you can also configure some of the sensor's network settings. The settings for IDS MC also include parameters such as the valid login credentials that IDS MC needs to access the sensor across the network. To configure the sensor's network settings using IDS MC, select Configuration>Settings>Identification. This screen enables you to configure the following parameters (see Figure 10-4):

- Sensor IP address
- Sensor NAT address
- Sensor host name
- Sensor group
- Sensor description
- User ID to access sensor
- Password to access sensor

Figure 10-4   *IDS MC Sensor Identification*

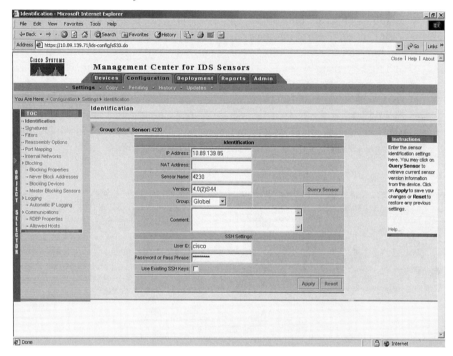

Most of these parameters in Figure 10-4 are self-explanatory, except for the sensor's NAT Address and the Query Sensor button. The sensor's NAT Address value is used when a device that performs Network Address Translation (NAT) is located between the IDS MC server and the sensor. In this situation, you use the NAT Address parameter to indicate the IP address that IDS MC connects to (public or NAT'ed address) communicate with the sensor, whereas the sensor IP address parameter indicates the actual address of the sensor (private address). The Query Sensor button enables you to retrieve the software version of the sensor directly from the sensor using SSH. To use this option, you must specify the following parameters:

- Sensor IP address
- User ID to access sensor
- Password to access sensor

NOTE   When using IDS MC, you can also configure the sensor's TLS settings and web server port by selecting Configuration>Settings>Communications>RDEP Properties.

Configuring Allowed Hosts

By default, your sensor only allows addresses on the 10.1.9.0 Class C subnet to connect to the command and control interface. After defining an IP address for your sensor, you need to configure your sensor to allow your management system and monitoring system to connect to the sensor. To enable your management systems to connect to the sensor, your initial sensor configuration included adding an access list via the **service host> networkAccess>accessList** CLI command. You can always allow other hosts through the sensor's CLI, or you can configure which systems are allowed to connect to your sensor through your management system. When using IDM, you can configure the allowed hosts by selecting Device>Sensor Setup>Allowed Hosts (see Figure 10-5).

Figure 10-5 *Configuring Allowed Hosts in IDM*

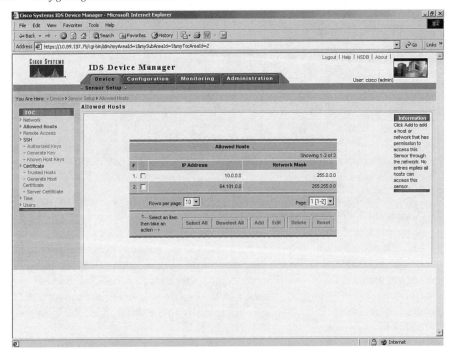

You can also easily configure the allowed hosts through IDS MC. When using IDS MC, you configure the allowed hosts by selecting Configuration>Communications>Allowed Hosts (see Figure 10-6).

Figure 10-6 *Configuring Allowed Hosts in IDS MC*

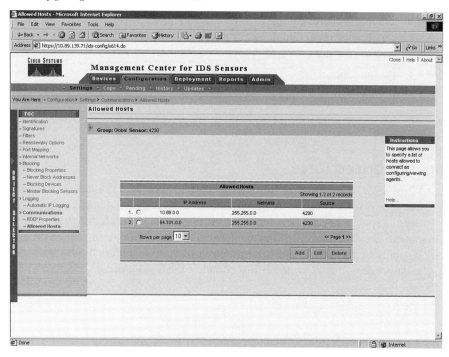

Remote Access

By default, your sensor enables you to interactively log in to the sensor using SSH. This traffic is encrypted, which protects the transmission of authentication credentials (and other information) across the network.

The sensor also supports Telnet to gain interactive access to the sensor. Using Telnet is normally considered insecure because it passes your login credentials in the clear across the network. If you decide to use Telnet for interactive access, you must enable this functionality. Through the IDM interface, you can enable Telnet access to your sensor by selecting Device>Sensor Setup>Remote Access and by selecting the Telnet check box.

NOTE	When running the **setup** command to initially configure your sensor, you can enable Telnet. You can also enable Telnet access from the sensor CLI using the **service host>networkParams>telnetOption** command.

Secure Shell (SSH) Properties

The default interactive communication enabled on the sensor is SSH. SSH provides a secure mechanism to communicate with your sensor. To use SSH effectively, however, you may need to configure some SSH properties, such as the following:

- Define authorized keys
- Generate a new host key
- Configure SSH known host keys

Defining Authorized Keys

When using SSH to log in to the sensor, you can use RSA/DSA authentication rather than using passwords. To use RSA/DSA authentication, each user generates a public/private key pair. The public key can be shared with other systems and used to encrypt information that can only be decrypted using the private key. The private key is protected by a passphrase. When using authorized keys, the user must enter the passphrase for the specified username to gain access to the private key and complete the login process.

Passphrase

A *passphrase* is a string of characters only the user knows that enables access to the user's private key. The private key is stored on the system and is encrypted to prevent unauthorized access. The passphrase is used to decrypt the private key so that the private key can be used to decrypt information encrypted using the user's public key.

When using IDS MC, you have the option of using authorized keys rather than a regular account password. During the addition of a new sensor, you specify the login credentials that IDS MC will use to connect to the sensor. The default credentials are a username and password, but you can also enable authorized keys if you have authorized keys installed on your sensor.

Although you can configure IDS MC to use authorized keys when you add a sensor to IDS MC, you can also enable authorized keys at any time by selecting Configuration>Settings> Identification. Then to enable IDS MC to access you sensor using authorized keys (rather than a username and password), you check the Use Existing SSH Keys check box, and enter the passphrase in the Password field (see Figure 10-7)

Figure 10-7 *Configuring Authorized Keys in IDS MC*

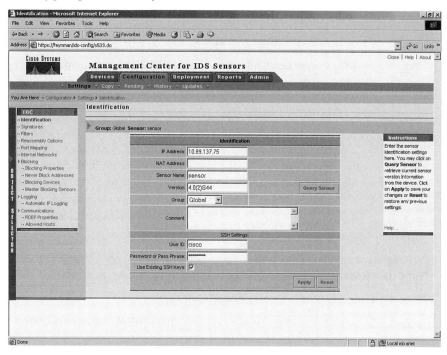

Before you change the sensor's configuration in IDS MC to use a passphrase, however, you need to perform the following two tasks:

- Generate the SSH key
- Import the SSH Key

Generating the SSH Key

To generate an SSH key on your IDS MC server, follow these steps:

Step 1 Log in to the server where IDS MC is installed.

Step 2 Choose Start>Run to access the Run command line.

Step 3 Enter **puttygen** in the command-line field and click OK. The PuTTY Key Generator window opens.

Step 4 Click Generate to accept the default values. Drag your mouse pointer over the blank area of the PuTTY Key Generator (to generate randomness) for the key generation process. The public key displays.

Step 5   Enter an SSH key passphrase in the Key Passphrase field.

Step 6   Enter the same passphrase again in the Confirm Passphrase field.

Step 7   Click Save Private Key. The Save Private Key As windows opens.

Step 8   Save the private key with the host name of the sensor that you are going to use passphrase authentication on in X:\Program Files\CSCOpx\MDC\bin\ids directory (where X is the default drive where IDS MC is installed).

NOTE   PuTTY is a free Windows-based SSH client. This software is provided with IDS MC. You can find out more information about this software at http://www.putty.nl/index.htm.

Importing the SSH Key

After generating the SSH public/private key pair, you still need to import the public key onto the sensor. To copy the public key to the sensor, follow these steps:

Step 1   Connect to the sensor CLI interface.

Step 2   Enter global configuration mode using the **configuration terminal** command.

Step 3   Enter the SSH key using the **ssh authorized-key** *{id} {modulus keylength} {public exponent} {modulus number}* command.

NOTE   Enter the modulus key length, public exponent, and modulus number parameters by copying them from the PuTTY Key Generator screen (Key field) to the sensor CLI. The first number in the Public Key field is the modulus key length. The next one is the public exponent. The last (and longest) number is the modulus number.

Generating a New Host Key

Normally, you do not need to change the SSH host key for your sensor. This key is automatically generated when you first start up your sensor after initial configuration. If you change certain sensor characteristics, however, such as the IP address, you will need to generate a new host key because the existing key will no longer match the host parameters (such as the IP address).

To generate a new host key using IDM, you select Device>Sensor Setup>SSH>Generate Key (see Figure 10-8). You can also perform the same operation from the sensor's CLI using the **ssh>generate-key** command, which is available without entering global configuration mode.

Figure 10-8 *Generating a New SSH Host Key*

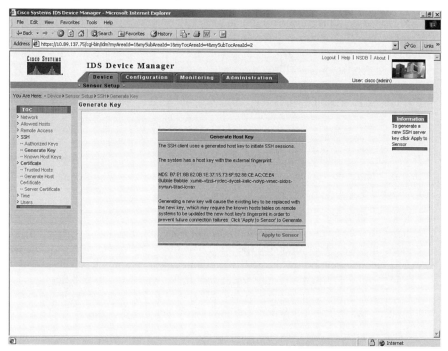

CAUTION	Do not generate another SSH host key unless it's necessary. The sensor's host key is stored on each system that accesses the sensor via SSH. When you generate another SSH host key, these systems need to be updated to use the new key before they will be able to access the sensor. It can also affect the devices that the sensor connects to for such things as blocking.

Configuring SSH Known Host Keys

Whenever your sensor communicates with another network device using SSH, it needs to have a public key (for that device) to validate the communication session. You need to add these keys to your sensor using the sensor's CLI or IDM. A common situation where this occurs is when you plan to communicate with a managed device using SSH. Before the sensor will be able to successfully communicate with the blocking device, you need to add an SSH host key for it on the sensor.

NOTE   Although you can connect to the sensor using both RSA (SSH version 1) and DSA keys (SSH version 2), the sensor communicates with other devices using only RSA keys (because the CLI commands currently support only the creation of RSA keys). This might seem like a security concern, because various vulnerabilities have been identified in SSH version 1. These vulnerabilities, however, have been corrected in the latest SSH implementations. Currently, the main difference between SSH version 1 and SSH version 2 is that SSH version 2 supports certificates and SSH version 1 does not.

If you do not know the public key information, you can use the **ssh host-key** global configuration command via the sensor's CLI to install the correct public key. The syntax for this command is as follows:

```
ssh host-key ip-address
```

When you specify an IP address with the **ssh host-key** command, your sensor attempts to connect to the SSH server on the specified IP address. This connection attempt retrieves the public key information for the SSH server and displays it on the screen so that you can verify that the information is the correct public key for that server. After the key is added, the sensor software can connect to the SSH server and be confident that it is connecting to a trusted device. The following command illustrates this process for host 10.89.138.79:

```
sensor(config)# ssh host-key 10.89.138.79
MD5 fingerprint is 8F:34:92:3C:63:1F:42:AA:87:CE:AD:10:62:C8:71:B4
Bubble Babble is xikos-padog-ticag-tebyz-vepog-gedib-zadag-nacub-nycem-bobab-lixyx
Would you like to add this to the known hosts table for this host?[yes]: yes
sensor(config)#
```

NOTE   To display the SSH host keys currently stored on the sensor, use the **show ssh host-key** command available in privileged exec mode. The syntax for this command is as follows:

```
show ssh host-key [ip-address]
```

Without the optional *ip-address* parameter, the command shows the IP addresses for all the host keys stored on the sensor. Adding the *ip-address* parameter displays the actual SSH host key for the IP address specified.

You can also add SSH public keys to your sensor using IDM. When using this management application, you need to specify the following pieces of information about the public key:

- IP address
- Key modulus
- Public exponent
- Public modulus

When adding SSH public keys using IDM, select Device>Sensor Setup>Known Host Keys. This displays the SSH Host Keys window in the content area, which shows the current SSH host keys defined on the sensor. If you want to add another SSH host key using IDM, follow these steps:

Step 1   Click the Device tab on the main IDM screen.

Step 2   Select Sensor Setup from the options bar.

Step 3   Select Known Host Keys from the TOC under SSH. This displays the SSH Host Keys window in the content area.

Step 4   Click Add to add a new public key. This displays the SSH Host Keys Adding window in the content area (see Figure 10-9).

Figure 10-9   *Adding SSH Host Keys in IDM*

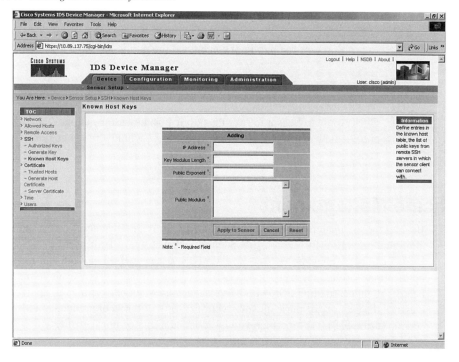

Step 5   In the IP Address field, enter the IP address of the SSH server that you are adding the SSH public key for.

Step 6   In the Key Modulus Length field, enter an ASCII decimal integer from 511 to 2048.

NOTE   The Key Modulus Length field indicates the number of significant bits in the modulus. The strength of the RSA key relies on the size of the modulus. The larger the key modulus length, the stronger the RSA key. A common value for many SSH clients is 1024.

Step 7   In the Public Exponent field, enter an ASCII decimal integer from 3 to 4294967296. The RSA algorithm uses this value to actually encrypt your session.

Step 8   In the Public Modulus field, enter an ASCII decimal integer in the range x, such that $2^{\wedge}$(key modulus length $- 1$) $< x < 2^{\wedge}$key modulus length. For instance, if your modulus length is 1024, the public modulus is between $2^{\wedge}1023$ and $2^{\wedge}1024$.

NOTE   The RSA algorithm uses the public exponent and the public modulus to encrypt your session.

Step 9   Click Apply to Sensor to save the public host key information. Your new entry is now displayed in the SSH Host Keys window in the content area.

Certificate Management

Besides the parameters for SSH, which are used for interactive access, you can also configure properties for the sensor's Secure Sockets Layer / Transport Layer Security (SSL/TLS) communications. You use SSL/TLS to access IDM on your sensor (and other applications through the web server port). In certain situations, however, your sensor also needs to connect to other SSL/TLS servers, such as when performing an upgrade. To enhance the security of these updates, your sensor will only communicate with SSL/TLS servers (using HTTPS) for which you have added a trusted host certificate.

Trusted Host Certificates

Before your sensor can connect to an SSL/TLS server, you must add a certificate for that system on your sensor. This certificate is then used to verify the identity of the server when the sensor communicates with it using SSL/TLS. Without this certificate, your sensor has no way to verify the identity of the server, which could enable another server to impersonate as the real server. An example of when you will need to add a trusted host certificate is when you plan to use a SSL/TLS web server to perform sensor upgrades.

To add a trusted host certificate using IDM, follow these steps:

Step 1   Click the Device tab on the main IDM screen.

Step 2   Select Sensor Setup from the options bar.

Step 3   Select Trusted Hosts from the TOC in the Certificates section. This
displays the Trusted Certificates window in the content area.

Figure 10-10   *Trusted Host Certificates in IDM*

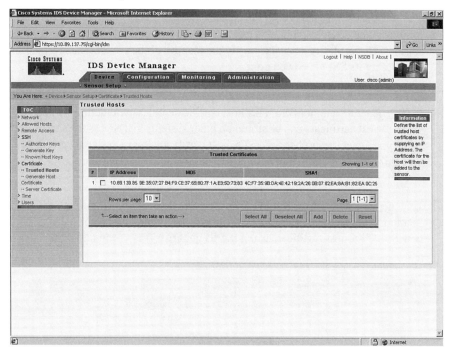

Step 4   Click the Add button to add another trusted host certificate. This displays
an Adding window in the content area.

Step 5   Enter the IP address of the SSL/TLS server that you want to trust.

Step 6   Click the Apply to Sensor button to add the trusted host certificate.

NOTE   The sensor will attempt to connect to port 443 on the specified server. If it cannot connect,
it will display an error message pop-up indicating that the socket connection failed. If the
connection succeeds, the certificate is automatically added to the list of trusted certificates.

Step 7 Verify the certificate's hash value via an out-of-band mechanism.

NOTE You can also add trusted host certificates from the sensor's CLI using the **tls trusted-host** command. Furthermore, using the command line, you can specify the port of the SSL/TLS server if it does not happen to use the default port of 443.

Generating a Host Certificate

Similar to the SSH host key, you can also generate a new SSL/TLS host certificate for the sensor. This certificate is used to verify the identity of the sensor whenever a user or device connects to its SSL/TLS web port.

CAUTION Do not generate another SSL/TLS host certificate unless you definitely need to. The sensor's host certificate can be stored on other systems that access the sensor via SSL/TLS. After you generate another SSL/TLS host certificate, these systems need to be updated to recognize the new certificate before they will be able to access the sensor.

To generate a new sensor SSL/TLS host certificate using IDM, you select Device>Sensor Setup>Certificate>Generate Host Certificate (see Figure 10-11). You can also generate a new SSL/TLS host certificate using the **tls generate-key** command on the sensor's CLI.

Figure 10-11 *Generating a New Server Certificate in IDM*

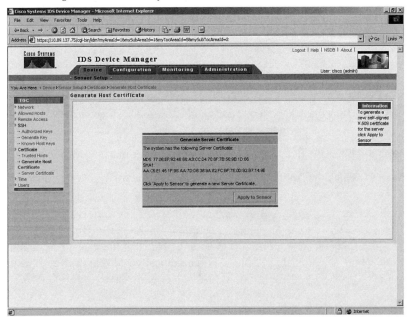

Viewing Server Certificate

To view the current hashes for your sensor's SSL/TLS certificate, select Device>Sensor Setup>Certificate>Server Certificate (see Figure 10-12). This functionality is also available from the sensor's command line using the **show tls fingerprint** command.

Figure 10-12   *Viewing the Server Certificate in IDM*

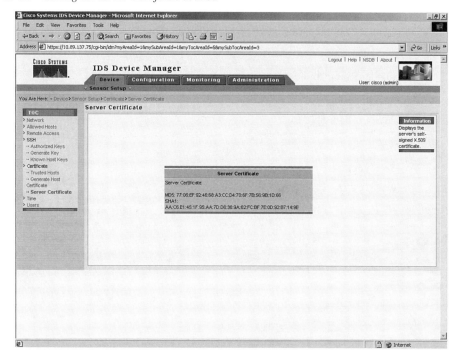

Following common security best practices, you need to obtain this information through an out-of-band connection (or secure in-band connection) to initially verify the identity of the sensor when you connect to the sensor for the first time from a management system.

Configuring Time

You have several options for configuring the regulation of time on your sensor. The time on your sensor is important because all the events stored (such as alarms) are marked with the current time to indicate when they occurred. You can configure the sensor's time settings from the sensor CLI or from IDM.

NOTE   When configuring the sensor's time properties using the CLI, you need to access **service host>timeParams**.

When using IDM to configure your sensor's time properties, you need to select Device>Sensor Setup>Time. This displays the Time Settings window in the content area and enables you to configure time based on the following functional categories (see Figure 10-13):

- Time Settings
- Standard Timezone
- NTP Server
- Daylight Savings Time
- Daylight Savings Time Duration

Figure 10-13 *Time Settings in IDM*

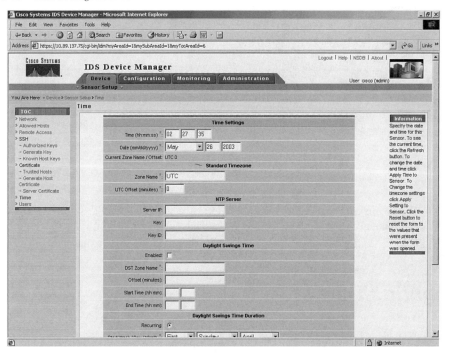

Setting the Time

Using IDM, you can manually set the time by configuring the following fields from the Time Settings window:

- Time
- Date

You configure the time by specifying the following three values:

- hh (current hour in the range 0–24)
- mm (current minute in the range 0–60)
- ss (current seconds in the range 0–60)

You configure the date using the following three fields:

- Month (select value from pull-down menu)
- Day (current day in month in the range 1-31)
- Year (current four-digit year)

After changing these parameters, you can update the sensor's time by clicking Apply Time to Sensor.

NOTE   While viewing the Time Settings window, you can update the time settings shown on the screen to reflect the sensor's current time by clicking the Refresh button at the bottom of the window.

Configuring the Time Zone

Besides specifying the time, you can also specify a time zone. The default time zone is Coordinated Universal Time (UTC), which is also known as Greenwich Mean Time (GMT) or Zulu time. Table 10-1 lists some other common time zones.

Table 10-1   *Common Time Zones*

Time Zone	Offset
EST (eastern standard time)	–5 hours (–300 minutes)
CST (central standard time)	–6 hours (–360 minutes)
PST (pacific standard time)	–8 hours (–480 minutes)
CET (central Europe time)	+1 hour (+60 minutes)
JST (Japan standard time)	+9 hours (+540 minutes)

To change the time zone, you specify a name for the time zone and a current offset for that zone. The offset represents the difference in time for the zone that you specify compared to GMT.

You can name your time zone anything that you want, because the offset value determines the time change. Nevertheless, it makes it easier to understand if you use one of the standard time zone abbreviations.

To apply your changes to your sensor, you need to click Apply Settings to Sensor. Changing the time zone requires you to reboot the sensor before the changes will take effect.

Configuring an NTP Server

Instead of specifying your time manually, you can also configure your sensor to automatically retrieve the time from a Network Time Protocol (NTP) server. By using an NTP server, you can more accurately synchronize the time on multiple sensors throughout your network. Then it is easier to correlate the events from those different sensors.

To configure an NTP server, you need to specify the following three parameters:

- Server IP address
- Key
- Key ID

The server IP address enables the sensor to communicate with the NTP server, and the key and key ID are used by your sensor to authenticate the NTP request received from the server. NTP clients usually enable you to define multiple NTP authentication keys. The key ID value specifies the number of the NTP key to use (in the range of 1 to 4294967295) and the key specifies a 32-character string that represents the secret key. NTP authentication is explained in RFC 1305, "Network Time Protocol."

After entering the NTP parameters, you need to click Apply Settings to Sensor. The changes require you to reboot the sensor for the changes to take effect.

Configuring Daylight Savings Time

Whether you use a manually configured time or an automatic time from an NTP server, you can configure your sensor to automatically adjust its time due to daylight savings time (see Figure 10-14). To enable daylight savings time, you need to click the Enable check box in the Daylight Savings Time section of the Time Settings window. You must also specify the following parameters:

- DST zone name
- Offset (in minutes)
- Start time
- End time

Figure 10-14   *Daylight Savings Time Settings in IDM*

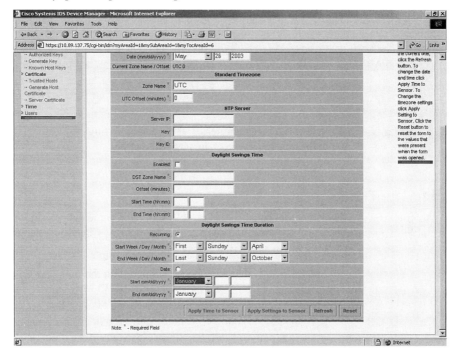

To identify when to apply daylight savings time changes, you must also configure when daylight savings time starts and ends using either of the following methods:

- Recurring
- Specific dates

Configuring Recurring Daylight Savings Time

In most situations, the exact dates when daylight savings time begins and ends are not fixed. For instance, it is defined as beginning on the first Sunday in April and ending on the last Sunday in October. To choose recurring daylight savings time, you need to check the Recurring check box in the Daylight Savings Time Duration on the Time Settings window. You also need to specify the following two parameters (see Figure 10-14):

- Start Week / Day / Month
- End Week / Day / Month

After entering the daylight savings parameters, click Apply Settings to Sensor. The changes require you to reboot the sensor for the changes to take effect.

Configuring Fixed Daylight Savings Time

Instead of recurring, you can also define daylight savings time to begin and end on fixed dates. To use fixed dates to define when daylight savings time begins and ends, you need to check the Date check box in the Daylight Savings Time Duration on the Time Settings window. You also need to specify the following two parameters (see Figure 10-14):

- Start mm/dd/yyyy
- End mm/dd/yyyy

After entering the daylight savings parameters, click Apply Settings to Sensor. The changes require you to reboot the sensor for the changes to take effect.

Correcting the Time

If you need to correct the time because you initially entered a value that was incorrect (such as 7:00 p.m. rather than 7:00 a.m.), you need to be careful when you correct the time if your sensor has already captured events in the Event Store.

If the Event Store contains events that have been stamped with the incorrect time, these events may appear to occur in the future when you correct the time. Suppose, for instance, that you initially configure the time to 9:00 p.m. rather than 9:00 a.m. You notice your mistake at 11:00 a.m. By this time, your Event Store contains numerous events all stamped with times ranging from 9:00 p.m. to 11:00 p.m. If you just correct the time, the new events will be stored with times of 11:00 a.m. and onward. Because this time is before the saved events, the new events will appear to have occurred before the originally saved events. An incorrect time value can also make it almost impossible to correlate events across multiple sensors.

To correct the time for your stored events that have the incorrect time stamp, you need to retrieve all the events from the Event Store, and then clear the Event Store using the **clear events** command on the sensor CLI.

Adding Users

When you initially configured your sensor, you probably added a couple of accounts via the CLI. The functionality to add, modify, and remove user accounts on the system is also available via IDM. With Cisco IDS version 4.0 sensors, you can create new accounts and define their privileges based on the following four user privilege roles:

- Viewer
- Operator
- Administrator
- Service

Each of these privilege roles defines the operations that the user is allowed to perform on the sensor. These user roles are explained in detail in Chapter 7, "Cisco IDS Network Sensor Installation." To add a new account on your sensor using IDM, follow these steps:

Step 1   Click the Device tab.

Step 2   Select Sensor Setup from the options bar.

Step 3   From the TOC, select Users. This brings up the Users window in the content area (see Figure 10-15). This window shows you the current users you have configured for the system.

Figure 10-15   *Users Window in IDM*

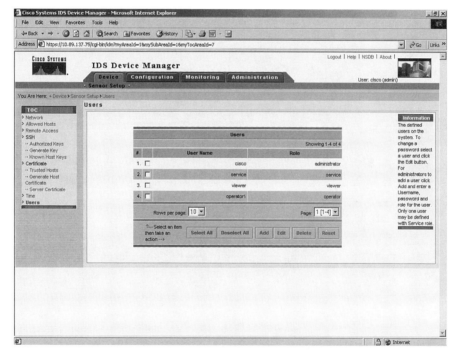

Step 4   Click Add. This displays the Users Adding window in the content area (see Figure 10-16).

Figure 10-16 *Adding Users in IDM*

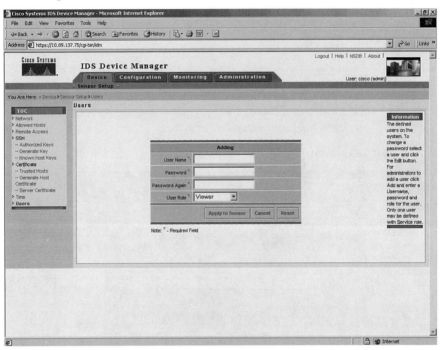

Step 5 Enter a unique name for the new account in the User Name field (1 to 16 alphanumeric characters).

Step 6 Assign the account a password by entering an alphanumeric value in the Password field (1 to 16 characters).

Step 7 For security purposes, the password is not displayed on the screen when you enter it. Therefore, you must re-enter the password in the Password Again field. If the two passwords do not match, you will be prompted to enter them again.

Step 8 Assign a user role to the new account using the drop-down menu for the User Role field. This role defines the privileges that the account has.

Step 9 Click the Apply to Sensor button to add the new account to the sensor.

NOTE To remove or edit an account, check the box next to an account name shown in the Users window (see Figure 10-15), and then click either the Delete or Edit button respectively.

Administrative Tasks

Sometimes your sensor might not operate as you expect. During these times, you will need to examine information about the sensor to determine why it does not work. You might also need to capture this information to assist the Cisco Technical Assistance Center (TAC) when they troubleshoot the operation of your sensor. When using IDM and the sensor CLI, you can use the following options to administer and troubleshoot the operation of your sensor:

- Viewing system information
- Viewing diagnostic information
- Rebooting the sensor

NOTE   The Cisco TAC website also has a large amount of information on troubleshooting and configuring Cisco equipment. You can access this information at http://www.cisco.com/en/US/support/index.html.

Viewing System Information

Sometimes you might want to check whether critical processes are running on your sensors. You might also want to examine the statistics showing the packets processed by your network interface. This information is available when you use the **show version** command on the sensor's CLI. You can also obtain this same information through the IDM user interface by following these steps:

Step 1   Click the Administration tab on the main IDM screen.

Step 2   Select Support from the options bar.

Step 3   Select System Information from the TOC. This displays the System Information window in the content area (see Figure 10-17).

Figure 10-17 *System Information Window in IDM*

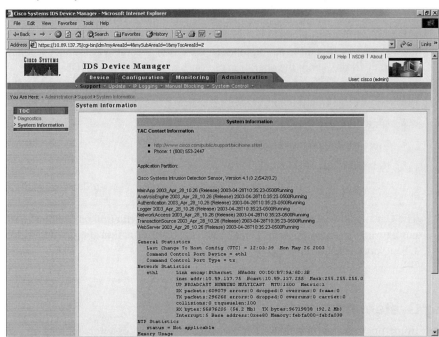

Viewing Diagnostic Information

To assist with troubleshooting sensor problems, you can use the **show tech-support** CLI command. This command provides a wealth of information about the sensor including the following:

- Current configuration
- Show version information
- System information (CidDump output)

NOTE   You probably want to run only the **show tech-support** command when you are actually diagnosing a problem with your sensor, because it can take up to 5 to 10 minutes to complete.

This information is vital when debugging the operation of your sensor. Besides the CLI, you can also access this information from the IDM interface. To view your sensor's diagnostic information, follow these steps:

Step 1   Click the Administration tab on the main IDM screen.

Step 2   Select Support from the options bar.

Step 3   Select Diagnostics from the TOC. This displays the Diagnostics pop-up in the content area (see Figure 10-18).

Figure 10-18   *Diagnostics Pop-up in IDM*

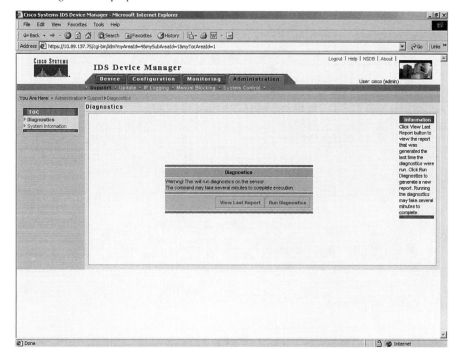

Step 4   Click the Run Diagnostics button to generate the diagnostics report. This will display a pop-up indicating that the report will take several minutes to complete. (You can click the Cancel button to abort the report creation.) The diagnostics report provides the same information as the **show tech-support** CLI command.

NOTE   If this is not the first time you have generated a diagnostics report, you will also have the
            option to view the last report you generated by clicking the View Last Report button.

Step 5   When the View Diagnostics Result window appears in the content area,
            the diagnostics report has been generated. To view the report, click the
            View Results button. The Diagnostics report appears in a separate
            browser window (see Figure 10-19).

Figure 10-19   *Diagnostics Report in IDM*

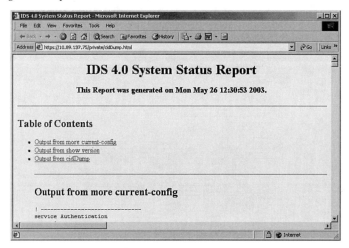

Rebooting the Sensor

Many configuration changes, such as changing the sensor's time zone or IP address, require
you do reboot the sensor. From the CLI you can accomplish this by using the **reset** CLI
command. The **reset** command shuts down the applications and processes on the sensor in
an orderly fashion and then reboots the sensor.

This same functionality is also available through the IDM user interface. To reboot the sensor using the IDM user interface, follow these steps:

Step 1   Click the Administration tab from the main IDM screen.

Step 2   Select System Control from the options bar. This displays the System Control window in the content area (see Figure 10-20).

Figure 10-20   *System Control in IDM*

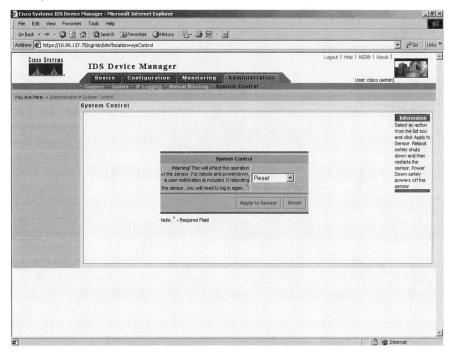

Step 3   From the drop-down menu, select either Reset (reboots the sensor) or Power Down (powers down the sensor without rebooting).

Step 4   Click the Apply to Sensor button to perform the selected operation.

Summary

Besides the basic configuration steps that you need to initially perform on you sensors, you will periodically need to perform various other sensor configuration tasks. Although you can perform these tasks from the sensor's CLI, it is usually easier to perform these tasks via your management tools (such as IDM and IDS MC). The sensor configuration tasks fall into the following categories:

- Adding sensors in IDS MC
- Configuring network settings
- Configuring remote access
- Configuring time
- Adding users
- Viewing diagnostic information
- Viewing system information
- Rebooting the sensor

Before using IDS MC to manage your sensors, you need to add the sensors so that IDS MC knows which sensors it is managing and how to communicate with those sensors. When adding sensors to IDS MC, you can place your sensors in sensor groups that enable you to perform configuration operations on the entire group or use certain group configuration settings.

Before external systems (clients or devices) can access the sensor, you must provide them access. By default, the sensor only allows connections from hosts whose IP addresses are on the 10.1.9.0 network (Class C network). You must enable access for every device or network that needs to access your sensor.

You use SSH to securely access the sensor's CLI. To enable your sensors to communicate with other devices securely across the network, you need to configure the SSH properties on your sensor. The SSH properties that you can configure are as follows:

- Define authorized keys
- Generate a new host key
- Configure SSH known host keys

Instead of using passwords, you can also define authorized keys to access the sensor's CLI via SSH. You essentially place the user's private key on the sensor. Then when the user logs in, he enters his passphrase to gain access to his private key to complete the authentication process. Configuring passphrase authentication requires the following two initial tasks:

- Generate the SSH key
- Import the SSH key to the sensor

For all the devices that your sensor needs to communicate with, such as blocking sensors, you need to add the SSH server's public key. If you do not add the SSH server's public key, the sensor will fail to connect to the SSH server on the target device because it will be unable to verify the authenticity of the server.

Your sensor has various time settings. The time on your sensor is important because the sensor uses this time to stamp each alarm event. Stamping alarms with an accurate time enables you to correlate events across your network. Some of the options that configure with respect to the sensor's time are as follows:

- Sensor's current time
- Sensor's time zone
- NTP server
- Daylight savings time parameters

To access your sensor, a user must have a valid account. You can add and remove accounts using IDM. Each account has specific privileges that are defined by the user role that is assigned to the user. You can assign each user one of the following roles:

- Administrator
- Operator
- Viewer
- Service

You can also retrieve information to troubleshoot the operation of your sensor. You can use the following two options to view information about your sensor:

- System information
- Diagnostics

Finally, you can also reboot or power down your sensor through the IDM interface.

Review Questions

The following questions test your retention of the material presented in this chapter. The answers to the review questions are in Appendix B, "Answers to Chapter Review Questions."

1 When adding a sensor to IDS MC, what is the minimum amount of information that you must provide?

2 What is an advantage of placing sensors into a sensor group in IDS MC?

3 By default, what network addresses are allowed to connect to the sensor?

4 What must you do on your sensor to enable it to communicate with an SSH server?

5 What are the four roles that you can assign a user account on your sensor?

6 What determines the privileges that an account on your sensor has?

7 What information is included in the **show tech-support** command?

8 What are the two ways to configure when daylight savings time starts and stops?

9 When making a significant time change on your sensor, what problem must you watch out for?

10 What are the two ways that you can configure time on the sensor?

11 What two methods of interactive access do you have to communicate with your sensor?

12 What is a common situation in which you need to add a known SSH host key?

13 What is a situation in which you would need to add a trusted host certificate to your sensor?

14 What are the two ways that IDS MC can authenticate to a sensor?

Upon completion of this chapter, you will be able to perform the following tasks:

- Identify the major sensor system variables
- Configure the sensor system variables
- Identify signature groups
- Explain event filters
- Configure event filters
- Tune existing signatures
- Explain custom signatures
- Identify steps involved in creating custom signatures
- Create custom signatures

CHAPTER 11

Signature Configuration

To minimize false positives, Cisco IDS uses various signature engines that enable you to tune signatures to your unique network environment. These signature engines use various parameters to define the behavior of the signatures, enabling you to easily create custom signatures especially suited for your own network architecture or tweak existing signatures to make them operate more effectively on your network.

Besides understanding the various signature engines themselves, you also need to understand what tools are available to actually tune existing signatures and enable you to create your own custom signatures. This chapter focuses on how you can use IDS Device Manager (IDM) and Management Center for IDS Sensors (IDS MC) to configure your IDS signatures. IDM (introduced in Chapter 9, "Cisco IDS Device Manager and Event Viewer") is provided with your sensor software and enables you to manage your sensors individually, one sensor at a time. IDS MC enables you to manage and configure up to 300 sensors (see Chapter 16, "Enterprise IDS Management").

Global Sensing Configuration

Before explaining the ways in which you can configure your Cisco IDS signatures, it is helpful to explain a couple of global sensing options that impact the way that your sensor actually captures and analyzes traffic. The two major global sensing configuration parameters are the following:

- Internal networks
- Reassembly options

Internal Networks

To help minimize the number of false positive alarms that you need to analyze, tune your IDS signatures and filter out known false positive situations. One way to accomplish this is by defining your internal networks. These networks are considered partially trusted and part of your protected network. By establishing filters on these internal networks (with respect to certain signatures), you can reduce the number of false positives that your security analyst must examine. You can easily define your internal networks using both IDM and IDS MC.

NOTE   You can also configure internal networks from the sensor's command-line interface (CLI) using the **service alarm-channel-configuration>tune-alarm-channel>systemVariables** commands. Internal networks are defined by the IN system variable.

Although you can specify IP address exclusions explicitly in your event filters, the IP addresses for internal networks tend to change as your network expands and changes. After each change, you need to update each filter that uses explicit IP addresses. By configuring internal networks instead, you have the ability to define filters with the IN and OUT keywords. Then, when your network changes, all you need to do is to modify the internal network parameter and all of your event filters will automatically reflect the addition of the new addresses.

When defining event filters, the IN keyword indicates that IP addresses configured by your internal network configuration parameters are considered valid matches. The opposite keyword, OUT, refers to addresses that have not been explicitly configured as being part of your protected network (via the internal network parameters).

NOTE   Through IDM, you can also configure several other system variables, such as DMZ1, SIG1, and USER-ADDRS1, which can also be used when creating event filters. These variables operate similar to the IN and OUT variables by providing you with various address and signature groups. Using these variables in your filters enables you to create filters that are easy to manage and self-documenting. When using any of the system variables in a filter, you need to precede the variable name with a dollar sign ($), such as $IN, $SIG1, and $DMZ1.

Defining Internal Networks Using IDS Device Manager (IDM)

IDM enables you to add and modify to the internal network configuration for a single sensor. When configuring your internal networks using IDM version 4.x, you need to modify the IN system variable. The steps to modify your internal networks are as follows:

Step 1   Click the Configuration tab on the main IDM screen.

Step 2   Select Sensing Engine from the options bar.

Step 3   From the TOC, select System Variables in the Alarm Channel Configuration section. This displays the System Variables window in the content area, showing the current configuration for your system variables (see Figure 11-1).

Figure 11-1 *Configuring Alarm Channel System Variables*

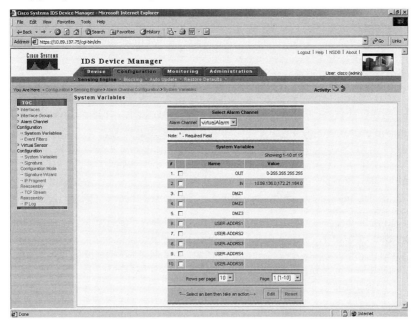

Step 4 Check the check box to the right of the IN system variable and then click the Edit button. This displays the System Variables Editing window in the content area.

Step 5 Enter the network or networks that you want to define as internal networks by entering these networks in the IN field.

NOTE   You can enter multiple networks by separating them with commas. You can also enter network ranges entering two IP addresses separated by a dash.

Step 6 Click the OK button to save you changes. You will see a pop-up window in the content area indicating that you need to commit your changes to make them take effect (see Figure 11-2).

Figure 11-2 *Commit Changes Pop-up Window*

NOTE	When you modify the system variables, you must commit the changes by clicking the Save Changes icon on the activity bar before you can perform other configuration changes to your sensor. You can also cancel your changes by clicking the Cancel Changes icon on the activity bar.

Defining Internal Networks Using Management Center for IDS Sensors (IDS MC)

You can also modify internal networks when using IDS MC. With IDS MC, however, you can modify the internal network configuration for a group of sensors or for an individual sensor. If you change the internal network configuration for the Global group, for instance, all of the sensors that IDS MC manages will use that configuration along with any additional internal networks specifically configured for a sensor or sensor group.

Figure 11-3 shows a configuration that includes two globally configured internal networks and one sensor-specific internal network. The globally configured values include the 10.89.137.0 network and the address range 172.21.16.10 through 172.21.16.200. The 10.89.136.0 network is specifically configured for the sensor labeled sensor. You can determine where the internal network is defined by looking at the Source field.

Figure 11-3   *The Internal Networks Window in IDS MC*

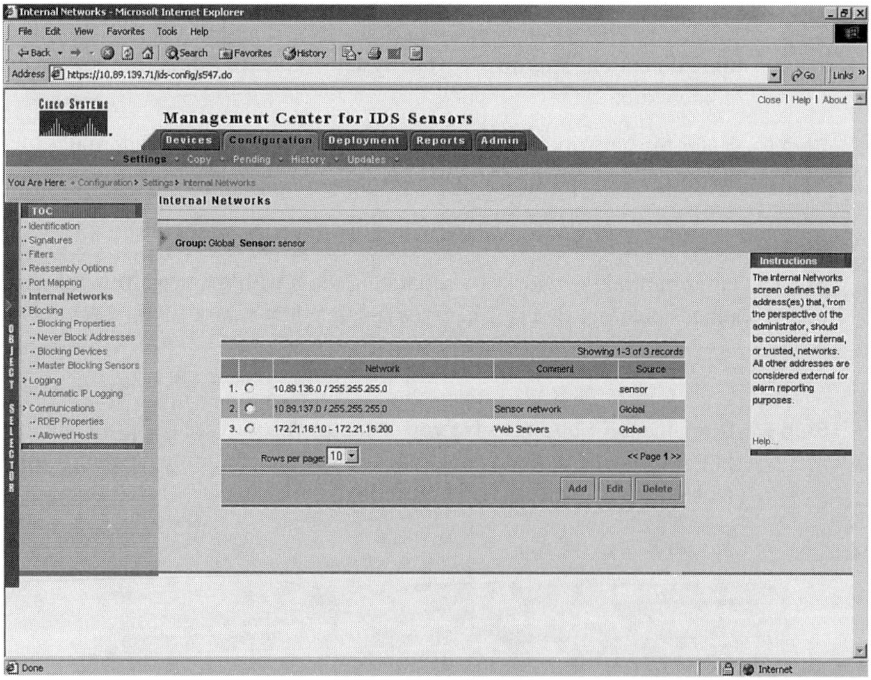

To add an internal network using IDS MC, follow these steps:

Step 1   Click the Configuration tab on the main IDS MC screen.

Step 2   Select Settings from the options bar (or in the content area).

Step 3   Click the object selector bar to select which group or specific sensor you want to apply your changes to.

Step 4   Select Internal Networks from the TOC to display the Internal Networks window in the content area (see Figure 11-3).

Step 5   Click the Add button to add an internal network. This will display Enter Network window in the content area (see Figure 11-4).

Figure 11-4   *Adding an Internal Network in IDS MC*

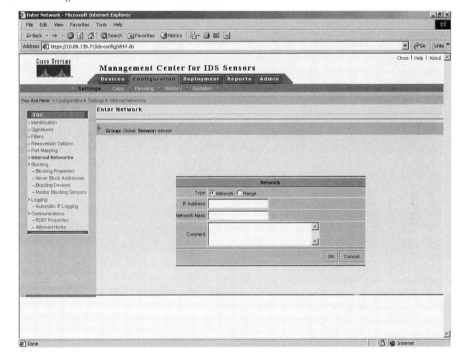

Step 6   Enter the IP address and network mask for the internal network being added. You can also enter a descriptive comment for this network.

NOTE   You can also enter an address range by clicking the Range radio button. The window changes to enable you to enter a starting and ending IP address, along with the comment (see Figure 11-5).

Figure 11-5 *Adding an Internal Address Range in IDS MC*

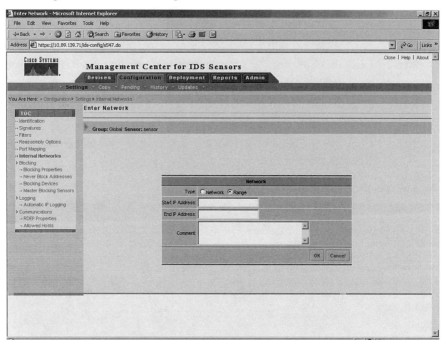

Step 7 Click the OK button to save your changes.

NOTE Before your changes are applied to the sensor configuration, you will need to deploy the changes (see Chapter 16).

Reassembly Options

Another global sensing task is to configure your sensor's reassembly options. These options impact the way in which your sensor processes IP fragments as well as TCP packets. The reassembly options fall into the following two categories:

- IP fragment reassembly
- TCP stream reassembly

CAUTION You should not change these parameters without performing a detailed analysis of your network traffic. Incorrectly altering these parameters can impact your sensor's performance and accuracy.

IP Fragment Reassembly

Different operating systems reassemble IP fragmented packets in slightly different ways. With IP fragment reassembly, you can configure your sensor to reassemble fragmented traffic the same as one of the following operating systems using the IP reassemble mode:

- NT (default)
- Solaris
- Linux
- BSD

Currently, when you configure this parameter, it applies to all the packets processed by your sensor. Therefore, you probably want to set it to an operating system that is representative of the most number of systems on your network.

To reassemble an IP fragmented datagram, your sensor must store the individual fragments until it has all of them for a single IP datagram. Then it can construct the reassembled IP datagram composed from all the individual fragmented packets. Because storing the fragments consumes sensor resources, an attacker might try to flood your sensor with incomplete IP fragmented datagrams. Therefore, you can also configure the length of time that the sensor waits before deleting fragments from an incomplete IP fragmented datagram. The Reassemble Timeout controls the time that your sensor stores incomplete IP fragments.

NOTE   If you use IDM, you can also configure the Maximum Reassemble Fragments parameter. This parameter controls the maximum number of fragmented packets that the sensor will store for a single IP fragmented datagram and is currently only configurable through IDM.

To configure IP fragment reassembly using IDM, follow these steps:

Step 1   Click the Configuration tab on the main IDM screen.

Step 2   Select Sensing Engine from the options bar.

Step 3   Select IP Fragment Reassembly from the Virtual Sensor Configuration section of the TOC. The IP Fragment Reassembly window appears in the content area (see Figure 11-6).

Figure 11-6   *IP Fragment Reassembly Window in IDM*

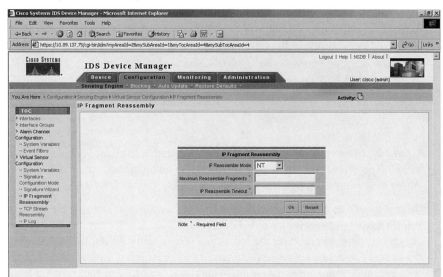

Step 4   Select the IP Reassemble Mode using the pull-down menu.

Step 5   Enter a value for the Maximum Reassemble Fragments field.

Step 6   Define how long (in seconds) fragmented packets that are part of incomplete IP datagrams are stored by entering a value in the IP Reassemble Timeout field. (A reasonable default value is 120 seconds.)

Step 7   Click the OK button to save your values.

NOTE   When you modify the IP fragment reassembly parameters, you must commit the changes by clicking the Save Changes icon on the activity bar before you can perform other configuration changes to your sensor. You can also cancel your changes by clicking the Cancel Changes icon on the activity bar.

TCP Stream Reassembly

Normal TCP traffic begins with a three-way handshake and ends with a FIN or an RST packet. Many attackers, however, will flood your network with traffic that appears to be valid TCP attack traffic with the intent to cause your IDS to generate alarms. This attack traffic, however, is not part of valid TCP sessions. By tuning your sensor's TCP reassembly options, you can control how your sensor responds to the TCP traffic that traverses your network. When configuring TCP reassembly, define the following parameters:

- Enable TCP three-way handshake
- TCP reassemble mode
- TCP open establish timeout
- TCP embryonic timeout

NOTE   When using IDM, you also need to specify the TCP max queue size parameter.

If you enable the TCP three-way handshake, your sensor only analyzes TCP streams that start with a complete three-way handshake. Although this can reduce the number of alarms generated by traffic that is not part of a valid TCP stream, it can also cause your sensor to potentially miss valid attacks against your network. For instance, TCP connections that are already established when the sensor is booted will not be analyzed because the three-way handshake will have already occurred. Essentially, any situation that causes your sensor to miss part of the initial three-way handshake will cause those connections not to be monitored.

Each IP packet in a TCP stream has sequence numbers that enable the destination host to put the packets into the correct order and identify missing packets. When using IDM, you can choose from one of the following two TCP reassembly modes depending on your network environment:

- Strict
- Loose

Strict TCP stream reassembly causes your sensor to ignore streams that are missing packets (based on the sequence numbers). When a gap in a TCP session is detected (a missing packet in the sequence), the sensor stops processing data for the TCP stream.

Loose TCP stream reassembly attempts to place the packets collected during a specific period of time in the correct sequence number order, but still processes the packets if missing packets never arrive. Because it allows gaps in the sequence number chain, using this option can lead to false positives because the TCP stream is incomplete.

NOTE	Using the sensor's CLI, you can configure a third TCP stream reassembly mode named asym. This mode can be used to monitor one half of an asymmetrically routed link. It disables the sequence number window enforcement because acknowledgements might not be available. Using this mode can open the sensor up to window evasion techniques so it should not be used unless required.

The TCP open establish timeout specifies the number of seconds that can transpire before the sensor frees the resources allocated to a fully established TCP session. This timeout is applied to sessions for which the sensor has not seen any traffic from the participating hosts involved in the session.

The TCP embryonic timeout specifies the number of seconds that can transpire before the sensor frees resources allocated for an initiated, but not fully established, TCP session.

To configure TCP stream reassembly using IDM, follow these steps:

Step 1 Click the Configuration tab on the main IDM screen.

Step 2 Select Sensing Engine from the options bar.

Step 3 Select TCP Stream Reassembly from the Virtual Sensor Configuration section of the TOC. The TCP Stream Reassembly window appears in the content area (see Figure 11-7).

Figure 11-7 *The TCP Stream Reassembly Window in IDM*

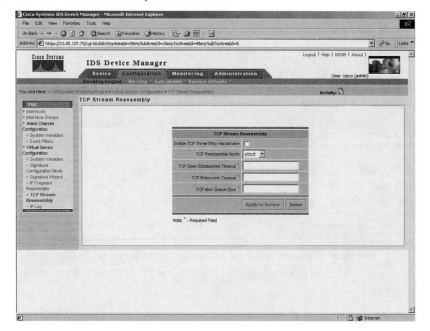

Step 4   Check the Enable TCP Three-way Handshake check box if you want to force the sensor to process TCP packets only from sessions that have completed the three-way handshake.

Step 5   Select the TCP Reassemble mode using the pull-down menu.

Step 6   Enter the TCP open establish timeout. The range is from 1 to 120 seconds. (A good default value is 90 seconds.)

Step 7   Enter the TCP embryonic timeout. The range is from 0 to 15 seconds. (A good default value is 15 seconds.)

Step 8   Enter the TCP maximum queue size.

Step 9   Click the Apply to Sensor button to save your values.

NOTE   When you modify the TCP stream reassembly parameters, you must commit the changes by clicking the Save Changes icon on the activity bar before you can perform other configuration changes to your sensor. You can also cancel changes by clicking the Cancel Changes icon on the activity bar.

Configuring Reassembly Options Using IDS MC

You can also configure your sensor's reassembly options using IDS MC. With IDS MC, however, both IP fragment reassembly and TCP stream reassembly are configured using the same screen. To configure your sensor's reassembly option using IDS MC, follow these steps:

Step 1   Click the Configuration tab on the main IDS MC screen.

Step 2   Select Settings from either the options bar or the content area.

Step 3   Select the sensor that you want to change the reassembly options on using the object selector bar.

Step 4   Select Reassembly Options from the TOC. The Reassembly Options IDS 4 window appears in the content area (see Figure 11-8).

Figure 11-8   *The Reassembly Options IDS 4 Window in IDM*

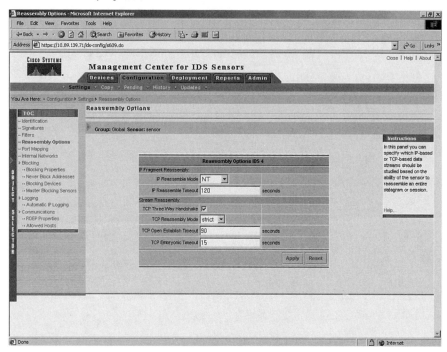

Step 5   Enter the values for both the IP fragment reassembly options and the TCP
stream reassembly options. (The current values are shown on the screen.)

Step 6   Click Apply to save your changes.

NOTE   Before changes are applied to your sensor configuration, you will need to deploy the
changes (see Chapter 16).

Signature Groups in IDM

To tune and customize your Cisco IDS signatures, you can examine signatures using
various signature groups. Using IDM, access the main signature groups screen by choosing
Configuration>Sensing Engine>Virtual Sensor Configuration>Signature Configuration
Mode (see Figure 11-9).

Figure 11-9   *Signature Groups in IDM*

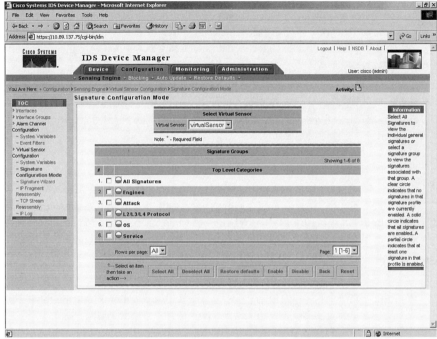

Each major signature group falls into one of the following six categories:

- Signature ID (all signatures)
- Signature Engine
- Attack type
- L2/L3/L4 Protocol
- Operating System (OS)
- Service

NOTE   Do not confuse the Service signature category with the service signature engines. This is a categorization of all the signatures based on the service that the signature impacts and includes all the Cisco IDS signatures. Some sample Service categories are File Sharing, Telnet, and R-Services. For more information on the Service signature category, refer to the "Service" section later in this chapter.

Each of these categories (major signature groups) also contains multiple signature groups. To display all the signatures for a specific category, just click the category name. Furthermore, all the signatures in each group share some common characteristic. One advantage of grouping signatures is that you can easily see which signatures are enabled or disabled. Furthermore, you can easily enable or disable all the signatures sharing a common attribute.

By examining the circle before the group name, it is easy to determine some quick information about the signatures in that group. A filled-in circle means that all the signatures in that group are enabled. An empty circle indicates that all the signatures in the group are disabled. When the circle is only half filled in, it indicates that a signatures are enabled and some signatures are disabled.

Signature ID

The All Signatures group enables you to access all the Cisco IDS signatures by their signature ID (see Figure 11-10). When you want to access a signature based on the signature ID, this is the most efficient way in which to access a signature. To get to a specific range of signature IDs, you can use the pull-down menu associated with the Page field.

NOTE   Beginning with version 4.1, the values in the pull-down menu indicate the beginning and ending signature ID for each successive page in the signature list.

Figure 11-10   *All Signatures Signature Group in IDM*

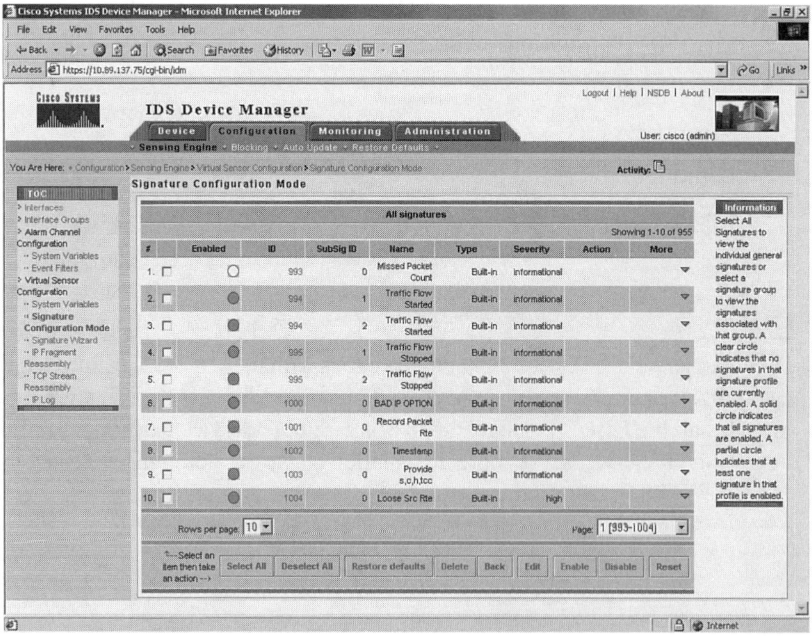

Signature Engine

When you want to add your own signatures, you need to use the Engines group (see Figure 11-11). This group enables you to access the Cisco IDS signatures grouped according to the signature engines on which they are based. (For a detailed description of the various signature engines, see Chapter 13, "Cisco IDS Alarms and Signatures.")

Figure 11-11   *Engines Signature Group in IDM*

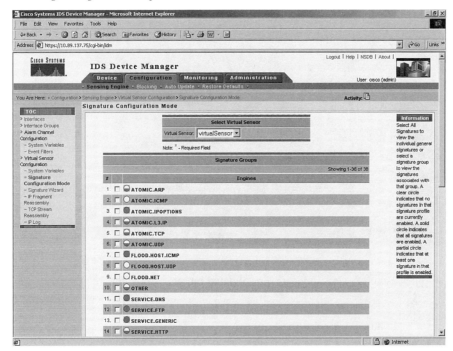

NOTE	To add your own custom signatures (using IDM), you must begin by selecting the specific signature engine that the signature is based on (see "Creating Custom Signatures" later in this chapter). Accessing signatures by any other signature group (such as Attack or OS signature groups) will not enable you to add new signatures, although you can use those signature groups to tune existing signatures.

Attack Type

The Attack signature group consolidates signatures based on the type of attack that the signature detects (see Figure 11-12).

Figure 11-12 *Attack Signature Group in IDM*

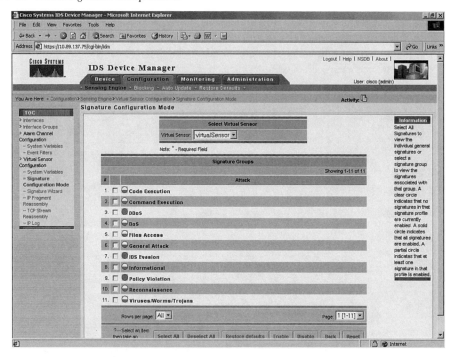

The Cisco IDS signatures are consolidated into the following attack types:

- Code Execution
- Command Execution
- DDos
- DoS
- File Access
- General Attack
- IDS Evasion
- Informational
- Policy Violation
- Reconnaissance
- Viruses/Worms/Trojans

L2/L3/L4 Protocol

Sometimes it is helpful to access signatures by the protocol that the signature is associated with. The L2/L3/L4 Protocol signature category groups the Cisco IDS signature into the following groups (see Figure 11-13):

- ARP
- General L2/L3/L4 Protocol
- General Protocol
- IP
- TCP/UDP Combo Sweeps

Figure 11-13 *L2/L3/L4 Protocol Signature Group in IDM*

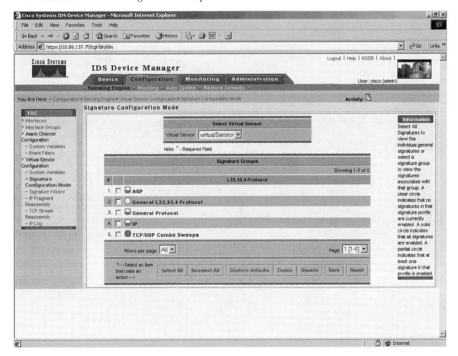

If you want to know which signatures are available to analyze a specific protocol layer, this grouping will provide this information for you. For instance, you can use the ARP group to examine all the Address Resolution Protocol (ARP) signatures that examine traffic at the link layer (Layer 2).

Operating System

Every network is unique. Your network might be homogeneous (such as all Windows systems or all UNIX systems) or it might be a heterogeneous collection of many different systems running many different operating systems. The OS signature group divides the Cisco IDS signatures into the following categories (see Figure 11-14):

- General OS
- IOS
- MacOS
- Netware
- UNIX
- Windows

Figure 11-14 *OS Signature Group in IDM*

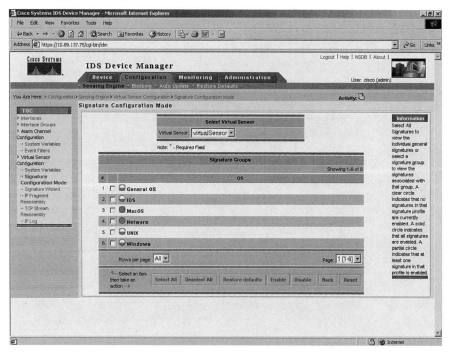

Suppose your network does not contain any systems that run MacOS. To reduce the amount of traffic analyzed by your monitoring application, you can choose to disable all of these signatures. You can easily accomplish this by disabling all the signatures in the MacOS signature group.

NOTE	Before disabling a particular signature, verify that the signature does not apply to your network. Otherwise, attacks can be launched against valid targets on your network, and your IDS will not indicate that they are occurring.

You can also use these groups to examine the signatures available for a specific operating system. Knowing the signatures that are available enables you to understand the protection provided by the Cisco IDS signatures and enables you to tune those signatures more effectively to match the operating systems running on your network.

Service

The Service signature group organizes the Cisco IDS signatures into the following categories (see Figure 11-15):

- DHCP
- DNS
- FTP
- File Sharing
- Finger
- General Service
- HTTP
- HTTPS
- IMAP
- Ident
- LPR
- NETBIOS/SMB
- NNTP
- NTP
- POP
- R-Services
- RPC
- SMTP
- SNMP
- SOCKS

- SQL
- SSH
- Telnet
- TFTP

Figure 11-15   *Service Signature Group in IDM*

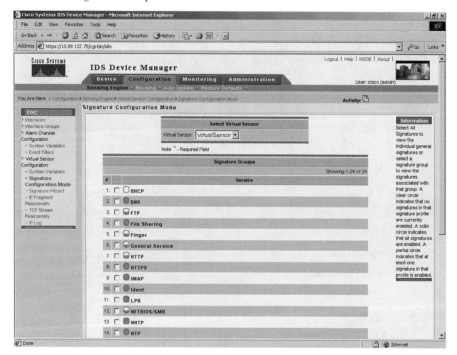

Almost all the categories in the Service signature group are protocols (except for categories such as File Sharing and General Service). Again, you can reduce the number of signatures that your sensor needs to process by disabling the signatures for protocols that you do not use on your network. If none of your systems use a specific protocol, you might not want your sensor to watch for attack traffic related to that protocol.

CAUTION   Disabling signature groups can reduce the number of signatures that your sensor has to process, but it also eliminates those signatures from alarming. If someone enables one of these protocols on your network, you will not see any attacks against that protocol.

Signature Groups in IDS MC

You can also use IDS MC to search through the supplied signatures using various signature groups by choosing Configuration>Settings>Signatures and using the drop-down menu to select the different categories (see Figure 11-16).

Figure 11-16 *Signatures Screen in IDS MC*

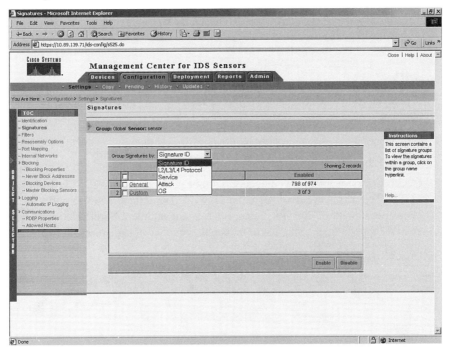

IDS MC provides groups similar to IDM. You can use the following signature groups using IDS MC to locate and tune the signatures provided with Cisco IDS:

- Signature ID
- L2/L3/L4 Protocol
- Service
- Attack Type
- Operating System

NOTE   To select the different categories of signature groups when using IDS MC, use the Group Signatures By pull-down menu.

Unlike IDM, IDS MC lists the total number of signatures in each group along with a count indicating the number of signatures in the group that are enabled. For instance, Figure 11-16 shows that there are 974 built-in signatures supplied with Cisco IDS. By default, 798 of those signatures are enabled. These values are from Cisco IDS sensor software version 4.0(2) S44 and will change with different releases of the Cisco IDS software.

NOTE   Regardless of the Cisco management software, the signatures enabled by default are the same.

Signature ID

When you choose the Signature ID group (see Figure 11-16), you have the following two options:

- General
- Custom

Clicking General enables you to access all the preloaded Cisco IDS signatures (see Figure 11-17). These are the default signatures provided with the Cisco IDS software, as opposed to custom signatures that you create. Because the number of preloaded signatures is large, you can apply a filter to the list to reduce the number of signatures that you view.

Figure 11-17   *The Signatures Screen in IDS MC*

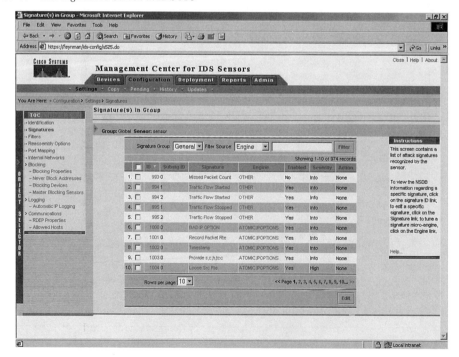

You can filter on the following signature characteristics:

- ID
- Subsig ID
- Signature
- Engine
- Enabled
- Severity
- Action

For instance, you can reduce the number of signatures displayed to only signatures based on the ATOMIC.ICMP engine by performing the following steps in the Signature(s) in a Group window (see Figure 11-17):

Step 1   Select Engine from the pull-down menu for the Filter Source field.

Step 2   Enter **ATOMIC.ICMP** in the text box next to the Filter button.

Step 3   Click the Filter button. This refines the signature list to only those based on the ATOMIC.ICMP signature engine (see Figure 11-18).

Figure 11-18   *Signatures Using the ATOMIC.ICMP Signature Engine*

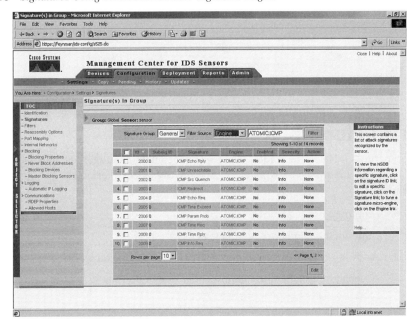

Besides viewing the preloaded signatures, you can also view and add your own custom signatures by clicking Custom on the Signatures screen (see Figure 11-19). You will see the custom signatures that you have already created and you can create a new custom signature by clicking the Add button. Adding custom signatures is discussed in detail in the "Creating Custom Signatures" section later in this chapter.

Figure 11-19 *Custom Signatures in IDS MC*

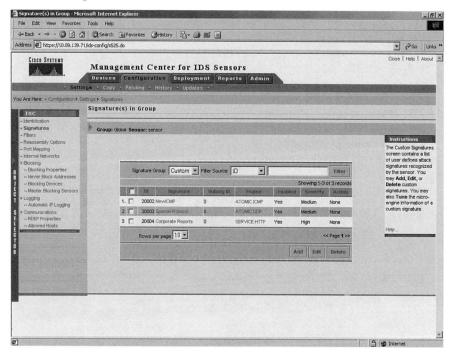

Signature Filtering

Sometimes it is helpful to filter when specific signatures trigger and generate alarm events based on your unique network configuration. Signature filtering can help in the following situations:

- Limiting false positives
- Limiting the number of alarms generated
- Allowing certain events to occur without generating an alarm
- Associating a signature with a specific source destination address via exclusion and inclusion filters

Defining an Event Filter

Normally, filtering an alarm means that the sensor will analyze the data stream but will not generate an alarm (except for inclusive filters). When using signature filtering, you place restrictions or limitations on specific signatures. This is accomplished by creating filtering qualifications based on the following signature fields:

- Signature
- Source Address
- Destination Address

You must also specify the filter type. The way you specify filter types is slightly different between IDM and IDS MC so each of these management platforms will be addressed separately.

Event Filter Types in IDS MC

When using IDS MC, you can create the following two types of filters:

- Include
- Exclude

When you create an exclude filter, attacks that match the parameters of your filter will not generate an alert. For instance, you might exclude the sweep signatures from a system that you regularly use to scan your network.

An include filter is used in conjunction with an existing exclude filter. You use the include filter to remove the exclusion for specific systems, but it is meaningless without first defining an exclude filter.

For instance, suppose you create a filter to exclude alarms from the 10.89.10.0 Class C address range. You might then want to include alarms for a specific address within that range, such as 10.89.10.100.

Event Filter Types in IDM

When using IDM, you can also create exclude and include filters, but the filters do not have a field in which you enter either exclude or include. Instead with IDM, the filters that you create are automatically exclusion filters.

To create an include filter, you define a filter and check a check box that is labeled Exception. So in IDM, an include filter is created as an exception to an existing filter.

Filtering Process

On the sensor, the attacks detected go through the following filtering process:

Step 1   Sensor detects an attack against the protected network by examining network traffic.

Step 2   The sensor's sensing engine checks to determine whether a signature filter exists.

Step 3   The sensor checks the filter parameters and compares them against the traffic that triggered the attack.

Step 4   The sensor then completes one of the following:

— If the traffic does not match the filter, the sensor generates an alert and performs any configured actions.

— If the traffic matches the filter and the filter is an exclusion, the sensor does not generate an alert (alarm event).

— If the traffic matches the filter and the filter is an inclusion, the sensor generates an alert and performs any configured actions.

Adding an Event Filter Using IDM

When using IDM, defining signature filters is accomplished through Configuration>Sensing Engine>Alarm Channel Configuration>Event Filters (see Figure 11-20). The Event Filters screen displays the filters that you have already configured. To apply a filter to a signature, you need to configure the following parameters:

- Signature ID
- Subsignature ID
- Source Addresses
- Destination Addresses
- Is This Filter an Exception

Figure 11-20 *Event Filters Screen in IDM*

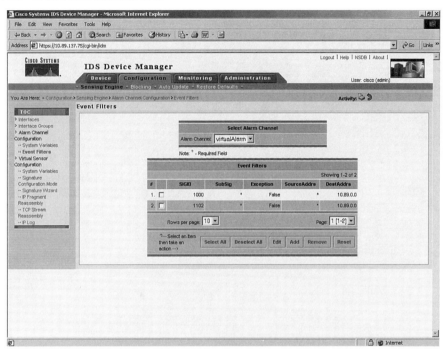

To add a filter using IDM, follow these steps:

Step 1 Click the Configuration tab on the main IDM screen.

Step 2 Select Sensing Engine from the options bar.

Step 3 Select Event Filters from the Alarm Channel Configuration section of the TOC. The Event Filters window appears in the content area (see Figure 11-20).

Step 4 Click the Add button. The Event Filters Adding window appears in the content area (see Figure 11-21).

Figure 11-21 *Adding an Event Filters in IDM*

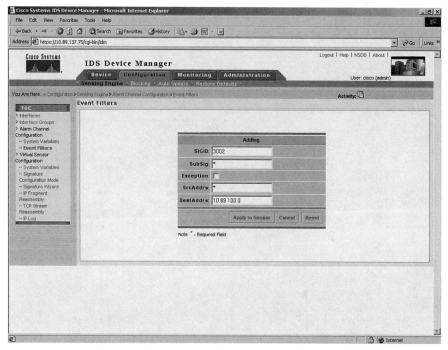

Step 5   Define the signature(s) to filter by entering values for the SIGID and SubSig ID fields. In this example, signature 3002 is filtered.

Wildcard Character

The wildcard character (*) can be used for any of the filter parameters. This enables you to match any value for a specific filtering parameter, such as applying a filtering to all signatures or source/destination addresses. You will commonly use this wildcard value for the SubSig field because it is required in the filter definition, but it is usually not used when creating new signatures.

Step 6   Check the Exception check box if this signature filter is an exception to an existing filter.

Step 7   Enter the source address or network to filter.

Step 8   Enter the destination address or network to filter. In this example, the filter only applies to hosts on the 10.89.100.0 subnet.

NOTE   Besides using actual addresses for the source and destination address, you can also use keywords such as $IN and $OUT.

Step 9   Click Apply to Sensor to save your filter.

NOTE   When you add or change a filter, you must commit the changes by clicking the Save Changes icon on the activity bar before you can perform other configuration changes to your sensor. You can also cancel your changes by clicking the Cancel Changes icon on the activity bar.

Adding an Event Filter Using IDS MC

When using IDS MC, defining signature filters is accomplished through Configuration>Settings>Filters (see Figure 11-22). The Filters screen displays the filters that you have already configured. To apply a filter to a signature, you need to configure the following parameters:

- Filter Name
- Signature(s)
- Source Addresses
- Destination Addresses
- Action

The Action field identifies whether the filter is an exclude or include filter. An exclude filter causes the sensor to not generate alarms if the detected traffic matches the parameters specified in the filter. An example of how this type of filter can be useful is with a host that your security team uses to periodically scan the network looking for vulnerabilities. By default, every time that you scan the network with this host, it generates various alarms for the different types of attacks that are generated to look for vulnerabilities. By creating an exclude filter for the scanning host, you can prevent your sensor from generating alarms based on the traffic from the authorized scanning host while still alarming on similar traffic from other systems.

Figure 11-22   *The Filters Screen in IDS MC*

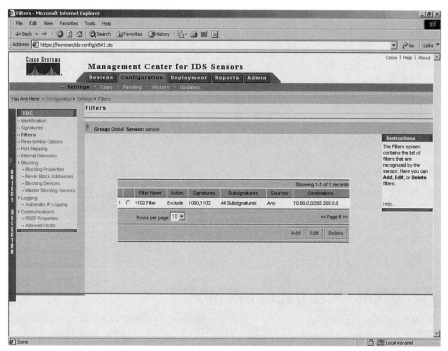

Include filters operate exactly the opposite of the exclude filters. With an include filter, you cause the sensor to alarm on the signature if the traffic includes the specified parameters. The include filters, however, only work in conjunction with an existing exclude filter. An example of how this type of filter is useful can be shown with NetBIOS traffic. Assume you want to allow NetBIOS traffic to traverse between machines on your protected network, but not between a machine outside your protected network to a machine on your protected network. First you set up an exclude filter that excludes all addresses from the NetBIOS signature. Then by setting up an include filter on the NetBIOS signature with the source address of OUT and the destination address defined as IN, you will cause your sensor to trigger the NetBIOS alarm only when the NetBIOS traffic originates from an external host to a host on your protected network.

To add a filter using IDS MC, follow these steps:

Step 1   Click the Configuration tab on the main IDS MC screen.

Step 2   Select Settings from either the options bar or content area.

Step 3   Select the sensor on which you want to add the filter by clicking the object selector followed by the sensor name.

Step 4   Select Filters from the TOC. The Filters window appears in the content area, showing the currently defined filters (see Figure 11-22).

Step 5   Click the Add button. The Enter Filter window appears in the content area (see Figure 11-23).

Figure 11-23   *Enter Filter Screen in IDS MC*

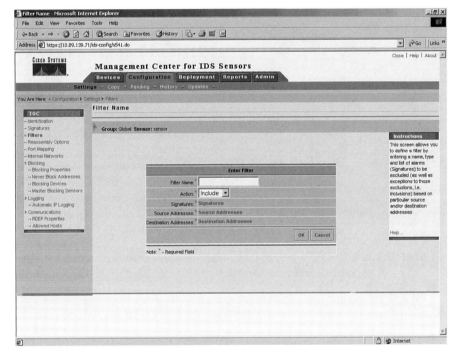

Step 6   Enter a name for the filter.

Step 7   Choose whether the filter is an include or exclude filter using the Action field pull-down menu.

Step 8   Select the signatures to be excluded by clicking Signatures. The Enter Signatures window appears in the content area (see Figure 11-24).

Step 9   Highlight the signatures to be added to the filter that will be applied, and then click the Add button to move the selected signatures from the Available Signatures list to the Selected Signatures list.

Figure 11-24 *The Enter Signatures Screen in IDS MC*

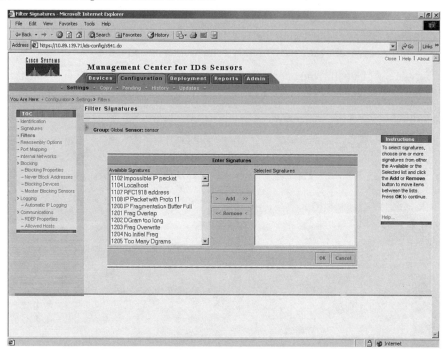

Step 10 Click the OK button when you have finished selecting signatures. This brings up the Enter Subsignatures screen in the content area (see Figure 11-25).

Step 11 Select the desired subsignatures (or select All Subsignatures), and then click the Add button to move the selected subsignatures to the Selected Subsignatures list.

NOTE Unless you want the filter to apply to a specific subsignature ID, it is recommended that you include all subsignatures to make the filter more flexible.

Step 12 Click the OK button when you are finished selecting subsignatures.

Step 13 Click Source Addresses to define the source addresses that the filter will match. This displays the Filter Source Addresses screen in the content area showing any configured source addresses for this filter.

Step 14 Click the Add button to add a source address to the filter. The Filter Source Addresses screen displays in the content area (see Figure 11-26).

Figure 11-25   *The Enter Subsignatures Screen in IDS MC*

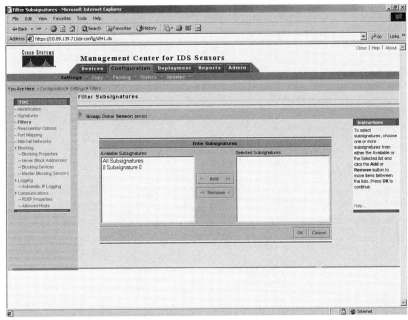

Figure 11-26   *The Enter Filter Address Screen in IDS MC*

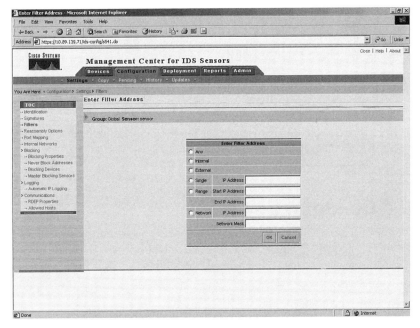

Step 15   Enter a source address for the filter. You have the following options to define a source address:

— Any (all source addresses)

— Internal addresses (IN)

— External addresses (OUT)

— Single IP address

— Range of IP addresses

— Network address and mask

NOTE   To use the internal and external address options, you must first define the IN and OUT system variables.

Step 16   Click OK to save the source address entry.

Step 17   Click the Add button to add additional source addresses to the filter if desired. When done adding source addresses, click the OK button to continue.

Step 18   Click Destination Addresses to define the destination addresses that the filter will use. The destination address is defined similarly to the source address. When you have finished adding destination addresses, click OK to continue.

Step 19   Click the OK button to save the filter.

NOTE   Before your changes are applied to your sensor configuration, you still need to deploy the changes (see Chapter 16).

Signature Configuration

Although Cisco IDS signatures are configured to operate efficiently in most network environments, you also have the ability to manipulate Cisco IDS signatures to customize them to your specific network topology. Configuring IDS signatures falls into the following two categories:

- Signature tuning
- Custom signatures

Signature Tuning

You can tune the characteristics for all the signatures in Cisco IDS. This tuning function-ality enables you to customize Cisco IDS to suit many different network environments. Because of the comprehensive list of available built-in signatures, most of your signature configuration will involve tuning existing signatures. When you perform one of the following operations on a signature, you are performing basic signature configuration:

- Enabling or disabling a signature
- Assigning a severity level
- Assigning a signature action

Because performing these operations does not change the manner in which the signature analyzes network traffic, they are not technically considered signature tuning. You can also change other signature characteristics to tune the built-in signatures to suit your environment. Tuning a built-in signature involves changing the way it operates to match the needs of your network environment. A simple example of tuning would be to change the AlarmThrottle from FireOnce to one of the alarm summarization modes (such as Global-Summarize) to reduce the quantity of alarms that your security operator needs to analyze (especially for certain low-severity signatures).

NOTE   Although most of the characteristics can be tuned for "built-in" signatures, certain parameters are protected and cannot be altered. Also, you can return a "built-in" signature to its default configuration by selecting the signature and clicking the Restore Defaults button.

Custom Signatures

Sometimes you need to create your own custom signatures to handle new exploits or signa-tures for traffic that is unique to your network (such as proprietary protocols). Instead of tuning an existing signature, when creating custom signatures, you actually create a brand new signature. This custom signature is processed by a specific signature engine and leverages the logic of that signature engine, which includes the individual engine param-eters that affect the analysis as well as the master signature parameters that all signatures can use. You can create custom signatures through both the IDM and IDS MC graphical interfaces and through the sensor's CLI.

NOTE   The valid signature ID range for custom signatures is 20000 through 50000.

Tuning a Signature

Using the signature configuration mode, you can view the hundreds of Cisco IDS signatures, either by signature ID or the various signature group categories. When viewing a list of built-in signatures using IDM you can quickly determine the following properties of a signature (see Figure 11-27):

- Status (enabled/disabled)
- ID
- Subsignature ID
- Name
- Type
- Severity
- Actions assigned

Figure 11-27 *Viewing Signatures in IDM*

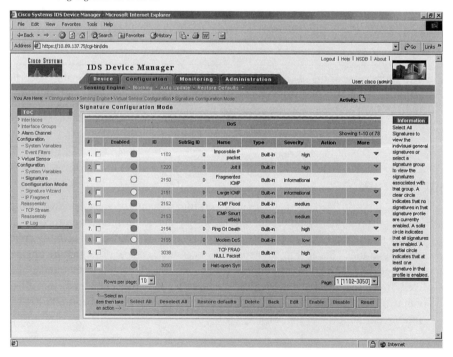

From the Signature Configuration Mode screen (see Figure 11-27) you can enable or disable a signature by clicking the check box next to one or more signatures and then clicking either the Enable or Disable button. Using the same process, you can delete custom signatures that you have created by clicking the Delete button and tune a signature using the Edit button.

NOTE   Although you can disable built-in signatures, you cannot delete the built-in signatures supplied with your Cisco IDS.

You can also view a list of signatures through IDS MC (see Figure 11-28). IDS MC enables you to quickly determine the following properties of a signature:

- Status (enabled/disabled)
- ID
- Subsignature ID
- Name
- Signature engine
- Severity
- Actions assigned

Figure 11-28   *Viewing Signatures in IDS MC*

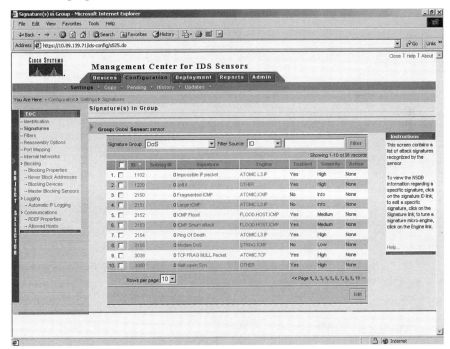

If you check the check box next to a signature, you can change the basic signature parameters by clicking the Edit button. To tune the signature, you need to click the Engine field on the signature to be tuned.

Suppose that you want to tune the characteristics of signature 6250, Auth Failure FTP. By default, this signature has the characteristics shown in Table 11-1.

Table 11-1   *Default Values for Signature 6250*

Parameter	Value
AlarmThrottle	Summarize
AlarmSeverity	Informational
MinHits	3
EventAction	None

On your network, you use an FTP server to store beta software that is downloaded by customers. Because of this, you decide that you want to closely monitor failed FTP login attempts and adjust the signature to match the following requirements:

- Trigger a high-severity alarm after two failed login attempts
- Generate an alarm every time the signature fires
- Terminate the TCP session that triggers the signature

To support these requirements, you need to adjust the values for signature 6250 to match the values shown in Table 11-2.

Table 11-2   *New Values for Signature 6250*

Parameter	Value
AlarmThrottle	FireAll
AlarmSeverity	High
MinHits	2
EventAction	Reset

The following two sections explain the steps that you need to perform to tune the 6250 signature using both IDM and IDS MC.

Tuning Signature 6250 Using IDM

To tune signature 6250 to support your new requirements using IDM, follow these steps:

Step 1   Click the Configuration tab on the main IDM screen.

Step 2   Select Sensing Engine from the options bar.

Step 3   Select Signature Configuration Mode from the Virtual Sensor Configuration section of the TOC. The Signature Groups window appears in the content area showing the major signature categories.

Step 4   Because you know the ID of the signature that you want to tune, select All Signatures.

Step 5   To locate the signature that you want to tune, use the Page drop-down menu.

NOTE   Beginning in version 4.1, this drop-down menu lists the beginning and ending signature IDs for each page in the list of signatures.

Step 6   When the signature is displayed on the screen, you need to check the check box next to the signature name and then click the Edit button. This displays the signatures parameters in the content window so that you can change them (see Figure 11-29). The values shown represent the current values for the signature.

Figure 11-29   *Tuning a Signature Using IDM*

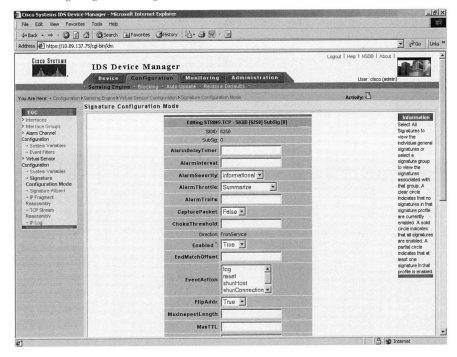

Step 7 For the AlarmSeverity field, use the drop-down menu to change the alarm's severity to High.

Step 8 For the AlarmThrottle field, use the drop-down menu to change to signature's alarming mode to FireAll.

Step 9 For the EventAction field, highlight Reset so that the signature resets the TCP connection.

Step 10 For the MinHits fields, change the value from 2 to 3.

Step 11 Click OK to save the updated signature configuration.

NOTE When you tune signatures, you must commit the changes by clicking the Save Changes icon on the activity bar before you can perform other configuration changes to your sensor. You can also cancel your changes by clicking the Cancel Changes icon on the activity bar.

Tuning Signature 6250 Using IDS MC

To tune signature 6250 to support your new requirements using IDS MC, follow these steps:

Step 1 Click the Configuration tab on the main IDS MC screen.

Step 2 Select the sensor that you want to configure using the object selector bar.

Step 3 Select Settings from either the options bar or the content area.

Step 4 Select Signatures from the TOC.

Step 5 Because you know the signature ID, select Signature ID using the Group Signatures By drop-down menu.

Step 6 Select the General group name.

Step 7 Enter 6250 in the text box next to the Filter button, and then click the Filter button to filter the display so that only signature 6250 displays (see Figure 11-30).

Step 8 Click String.TCP in the Engine field for the signature. This brings up the Signature Tuning screen in the content area (see Figure 11-31).

Figure 11-30 *Displaying Signature 6250 Using IDS MC*

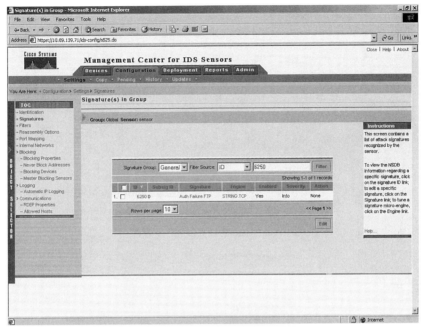

Figure 11-31 *The Signature Tuning Screen*

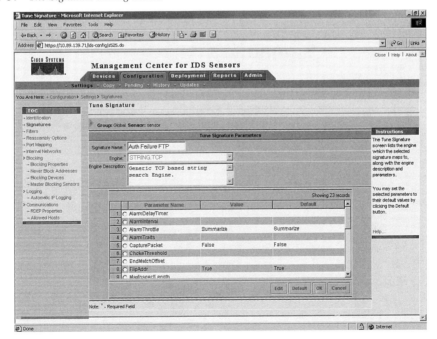

Step 9   Click the AlarmThrottle radio button and click the Edit button. The Signature Parameter window displays in the content area.

Step 10   Change the Value field from Summarize to FireAll.

Step 11   Click OK to save your changes.

Step 12   Click the MinHits radio button and click the Edit button. The Signature Parameter window displays in the content area.

Step 13   Change the Value field from 3 to 2.

Step 14   Click OK to save your changes.

Step 15   Click OK to return to the Signature(s) in a Group screen.

Step 16   Select the check box next to signature 6250 and click the Edit button. The Edit Signatures page displays in the content area.

Step 17   Select High from the Severity drop-down menu.

Step 18   Select the Reset check box.

Step 19   Click OK to save your changes.

NOTE   Before your changes are applied to your sensor configuration, you will need to deploy the changes (see Chapter 16).

Creating Custom Signatures

With the wealth of different signatures supplied by Cisco IDS, you should rarely need to create your own custom signatures. You can usually modify or tune existing signatures to meet your intrusion detection needs. Sometimes, however, custom signatures are necessary. When creating custom signatures, you must perform the following tasks:

- Choose a signature engine
- Verify existing functionality
- Define signature parameters
- Test signature effectiveness

Choose a Signature Engine

The various Cisco IDS signature engines enable you to create a wide range of custom signatures. When choosing which signature engine to use for a new signature, you need to consider several factors, such as the following:

- Network protocol
- Target address
- Target port
- Attack type
- Inspection criteria

Network Protocol

Before creating a new signature, you must first determine the network protocol that needs to be examined to locate the intrusive traffic. Normally, for instance, you specify the protocol for your signatures using the Protocol Master Engine parameter. If you want to create an EIGRP routing protocol signature, this parameter will only enable you to specify IP. Therefore, you need to identify a signature engine that enables you to specify the IP protocol number, because EIGRP uses IP protocol number 88.

A quick examination of the signature engines reveals that the ATOMIC.L3.IP engine enables you to specify the IP protocol number using the ProtoNum parameter. Therefore, this engine is probably a good candidate for your new signature.

Target Address

Attacks are directed at specific systems on your network. Some attacks target a specific host while others target many hosts on the network. For instance if you create a signature to detect an attack that floods your network with ICMP traffic, you will probably use a FLOOD signature engine. If the target is a single host, then you will use the FLOOD.HOST.ICMP signature engine. If on the other hand, you are concerned about a flood of traffic against your network, you will use the FLOOD.NET signature engine.

Target Port

Determine the anticipated port or ports that the attack traffic will be sent to. For instance, the SWEEP.PORT.UDP signature engine enables you to detect UDP connections to a single UDP port or multiple UDP ports.

Attack Type

Sometimes, the type of attack that you want to detect will lead you toward the appropriate signature engine. The flood signature engines, for instance, are almost always used to detect denial-of-service (DoS) attacks. Similarly, the sweep signature engines are usually used to detect reconnaissance attacks against your network.

NOTE   Although the various engines were designed to detect specific types of attacks, they are not limited to those attacks. For instance, some DoS attacks are detected using atomic signature engines.

Inspection Criteria

Some signatures detect specific packet characteristics, such as IP addresses and ports or header length fields. Other signatures require the signature engine to analyze the payload of a packet for a specific string pattern. Many signature engines enable you to specify a string pattern that the signature will trigger on when it is detected in network traffic. The string signature engines enable you to search for a specific pattern in various types of network traffic using regular expressions. (For more information on regular expressions, see Chapter 13.)

Verify Existing Functionality

After you have determined the signature engine that provides the functionality your custom signature needs, you need to verify that an existing signature does not already perform the functionality you desire. You can do this by examining all the signatures supported by the engine that you have chosen to determine whether any of them already do what you want your new signature to accomplish. In some situations, you might be able to easily tune an existing signature to gain the new functionality that you desire.

Suppose you want to create a signature that detects an attacker searching for systems that are listening on TCP port 34560 using a FIN sweep. This functionality closely matches a host sweep. By default, Cisco IDS comes with the following eight TCP host sweep signatures:

- Signature 3030, TCP SYN Host Sweep
- Signature 3031, TCP FRAG SYN Host Sweep
- Signature 3032, TCP FIN Host Sweep
- Signature 3033, TCP FRAG FIN Host Sweep
- Signature 3034, TCP NULL Host Sweep
- Signature 3035, TCP FRAG NULL Host Sweep

- Signature 3036, TCP SYN/FIN Host Sweep
- Signature 3037, TCP FRAG SYN/FIN Host Sweep

Signature 3032 generates alarms based on host sweeps using TCP FIN packets. This signature, however, triggers based on traffic to any TCP ports, not just port 34,560. Using this signature as a starting point, you can modify the signature parameters to create a custom signature that triggers solely on TCP port 34,560 traffic.

Define Signature Parameters

After selecting a signature engine, you need to decide the parameters that you will use for the required parameters, as well as determine which optional parameters you need to configure to match the intrusive traffic that you want to detect. When defining parameters, you need to try to consider situations in which the new signature can accidentally alarm on normal user activity. Minimizing false positives is a key consideration when developing custom signatures.

Continuing with the example, you have created a custom signature based on signature 3032. By default, this signature triggers on TCP traffic to any port. To limit the analysis to only port 34,560, you need to alter the PortOfInterest parameter. The value of this parameter limits the signature's analysis as follows:

- **0**—Match traffic to any TCP port
- **1**—Match traffic on TCP ports from 1 to 1023
- **2**—Match traffic on TCP ports from 1024 to 65,535
- **3 to 65,535**—Match traffic only on TCP port specified

Therefore, by setting the PortOfInterest parameter to 34,560, your custom signature will only trigger on traffic to TCP port 34,560. You might also want to adjust the Unique parameter to indicate how many connections are required for the signature to trigger. (The default is five.)

Test Signature Effectiveness

After you have created a custom signature, you need to test the signature on your live network. The first test is to verify that the signature will actually detect the intrusive traffic that you built it to detect. Next, you might observe that the new signature alarms on traffic that you did not consider. You also want to make sure that your new signature does not significantly impact the performance of your sensor or your network. Event actions, such as reset and IP blocking, can potentially impact your network's performance if configured incorrectly.

Custom Signature Scenario

Suppose that your web server contains sensitive files that are located in a directory called CorporateReports. You might want to create a custom signature that alarms when HTTP requests are crafted to attempt to access this directory.

NOTE   To minimize false positives, you will also probably want to establish signature filters that prevent the signature from triggering when the CorporateReports directory is accessed from legitimate systems or networks.

To define your custom signature, you need to first choose the signature engine that best fits the functionality required. In this situation, you need to search for HTTP requests that access a specific directory on your web server. The SERVICE.HTTP signature engine contains a parameter named UriRegex that enables you to define a search pattern that examines the URI portion of an HTTP request. That is exactly the functionality that you need. Besides the default values, your custom signature will use the following parameters:

- SIGID (34000)
- Subsig (0)
- SigName (Corporate Reports)
- AlarmSeverity (High)
- UriRegex ([/\\][Cc][Oo][Rr][Pp][Oo][Rr][Aa][Tt][Ee][Rr][Ee][Pp][Oo][Rr][Tt][Ss])

NOTE   By default, the custom signature examines traffic to the following TCP ports: 80, 3128, 8000, 8010, 8080, 8888, and 24,326. These ports represent the common values used for web-based traffic.

Creating Custom Signatures Using IDM

To create the example custom signatures using IDM, follow these steps:

Step 1   Click the Configuration tab on the main IDM screen.

Step 2   Select Sensing Engine from the options bar.

Step 3   Select Signature Configuration Mode from the Virtual Sensor Configuration section of the TOC. The Signature Groups window appears in the content area.

Step 4   Click Engines to show the various signature engines that you can use to construct signatures.

Step 5   Click SERVICE.HTTP to display a list of the existing signatures supported by this engine.

Step 6   Click the Add button to create a new signature based on the SERVICE.HTTP signature engine. The Adding SERVICE.HTTP window appears in the content area (see Figure 11-32).

Figure 11-32   *Adding the SERVICE.HTTP Signature Using IDM*

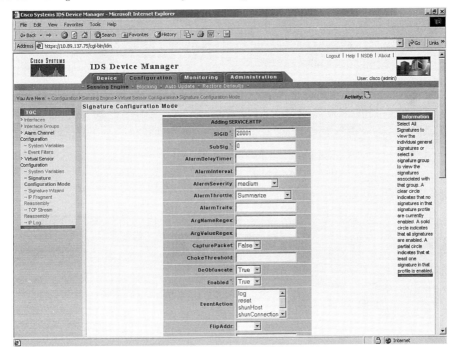

Step 7   Enter **34000** for the SIGID field.

Step 8   Change the value of the SigName field from SERVICE.HTTP to **Corporate Reports**.

Step 9   Change the AlarmSeverity from the default of Medium to High using the drop-down menu.

Step 10   Change the value of the UriRegex field to [/\\][Cc][Oo][Rr][Pp][Oo][Rr] [Aa][Tt][Ee][Rr][Ee][Pp][Oo][Rr][Tt][Ss].

Step 11   Click the OK button to save the new custom signature.

NOTE   When you add a custom signature, you must commit the changes by clicking the Save Changes icon on the activity bar before you can perform other configuration changes to your sensor. You can also cancel your changes by clicking the Cancel Changes icon on the activity bar.

Creating Custom Signatures Using IDS MC

To create the example custom signatures using IDS MC, follow these steps:

Step 1   Click the Configuration tab on the main IDS MC screen.

Step 2   Select the sensor that you want to configure using the object selector bar.

Step 3   Click Settings from either the options bar or the content area.

Step 4   Select Signatures from the TOC. The Signatures window appears in the content area.

Step 5   Use the Group Signatures By drop-down menu to select Signature ID.

Step 6   Click Custom in the content area. The current defined custom signatures then display in the content area (see Figure 11-33).

Figure 11-33   *Custom Signatures in IDS MC*

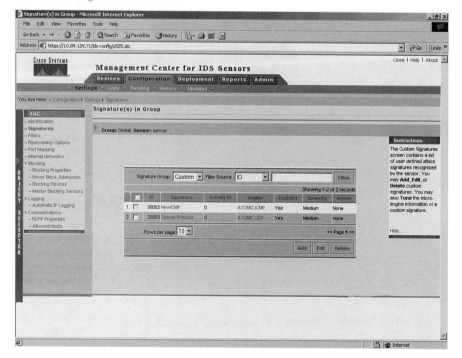

Step 7   Click the Add button to add a new custom signature. The Tune Signature Parameters window displays in the content area (see Figure 11-34).

Figure 11-34   *The Tune Signature Parameters Window in IDS MC*

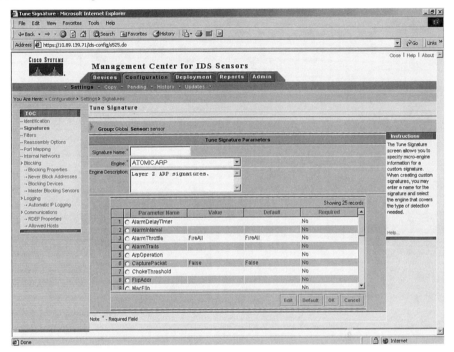

NOTE   With IDS MC, the signature just receives the next available SIGID value. You cannot set it directly.

Step 8   From the Engine drop-down menu, select SERVICE.HTTP.

Step 9   Enter **Corporate Reports** in the Signature Name field.

Step 10   Click the radio button next to the UriRegex field and click the Edit button. The Signature Parameter window appears in the content area (see Figure 11-35).

Figure 11-35 *The Signature Parameter Window in IDS MC*

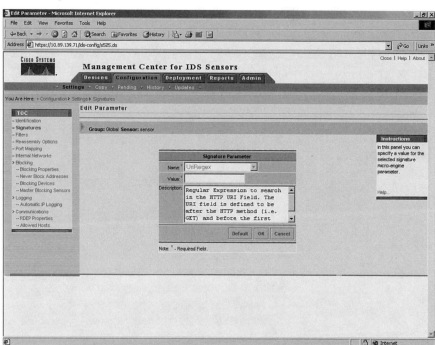

Step 11 Change the contents of the Value field to [/\\][Cc][Oo][Rr][Pp][Oo][Rr]
[Aa][Tt][Ee][Rr][Ee][Pp][Oo][Rr][Tt][Ss].

Step 12 Click the OK button to save you changes. The Tune Signature Parameters
window appears in the content area.

Step 13 Click the OK button to save your changes. The list of custom signatures
appears in the content area.

Step 14 Check the check box next to the new signature and click the Edit button.
The Edit Signatures window appears in the content area (see Figure 11-36).

Step 15 Change the Severity to High using the drop-down menu.

Step 16 Verify that the Enable check box is checked. If not, check it to enable the
signature.

Step 17 Click the OK button to save the changes.

NOTE   Before your changes are applied to your sensor configuration, you will need to deploy the
changes (see Chapter 16).

Figure 11-36 *The Edit Signatures Window in IDS MC*

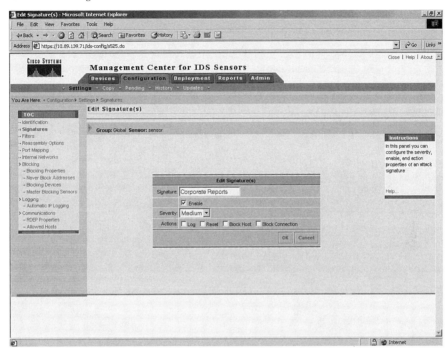

Using the IDM Signature Wizard

With IDM version 4.1, you can also create the custom signature using the Signature Wizard. The purpose of the Signature Wizard is to walk you through the definition of the following signature components:

- Signature type
- Signature identification
- Engine-specific parameters
- Alert response
- Alert behavior

To create the example custom signature using the Signature Wizard in IDM, follow these steps:

Step 1   Click the Configuration tab on the main IDM screen.

Step 2   Select Sensing Engine from the options bar.

Step 3   Select Signature Wizard from the Virtual Sensor Configuration section of the TOC. A warning appears in the content area explaining that custom signatures can impact the performance of your sensor.

Step 4   Click the Start the Wizard button to begin the creation of your custom signature. The Signature Type window appears in the content area (see Figure 11-37).

Figure 11-37   *The Signature Type Window*

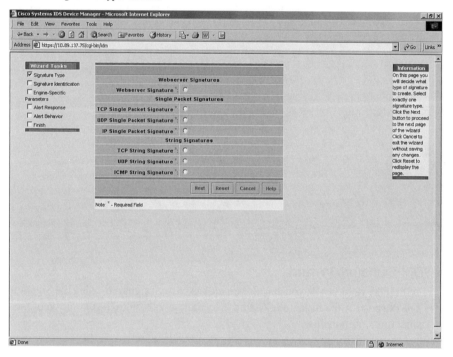

Step 5   Click the Webserver Signature radio button, and then click the Next button to continue. The Signature Identification window appears in the content area (see Figure 11-38).

Step 6   Enter **34000** in the Signature ID field.

Step 7   Enter **Corporate Reports** in the Signature Name field.

Step 8   Click the Next button to continue. The Webserver Service Ports window appears in the content area (see Figure 11-39).

Figure 11-38 *The Signature Identification Window*

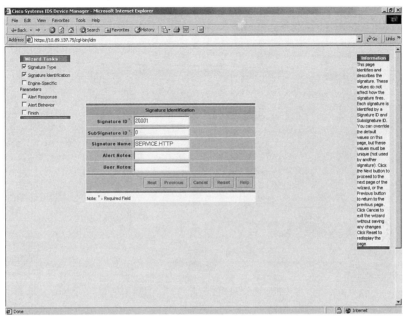

Figure 11-39 *The Webserver Service Ports Window*

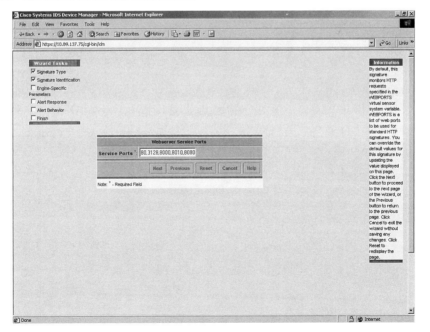

Step 9 Because you are not adding any new service ports, click the Next button to continue. The Webserver Regular Expressions window appears in the content area (see Figure 11-40).

Figure 11-40 *The Webserver Regular Expressions Window*

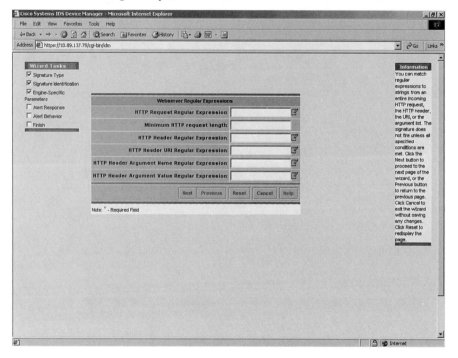

Step 10 Change the value of the HTTP Header URI Regular Expression field to [/\][Cc][Oo][Rr][Pp][Oo][Rr][Aa][Tt][Ee][Rr][Ee][Pp][Oo][Rr][Tt][Ss].

Step 11 Click the Next button to continue. The Webserver Buffer Overflow Checks window appears in the content area (see Figure 11-41).

Step 12 Click the Next button to continue. The Alert Response Actions window appears in the content area (see Figure 11-42).

Figure 11-41   *The Webserver Buffer Overflow Checks Window*

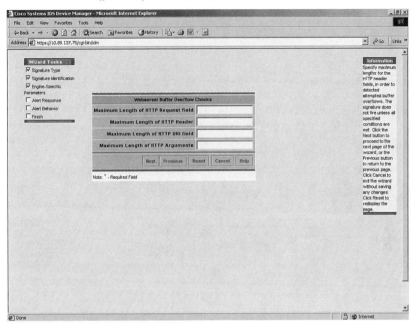

Figure 11-42   *The Alert Response Actions Window*

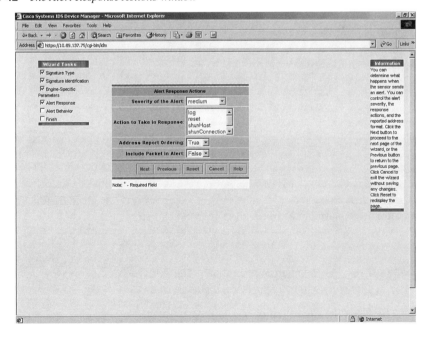

NOTE   By not configuring any of the maximum length parameters, your new signature will not generate an alarm for HTTP requests based on the length of the HTTP requests.

Step 13   Using the Severity of the Alert drop-down menu, set the value to High.

Step 14   Click the Next button to continue. The Default Alert Behavior screen appears in the content area (see Figure 11-43).

Figure 11-43   *The Default Alert Behavior Window*

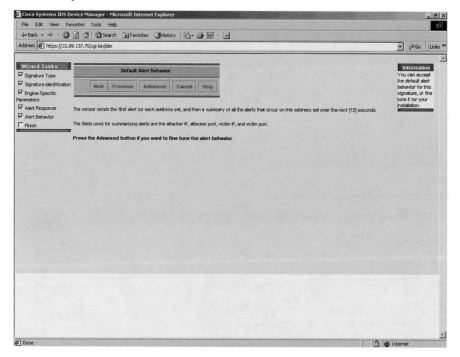

NOTE   If you want to change the default alert behavior, click the Advanced button. You can then customize the alarming characteristics for your signature.

Step 15   Click the Next button to continue. The Ready to Create the New Signature window appears in the content area.

Step 16   Click the Create button to add the new signature.

Step 17 After the Wizard Completed window appears, the signature has been created. Click the OK button to continue.

NOTE To actually add the new signature to the sensor's configuration, you will need to click the Save Changes icon on the activity bar. You can also cancel your changes by clicking the Cancel Changes icon on the activity bar.

Summary

Signatures form the heart of the Cisco IDS solution. Multiple signature engines enable Cisco IDS to process various types of attack traffic very efficiently and effectively. Cisco IDS uses multiple signature engines to support its numerous signatures (see Chapter 13). When processing network traffic, the following global sensor sensing parameters impact the operation of your sensor:

- Internal networks
- IP fragment reassembly
- TCP stream reassembly

To efficiently locate, enable, and disable signatures based on their functional characteristics, you can view Cisco IDS signatures based on the following different categories:

- Signature ID
- Attack Type
- L2/L3/L4 Protocol
- Operating System
- Service

To reduce false positives, you can add signatures to a filter and apply the filter to your sensor to minimize the systems that can trigger certain signatures. When defining filters you need to specify the following parameters:

- Signature
- Source IP address
- Destination IP address
- Filter type

You can define two types of filters. By default, filters exclude specific addresses from generating a specific alarm. Sometimes, however, you might want to remove the filter exclusion for a specific address. Include filters enable you to include an address that has been previously excluded by an existing exclude filter. An include filter essentially represents an exception to your previously defined filter.

Signature configuration is an important aspect of customizing Cisco IDS to your unique network environment. Signature configuration falls into the following two categories:

- Tuning existing signatures
- Creating custom signatures

Tuning signatures involves altering the characteristics of existing signatures to more closely suite your network environment. An example might include changing the MinHits parameter or adding to an existing list of ports via the ServicePorts parameter.

In some situations, you might need to actually create your own custom signatures. Creating a custom signature involves various tasks, but can be summarized into the following major operations:

- Choose the appropriate signature engine
- Verify existing functionality
- Define engine parameters
- Test the operation of the new signature

Choosing an appropriate signature engine is crucial to creating an effective and efficient custom signature. The major tasks involved in choosing a signature engine depend on identifying the following characteristics of the attack traffic being monitored:

- Network protocol
- Target address(es)
- Target port(s)
- Attack type
- Inspection criteria

Review Questions

The following questions test your retention of the material presented in this chapter. The answers to the review questions are in Appendix B, "Answers to Chapter Review Questions."

1 What are the two major global sensing parameters that impact the way that your sensor actually captures and analyzes traffic?

2 What are the two types of reassembly options that you can configure on your sensor?

3 What is the purpose of defining internal networks?

4 What are the two TCP stream reassembly modes?

5 What are the main categories by which your can view the various signature groups?

6 How does strict TCP stream reassembly work?

7 What is the main benefit of creating signature filters?

8 How does loose TCP stream reassembly differ from *strict* TCP stream reassembly?

9 What are the two types of signature filters that you can define?

10 What does an include (or exception) filter do?

11 What are the two major tasks involved with respect to signature configuration?

12 When tuning signatures, what are the three tasks that are considered basic signature configuration?

13 What are some of the factors that impact the selection of a signature engine for a custom signature?

14 What are the steps involved in creating a custom signature?

15 What is the difference between the TCP embryonic timeout and the TCP open establish timeout?

16 What are the major categories by which you can view the Cisco IDS built-in signatures?

17 What does the IP fragment reassemble timeout parameter control?

18 When viewing the Cisco IDS signatures using the Service category, what are most of the major signature groups based on?

19 What are the major fields you need to configure to define a signature filter?

20 Why is it important to test your custom signatures?

Upon completion of this chapter, you will be able to perform the following tasks:

- Define IP blocking
- Identify the types of managed devices
- Identify the factors that impact IP blocking usage
- Configure IP blocking using IDS Device Manager (IDM)
- Configure IP blocking using Management Center for IDS sensors (IDS MC)
- Define the master blocking sensor
- Configure manual blocking using IDM
- Configure IP logging using IDM
- Configure IP logging using IDS MC
- Define the TCP reset action

CHAPTER 12

Signature Response

Signature Response Overview

By default, your Cisco IDS sensors analyze network traffic and generate alarms that your monitoring application retrieves and displays in a graphical interface. In some situations, however, it is beneficial to respond to intrusive traffic instead of simply passively detecting the intrusive traffic. Cisco IDS provides several signature responses that you can configure to enable your network sensors to react to attacks against devices on your network. Cisco IDS supports the following signature responses at the network level:

- IP blocking
- TCP resets
- IP logging

This chapter explains in detail how to use and configure the signature responses using both IDS Device Manager (IDM) and the Management Center for IDS sensors (IDS MC). Step-by-step examples highlight the major configuration tasks needed to successfully use signature response actions on your network. IP blocking is the most common and widely deployed signature response action. The majority of the chapter is devoted to explaining this useful feature. Before you can use it, however, you must understand what IP blocking is and the factors that impact its operation.

IP Blocking

IP blocking enables you to halt future traffic from an attacking host's IP address for a specified period of time, thereby limiting the attacker's access to your network. You have the following two options with respect to IP blocking:

- shunHost
- shunConnection

The shunHost action causes the sensor to block all traffic coming from the host that triggered the signature. This is very effective at protecting your network, because all the traffic from the attacking system is prevented from entering your network. The drawback is that if the alarm is a false positive, you will cause a self-inflicted denial-of-service (DoS) attack until you have time to analyze the situation and remove the block. If an attacker can spoof the source address of the attack, the attack traffic can also be used to deny service to legitimate systems on your network.

The shunConnection action, however, only blocks traffic (from the host that triggered the signature) to the destination port and destination IP address of the traffic that triggered the signature. If an attacker targets a specific service on systems across your network, this would not prevent the attack from proceeding. The attacker would still be able to send traffic to other services or ports on the original destination host, as well as send traffic to all ports on other systems throughout your network. Now in a false positive situation, you only deny a user's system from connecting to a single service (port number) on a specific system. This is still a DoS situation, but not as severe as denying all traffic from the user's system.

NOTE   Both blocking actions can also be manually initiated from the sensor command-line interface (CLI) and the management interface.

You configure IP blocking on an individual signature basis. This section focuses on explaining the following topics:

- IP blocking devices
- Blocking guidelines
- Blocking process
- ACL considerations

But first, it is helpful to review some of the terminology that is used in conjunction with IP blocking.

IP Blocking Definitions

Before describing IP blocking in detail, it is helpful to explain a few terms that you need to know. Table 12-1 lists the terms commonly used in conjunction with IP blocking.

Table 12-1   *Common IP Blocking Terms*

Term	Definition
Active ACL	The active access control list (ACL) is the dynamically created ACL that the sensor applies to the managed device.
Blocking sensor	A sensor that you have configured to control one or more managed devices.
Device management	The capability of a sensor to interact with certain Cisco devices and dynamically reconfigure them to block the source of an attack using an ACL, VACL, or the **shun** command on the PIX.

Table 12-1   *Common IP Blocking Terms (Continued)*

Term	Definition
Blocking	A feature of Cisco IDS that enables your sensor to block traffic from an attacking system that has triggered a signature that is configured for blocking. (IP blocking is also called *shunning*.)
Interface/direction	The combination of the interface and direction on the interface (in or out) determines where a blocking ACL is applied on the managed device. You can configure the sensor to shun a total of 10 interface/ direction combinations (across all devices on the sensor).
Managed device	The Cisco device that actually blocks the source of an attack after being reconfigured by the blocking sensor.
Managed interface	The interface on the managed device on which the sensor applies the dynamically created ACL (also known as the *blocking interface*).

IP Blocking Devices

You can configure your sensor to perform device management on a variety of Cisco devices. You can use the following types of devices to serve as managed devices:

- Cisco routers
- Cisco Catalyst 6000 switches
- Cisco PIX firewalls and the Firewall Switch Module (FWSM)

Cisco Routers

The following Cisco routers have been tested and approved to serve as blocking devices:

- Cisco routers running Cisco IOS Software Release 11.2 or later
- Catalyst 5000 switches with a Route Switch Module (RSM)
- Catalyst 6000 with a Multilayer Switch Feature Card (MSFC)

Each sensor can control up to 10 interfaces on any of the supported devices.

When using IP blocking, your sensor must be able to communicate with the managed device in order to reconfigure the device to block the traffic from the attacking system. Your sensors log in to the managed device and dynamically apply an ACL. The sensor also removes the block after a configured amount of time. To manipulate the ACLs on the managed device, you must configure the following on your managed devices:

- Telnet access (vty) enabled
- Line password assigned to vty
- Secure Shell (SSH) access allowed from sensor (or Telnet)
- Router's enable password assigned

NOTE	When enabling access to your router, you can either use local user accounts or configure your router to use an authentication, authorization, and accounting (AAA) server to manage access to the router. Using a AAA server provides centralized management for access to your devices as well as tighter control over the operations that each user is allowed to perform on your devices.

Cisco Catalyst 6000 Switches

Some Catalyst 6000 switches do not support ACLs (those without the MSFC). You can still use these devices to perform device management by using VLAN access control lists (VACLs) if you have a Policy Feature Card (PFC) and you run CatOS.

NOTE	To support ACLs on your Catalyst 6000 switch, you must have an MSFC installed on the switch. If your Supervisor Module contains a Policy Feature Card (PFC), your Catalyst 6000 switch supports VACLs. If you do not have either a PFC or MSFC, your Catalyst 6000 switch does not support either VACLs or ACLs and cannot be used for IP blocking.

To manipulate the VACLs on the Catalyst 6000 switch device, you must configure the following on your Catalyst switch:

- Telnet access (vty) enabled
- Line password assigned to Vty
- SSH access allowed from sensor (or Telnet)
- Switch's enable password assigned

NOTE	When enabling access to your router, you can either use local user accounts or configure your router to use an authentication, authorization, and accounting (AAA) server to manage access to the router. Using a AAA server provides centralized management for access to your devices as well as tighter control over the operations that each user is allowed to perform on your devices.

NOTE	If your Catalyst 6000 switch has an MSFC and you are running CatOS on your switch, you have the option of using ACLs or VACLs when implementing IP blocking.

Cisco PIX Firewalls

Besides Cisco routers and Catalyst 6000 switches, you can also use Cisco PIX firewalls to serve as managed devices. Instead of updating an ACL on the router, however, the sensor uses the PIX's **shun** command to block the traffic from the attacking system. Because the **shun** command was introduced in version 6.0 of the PIX operating system, any of the following PIX models running version 6.0 or higher can serve as a managed device:

- 501
- 506E
- 515E
- 525
- 535

In addition to the PIX firewalls, the FWSM can also serve as a managed device, because the initial version of the FWSM supports the PIX 6.0 feature set. The FWSM is a firewall that resides on a Catalyst 6500 line card. Like the PIX firewalls, the FWSM blocks traffic using the **shun** command.

---

shun Command

The PIX **shun** command provides a dynamic response to attacks by enabling the PIX to prevent new connections from an attacking system and to disallows packets for existing connections from an attacking system. For more information on the **shun** command, refer to the Cisco PIX Firewall Command Reference, Version 6.3.

Just as with the Cisco routers that serve as blocking devices, your sensor must be able to communicate with the PIX firewall or FWSM for it to serve as a blocking device. To communicate with the PIX firewall or FWSM, you must enable one of the following communication vehicles:

- Telnet
- SSH

NOTE   Although Telnet is available, SSH access to your PIX firewall (or FWSM) is preferred because the communication with the firewall is encrypted (preventing someone on the network from sniffing your login credentials). This is especially important for access to your PIX firewall because the firewall is installed to protect your network.

No matter which of these communication vehicles you decide to use, you must assign an enable password to your PIX firewall or FWSM.

NOTE	When enabling access to your firewall, you can either use local using accounts or configure your router to use an authentication, authorization, and accounting (AAA) server to manage access to the router. Using a AAA server provides centralized management for access to your devices as well as tighter control over the operations that each user is allowed to perform on your devices.

Blocking Guidelines

The IP blocking functionality incorporated into Cisco IDS provides a powerful tool to protect your network. If used incorrectly, however, a knowledgeable attacker can use this functionality against your network in a DoS attack.

The IP blocking feature generates ACLs (or PIX **shun** commands) that are based on IP addresses. The sensor has no mechanism to determine whether the address being blocked is a critical server on your network or the address of a legitimate attacker. Therefore, implementing IP blocking requires careful planning and analysis. Some of the important items that you need to consider when designing and implementing IP blocking are as follows:

- Antispoofing mechanisms
- Critical hosts
- Network topology
- Entry points
- Signature selection
- Blocking duration
- Device login information
- Interface ACL requirements

Antispoofing Mechanisms

Attackers will usually forge packets with IP addresses that are either private addresses (refer to RFC 1918) or addresses of your internal network. The attacker's goal is to have Cisco IDS block legitimate IP addresses, thus causing a denial of service. If you implement proper antispoofing mechanisms, however, Cisco Secure IDS will not block these valid addresses.

An excellent reference on IP address filtering is RFC 2827, "Network Ingress Filtering: Defeating Denial of Service Attacks Which Employ IP Source Address Spoofing." This reference explains how you can apply basic filtering to your router interfaces. Following these recommendations should significantly help mitigate the IP spoofing attacks directed against your network.

Basically, you want to make sure that all the traffic leaving your protected network comes from a source IP address that represents a valid address on your protected network. Consequently, for traffic entering your protected network, you want to make sure that the source IP address is not one of your valid internal addresses. Addresses that violate these criteria are probably spoofed and need to be dropped by your router.

Critical Hosts

Many hosts on your network perform critical tasks. To prevent any possible disruption to the operation of your network, these systems should not be blocked. Some of the critical components that should not be blocked include the following:

- Cisco IDS sensors
- AAA server
- Perimeter firewall
- DNS servers

By establishing *never-block addresses* (see "Defining Addresses Never to Block" later in the chapter) for these critical systems, you can prevent IP blocking from disrupting the operation of these important systems (either accidentally or during a deliberate attack).

Network Topology

Your network topology impacts your implementation of IP blocking. You will have sensors deployed throughout your network, but a single managed device can only be controlled by one sensor. You need to decide which sensors will control which managed devices. Furthermore, a single sensor can only perform IP blocking on a maximum of 10 interfaces across one or more managed devices.

Entry Points

Many networks have multiple entry points to provide redundancy and reliability. These entry points provide multiple avenues for an attacker to access your network. You need to decide whether all of these entry points need to participate in IP blocking. Furthermore, you need to make sure that when IP blocking is initiated on one entry point, an attacker cannot bypass the block by using another entry point. If multiple sensors are performing blocking on your network, you need to configure master blocking sensors to coordinate blocking between these various sensors.

Signature Selection

Cisco IDS supports hundreds of signatures. It is not feasible or manageable to perform IP blocking on all of these signatures. Some signatures are more susceptible to spoofing than others. If you implement IP blocking on a User Datagram Protocol (UDP) signature, for instance, an attacker may be able to impersonate one of your business partners, causing you to generate a DoS attack against your own network. Transport Control Protocol (TCP) signatures are usually better candidates for IP blocking because the connection-oriented nature of TCP makes spoofing attacks much more difficult.

Other signatures are prone to false positives. Implementing IP blocking on these signatures can disrupt normal user traffic because the sensor has no way to distinguish a false positive from a real attack.

Deciding which signatures you want to configure to perform IP blocking and whether the blocking will be for the destination port and destination address only (shunConnection) or all traffic (shunHost) is one of the major configuration tasks that you must tackle when implementing IP blocking on your network.

Blocking Duration

The default blocking duration is 30 minutes. You need to decide whether this value is appropriate for your network environment. IP blocking is designed to stop traffic from an attacking host to enable you to analyze what is happening and give you time to take more long-term blocking actions if appropriate.

If your blocking duration is too short, the attacker will regain access to your network before you have had a chance to fully examine the extent of the attack and take appropriate actions. If the initial attack compromises a system, the attacker's subsequent access (after the blocking duration expires) may appear to be normal user traffic and not trigger any of your IDS signatures. So it is important to thoroughly analyze the attack before the attacker can regain access to your network.

Setting your blocking duration to high, however, also has its drawbacks. Setting the blocking duration to a very high value creates a DoS situation when the block occurs because of a false positive. Because the block duration is long, it will impact the normal user for a longer period of time (usually until you have analyzed the circumstances and determined that the alarm was a false positive). You must carefully consider what the appropriate blocking duration is for your network environment.

Device Login Information

When implementing IP blocking, your sensor must be able to log in to the managed device and dynamically apply an ACL (or other IP blocking feature). Therefore, your sensor needs to have privileged credentials to this device. Some devices support SSH, whereas others may support only Telnet. When connecting via Telnet, the connection should traverse a secure network (such as an out-of-band network) to prevent an attacker from capturing your username and password information. SSH access has a little more flexibility because it was designed to traverse untrusted networks.

Interface ACL Requirements

An interface on your Cisco router serving as a managed device can only have one ACL applied to it for a specific traffic direction (either inbound to the interface or outbound from the interface). If you already have existing ACL entries on a given interface for a specified traffic direction (besides the shun entries generated by the sensor), you need to configure these entries in either a PreShun ACL or PostShun ACL (or both) on your managed device.

When the sensor generates a blocking ACL for a device, it first includes all the entries from the PreShun ACL. Then it adds the shun entries that it dynamically creates. Finally, it adds the entries from the PostShun ACL. This is the complete ACL that is applied to the managed device.

Blocking Process

Blocking is initiated when a signature configured for IP blocking triggers an alarm or a manual blocking event is generated. This causes the sensor to create the appropriate blocking ACLs (or sets of configurations) and pushes this information to all the managed devices that it controls. At the same time, an alarm is sent to the Event Store. When the shun duration expires, the sensor updates the ACLs (or configurations) to remove the shun from each controlled device.

The sensor controls starting and stopping shuns on routers, switches, PIX firewalls, and FWSMs. A shun is initiated when one of the following two events occurs:

- A signature configured with the shun action triggers
- You manually initiate a shun (from a management interface such as the CLI, IDM, or IDS MC)

NOTE   Usually, shuns expire after a configured amount of time. You can also configure the sensor to initiate a permanent shun that does not expire until you remove it by manually blocking a specific system (see "Manual Blocking" later in the chapter). In this case, the sensor initiates a persistent connection with your managed device until you remove the shun. This also applies to shuns initiated from the sensor CLI.

The blocking process involves the following sequence of operations:

Step 1   The sensor detects an event or action that is configured for shunning.

Step 2   The sensor pushes a new set of configurations or ACLs (one for each interface and associated traffic direction) to each controlled device. It applies the shun to each of the devices and interfaces that the sensor is configured to control.

Step 3   For alarm events, the alarm is sent to the Event Store at the same time that the shun is applied. Each of these events happens independently of each other.

Step 4   When the configured shun duration expires, the sensor updates the configurations or ACLs to remove the shun.

Access Control List (ACL) Placement Considerations

When applying ACLs on your network, consider your operational requirements and network topology. You have several options when applying ACLs to one of your network devices. The ACL might be applied on either the external or internal interface of the router. It can also be configured for inbound or outbound traffic on each of these two interfaces (when using ACLs). Although you can choose inbound or outbound (with respect to the router interface, not your network) on each physical interface, the most common combinations are illustrated in Figure 12-1.

Figure 12-1 *ACL Placement*

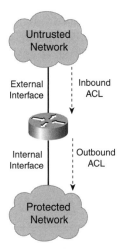

When deciding where to apply your ACLs, you need to understand the various options available to you. These options are as follows:

- Traffic direction
- External interface
- Internal interface

NOTE   If you use VACLs, you do not have a concept of traffic direction. You can only limit traffic without regard to the direction (on a specific interface) that it is traversing. There is no concept of inbound or outbound traffic on an interface. VACLs just capture the traffic passing through the switch that matches their specified characteristics.

The *traffic direction* specifies whether the ACL is applied to traffic entering or leaving the specified interface. You can allow certain traffic into an interface while denying this same traffic from leaving the interface. You must apply a traffic direction when creating an ACL for a given interface on your network.

The *external interface* is located on the unprotected side of your network device (see Figure 12-1). Applying your ACL to your external interface for inbound traffic provides the best protection against attacks originating from outside your network because the traffic is denied before it enters the router.

The *internal interface* resides on the protected side of your network device (see Figure 12-1). Applying your ACL to your internal interface for outbound traffic does not block traffic from reaching the router itself. This prevents you from accidentally blocking traffic that your router needs.

External versus Internal

Applying the ACL to the external interface in the inward direction denies a host access before the router processes the packets. If the attacker generates a large amount of traffic (common for DoS attacks), this reduces the performance impact on your router.

Applying the ACL to the internal interface in the outbound direction denies traffic from a host to the devices on your protected network, but allows the packets to be processed by the router. This scenario is less desirable, but it does have the benefit of preventing you from accidentally denying traffic that the router needs, such as routing updates.

Each network configuration has its own specific requirements. You must decide, based on your unique network architecture, which configuration meets your needs for security and user functionality.

Access Control Lists (ACLs) Versus VLAN Access Control Lists (VACLs)

In most situations, you do not have a choice between using either ACLs and VACLs. If you have a Catalyst 6000 running CatOS and a MSFC, however, you can choose to use either VACLs or ACLs. Therefore, it is helpful to understand the benefits of each of these access control mechanisms.

VACLs are directionless. You can't specify a direction like you can when defining ACLs. This means that if direction is important when blocking the traffic, using an ACL is the only choice.

ACLs are applied to the MSFC on the switch. The MSFC is essentially a router integrated into the switch. Being a router, however, any ACLs that you define on it are only used to restrict the flow of traffic between different VLANs or broadcast domains. ACLs cannot be used to restrict traffic between systems on the same network segment (because the traffic is transmitted at the link layer). A VACL, however, is applied at the link layer on the switch (which is one of the reasons that VACLs are directionless). This means that VACLs can restrict traffic between systems that are on the same network segment (or VLAN).

Using Existing ACLs

In some situations, you might need to configure IP blocking on an interface for traffic traveling in a direction on which you already have an existing ACL. If you just configure your sensor to generate shuns using that device (and interface), your existing ACL will no longer be applied to the managed device's interface because the blocking sensor takes control of the interface and applies its own ACL. Therefore, to use blocking on an interface (for traffic in a specific direction) that has an existing ACL, you need to define the following extra sensor configuration variables that identify ACLs that you have configured on your managed device:

- PreShun ACL
- PostShun ACL

NOTE   The PreShun and PostShun ACL sensor variables identify the names of ACLs that you have configured on the managed device. The system variables represent either numbered or named ACLs that the sensor uses when building the complete ACL that will be applied to the managed interface.

When you configure a sensor as a blocking sensor, it takes control of the ACL for the specified interface and traffic direction on the managed device. If you configure either a PreShun or PostShun ACL, the sensor applies these entries to the managed device by creating a single ACL composed of the PreShun and PostShun entries. When a blocking event occurs, the sensor creates a new single ACL to perform the blocking. This ACL is composed of the PreShun ACL entries followed by the dynamically created shun entries and ending with the PostShun entries.

NOTE   You need to consider carefully which entries you place in you PreShun ACL. The addresses allowed by the PreShun ACL will come before the dynamically created shun entries (in the ACL that is applied to the managed device). That means that these entries cannot be blocked by the shun entries because the router only looks for the first match in the ACL.

Suppose that you configure the following entries in your PreShun ACL:

```
permit ip host 192.168.20.38 host 192.168.20.66
deny ip 173.60.10.0 0.0.0.255 any
```

Next assume that that the following entry is in your PostShun ACL:

```
permit ip 172.20.0.0 0.0.255.255 any
```

Finally, assume that the following hosts are configured as never-block addresses:

- 10.300.l0.20
- 10.300.100.10

Now your sensor takes this information and generates the following ACL that is always applied to the managed device's managed interface:

```
permit ip host 10.300.10.20
permit ip host 10.300.100.10
permit ip host 192.168.20.38 host 192.168.20.66
deny ip 173.60.10.0 0.0.0.255 any
permit ip 172.20.0.0 0.0.255.255 any
```

If your sensor detects traffic from 172.20.10.10 that triggers a signature configured for blocking, the sensor needs to update the ACL on the managed device. The updated ACL includes the entries needed to block the attacker's traffic. The resulting blocking ACL that also denies traffic from 172.20.10.10 is as follows:

```
permit ip host 10.300.10.20
permit ip host 10.300.100.10
permit ip host 192.168.20.38 host 192.168.20.66
deny ip 173.60.10.0 0.0.0.255 any
deny ip host 172.20.10.10 any
permit ip 172.20.0.0 0.0.255.255 any
```

Master Blocking Sensor

Depending on your network configuration, you can have multiple entry points into your network. When one of your sensors initiates a blocking event, it prevents further intrusive traffic from entering your network from that same source address. If more than one of your sensors is configured for IP blocking, you probably want these sensors to coordinate their blocking actions with each other so that all entry points into you network are blocked when an attack is noticed by any of your sensors. This coordination is handled by configuring a *master blocking sensor.*

It is perhaps easiest to explain the master blocking sensor through an example. Figure 12-2 illustrates a network that is connected to the Internet through multiple Internet service providers (ISPs). A Cisco IDS sensor monitors each of the entry points into this network. Furthermore, each of the sensors is configured to perform device management on its associated border or perimeter router.

Figure 12-2 *Master Blocking Sensor*

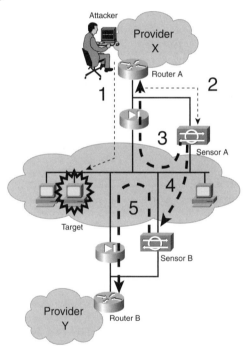

First, an attacker attempts to compromise a host on the protected network (Step 1 in Figure 12-2). This usually involves the attacker launching an exploit against the target machine.

When Sensor A detects the attack, it fires one of the signatures in its database (Step 2 in Figure 12-2). Because the signature is configured for blocking, Sensor A Telnets (or uses SSH) into Router A and updates the ACL to block the traffic from the attacker's host along with generating the alarm event (Step 3 in Figure 12-2).

The ACL on Router A will prevent the attacker from sending traffic into the network through Provider X's network (see Figure 12-2). Because there are two entry points into the network, however, the attacker can reroute the traffic through Provider Y, because it still currently allows traffic from the attacker's host. Therefore, to completely protect the network from the attacker, Sensor B is also configured as a master blocking sensor.

After blocking the attacker's traffic at Router A, Sensor A then tells Sensor B to also block the attacker's traffic (Step 4 in Figure 12-2). Because Sensor B is configured as the master blocking sensor (for Sensor A), Sensor B accepts Sensor A's request and Telnets (or uses SSH) into Router B (Step 5 in Figure 12-2) to update the ACL to also block the attacker's traffic. At this point, both entry points into the network are now protected from the attacker.

NOTE   A savvy network security administrator will configure Sensor A to command Sensor B to block traffic from Provider Y's router. This will protect from attacks initiated through Provider X's network. Then to complete the security configuration, the administrator also needs to configure Sensor A as the master blocking sensor for Sensor B. Therefore, if an attacker comes from either Provider X or Provider Y, both entry points into the network are protected.

Configuring IP Blocking

When configuring IP blocking, you need to perform numerous configuration operations. These operations fall into the following actions:

- Assigning the block action
- Setting blocking properties
- Defining addresses never to block
- Setting up logical devices
- Defining blocking devices
- Defining master blocking sensors

Assigning the Block Action

Before your sensor will initiate IP blocking, you need to configure one or more of your Cisco IDS signatures with the shun action. In IDM version 4.0, you configure the actions for a signature by editing the EventAction field of a signature (see Figure 12-3).

Figure 12-3 *Editing a Signature's Properties*

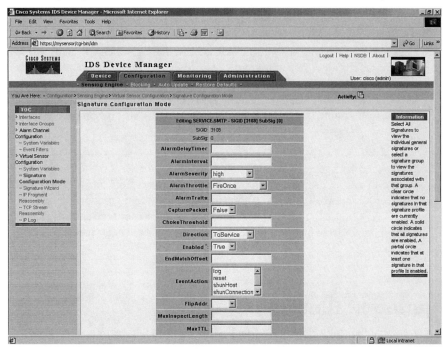

When using IDS MC, you configure the actions for a signature by selecting Configuration>
Settings>Signatures and then selecting either the Block Host or Block Connection check
boxes (see Figure 12-4).

Configuring signatures is explained in detail in Chapter 11, "Signature Configuration."

NOTE   For TCP-based signatures, you can cause your sensor to reset the TCP connection from the
attacking host by selecting the reset action (or checking the Reset check box in IDS MC).
This response does not require any other configuration because it just resets the attacker's
current TCP connection.

Figure 12-4 *Setting a Signature's Actions*

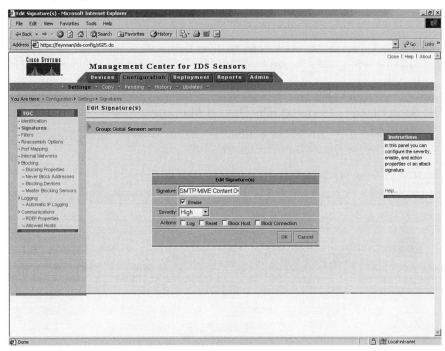

Setting Blocking Properties

Certain blocking properties apply to signatures that are configured with the block action. The following blocking parameters apply to all automatic blocks that the sensor initiates:

- Maximum block entries
- Allow the sensor IP to be blocked
- Block duration

The Maximum Block Entries parameter specifies the maximum number of dynamically created shun entries that the blocking sensor can place into the ACL to block attacking hosts. This value prevents the sensor from generating an ACL that contains an abnormally large number of entries, which could impact the performance of the managed device. The default value is 100 entries.

The Blocking Properties screen contains a check box that is labeled similar to Allow the Sensor IP to Be Blocked (this varies slightly between management systems). Not checking this box causes the sensor to place a permit entry for the sensor's IP address at the beginning of the dynamically created shun entries. Because this **permit** statement is processed before any deny entries, traffic to the sensor's IP address cannot be blocked by the blocking ACL.

This prevents an attack from blocking the sensor's access to the managed device. If the sensor is somehow blocked from access to the managed device, it will not be able to change the blocking ACL after it has been applied.

The block duration (or block time) specifies the length of time that your blocking sensor will wait before removing the blocking ACL. The default block duration is 30 minutes.

Setting Blocking Properties Using IDS Device Manager (IDM)

When using IDM, you set the blocking properties by selecting Configuration> Blocking>Block Properties (see Figure 12-5).

Figure 12-5 *IDM Blocking Properties Screen*

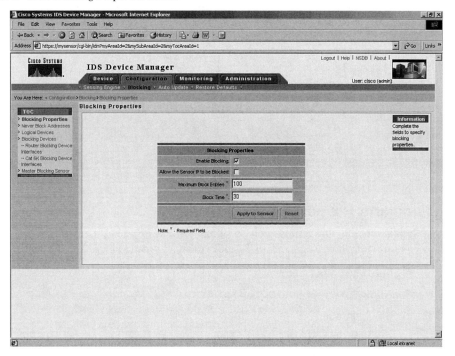

| NOTE | In version 4.0 of the appliance software, the Blocking Properties screen did not have the Block Time field. If you run 4.0, to set the block duration, you must use the CLI. Then you use service virtual-sensor-configuration virtual (Sensor>Tune Micro-engines>ShunEvent> ShunTime) to change the default block duration. |

To set the blocking properties through IDM, follow these steps:

Step 1 Click the Configuration tab from the IDM main screen.

Step 2 Select Blocking from the options bar.

Step 3 Select Blocking Properties from the TOC. This displays the Blocking Properties window.

Step 4 Enter the maximum number of entries allowed in the blocking ACL by entering a value in the Maximum Block Entries field.

Step 5 Check the box next to Allow the Sensor IP to Be Blocked if you want the blocking ACL to be able to block the sensor's IP address.

Step 6 Enter the length of time before the blocking ACL will expire.

Step 7 Click Apply to Sensor to save the changes.

| NOTE | You must commit the changes by clicking the Save Changes icon on the activity bar before you can perform other configuration changes to your sensor. You can also cancel changes by clicking the Cancel Changes icon on the activity bar. |

Setting Blocking Properties Using Management Center for IDS Sensors (IDS MC)

When using IDS MC, set the blocking properties by selecting Configuration>Settings>Blocking>Block Properties (see Figure 12-6).

Figure 12-6 *IDS MC Blocking Properties Screen*

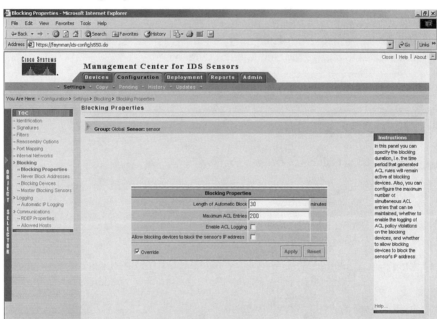

To set the blocking properties through IDS MC, follow these steps:

Step 1 From the IDS MC main screen, click the Configuration tab.

Step 2 Select the sensor or sensor group that you want to set the blocking properties for by using the object selector bar.

Step 3 Select Settings from the options bar.

Step 4 Select Blocking Properties from the TOC. The Blocking Properties window displays in the content area.

Step 5 Enter the length of time (in minutes) before the blocking ACL will expire in the Length of Automatic Block field.

Step 6 Enter the maximum number of entries allowed in the blocking ACL by entering a value in the Maximum ACL Entries field.

Step 7 To enable your managed device to generate syslog messages caused by failures to the blocking ACL, check the Enable ACL Logging check box. This causes the sensor to place the keyword **log** on the blocking access control entries that are created.

| NOTE | Besides enabling logging for the blocking ACL, you must also define a syslog data source (on your sensor) to accept syslog messages from the managed device. For more information on the Syslog protocol, refer to RFC 3195, "Reliable Delivery for Syslog," and RFC 3164, "The BSD Syslog Protocol." |

Step 8 Check the box next to Allow Blocking Devices to Block the Sensor's IP Address if you want the blocking ACL to be able to block the sensor's IP address.

Step 9 Click Apply to save the blocking properties that you have entered.

| NOTE | To actually update the configuration on your sensor, you must first save the changes to the IDS MC database (using Configuration>Pending), and then generate and deploy the updated configuration files using the options under the Deployment tab (see Chapter 16, "Enterprise IDS Management"). |

Defining Addresses Never to Block

To prevent your blocking sensor from blocking traffic to critical systems on your network (either accidentally or due to a deliberate attack), you can configure which IP addresses your blocking device should never block.

| NOTE | The never-block entries are added (as **permit** statements) before the dynamically created blocking entries generated by the sensor. Because these entries come before any blocking entries, these addresses cannot be blocked by the blocking ACL. |

Defining Never-Block Addresses in IDM

To configure *never-block addresses* in IDM, you need to select Configuration> Blocking>Never Block Addresses (see Figure 12-7).

Figure 12-7   *IDM Never Block Addresses Screen*

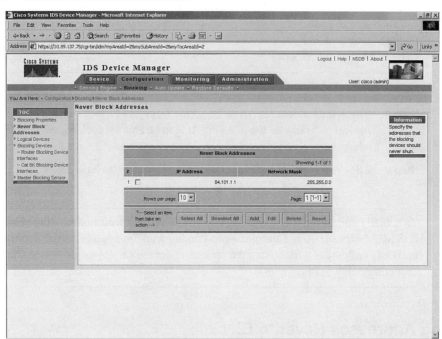

To configure which addresses cannot be blocked by the blocking ACL generated by your blocking sensor when using IDM, follow these steps:

Step 1   Click the Configuration tab on the IDM main screen.

Step 2   Click Blocking from the options bar.

Step 3   Click Never Block Addresses from the TOC. The Never Block Addresses window appears in the content area.

Step 4   Click Add. The Never Block Addresses Adding window appears in the content area.

Step 5   Enter the IP address and netmask for the address that should never be blocked.

Step 6   Click Apply to Sensor to save the never-block address entry.

NOTE   You must commit the changes by clicking the Save Changes icon on the activity bar before you can perform other configuration changes to your sensor. You can also cancel your changes by clicking the Cancel Changes icon on the activity bar.

NOTE   From the Never Block Addresses screen, you can manipulate existing entries by clicking the check box next to the entry that you want to modify and then clicking either Edit or Delete.

Defining Never-Block Addresses in IDS MC

To configure which addresses cannot be blocked by the blocking ACL generated by your blocking sensor when using IDS MC, select Configuration>Settings>Blocking>Never Block Addresses (see Figure 12-8).

Figure 12-8 *IDS MC Never Block Addresses Window*

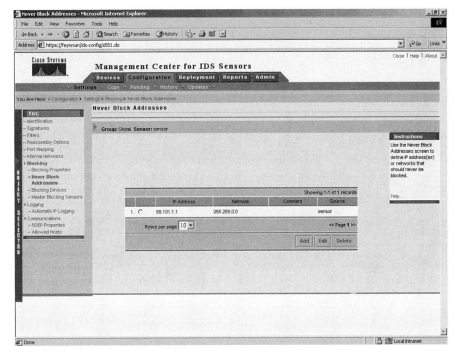

When defining addresses that should not be blocked, follow these steps:

Step 1   From the IDS MC main screen, click the Configuration tab.

Step 2   Click Never Block Addresses under the Blocking section in the TOC. This displays the Never Block Addresses screen in the content area.

Step 3 Click Add to enter an IP address that should not be blocked. This displays the Enter Network screen.

Step 4 Enter the IP address and netmask for the address that should never be blocked.

Step 5 Click OK to save the never-block address entry.

NOTE To actually update the configuration on your sensor, you must first save the changes to the IDS MC database (using Configuration>Pending) and then generate and deploy the updated configuration files using the options under the Deployment tab (see Chapter 16).

NOTE From the Never Block Addresses screen, you can manipulate existing entries by clicking the check box next to the entry that you want to modify and then clicking either Edit or Delete.

Setting Up Logical Devices

If you use IDM to manage your sensors, you configure *logical devices*. A logical device enables you to group blocking devices that share the following authentication parameters:

- Username
- Password
- Enable password

When you create a blocking device, you associate the appropriate logical device with it. This logical device can be associated to multiple blocking devices.

To configure a logical device in IDM, follow these steps:

Step 1 Select the Configuration tab from the main IDM screen.

Step 2 Select Logical Devices from the options bar. This displays the Logical Device Configuration window in the content area.

Step 3 Click Add. The Logical Devices Adding window is displayed in the content area.

Step 4 Enter a name for the logical device in the Name field.

Step 5 Enter the enable password for the device in the Enable Password field.

Figure 12-9 *Logical Device Configuration Screen*

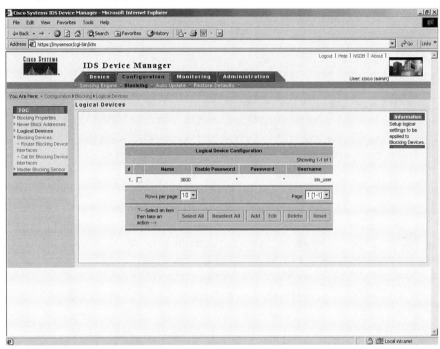

Step 6   Enter the login password in the Password field.

Step 7   Enter the username in the Username field.

Step 8   Click Apply to Sensor to save the logical device.

NOTE   You must commit the changes by clicking the Save Changes icon on the activity bar before you can perform other configuration changes to your sensor. You can also cancel your changes by clicking the Cancel Changes icon on the activity bar.

NOTE   When using IDS MC, it does not enable you to define logical devices. Instead, the authentication credentials for the blocking device are entered when you are configuring the blocking device parameters.

Defining Blocking Devices

Cisco IDS supports the following three different types of blocking devices:

- Cisco IOS routers
- Catalyst 6000 switches with a PFC (running CatOS)
- PIX firewalls

NOTE When configuring an FWSM as a blocking device, you follow the steps for configuring a PIX firewall, because the FWSM supports the PIX 6.0 feature set. There is not a separate configuration option for the FWSM.

Each of these blocking devices uses a slightly different mechanism to block traffic on the network. The routers use ACLs to restrict traffic flow. The Catalyst switch uses VACLs to restrict traffic, and the PIX (or FWSM) uses the **shun** command to restrict traffic. Therefore, configuring each of these different types of blocking devices is slightly different.

NOTE It is important to choose the correct device type when defining a blocking device. The sensor creates the commands to initiate blocking based on this device type. Using the wrong device type (especially with respect to the operating system running on the Catalyst switch) will prevent blocking from operating correctly.

Defining Blocking Devices Using IDM

When using IDM, defining a blocking device is a two-step process. You must first define the blocking device. Then you define one of the following interfaces that you associate with a blocking device:

- Router blocking device interface
- Cat6K blocking device interface

NOTE You do not need to create an interface when you are using a PIX (or FWSM) as your blocking device. The PIX (and FWSM) performs the blocking via its **shun** command, so you do not need to specify an interface. Therefore, with PIX-managed devices, you only need to define the blocking device itself.

You define blocking devices through IDM by clicking Add on the Configuration> Blocking>Blocking Devices screen (see Figure 12-10) and defining the fields shown in Table 12-2.

Figure 12-10   *IDM Blocking Devices Screen*

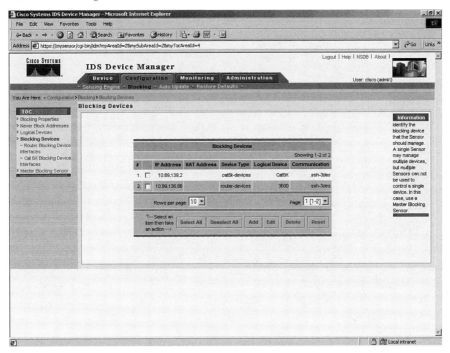

You can also edit or delete an existing blocking device by clicking the check box next to the blocking device that you want to modify and then clicking either Edit or Delete.

Table 12-2   *IDM Blocking Device Fields*

Field	Description
IP Address	The IP address that the sensor will use to communicate with the blocking device.
NAT Address	The NAT address of the blocking device.
Apply Logical Device	Pull-down menu that enables you to select a logical device that defines the login credentials for the blocking device.
Device Type	Pull-down menu to select the blocking device type. Valid options are Cisco Router, Catalyst 6000 VACL, and PIX.
Communication	The communication vehicle that you plan to use to communicate with the blocking device. Valid options are SSH DES, SSH 3DES, and Telnet.

NOTE   If you choose SSH DES or SSH 3DES, you need to use the CLI command **ssh host-key** to add the router to the list of valid SSH servers before the sensor will be able to successfully communicate with your blocking device. The sensor currently uses SSH version 1 to communicate with the blocking device.

To add a blocking device using the IDM interface, follow these steps:

Step 1 Click the Configuration tab on the IDM main screen.

Step 2 Click Blocking on the option bar.

Step 3 Click Blocking Devices in the TOC. The Blocking Devices window appears in the content area.

Step 4 Click Add in the Blocking Devices window. The Blocking Devices Adding window appears in the content area.

Step 5 Define your blocking device fields (see Table 12-2).

Step 6 Click Apply to Sensor to save your blocking device.

NOTE   You must commit the changes by clicking the Save Changes icon on the activity bar before you can perform other configuration changes to your sensor. You can also cancel your changes by clicking the Cancel Changes icon on the activity bar.

Defining Router Blocking Devices Interfaces Using IDM

Your blocking sensor needs to know to which interface on your router that you want to apply the blocking ACL. You configure this information by defining a router device blocking interface entry using the Configuration, Blocking>Blocking Properties>Router Blocking Devices screen (see Figure 12-11). In the Router Interfaces window, your currently defined router interfaces are displayed and you can create a new one by clicking Add. When defining a new router interface, you need to specify the fields listed in Table 12-3. You can also edit or delete an existing router interface entry by clicking the check box next to the router interface entry to be modified and then clicking Edit or Delete.

Table 12-3   *IDM Router Interface Fields*

Field	Description
IP Address	The IP address that the sensor will use to communicate with the blocking device. You select this entry from a pull-down that lists the addresses of the router blocking devices that you have defined.
Blocking Interface	The interface on the blocking device where the blocking sensor will apply the blocking ACL.
Blocking Direction	Determines whether the blocking ACL will be applied on inbound or outbound traffic on the blocking interface. You select either In or Out from the pull-down menu.
Pre-Block ACL Name	Name of the ACL (on the blocking device) whose entries will be inserted at the beginning of the blocking ACL.
Post-Block ACL Name	Name of the ACL (on the blocking device) whose entries will be placed at the end of the blocking ACL.

Figure 12-11   *IDM Router Interfaces Screen*

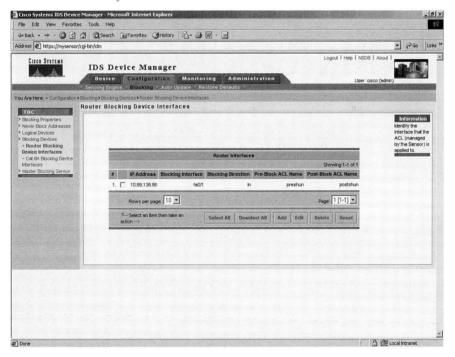

To add a router interface using the IDM interface, follow these steps:

Step 1   Click the Configuration tab on the IDM main screen.

Step 2   Click Blocking on the option bar.

Step 3   Click Router Blocking Device Interfaces in the TOC. The Router
Interfaces window appears in the content area.

Step 4   Click Add in the Router Interfaces window. The Router Blocking Device
Interfaces Adding window appears in the content area.

Step 5   Define your router interface using the fields shown in Table 12-3.

Step 6   Click Apply to Sensor to save the router interface entry.

NOTE   You must commit the changes by clicking the Save Changes icon on the activity bar before
you can perform other configuration changes to your sensor. You can also cancel your
changes by clicking the Cancel Changes icon on the activity bar.

Defining Cat6K Blocking Devices Interfaces Using IDM

Your blocking sensor needs to know to which VLAN on your Catalyst 6000 switch you
want to apply the blocking VACL. You configure this information by defining a Catalyst
6000 device blocking interface entry using the Configuration>Blocking>Blocking
Properties>Cat6K Blocking Devices screen (see Figure 12-12). In the Cat 6k Interfaces
window, your currently defined Cat 6k interfaces are displayed and you can create a new
one by clicking Add. When defining a new Cat 6k interface, you need to specify the fields
listed in Table 12-4. You can also edit or delete an existing Cat 6k interface entry by clicking
the check box next to the Cat 6k interface entry to be modified and then clicking Edit or
Delete.

Table 12-4   *IDM Cat6k Interface Fields*

Field	Description
IP Address	The IP address that the sensor will use to communicate with the blocking device. You select this entry from a pull-down that lists the addresses of the Cat6k blocking devices that you have defined.
VLAN Number	The VLAN on the blocking device where the blocking sensor will apply the blocking VACL.
Pre-Block VACL Name	Name of the VACL (on the blocking device) whose entries will be inserted at the beginning of the blocking ACL.
Post-Block VACL Name	Name of the VACL (on the blocking device) whose entries will be placed at the end of the blocking ACL.

Figure 12-12 *IDM Cat6k Interfaces Screen*

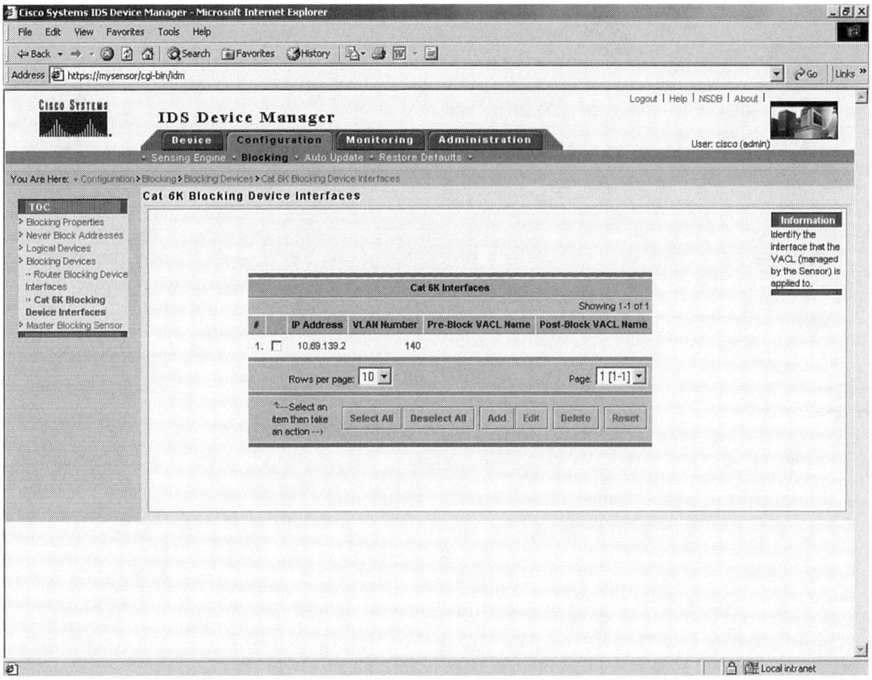

To add a Cat6k interface using the IDM interface, follow these steps:

Step 1 Click the Configuration tab on the IDM main screen.

Step 2 Click Blocking on the option bar.

Step 3 Click Cat 6k Blocking Device Interfaces in the TOC. The Cat 6k Interfaces window appears in the content area.

Step 4 Click Add in the Cat 6k Interfaces window. The Cat 6k Blocking Device Interfaces Adding window appears in the content area.

Step 5 Define your router interface using the fields shown in Table 12-4.

Step 6 Click Apply to Sensor to save the router interface entry.

NOTE You must commit the changes by clicking the Save Changes icon on the activity bar before you can perform other configuration changes to your sensor. You can also cancel your changes by clicking the Cancel Changes icon on the activity bar.

Defining Blocking Devices Using IDS MC

When using IDS MC, you can also define following three types of blocking devices:

- Router blocking device interface
- Cat6K blocking device interface
- PIX blocking device

NOTE   When configuring an FWSM as a blocking device, you must follow the steps for configuring a PIX firewall, because the FWSM supports the PIX 6.0 feature set. There is not a separate configuration option for the FWSM.

When defining one of these blocking devices, specify its characteristics using various fields like in IDM, but IDS MC does not have logical devices or separate device interface entries. Instead, IDS MC incorporates the authentication parameters and interface information into the actual blocking device definition.

You define blocking devices through IDS MC by clicking Add on the Configuration>Settings>Blocking>Blocking Devices screen (see Figure 12-13) and defining the fields shown in Table 12-5. You can also edit or delete an existing blocking device by clicking the check box next to the blocking device that you want to modify and then clicking either Edit or Delete.

Table 12-5   *IDS MC Blocking Device Fields*

Field	Description
Device Type	Specifies the type of blocking device that you want to define. The pull-down menu enables you to specify Cisco Router, PIX, or Catalyst 6000 VACL.
IP Address	The IP address that the sensor will use to communicate with the blocking device.
NAT Address	(Optional) The NAT address of the blocking device.
Comment	(Optional) A text field that enables you to provide a description of the blocking device.
Username	(Optional) Username that the blocking sensor will use to log in to the managed device.
Password	Password for the username that enables the blocking sensor to access the managed device.
Enable Password	Password that enables the blocking sensor to gain privileged access to the managed device.

Table 12-5   *IDS MC Blocking Device Fields (Continued)*

Field	Description
Secure Communications	Identifies the communication vehicle that you plan to use to communicate with the blocking device. Valid options are none, SSH, and SSH 3DES. (None implies Telnet access.)
Interfaces	This field enables you to specify the interfaces for your managed device by clicking Edit Interfaces. When defining a PIX blocking device, you do not receive this field because the PIX uses the **shun** command to block the traffic.

NOTE   If you choose SSH DES or SSH 3DES, you need to use the CLI command **ssh host-key** to add the router to the list of valid SSH servers before the sensor will be able to successfully communicate with your blocking device.

Figure 12-13   *IDS MC Blocking Devices Screen*

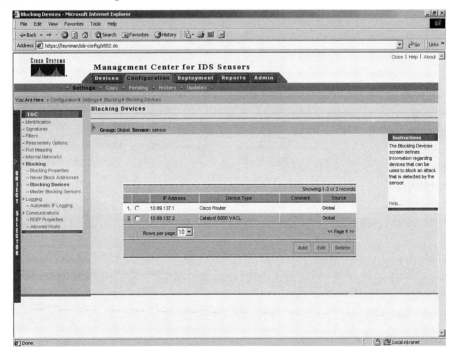

Defining Router Blocking Devices Using IDS MC

When defining a router blocking device using IDS MC, besides the basic blocking device characteristics, you must specify the interface that the blocking ACL will be applied on. The blocking interface is specified using the fields listed in Table 12-6.

Table 12-6 *IDS MC Router Interface Fields*

Field	Description
Blocking Interface Name	This field identifies the name of the interface on the router that the sensor will apply the blocking ACL to. Sample interfaces include fa0/1, e0, and fa1/1.
Blocking Direction	The blocking direction identifies whether the ACL is applied to traffic entering the interface or traffic leaving the interface. Valid options are Inbound and Outbound (selected by the pull-down menu).
Pre-block ACL Name	Name of an ACL on the managed device containing entries that will be placed at the beginning of the blocking ACL (before the dynamically created shun entries).
Post-block ACL Name	Name of an ACL on the managed device containing entries that will be placed at the end of the blocking ACL (after the dynamically created shun entries).

To define a router blocking device using IDS MC, follow these steps:

Step 1 Click the Configuration tab on the main IDS MC screen.

Step 2 Click Settings on the option bar.

Step 3 Click Blocking Devices in the TOC. This displays the Blocking Devices window in the content area.

Step 4 Click Add to define a new blocking device. This displays the Enter Blocking Device window (see Figure 12-14).

Step 5 Select Cisco Router for the Device Type.

Step 6 Define the blocking device using the fields listed in Table 12-5.

Step 7 Click Edit Interfaces to enter the interface information for the blocking device. This brings up the Enter Blocking Device Interfaces window (see Figure 12-15). This window displays the currently defined interfaces for the blocking device (currently blank because no interfaces have been defined yet).

Figure 12-14   *IDS MC Enter Blocking Device Screen*

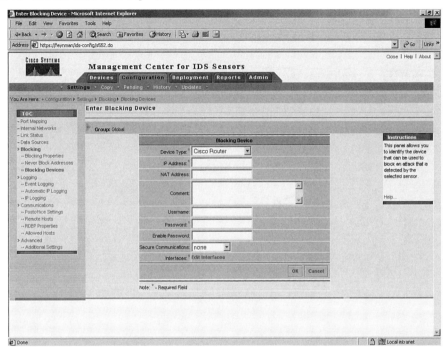

Step 8   Click Add to add a new interface entry. The Enter Blocking Device Interface window appears in the content area.

Step 9   Define the interface that the blocking ACL will be applied to by the blocking sensor.

Step 10   Define the traffic direction on the interface (either inbound or outbound).

Step 11   Define the Pre-block ACL Name and Post-block ACL Name.

Step 12   Click OK to save the interface information. This redisplays the Blocking Device Interfaces window.

Step 13   Click OK to exit the Enter Blocking Device Interfaces window. This redisplays the Enter Blocking Device window.

Step 14   Click OK to save the Blocking Device definition. This redisplays the Blocking Devices window.

NOTE   To actually update the configuration on your sensor, you must first save the changes to the IDS MC database (using Configuration>Pending) and then generate and deploy the updated configuration files using the options under the Deployment tab (see Chapter 16).

Figure 12-15 *IDS MC Enter Blocking Device Interfaces Screen (for Routers)*

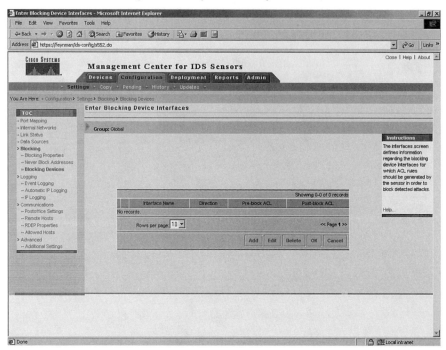

Defining Catalyst 6000 Blocking Devices Using IDS MC

When defining a Catalyst 6000 VACL blocking device using IDS MC, besides the basic blocking device characteristics, you must specify the VLAN that the blocking VACL will be applied on. The blocking interface is specified using the fields listed in Table 12-7.

Table 12-7 *IDS MC Catalyst 6000 Interface Fields*

Field	Description
VLAN Number	This field identifies the name of the VLAN on the Catalyst 6000 switch that the sensor will apply the blocking VACL to.
Pre-block ACL Name	Name of an ACL on the managed device containing entries that will be placed at the beginning of the blocking ACL (before the dynamically created shun entries).
Post-block ACL Name	Name of an ACL on the managed device containing entries that will be placed at the end of the blocking ACL (after the dynamically created shun entries).

To define a Catalyst 6000 VACL blocking device using IDS MC, follow these steps:

Step 1   Click the Configuration tab on the main IDS MC screen.

Step 2   Click Settings on the option bar.

Step 3   Click Blocking Devices in the TOC. This displays the Blocking Devices window in the content area.

Step 4   Click Add to define a new blocking device. This displays the Enter Blocking Device window.

Step 5   Select Catalyst 6000 VACL for the Device Type.

Step 6   Define the blocking device using the fields listed in Table 12-5.

Step 7   Click Edit Interfaces to enter the interface information for the blocking device. This brings up the Enter Blocking Device Interfaces window (see Figure 12-16). This window displays the currently defined interfaces for the blocking device (currently blank because no interfaces have been defined yet).

Figure 12-16   *IDS MC Enter Blocking Device Interfaces Screen (for Catalyst 6000 VACL)*

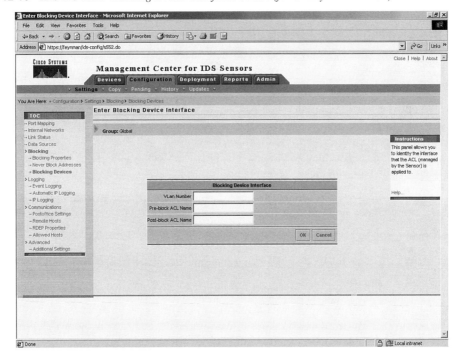

Step 8   Click Add to add a new interface entry. The Enter Blocking Device Interface window appears in the content area.

Step 9   Define the VLAN that the blocking VACL will be applied to by the blocking sensor.

Step 10   Define the Pre-block ACL Name and Post-block ACL Name.

Step 11   Click OK to save the interface information. This redisplays the Blocking Device Interfaces window.

Step 12   Click OK to exit the Enter Blocking Device Interfaces window. This redisplays the Enter Blocking Device window.

Step 13   Click OK to save the Blocking Device definition. This redisplays the Blocking Devices window.

NOTE   To actually update the configuration on your sensor, you must first save the changes to the IDS MC database (using Configuration>Pending) and then generate and deploy the updated configuration files using the options under the Deployment tab (see Chapter 16).

Defining PIX Blocking Devices Using IDS MC

Unlike the other blocking devices, you do not need to specify an interface when using a PIX as a blocking device. All you need to do is specify the normal blocking device parameters. To configure a PIX blocking device, follow these steps:

Step 1   Click the Configuration tab on the main IDS MC screen.

Step 2   Click Settings on the option bar.

Step 3   Click Blocking Devices in the TOC. This displays the Blocking Devices window in the content area.

Step 4   Click Add to define a new blocking device. This displays the Enter Blocking Device window.

Step 5   Select PIX for the Device Type.

Step 6   Define the blocking device using the fields listed in Table 12-5.

Step 7   Click OK to save the interface information. This redisplays the Blocking Device Interfaces window.

Step 8   Click OK to exit the Enter Blocking Device Interfaces window. This redisplays the Enter Blocking Device window.

Step 9   Click OK to save the Blocking Device definition. This redisplays the Blocking Devices window.

NOTE   To actually update the configuration on your sensor, you must first save the changes to the IDS MC database (using Configuration>Pending) and then generate and deploy the updated configuration files using the options under the Deployment tab (see Chapter 16).

Defining Master Blocking Sensors

One sensor can initiate blocking on multiple managed devices on your network. Only one sensor, however, can initiate blocking on a specific managed device. If you use multiple sensors to perform IP blocking on your network, you will need to define master blocking sensors to coordinate your blocking so that all entrances into your network are protected.

Configuring a Master Blocking Sensor in IDM

When defining a master blocking sensor using IDM, you need to specify the parameters listed in Table 12-8.

Table 12-8   *IDM Master Blocking Sensor Fields*

Field	Description
IP Address	This field specifies the IP address of the sensor that will actually apply the blocking requests to the managed device.
Port	Indicate the port that the sensor will connect to when communicating with the master blocking sensor.
Username	Username of the account that the sensor will use when connecting to the master blocking sensor.
Password	Password of the account that the sensor will use when connecting to the master blocking sensor.
Use TLS	Check box indicating whether the communication with the master blocking sensor is over an encrypted channel.

To add a master blocking sensor using IDM, follow these steps:

Step 1   Click the Configuration tab on the main IDM screen.

Step 2   Click Blocking on the options bar.

Step 3   Click Master Blocking Sensor in the TOC. This displays the Master Blocking Sensor window in the content area. This window displays your currently configured master blocking sensors.

Step 4   Click Add to add a new master blocking sensor. This brings up the Master Blocking Sensor Adding window.

Step 5   Enter the IP address of the master blocking sensor that the current sensor will forward blocking requests to.

Step 6   Specify the port that the sensor will use to communicate the blocking requests.

Step 7   Specify the username and password that the sensor will need to use to log in to the master blocking sensor.

Step 8   If you are using encrypted communication to the master blocking sensor, make sure that the Use TLS check box is checked.

Step 9   Click Apply to Sensor to save your master blocking sensor definition.

NOTE   You must commit the changes by clicking the Save Changes icon on the activity bar before you can perform other configuration changes to your sensor. You can also cancel your changes by clicking the Cancel Changes icon on the activity bar.

Configuring Master Blocking Sensor in IDS MC

Because IDS MC has a view of multiple sensors across your network, defining a master blocking sensor is easier than using IDM. With IDS MC, you only need to specify the IP address of the master blocking sensor from a list of potential master blocking sensors.

To configure master blocking sensors using IDS MC, follow these steps:

Step 1   Click the Configuration tab on the main IDS MC screen.

Step 2   Select the sensor that you want to configure a master blocking sensor for by using the object selector bar.

Step 3   Click Settings on the option bar.

Step 4   Click Master Blocking Sensors from the TOC. The Master Blocking Sensors window appears in the content area.

Step 5   Click Add to add a master blocking sensor. This displays the Enter Master Blocking Sensor window.

Step 6   From the list of available sensors, choose the sensor that will serve as a master blocking sensor.

Step 7   Click OK to save the master blocking sensor configuration.

NOTE   To actually update the configuration on your sensor, you must first save the changes to the IDS MC database (using Configuration>Pending) and then generate and deploy the updated configuration files using the options under the Deployment tab (see Chapter 16).

Manual Blocking

Using IDM, you can manually initiate block requests. You have the option of initiating manual blocks for a single host or for a specific network.

Blocking Hosts

When defining a manual block against a single host, you need to define the fields shown in Table 12-9.

Table 12-9   *IDM Host Manual Block Fields*

Field	Description
Source Address	The source address that will be blocked by the block request.
Source Port	(Optional) The source port of the traffic to be blocked.
Destination Address	(Optional) The destination address of the traffic to be blocked.
Destination Port	(Optional) The destination port of the traffic to be blocked.
Protocol	(Optional) The protocol to be blocked. Valid options are None, TCP, and UDP.
Connection Shun	(Optional) When this box is checked, it causes the shun to be applied only to connections that match the source address, destination address, destination port, and protocol specified.
Timeout (Minutes)	The length of time that you want the shun to remain in effect.

NOTE   Specifying a protocol of None implies IP traffic. This option is used when you want to deny all traffic from a specified source address. Specifying a protocol of either TCP or UDP enables you to restrict your block traffic matching a single port for a specific transport protocol (in conjunction with the specified source and destination addresses).

To initiate a manual host block, follow these steps:

Step 1   Click the Administration tab on the main IDM screen.

Step 2   Click Manual Blocking on the options bar.

Step 3   Select Host Manual Blocks from the TOC. This displays the Host Manual Blocks window in the content area. Any host blocks currently in effect will be displayed.

Step 4   Click Add to enter a new host block. The Hosts Manual Blocks Adding window appears.

Step 5   Enter the appropriate manual block fields listed in Table 12-9 that define your block request.

Step 6   Click Apply to Sensor to initiate the block.

NOTE   You can remove current manual host blocks by clicking the check box next to a host entry (on the Host Manual Blocks window) and then selecting Delete.

NOTE   You must commit the changes by clicking the Save Changes icon on the activity bar before you can perform other configuration changes to your sensor. You can also cancel your changes by clicking the Cancel Changes icon on the activity bar.

Blocking Networks

When defining a manual block against a network, you need to define the fields shown in Table 12-10.

Table 12-10   *IDM Network Manual Block Fields*

Field	Description
IP Address	The source IP address that will be blocked by the block request
Netmask	The netmask that defines which bits in the IP address are part of the network address that will be blocked
Timeout (Minutes)	The length of time that you want the shun to remain in effect

To initiate a manual network block, follow these steps:

Step 1   Click the Administration tab on the main IDM screen.

Step 2   Click Manual Blocking on the options bar.

Step 3   Select Network Manual Blocks from the TOC. This displays the Network Manual Blocks window in the content area. Any network blocks currently in effect will be displayed.

Step 4   Click Add to enter a new network block. The Network Manual Blocks Adding window appears.

Step 5   Enter the appropriate manual block fields listed in Table 12-10 that define your block request.

Step 6   Click Apply to Sensor to initiate the block.

NOTE   You must commit the changes by clicking the Save Changes icon on the activity bar before you can perform other configuration changes to your sensor. You can also cancel your changes by clicking the Cancel Changes icon on the activity bar.

NOTE   You can remove current manual network blocks by clicking the check box next to a network entry (on the Network Manual Blocks window) and then selecting Delete.

IP Logging

IP logging enables you to capture the actual packets that an attacking host sends to your network. You can then analyze these packets using a packet analysis tool, such as Ethereal, to determine exactly what an attacker is doing.

You can capture traffic using IP logging both in response to signature configured with the IP logging action, as well as manually initiated IP logging requests.

IP Logging Parameters in IDM

When using IDM, you configure the IP logging parameters through the Configuration>Sensing Engine>Virtual Sensor Configuration>IP Log (see Figure 12-17).

Figure 12-17 *IDM IP Logging Window*

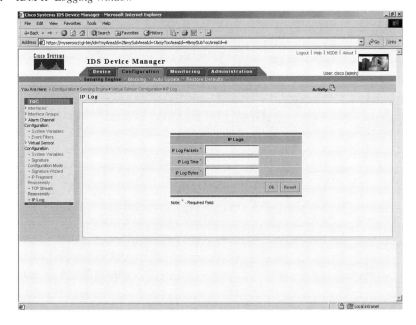

You can configure the amount of traffic logged by specifying one or more of the following parameters:

- Number of packets
- Duration in seconds
- Number of bytes

These parameters affect the amount of traffic that your signatures configured for IP logging will generate, but does not affect the amount of traffic on the network.

IP Logging Parameters in IDS MC

When using IDS MC, you configure the automatic IP logging parameters through the Configuration>Settings>Logging>Automatic IP Logging (see Figure 12-18).

Figure 12-18 *IDS MC Automatic IP Logging Window*

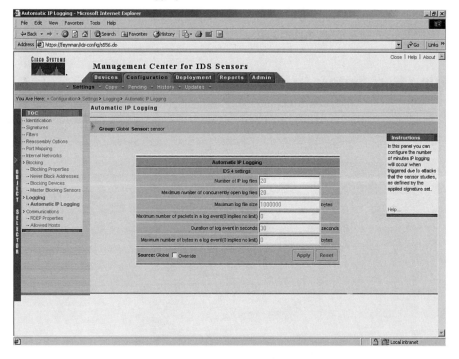

You can configure the amount of traffic logged by specifying one or more of the following parameters:

- Number of IP log files
- Maximum number of open IP log files
- Maximum log file size
- Number of packets
- Duration in seconds
- Number of bytes

These parameters affect the amount of traffic that your signatures configured for IP logging will generate but does not affect the amount of traffic on the network.

NOTE   The first three parameters (number of IP log files, maximum number of open IP log files, and maximum log file size) are ignored with Cisco IDS version 4.0 sensors because these sensors use a circular queue for log file information. If the queue becomes full, the newer IP log information just overwrites the oldest information in the IP log queue.

Manual IP Logging

Sometimes you might want to capture the actual traffic from a specific source address. You can specify the amount of traffic to capture using one of the following characteristics:

- Duration (minutes)
- Number of packets
- Number of bytes

NOTE   The duration for automatically initiated IP logging is specified in seconds. This is different from manually initiated IP logging in which the duration is specified in minutes.

To manually initiate IP logging using IDM, follow these steps:

Step 1   Click the Administration tab on the main IDM screen.

Step 2   Click IP Logging on the options bar. This displays the IP Logging Adding window in the content area (see Figure 12-19).

Figure 12-19 *IDM Manual IP Logging Window*

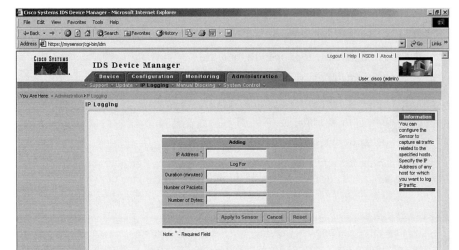

Step 3 Enter the source IP address of the traffic to be logged.

Step 4 Optionally specify the amount of traffic to be logged by specifying one or more of the following parameters: duration of capture, number of packets to capture, and the number of bytes to capture.

Step 5 Click Apply to Sensor to start logging the specified traffic.

NOTE You must commit the changes by clicking the Save Changes icon on the activity bar before you can perform other configuration changes to your sensor. You can also cancel your changes by clicking the Cancel Changes icon on the activity bar.

TCP Reset

The TCP reset response essentially terminates the current TCP connection from the attacker by sending a *TCP reset packet*. This response is effective only for TCP-based connections. UDP traffic, for example, is unaffected by TCP resets. If you configure the reset action for a UDP-based signature, it will be ignored when the signature triggers.

TCP Reset Packet

The Transmission Control Protocol (TCP) provides a connection-oriented communication mechanism. The connection is established through a three-way handshake. To terminate a connection, each side of the connection can send a packet with the FIN bit set, signaling the end of the connection. It is also possible, however, for one side of the connection to abruptly terminate the connection by sending a reset packet (packet with the RST flag set) to the other side. The sensor uses this approach to terminate an attacker TCP connection. For a detailed explanation of TCP/IP protocols refer to *TCP/IP Illustrated Volume 1: The Protocols*, by W. Richard Stevens (Addison-Wesley, 1994).

To configure a signature (TCP-based) to perform the TCP reset response action, you only need to configure the reset action for the specific signature. Then, when a specific TCP connection triggers the signature, the sensor will send TCP resets to both ends of the connection and cause it to terminate. Although this ends the attacker's connection with your network, it does not prevent the attacker from initiating another connection into your network. This new connection will work until another signature triggers that either resets the connection or initiates a blocking response.

Summary

Cisco IDS enables you to take several actions in response to detecting intrusive activity on your network. These responses fall into the following categories:

- IP blocking
- TCP resets
- IP logging

IP blocking enables you to block traffic from a specific address for a specified period of time. You can two types of blocking or shunning:

- shunHost
- shunConnection

Shunning a host causes your sensor to block all traffic coming from the attacking system. Sometimes, however, you want to be more selective in the traffic that you are blocking. Therefore, by shunning a connection you cause the sensor to only block the traffic from the attacking system to the destination port and destination IP address of the traffic that caused the shun to be initiated.

Before instituting IP blocking, you must understand certain guidelines that will help you successfully configure IP blocking. These guidelines fall into the following categories:

- Antispoofing mechanisms
- Critical hosts
- Network topology
- Entry points
- Signature selection
- Blocking duration
- Device login information
- Interface ACL requirements

When performing blocking, your sensor must communicate with another device (called the managed device) that performs the actual shunning. The following types of devices can serve as managed devices:

- Cisco routers
- Cisco Catalyst 6000 switches
- Cisco PIX firewalls (and FWSMs)

Each sensor that you use to initiate IP blocking can manage up to 10 managed interfaces across one or more managed devices. The type of managed device dictates the manner in which the actual blocking is accomplished.

When performing shunning on a router, the blocking sensor connects to the managed device and places an ACL on a specific interface.

Catalyst 6000 switches use VACLs to implement the blocking functionality. When you use a Catalyst 6000 as your managed device, you specify the VLAN that the VACL will be applied to, but you can't specify the traffic direction.

Finally, when using PIX (or FWSM)-managed devices, the blocking is performed using the **shun** command.

Only one sensor can initiate shuns on a specific managed device. You may need to have one sensor that detects an attack initiate shuns on a device that is already managed by another sensor. In this situation, you need to define a master blocking sensor.

A master blocking sensor receives blocking requests from other sensors and then performs these blocking requests on the managed devices that it controls.

To prevent shunning from impacting critical systems on your network, you can define never-block addresses that represent systems on your network and that should never be blocked by your shunning.

Some blocking properties apply to every signature that is configured to initiate IP blocking. The global blocking properties are as follows:

- Maximum block entries
- Allow the sensor IP to be blocked
- Block duration

Besides the automatic blocking and IP logging, you can also configure manual shunning and IP logging when you use IDM. Through the IDM interface, you can initiate a manual shun on either a single host or on a network.

IP logging enables you to capture the actual packets from a specific system. You can initiate IP logging in response to a specific signature. You can configure global parameters that apply to automatic IP logging based on signatures configured for IP logging. These parameters, such as the following, enable you to limit the amount of traffic collected by IP logging:

- Duration (seconds)
- Number of packets
- Number of bytes

If you use IDM, you can also manually initiate IP logging. When manually logging traffic from specific systems, you can also limit the amount of traffic captured by specifying the following traffic limitations on a per-host basis:

- Duration (minutes)
- Number of packets
- Number of bytes

When configuring the TCP reset response, all you need to do is configure a TCP-based signature with the reset action. You do not need to configure any other parameters.

Review Questions

The following questions test your retention of the material presented in this chapter. The answers to the review questions are in Appendix B, "Answers to Chapter Review Questions."

1 What are the three signature responses supported by the Cisco IDS network appliance software (besides alarming)?

2 What are the two ways that you can shun traffic in response to a signature firing?

3 What are the two types of shuns that you can configure for a signature?

4 What is a blocking sensor?

5 What are the three types of managed devices supported by Cisco IDS?

6 How does you blocking sensor perform blocking on a PIX-managed device?

7 Which type of managed device uses VACLs to block the traffic?

8 What is the managed interface?

9 What are the two ways that your blocking sensor communicates with your managed devices?

10 Can you specify a traffic direction when blocking traffic using a VACL?

11 Why is it advantageous to place your ACLs on your external router interface?

12 What is the PreShun ACL?

13 What is the PostShun ACL?

14 What is a master blocking sensor?

15 How many interfaces can a single sensor manage for IP blocking?

16 If you use SSH to communicate with your managed devices, what do you need to configure from the sensor's command line to enable this communication to take place successfully?

17 How can you limit the amount of traffic captured when you initiate manual IP logging?

18 When initiating manual blocking through IDM, what are your two options?

19 What is device management?

20 On which signatures can you effectively configure the reset response?

Upon completion of this chapter, you will be able to perform the following tasks:

- Identify the major categories of signature engines
- Explain the different alarming modes
- Identify the master signature parameters
- Explain regular expression string matching
- Identify the Atomic signature engines
- Identify the Flood signature engines
- Identify the Service signature engines
- Identify the State signature engines
- Identify the Sweep signature engines

CHAPTER 13

Cisco IDS Alarms and Signatures

To identify malicious activity, Cisco IDS monitors network traffic and generates alarms when traffic matching specific signatures is detected. A *signature* is basically a description of network traffic that attackers use while conducting network-based attacks. To support a wide range of signatures and enable users to develop their own custom signatures, Cisco IDS uses a set of signature engines. Each signature engine examines network traffic for intrusive activity with similar characteristics (such as the TCP-based String engines, which handle signatures that look for specific textual strings in TCP traffic). These signature engines parse a list of signature definitions and then search for traffic matching those signatures in the network traffic stream.

Cisco IDS Signatures

Because signature engines and signatures are the foundation of Cisco IDS, Cisco security engineers continually research and develop these components. The signature engines are designed to perform a wide range of different functions, such as pattern matching, stateful pattern matching, protocol decodes, and other heuristic methods. Furthermore, new signature engines are being added to efficiently support a larger range of signatures. Between Cisco IDS version 3.1 and version 4.0, the number of signature engines increased dramatically.

Before covering signature engines and alarms in more detail, it is helpful to provide a quick explanation about the following topics that are useful to understanding signatures:

- Alarm modes
- Regular expression string matching

Alarm Throttle Modes

Managing alarms efficiently is vital to the success of your Cisco IDS deployment. To enhance your ability to control the volume of alarms generated by your sensors, Cisco IDS supports several alarming modes (specified by the AlarmThrottle master signature parameter). Each of the following alarm throttle modes is designed to assist you in regulating the number of alarms generated by intrusive traffic in different situations:

- FireOnce
- FireAll
- Summarize
- GlobalSummarize

Besides the alarming mode, the SummaryKey parameter also impacts the number of alarms generated. This parameter determines which alarms are considered a duplicate or the same and can be based on the source and destination IP address as well as the source and destination port (for a given signature). The various alarming modes regulate the number of alarms generated, but you need to be able to determine which instances of an attack are considered a duplicate of an alarm that has already been generated. The SummaryKey can be one of the following values listed in Table 13-1.

Table 13-1   *SummaryKey Values*

Value	Description
AaBb	Duplicates alarms based on both the source and destination IP addresses as well as the source and destination ports.
AxBx	Duplicates alarms based only on the source and destination IP addresses.
Axxb	Duplicates alarms based on the source IP address and the destination port.
Axxx	Duplicates alarms based only on the source IP address.
xxBx	Duplicates alarms based only on the destination IP address.
xxxx	Any combination of source and destination IP address or source and destination port is considered a duplicate alarm.

For instance, assume that you have the alarms listed in Table 13-2.

Table 13-2   *Alarms*

Alarm	Source IP Address	Source Port	Destination IP Address	Destination Port
1	10.89.100.10	3201	10.90.10.100	25
2	10.89.100.10	3201	10.90.10.200	25
3	10.89.100.10	3201	10.90.10.100	25
4	10.91.10.100	2500	10.90.10.200	512
5	10.89.100.10	2300	10.90.15.100	25
6	10.89.100.10	100	10.90.10.100	80

Assuming that a specific signature is configured with the different values for the SummaryKey, the following alarms would be considered duplicate alarms:

- Alarms 1, 2, 3, 5, and 6 for SummaryKey Axxx
- Alarms (1, 3, and 6) and (2 and 4) for SummaryKey xxBx
- Alarms 1, 3, and 5 for SummaryKey Axxb
- Alarms 1 and 3 for SummaryKey AaBb
- Alarms 1, 3, and 6 for SummaryKey AxBx
- Alarms 1 through 6 for SummaryKey xxxx

NOTE   The different alarm modes base their determination of duplicate alarms only for instances of the same signature.

FireOnce

A signature configured with the FireOnce option will trigger a single alarm for a configured SummaryKey value and then wait a predefined period of time (usually specified by the ThrottleInterval parameter) before triggering another duplicate alarm for the same signature.

For instance, assume the SummaryKey value is set to Axxx. If host A causes the signature to fire, the same signature will not trigger from host A again until the time specified by the ThrottleInterval has expired.

FireAll

Configuring a signature with the FireAll option causes the signature to trigger an alarm every time activity that matches the signature's characteristics is detected. This is effectively the opposite of the FireOnce option and can generate a considerably large number of alarms during an attack.

Summarize

Like FireOnce, the Summarize mode limits the number of alarms generated and makes it difficult for an attacker to overload the sensor with alarms. With the Summarize mode, however, you also receive information on the number of times an activity that matches a signature's characteristics was observed during a specific period of time.

When using the Summarize mode, the first instance of intrusive activity triggers a normal alarm. Then, other instances of the same activity (duplicate alarms) are counted until the end of the signature's ThrottleInterval. When the length of time specified by the ThrottleInterval has elapsed, a summary alarm is sent, indicating the number of alarms that occurred during the time interval specified by the ThrottleInterval parameter.

GlobalSummarize

The GlobalSummarize mode operates similarly to the Summarize mode in that the first instance of the intrusive activity generates a normal alarm. Then, when the length of time specified by the ThrottleInterval has elapsed, a summary alarm is sent, indicating the number of alarms that occurred during the time interval specified by the ThrottleInterval parameter. The difference, however, is that the GlobalSummarize mode is based on the xxxx SummaryKey, which consolidates alarms for all address and port combinations.

Summary Mode Escalation

The variable alarming modes provide you the flexibility of having signatures that alarm on every instance of a signature, but then reduce the number of alarms generated when the number of alarms would start to significantly impact the resources on the IDS and the ability of the network security administrator to analyze the alarms being generated.

Setting the ChokeThreshold parameter enables a signature to use variable alarm summarization. In this mode, the signature needs to be configured to use one of the following initial AlarmThrottle modes:

- FireAll
- Summarize

When traffic causes the signature to trigger, the alarms are generated according to the initial AlarmThrottle mode (see Figure 13-1). If the number of alarms for the signature exceeds the value configured for the ChokeThreshold parameter (during a ThrottleInterval), the signature automatically switches to the next higher alarming mode (generating fewer alarms). If the number of alarms for the signature exceeds twice the ChokeThreshold (still during the same ThrottleInterval), the signature switches to GlobalSummarize (if not already at this level, because this is the maximum level of alarm consolidation). At the end of the ThrottleInterval, the signature reverts back to its configured alarming mode.

Figure 13-1 *Automatic Alarm Summarization*

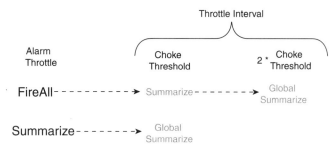

For instance, suppose that you have a signature with the following values:

- **ChokeThreshold**—10
- **ThrottleInterval**—5 seconds
- **AlarmThrottle**—FireAll
- **SummaryKey**—AxBx

Initially, every time the signature is triggered (between the same two hosts) an alarm is generated. Then if the number of alarms for the signature exceeds 10 (during a 5-second period), the signature automatically switches to Summarize mode. Finally, if the number of alarms exceeds 20 (during the same 5-second period), the signature automatically switches to GlobalSummarize mode. At the end of the ThrottleInterval (after 5 seconds), the signature reverts back to the FireAll alarming mode. After switching to one of the summarization modes, a summary alarm is generated at the end of the ThrottleInterval, indicating the number of alarms that were detected during the summarization period.

Regular Expression String Matching

Many signatures look for intrusive activity by searching for patterns in the analyzed traffic. These patterns are specified as regular expressions. You create regular expressions (regex) using a powerful and flexible notational language that enables you to describe simple and complex textual patterns. Using various special characters, you can easily specify succinct expressions that search for almost any arbitrary pattern. The regular expression syntax options (for Cisco IDS version 4.0) are shown in Table 13-3.

Table 13-3 *Regular Expression Syntax*

Meta-character	Name	Description
?	Question Mark	Repeat 0 or 1 time
*	Star, asterisk	Repeat 0 or more times
+	Plus	Repeat 1 or more times

continues

Table 13-3   *Regular Expression Syntax (Continued)*

Meta-character	Name	Description
{x}	Quantifier	Repeat exactly x times
{x,}	Minimum quantifier	Repeat at least x times
.	Dot	Matches any one character except a new line (0x0A)
[abc]	Character class	Matches any character listed
[^abc]	Negated character class	Matches any character not listed
[a–z]	Character range class	Any character listed in the range (inclusive) matches
()	Parenthesis	Used to limit the scope of other meta-characters
|	Alternation, or	Matches either expression that it separates
^	Caret	Forces match to occur at the beginning of a line
\char	Escaped character	Matches the literal character (even for meta-characters)
char	Character	Matches the literal character (unless character is a meta-character)
\r	Carriage return	Matches the carriage return (0x0D)
\n	New line	Matches the new line character (0x0A)
\t	Tab	Matches the tab character (0x09)
\f	Form feed	Matches the form feed character (0x0C)
\xNN	Escaped hexadecimal character	Matches character with the hexadecimal value specified by NN (where 0<=N<=F)
\NNN	Escaped octal character	Matches character with the octal value specified by NN (where 0<=N<=7)

Understanding regular expressions can be confusing if you are not familiar with them. To help clarify how regular expressions operate, Table 13-4 outlines numerous regular expressions in conjunction with the patterns that they try to match.

Table 13-4   *Sample Regular Expressions*

Regular Expression	String to Match
Attacker	Attacker
[Aa]ttacker	Attacker or attacker
c(ar)+s	Variations of cars, carars, carararars

Table 13-4 *Sample Regular Expressions (Continued)*

Regular Expression	String to Match
foo.*bar	foo and any number of intervening characters (except a new line) between the word bar
Earl|Jim	Either Earl or Jim
(ball|m)oon	Either balloon or moon
\[ABC\]	[ABC]
{XY}3	XYXYXY

NOTE   When creating regular expressions, the case matters. Plus, hastily creating regular expressions with wildcards can potentially lead to a large number of false positives.

Cisco IDS Alarms

Cisco IDS sensors generate an alarm when a signature is triggered. These alarms are stored on the sensor until you retrieve them with a management application (such as IDS Event Viewer [IEV] or Security Monitor). Each alarm is assigned a severity level to help prioritize the seriousness of the alarms. To indicate the changes in the flow of network traffic to your sensor, you can also see sensor status alarms.

Severity Levels

To help the network security administrators determine the potential severity of a signature when detected, each signature has an associated alarm level. These alarm levels indicate the relative seriousness of the traffic that has been detected. The defined severity levels for Cisco IDS from lowest to highest are as follows:

- Informational
- Low
- Medium
- High

NOTE   In Cisco IDS 3.x terminology, "disabled" was also considered an alarm severity level.

Sensor Status Alarms

Besides using alarms to indicate when your network is being attacked, Cisco IDS also uses specific alarms to indicate status information about the sensors on your network. The status alarms are listed in Table 13-5.

Table 13-5 *Sensor Status Alarms*

ID	Subsignature ID	Signature Name	Description
993	0	Missed Packet Count	The sensor's monitoring interface was unable to capture all the traffic on the network. This usually indicates that the monitoring interface is saturated. The alarm includes the percent of packets dropped.
994	1	Traffic Flow Started	The sensor's monitoring interface is capturing network traffic. This alarm is generated once every time the sniffing interface receives traffic. It will not trigger again until after a break in traffic (such as a 995 alarm).
994	2	Traffic Flow Started	The sensor's monitoring interface link status went from a down to an up or active state.
995	1	Traffic Flow Stopped	The sensor's monitoring interface is up and operational, but does not detect any network traffic.
995	2	Traffic Flow Stopped	The sensor's monitoring interface link status went down. This could indicate that the interface is unplugged.

These status alarms provide invaluable information about the operation of your IDS sensors, which represent the eyes and ears of your network monitoring capability. If a sensor's network connection is unplugged, for instance, you will receive notification by a 995 alarm (subsignature ID 2). This will enable you to take corrective action.

NOTE   The status alarms available in version 3.1 (such as Route Up and Down and Daemon Down) are no longer available because version 4.0 uses Remote Data Exchange Protocol (RDEP) for communication rather than PostOffice.

Cisco IDS Signature Engines

Cisco IDS monitors network traffic with a suite of signature engines. By spreading signature processing across distinct categories where all the signatures for a category share similar characteristics, you can analyze network traffic more efficiently and add your own custom signatures more easily. The signature engines fall into the categories shown in Table 13-6.

Table 13-6 *Signature Engine Categories*

Engine Category	Usage
Atomic	Used for single-packet conditions
Flood	Used to detect denial-of-service (DoS) attempts
Service	Used when services at OSI Layers 5, 6, and 7 require protocol analysis
State	Used when stateful inspection is required
String	Used for string pattern matching
Sweep	Used to detect network reconnaissance scans
Miscellaneous	Various assorted signature engines (such as Trojan and Traffic engines)

Understanding the capabilities of each of the signature engines is crucial to tuning built-in signatures and developing custom signatures that are unique to your own network environment. This section explains the various signature engines and highlights many of the parameters that you need to use to both tune built-in signatures and develop your own custom signatures. Before examining the different engines, it is helpful to understand the parameters used to define a signature.

Signature Parameters

To identify the traffic that a specific signature looks for, each signature is defined by specifying a set of parameters. Some parameters are unique to a specific signature engine, whereas other parameters are common to all signatures. All the parameters are stored in configuration files for each signature engine to parse. Each parameter falls into one of the following two groups:

- Master signature parameters
- Engine-specific parameters

NOTE   Besides creating custom signatures, end users can also *tune* the default signatures that are supplied with Cisco IDS. Therefore, the explanation of various parameters will be qualified by the following attributes:

- Protected

- Required

The *protected* attribute indicates that a parameter is part of the fundamental definition of a signature (usually these parameters are specified when a signature is initially created and then are not changed from that point on). The *required* attribute indicates that the parameter must be included as part of a signature's definition (for instance, the signature ID).

Master Signature Parameters

Master signature parameters identify characteristics common to all signatures, such as the signature ID. These parameters are individually configurable on most, if not all signatures, and are not limited to any specific signature engine. The major master signature parameters are listed in Table 13-7. (For a comprehensive list of master signature parameters, refer to the documentation on the Cisco website at http://www.cisco.com/univercd/cc/td/doc/product/iaabu/csids/csids9/idmiev/swappa.htm.)

Table 13-7   *Major Master Signature Parameters*

Parameter Name	Values	Attributes	Description
AlarmDelayTimer	1–3000	None	The number of seconds to delay further signature inspection after the signature is triggered.
AlarmInterval	2–1000 seconds	None	Defines the alarm summarization period for sliding window mode.
AlarmSeverity	High Medium Low Informational	None	The severity of the alert generated.
AlarmThrottle	FireAll FireOnce Summarize GlobalSummarize	None	Controls how many alarms are generated by the signature with the following options: **FireAll**—Sends all alarms **FireOnce**—Sends first alarm and then deletes the inspector **Summarize**—Sends an IntervalSummary alarm **GlobalSummarize**—Sends a GlobalSummary alarm

Table 13-7   *Major Master Signature Parameters (Continued)*

Parameter Name	Values	Attributes	Description
AlarmTraits	0–65535	None	User-defined trait that further describes this signature's alarm severity based on a user-defined severity scale.
ChokeThreshold	0–2147483647	None	Specifies a count of alarms that triggers variable alarm summary mode.
Enabled	True False	Required	True if signature is enabled, false otherwise.
EventAction	Log Reset ShunHost ShunConnection ZERO	None	The action(s) to be performed when the signature fires.
FlipAddr	True False	None	Swaps the source and destination information in an alarm event when set to true.
MaxInspectLength	0–2147483647	None	Defines the maximum number of bytes to inspect.
MaxTTL	0–1000	None	The maximum number of seconds to inspect a logical stream.
MinHits	0–2147483647	None	Defines the minimum number of instances of the desired traffic that must be detected before triggering the signature.
Protocol	Frag IP TCP UDP ICMP ARP Cross Zero Custom	Required	Defines the protocol to be inspected.

continues

Table 13-7 *Major Master Signature Parameters (Continued)*

Parameter Name	Values	Attributes	Description
ResetAfterIdle	2–1000	None	Defines the number of seconds to wait to reset signature counts after no traffic is seen between the hosts.
ServicePorts	Numeric	None	Comma-separated list of ports or port ranges where the target service can reside.
SigComment		None	User information about this signature.
SIGID	993–50000	Required	Numeric ID for the signature. **993–19999**—Range for default (built-in) signatures **20000–50000**—Range for custom (user-defined) signatures
SigName	<String>	None	Descriptive name for a signature.
SigStringInfo		None	Extra information included in the alarm information.
SubSig	0–65535	Required	Numeric sub-ID for a signature. Denotes a specific variant of the signature.
SummaryKey	Axxx xxBx AxBx AaBb Axxb	Required	Determines the address parameters used to constitute duplicate alarms for a specific signature.
ThrottleInterval	0–1000 seconds	None	Defines the alarm summarization period when not using the sliding window mode.
WantFrag	True False blank	None	Controls the inspection of fragmented packets. **True**—Fragment is desired **False**—Fragment not desired **blank**—Accept both

By default, Cisco IDS treats the source IP address of the intrusive traffic as the attacker's IP address. The FlipAddr parameter is useful in situations in which the traffic that the signature is matching comes from the target system (instead of the attacker's system). In these situations, by setting the FlipAddr parameter to true, you can override the signature's default behavior and correctly identify the destination IP address of the offending traffic as the attacker.

Sometimes, you want to limit the search for your intrusive traffic within a data stream. The MaxInspectLength parameter enables you to limit your search within a data stream to a specified maximum number of bytes from the beginning of the data stream.

Engine-Specific Parameters

Along with the parameters common to every signature, each signature engine also has its own specific signature parameters. These parameters enable the efficient creation of signatures without an unwanted number of extra and unnecessary parameters being tagged onto every signature that you create. The following sections explain some of the major engine-specific parameters and describe the signature engines themselves.

Atomic Signature Engines

The six different signature engines shown in Table 13-8 handle all the Atomic signatures. Each of these engines is designed to efficiently support signatures that trigger based on information in a single packet. Whenever a packet that matches a configured signature is detected, the appropriate signature engine triggers an alarm. The different Atomic engines are each constructed to efficiently handle searching different types of traffic streams (such as ICMP, TCP, and UDP).

Table 13-8   *Atomic Signature Engines*

Engine	Description
ATOMIC.ARP	ARP simple and cross-packet signatures
ATOMIC.ICMP	ICMP alarms based on these ICMP parameters: type, code, sequence, and ID
ATOMIC.IPOPTIONS	Alarms based on the decoding of Layer 3 options
ATOMIC.L3.IP	Layer 3 IP alarms
ATOMIC.TCP	TCP packet alarms based on these parameters: port, destination, flags, and simple packet regular expressions
ATOMIC.UDP	UDP packet alarms based on these parameters: port, direction, and data length

NOTE   The Atomic signature engines ignore the ResetAfterIdle and MaxInspectLength master
signature parameters.

Because these Atomic signature engines examine single packets, they do not need to
maintain state. Therefore, the Atomic engines do not store any persistent data across
multiple data packets.

ATOMIC.ARP Engine Parameters

ATOMIC.ARP enables you to support basic Layer 2 Address Resolution Protocol (ARP)
signatures (refer to RFC 826, "An Ethernet Address Resolution Protocol"). Numerous tools
are available that enable an attacker to attack your network at the link layer, such as dsniff
and ettercap. The ATOMIC.ARP signature engine enables Cisco IDS to easily detect the
usage of these tools on your network and is a new feature of version 4.0. To tune existing
ATOMIC.ARP signatures or create your own custom signatures, you need to understand
the parameters shown in Table 13-9.

Table 13-9   *ATOMIC.ARP Engine Parameters*

Parameter Name	Values	Attributes	Description
ArpOperation	0–255	None	The ARP operation code that this signature will match on
MacFlip	0–65535	None	Fires an alarm when the MAC address for an IP address changes more than this number of times
RequestInbalance	0–65535	None	Fires an alarm when there are this many more ARP requests than replies for an IP address
wantDstBroadcast	True False	None	If true, fires an alarm for this signature when an ARP message has a destination Ethernet address of FFFFFF
wanSrcBroadcast	True False	None	If true, fires an alarm for this signature when an ARP message has a source Ethernet address of FFFFFF

NOTE   Although none of the ATOMIC.ARP engine parameters are required, in practice, you need
to specify at least one parameter to make a useful signature. If you do not specify any of the
parameters, the signature will match on every ARP packet that is processed.

The ArpOperation enables you to create alarms based on a specific ARP operation code. The normal two ARP operations codes are as follows:

- ARP request (1)

- ARP reply (2)

The RequestInBalance causes a signature to trigger if more ARP requests than replies are detected for a specific IP address. Normally, the requests and replies are matched up one to one so an imbalance can indicate malicious activity.

A normal ARP request is sent to the broadcast Ethernet address so that every system on a segment can see the request and potentially respond. Seeing a broadcast Ethernet address in any other situation (such as in the Ethernet source address) is probably an indication of potential intrusive activity and should be investigated. The wantDstBroadcast and wantSrcBroadcast enable you to create ARP signatures that look for traffic in which either the destination or source Ethernet address is the broadcast address.

ATOMIC.ICMP Engine Parameters

The ATOMIC.ICMP engine is specialized to support signatures that inspect Internet Control Message Protocol (ICMP) packets. The major parameters are listed in Table 13-10.

Table 13-10   *ATOMIC.ICMP Engine Parameters*

Parameter Name	Values	Attributes	Description
IcmpCode	0–255	None	The value for the ICMP header Code to match
IcmpId	0–65535	None	The value for the ICMP header Identifier to match
IcmpMaxCode	0–255	None	ICMP Code values above this value trigger alarms
IcmpMaxSeq	0–65535	None	ICMP Seq values above this value trigger alarms
IcmpMinCode	0–255	None	ICMP Code values below this value trigger alarms
IcmpMinSeq	0–65535	None	ICMP Seq values below this value triggers alarms
IcmpSeq	0–65535	None	The value for the ICMP header Sequence to match
IcmpType	0–255	None	The value for the ICMP header Type to match
IpTOS	0–255	None	The value for the IP header Type Of Service (TOS) to match

This engine has many parameters that enable you to efficiently detect specific ICMP traffic on your network. The parameters are divided into single-value parameters as well as boundary values that enable you to specify a minimum of maximum value. None of the ATOMIC.ICMP engine parameters are required, so you can easily create a signature from the simple "any ICMP packet" to very complex signatures.

You can specify single values for the following ICMP header fields:

- Code
- Identifier
- Sequence
- Type

NOTE   For more information on ICMP codes and types, see the "FLOOD.HOST.ICMP Engine Parameters" section later in this chapter.

Besides the ICMP header fields, you can also specify a single value for the Type Of Service (TOS) field in the IP header. These signatures look for packets in which the specified single value matches the field in the packet being inspected. You can use all the single values in a single packet, but it is not very practical unless there is a reason to alarm on an ICMP packet in which all the individual fields must match specific values.

In some situations, you want to create signatures that trigger on a range of values for a specific field rather than a single value. You can specify a range of values for the following two ICMP header fields:

- Code
- Sequence

You configure a range by specifying a minimum value and or a maximum value. ICMP packets, in which the actual value is less than the configured minimum value or greater than the configured maximum value, cause the signature to trigger.

ATOMIC.IPOPTIONS Engine Parameters

ATOMIC.IPOPTIONS is a simple engine that decodes Layer 3 (IP) options. The major parameters for this engine are listed in Table 13-11.

Table 13-11   *ATOMIC.IPOPTIONS Engine Parameters*

Parameter Name	Values	Attributes	Description
HasBadOption	True False	None	If true, matches when a packet with malformed options is detected
IpOption	0–255	None	The IP option code to match

IP options provide optional information for the IP datagram. The major options are as follows:

- Security and handling restrictions (IP option 2)
- Record route (IP option 7)
- Time stamp (IP option 4)
- Loose source routing (IP option 3)
- Strict source routing (IP option 9)

You can specify a specific IP option to search for using the IpOption parameter. The only other option is the HasBadOption parameter. By setting this parameter to true, you cause the signature to trigger when a packet with an invalid option is detected (refer to RFC 1812).

ATOMIC.L3.IP Engine Parameters

The ATOMIC.L3.IP signature engine is a general-purpose engine that inspects network packets at the Internet Protocol (IP) layer (Layer 3). The major engine parameters are shown in Table 13-12.

Table 13-12 *ATOMIC.L3.IP Engine Parameters*

Parameter Name	Values	Attributes	Description
MaxDataLen	0–65535	None	Triggers an alarm if the IP data length exceeds this value.
MaxProto	0–255	None	Triggers an alarm if the IP protocol value is greater than this value.
MinDataLen	0–65535	None	Triggers an alarm if the IP data length is less than this value.
MinProto	0–255	None	Triggers an alarm if the IP protocol value is less than this value.
isIcmp	True False	None	Only examines ICMP packets.
isImpossiblePacket	True False	None	Triggers an alarm if the source IP address of the packet equals the destination IP address.
isLocalhost	True False	None	The local host IP address (127.0.0.1) is seen in an IP packet.
isOverrun	True False	None	Triggers an alarm when a fragment overrun is detected.
isRFC1918	True False	None	Triggers an alarm if an IP address in the packet is a reserved IP address specified by RFC 1918.

This engine inspects specific fields in the IP header, such as the following:

- IP Packet Length
- IP Protocol
- Source IP Address
- Destination IP Address

You can search for packets that contain IP protocol values outside of a specific range (defined by the MaxProto and MinProto parameters). You can also search for packets in which the size falls outside a specified range (defined by the MaxDataLen and MinDataLen parameters).

Besides ranges, you can also specify several address checks that search for packets in which the IP addresses match certain known conditions, such as the following:

- IsImpossiblePacket (source equals destination)
- IsLocalhost (127.0.0.1 IP address)
- isRFC1918 (nonroutable addresses)

You can also use the isOverrun parameter to create signatures that search fragmented packets to find situations in which the fragments overlap.

ATOMIC.TCP Engine Parameters

The ATOMIC.TCP signature engine is designed to support TCP signatures. These signatures identify traffic based on the various TCP fields, such as source and destination ports, or the contents of the packet's data. The major parameters associated with this signature engine are listed in Table 13-13.

Table 13-13 *ATOMIC.TCP Engine Parameters*

Parameter Name	Values	Attributes	Description
DstPort	0–65535	None	A single destination port to match.
Mask	FIN SYN RST PSH ACK URG ZERO	Required	The mask used when checking the TCP flags. This field indicates the TCP flags that you want to include in your checking.

Table 13-13 *ATOMIC.TCP Engine Parameters (Continued)*

Parameter Name	Values	Attributes	Description
PortRange	0–2	None	Specifies the destination port range to match: **0**—All ports **1**—Only low ports (0–1024) **2**—Only high ports (1025–65535)
PortRangeSource	0–2	None	Specifies the source port range to match: **0**—All ports **1**—Only low ports (0–1024) **2**—Only high ports (1025–65535)
SinglePacketRegex	\<string\>	None	A regular expression to search for in a single TCP packet.
SrcPort	0–65535	None	A single source port to match.
TcpFlags	FIN SYN RST PSH ACK URG ZERO	Required	The TCP flags (out of the flags included in the mask) that need to be set for the signature to trigger.

When specifying signatures with the ATOMIC.TCP signature engine, you must specify the Mask and TcpFlags parameters. The Mask parameter essentially identifies the TCP flags that you are interested in, whereas the TcpFlags parameter indicates which of the TCP flags need to be set. Any TCP flags that you do not include in the mask cannot have an impact on whether the signature triggers. For instance, assume that you set the Mask parameter to include FIN and ACK and the TcpFlags parameter to include only FIN. The signature will trigger only based on the values of the FIN and ACK flags in the packets. (All the other TCP flags in the packet are ignored.) Packets will trigger the signature as follows:

- If the ACK and FIN flags are set, the signature will not trigger.
- If the FIN flag is set and the ACK flag is not set, the signature will trigger (regardless of the settings for the other TCP flags).
- If the FIN flag is not set, the signature will not trigger.

ATOMIC.UDP Engine Parameters

The ATOMIC.UDP signature engine is specially designed to support User Datagram Protocol (UDP) signatures. These are Layer 4 or transport layer signatures. The major signature engine parameters are shown in Table 13-14.

Table 13-14   *ATOMIC.UDP Engine Parameters*

Parameter Name	Values	Attributes	Description
DstPort	0–65535	None	A single destination port to match
MinUDPLength	0–65535	None	Triggers an alarm if a UDP packet with a length less than this is detected
ShortUDPLength	True False	None	Fires an alarm if the UDP length in the packet indicates a size smaller than specified by the IP packet length
SrcPort	0–65535	None	A single source port to match

This basic engine provides the capability to examine ports and packet lengths. You can search for specific ports using the DstPort and SrcPort parameters. You can also search for UDP packets that are smaller than a specified size using the MinUDPLength parameter.

A UDP packet contains two length fields, a length in the IP header that indicates the entire length of the IP packet along with a length in the UDP header that indicates the size of the UDP payload. Using the ShortUDPLength parameter, you can create signatures that trigger on packets in which the length in the IP header indicates that the length in the UDP header should be larger than it is.

Because none of the parameters are required, you can easily create signatures from the basic "any UDP packet" to more complex signatures.

NOTE   Although none of the parameters for the ATOMIC.UDP signature engine are required, you must at least specify one of the parameters when creating a signature.

Flood Signature Engines

The Flood engines fall into the following two categories:

- Host
- Net

The Host Flood engines analyze traffic directed at one specific destination host from many source hosts. They attach a packets-per-second (PPS) rate counter to a specific destination address, with the sampling being done on a per-second basis.

The FLOOD.NET engine analyzes the aggregate traffic on the entire network segment. These signatures are many to many and generate a PPS counter for a sensor rather than a specific address. Sampling is also done on a per-second basis.

The Flood engines ignore the WantFrag, MaxInspectLength, and ResetAfterIdle master signature parameters.

The Flood signature engines are shown in Table 13-15.

Table 13-15 *Flood Signature Engines*

Engine	Description
FLOOD.HOST.ICMP	Flood signatures based on ICMP packets
FLOOD.HOST.UDP	Flood signatures based on UDP traffic that enables you to exclude up to three source and destination ports from signature analysis
FLOOD.NET	Flood signatures that use Gap, Peaks, and Rate to trigger a flood of TCP, UDP, and ICMP traffic

FLOOD.HOST.ICMP Engine Parameters

The FLOOD.HOST.ICMP signature engine supports signatures that detect ICMP traffic coming from many source hosts to a single destination host. The major engine-specific parameters are shown in Table 13-16.

Table 13-16 *FLOOD.HOST.ICMP Engine Parameters*

Parameter Name	Values	Attributes	Description
IcmpType	0–255	None	The value to match for the ICMP header TYPE
Rate	0–2147483647	Required	The maximum PPS required to trigger a flood

These signatures identify traffic floods based on either all ICMP traffic if you do not specify the IcmpType parameter or specific ICMP traffic floods based on one of the following ICMP types:

- Echo reply (Type 0)
- Destination unreachable (Type 3)
- Source quench (Type 4)
- Redirect (Type 5)

- Echo request (Type 8)
- Router advertisement (Type 9)
- Router solicitation (Type 10)
- Time exceeded (Type 11)
- Parameter problem (Type 12)
- Time stamp request (Type 13)
- Time stamp reply (Type 14)
- Information request (Type 15)
- Information reply (Type 16)
- Address mask request (Type 17)
- Address mask reply (Type 18)

You must specify the maximum rate (using the Rate parameter) required for the specified ICMP traffic to trigger an alarm.

FLOOD.HOST.UDP Engine Parameters

The FLOOD.HOST.UDP signature engine supports signatures that detect floods of UDP traffic to a specific host on your network. The major engine-specific parameters are shown in Table 13-17.

Table 13-17   *FLOOD.HOST.UDP Engine Parameters*

Parameter Name	Values	Attributes	Description
ExcludeDst1	0–65535	None	The destination port to be excluded from analysis by the flood signature
ExcludeDst2	0–65535	None	The destination port to be excluded from analysis by the flood signature
ExcludeDst3	0–65535	None	The destination port to be excluded from analysis by the flood signature
ExcludeSrc1	0–65535	None	The source port to be excluded from analysis by the flood signature
ExcludeSrc2	0–65535	None	The source port to be excluded from analysis by the flood signature
ExcludeSrc3	0–65535	None	The source port to be excluded from analysis by the flood signature
Rate	0–2147483647	Required	The maximum PPS required to trigger a flood

To help reduce the number of false positives, you can specify three excluded source ports and three excluded destination ports. Traffic coming from or going to these excluded ports is excluded from analysis by the FLOOD.HOST.UDP signature engine.

Besides the optional excluded ports, the only required parameter at the engine level is the Rate parameter. You need to specify the maximum amount of traffic (in PPS) required to indicate intrusive or abnormal activity that generates an alarm and should be analyzed.

FLOOD.NET Engine Parameters

The final Flood signature engine is the FLOOD.NET signature engine that is designed to support flood signatures that are triggered by a flood of traffic against your entire network (as opposed to a single host). The major engine-specific parameters are shown in Table 13-18.

Table 13-18   *FLOOD.NET Engine Parameters*

Parameter Name	Values	Attributes	Description
Gap	0–2147483647	None	Defines an interval (in seconds) at which the peak count is reset to 0 if the matched traffic remains below the defined rate.
IcmpType	0–255	None	The value to match for the ICMP header Type. This parameter is only valid if the Protocol master signature parameter is set to ICMP.
Peaks	0–2147483647	None	Defines the maximum period of time (above the specified rate) necessary to trigger the signature.
Rate	0–2147483647	Required	The maximum PPS required to trigger a flood.

When defining signatures for this engine, you need to first determine which type of traffic you will monitor. You specify the traffic type using the Protocol master engine parameter. If you set this value to be ICMP, you can also specify a specific type of ICMP traffic using the IcmpType parameter.

Next you need to the following three parameters that define the amount of traffic that constitutes a flood:

- Gap
- Peaks
- Rate

With the Rate parameter, you specify the maximum time interval that the monitored traffic is allowed to exceed the specified rate before triggering the signature. The parameter works in conjunction with the Peaks parameter. The Peaks parameter defines the maximum period of time in seconds (during a given ThrottleInterval) that the monitored traffic must remain above the specified rate to trigger the signature. The final parameter, Gap, indicates how long the monitored traffic must remain below the specified rate before the peak count is reset to zero (during a ThrottleInterval).

When setting the parameters for a FLOOD.NET signature, the hardest task is determining the appropriate values to use for the Rate parameter because it varies from one network to the next. Therefore, to assist you in calculating the rate, you can run the signature in diagnostic mode or feedback mode.

Diagnostic Mode

Determining the rate at which certain traffic normally occurs on the network can be a very challenging task because it varies from network to network. Therefore, by specifying a rate of zero, you can place a Flood.Net signature in diagnostic mode. In this mode, the signature will trigger informational alarms that indicate the rate of traffic observed (that matches the signature) during each ThrottleInterval. This information will be provided in the Alarm details field (as a textual string such as MaxPPS=xyz). By running the signature in diagnostic mode over a period of time, you can determine what the normal rate of the traffic is for each FLOOD.NET signature. Then you can define a rate that is above the measured normal rate so that the flood signatures will indicate abnormal network activity that needs to be investigated.

OTHER Signature Engine

The OTHER signature engine handles signatures that do not fit into the other protocol engine decoders. The OTHER engine enables you to specify parameters (similar to other engines) that are then used by specialized processors in the system. Some common examples of these signatures are the sensor status alarms that indicate changes in the flow of traffic to the sensor. The major engine-specific parameters are shown in Table 13-19.

Table 13-19 *OTHER Engine Parameters*

Parameter Name	Values	Attributes	Description
HijackMaxOldAck	0–2147483647	None	Defines the maximum number of old, dateless client-to-server ACKs allowed before triggering a Hijack signature
HijackReset	True False	None	If true, requires a reset to be detected by the Hijack signature

Table 13-19 *OTHER Engine Parameters (Continued)*

Parameter Name	Values	Attributes	Description
ServicePorts	<port list>	None	A comma-separated list of ports or port ranges at which the Secure Shell [SSH] service can reside
SynFloodMaxEmbrionic	0–2147483647	None	The maximum number of simultaneous embryonic connections allowed to any service needed to trigger the signature
TrafficFlowTimeout	0–2147483647	None	The number of seconds that must expire without any traffic to trigger the signature

NOTE You cannot define custom signatures for the OTHER engine because these signatures are supported by custom code.

Service Signature Engines

The Service signature engines analyze traffic above the basic UDP and TCP transport layers. Each of these signature engines has detailed knowledge of the service that it examines. This includes decoding application layer protocols such as Remote Procedure Call (RPC), Simple Mail Transport Protocol (SMTP), and Network Time Protocol (NTP). By decoding the traffic payloads similar to the actual applications, the Service signature engines can accurately detect attack traffic while minimizing false positives. The various Service signature engines are shown in Table 13-20.

Table 13-20 *Service Signature Engines*

Engine	Description
SERVICE.DNS	Examines TCP and UDP DNS packets
SERVICE.FTP	Examines File Transfer Protocol (FTP) port command traffic
SERVICE.GENERIC	Emergency response engine to support rapid signature response
SERVICE.HTTP	Examines Hypertext Transport Protocol (HTTP) traffic using string-based pattern matching
SERVICE.IDENT	Examines IDENT protocol (RFC 1413) traffic
SERVICE.MSSQL	Examines traffic used by Microsoft SQL Server
SERVICE.NTP	Examines NTP traffic

continues

Table 13-20   *Service Signature Engines (Continued)*

Engine	Description
SERVICE.RPC	Examines RPC traffic
SERVICE.SMB	Examines Server Message Block (SMB) traffic
SERVICE.SMTP	Examines SMTP traffic
SERVICE.SNMP	Examines Simple Network Management Protocol (SNMP) traffic
SERVICE.SSH	Examines SSH traffic

NOTE   The Service engines do not use the ResetAfterIdle, WantFrag, or MaxInspectLength master engine parameters.

The SERVICE.SMTP engine is actually a predefined state machine that enables you to configure pattern matches for different states in the SMTP protocol. Therefore, this engine is explained in the "State Signature Engines" section later in this chapter.

SERVICE.DNS Engine Parameters

The SERVICE.DNS signature engine performs advanced decodes of DNS traffic. This includes detecting various anti-evasion techniques such as following multiple jumps in the DNS payload. This engine is a consolidation of the SERVICE.DNS.TCP and SERVICE.DNS.UDP signature engines that were available in the 3.x releases. The Protocol master engine parameter enables you to select between UDP and TCP signatures. The major engine-specific signature parameters for the SERVICE.DNS signature engine are shown in Table 13-21.

Table 13-21   *SERVICE.DNS Engine Parameters*

Parameter Name	Values	Attributes	Description
QueryChaosString	<string>	None	Defines the DNS query class chaos string to match
QueryClass	0–65535	None	Defines the DNS query class 2-byte value to match
QueryInvalidDomainName	True False	None	If true, matches when the DNS query length > 255
QueryJumpCountExceeded	True False	None	DNS compression counter

Table 13-21 *SERVICE.DNS Engine Parameters (Continued)*

Parameter Name	Values	Attributes	Description
QueryOpcode	0–255	None	Defines the DNS query opcode value.
QueryRecordDataInvalid	True False	None	If true, matches when the DNS record data is incomplete.
QueryRecordDataLength	0–2147483647	None	Determines the DNS response data length.
QuerySrcPort53	True False	None	If true, matches if the DNS query comes from port 53. If false, matches if the DNS query does not come from port 53.
QueryStreamLen	0–2147483647	None	Matches when the DNS packet length is greater than this value.
QueryType	0–65535	None	Defines the DNS query type to match.
QueryValue	True False	None	If true matches when the DNS request is a query. When false, matches when the DNS request is a response.

The engine-specific parameters for the SERVICE.DNS engine enable you to specify specific values for the following DNS fields:

- Chaos String
- Class
- Opcode
- Type

You can apply your signatures to either DNS response packets or DNS request packets using the QueryValue parameter. If this parameter is set to true, the signature triggers if the traffic is a DNS request. Similarly, you can determine whether a DNS query originates from port 53 using the QuerySrcPort53 parameter.

You can check the size of the domain name using the QueryInvalidDomainName parameter. If this parameter is set to true, the signature triggers if the domain name is greater than 255 characters.

Finally, you can also create signature DNS signatures that trigger if the DNS packet length is greater than a certain value. You define this value by using the QueryStreamLen parameter.

SERVICE.FTP Engine Parameters

The STRING.TCP engine is useful for creating many string-based FTP signatures. Certain signatures, however, are not appropriate for the String signature engines. The SERVICE.FTP signature fills this gap by providing an engine that supports signatures specifically centered on the FTP **port** command. This engine decodes FTP **port** commands and traps invalid **port** commands or attacks based on the **port** command. The control traffic is only examined on port 21 traffic because port 20 is used by FTP to transport only data traffic. The major engine-specific parameters for the SERVICE.FTP signature engine are shown in Table 13-22.

Table 13-22 *SERVICE.FTP Engine Parameters*

Parameter Name	Values	Attributes	Description
BadPortCmdAddress	True False	None	If true, matches when an invalid address is specified in a **port** command.
BadPortCmdPort	True False	None	If true, matches when an invalid port is specified in a **port** command.
BadPortCmdShort	True False	None	If true, matches when the **port** command is malformed (too short).
Direction	ANY FromService ToService	None	ToService or FromService determines whether the signature matches on traffic to or from the FTP service port. ANY matches for traffic in both directions.
ServicePorts	<port list>	None	A comma-separated list of ports or port ranges on which to look for the FTP traffic.
IsPASV	True False	None	If true, matches when a port spoof is detected.

The ServicePorts parameter enables you to define on which ports the signature engine will perform its analysis. By default this parameter is set to port 21, but you can alter it if you happen to use other ports for the FTP protocol. In conjunction with this parameter, you can use the Direction parameter to indicate whether the signature will trigger on traffic to the service port, from the service port, or in either direction.

You can specify the following three Boolean parameters that relate to the validity of the actual FTP **port** commands analyzed by the engine:

- BadPortCmdAddress
- BadPortCmdPort
- BadPortCmdShort

Finally, you can use the IsPASV parameter to cause your signature to trigger when a PASV port spoof is detected in the analyzed traffic.

SERVICE.GENERIC Engine Parameters

The SERVICE.GENERIC is an unusual signature engine. You will not use this engine to create regular custom signatures. Instead, this signature engine is designed as an emergency-response engine that supports rapid signature response. The major engine-specific parameters are shown in Table 13-23.

Table 13-23 *SERVICE.GENERIC Engine Parameters*

Parameter Name	Values	Attributes	Description
DstPort	0–65535	None	The destination port of interest for this signature.
IntermediateInstructions	<string>	Protected	Assembly or machine code in string form. This field is for expert use only.
PayloadSource	FullTcpStream ICMPData L2Header L3Header L4Header TCPData UDPData	None	Identifies where to begin payload search.
SrcPort	0–65535	None	The source port of interest for this signature.

The signatures supported by this engine use assembly language and machine code to define how the signatures process different parts of the analyzed packets. These signatures can search various payload sources to locate intrusive activity.

CAUTION	Creating signatures using the SERVICE.GENERIC signature engine requires an expert level of understanding to create the appropriate assembly language instructions and is not intended for use by normal users.

SERVICE.HTTP Engine Parameters

The SERVICE.HTTP signature engine provides regular expression, based pattern inspection specifically designed to analyze HTTP. The major engine-specific parameters are shown in Table 13-24.

Table 13-24   *SERVICE.HTTP Engine Parameters*

Parameter Name	Values	Attributes	Description
UriRegex	<string>	Protected	The regular expression used to search for a pattern in the URI section of the HTTP request. The URI is after the valid HTTP method and before the first <cr><lf> or argument delimiter (?&).
ArgNameRegex	<string>	Protected	The regular expression used to search for a pattern in the Arguments section.
ArgValueRegex	<string>	Protected	The regular expression used to search for a pattern in the Arguments section after the ArgNameRegex is matched.
HeaderRegex	<string>	Protected	The regular expression used to search for a pattern in the header section.
RequestRegex	<string>	Protected	The regular expression used to search for a pattern anywhere in the entire HTTP request.
MaxUriFieldLength	0–4294967295	None	Specifies the maximum URI length considered normal.
MaxArgFieldLength	0–4294967295	None	Specifies the maximum Argument field length considered normal.

Table 13-24   *SERVICE.HTTP Engine Parameters (Continued)*

Parameter Name	Values	Attributes	Description
MaxHeaderFieldLength	0–4294967295	None	Specifies the maximum header field length considered normal.
MaxRequestFieldLength	0–4294967295	None	Specifies the maximum HTTP request length considered normal.
Deobfuscate	True False	None	Determines whether to perform anti-evasion HTTP de-obfuscation before examining the HTTP request.
ServicePorts	<port list>	Required	A comma-separated list of ports or port ranges to search for the HTTP traffic.
MinRequestMatchLength	0–4294967295	None	The minimum number of bytes that the UriRegex must match.

The pattern-matching functionality provided by the SERVICE.HTTP signature engine is enabled through the implementation of various regex strings. These regex strings search the following different portions of a regular HTTP message (see Figure 13-2):

- Entire HTTP request
- HTTP header
- URI
- Arguments and Entity body

Figure 13-2   *Sample HTTP Request*

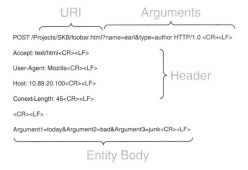

The URI identifies the file or resource that the HTTP request attempts to access. The UriRegex parameter specifies a regular expression that searches this field. The URI begins after the HTTP method (such as GET or POST) and goes up to the first <CR><LF> or argument delimiter (? or &) that is detected.

Setting the HeaderRegex results in searches of the HTTP header for the specified pattern. The header section begins after the first <CR><LF> and ends when a double <CR><LF> combination is detected.

Searching the Arguments section involves the following two parameters:

- ArgNameRegex
- ArgValueRegex

The ArgNameRegex is a regex that identifies the name of the argument that you look for in the HTTP request. If the ArgNameRegex is found, the signature uses the ArgValueRegex regular expression to search for a specific value after the argument is located. These two regular expressions search for arguments in the following two places (see Figure 13-2):

- After the URI, beginning with the argument delimiter (? or &) and ending at the first <CR><LF>
- The Entity body section of the HTTP request

You can also specify the RequestRegex parameter. This regex identifies a pattern that the signature will search for anywhere in the entire HTTP request. Sometimes you want the signature to trigger if the pattern matched by the RequestRegex regular expression is larger than a specified size. Using the MinRequestMatchLength, you cause the signature to only trigger if the RequestRegex is found and the size of the pattern matched is larger than the value specified by the MinRequestMatchLength parameter.

NOTE   The MinRequestMatchLength parameter is only applicable when the RequestRegex contains an iterator (* or +) that enables the pattern to match on variable-length patterns.

Besides pattern matching, you can also specify the following parameters that indicate maximum field values:

- MaxUriFieldLength
- MaxArgFieldLength
- MaxHeaderFieldLength
- MaxRequestFieldLength

If the length of any of these fields exceeds the specified value, the signature will trigger. These parameters enable you to generate alarms if any of these fields are abnormally large in an HTTP request.

The ServicePorts parameter enables you to indicate on which ports the signature should look for HTTP traffic. By default, web servers run on port 80, but many people use various other ports, such as 8080. You need to configure this parameter based on your network configuration.

NOTE Because HTTP pattern matching requires a lot of sensor resources (memory and CPU), if a valid HTTP method (GET, HEAD, or POST) is not detected in the first 20 bytes of the HTTP request, HTTP inspection processing is stopped for the entire data stream.

SERVICE.IDENT Engine Parameters

The Identification protocol (IDENT) is defined by RFC 1413. Basically, it is a service that enables a remote system to gain information about the user who attempts to make a TCP connection with it. Numerous security problems have been associated with this protocol, which normally runs on port 113. The major engine-specific parameters for the SERVICE.IDENT engine are shown in Table 13-25.

Table 13-25   *SERVICE.IDENT Engine Parameters*

Parameter Name	Values	Attributes	Description
Direction	FromService ToService	None	Determines whether the signature matches on traffic to the service port or from the service port.
MaxBytes	0–65535	None	Defines the maximum number of bytes in the payload that is considered normal.
ServicePorts	<port list>	None	Comma-separated list of ports or port ranges on which the service can reside.
HasBadPort	True False	None	If true, the signature matches when a bad port number is detected in the payload.
HasNewLine	True False	None	If true, the signature matches when a nonterminating, new line character is detected in the payload.

The SERVICE.IDENT signature performs a basic decode of the IDENT protocol and enables you to look for abnormal IDENT packets. Setting the HasBadPort parameter to true causes the signature to trigger if the packet contains a bad port number. Similarly, setting

HasNewLine to true causes the signature to trigger if the packet contains any new line characters besides the one signaling the end of the IDENT request.

Like SERVICE.HTTP, you can specify the ports on which the IDENT traffic can be found. The SERVICE.IDENT signatures examine all traffic for the ports specified by the Service-Ports parameter. Using the Direction parameter, you control whether the signature checks for traffic to the service port or from the service port.

Finally, you can check for buffer overflow attacks by using the MaxBytes parameter. Any IDENT request that is larger than this value causes your signature to trigger.

SERVICE.MSSQL Engine Parameters

The SERVICE.MSSQL signature engine inspects the protocol used by Microsoft SQL Server (MSSQL). The major engine-specific parameters are listed in Table 13-26.

Table 13-26 *SERVICE.MSSQL Engine Parameters*

Parameter Name	Values	Attributes	Description
SqlUsername	<string>	None	Determines the username (exact match) to match for a user logging in to the MSSQL service
PasswordPresent	True False	None	If true, the signature matches if a password is not provided in the MSSQL login request

Using the SqlUsername parameter, you can specify a username that will cause the signature to trigger if the engine detects this username in a login request sent to the SQL Server. This parameter is the exact username (specified as a string and not as a regular expression) that will cause the signature to trigger.

You can also use the PasswordPresent parameter to search for login attempts that do not specify a password. If this parameter is set to true, the signature triggers on any login attempts to the SQL Server that do not specify a password.

SERVICE.NTP Engine Parameters

The SERVICE.NTP signature engine inspects Network Time Protocol (NTP) traffic. NTP enables systems on your network to synchronize their system clocks and is defined by RFC 1305. The major engine-specific parameters are shown in Table 13-27.

Table 13-27   *SERVICE.NTP Engine Parameters*

Parameter Name	Values	Attributes	Description
Mode	0–0xffff	None	Specifies the mode of operation for the NTP packets (RFC 1305) to match. (0–7 are normal defined values).
MaxSizeOfControlData	0–0xffff	None	Maximum amount of data in a control packet that is considered normal.
ControlOpCode	0–0xffff	None	The opcode number of an NTP control packet to match.
IsInvalidDataPacket	True False	None	If true, signature matches when the structure of the NTP data packet is incorrect.
IsNonNtpTraffic	True False	None	If true, signature matches when the traffic examined is not NTP traffic.

Using the Mode parameter, you can create signatures that check the mode of operation specified in the packet. The NTP modes (from RFC 1305) are as follows:

- Unspecified (Mode 0)
- Symmetric Active (Mode 1)
- Symmetric Passive (Mode 2)
- Client (Mode 3)
- Server (Mode 4)
- Broadcast (Mode 5)
- NTP Control Message (Mode 6)
- Reserved (Mode 7)

The ControlOpCode parameter configures your signature to trigger based on specific NTP commands. The NTP commands are as follows:

- Read Status (Opcode 1)
- Read Variables (Opcode 2)
- Write Variables (Opcode 3)
- Read Clock Variables (Opcode 4)
- Write Clock Variable (Opcode 5)
- Set Trap Address/Port (Opcode 6)
- Trap Response (Opcode 7)

Setting the IsNonNtpTraffic parameter to true causes your signature to trigger when the traffic being analyzed is not NTP traffic. Similarly, setting the IsInvalidDataPacket parameter to true causes the signature to trigger if the structure of the NTP message is malformed (but is still recognizable as an NTP message).

Finally, you can search for abnormally large NTP messages using the MaxSizeOfControlData parameter. It enables you to define the maximum size of an NTP message before the signature triggers an alarm.

SERVICE.RPC Engine Parameters

Remote Procedure Call (RPC) is a protocol that one program can use to request a specific service from a program located on another computer across the network (refer to RFC 1057). The SERVICE.RPC engine provides signatures for detecting attacks against UNIX systems with the SUNRPC (Sun Microsystem's Remote Procedure Call) protocol enabled. The major engine-specific parameters for the SERVICE.RPC engine are shown in Table 13-28.

Table 13-28 *SERVICE.RPC Engine Parameters*

Parameter Name	Values	Attributes	Description
Direction	ToService FromService	None	ToService or FromService specifies whether traffic is matched going to or from the service port.
PortMapProgram	0–99999	None	The program number sent to the portmapper that this signature is interested in.
RpcMaxLength	0–99999	None	Defines the maximum RPC message length considered normal.
RpcProcedure	0–65535	None	The RPC procedure number that this signature will match on.
RpcProgram	0–99999	None	The RPC program number that this signature will match on.
ServicePorts	<port list>	None	Comma-separated list of ports or port ranges on which the service can reside.
Unique	2–40	None	Identifies the number of unique port connections allowed until the signature fires. To be valid, the isSweep parameter must be set to true.
IsPortMapper	True False	None	True means the signature is interested in port 111 traffic (portmapper), false if it is not.

Table 13-28 *SERVICE.RPC Engine Parameters (Continued)*

Parameter Name	Values	Attributes	Description
IsSpoolSrc	True False	None	Matches when the source address is 127.0.0.1.
IsSweep	True False	None	True if this is a sweep signature, false otherwise. Must be set to true for the Unique parameter to be valid.

NOTE   The SERVICE.RPC signature engine consolidates the following 3.x signature engines:

- SERVICE.RPC
- SERVICE.PORTMAP
- SWEEP.RPC

RPC has a utility that provides the port numbers for various services that run on a system. RPC-based sweep signatures are signatures that involve an attacker attempting to send RPC traffic for a single RPC program number to multiple ports on a single target system.

When configuring the RPC sweep signatures, you need to configure three parameters:

- RpcProgram
- Unique
- isSweep

The isSweep parameter needs to be set to true to indicate that the signature is a sweep. The RpcProgram is just a number that indicates the unique RPC program number that the signature will match on, whereas the Unique parameter specifies the maximum number of RPC packets (for the specified RPCProgram number to different destination ports) that constitute an attack. For instance, if you create a signature with a value of 100003 for the RpcProgram parameter and a Unique value of 6, any time that a single host receives RPC packets to six different destination ports in which the RPC program is 100003, the signature will fire. These signatures are similar to regular port sweep signatures, except that instead of triggering on connection requests to multiple ports on the target system, the signature fires on multiple RPC packets (with the same RPC program number) being sent to multiple ports on the target system. The attacker is trying to bypass the portmapper program and locate RPC services directly.

The PortMapProgram parameter enables you to create signatures to look for client requests to the portmapper program that are requesting the port for a specific RPC service (identified by a single RPC program number). For instance, if you want to create a signature that watches for requests to the ypbind service, you set the PortmapProgram to 100007. Then, anytime that the sensor detects a client request to the portmapper program with a value of 100007, the signature will trigger an alarm.

You can also create signatures that examine generic RPC traffic. Using the RpcProgram and RpcProcedure parameters, you can create signatures that decode the RPC header, which enables the signatures to trigger on a specified RPC program number and RPC procedure. For instance, you can create a signature that looks for RPC traffic to a specific procedure within ypbind by creating a custom signature that specifies an RpcProgram value of 100007 (along with defining the value for the RPC procedure that you are interested in).

SERVICE.SMB Engine Parameters

The SERVICE.SMB signature engine decodes the Server Message Block (SMB) protocol. Unlike other signature engines, you cannot add custom signatures to the SERVICE.SMB signature engine. Instead, this engine contains a list of built-in signatures. These built-in signatures can vary with each signature update. The built-in signatures for version 4.0 are as follows:

- **3303**—Login successful with guest privileges
- **3304**—NULL login attempt
- **3305**—Windows 95/98 password file access
- **3306**—Remote Registry attempt
- **3307**—RedButton reconnaissance
- **3308**—Remote isarpc service access attempt
- **3309**—Remote srvsvc service access attempt
- **6255**—SMB login failure

Because you cannot create custom signatures for this engine, the engine parameters (shown in Table 13-29) enable you to tune how the built-in signatures for the SERVICE.SMB signature engine operate.

Table 13-29   *SERVICE.SMB Engine Parameters*

Parameter Name	Values	Attributes	Description
ScanInterval	1–131071	None	The time interval in seconds that is used to determine alarm rates (for signature 6255 only)
HitCount	1–65535	None	The number of occurrences in the ScanInterval that causes the signature to fire (for signature 6255 only)

Table 13-29 *SERVICE.SMB Engine Parameters (Continued)*

Parameter Name	Values	Attributes	Description
PipeName	<string>	None	String (maximum of 260 bytes) that identifies the name of the pipe to watch for in NT_CREATE_ANDX (not implemented for user signatures)
AccountName	<string>	None	String (maximum of 260 bytes) that identifies the account name to look for during login attempts (not implemented for user signatures)
FileName	<string>	None	String (maximum of 260 bytes) that identifies the filename that triggers the signature when detected in open attempts (not implemented for user signatures)

SERVICE.SNMP Engine Parameters

The SERVICE.SNMP signature engine supports signatures that examine SNMP traffic (see RFC 3412). The major engine-specific parameters are shown in Table 13-30.

Table 13-30 *SERVICE.SNMP Engine Parameters*

Parameter Name	Values	Attributes	Description
CommunityName	<string>	None	The SNMP password (community string) that the signature matches on.
ObjectId	<string>	None	The object identifier that the signature will match on.
BruteForceCount	1–32	None	Defines the number of unique community names seen between a pair of addresses to constitute a brute-force attempt.
IsBruteForce	True False	Protected	If true, the BruteForceCount becomes a valid parameter.
IsInvalidPacket	True False	Protected Required	If true, the signature matches traffic that is an invalid SNMP packet.
IsNonSnmpTraffic	True False	Protected	If true, the signature matches non-SNMP traffic to UDP port 161.

The SERVICE.SNMP signature engine has the following three Boolean values:

- IsBruteForce
- IsInValidPacket
- IsNonSnmpTraffic

When you set the IsNonSnmpTraffic parameter to true, the signature triggers when the traffic examined does not represent a valid SNMP packet. Similarly, setting the IsInvalid-Packet to true causes the signature to trigger when the traffic appears to be an SNMP packet but the data is malformed in some fashion.

You can check for brute-force attempts to guess a valid community name using the following parameters:

- IsBruteForce
- BruceForceCount

Setting the IsBruteForce parameter to true causes the signature to trigger if it detects a single system using more unique community names against a single target system than the value specified by the BruteForceCount parameter. If the BruteForceCount is set to 4 and IsBruteForce is set to true, for example, the signature will trigger if host A sends 4 or more SNMP requests (with different community name strings) to host B.

You can also create signatures that search for specific community names or object IDs by setting the CommunityName and ObjectID parameters.

NOTE   The SERVICE.SNMP signature engine only inspects traffic for SNMP version 1.

SERVICE.SSH Engine Parameters

The SERVICE.SSH signature engine supports signatures that examine SSH traffic. Because everything except the initial setup fields are encrypted in an SSH session, these signatures only examine the setup fields. The major parameters for this engine are listed in Table 13-31.

Table 13-31   *SERVICE.SSH Engine Parameters*

Parameter Name	Values	Attributes	Description
Direction	Any ToService FromService	None	ToService and FromService cause the signature to match traffic to or from the service port. Any matches traffic in both directions.
KeyLength	0–65535	None	Defines the RSA key length to match.
PacketDepth	0–65535	None	Defines the number of packets to watch before determining that a session key was missed.
ServicePorts	<port list>	None	A comma-separated list of ports or port ranges at which the SSH service can reside.
UserLength	0–65535	None	Usernames larger than this length trigger a USERNAME overflow.

Using the SERVICE.SSH signature engine, you can examine the following setup fields:

- RSA Key Length
- Username Length

The Direction parameter indicates whether the signature examines traffic to the service (ToService), from the service (FromService), or in either direction (any). On the other hand, the ServicePorts parameter defines the ports on which the signature will process traffic.

NOTE   You can tune the signatures that are provided with the SERVICE.SSH signature engine, but you cannot create your own custom signatures using this signature engine. In addition, this engine currently supports only SSH version 1.

SERVICE.SYSLOG Engine Parameters

The SERVICE.SYSLOG signature engine analyzes traffic directed at the syslog port (514 UDP). The major engine-specific parameters are shown in Table 13-32.

Table 13-32   *SERVICE.SYSLOG Engine Parameters*

Parameter Name	Values	Attributes	Description
AclDataSource	\<string\>	None	A comma-separated list of IP addresses that are valid sources of access control list (ACL) policy violations
AclFilterName	\<string\>	• None	Identifies the name of the ACL filter
Facility	\<number\>	• None	Defines the syslog facility level to match
Priority	\<number\>	• None	Defines the syslog priority level to match

This engine specifically looks for syslog messages that match a predetermined format that indicates a Cisco ACL policy violation. The AclFilterName identifies the ACL that the signature searches for in the syslog traffic. To minimize false positives, you can use the AclDataSource parameter to indicate IP addresses that should not trigger the signature. Any policy violations (syslog messages) detected for these addresses will not trigger the signature.

NOTE   When you create a Cisco ACL, you can specify the **log** keyword as shown in the following ACL entry:

```
access-list 101 deny 10.0.1.0 0.0.0.255 any log
```

The **log** keyword causes matches to the entry (traffic that is denied) to generate a syslog message. These syslog messages are considered Cisco ACL policy violations.

State Signature Engines

A State machine consists of a starting state and a list of valid state transitions. Cisco IDS supports the following three State machine engines:

- SERVICE.SMTP
- STATE.STRING.CISCOLOGIN
- STATE.STRING.LPRFORMAT

Each of these engines has a set of valid states. To use these State machine engines, use the parameters defined by the STATE.STRING signature engine.

NOTE   Although SERVICE.SMTP is named like other Service signature engines (such as SERVICE.SSH), this engine is actually a State machine engine.

STATE.STRING Engine Parameters

Each of the State machine engines uses the engine parameters listed in Table 13-33.

Table 13-33   *State Machine Engine Parameters*

Parameter Name	Values	Attributes	Description
Direction	ToService FromService	Protected Required	Indicates whether to inspect traffic to the service (ToService) or from the service (FromService)
EndMatchOffset	1–4294967295	Protected	The exact stream offset (in bytes) in which the RegexString must report a match
MinMatchLength	1–4294967295	Protected	The minimum number of bytes the RegexString must match from the start to the end of the match
RegexString	<string>	Protected Required	The regex that specifies the pattern to search for
ServicePorts	<port list>	Protected Required	A comma-separated list of ports or port ranges at which the service may reside
StateName	ENUM	Protected Required	The name of state in the StateMachine to restrict the match of the regex string

The StateName parameter indicates the state that the State machine must be in for the signature to begin searching for the pattern specified by the RegexString parameter. If a match is found in the correct state, the signature triggers.

You can restrict the pattern matching by using the EndMatchOffset and MinMatchLength parameters. The MinMatchOffset parameter limits the searching to a range starting at the beginning of the stream and going the specified number of bytes. The MinMatchLength specifies a minimum number of bytes that the RegexString parameter must match for the signature to trigger.

SERVICE.SMTP Engine State Transitions

Table 13-34 shows the transitions defined for the SERVICE.SMTP signature engine. These states relate to the Simple Mail Transport Protocol (SMTP) and are not configurable by the user. You can use these transitions (in conjunction with the StateName parameter) to create signatures that check for specific patterns at different states in the SMTP protocol.

Table 13-34   *SERVICE.SMTP Engine Transitions*

Regex String	Required State	Next State	Direction
[\r\n]250[ ]	START	SmtpCommands	FromService
250[ ][^\r\n][\x7f-\xff]*SNMP	START	SmtpCommands	FromService
(HE|EH)LO	START	SmtpCommands	ToService
[\r\n](235|220.*TLS)	START	ABORT	FromService
[\r\n](235|220.*TLS)	SmtpCommands	ABORT	FromService
[Dd][Aa][Tt][Aa][Bb][Dd][Aa][Tt]	SmtpCommands	MailHeader	ToService
[\r\n]354	SmtpCommands	MailHeader	FromService
[\r\n][.][\r\n]	MailHeader	SmtpCommands	ToService
[\r\n][2][0–9][0–9][ ]	MailHeader	SmtpCommands	FromService
([\r\n]|[\n][\r]){2}	MailHeader	MailBody	ToService
[\r\n][.][\r\n]	MailBody	SmtpCommands	ToService
[\r\n][2][0-9][0-9][ ]	MailBody	SmtpCommands	FromService

STATE.STRING.CISCOLOGIN Engine State Transitions

Table 13-35 shows the transitions defined for the STATE.STRING.CISCOLOGIN signature engine. These states relate to interactive Telnet logins to Cisco devices and are not configurable by the user. You can use these transitions (in conjunction with the StateName parameter) to create signatures that check for specific patterns at different states in the Cisco login process.

Table 13-35 *STATE.STRING.CISCOLOGIN Engine Transitions*

Regex String	Required State	Next State	Direction
User[ ]Access[ ]Verification	START	CiscoDevice	FromService
Cisco[ ]Systems[ ]Console	START	CiscoDevice	FromService
assword[:]	CiscoDevice	PassPrompt	FromService
\x03	PassPrompt	ControlC	ToService
(enable)	ControlC	EnableBypass	FromService
\x03[\x00–\xFF]	ControlC	PassPrompt	ToService

STATE.STRING.LPRFORMAT Engine State Transitions

Table 13-36 shows the transitions defined for the STATE.STRING.LPRFORMAT signature engine. These regex strings are not configurable by the user.

Table 13-36 *STATE.STRING.LPRFORMAT Engine Transitions*

Regex String	End Offset	Required State	Next State	Direction
[1–9]	1	START	ABORT	ToService
%		START	FormatChar	ToService
[\x0a\x0d]		FormatChar	ABORT	ToService

String Signature Engines

The String signature engines support regex pattern matching and alarm functionality for multiple protocols including ICMP, UDP, and TCP. Each of these engines shares the common engine-specific parameters shown in Table 13-37.

Table 13-37 *Common String Engine Parameters*

Parameter Name	Values	Attributes	Description
Direction	ToService FromService	Protected Required	Indicates whether to inspect traffic to the service (ToService) or from the service (FromService).
EndMatchOffset	1–4294967295	Protected	The exact stream offset (in bytes) in which the regex string must report a match.

Table 13-37 *Common String Engine Parameters (Continued)*

Parameter Name	Values	Attributes	Description
MinMatchLength	1-4294967295	Protected	The minimum number of bytes the regex string must match from the start to the end of the match.
RegexString	<string>	Protected Required	The regex that specifies the pattern to search for.
ServicePorts	<port list>	Required	A comma-separated list of ports or port ranges at which the service can reside.
StripTelnetOptions	True False	Protected	If true, any Telnet options are stripped off before a regex pattern match is performed on the data.

The String signature engines are divided into the following three signature engines:

- STRING.ICMP
- STRING.TCP
- STRING.UDP

Each of the engines supports signatures that search their specific protocol for configured patterns.

Sweep Signature Engines

The Sweep signature engines identify situations in which one system either makes connections to multiple hosts or multiple ports. Typically, these signatures detect the initial reconnaissance performed by an attacker against your network. The Sweep engines are shown in Table 13-38.

Table 13-38 *Sweep Signature Engines*

Engine	Description
SWEEP.HOST.ICMP	Single source scanning multiple network addresses using ICMP packets
SWEEP.HOST.TCP	Single source scanning multiple network addresses using TCP packets
SWEEP.MULTI	UDP and TCP combined port sweeps
SWEEP.OTHER.TCP	Odd sweeps and certain NMAP scans
SWEEP.PORT.TCP	TCP connections to multiple destination ports between two network addresses
SWEEP.PORT.UDP	UDP connections to multiple destination ports between two network addresses

NOTE	The Sweep signature engines use the ResetAfterIdle master engine parameter to clear the current value of the unique counter when the traffic being monitored between the hosts has been idle for the period of time specified by the ResetAfterIdle parameter.

SWEEP.HOST.ICMP Engine Parameters

The SWEEP.HOST.ICMP signature engine supports signatures that trigger when one host sends ICMP traffic to multiple destination systems. The engine-specific parameters are shown in Table 13-39.

Table 13-39 *SWEEP.HOST.ICMP Engine Parameters*

Parameter Name	Values	Attributes	Description
IcmpType	0–255	None	The IcmpType that this signature matches
Unique	2–40	Required	Identifies the number of unique connection allowed until the signature fires

You use the IcmpType to define which type of ICMP traffic you want the signature to trigger on. Then you use the Unique parameter to indicate how many instances of the ICMP traffic are required to trigger the signature. The ResetAfterIdle master engine parameter controls the period of time that the host must not send ICMP traffic to clear the unique counter.

NOTE	If you do not specify a value using the IcmpType parameter, the signature uses all ICMP traffic.

SWEEP.HOST.TCP Engine Parameters

The SWEEP.HOST.TCP signature engine supports signatures that trigger when one host sends TCP traffic to multiple destination systems. The engine-specific parameters are shown in Table 13-40.

Table 13-40 *SWEEP.HOST.TCP Engine Parameters*

Parameter Name	Values	Attributes	Description
Mask	FIN SYN RST PSH ACK URG ZERO	Required	The mask used when checking the TCP flags. This field indicates the TCP flags that you want to include in your checking.
TcpFlags	FIN SYN RST PSH ACK URG ZERO	Required	The TCP flags (out of the flags included in the mask) that need to be set for the signature to match.
Unique	2–40	Required	Identifies the number of unique connections allowed until the signature fires.

You need to specify which type of TCP traffic you want the signature to match on using the following parameters:

- Mask
- TcpFlags

The Mask parameter essentially identifies the TCP flags that you are interested in, whereas the TcpFlags parameter indicates which of the TCP flags need to be set. Any TCP flags that you do not include in the mask cannot have an impact on whether the signature triggers. For instance, assume that you set the Mask parameter to include FIN and RST and the TcpFlags parameter to include only RST. The signature will trigger only based on the values of the FIN and RST flags in the packets. (All the other TCP flags in the packet are ignored.) Packets will trigger the signature as follows:

- If the RST and FIN flags are set, the signature will not trigger.
- If the RST flag is set and the FIN flag is not set, the signature will trigger (regardless of the value for the other TCP flags).
- If the RST flag is not set, the signature will not trigger.

Again the Unique parameter indicates the number of unique connections required to trigger the signature, and the ResetAfterIdle master engine parameter controls the clearing of the unique counter after an idle period.

SWEEP.MULTI Engine Parameters

The SWEEP.MULTI signature engine is designed to support sweeps that involve both TCP and UDP traffic. The engine-specific parameters are shown in Table 13-41.

Table 13-41   *SWEEP.MULTI Engine Parameters*

Parameter Name	Values	Attributes	Description
TcpInterest	1–2	None	The predefined TCP ports that the signature matches on. 1 = SATAN normal 2 = SATAN heavy
UdpInterest	1–2	None	The predefined UDP ports that the signature matches on. 1 = SATAN normal 2 = SATAN heavy
UniqueTcpPorts	2–40	None	Identifies the number of unique TCP connections allowed until the signature fires.
UniqueUdpPorts	2–40	None	Identifies the number of unique UDP connections allowed until the signature fires.

The TcpInterest and UdpInterest parameters enable a signature to trigger when the signature detects traffic that matches the ports used by the SATAN scanning tool.

The UniqueTcpPorts and UniqueUdpPorts parameters support signatures that trigger based on a mix of TCP and UDP connections.

SWEEP.OTHER.TCP Engine Parameters

The SWEEP.OTHER.TCP signature engine supports signatures that trigger when a mix of TCP packets (with different flags set) is detected on the network. The engine-specific parameters for this engine are shown in Table 13-42.

Table 13-42   *SWEEP.OTHER.TCP Engine Parameters*

Parameter Name	Values	Attributes	Description
PortRange	0–2	None	Specifies the destination port range to match: **0**—All ports **1**—Only low ports (0–1024) **2**—Only high ports (1025–65535))
TcpFlags1	FIN SYN RST PSH ACK URG ZERO	None	The TCP flags that need to be set for equality comparison (1 of 4).
TcpFlags2	FIN SYN RST PSH ACK URG ZERO	None	The TCP flags that need to be set for equality comparison (2 of 4).
TcpFlags3	FIN SYN RST PSH ACK URG ZERO	None	The TCP flags that need to be set for equality comparison (3 of 4).
TcpFlags4	FIN SYN RST PSH ACK URG ZERO	None	The TCP flags that need to be set for equality comparison (4 of 4).

The PortRange parameter identifies the ports that are valid for the signature to process. You have the following options when specifying valid ports:

- **0**—All ports
- **1**—Low ports (1–1024)
- **2**—High ports (1025–65535)

You can specify up to four different sets of TCP flag combinations. Each of the TCP flag combinations that you specify must be detected before the signature triggers. Unlike other TCP-based engines, this engine does not have a Mask parameter. In this situation, the signature only looks for the flags specified in the TcpFlags parameter and ignores any other TCP flags. Suppose, for instance, that you set the TcpFlags parameters to the following values:

- **TcpFlags1**—SYN,FIN
- **TcpFlags2**—FIN,RST
- **TcpFlags3**—RST,PSH

The signature will not trigger until it sees at least three different packets in which each packet matches one the following criteria:

- Packet with at least the SYN and FIN flags set
- Packet with at least the FIN and RST flags set
- Packet with at least the RST and PSH flags set

This engine is useful for detecting attacks from various scanning tools (such as NMAP and queso) that send TCP packets with weird flag combinations in an attempt to identify the target operating system.

SWEEP.PORT.TCP Engine Parameters

The SWEEP.PORT.TCP signature engine supports signatures that detect when a single host attempts to connect to multiple TCP ports on the same target system. The engine-specific parameters are shown in Table 13-43.

Table 13-43   *SWEEP.PORT.TCP Engine Parameters*

Parameter Name	Values	Attributes	Description
InvertedSweep	True False	None	If true, the signature uses the source port rather than the destination port to count unique connections.
Mask	FIN SYN RST PSH ACK URG ZERO	Required	The mask used when checking the TCP flags. This field indicates the TCP flags that you want to include in your checking.
PortRange	0–2	Required	Specifies the destination port range to match: **0**—All ports **1**—Only low ports (0–1024) **2**—Only high ports (1025–65535)
SuppressReverse	True False	None	Do not trigger the signature when a sweep is detected in the reverse direction on this address set.
TcpFlags	FIN SYN RST PSH ACK URG ZERO	Required	The TCP flags (out of the flags included in the mask) that need to be set for the signature to match.
Unique	2–40	None	Identifies the number of unique connections allowed until the signature fires.

Like other engines (such as SWEEP.HOST.TCP), you need to specify the TCP flags that you want to be included in your processing using the Mask and TcpFlags parameters, and the Unique parameter indicates how many connections are needed to trigger the signature. The SWEEP.PORT.TCP signature engine, however, has the following new parameters:

- InvertedSweep
- SuppressReverse

When you set the InvertedSweep parameter to true, the signature triggers on the source port rather than the destination port when counting unique connections. Similarly, the Suppress-Reverse parameter controls whether the signature attempts to automatically trigger in the reverse direction. When set to true, the reverse direction is not checked.

SWEEP.PORT.UDP Engine Parameters

The SWEEP.PORT.UDP signature engine supports signatures that detect when a single host attempts to connect to multiple UDP ports on the same target system. The engine-specific parameters are shown in Table 13-44.

Table 13-44 *SWEEP.PORT.UDP Engine Parameters*

Parameter Name	Values	Attributes	Description
PortsInclude	<port list>	None	A comma-separated list of ports or port ranges that are included in the sweep analysis
Unique	2–40	None	Identifies the number of unique connections allowed between two hosts until the signature fires

For this engine, the new parameter is the PortsInclude parameter. It enables you to specify a comma-separated list that indicates which UDP ports the signature will use when looking for unique connections. Ports not included in the list have no impact on the signature.

Traffic Signature Engine

The TRAFFIC.ICMP signature supports signatures that trigger on nonstandard usage of the ICMP protocol. Tools that exploit ICMP traffic include Tribe Flood Network (TFN and TFN2K), Stacheldraht, and Loki. The engine-specific parameters for this engine are shown in Table 13-45.

Table 13-45 *TRAFFIC.ICMP Engine Parameters*

Parameter Name	Values	Attributes	Description
ReplyRatio	0–2147483647	None	Defines how large the imbalance of ICMP replies to ICMP requests can grow before the signature triggers.
WantRequest	Any False True	None	If true, must detect an echo request before the signature triggers. If false, signature will not trigger if an echo request is detected. Any does not care.

Table 13-45   *TRAFFIC.ICMP Engine Parameters (Continued)*

Parameter Name	Values	Attributes	Description
IsLoki	True False	None	This signature matches on the original Loki tool.
IsModLoki	True False	None	This signature will match on the modified Loki tool.

Loki is a backdoor Trojan program. It enables an attacker to execute commands and receive information from the infected machine through an ICMP tunnel. There is also a modified version of the Loki program. Both these types of traffic can cause your signature to trigger if you set the isLoki and isModLoki parameters to true.

NOTE   You cannot add custom signatures to the TRAFFIC.ICMP engine. If you try to add custom signatures, you will receive an error message.

Trojan Signature Engine

Attackers can place various backdoor Trojan programs on systems in your network to enable them to operate from those systems. Cisco IDS has three signature engines specifically designed to detect the presence of Trojan programs on your network (see Table 13-46).

Table 13-46   *Trojan Signature Engines*

Engine	Description
TROJAN.BO2K	Detects the presence of BO2K using the TCP protocol
TROJAN.TFN2K	Detects the presence of the TFN2K Trojan by examining UDP, TCP, and ICMP traffic
TROJAN.UDP	Detects the presence of BO and BO2K using the UDP protocol

---

NOTE   You cannot add custom signatures to any of the Trojan signature engines, and the engines do not have any user-configurable engine-specific parameters. You can tune only the master signature parameters for these signature engines.

Summary

Cisco IDS signatures analyze network traffic and detect intrusive activity on your network. The signatures are built from various signature engines designed to handle specific types of intrusive activity. Besides the signatures themselves, Cisco IDS provides a very robust alarming capability that you can use to regulate the number of alarms you need to process.

Cisco IDS supports the following different alarm throttle modes for each signature:

- FireOnce
- FireAll
- Summarize
- GlobalSummarize

Besides the two fixed alarm summarization modes, you can also configure summary mode escalation that causes the signature to alter the alarm throttle mode based on the rate at which the attack traffic is detected on the network. The ChokeThreshold parameter is used to indicate when the summary mode escalation starts.

Each alarm generated has one of the following severity levels:

- Informational
- Low
- Medium
- High

In conjunction with the signatures that detect intrusive activity, Cisco IDS supports various signatures that report information about the health of your sensors. These signatures enable you to quickly discover when your sensor does not receive network traffic correctly.

When tuning Cisco IDS signatures (or creating custom signatures), you need to define the characteristics of the signatures using the following types of parameters:

- Master engine parameters
- Engine-specific parameters

The master engine parameters are global parameters common to most if not all signatures. These parameters include such items as the protocol and signature ID. Engine-specific parameters, on the other hand, are parameters specific to the engine that the signature is based on. These parameters vary from one signature engine to another.

Cisco IDS divides the signature processing into the following major categories of signature engines:

- Atomic
- Flood

- Service
- State
- String
- Sweep
- Miscellaneous

The Atomic signature engines detect attacks that occur in a single packet. Because these signatures trigger based on the contents of a single packet, these engines do not need to maintain any state information. Atomic signature engines based on the following protocols can detect various attacks:

- ARP
- ICMP
- TCP
- UDP
- IP

The Flood signature engines trigger when a flood of traffic enters your network. These engines detect floods of traffic directed at a single host on your network as well as floods of traffic against the entire network.

To analyze different services and protocols, Cisco IDS provides numerous Service signature engines. These engines perform protocol decodes and essentially process traffic similar to the way actual systems on the network would. The analytical capability provides very powerful attack detection capability. Cisco IDS has separate service engines for the following protocols:

- DNS
- FTP
- HTTP
- IDENT
- MSSQL
- NTP
- RPC
- SMB
- SNMP
- SSH
- Syslog

Some protocols have different states. Searching for specific patterns at these various states enables you to create very robust signatures. Cisco IDS provides the following predefined state engines:

- SERVICE.SMTP
- STATE.STRING.CISCOLOGIN
- STATE.STRING.LPRFORMAT

Cisco IDS supports various Sweep signature engines that detect the following types of sweeps against your network:

- Host
- Port

A host sweep involves a single host attempting to access multiple destination hosts on your network. This access can be through one of the following protocols:

- ICMP
- TCP

A port sweep involves a single host attempting to access multiple ports on a single target system. The ports can be accessed via one of the following protocols:

- TCP
- UDP

Cisco IDS also supports some specialized signature engines that specifically detect certain Trojan programs being used on your network. The three Trojan engines are as follows:

- TROJAN.BO2K
- TROJAN.TFN2K
- TROJAN.UDP

One final specialized signature engine is the TRAFFIC.ICMP signature engine that detects nonstandard usage of the ICMP protocol.

Review Questions

The following questions test your retention of the material presented in this chapter. The answers to the review questions are in Appendix B, "Answers to Chapter Review Questions."

1 What are the four basic alarming modes?

2 How does the FireOnce alarm mode work?

3 What is the difference between the Summarize and GlobalSummarize alarming modes?

4 What is variable alarm summarization?

5 Which master parameter do you need to configure to enable variable alarm summarization?

6 What are master engine parameters?

7 What master engine parameter do you use to configure the signature's alarm mode?

8 What is an atomic signature?

9 Which Atomic signature engine examines Layer 2 traffic?

10 What do the Flood signature engines detect?

11 How do you enable the diagnostic mode for a signature based on the FLOOD.NET signature engine?

12 Which type of signature engine provides protocol decode capability for various network protocols?

13 What is a host sweep?

14 What is a port sweep?

15 What are the two Host Sweep engines?

16 Which master engine parameter do you configure to cause the sweep signature to reset the counter of unique connections seen (after an idle time between the host[s] involved)?

17 What is the SummaryKey (master engine parameter)?

18 Which SummaryKey value uses only the source IP address to determine multiple instances of the same alarm?

19 What functionality do signatures based on the String signature engines provide?

20 Which signature engine specifically supports detecting scans from the SATAN scanning tools?

21 Which engine enables you to generate an alarm based on a specific IP protocol number that should not be present on your network.

22 What is the sampling rate used by the flood signatures?

Upon completion of this chapter, you will be able to perform the following tasks:

- Understand endpoint protection requirements
- Identify Cisco Security Agent (CSA)-supported platforms
- Understand CSA policies
- Configure CSA policies
- Monitor host events using the Management Center for CSA (CSA MC)
- Understand basic event reports using CSA MC
- Understand how to build and deploy agent kits
- Configure groups and hosts using CSA MC
- Explain the purpose of the Profiler tool

CHAPTER 14

Host Intrusion Prevention

Network security devices, such as firewalls and intrusion detection systems, enhance the security posture of your network. You must also, however, provide security protection at the endpoint or host level. With the Okena acquisition, Cisco enhanced its endpoint security capability with the StormWatch product. The product is now the Cisco Host Intrusion Prevention (HIP) solution and complements the overall Cisco intrusion protection strategy.

Endpoint Protection

Traditional network security devices are important to your overall network security solution, but they have several deficiencies with respect to protecting the endpoints on your network. Some of the problems that you need to address at the host level include the following:

- Zero-day protection
- Data protection
- Server and desktop maintenance

Zero-Day Protection

Many host security protection products (such as antivirus software) provide signature-based security protection. When a new attack is published, the manufacturers of these products update their devices to handle this new attack. There is a delay, however, between the release of the attack and the release of this new signature during which your system is unprotected.

Zero-day protection refers to the capability of protecting your system against attacks as soon as they are released. Rapidly spreading worms and viruses can wreak havoc on your network before you have a chance to manually update your security products.

Usually, zero-day protection is not available with signature-based security products. Instead, you need to use an anomaly or behavior-based security product. Because these products use a definition of what is normal system behavior, they can react when operations deviate from this norm.

Data Protection

The systems on your network house a wealth of information vital to your business. Protecting this information from deletion is very important. Many viruses destroy information on your systems and cause a significant impact to your company's productivity while the systems are restored to their original condition. Other viruses disclose sensitive information by making private emails public. The bottom line is that you need to protect the data that resides on the many systems on your network.

Server and Desktop Maintenance

Security vulnerabilities are uncovered daily. Patching your systems to protect against these security vulnerabilities becomes a never-ending race that consumes tremendous resources. As your network grows, this maintenance process involves updating hundreds or thousands of individual systems. Furthermore, if you happen to miss any systems, your network has a weak point that is more susceptible to being attacked.

Cisco Security Agent (CSA)

Cisco Security Agent (CSA) provides a distributed mechanism with which to secure the hosts across your entire enterprise. By deploying agents on each individual system, CSA technology can effectively defend against the proliferation of attacks across your network. Besides defending against known malicious behavior, these agents also enforce policies that you have defined for each system.

The CSA software is installed on each endpoint system and intercepts operations on that system. The software is comprised of the following interceptors that analyze the operations on a given system:

- File system interceptor
- Network interceptor
- Configuration interceptor
- Execution space interceptor

The operations on the protected host are analyzed and compared to the agent's policy rules to identify policy violations.

Attack Protection

CSAs are deployed throughout your network and each agent focuses on preventing malicious activity on a single host. This malicious activity falls into the following categories:

- Known malicious behavior
- Policy violations
- Application profiling

The agents running on your system determine to which of these categories the specific actions belong by following both default and user-defined, rule-based policies. These rule-based policies use the following factors to categorize the traffic:

- Resource being accessed
- Operation being invoked
- Application initiating the action

Known Malicious Behavior

Known malicious behavior is activity that in all situations represents intrusive activity that should not occur on your network. The default policies do not permit these actions to occur on your protected systems.

Policy Violations

Besides activity that is always bad, certain activity is not allowed because of the *security policy* that you have created for your network. By creating CSA policies that enforce the requirements of your security policy, you can determine when users violate the rules that you have established.

Security Policy

A security policy is a formal statement that outlines the rules by which access to your network is controlled. All access to your information assets must abide by these rules. When installing security components on your network, these rules also establish a framework that defines what you need to check for, the restrictions that you need to impose on network traffic, and the applications allowed on the network. An excellent reference to learn more about security policies is RFC 2196, "Site Security Handbook."

CSA Policy

The CSA on each individual host uses a set of rules that identifies permissible operations that are known as *CSA policies*. Each agent can be configured with its own CSA policy, or you can use the same CSA policy for a group of systems. The CSA policies used on the host throughout your network should reflect your formal security policy.

Application Profiling

Finally, you may want to know when a specific application does something that is outside its normal range of activity for an application. Using the Profiler (see the "Profiler" section later in the chapter), you can determine the operations that an application performs to accomplish its normal tasks. Then basing rules on this observed behavior, you can create a custom policy that will indicate if the application attempts an operation that would be considered abnormal.

Deployment Overview

You deploy and manage CSAs throughout your network using the Management Center for Cisco Security Agents (CSA MC). CSA MC is part of the CiscoWorks VPN/Security Management Solution (VMS) product. The CSA MC software suite is comprised of the following major components:

- Management Center for Cisco Security Agents (CSA MC)
- Cisco Security Agents

Using CSA MC, you organize your network into groups of systems that share similar characteristics and then apply security policies to those groups. All configuration operations are performed on CSA MC using a web-based interface. These configuration changes are then automatically deployed to the individual systems by updating the individual agents on those systems.

CSA Supported Platforms

Currently you can use CSA software on the following systems:

- Windows XP (Professional, English, 128-bit encryption) with Service Pack 0 or 1
- Windows 2000 (Professional, Server, or Advanced Server) with Service Pack 0, 1, 2, or 3
- Windows NT (Workstation, Server, or Enterprise Server) with Service Pack 5 or higher
- Solaris 8

NOTE   Citrix Metaframe and Citrix XP are also supported, as well as Terminal Services on Windows XP and Windows 2000. Terminal Services on Windows NT is *not* supported. To determine the latest CSA-supported platforms, refer to the Cisco documentation.

Each system on which you install the agent software must meet certain system requirements. The system requirements for Windows systems are as follows:

- Intel 200-MHz processor or higher
- Minimum 128 MB memory
- NTFS file system
- 15 MB or higher free space on hard disk
- Ethernet or dialup network connection

The Solaris systems on which you install the agent software should meet the following system requirements:

- UltraSPARC 500-MHz processor or higher
- Minimum 256 MB memory
- 15 MB or higher free space on hard disk
- Ethernet or dialup network connection

NOTE   Based on market requirements, Cisco will periodically add other operating systems to the list of supported operating systems.

CSA Installation

Installing the agent software on your systems is a simple task. First, you distribute the URL where the end user can retrieve the agent kit. The end user can then download the agent kit and install the agent software on the system. After the agent software has been installed, it automatically registers with CSA MC, regularly polls for policy updates and forwards events to the CSA MC database. For more information on agents kits, see the "Agent Kits" section later in this chapter.

NOTE   To install the agent kit on the system, the user must have local administrative privileges.

Management Center for Cisco Security Agents

The CSA MC is the central management software that maintains the database for all the policies and system nodes on which you have installed the CSA software. CSA MC is a component of the CiscoWorks VMS product. You must have CiscoWorks Common Services installed on the system on which you are installing CSA MC (refer to the Cisco documentation on installing the CiscoWorks Common Services). Furthermore, you must have VMS version 2.2 to install CSA MC.

The agent software on each of your endpoint systems registers with CSA MC. After CSA MC verifies the agent software, CSA MC deploys the configured policy either for that specific system or for the group to which the system belongs.

Besides monitoring the activity on the local system, the agent software regularly polls CSA MC to check for policy updates. Whenever it detects alerts at the local level, the agent's event manager passes these alerts to the global event manager on CSA MC. The global event manager examines these events, which may trigger an alert notification to the administrator or cause the agent to take a particular action in response to the activity.

Using Management Center for Cisco Security Agents

CSA MC provides a centralized facility to manage your CSAs. Using CSA MC, you can deploy customized, role-based policies to specific groups or individual systems throughout your network. Furthermore, you can monitor the alerts generated by your various agents. To use CSA MC effectively, you must understand the following operations:

- Defining security policies
- Role-based administration
- Deploying CSA policies

Defining Security Policies

Before attempting to protect your network using CSAs, you must have a well-planned and well-defined network security policy. This security policy provides the framework against which you build the roles for your agent software, because it defines which network services and resources you need to protect as well as the level of protection required for each of these resources.

A CSA policy is a collection of rules. You need to analyze your various systems to determine the level of security protection that they require and then develop policies that provide the appropriate level of security protection. CSA MC comes with a variety of templates and preconfigured policies that you can use or customize if necessary to easily match your individual requirements.

Besides defining different CSA policies for different security environments, you can also group systems. Therefore, you can apply a single CSA policy to an entire group of systems that all have similar security needs. This makes the management of those agents much easier because you can change the CSA policy for the entire group of machines as opposed to configuring each individual system separately.

When first creating and deploying your CSA policies, it is helpful to verify the impact that the policy has on your systems. To accomplish this goal, you can initially deploy your CSA policies in test mode. While in test mode, the CSA policies log events that would normally trigger a deny or query rule (see the section "Policy Components" later in this chapter), but not actually perform the deny or query actions. Therefore, you can analyze the logs to determine what the impact on your endpoint systems will be when you actually enforce the CSA policy. When you are satisfied with the CSA policy, you can then enable it so that it becomes active.

Role-Based Administration

You control access to CSA MC by creating CiscoWorks users. You can assign the privilege roles shown in Table 14-1 to the CiscoWorks users you create.

Table 14-1   *CiscoWorks User Roles*

User Role	Description
Help Desk	Read-only for the entire system
Approver	Read-only for the entire system and includes the configuration approval privileges
Network Operator	Read-only for the entire system, generates reports, and includes configuration deployment privileges
Network Administrator	Read-only for the entire system and includes privileges to edit devices and device groups
System Administrator	Performs all operations

When using CSA MC, you can assign different users to perform different configuration tasks within CSA MC. A user's ability to configure CSA MC depends on the user's access to the CSA MC database. You basically have the following three configuration tasks associated with CSA MC:

- **Configure**—Provides full read and write access to the CSA MC
- **Deploy**—Provides full read and partial write access to the CSA MC so that the user can manage hosts and groups, attach policies, create kits, schedule software updates, and perform all monitoring operations
- **Monitor**—Provides read access to the CSA MC database so that the user can create reports, alerts, and event sets

Table 14-2 shows the correlation between CiscoWorks user roles and their capability to perform the three configuration tasks associated with CSA MC.

Table 14-2 *CSA MC User Roles*

Configuration Task	CiscoWorks User Role Required
Configure	Network Administrator or System Administrator
Deploy	Network Operations
Monitor	Any privilege besides those required for configuring and deploying user roles

Deploying CSA Policies

When setting up CSA MC to protect your endpoint systems, you need to perform various tasks to effectively deploy the agent software to your various systems. The major tasks associated with deploying the agent software are as follows:

- Create groups
- Build and distribute agent kits
- Configure policies
- Attach policies to groups
- Generate rules

Create Groups

Each system that you want to protect with CSA must download the agent software and register with CSA MC in order to receive the appropriate policies that you have built for them. Managing these policies can become very labor intensive if you have an individual policy for each system on your network.

Instead of defining policies for individual systems, it is easier to define policies for a class or group of systems that share similar security needs. Then, when you need to change the policy, your changes apply to an entire group of systems, rather than just a specific system. Some of the criteria that you may use to group systems include the following:

- System function (such as web servers)
- Business group (such as Finance or Engineering)
- Geographical location
- Topological location (such as subnet)
- Importance to your organization (such as mission critical or end user)

For more information on establishing groups, see the section "Configuring Groups and Managing Hosts" later in the chapter.

Build and Distribute Agent Kits

To reduce the administrative burden of installing the agent software on the systems throughout your network, you can build CSA installation kits. These kits make it trivial for end users to install the agent software on their system. Then when the agent is running, it can register with CSA MC and automatically receive CSA policy updates. Furthermore, the agent kit can associate a specific system with a defined group or groups. For more information on building and distributing agent kits, see the section "Agent Kits" later in this chapter.

Configure CSA Policies

CSA policies form the heart of your CSA MC system. They enforce your overall corporate security policy and define the level of protection required on your various systems. Your security policy, however, is a dynamic entity and changes over time as your network evolves and your security requirements change.

Initially developing your CSA policies on a well-thought-out security policy will definitely assist you in enabling your agents to provide a solid security foundation for your network. The section "CSA Policies" later in this chapter provides detailed information on how to configure the policies that regulate your deployed agents. The section "Using Management Center for Cisco Security Agents 4.0" also provides extensive information on creating CSA policies.

Associating Policies to Groups

Your policies define access rules and system correlation rules. These rules are grouped together under a common policy name. To use your own custom policies (or the preconfigured policies), you need to associate the policy with specific groups of systems on your network. When you attach a policy to a specific group, it then determines the actions that are allowed and denied on those systems. For more information on attaching policies to groups, see the section "Attaching Policies to Groups" later in this chapter.

Generate Rules

When you make change to your policies, they are saved in the CSA MC database. These changes, however, are not automatically distributed to your agents. Instead, these changes are marked as nondistributed database items (with the name of the administrator who made the changes). You then have the ability to modify these changes or even delete them. If you choose to propagate these changes to your agents, you must regenerate the rules, and this causes them to be redistributed to the agents that are distributed throughout your network.

Monitoring CSA Events

The agents deployed throughout your network will generate various events and messages. Besides keeping abreast of the activity on your network, monitoring this information enables you to supplement the rules already in place on your agents by configuring CSA MC to send an email message, issue Simple Network Management Protocol (SNMP) traps, generate a text-based pager message, log to a text file, or even execute custom programs. You can also control the type of alert sent based on the following criteria:

- Severity of the logged event
- Specific event
- Host that generated the event

Using the Monitor category from the CSA MC main menu bar, you can access the various monitoring operations. The options available are as follows:

- Status Summary
- Event Log
- Event Log Management
- Event Sets
- Alerts

Status Summary

Using the Status Summary option, you can observe a quick overview of status information concerning CSA MC (see Figure 14-1). Some of the information shown on this status screen includes the following:

- Events recorded in the past 24 hours
- Active hosts with the current configuration
- Active hosts running an old configuration
- Active hosts running with old software
- Active hosts with software update pending
- Unprotected hosts
- Hosts running in test mode
- Hosts not actively polling (unknown status)
- Groups with no policy attached

Figure 14-1 *Status Summary Screen*

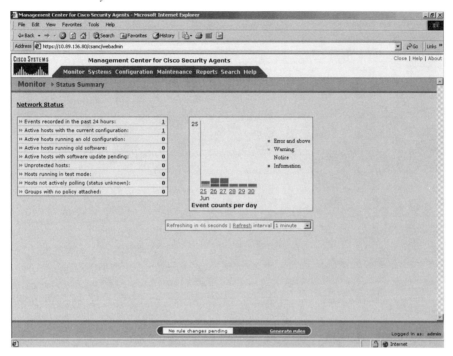

Event Log

The Event Log view enables you to view the events generated by your registered agents (see Figure 14-2). By default, the event log displays all events for all hosts, regardless of the severity or policy that generated the alert.

Figure 14-2   *Event Log Screen*

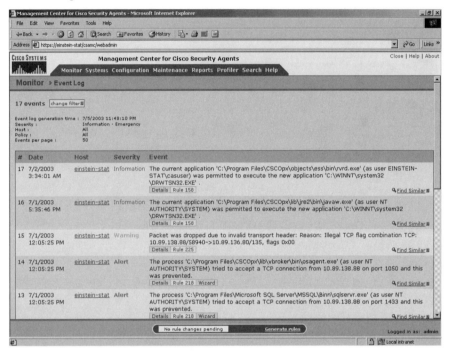

You can regulate the information displayed by either specifying the specific types of events that you want to see or by defining a filter based on the following criteria:

- Event log generation time
- Time range
- Severity
- Host
- Rule ID
- Events per page

NOTE   To view the specific details for any of the events displayed, you can click Details under the event description. This displays a pop-up window with the event's detailed information (see Figure 14-3).

Figure 14-3 *Event Details Pop-Up Window*

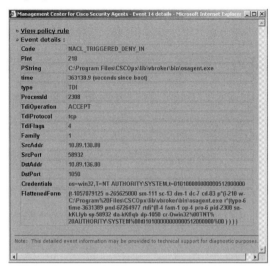

Filtering by Event Characteristics

You can regulate the information displayed in the event log by defining the events in which you are interested. You can do this through the following two mechanisms:

- Predefined event set
- Custom event set

Using the predefined event set, you can filter the events displayed using various options such as the following:

- All events
- All events in the last 24 hrs
- Configuration errors
- Events from critical systems
- Globally correlated events
- Significant network events

You can also define a custom event set. Creating custom event sets is explained in the "Event Sets" section later in this chapter.

To change the event set criteria used to display the event log, follow these steps:

Step 1   Select Monitor from the main menu bar on the Management Center for Cisco Security Agents screen.

Step 2   Select Event Log from Menu Options. This displays the Event Log screen.

Step 3   Click Change Filter (see Figure 14-2). A pop-up window displays enabling you to filter the information displayed by the event log (see Figure 14-4).

Figure 14-4   *Change Filter Pop-Up Screen*

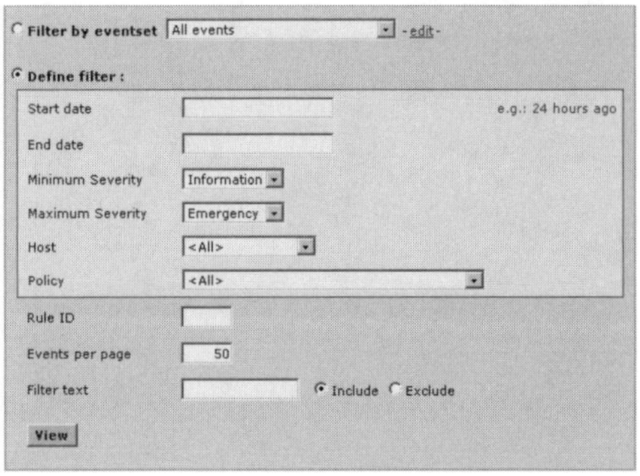

Step 4   Check the Filter by eventset radio box.

Step 5   Specify a predefined event set (or previously defined custom event set), using the Filter by eventset pull-down menu.

Step 6   Click View to update the event log display.

Defining a Filter

To define a filter for the event log, follow these steps:

Step 1   Select Monitor from the main menu bar on the Management Center for Cisco Security Agents screen.

Step 2   Select Event Log from Menu Options. This displays the Event Log screen.

Step 3   Click Change Filter (see Figure 14-2). A pop-up window displays enabling you to filter the information displayed by the event log (see Figure 14-4).

Step 4   Check the Define Filter radio box.

Step 5   Enter the start date (if desired).

Step 6   Enter the end date (if desired).

Step 7   Enter the minimum event severity to be displayed using the Minimum Severity pull-down menu.

Step 8   Enter the maximum event severity to be displayed using the Maximum Severity pull-down menu.

Step 9   Select the host for which you want to view the events using the Host pull-down menu.

Step 10   Select the policy for which you want to view the events using the Policy pull-down menu.

Step 11   Enter a specific rule ID to be displayed (if desired).

Step 12   Define how many events you want to display per page on the display by entering a value in the Events per Page field.

Step 13   Enter a textual string in the Filter Text field that you want to be either included or excluded from the event log display, and then click either the Include or Exclude radio button.

NOTE   Using the Filter Text field and the Include and Exclude radio buttons, you can define text that you want your event filter to either include or exclude from the list of displayed events based on the textual information in the event description. If you do not want to see events that contain the word "shutdown" in the event description, for example, you can specify shutdown for the Filter Text field and click the Exclude radio button.

Step 14   Click View to use the defined filter.

Event Log Management

The Event Log Management feature enables you to create event database management tasks to manage the size of your event log. As your event log grows, specifying parameters for deleting events will help prevent this log from growing too large and from maintaining stale information. You can create management tasks for the event log based on the following criteria:

- Age in days
- Event severity
- Defined system group

By default, no management tasks are defined for your event log. To define management tasks for your event log, follow these steps:

Step 1   Select Monitor from the main menu bar on the Management Center for Cisco Security Agents screen.

Step 2   Select Event Log Management from Menu Options. This displays the Event Managing Tasks screen (see Figure 14-5).

Figure 14-5   *Event Managing Tasks Screen*

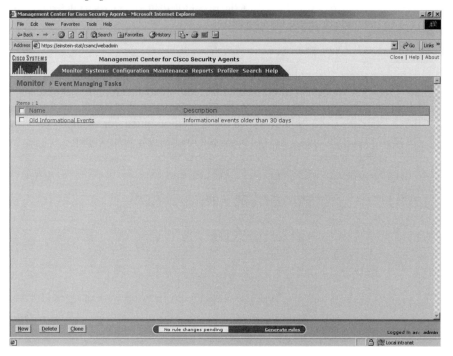

Step 3 Click New to create a new management task for the event log information. The screen displays the management task parameters (see Figure 14-6).

Figure 14-6 *Management Task Parameters Screen*

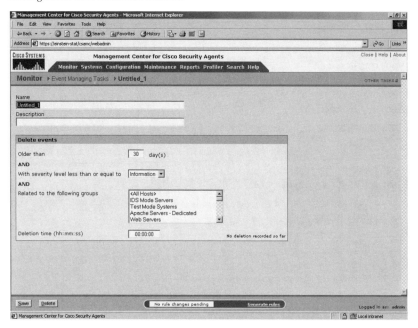

Step 4 Enter the name of the new management task in the Name text box.

Step 5 Enter a description for the new management task in the Description text box.

Step 6 Enter the age (in days) at which to remove events by entering a value in the Older Than text box. (The default is 30 days.)

Step 7 Enter the maximum severity of the events to be removed by using the With Severity Level Less Than or Equal To pull-down menu. All events with a severity equal to or less than this value will be removed.

Step 8 Define the groups for which the events will be removed by selecting group(s) from the Related to the Following Groups list box.

NOTE To select multiple items in the list box, hold down the Ctrl key while clicking the groups. You can also select a contiguous block of items by selecting an item and then holding down the Shift key while selecting the ending item of the block.

Step 9 Define the time at which you want the deletion to occur by specifying a deletion time in the following format: hh:mm:ss.

Step 10 Click Save to save the new management task.

Event Monitor

Similar to the event log, the Event Monitor enables you to view the events generated by your registered agents (see Figure 14-7). The main difference between the two views is that the events displayed by the Event Monitor are automatically updated every 15 seconds.

Figure 14-7 *Event Monitor Screen*

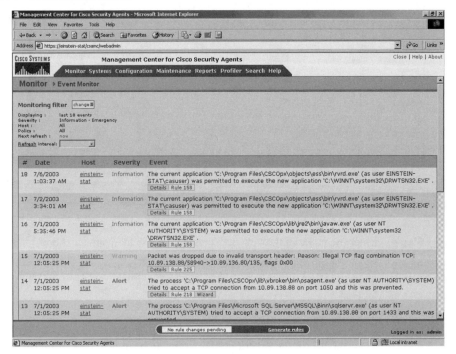

NOTE The steps to filter the information displayed by the Event Monitor are similar to those used to change the event log display, so refer to the section "Event Log" for information on how to filter events for the Event Monitor.

Event Sets

Event sets are similar to system variables in that they enable you to specify or filter the events used by other CSA MC components. More specifically, event sets are used when defining the events that impact specific alerts and reports.

Selecting the Event Sets menu option enables you to view the event sets configured on your system (see Figure 14-8). This display contains the predefined event sets along with any custom event sets that you have created.

Figure 14-8 *Event Sets Screen*

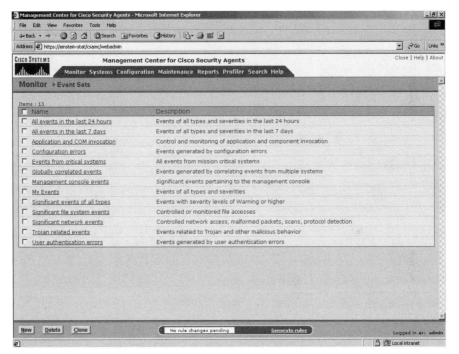

The predefined event sets are shown in Table 14-3.

Table 14-3 *Predefined Event Sets*

Event Set	Description
All events	Events of all types and severities
All events in the last 24 hrs	Events of all types and severities in the last 24 hours
All events in the last 7 days	Events of all types and severities in the last 7 days
Application and COM invocation	Control and monitoring of application and component invocation

continues

Table 14-3   *Predefined Event Sets (Continued)*

Event Set	Description
Configuration errors	Errors generated by configuration problems
Events from critical systems	All events from mission-critical systems
Globally correlated events	Events generated by correlating events from multiple systems
Management console events	Significant events related to the management console
Significant events of all types	Events with a severity level of warning or higher
Significant file system events	Controlled or monitored file accesses
Significant network events	Controlled network access, malformed packets, scans, and protocol detection
Trojan-related events	Events related to Trojans or other similar malicious behavior
User authentication errors	Events generated by user authentication errors on the CSA protected system

From the Event Sets screen, you can perform the following three operations:

- Create new event sets
- Delete existing event sets
- Clone existing event sets

To create a new event set, you just click New and enter the parameters shown in Table 14-4 to define the event set. To either delete or clone an existing event set, you must first check the check box next to the appropriate event set and then click either Delete or Clone.

Table 14-4   *Event Specification Parameters*

Parameter	Description
Event Type	The type of events that you want displayed
Severity Level	The severity level of the events that you want displayed
Groups	The groups (that generated the events) that you want displayed
Policies	The policies (that triggered the events) that you want displayed
Timestamps	The time range for which you want to display the events

Alerts

You can configure CSA MC to take various actions in response to a policy triggering an event. The actions that you can specify are as follows:

- Send an email message
- Generate a pager message

- SNMP notification
- Log information to a file
- Run a custom program

By default, CSA MC does not have any predefined alerts. To add an action for a specific event, follow these steps:

Step 1   Select Monitor from the main menu bar on the Management Center for Cisco Security Agents screen.

Step 2   Select Alerts from Menu Options. This displays the Alerts screen (see Figure 14-9).

Figure 14-9   *Alerts Screen*

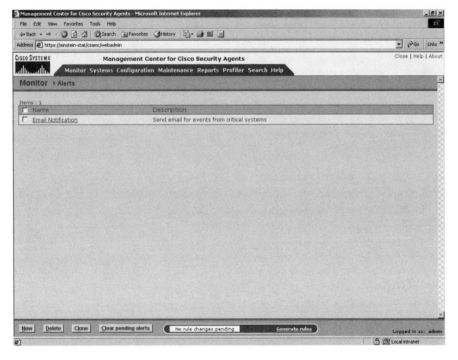

Step 3   Click New. The Alert specification screen displays (see Figure 14-10).

Figure 14-10 *Alert Specification Screen*

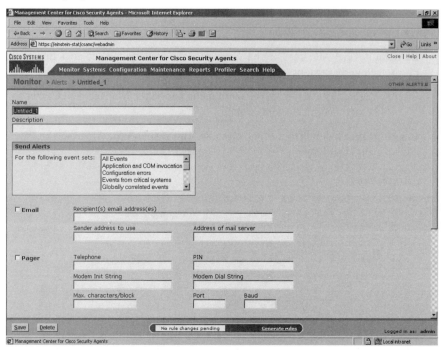

Step 4 Define which events will generate the alert by selecting an event set from the For the Following Event Sets list box.

NOTE To select multiple items in the list box, hold down the Ctrl key while clicking the groups. You can also select a contiguous block of items by selecting an item and then holding down the Shift key while selecting the ending item of the block.

Step 5 Check the radio box next to the alert type to be used (email, page, SNMP, log, or custom program).

Step 6 Specify the parameters required for the specified action.

Step 7 Click Save to save your new alert.

Configuring Groups and Managing Hosts

Maintaining individual policies for each system on your network represents a large administrative burden. Instead, it is easier to group systems that share similar security requirements. Some of the benefits of using host groups are as follows:

- Enables you to consistently apply the same policy across multiple systems
- Enables you to easily use the alert mechanism to cause actions based on events from any system in the group
- Enables you to use the test mode (for new policies) for a group of systems

Each network is unique. Therefore, the manner in which you group your systems will vary from network to network. Among others, you can use the following criteria to group systems:

- System function (such as web servers)
- Business group (such as Finance or Engineering)
- Geographical location
- Topological location (such as subnet)
- Importance to your organization (such as mission critical or end user)

Configuring Groups

After you install agent software on your systems, they automatically register with CSA MC. Hosts inherit the group membership associated with the agent kits that they initially used to load the agent software onto their system. The initial agent kit also identifies the location of the CSA MC server that the CSA needs to communicate with after the agent software has been installed.

CSA MC provides you with various default groups that you can assign to your agent kits (see Figure 14-11). The default groups are divided into the following categories based on operating system:

- UNIX
- Windows

Figure 14-11   *Groups Screen*

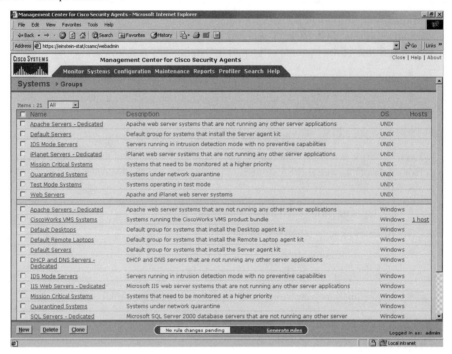

Some of the default groups include the following:

- Mission-critical systems
- Web servers
- Test mode systems
- Default servers

If the supplied groups do not fit your network requirements, you can also define your own custom groups. To configure a host group, follow these steps:

Step 1   Select Systems from the main menu bar on the Management Center for Cisco Security Agents screen. The Systems Menu Options display (see Figure 14-12).

Figure 14-12 *Systems Screen*

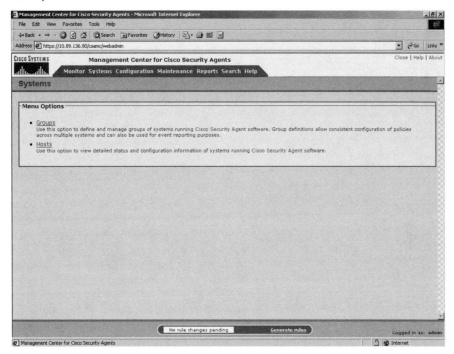

Step 2   Select Groups. The Groups screen displays (see Figure 14-11).

Step 3   Click New. This displays a pop-up prompt that asks you to specify the operating system of the group being created.

Step 4   Click either UNIX or Windows (depending on the operating system of the group being created). The Groups Definition screen then displays (see Figure 14-13). For this example, Windows was chosen from the pop-up prompt.

Figure 14-13 *Windows Group Definition Screen*

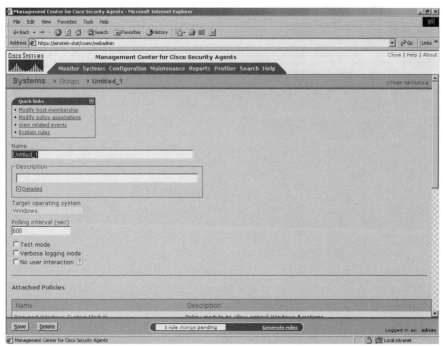

Step 5 Enter a name for the new group in the Name text box.

Step 6 Enter a description for the new group in the Description text box.

Step 7 Define how often the systems in the group will poll CSA MC checking for policy updates by entering a value in the Polling Interval field. (The default is 600 seconds.)

Step 8 If you want the group to operate in test mode, check the Test Mode check box.

Step 9 If you want to enable verbose logging, check the Verbose Logging Mode check box.

Step 10 If you do not want the end user to be able to interact with CSA MC or receive any pop-up queries, check the No User Interaction check box.

Step 11 To define which policies are attached to your new group, click Modify Policy Associations. This displays the Add Policies screen (see Figure 14-14).

Figure 14-14 *Add Policies to a Group*

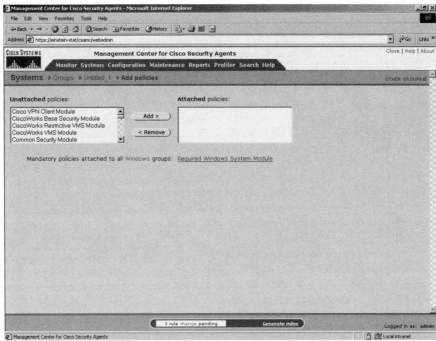

Step 12 Click the policy to be added in the Unattached Policies list box, and then click Add to add the policy to the group definition.

NOTE Some policies are mandatory and cannot be removed from the group definition, such as the Required Windows System Module (for Windows groups).

Step 13 Click Generate Rules to save the changes that you made. The Generate Rule Programs screen displays (see Figure 14-15).

Figure 14-15 *Generate Rule Programs Screen*

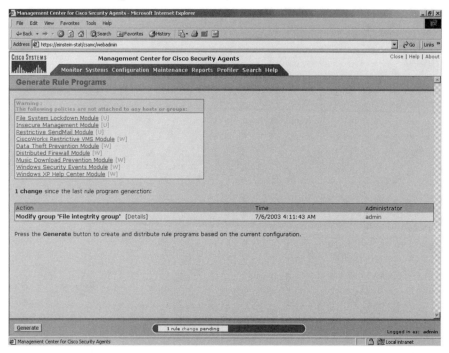

Step 14 Click Generate. This updates your rules based on the new changes and
then distributes those changes to affected systems.

Hosts

The Hosts menu option enables you to check the status of the systems that have registered
with CSA MC (see Figure 14-16). The last field for each host entry displays information
about the system based on the value of the pull-down menu. You can select the following
options from the pull-down menu:

- Active

- Protected

- Latest Software

- Test Mode

- Last Poll

Figure 14-16 *Hosts List Screen*

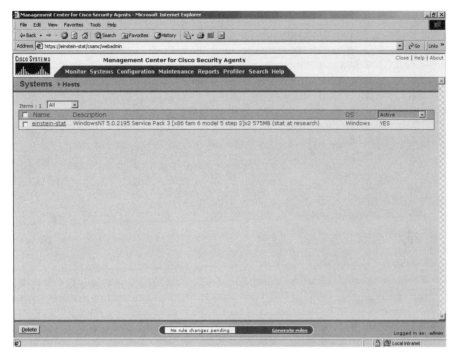

Determining Active Hosts

The default value for the pull-down field is Active. Therefore, the Hosts List screen enables you to quickly determine which agents have successfully registered with CSA MC. All registered agents will have a value of Yes in the Active field. Hosts for which the agent has not registered are listed with a value of No in the Active field.

The hosts with a value of No in the Active field indicate systems that have registered with CSA MC in the past but are currently not communicating with CSA MC. The systems might be turned off or they might be laptops that are not currently connected to the network.

Determining Protected Hosts

By changing the pull-down field to Protected, you can determine which hosts are protected by a specific policy. If the Protected field has a value of Yes, the host belongs to a group that has a policy associated with it. If the Protected field has a value of No, the host either does not belong to a group or the group to which it belongs does not have a policy attached to it.

Verifying Agent Software

To ensure the highest level of protection, your agents need to run current software. When you change the value of the pull-down field to Latest Software, hosts that have a value of Yes run the latest agent software (based on the software available on the CSA MC server). Any hosts with a value of No in the Latest Software field are running older software and should be upgraded to the latest software after adequate testing has been performed on the new software.

Identifying Agents Running in Test Mode

When you initially create your policies, you can run them in test mode, to verify their impact on your network before you actually enable them. By changing the pull-down field to Test Mode, you can identify hosts that run policies that are in test mode. Hosts with a value of Yes run in test mode, whereas hosts with a value of Off not run in test mode.

Viewing the Agent's Last Poll Time

Your agents are continually polling CSA MC to check for new policy updates. By changing the pull-down field to Last Poll you can view the last time that each of the agents polled CSA MC.

CSA Policies

CSA policies are constructed based on rules that regulate the behavior allowed on your systems. Therefore, understanding policies and deploying policies to the agents is vital to successfully using CSA MC. Some of the items that you need to understand with respect to CSA policies are as follows:

- Policy components
- Configuring policies
- Configuring rules
- Using configuration variables
- Configuring application classes
- Global event correlation

CSA Policy Components

Each of your CSA policies is comprised of one or more access rules. When configuring these access rules, you must consider the following rule components:

- Allow versus Deny
- Secondary precedence
- Monitoring access
- Mandatory policies

Allow vs. Deny

When you write your rules, each of them must be assigned an action, which can be one of the following:

- Allow
- Deny
- Query (Default Allow)
- Query (Default Deny)

Furthermore, CSA MC processes rules in a defined order based on their priority. The highest priority rule is 1 and these rules are always checked first. In this way, a higher-priority rule can trigger on an event and prevent a lower-priority rule from being processed. The priority scheme that CSA MC uses is shown in Table 14-5.

Table 14-5   *CSA MC Rule Priorities*

Priority	Rule Type
1	Add Process to Application
2	High-Priority Deny
3	Allow
4	Query User (Default Allow)
5	Query User (Default Deny)
6	Deny
7	Default Action (Allow)

NOTE   Although the Add Process to Application is the highest-priority rule type, it does not override other lower-priority rules. Instead, its action is to build a dynamic application for any rules that use it (see the section "Dynamic Application Classes" later in this chapter).

For every CSA policy that you configure, the default action of that policy is Allow. Therefore, every CSA policy that you create allows all system actions until you specifically write a rule to deny a specific action. This means that it is unlikely that you will create rules with the Allow action unless they are exceptions to an existing rule with the Deny action.

When creating CSA policies, it is easiest to work from the lowest-priority rule and work upward to higher-priority rules. Initially, everything is allowed by default. Therefore, the first rule that you will need to add is some type of Deny rule. Then, you can add any Allow rules that are needed to build exceptions to the Deny rule.

NOTE   When creating a high-priority Deny rule, you probably want to place it in its own standalone CSA policy. This enables you to then attach the policy to several groups. With high-priority Deny rules, you can easily restrict access to resources from specific groups or from all systems on your network.

CAUTION   The Deny rules can potentially restrict access to legitimate users and processes, so take care when defining these rules.

Secondary Precedence

The rule actions (Allow and Deny) form the initial precedence used by CSA MC. You can also use logging to establish precedence between rules of the same type. If you have two Allow rules, for example, the Allow rule that has logging enabled takes precedence over an Allow rule that has logging disabled.

Sometimes, however, this secondary precedence produces undesirable results. Therefore, most rules have a check box labeled Take Precedence over Other *<action>* Rules. This check box enables you to override the secondary precedence based on logging and specify which rules of a given type are processed first.

Suppose, for instance, that you have the two rules with the following characteristics:

- Log, Deny, all applications, acting as server for TCP/1-32000
- No log, Deny, all applications, acting as server for TCP/1200

In this situation, both rules perform the Deny action. Therefore, the first rule (with logging enabled) takes precedence. This causes activity to TCP port 1200 to be both denied and logged. Your second rule disables logging for TCP port 1200, but this action is overridden by the first rule. Therefore, by using the Take Precedence Over Other *<action>* Rules option, you can cause the second rule to take precedence and prevent the logging activity.

Monitoring Access

Normally you do not need to create Allow rules unless you make an exception to a Deny rule that you have created. One other situation in which you can use an Allow rule is when you want to monitor specific events. Sometimes you want to know when specific events occur, but you do not want to deny them. In this situation, you can create an Allow rule with logging enabled. This causes the event to be logged even though the action is not denied.

NOTE	Logging common valid events can potentially generate massive amounts of log entries.

Mandatory Policies

Normally you need to attach a CSA policy to a specific group to make it apply to that group. Sometimes you want to make a CSA policy that should be applied to all groups. You can manually apply a CSA policy to every group, but this is time-consuming, and you might forget to apply it to new groups as you create them. Therefore, a better way is to make a CSA policy mandatory (when creating the policy). Then the policy is automatically applied to all groups.

Querying the User

For Windows systems, you can choose to implement rules that query the user for whether to deny or allow a specific event. When the specific activity is detected, the user is presented with a pop-up window enabling him to allow or deny the activity (see Figure 14-17). These query rules also have an associated Deny or Allow action. This action will be performed automatically if the user does not answer the query within 5 minutes.

Figure 14-17 *User Query Pop-up*

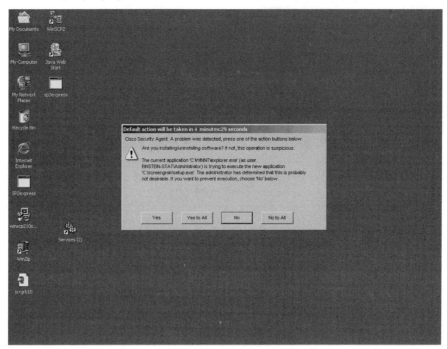

NOTE	For UNIX rules, you do not have the ability to query the user. Furthermore, if you check the No User Interaction check box when creating a group, no query messages are sent to the user. Instead, the actions are immediately performed.

Configuring Policies

A CSA policy is basically a set of rules organized under a common name. You then use this name to assign the policy to different groups of systems. Then the rules in the CSA policy control the actions allowed on those systems.

CSA MC comes with numerous predefined policies that you can use to protect the systems on your network. You can assign these policies to your defined groups. If the predefined CSA policies do not meet your requirements, you can also define your own custom policies by performing the following steps:

Step 1 Select Configuration from the main menu bar on the Management Center for Cisco Security Agents screen. The Configuration Menu Options display (see Figure 14-18).

Figure 14-18 *Configuration Menu Options*

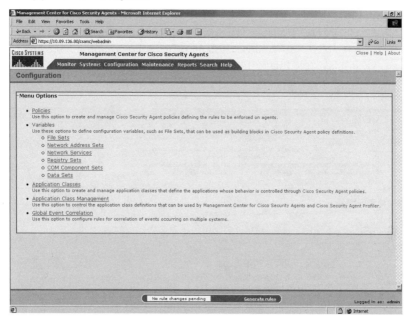

Step 2   Select Policies. The Policies screen displays (see Figure 14-19).

Figure 14-19 *Policies Screen*

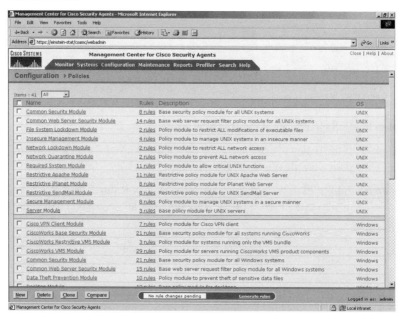

Step 3 Click New. A pop-up window displays, and you must select the operating system to which the policy will be applied.

Step 4 Click either UNIX or Windows, based on your requirements. (This example is for Windows systems). The Policy Definition screen displays (see Figure 14-20).

Figure 14-20 *Policy Definition Screen*

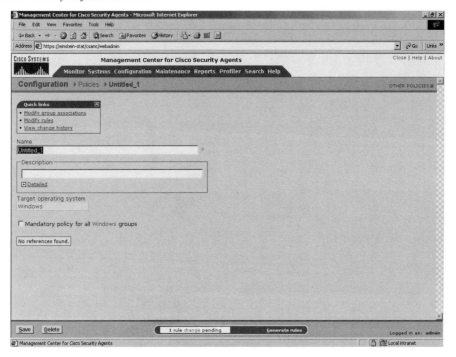

Step 5 Enter a name for the new policy in the Name text box.

Step 6 Enter a description for the new policy in the Description text box.

Step 7 If the policy is mandatory for all Windows groups, check the Mandatory policy for all Windows groups check box.

Step 8 Add rules to the policy by clicking Modify Rules. The Rules page displays (see Figure 14-21). Initially no rules are assigned to your policy.

Step 9   Click Add Rule to add a rule to your policy (see Figure 14-21) and select the type of rule that you want to add from menu of rules. (See the section "Understanding Rules" later in this chapter for more information on the types of rules.)

Figure 14-21   *Adding a Rule*

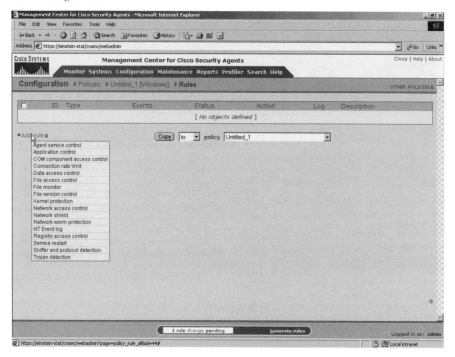

Step 10   Define the parameters for the specific rule.

Step 11   Add groups to the policy by clicking Modify Groups Associations. The Attach to Groups page displays (see Figure 14-22). Initially no rules are assigned to your policy.

Figure 14-22 *Adding Groups to a Rule*

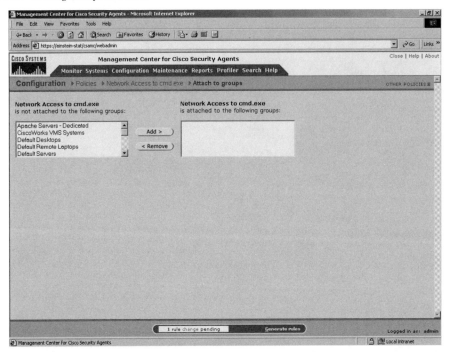

☯ **Step 12** Click a group in the list box on the left and click Add to attach the group to the policy. You can also remove groups using the Remove button and reversing the process.

Step 13 Click Save.

Step 14 Click Generate Rules to save the changes that you made. The Generate Rule Programs screen displays.

Step 15 Click Generate. This updates your rules based on the new changes and then distributes those changes to affected systems.

Understanding Rules

When defining a new policy, you need to build it from the various available rule types. Some rules are common to both UNIX and Windows systems, whereas others are unique to only one of these operating systems. Understanding the different rules enables you to create effective policies that enforce your overall security policy.

NOTE The following rules sections are meant to serve as an overview of the type of rules that you can use in your policies. For detailed information on the configuration of these rules, refer to the "Using Management Center for Cisco Security Agents 4.0" documentation.

Rules Common to Windows and UNIX

Table 14-6 shows the rules common to both Windows and UNIX systems.

Table 14-6 *Common Rules*

Rule Name	Description
Agent Service Control	Controls whether users are allowed to suspend agent security, which disables all rules until security is manually resumed or the system is rebooted
Application Control	Controls which applications are allowed to run on the designated systems
Connection Rate Limit	Controls the number of network connections that can be received or sent by the designated system within a specified period of time
Data Access Control	Detects malformed web server requests
File Access Control	Controls whether selected applications can perform read or write operations
File Monitor	Tracks read and/or write access to a specified file of files
Network Access Control	Controls access to specified network services or addresses

Windows-Only Rules

Some rules can only be applied to Windows systems. Table 14-7 shows the rules that are unique to Windows systems.

Table 14-7 *Windows-Specific Rules*

Rule Name	Description
COM Component Access Control	Controls whether specified applications can access specific COM components
File Version Control	Prevents users from running specified versions of defined applications on their system
Kernel Protection	Prevents unauthorized access to the operating system (such as preventing device drivers from dynamically loading after system startup)
NT Event Log	Enables you to cause specified Windows NT event log entries to appear in the CSA MC event log

continues

Table 14-7 *Windows-Specific Rules (Continued)*

Rule Name	Description
Registry Access Control	Controls whether specified applications can write to specified Registry keys
Service Restart	Enables the agent to restart Windows NT services that have stopped or are no longer responding to service requests
Sniffer and Protocol Detection	Causes the detection of non-IP programs and packet-sniffer programs to be logged

COM

Microsoft's Component Object Model (COM) enables applications (both local and remote) to interact using objects. Applications such as Microsoft Word use this functionality to create macros and utility scripts. Although COM provides useful functionality, it has also been used maliciously to attack systems.

UNIX-Only Rules

Some rules can only be applied to UNIX systems. Table 14-8 shows the rules that are unique to UNIX systems.

Table 14-8 *UNIX-Specific Rules*

Rule Name	Description
Network Interface Control	Controls whether specified applications can open the network interface in promiscuous mode.
Resource Access Control	Prevents suspicious symbolic links from being followed.
Rootkit / Kernel Protection	Prevents unauthorized access to the operating system (such as preventing device drivers from dynamically loading after boot time)
Syslog Control	Enables you to cause specified syslog entries to appear in the CSA MC event log.

Suspicious Symbolic Link

A suspicious symbolic link is one that meets the following criteria:

- Parent directory is a temporary directory such as /tmp or /usr/tmp.
- Symbolic link's owner is different from parent directory's owner.
- Symbolic link's owner is different from the effective user ID (UID) of the process.

Using Configuration Variables

Variables enable you to more effectively supply information to the access control rules that you define. Figure 14-23 illustrates the relationship between the system variables and other system components such as access control rules.

Figure 14-23   *Adding Groups to a Rule*

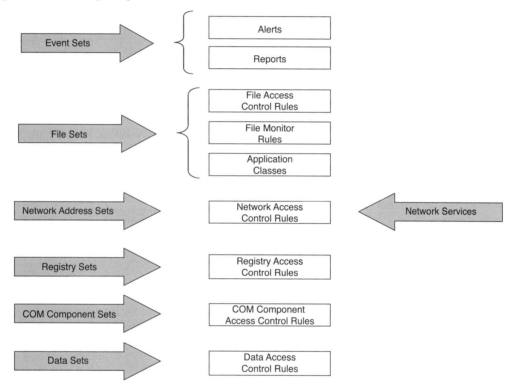

System variables fall into the following categories:

- File sets
- Network address sets
- Network services
- Registry sets
- COM component sets
- Data sets

NOTE   You can make your system administration duties easier by using system variables, but they are not required. Instead of using the variables, you can enter the information directly into corresponding rule configuration fields. Entering this information directly, however, is much more prone to input error.

File Sets

You use file sets with the following three components:

- File access control rules
- File monitor rules
- Application classes

The file set enables you to group individual files and directories under a single name. Then you can use this name in rules that control file permissions and restrictions to apply the controls to all the files in the file set.

Network Address Sets

Network address sets enable you to define a list of IP addresses. This list of addresses can then be used in network access control rules in which you impose restrictions on certain IP addresses. Instead of specifying all the addresses in the rule itself, you just need to specify the name of the network address set.

Network Services

Configuring network services enables you to define the characteristics for a network service. These properties can then be used by network access control rules. When defining a network service, you can define the following characteristics:

- Ports used for initial connections
- Subsequent ports used by client-initiated connections
- Subsequent ports used by server-initiated connections

Registry Sets

Many viruses invoke themselves by altering Registry keys. You can develop rules by specifying these common Registry keys manually, but you can also create a Registry set that defines multiple Registry key values. Then you can use a single name inside of your Registry access control rules. This enables you to use the same Registry key values easily and consistently for multiple rules.

COM Component Sets

COM component sets are listings of COM program IDs (PROGIDs) and COM class IDs (CLSIDs) referenced by a single name. This name can then be used in COM component access rules to limit access to all the specified objects in the set.

Data Sets

Data sets are used to provide input to data access control rules and are essentially a list of data strings under one common name. These strings represent patterns that will be compared against the URI portion of HTTP requests.

CSA MC provides you with various preconfigured data sets. The predefined data sets match patterns based on the following criteria:

- Certain meta-character usage
- Known classes of attacks
- Web server–specific exploits

Configuring Application Classes

Your access control rules are application-centric. When creating your access control rules, you must define which applications the defined rules will apply to. You do this by using application classes. Application classes fall into the following two categories:

- Static application classes
- Dynamic application classes

Static Application Classes

Static application classes essentially categorize their applications based on the names of the executables that launch the applications. Processes belong to a configured application class while they are running. When the application stops, it is removed from the application class. Therefore, application classes are ephemeral and constantly being reevaluated and classified by the agent software.

CSA MC provides numerous predefined application classes for both UNIX and Windows systems. These application classes appear in brackets in the rule Application Classes Selection list box when you are creating new rules (see Figure 14-24).

Figure 14-24 *Application Classes Selection List Box*

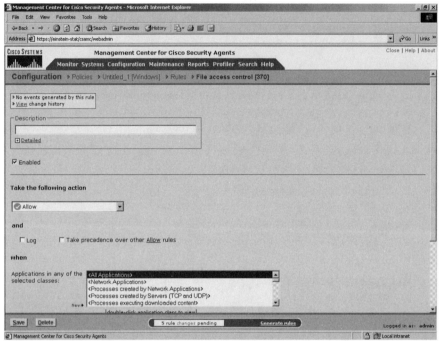

To view the currently configured application classes, you select Application Classes from the Configuration menu options (see Figure 14-25). You can view the current settings for an existing application class by clicking the class name. You can also create your own application classes by clicking New.

Dynamic Application Classes

Besides defining static application classes based on the names of the executables and processes, you can also create dynamic application classes. These classes categorize applications based on their behavior rather than the names of their executables. The advantage to dynamic application classes is that they apply to specific behavior and not specific executables or processes.

Figure 14-25 *Application Classes Screen*

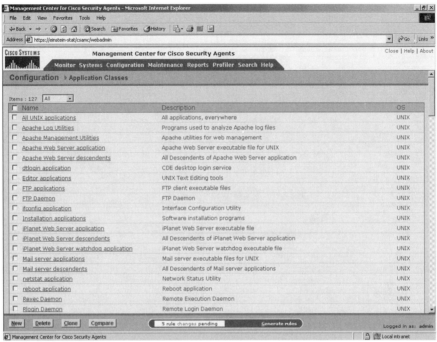

An example of a situation in which a dynamic application class is useful would be if you want to create a rule that applies to email clients. You can have numerous email clients in use across your network. By creating a dynamic application class, you can easily apply the rule to any application that exhibits the behavior of an email client.

You configure a dynamic application class using the same process as creating a static application class, but instead of specifying the name of the executables, you check the When Dynamically Defined by Policy Rules check box. Then you need to define an application-builder rule that will determine which applications will become members of the dynamic application class.

To create an application-builder rule, you need to define a new rule, such as a file access control rule. Then you need to set the rule action to Add Process to Application Class and choose the name of the dynamic application class using the pull-down menu (see Figure 14-26). You also need to configure the other rule parameters. Then this rule takes precedence over other rules and is used to determine which applications will become members of your dynamic application class.

Figure 14-26 *Application-Builder Rule Creation*

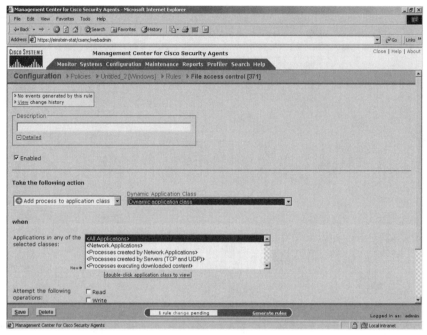

Global Event Correlation

In some situations you need to correlate events from multiple agents across your network. A situation in which this proves useful is if activity is detected on several of your systems and you want CSA MC to automatically update the policies on all of your agents to prevent further occurrences of this activity across your network.

CSA MC comes with several rules that you can use to perform global event correlation. Some examples of the rules that enable you to correlate events from multiple agents include the following:

- Network shield rule
- Network worm rule
- Trojan detection rule

Agent Kits

To reduce your administrative burden, CSA MC enables you to create custom CSA installation kits to install the agent software on your endpoint systems. After the agent has been installed on the system, it automatically registers with CSA MC. At that point, policy updates can be automatically deployed to the operational agents.

NOTE   CSA MC has numerous preconfigured agent kits that you can use to deploy agent software to the systems on your network. These kits place your hosts in groups that have policies already associated with them.

Building Agent Kits

If the predefined agent kits do not meet your requirements, you can create your own custom agent kits. To create an agent kit, follow these steps:

Step 1   Select Maintenance from the main menu bar on the Management Center for Cisco Security Agents screen. The Maintenance Menu Options are displayed (see Figure 14-27).

Figure 14-27   *Maintenance Menu Options*

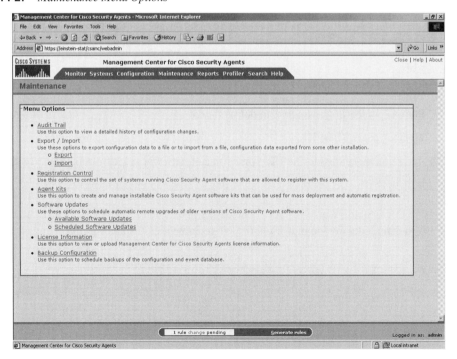

Step 2   Select Agent Kits from the Maintenance Menu Options. The configured
agent kits display onscreen (see Figure 14-28).

Figure 14-28   *Agent Kits Screen*

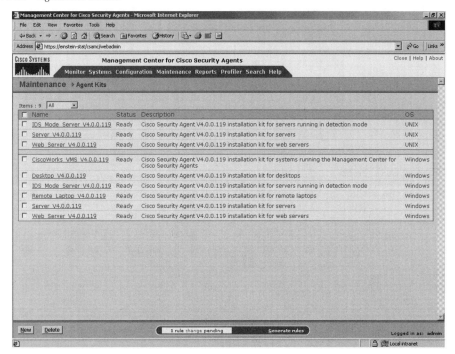

Step 3   Click New. The Adding an Agent Kit screen displays (see Figure 14-29).

Step 4   Enter the parameters to define the kit.

Step 5   Click Make Kit.

After you make the kit, the URL that you can retrieve the kit from is shown on the screen
(see Figure 14-30).

NOTE   You cannot deploy the new kit until you generate the outstanding rule changes.

Figure 14-29   *Adding an Agent Kit Screen*

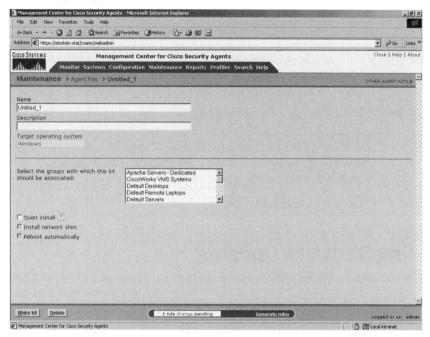

Figure 14-30   *Agent Kit Download Location*

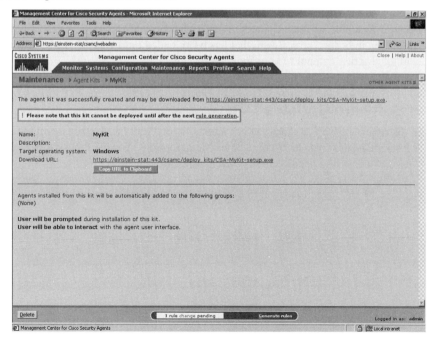

Controlling Agent Registration

To prevent rogue agents from connecting with your CSA MC server, you can limit which IP addresses are allowed to connect to CSA MC. By default, all IP addresses are allowed to connect to your CSA MC server. To change this, follow these steps:

Step 1   Select Maintenance from the main menu bar on the Management Center for Cisco Security Agents screen. The Maintenance Menu Options display (see Figure 14-27).

Step 2   Select Registration Control from the Maintenance Menu Options. In the text box, enter the valid IP address ranges that are allowed to connect to your CSA MC server. Enter each IP address range on a different line and separate the IP addressees defining the range by a dash (such as 10.89.0.0-10.89.255.255).

Step 3   Click Save to save your changes.

Distributing Software Updates

Cisco provides software updates via its website (www.cisco.com) for both CSA MC and your agents. By downloading and installing these updates on CSA MC, you can distribute new software to your agents as easily as you deploy new rules.

Available Software Updates

You can view the software updates available to deploy on your agents by selecting Software Updates>Available Software Updates from the Maintenance Menu Options (see Figure 14-31). The screen indicates the software that has been loaded onto your CSA MC server and is available for deployment to your individual agents.

Scheduled Software Updates

To distribute software updates to your agents, select Software Updates>Scheduled Software Updates from the Maintenance Menu Options. You click New to schedule a software update for specific groups (see Figure 14-32).

Figure 14-31 *Available Software Updates*

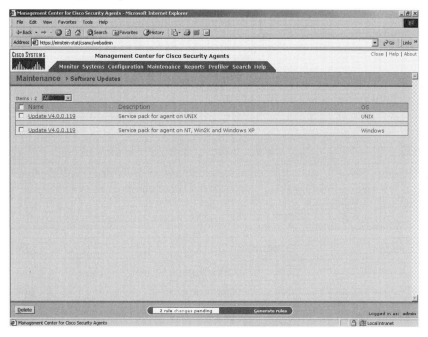

Figure 14-32 *Scheduling Software Updates*

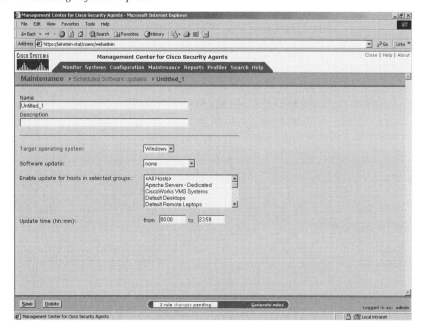

When scheduling a software update, you need to configure the following information:

- Target operating system
- Software update
- Groups to which the update will be applied
- Time frame to perform update

Reports

Using CSA MC, you can generate various reports based on the events that have been logged as well as information about your CSA MC configuration. You can generate the reports shown in Table 14-9.

Table 14-9   *CSA MC Reports*

Report	Description
Events by Severity	Generate a report based on the severity of the events
Events by Group	Generate a report that shows the events from a specific group
Host Detail	Generate an in-depth report providing information on the hosts in one or more groups
Policy Detail	Generate an in-depth report on one or more selected policies
Group Detail	Generate an in-depth report on one or more selected groups

Profiler

For common applications, the preconfigured policies perform well when protecting your systems. Sometimes, however, you might have custom applications for which you need to create a policy. Without in-depth knowledge of the application, it can be difficult to create a policy that does not break existing functionality.

To enable you to efficiently create policies that do not break these applications, you can use the CSA Profiler software. This software monitors the actions of designated applications to determine the resources that they access during their normal operation. It then uses this information to provide you detailed information so that you can develop a custom policy for the application.

To use the Profiler, you essentially configure an analysis job for a specific application. This analysis job is sent to a host running CSA, and when the analysis job runs, all operations for the application being profiled are logged. This log information is then sent to CSA MC. By examining the log information, the Profiler on CSA MC can generate an appropriate CSA policy for the specific application. For more information on the Profiler, refer to the "Management Center for Cisco Security Agents 4.0" documentation.

Summary

Network security devices are only part of a complete security solution for your network. You need to provide security protection all the way to the individual hosts on your network. The Cisco Host Intrusion Protection (HIP) solution provides a behavior-based security solution that protects your network and provides the following benefits:

- Zero-day protection
- Data protection
- Simplified server and desktop maintenance

Cisco Security Agent (CSA) provides a distributed mechanism with which to secure the hosts across your entire enterprise. The attack protection provided by CSA includes the following levels:

- Known malicious behavior
- Policy violations
- Application profiling

The agents running on your system analyze traffic and processes based on sets of application-centric rules. These rule-based policies use the following factors to categorize the traffic:

- Resource being accessed
- Operation being invoked
- Application initiating the action

You deploy and manage Cisco Security Agents throughout your network using the Management Center for Cisco Security Agents. This software suite is comprised of the following major components:

- Cisco Security Agents Management Center (CSA MC)
- Cisco Security Agents

Using CSA MC, you organize your network into groups of systems that share similar characteristics and then apply security policies to those groups. All configuration operations are performed on CSA MC using a web-based interface. You then deploy these configuration changes to the individual systems by updating the individual agents on those systems.

When setting up CSA MC to protect your endpoint systems, you need to perform various tasks to effectively deploy the agent software to your various systems. The major tasks associated with deploying the agent software are as follows:

- Create groups
- Build and distribute agent kits
- Configure policies

- Attach policies to groups
- Generate rules

Some of the criteria that you can use to group systems include the following:

- System function (such as web servers)
- Business group (such as Finance or Engineering)
- Geographical location
- Topological location (such as subnet)
- Importance to your organization (such as mission critical or end user)

When defining your CSA policies, you should use your own security policy as a framework. Therefore, your agents help enforce the security policy that matches your network environment. Each policy is comprised of various rules. The agent software uses these rules to determine which activity on the system is allowed or denied. By default, all activity on the system is allowed unless denied by a specific rule.

Instead of entering information directly via the configuration screens, you can also create different system variables that can be used when configuring CSA MC. These variables can be used to more efficiently configure your access rules and policies. These variables fall into the following categories:

- File sets
- Network address sets
- Network services
- Registry sets
- COM component sets
- Data sets

You can use CSA MC to correlate events from multiple agent systems. Using this information, you can automatically update the policies across your network to halt the spread of malicious programs such as worms and Trojan horses.

The agents deployed throughout your network will generate various events and messages. Besides keeping abreast of the activity on your network, monitoring this information enables you to supplement the rules already in place on your agents by configuring CSA MC to send an email message, issue SNMP traps, generate text-based messages to pagers, log to a text file, or even execute custom programs. You can control the alerts sent out based on the following criteria:

- Severity of the logged event
- Specific event
- Host that generated the event

When viewing the events generated by your agents, you can use either the Event Log view or the Event Monitor view. The main difference between the two views is that the information displayed by the Event Monitor is refreshed regularly (default every 15 seconds). You can filter the information displayed by both event viewers using the following criteria:

- Event log generation time
- Time range
- Severity
- Host
- Rule ID
- Events per page

Besides viewing event information on the screen, you can also generate reports based on the event data as well as your CSA MC configuration. The reports fall into the following categories:

- Events by Severity
- Events by Group
- Host Detail
- Policy Detail
- Group Detail

Review Questions

The following questions test your retention of the material presented in this chapter. The answers to the review questions are in Appendix B, "Answers to Chapter Review Questions."

1 What are some of the problems faced when securing your endpoints?

2 What three levels of application protection does CSA provide?

3 What are the factors used by the agents when using rule-based policies to categorize traffic?

4 Which three Windows operating systems are supported agent platforms?

5 Which UNIX operating system is a currently supported agent platform?

6 Which CiscoWorks user role can manage hosts and groups, attach policies, and only has partial write access to the CSA MC database?

7 What are the three configuration tasks associated with CSA MC that require different privileges?

8   What are some of the criteria that you can use to group systems?

9   What is major difference between the event log and the Event Monitor?

10   What actions (alerts) can CSA MC take in response to events?

11   What is test mode?

12   Which rules can you use file sets with?

13   Which network services are data sets associated with?

14   What two types of application classes can you configure?

15   List some rules that enable global event correlation?

16   What is the Profiler program?

Upon completion of this chapter, you will be able to perform the following tasks:

- Explain the IDS software file format
- Identify the types of software updates
- Identify the major ways to update sensor software
- Explain the basic troubleshooting commands available through the sensor command-line interface (CLI)

CHAPTER 15

Cisco IDS Maintenance and Troubleshooting

New vulnerabilities that pose a threat to networks and hosts are discovered every day. Cisco regularly releases signature updates to enhance the capability of your sensors to detect these new attacks by adding new attacks to each sensor's signature database. Cisco also releases service packs to improve each sensor's intrusion detection capabilities.

You can install these software updates either automatically or manually using a sensor's CLI. Besides software updates, you might periodically need to troubleshoot the operation of your sensor. The sensor's CLI provides several commands that inform you about the operation of your sensor and enables you to perform some basic troubleshooting on your sensor.

Software Updates

Cisco is continually enhancing the capabilities of its IDS software. New signatures are being added to address new attacks as they are discovered. These improvements are deployed via the following types of software releases:

- Major software updates
- Minor software updates
- Service packs
- Signature updates
- Appliance Recovery Partition Image files

The file format of new software releases indicates the type of software update along with its version information. Plus you have several ways in which you can retrieve and install the updates on your sensors.

Cisco Active Update Notification System

To keep current with new software updates and other important Cisco IDS information, you can subscribe to the Cisco Active Update Notification System at http://www.cisco.com/warp/public/779/largeent/it/ids_news/subscribe.html.

This mailing list provides a vehicle to quickly disseminate information on new software updates as well as important new signature update information. You can also view these notifications on the Cisco website.

IDS Software File Format

The Cisco IDS software releases have a filename that is comprised of the following components (see Figure 15-1):

- Software type
- Cisco IDS version
- Service pack level
- Signature version
- Extension

Figure 15-1 *Cisco IDS Software Release Filename Components*

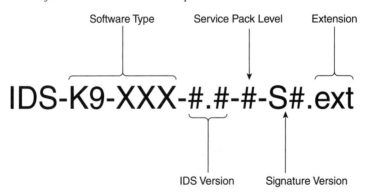

The following are examples of files that demonstrate the naming conventions:

- IDS-sig-4.0-2-S42.rpm.pkg
- IDS-K9-sp-4.0-2-S42.rpm.pkg
- IDS-K9-sp-4.0-2-S42.readme.txt
- IDS-K9-min-4.1-1-S47.rpm.pkg

Software Type

Major software updates, minor software updates, and service packs represent updates to the actual sensor software. They enhance the functionality of your sensor's software by adding new capabilities and addressing any known bugs. A major software update is recognizable by the keyword *maj* in the filename. Minor software updates utilize the *min* keyword, and a service pack is recognizable by the keyword *sp* in the filename.

Unlike a service pack, signature updates do not add new features to your sensor's software. They are released to add new signatures to your sensor. Because Cisco IDS uses multiple signature engines, it is easy to add new signatures without actually changing the software that the sensor runs. A signature update is recognizable by the keyword *sig* in the filename.

NOTE	Signature and software updates must be applied to the correct IDS version. For instance, 4.0-1-sig-S42 cannot be applied to a sensor running version 4.1-1-S43. Similarly, a version 3 update (such as 3.1-4-S54) cannot be applied to a version 4 sensor

If you need to re-image the software on your sensor, you can perform the software reload using the software located on the recovery partition. Using the Appliance Recovery Partition Image files, you can regularly update your recovery partition similar to the way in which you update your sensor software. A sample recovery image filename is IDS-42XX-K9- r-1.2-a-4.1-1-S47.tar.pkg.

Cisco IDS Version

The Cisco IDS version is comprised of the following two numbers:

* Major version
* Minor version

The major version is listed first followed by the minor version. The two numeric values are separated by a decimal. For instance, if the Cisco IDS version is 4.1, the major version is 4 and the minor version is 1.

NOTE	Besides the major and minor version numbers, you will also see major and minor software releases indicated by the keywords *maj* and *min* in the software's filename (as explained in the "Software Types" section earlier in this chapter).

Service Pack Level

Between major and minor software releases, Cisco releases service packs. Service packs are usually released to patch the Cisco IDS software. These updates are incremental improvements to the Cisco IDS software. For instance, 4.0-2 indicates that there has been one service pack for the 4.0 software release (the first version starts at 1).

Signature Version

As signatures are added to Cisco IDS, it is important to know which signatures are included in which software versions. Therefore, the software updates include a signature version that indicates which signatures are included in the update. The signature version is a number such as 42 (preceded by an *S*).

Extension

The extension can be one of the following values:

- rpm.pkg
- readme or readme.txt
- zip

The *rpm.pkg* extension contains an executable file that either contains a signature update or a new service pack.

The *readme* (or *readme.txt*) extension is a text file that provides you with relevant information about a specific service pack or signature update. Reading this information before you update your sensor is important to maintaining the correct operation of your Cisco IDS because it indicates problems associated with the new software. The readme files also indicate hardware requirements.

The *zip* extension is used by the updates that you need to apply to IDS MC so that IDS MC can understand the new signatures that are added to a sensor. IDS MC needs this information because it maintains a copy of the sensor's configuration that the user modifies.

Software Update Guidelines

To ensure the correct operation of your Cisco IDS sensors, you need to follow several guidelines when updating your sensor software. The guidelines fall into the following tasks:

- Read the release notes.
- Download the appropriate updates to your server.
- Install the software update on the sensor.

- If using IDS MC, install the updates on IDS MC first and use IDS MC to push the updates to your sensors.
- If using IDS Event Viewer (IEV), update your IEV software when necessary.

An important step in updating your sensors is to read the release notes. These documents contain important caveats and known issues that apply to the software update. By understanding these issues beforehand, you can make an intelligent decision as to whether these factors impact your decision to install the new software.

When using IDS MC, it is also important to realize that you need to install your sensor software updates through IDS MC itself. If you do not follow this procedure, you can run into configuration problems because IDS MC stores its own copy of the sensor's configuration in its database. To resolve such a configuration problem, however, you can always delete the sensor in IDS MC and add it again.

When using IEV to monitor alarms, an update to your sensor software usually requires you to update your IEV software. Because IEV monitors alarms generated by your sensor, it needs to understand all the alarms that your sensor can generate. Therefore, as you apply software updates to your sensor, you will also need to apply software updates to IEV. For signature updates, updating IEV is necessary to keep the Network Security Database (NSDB) information in IEV in line with the signatures available on the sensor.

NOTE   Service pack updates and signature updates must be applied to the correct base IDS software, but are cumulative updates. For instance, you can apply the sig-4.0-2-S42 signature update to any sensor with 4.0.2 software that has a signature level less than S42. You could not apply this update, however, if your sensor's software version is 4.0.1.

Upgrading Sensor Software

You can upgrade your sensor software through the following three mechanisms:

- Sensor's CLI
- IDS Device Manager (IDM)
- Management Center for IDS sensors (IDS MC)

Software Installation via the Command-Line Interface (CLI)

To upgrade the sensor software from the sensor's CLI, you first need access to the update file. Using the CLI, you have the following methods to access the update file:

- FTP
- HTTP/HTTPS
- Secure Copy (SCP)

Next you need to log in to the sensor with an account that has been assigned the Administrator role, because running the **upgrade** command requires administrative privileges. The syntax of the **upgrade** command is as follows:

```
upgrade <source URL of update>
```

Using this single command, you can apply both service packs as well as signature updates and recovery partition updates. The source URL indicates where the update file is stored. The URL syntax varies slightly depending on the type of server where the update resides. Use the following guidelines when designating the source of the update file:

- ftp://username@ipaddress/RelativeDirectory/filename
- ftp://username@ipaddress//AbsoluteDirectory/filename
- https://username@ipaddress/directory/filename
- http://username@ipaddress/directory/filename
- scp://username@ipaddress/RelativeDirectory/filename
- scp://username@ipaddress//AbsoluteDirectory/filename

Relative directories are based on the home directory of the account that you specified in the URL. For instance, assume the following parameters:

- Username is IDS.
- IDS's home directory is /home/IDS.
- System IP address is 10.10.10.10.

If the update file is located at /home/IDS/updates/IDS-sig-4.0-2-S42.rpm.pkg, to access upgrade using this file via SCP, you can you use either of the following URLs:

- scp://IDS@10.10.10.10/updates/IDS-sig-4.0-2-S42.rpm.pkg
- scp://IDS@10.10.10.10//home/IDS/updates/IDS-sig-4.0-2-S42.rpm.pkg

---

NOTE   The sensor cannot download signature updates and service packs directly from the Cisco website. You must download the signature update or service pack from the Cisco website to your server, and then configure the sensor to download them from your server.

The **upgrade** command prompts you for the password required to authenticate the file transfer. Instead of specifying all the parameters, you can also just supply the server type such as the following:

```
upgrade ftp:
```

When you just specify the server type, you are prompted for the rest of the fields as in the following command sequence:

```
sensor(config)# upgrade ftp:
User: stat
Server's IP Address: 10.89.152.40
Port[21]:
File name: /IDS/IDS-K9-min-4.1-1-S47-.rpm.pkg
Password: *****
Warning: Executing this command will apply a minor version upgrade to the
  application partition. The system may be rebooted to complete the upgrade.
Continue with upgrade? : yes
```

Software Installation Using IDS Device Manager (IDM)

Instead of using the sensor's CLI, you can also use the IDM interface to apply software and signature updates to your sensor. Again, you need to first download the update to your own server. Then follow these steps when using IDM to apply software updates to your sensor:

Step 1   Click the Administration tab on the main IDM interface.

Step 2   Select Update from the options bar. The Update Settings window appears in the content area (see Figure 15-2).

Figure 15-2   *Update Settings Window in IDM*

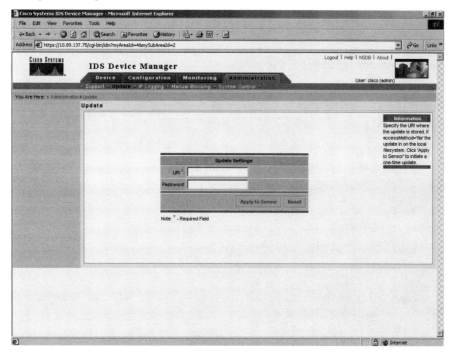

Step 3   In the URI field, enter the source URL of the update (the same URL as used by the **upgrade** command).

Step 4   In the Password field, enter the password required to access the update file using the username specified in the URI field.

Step 5   Click the Apply to Sensor button to apply the software update to your sensor.

Using IDM, you can also configure your sensor to automatically update its software. You basically configure your sensor to check a specific server on a regular basis using one of the following methods:

- Hourly
- Specific day of the week

If you choose to update hourly, you must specify a frequency (in hours) at which the sensor will check for new software updates. Your other option is to specify a specific day of the week on which to check for new software updates. For both of these options, you must also specify the time of day at which you want the actual update to be performed. When a new software update is found on the server, the sensor will wait to apply the software update until the time of day that you have specified.

NOTE   You still need to download the software updates and place them on your server (then being checked by your sensors). Then whenever new software is available on your update server, your sensors can automatically retrieve and install this software.

To use the automatic update mechanism configurable via IDM, follow these steps:

Step 1   Click the Configuration tab on the main IDM interface.

Step 2   Select Auto Update from the options bar. The Auto Update window appears in the content area (see Figure 15-3).

Step 3   Check the Enable Auto Update checkbox to enable the Auto Update feature.

Step 4   Enter the IP address of the server where the updates can be retrieved.

Step 5   Enter the directory where the updates will be located.

Step 6   Specify the username and password to be used to access the server and retrieve the updates.

Step 7   Choose the retrieval method using the File Copy Protocol pull-down menu. (You can choose either FTP or SCP.)

Figure 15-3 *Auto Update Window in IDM*

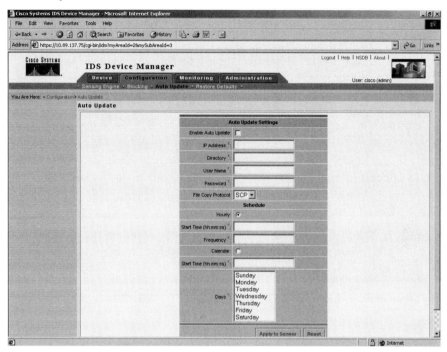

Step 8   Choose to check for new updates either hourly or on a specific day of the week by selecting either the Hourly or Calendar radio buttons.

Step 9   If choosing hourly, specify the start time and the frequency (number of hours between checks). You can specify a number between 1 and 8670 for the frequency.

Step 10 If choosing Calendar, specify the start time and the day of the week on which you want to check for new software updates.

Step 11 Click the Apply to Sensor button to apply the changes to the sensor.

Software Installation Using IDS MC

You can also use the IDS MC interface to apply service packs and signature updates to your sensor. Because IDS MC maintains sensor configuration files in its database, and pushes configuration information to the sensor itself, you must place the software update files on your IDS MC server. Then you can update the configuration of your sensors.

When using IDS MC to apply software updates to your sensor, follow these steps:

Step 1 Download the IDS MC updates from Cisco.com.

Step 2 You need to place these files into the following directory on your IDS MC
server (where X represents the drive where you installed the IDS MC
software):

— X:\Program Files\CSCOpx\MDC\etc\ids\updates

Step 3 Click the Configuration tab from the main IDS MC screen.

NOTE To launch the IDS MC interface, you must first log in to the CiscoWorks.

Step 4 Select Updates from either the options bar or the content area. The
Updates window appears in the content area (see Figure 15-4).

Figure 15-4 *Updates Window in IDS MC*

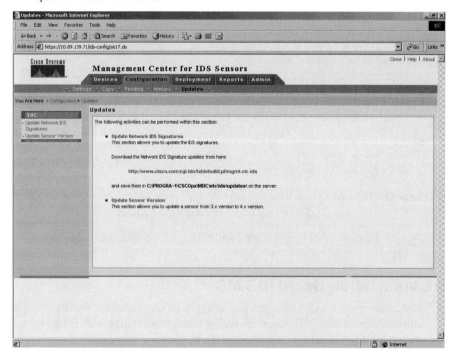

Step 5   Select Update Network IDS Signatures from the TOC. This displays the
Update Network IDS Signatures window in the content area (see Figure 15-5).

Figure 15-5   *Network IDS Signatures Window in IDS MC*

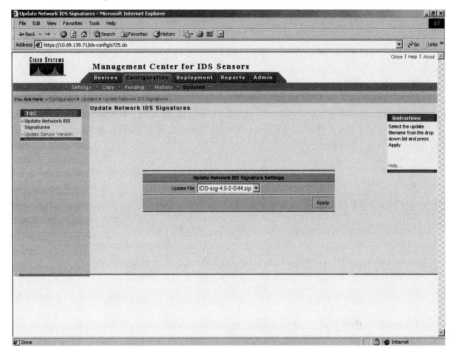

Step 6   Select the correct software or signature update from the drop-down menu
and click the Apply button to apply the update to IDS MC.

Step 7   Use the Upgrade Sensor Version option from the TOC to apply the update
to your actual sensors (see Figure 15-4).

Downgrading an Image

In some situations, you might need to return to a previous sensor software version or
signature release. This capability enables you to test a new software release on your sensor,
but provides the protection that you can always revert to your previous sensor software
version if you have any problems. The **downgrade** sensor CLI command provides this
functionality. The syntax for this command is as follows:

```
downgrade
```

When you run the **downgrade** command, it removes the software installed by the most
recent use of the **upgrade** command. This can also alter the configuration on your sensor

because the new software might have introduced new features or signatures onto your sensor that will be unavailable after the downgrade.

NOTE   You can determine which software the **downgrade** command will remove by running the **show version** command on the sensor's CLI and examining the Upgrade History section.

CAUTION   If you use IDS MC to manage your sensors, the IDS MC software will be unaware of the change in the software version on your sensor (after using the **downgrade** command). You will need to manually change the sensor's version in IDS MC or query the sensor for the new software version.

Image Recovery

If your sensor's software becomes corrupt, you will need to re-image your sensor to restore its software to its correct operational condition. When you re-image a sensor, all accounts are removed and the default Cisco account is reset to the default password (cisco). You must also initialize the sensor again by running the **setup** command.

NOTE   Before re-imaging your sensor, you should back up the current configuration. You can use the CLI command **copy current-config** *<destination URL>*. The beginning of the destination URL indicates the transfer protocol used, such as **scp:** for Secure Copy. The URLs for supported transfer protocols are shown in the "Upgrading Sensor Software" section earlier in this chapter.

When using the **recover** CLI command, you replace all the applications on your sensor from copies of these programs stored on the recovery partition. After using the **recover** command, all of your configuration information on the sensor is removed except for the network parameters, such as the IP address.

NOTE   Signature updates and service packs are not automatically applied to the recovery partition. Therefore, you need to keep your recovery partition updated in addition to applying signature and service packs. Otherwise, you will need to use the **upgrade** command (after using the **recover** command) to reapply the signature updates and service packs. To update your recovery partition, you need to apply the appropriate Appliance Recovery Partition Image file (using the **upgrade** command). This image is a separate image that you download in addition to your normal sensor software update.

Basic Troubleshooting

Using the sensor's CLI, you can also perform various commands that enable you to perform some basic troubleshooting operations on your sensor. The following **show** commands are useful in checking the operation of your sensor:

- **show version**
- **show interface**
- **show tech-support**
- **show statistics**
- **show events**

show version

The **show version** command displays the version information for all the installed operating system packages, signature packages, and IDS processes running on the system. The syntax for this command is as follows:

```
show version
```

Using this command, you can quickly determine the status of the major IDS processes, as shown in the following sample run of the **show version** command:

```
sensor# show version
Application Partition:

Cisco Systems Intrusion Detection Sensor, Version 4.1(1)S42(1)

OS Version 2.4.18-5smpbigphys
Platform: IDS-4210
Sensor up-time is 11 days.
Using 192937984 out of 244531200 bytes of available memory (78% usage)
Using 627M out of 7.8G bytes of available disk space (9% usage)


MainApp            2003_Apr_28_10.26   (Release)   2003-04-28T10:35:23-0500   Running
AnalysisEngine     2003_Apr_28_10.26   (Release)   2003-04-28T10:35:23-0500   Running
Authentication     2003_Apr_28_10.26   (Release)   2003-04-28T10:35:23-0500   Running
Logger             2003_Apr_28_10.26   (Release)   2003-04-28T10:35:23-0500   Running
NetworkAccess      2003_Apr_28_10.26   (Release)   2003-04-28T10:35:23-0500   Running
TransactionSource  2003_Apr_28_10.26   (Release)   2003-04-28T10:35:23-0500   Running
WebServer          2003_Apr_28_10.26   (Release)   2003-04-28T10:35:23-0500   Running
CLI                2003_Apr_28_10.26   (Release)   2003-04-28T10:35:23-0500

Upgrade History:


* IDS-K9-maj-4.0-1-S36                   12:10:10 UTC Sat May 17 2003
   IDS-K9-min-4.1-1-S42-1-.rpm.pkg   22:50:02 UTC Sat May 17 2003

Recovery Partition Version 1.1 - 4.0(1)S37
```

This command also shows you the software images and updates that you have installed on your sensor in the Upgrade History section. This information proves very useful if you need to use the **downgrade** command because you can see to which software version your sensor will revert.

All users can execute this command.

show interfaces

Using the **show interfaces** command, you can view the statistics for the interfaces on your sensor. Without any arguments, this command displays the statistics for all the interfaces on your sensor.

The syntax for the **show interfaces** command is as follows:

```
show interfaces [clear]
```

Using the **clear** keyword, you can clear the current diagnostic information for all the interfaces on your sensor. This can prove very useful if you want to check how the interface statistics are changing. Instead of writing down the current information and then running the command again to determine the changes, you can just clear the statistics first. Then when you run the **show interfaces** command the second time, you will immediately see the updated values.

The following shows a sample output stream from the **show interfaces** command:

```
sensor# show interfaces
command-control is up
  Internet address is 10.89.137.75, subnet mask is 255.255.255.0, telnet is disabled.
  Hardware is eth1, tx


Network Statistics
    eth1      Link encap:Ethernet  HWaddr 00:D0:B7:9A:8D:3B
              inet addr:10.89.137.75  Bcast:10.89.137.255  Mask:255.255.255.0
              UP BROADCAST RUNNING MULTICAST  MTU:1500  Metric:1
              RX packets:798889 errors:0 dropped:0 overruns:0 frame:0
              TX packets:328621 errors:0 dropped:0 overruns:0 carrier:0
              collisions:0 txqueuelen:100
              RX bytes:64461367 (61.4 Mb)  TX bytes:90717184 (86.5 Mb)
              Interrupt:5 Base address:0xee80 Memory:febfa000-febfa038

  Group 0 is up
    Sensing ports int0
    Logical virtual sensor configuration: virtualSensor
    Logical alarm channel configuration:  virtualAlarm

  VirtualSensor0
    General Statistics for this Virtual Sensor
        Number of seconds since a reset of the statistics = 525184
        Measure of the level of resource utilization = 0
        Total number of packets processed since reset = 853297
        Total number of IP packets processed since reset = 247388
        Total number of packets that were not IP processed since reset = 605909
        Total number of TCP packets processed since reset = 206841
        Total number of UDP packets processed since reset = 40484
```

```
        Total number of ICMP packets processed since reset = 63
       Total number of packets that were not TCP, UDP, or ICMP processed since reset = 0
        Total number of ARP packets processed since reset = 63086
        Total number of ISL encapsulated packets processed since reset = 0
        Total number of 802.1q encapsulated packets processed since reset = 0
        Total number of packets with bad IP checksums processed since reset = 154779
       Total number of packets with bad layer 4 checksums processed since reset = 154779
        Total number of bytes processed since reset = 99808723
        The rate of packets per second since reset = 1
        The rate of bytes per second since reset = 190
        The average bytes per packet since reset = 116
     Fragment Reassembly Unit Statistics for this Virtual Sensor
        Number of fragments currently in FRU = 0
        Number of datagrams currently in FRU = 0
        Number of fragments received since reset = 0
        Number of complete datagrams reassembled since reset = 0
        Number of incomplete datagrams abandoned since reset = 0
        Number of fragments discarded since reset = 0
     Statistics for the TCP Stream Reassembly Unit
        Current Statistics for the TCP Stream Reassembly Unit
           TCP streams currently in the embryonic state = 0
           TCP streams currently in the established state = 0
           TCP streams currently in the closing state = 0
           TCP streams currently in the system = 0
           TCP Packets currently queued for reassembly = 0
        Cumulative Statistics for the TCP Stream Reassembly Unit since reset
           TCP streams that have been tracked since last reset = 2456
           TCP streams that had a gap in the sequence jumped = 0
           TCP streams that was abandoned due to a gap in the sequence = 1
           TCP packets that arrived out of sequence order for their stream = 87
           TCP packets that arrived out of state order for their stream = 20280
           The rate of TCP connections tracked per second since reset = 0
     The Signature Database Statistics.
        The Number of each type of node active in the system (can not be reset)
           Total nodes active = 12
           TCP nodes keyed on both IP addresses and both ports = 0
           UDP nodes keyed on both IP addresses and both ports = 2
           IP nodes keyed on both IP addresses = 2
        The number of each type of node inserted since reset
           Total nodes inserted = 36928
           TCP nodes keyed on both IP addresses and both ports = 2326
           UDP nodes keyed on both IP addresses and both ports = 2877
           IP nodes keyed on both IP addresses = 8131
        The rate of nodes per second for each time since reset
           Nodes per second = 0
           TCP nodes keyed on both IP addresses and both ports per second = 0
           UDP nodes keyed on both IP addresses and both ports per second = 0
           IP nodes keyed on both IP addresses per second = 0
        The number of root nodes forced to expire because of memory constraints
           TCP nodes keyed on both IP addresses and both ports = 0
     Alarm Statistics for this Virtual Sensor
        Number of alarms triggered by events = 2
        Number of alarms excluded by filters = 0
        Number of alarms removed by summarizer = 0
        Number of alarms sent to the Event Store = 2


Sensing int0 is up
  Hardware is eth0, TX
  Reset port

sensor#
```

You can also limit which interfaces you display information on using one of the following commands:

- **show interfaces command-control**
- **show interfaces sensing**
- **show interfaces group**

All users can execute all the **show interfaces** commands.

show interfaces command-control

To display the statistics for the command and control interface only, you can use the **show interfaces command-control**. The syntax for this command is as follows:

```
show interfaces command-control
```

The first line of the output indicates whether the interface is up or down, as shown in the following output from the **show interfaces command-control** command:

```
sensor# show interfaces command-control
command-control is up
  Internet address is 10.89.137.75, subnet mask is 255.255.255.0, telnet is disabled.
  Hardware is eth1, tx

Network Statistics
    eth1     Link encap:Ethernet  HWaddr 00:D0:B7:9A:8D:3B
             inet addr:10.89.137.75  Bcast:10.89.137.255  Mask:255.255.255.0
             UP BROADCAST RUNNING MULTICAST  MTU:1500  Metric:1
             RX packets:797998 errors:0 dropped:0 overruns:0 frame:0
             TX packets:328156 errors:0 dropped:0 overruns:0 carrier:0
             collisions:0 txqueuelen:100
             RX bytes:64394258 (61.4 Mb)  TX bytes:90665384 (86.4 Mb)
             Interrupt:5 Base address:0xee80 Memory:febfa000-febfa038
sensor#
```

NOTE   The command and control interface on your sensor should always be in the up state.

---

show interfaces sensing

Using the **show interfaces sensing** command, you can view the status for one of your sensing interfaces. The syntax for this command is as follows:

```
show interfaces sensing interface
```

The *interface* parameter indicates the logical interface for which you want to view the information. Common interface names are int0 and int1. A sample status for int0 is as follows:

```
sensor# show interfaces sensing int0
Sensing int0 is up
  Hardware is eth0, TX
  Reset port

sensor#
```

show interfaces group

In Cisco IDS version 4.0, you can group interfaces into a logical group. Using the **show interfaces group** command, you can display the statistics for an interface group. The syntax for this command is as follows:

```
show interfaces group [number]
```

number indicates the logical number for the interface group. Valid values range from 0 through 7. The default logical group is 0.

NOTE   If you do not provide an interface group number on the command line, the **show interfaces group** command will display the statistics for all the groups on your sensor.

The output for this command is similar to the following:

```
sensor# show interfaces group 0
Group 0 is up
  Sensing ports int0
  Logical virtual sensor configuration: virtualSensor
  Logical alarm channel configuration:  virtualAlarm


VirtualSensor0
  General Statistics for this Virtual Sensor
    Number of seconds since a reset of the statistics = 525813
    Measure of the level of resource utilization = 0
    Total number of packets processed since reset = 854072
    Total number of IP packets processed since reset = 247437
    Total number of packets that were not IP processed since reset = 606635
    Total number of TCP packets processed since reset = 206841
    Total number of UDP packets processed since reset = 40533
    Total number of ICMP packets processed since reset = 63
   Total number of packets that were not TCP, UDP, or ICMP processed since reset = 0
    Total number of ARP packets processed since reset = 63164
    Total number of ISL encapsulated packets processed since reset = 0
    Total number of 802.1q encapsulated packets processed since reset = 0
    Total number of packets with bad IP checksums processed since reset = 154779
   Total number of packets with bad layer 4 checksums processed since reset = 154779
    Total number of bytes processed since reset = 99867131
    The rate of packets per second since reset = 1
    The rate of bytes per second since reset = 189
    The average bytes per packet since reset = 116
  Fragment Reassembly Unit Statistics for this Virtual Sensor
    Number of fragments currently in FRU = 0
    Number of datagrams currently in FRU = 0
    Number of fragments received since reset = 0
    Number of complete datagrams reassembled since reset = 0
    Number of incomplete datagrams abandoned since reset = 0
    Number of fragments discarded since reset = 0
  Statistics for the TCP Stream Reassembly Unit
    Current Statistics for the TCP Stream Reassembly Unit
      TCP streams currently in the embryonic state = 0
      TCP streams currently in the established state = 0
      TCP streams currently in the closing state = 0
      TCP streams currently in the system = 0
```

```
            TCP Packets currently queued for reassembly = 0
        Cumulative Statistics for the TCP Stream Reassembly Unit since reset
            TCP streams that have been tracked since last reset = 2456
            TCP streams that had a gap in the sequence jumped = 0
            TCP streams that was abandoned due to a gap in the sequence = 1
            TCP packets that arrived out of sequence order for their stream = 87
            TCP packets that arrived out of state order for their stream = 20280
            The rate of TCP connections tracked per second since reset = 0
    The Signature Database Statistics.
        The Number of each type of node active in the system (can not be reset)
            Total nodes active = 11
            TCP nodes keyed on both IP addresses and both ports = 0
            UDP nodes keyed on both IP addresses and both ports = 1
            IP nodes keyed on both IP addresses = 2
        The number of each type of node inserted since reset
            Total nodes inserted = 36959
            TCP nodes keyed on both IP addresses and both ports = 2326
            UDP nodes keyed on both IP addresses and both ports = 2881
            IP nodes keyed on both IP addresses = 8140
        The rate of nodes per second for each time since reset
            Nodes per second = 0
            TCP nodes keyed on both IP addresses and both ports per second = 0
            UDP nodes keyed on both IP addresses and both ports per second = 0
            IP nodes keyed on both IP addresses per second = 0
        The number of root nodes forced to expire because of memory constraints
            TCP nodes keyed on both IP addresses and both ports = 0
    Alarm Statistics for this Virtual Sensor
        Number of alarms triggered by events = 2
        Number of alarms excluded by filters = 0
        Number of alarms removed by summarizer = 0
        Number of alarms sent to the Event Store = 2
sensor#
```

show tech-support

Using the **show tech-support** command, you can display a comprehensive list of status and system information about your sensor. This command consolidates the output from the following individual commands and other data sources:

- **more current-config**
- **show version**
- Debug logs

NOTE   Beginning with version 4.1, besides the **more current-config** command you can also use **show configuration**.

The Technical Assistance Center (TAC) frequently uses the output from this command to debug problems with the operation of your sensor. The syntax for the **show tech-support** command is as follows:

```
show tech-support [page][password][destination destination-url]
```

Table 15-1 explains the parameters for the **show tech-support** command.

Table 15-1   **show tech-support** *Parameters*

Parameter	Description
page	(Optional) Causes the output to display one page of information at a time. You can then display the next line of output using the Enter key, or page through the information with the Spacebar.
password	(Optional) Leaves password and other security information in the output. If password is not used, passwords and other sensitive security information in the output are replaced with the label *<removed>*. This is the default.
destination	(Optional) Tag indicating that the information should be formatted as HTML and sent to the destination following the tag.
destination-url	Indicates the destination for the HTML-formatted output. (Required if the **destination** parameter is specified.)

When specifying a destination for the **show tech-support** command output, you can choose one of the following destination formats:

- ftp://username@ip_address/RelativeDirectory/filename
- ftp://username@ip_address//AbsoluteDirectory/filename
- scp://username@ip_address/RelativeDirectory/filename
- scp://username@ip_address//AbsoluteDirectory/filename

Instead of specifying all the options on the command line, you can also specify just the server type. In this situation, you are prompted for the individual parameters, as in the following sample output:

```
sensor# show tech-support destination scp:
User: IDS
Server's IP Address: 10.89.156.78
Port[22]:
File name: Sensor4230.out
Password: ********
```

Because this command has the capability to display passwords and other sensitive information, you can only execute this command using an account that has been assigned the Administrator role.

CAUTION   Generating all the information used by the **show tech-support** command can take up to 5 to 10 minutes to complete. During this time, you will not be able to use your console.

---

show statistics

Besides interface statistics, you can also display statistics about various processes on your sensor using the **show statistics** command. The syntax for this command is as follows:

```
show statistics {Authentication |EventServer |EventStore |Host |Logger |
    NetworkAccess |TransactionServer |TransacationSource |WebServer} [clear]
```

Table 15-2 shows the parameters for this command.

Table 15-2   **show statistics** *Parameters*

Parameter	Description
clear	Clears the statistics after they are retrieved (not available for host or network access statistics).
Authentication	Displays the authorization and authentication statistics.
EventServer	Displays the Event Server statistics.
EventStore	Displays the Event Store statistics.
Host	Displays host (main) statistics.
Logger	Displays logger statistics.
NetworkAccess	Displays network access controller statistics.
TransactionServer	Displays transaction server statistics.
TransactionSource	Displays transaction source statistics.
WebServer	Displays web server statistics.

If you want to view the information about the web server on your sensor, for instance, you can use the **show statistics WebServer** command. A sample of the output from this command is as follows:

```
sensor# show statistics WebServer
listener-443
   session-8
      remote host = 10.89.139.71
      session is persistent = yes
      number of requests serviced on current connection = 708
      last status code = 200
      last request method = GET
      last request URI = cgi-bin/event-server
      last protocol version = HTTP/1.1
      session state = processingGetServlet
   number of server session requests handled = 2137
   number of server session requests rejected = 0
   total HTTP requests handled = 19478
   maximum number of session objects allowed = 40
   number of idle allocated session objects = 9
   number of busy allocated session objects = 1
crypto library version = 6.0.3
sensor#
```

All users can execute this command.

show events

Sometimes you want to verify that your sensor is generating events. Using the **show events** command, you can display the local event log contents. The syntax for this command is as follows:

```
show events [{[alert[informational][low][medium][high]]|error[warning |fatal]
    |log |NAC|status}][hh:mm:ss[month day[ year]]]
```

Table 15-3 shows the parameters for this command.

Table 15-3   **show events** *Parameters*

Parameter	Description
alert	Displays the alerts that the sensor generates in response to suspicious activity on your network. If no alert level is specified (informational, low, medium, high), all alert events display.
error	Displays the error events that are generated by the various IDS services when error conditions are encountered. If no level is selected (error, warning, fatal), all error events display.
log	Displays the log events that are generated whenever a transaction is received and responded to by an application.
NAC	Displays network access control requests (block/shun requests).
status	Displays status events.
hh:mm:ss	Starts time in 24-hour time format.
day	Starts date of the month.
month	Starts month (specified using the name of the month).
year	Starts year (not abbreviated; for instance, January not Jan).

Although you can refine the output of the **show events** command, you can also just enter the command without any parameters. This will display the various events (including IDS alarms and errors) in real time on your sensor. The following output shows some sample events displayed using the **show events** command:

```
evError: eventId=1053192449236514001 severity=warning
  originator:
    hostId: sensor
    appName: sensorApp
    appInstanceId:
  time: 2003/05/17 17:27:37 2003/05/17 17:27:37 UTC
  errorMessage: name=errUnclassified Generating new Analysis Engine configuration
file.


evLogTransaction: command=getHostConfig eventId=1053192449236514002 successful=true
  originator:
    hostId: sensor
    appName: mainApp
```

```
        appInstanceId: 661
     time: 2003/05/17 17:27:39 2003/05/17 17:27:39 UTC
     requestor:
       user:
       application:
         hostId:
         appName: nac
         appInstanceId: 911


  evStatus: eventId=1053192449236514003
    originator:
      hostId: sensor
      appName: nac
      appInstanceId: 911
    time: 2003/05/17 17:27:39 2003/05/17 17:27:39
  UTC<shunningDisabled><description>Shunning disabled</description></shunningDis
  abled>
```

NOTE   The **show events** command continues to display events to the screen until you press Ctrl+C.

All users can execute the **show events** command.

Summary

New vulnerabilities that pose a threat to networks and hosts are discovered every day. Cisco regularly releases signature updates and service packs to enhance the capability of your sensors to detect these new attacks. Maintaining the current software on your sensor is crucial to keeping your Cisco IDS in peak operational condition.

Service packs and other software updates enhance the functionality of your sensor software. These updates are comprehensive and do not have to be applied incrementally (but they do need to applied to the correct base software version). Software updates use a file format that quickly enables you to distinguish software updates from signature updates. Examining the filename for a software update, you can easily determine the following information:

- Software type
- Cisco IDS version
- Service pack level
- Signature version
- Extension

You can update the software on your sensor using the following three management platforms:

- Sensor's CLI
- IDM
- IDS MC

Using the CLI, you use the **upgrade** command to update the software on your sensor and you have the following methods to access the update file:

- FTP
- HTTP/HTTPS
- SCP

When using IDS MC, not only must you update the software on your sensor, you must also update IDS MC itself. Because IDS MC maintains a copy of your sensor's configuration, it also needs to know the signatures that are available on your sensor.

If you need to revert to a previous software version, you can use the sensor's **downgrade** CLI command to remove the last software that you installed on the sensor using the **upgrade** command.

NOTE   If you use IDS MC, it will not know that the sensor has been downgraded. IDS MC will think that the sensor is still running the previous software version that is stored in IDS MC. You will need to delete and re-add the affected sensor.

From the sensor's CLI, you can obtain a wealth of troubleshooting information using various **show** commands. Some of the commands that you can use to troubleshoot your sensor are as follows:

- **show version**
- **show interface**
- **show tech-support**
- **show statistics**
- **show events**

Review Questions

The following questions test your retention of the material presented in this chapter. The answers to the review questions are in Appendix B, "Answers to Chapter Review Questions."

1   What two types of software updates do you regularly apply to your sensors?

2   What is the difference between the two types of software updates?

3   Which command do you use on the sensor's CLI to update the sensor's software?

4   When using the sensor CLI, which server types can you use to retrieve the sensor software from?

5   What command do you use to revert to the previous software version on your sensor?

6   What CLI command can you use to re-image your sensor?

7   What CLI command enables you to see the status of the IDS processes running on your sensor?

8   What CLI command can you use to view the statistics for only the command and control interface on your sensor?

9   What is the default interface group on the sensor?

10   Which CLI command displays the statistics for all the interfaces on your sensor?

11   Which user roles are allowed to run most of the **show** CLI commands on the sensor?

12   Which **show** CLI command requires administrator privileges to be run?

13   The TAC typically uses the output from which command to debug operational problems with your sensor?

14   Which CLI command enables you to view the alerts that are being generated by your sensor?

15   Which CLI command would you use to show the information about your sensor's web server (such as persistent connections)?

Upon completion of this chapter, you will be able to perform the following tasks:

- Explain the enterprise Cisco intrusion protection system management solution
- Explain the Management Center for IDS Sensors (IDS MC) architecture
- Identify the system requirements for the IDS MC server
- Identify the system requirements for the IDS MC client systems
- Install the IDS MC server software
- Explain the major components of the IDS MC user interface
- Explain the process used to deploy changes to your sensor configurations using IDS MC

CHAPTER 16

Enterprise IDS Management

Managing a large number of Cisco sensors one at a time using IDS Device Manager (IDM) is not practical. If you deploy a large number of sensors on your network, you need an efficient mechanism to configure and manage these devices. The Management Center for IDS Sensors (IDS MC) provides this capability. IDS MC is a component of the CiscoWorks Virtual Private Network (VPN)/Security Management Solution (VMS) bundle. The VMS bundle (version 2.2) integrates various applications that provide the following functionality:

- VPN monitoring
- VPN router management
- Firewall management
- IDS management
- Host agent management
- Security monitoring
- Operational management

This chapter provides a detailed examination of the IDS MC software by providing in-depth information on the following aspects of IDS MC:

- Architecture
- Server requirements
- Client requirements
- User interface components
- Accessing online help
- Configuration change deployment

CiscoWorks

CiscoWorks is the heart of the Cisco family of comprehensive network management tools that enable you to easily access and manage the advanced capabilities of the Cisco Archicture for Voice, Video, and Integrated Display (AVVID). It provides the foundation that IDS MC is built upon. Therefore, before you can access the IDS MC application, you must first log in to CiscoWorks. CiscoWorks also manages access to all the applications in the VMS bundle. To use IDS MC, you need to understand the following CiscoWorks components:

- Login process
- Authorization roles
- Adding users

NOTE   Because your CiscoWorks server is a key component in your overall network security solution, you need to take extra measures to ensure that it is protected from attack. One way to help secure your CiscoWorks server is to minimize access to it. By dedicating a server solely to CiscoWorks (instead of using the server for other purposes as well), you can minimize user access. This also limits the services available to an attacker.

Login Process

To access the applications supported by CiscoWorks, such as IDS MC and the Monitoring Center for Security (Security Monitor), you must first log in to the CiscoWorks server desktop. The CiscoWorks server desktop is the interface used for CiscoWorks network management applications, such as IDS MC.

To log in to CiscoWorks, you connect to the CiscoWorks desktop via your web browser. By default, the CiscoWorks web server is listening on port 1741. So if your CiscoWorks desktop is on a machine named CW2000.cisco.com through your Domain Name System (DNS) with an IP address of 10.89.139.71, you could connect to it by entering either of the following URLs:

- http://CW2000.cisco.com:1471/
- http://10.89.139.71:1741/

NOTE   If you are on the actual CiscoWorks server, you can also access CiscoWorks by using the following URL:

   - http://127.0.0.1:1741/

You can also enable CiscoWorks to use HTTPS (rather than HTTP). Some management centers (such as the Management Center for Cisco Security Agents) enable HTTPS on CiscoWorks automatically when you install them. When HTTPS is enabled, you need to connect to port 1742.

At the initial CiscoWorks screen, you need to log in to CiscoWorks by entering a valid username and password (see Figure 16-1).

Figure 16-1   *CiscoWorks Login Screen*

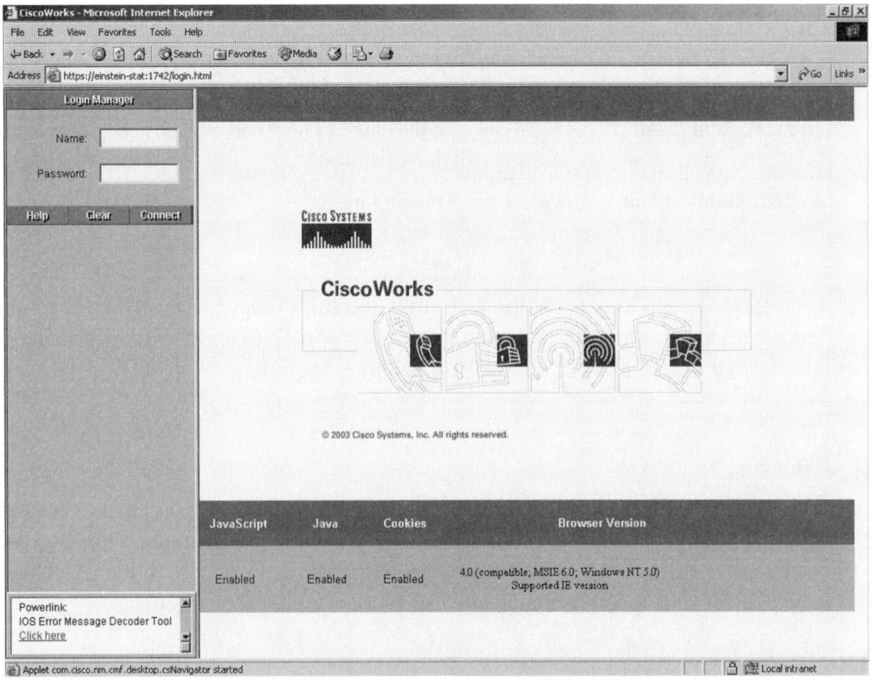

JavaScript	Java	Cookies	Browser Version
Enabled	Enabled	Enabled	4.0 (compatible; MSIE 6.0; Windows NT 5.0) Supported IE version

---

NOTE   Initially, you can log in using the administration account created during installation. The default value is admin for both the username and password (unless you changed these values during the installation process). For security reasons, you should change these values.

Authorization Roles

CiscoWorks enables you to define different roles for different users. These roles enable the user to perform specific operations when using CiscoWorks and any of the applications that are built upon CiscoWorks (such as IDS MC and Security Monitor). CiscoWorks supports five different user roles that are relevant to IDS MC operations (see Table 16-1):

Table 16-1   *CiscoWorks User Roles*

User Role	Description
Help Desk	Read-only for the entire system
Approver	Read-only for entire system and includes the configuration approval privileges

continues

Table 16-1 *CiscoWorks User Roles (Continued)*

User Role	Description
Network Operator	Read-only for the entire system, generates reports, and includes configuration deployment privileges
Network Administrator	Read-only for the entire system and includes privileges to edit devices and device groups
System Administrator	Performs all operations

NOTE   You can assign each user multiple authorization roles (depending on their responsibilities). CiscoWorks also supports two other roles of Export Data and Developer. These roles are not relevant to the IDS MC or Security Monitor operations.

Adding Users

As part of your IDS MC and Security Monitor configuration, you need to configure accounts for the various users that need to access these applications. The CiscoWorks Add User screen enables you to create new accounts that have access to the CiscoWorks applications. To create a new account in CiscoWorks, follow these steps:

Step 1   Log in to the CiscoWorks desktop.

Step 2   Choose Server Configuration>Setup>Security>Add Users. The Add user window appears (see Figure 16-2).

Figure 16-2 *CiscoWorks Add User Window*

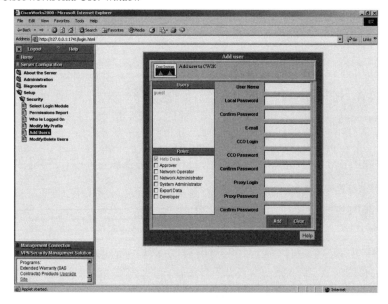

Step 3   Enter values for the new user. Table 16-2 describes these various fields.

Table 16-2   *CiscoWorks Add User Fields*

Field	Description
User Name	Username of the account being added.
Local Password	Password for the new user.
Confirm Password	Confirmation of the user's password.
E-Mail	(Optional) User's email address.
CCO Login	(Optional) User's Cisco.com registered user login name.
CCO Password	User's Cisco.com registered user password (only required if CCO login is specified).
Confirm Password	Confirmation of user's Cisco.com registered user password (only required if the CCO password is entered).
Proxy Login	(Optional) Enter the user's proxy login. Required if your network requires use of a proxy server.
Proxy Password	User's proxy password (only required if proxy login is specified).
Confirm Password	Confirmation of user's proxy login (only required if proxy login is specified).

Step 4   Using the Roles section of the Add Users window, select the roles associated with the user's responsibilities. You can assign multiple roles to a single user.

Step 5   Click Add to complete the addition of the user to the CiscoWorks database.

Management Center for IDS Sensors (IDS MC)

IDS MC is a web-based application that centralizes and accelerates the deployment and management of multiple devices. It enables you to easily update the configuration of multiple sensors by creating logical sensor groups. Furthermore, multiple people are able to access IDS MC via the CiscoWorks server (unlike IDM, which only allows a single user to connect to the sensor at a time). Figure 16-3 outlines the basic IDS MC deployment configuration.

Figure 16-3 *IDS MC Setup*

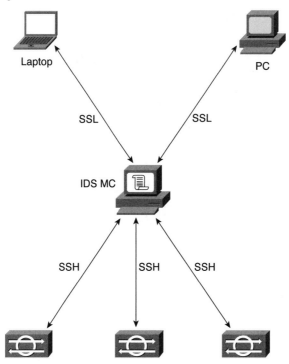

IDS MC version 1.2 can manage the following types of sensors:

- **Sensor appliance**—Requires software version 3.0 or higher
- **IDS Module**—Requires software version 3.0(5) or higher

NOTE   IDS MC has its own version number that is not the same as the VMS version. VMS version 2.2 includes IDS MC version 1.2. Version 2.2 refers to the CiscoWorks version, not the version of the individual components supplied in the VMS bundle.

Your can manage up to 300 sensors with IDS MC. By grouping sensors, you can efficiently manage multiple sensors that share a common configuration. You can even import the configuration from sensors that have been configured by other management applications, such as IDM. Furthermore, you can easily push signature updates and sensor software updates to individual sensors or sensor groups through IDS MC.

Architecture Overview

The IDS MC enables you to manage multiple sensors. The IDS MC application is built upon the underlying CiscoWorks foundation. This foundation provides a data store for all the CiscoWorks applications. In addition, IDS MC and Security Monitor share another data store that is used to house the alarm events and other configuration information. Figure 16-4 provides a high-level architecture overview of IDS MC.

Figure 16-4   *IDS MC Architecture Overview*

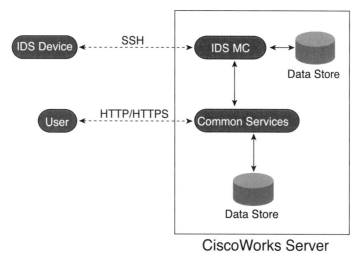

CiscoWorks provides a set of Common Services used by all the applications built on Cisco-Works, such as the IDS MC and the Security Monitor. Because each application built on CiscoWorks uses some of the same basic operations, this functionality is built into the Common Services. The features supported by the Common Services are listed in Table 16-3.

Table 16-3   *Common Services Features*

Feature	Description
Data storage and management	The data store is contained within a Sybase 7.0 SQL server. Common Services provides management for this data to enable backups and restores. In addition, Common Services incorporates the functionality to enable automatic repairs of the database to prevent corruption.
Web interface	An Apache web server provides the HTTP interface that enables users to connect to CiscoWorks. Access to IDS MC uses HTTPS. Tomcat is used to communicate with the Java servlets for the user interface.

continues

Table 16-3 *Common Services Features (Continued)*

Feature	Description
Session management	Manages sessions to enable multiple users to access IDS MC without losing or corrupting data.
User authentication/ authorization management	Manages permissions based on the authorization roles assigned to each user. These accounts and roles are created and managed via the Common Services.
Common environment for IDS MC	Enables multiple management consoles to operate independently within their own range of operation, while each use the features provided by Common Services.

Directories

The IDS MC places various files on the CiscoWorks server during installation. The majority of these files are located in several directories that are located under one common installation directory. Some of the major directories are shown in Figure 16-5. The home directory is typically X:\Program Files\CSCOPx\MDC (with X being the drive letter where the software is installed).

Figure 16-5 *IDS MC Directories*

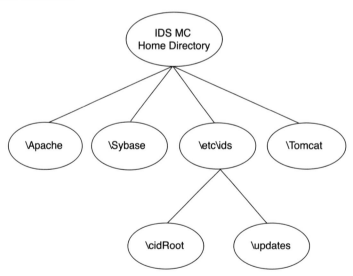

The various IDS MC files are logically divided into directories based on the various applications and functionality provided by IDS MC. When you update the network signatures known to IDS MC, for instance, you place the Signature update files in the etc\ids\upgrade directory.

Processes

During its operation, IDS MC uses various processes to perform its functionality. During troubleshooting, it is often helpful to know the names of these different processes and the basic functionality that they provide. Table 16-4 highlights the major IDS MC processes.

Table 16-4   *IDS MC Processes*

Process Name	Description
IDS_Analyzer	Defines event rules and requests user-specified notifications when appropriate
IDS_Backup	Performs the backups and restores of the IDS MC database
IDS_DbAdminAnalyzer	Periodically applies the active database rules to the current state of the server
IDS_DeployDaemon	Manages all configuration deployments
IDS_Notifier	Retrieves notification requests (script, email, and/or console) from other subsystems and performs the requested notification
IDS_Receiver	Receives Cisco IDS alarms and syslog security events and stores them in the database
IDS_ReportScheduler	Generates all scheduled reports

NOTE   You can view the status of these processes by choosing Server Configuration>Administration>Process Management>Process Status from the CiscoWorks main menu.

Windows Installation

When installing IDS MC, you need to understand the hardware and software requirements for the different components. The major components involved in an IDS MC Windows installation are as follows:

- CiscoWorks Common Services server
- Client systems
- Sensors

Because the sensors are appliances, the software and hardware are fairly fixed. The other two components, however, are built on your own machines. To ensure an operable installation, these systems must match some minimum requirements.

Server Requirements

To support all the functionality provided by IDS MC and the underlying CiscoWorks foundation, your CiscoWorks server needs to match the following requirements:

- IBM PC-compatible computer
- 1-GHz processor or faster
- Color monitor with video card capable of viewing 16-bit color
- CD-ROM drive
- 10BASE-T or faster network connection
- Minimum of 1 GB RAM
- 2 GB virtual memory
- Minimum of 9 GB free hard drive space (NTFS)
- Windows 2000 Professional, Server, or Advanced Server (with Service Pack 3)

NOTE   Requirements for the CiscoWorks server are frequently updated. For the latest server requirements, refer to the documentation on the Cisco website (such as the "Quick Start for VPN/Security Management Solution").

CAUTION   Do not attempt to install IDS MC with Security Monitor on a system that has Cisco Secure Policy Manager (CSPM) installed on it. The installer for Security Monitor attempts to install the Cisco IDS PostOffice software in a second location on the host, causing it to function incorrectly.

Installation Process

VMS Common Services is required for the IDS MC software. VMS Common Services provides the CiscoWorks server base components, software libraries, and the software packages specifically developed for the IDS MC. For more information on VMS, refer to the "Quick Start Guide for VPN Security Management Solution" and other documentation on the Cisco website.

After you have installed the VMS Common Services, you can then install the IDS MC Windows software using the following steps:

Step 1   Insert the Cisco IDS MC CD into the CD-ROM drive on your server. The Welcome window appears.

| **NOTE** | If autorun is enabled, the installation process should begin automatically. If it does not start automatically, you can begin the installation process by locating and executing setup.exe. |

Step 2   Click Next. The Software License Agreement window appears.

Step 3   If you agree with the license agreement, click Yes to continue with the installation. The Setup Type window appears.

| **NOTE** | If you click No, the installation process will stop. |

Step 4   Select Typical Installation as the installation type, and then click Next to continue. The System Requirements window appears.

| **NOTE** | If you want to install only IDS MC or the Security Monitor, you can choose Custom Installation and specify which component you want to install. |

Step 5   Click Next. The Verification window appears.

Step 6   Click Next. The Select Database Location window appears.

Step 7   The default database location is within the directory where VMS Common Services is installed. Click Next to accept the default directory. The Select Database Password window appears.

Step 8   Enter a password to secure access to the Sybase SQL database used by the IDS MC to store sensor information. You must type the password in two locations to verify that you typed it correctly. Click Next. The Select CW2000 Syslog Port Window appears.

| **NOTE** | The IDS MC database password must be at least four characters in length. If you enter a password that has fewer than four characters, you receive a pop-up error message indicating that your password is too short. You should also not make the password a dictionary word, to make it more difficult for an attacker to guess your password. For more information about creating strong passwords, refer to one of the numerous references available on the Internet, such as http://www.uni.edu/its/us/faqs/security/PasswordsStrong.htm. |

Step 9 The Security Monitor runs a different syslog server than the standard CiscoWorks syslog server. Either enter a new port number (1–65535) in the Server Port field or accept the default port for the CiscoWorks syslog server, and then click Next to continue. The Configure Communications Properties window appears.

Step 10 Enter the PostOffice communication parameters (see Table 16-5). After you have entered any necessary changes to the default values, click Next to continue. After the IDS MC software is installed, the Restart window appears.

Table 16-5 *IDS MC Processes*

Parameter	Description and Default Value
Host ID	The host identity of the Security Monitor's PostOffice service. The default is the last octet of the server's IP address.
Organization ID	The organization identity of the Security Monitor's PostOffice service. The default is 100.
IP Address	The IP address of the Security Monitor.
Host Name	The host name of the Security Monitor.
Organization Name	The organization name of the Security Monitor.

Step 11 Select Yes, I Want to Restart My Computer Now to finish the installation process.

Solaris Installation

Besides the Windows version, you can install IDS MC on a Solaris server. Just as in the Windows example, when installing IDS MC on Solaris, you need to understand the hardware and software requirements for the different components. The major components involved in an IDS MC Solaris installation are as follows:

- CiscoWorks server
- Client systems
- Sensors

Because the sensors are appliances, the software and hardware are fairly fixed. The other two components, however, are built on your own machines. To ensure an operable installation, these systems must match some minimum requirements.

Server Requirements

To support all the functionality provided by IDS MC and the underlying CiscoWorks foundation, your Solaris CiscoWorks server needs to match the following requirements:

- Sun UltraSPARC 60MP with 440-MHz or faster processor
- UltraSPARC III
- Solaris 2.8
- Minimum of 1 GB RAM

NOTE   Requirements for the CiscoWorks server are frequently updated. For the latest server requirements, refer to the documentation on the Cisco website (such as the "Quick Start for VPN/Security Management Solution").

Installation Process

VMS Common Services is required for the IDS MC software. VMS Common Services provides the CiscoWorks server base components, software libraries, and the software packages specifically developed for the IDS MC. For more information on VMS, see the "Quick Start Guide for VPN Security Management Solution" and other documentation on the Cisco website.

After you have installed the VMS Common Services, you can then install the IDS MC Solaris software using the following steps:

Step 1   Insert the Cisco IDS MC CD into the CD-ROM drive on your server.

Step 2   Log in as root on the system on which you have already installed CiscoWorks Common Services.

Step 3   Mount the CD-ROM on the system.

Step 4   Run the installation program by executing the following commands:

```
# cd /cdrom/cdrom0
# ./setup.sh
```

NOTE   You can also install the software from a remote directory location. To accomplish this, you use the **cd** command to change to the remote directory (instead of /cdrom/cdrom0) and then execute the installation program.

Step 5 Press Enter to read the license agreement and press Y to accept the license agreement and continue with the installation.

Step 6 Select the components to install (IDS MC, Security Monitor, or both).

Step 7 Enter the IDS MC database password and confirm it by entering it again.

Step 8 If installing IDS MC, enter the following information: database password, database location, and host IP address.

Step 9 If installing the Security Monitor, enter the PostOffice parameters shown in Table 16-5.

NOTE   After the installation completes, you must reboot the system for IDS MC and Security Monitor to operate correctly.

Client Requirements

Your users access IDS MC (both Windows and Solaris versions) via a browser on their system. These systems, however, should also meet certain minimum requirements to ensure successful system operation. Your client systems should meet the following requirements:

- IBM PC-compatible computer
- 300-MHz or faster processor
- Minimum 256 MB RAM
- 400 MB virtual memory (free space on hard drive)

Along with these requirements, your clients need to run one of the following operating systems:

- Windows 2000 Professional or Server with Service Pack 3
- Windows XP Professional (Service Pack 1) with Microsoft Virtual Machine
- Solaris SPARCstation or Sun Ultra 10 (running Solaris 2.8)

One final requirement is that your client systems need to use one of the following web browsers:

- Internet Explorer 6.0 (Service Pack 1) with Microsoft Virtual Machine
- Netscape Navigator 4.79

NOTE   Requirements for the CiscoWorks clients are frequently updated. For the latest client requirements, refer to the documentation on the Cisco website (such as the "Quick Start for VPN/Security Management Solution").

Launching IDS MC

You access the IDS MC software from the CiscoWorks main menu. After logging in to CiscoWorks, you need to follow these steps to access the IDS MC software:

Step 1   Click the VPN/Security Management drawer to expand it and reveal the folders within it.

Step 2   Click the folder named Management Center to expand this folder.

Step 3   Click IDS Sensors to launch the IDS MC software. The IDS MC launches in a new browser window (see Figure 16-6).

Figure 16-6   *Launching IDS MC Software*

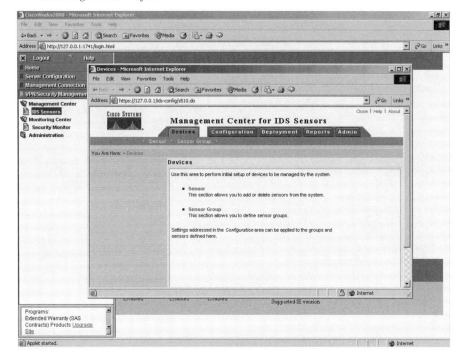

IDS MC Interface

Although the IDS MC user interface is graphical and easy to use, it is helpful to understand how the interface is structured. The IDS MC user interface is composed of the following major sections (see Figure 16-7):

- Configuration tabs
- Options bar

- Table of contents (TOC)
- Path bar
- Instructions box
- Content area
- Object bar
- Object selector handle
- Tools bar

Figure 16-7 *IDS MC User Interface*

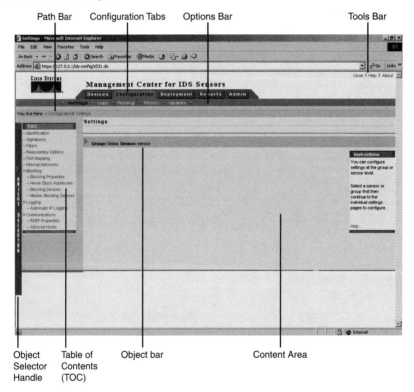

Configuration Tabs

The configuration tasks are broken down into the following five major categories:

- **Devices**—Enables you to perform initial setup of devices to be managed by the system

- **Configuration**—Enables you to change the operational configuration of the devices managed by the system

- **Deployment**—Enables you to generate configuration files, manage sensor configuration files, and submit or manage new jobs
- **Reports**—Enables you to generate reports, view scheduled reports, and view reports
- **Admin**—Enables you to configure system settings

To access one of the categories, you click the tab labeled with the appropriate name. The tabs are located across the top of the IDS MC display.

Options Bar

After clicking one of the major configuration tabs, the options for that selection display in a list that is located on the screen just below the configuration tabs. Figure 16-7 shows a screen in which the user clicked the Configuration tab. The options associated with the Configuration tab are as follows:

- Settings
- Copy
- Pending
- History
- Updates

Clicking any of these options causes a menu of available choices to display on the left side of the IDS MC interface (known as the TOC).

IDS MC Table of Contents (TOC)

The table of contents (TOC) is a menu of choices that displays down the left side of the IDS MC interface. It represents the list of suboptions that you can select (based on the option chosen). Figure 16-7 shows that the Configuration>Settings option has the following selections:

- Identification
- Signatures
- Reassembly Options
- Port Mapping
- Internal Networks
- Blocking
- Logging
- Communications

Path Bar

The path bar provides a visual road map indicating where you are with respect to the IDS MC interface. It is located above the TOC and below the options bar and begins with the text "You Are Here."

Figure 16-7 shows a situation in which the path bar's value is Configuration>Settings. This indicates that you performed the following steps to reach the current screen:

Step 1   Clicked the Configuration tab.

Step 2   Clicked the Settings option.

Instructions Box

Some pages provide you with an instructions box on the right side of the IDS MC display. This box (when displayed) provides you with a brief overview of the page that you have selected. This information is less than the amount of information provided through the Help option on the tools bar.

Content Area

The content area displays the information associated with the selection that you click on the TOC menu.

Object Bar

The object bar displays the object or objects that you have selected via the object selector. Figure 16-7 shows a situation in which you have selected the sensor named sensor from the global sensor group. When you perform configuration changes, the device or devices listed by the objects bar indicate which devices will receive updated configuration information.

Object Selector Handle

When making configuration changes via IDS MC, you need to specify which device or devices you want to apply those changes to. By clicking the object selector handle, you can select individual sensors or sensor groups. Any changes that you specify will then be applied to that sensor or sensor group. The object bar indicates the device or devices that you have currently selected.

Tools Bar

Located at the upper-right portion of the IDS MC interface is the tools bar. From the tools bar, you can access the following items:

- Close
- Help
- About

Clicking Close will log out your current IDS MC user session. Selecting Help opens up another browser window that displays detailed context-sensitive help information for using IDS MC. Finally, the About option displays information about the version of IDM that you use.

Accessing Online Help in IDS MC

IDS MC provides online documentation to assist in using the functionality provided. To access the IDS MC online help, choose Help from the IDS MC tools bar. A help window displays in a separate browser window. The IDS MC help browser window is composed of the following major components (see Figure 16-8):

- Content tab
- Index tab
- Search tab
- Information area

The information area initially displays context-sensitive help based on the window from which you invoked help. The Content tab enables you to view an index of relevant help topics that you can examine. The Index tab provides you with an alphabetic index of topics that you can obtain information on by scrolling through the list and clicking an item.

Sometimes you want to find help on a specific topic. Instead of searching either the content list or the index, you can also use the Search tab. Clicking this tab brings up a search box that you can use to search for help on a specific item.

Figure 16-8   *IDS MC Online Help*

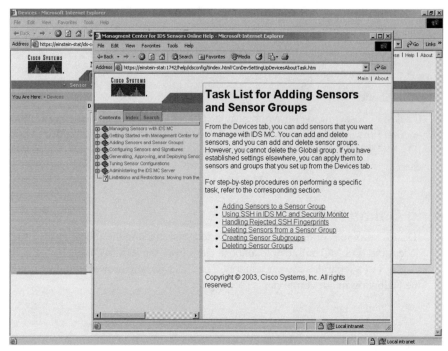

IDS Configuration File Deployment

The IDS MC software enables you to configure sensors as well as groups of sensors. When you make changes, however, they are not immediately propagated to your sensors. Instead, you must follow a distinct process to deploy your changes to the appropriate sensors. First, you commit these changes to the IDS MC database. Then you deploy these changes to your sensors or sensor groups. Deploying configuration changes is managed through the Deployment configuration tab and involves the following tasks (see Figure 16-9):

- Generate
- Approve
- Deploy

Figure 16-9 *Deployment Options*

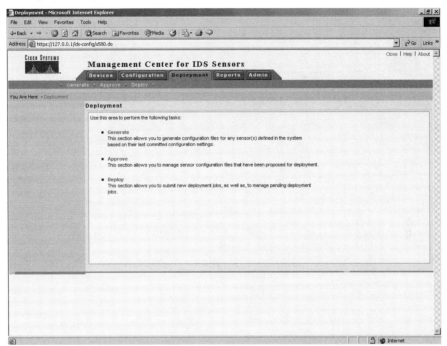

Deployment and Generate

After you make configuration changes to your sensors, you need to cause IDS MC to transfer those changes from the configuration information stored in the IDS MC database to the configuration files on your actual sensors. The first step in the deployment of the configuration changes is to use the Deployment>Generate option to generate the updated configuration files from the IDS MC database (see Figure 16-10).

Figure 16-10 *Deployment>Generate Option*

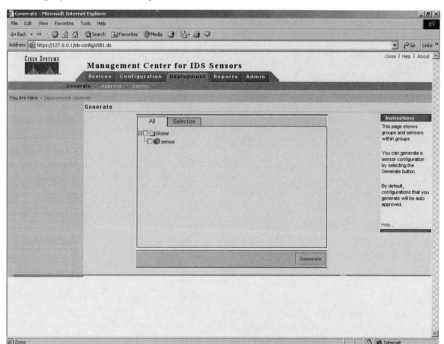

You select the sensor or sensor group on which the configuration has changed. Then you click Generate to enable the IDS MC software to identify the changes that need to be propagated to your sensors and create the updated configuration files.

Deployment and Approve

By default, you do not need to approve your configuration changes. After you generate the appropriate configuration changes, you can immediately deploy those changes to your sensors.

Depending on your environment, you might want to require the approval of configuration changes. You can enable the manual approval of configuration changes by choosing Admin>System Configuration>Configuration File Management and then selecting Enable Manual Configuration File Change Approval (see Figure 16-11).

Figure 16-11   *Enabling Manual File Change Approval*

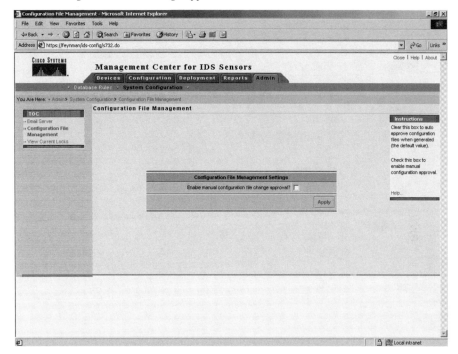

Deployment and Deploy

The final step in pushing your configuration changes out to your sensors is to use the Deployment>Deploy option to schedule the update of the sensor's configuration files. After choosing the sensors whose configurations have changed and selecting the Deployment>Deploy option, you have the following two options (see Figure 16-12):

- Submit
- Pending

Deployment>Deploy>Submit Option

The Submit option enables you to schedule the deployment of pending configuration updates. After selecting the desired changes (created by the Generate option), you need to tell IDS MC when you want those changes pushed out to your sensors. You accomplish this by creating a job that will run at a specified time and update the configuration on the appropriate sensors. You configure the properties of the job based on the fields listed in Table 16-6 (see Figure 16-13).

Figure 16-12 *Deploy Options*

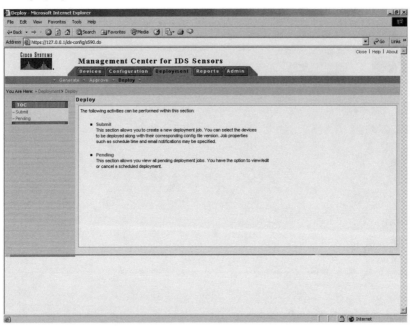

Figure 16-13 *Enter Job Properties Window*

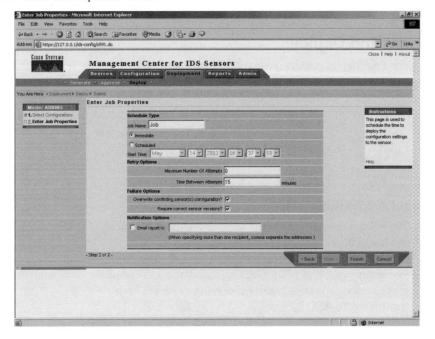

Table 16-6   *Job Properties*

Property	Description
Job Name	Name of the deployment job.
Immediate	Update the configuration files immediately.
Scheduled	Schedule the configuration update for a specified time in the future.
Maximum Number of Attempts	(Optional) Change the number of attempts that IDS MC will attempt to spawn an update on the sensors. The default is 0.
Time Between Attempts	(Optional) Change the number of minutes between attempts to spawn an update on the sensors. The default is 15.
Overwrite Conflicting Sensors Configuration	(Optional) Check this option to enable the configuration of the sensors to be overwritten.
Require Correct Sensor Versions	(Optional) Check this option to require the sensor's version to match the version listed by IDS MC.
Email Report To	(Optional) Check this option and specify an email address to receive status updates on the job deployments (configuration updates) that are pending.

Deploy>Pending Option

The Pending option enables you to monitor the status of pending configuration updates (job deployments). It provides you with a list of pending changes (see Figure 16-14). Besides editing or deleting the existing jobs, you can see the values of the Job fields shown in Table 16-7 for each job entry.

Figure 16-14   *Deploy>Pending Window*

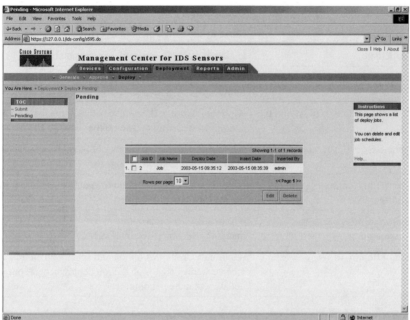

Table 16-7   *Pending Job Fields*

Field	Description
Job ID	Numeric ID associated with the job
Job Name	Alphanumeric description of the job
Deploy Date	Shows when the job will execute
Insert Time	Shows when the job was created
Insert By	Shows which user created the job

Summary

In enterprise environments, you need the ability to configure and manage a large number of sensors efficiently and easily. The Management Center for IDS Sensors (IDS MC) is a management interface that enables you to manage up to 300 sensors from a single server.

IDS MC runs on the following two different server platforms:

- Windows 2000 Server
- Solaris

The IDS MC software is built upon the CiscoWorks software and requires the VMS Common Services in conjunction with the IDS MC software. The VMS Common Services feature set provides the following functionality:

- Data storage and management
- Web interface
- Session management
- User authentication/authorization management
- Common environment for IDS MC

You create user accounts and roles via the underlying CiscoWorks software. The user roles (authorization roles) enable you to give users privileges to perform specific configuration tasks. The following user roles are relevant to accounts that you create to operate your IDS MC software.

- Help Desk
- Approver
- Network Operator
- Network Administrator
- System Administrator

The IDS MC user interface is graphical and divided into the following areas to make it easy for you to operate the IDS MC software:

- Configuration tabs
- Options bar
- TOC
- Path bar
- Instructions box
- Content area
- Object bar
- Object selector handle
- Tools bar

When pushing configuration updates to your sensors, you go through the following three-step deployment process (after the changes have been saved to the IDS MC database):

- Generate
- Approve
- Deploy

The Generate step determines the changes that have been made to the sensor or sensor group. The Approve step is automatic by default (although you can change it to manual if desired). The Deploy process enables you to schedule when the updates will occur (on the actual sensors) and enables you to monitor the progress of pending updates.

Review Questions

The following questions test your retention of the material presented in this chapter. The answers to the review questions are in Appendix B, "Answers to Chapter Review Questions."

1 How many sensors can you manage from one IDS MC server?

2 What is the foundation that IDS MC is built on?

3 What authorization roles can you assign to users who use IDS MC?

4 What two operating systems do IDS MC servers run on?

5 What features does the VMS Common Services provide?

6 What two browsers can you use to access IDS MC?

7 What privileges does a user receive from the Network Operator role?

8 Which software handles user authentication and authorization for IDS MC?

9 Which authorization role enables a user to perform all operations within IDS MC?

10 How do client systems access your IDS MC server?

11 How much RAM is recommended on your IDS MC server (for both Windows and Solaris deployments)?

12 Can you install IDS MC and Security Monitor on a machine that already has CSPM installed on it?

13 What is the path bar on the IDS MC interface?

14 What three steps are required to deploy updated configuration files when using IDS MC?

15 Which step in the deployment of an updated sensor configuration happens automatically by default?

Upon completion of this chapter, you will be able to perform the following tasks:

- Identify the server requirements for the Monitoring Center for Security (Security Monitor)
- Identify the client requirements for the Security Monitor
- Identify the major sections of the Security Monitor user interface
- Monitor alarms using the Security Monitor Event Viewer
- Manipulate the Security Monitor Event Viewer display
- Configure the Security Monitor Event Viewer preferences
- Administer the Security Monitor
- Graph alarm information using the Security Monitor Event Viewer
- Generate reports using the Security Monitor

CHAPTER 17

Enterprise IDS Monitoring and Reporting

When deploying a large number of Cisco IDS sensors, you need an efficient way by which to monitor the alerts from these devices. The Monitoring Center for Security (Security Monitor) provides this functionality.

Using Security Monitor, you can correlate and analyze alerts from the sensors deployed throughout your network using a graphical interface.

Monitoring Center for Security

The Security Monitor is a component of the CiscoWorks Virtual Private Network (VPN)/ Security Management Solution (VMS) product. VMS integrates numerous security applications into a single solution, such as the following:

- Management Center for IDS Sensors (IDS MC)
- Monitoring Center for Security (Security Monitor)
- VPN Monitor
- Management Center for VPN Routers
- Management Center for Firewalls
- VMS Common Services

Security Monitor provides numerous features such as the following:

- Device monitoring
- Web-based monitoring platform
- Custom reporting capability
- Email notification

Using Security Monitor, you can receive IDS events from up to 300 Cisco IDS–capable devices such as the following:

- Sensor appliances
- IDS modules
- Router modules

- Cisco IOS routers
- PIX firewalls

Using a standard web browser, you can access the Security Monitor to administer and monitor the alerts from your IDS devices. Furthermore, you can easily use an extensive list of common reports to support your reporting requirements.

NOTE   Installation of Security Monitor, as well as an explanation of CiscoWorks, is covered in Chapter 16, "Enterprise IDS Management."

Server Requirements

To support all the functionality provided by Security Monitor and the underlying Cisco-Works foundation, your CiscoWorks server needs to match certain requirements. The requirements for a Windows server are as follows:

- IBM PC-compatible computer
- 1-GHz processor or faster
- Color monitor with video card capable of viewing 16-bit color
- CD-ROM drive
- 10BASE-T or faster network connection
- Minimum of 1 GB RAM
- 2 GB virtual memory
- Minimum of 9-GB free hard drive space (NTFS)
- Windows 2000 Professional, Server, or Advanced Server with Service Pack 3

NOTE   Requirements for the CiscoWorks server are frequently updated. For the latest server requirements, refer to the documentation on the Cisco website (such as the "Quick Start for VPN/Security Management Solution").

You can also run your CiscoWorks server on Solaris. The requirements for the Solaris CiscoWorks server are as follows:

- Sun UltraSPARC 60MP with 440-MHz or faster processor
- UltraSPARC III
- Solaris 2.8
- Minimum of 1 GB RAM

NOTE Do not attempt to install Security Monitor on a system that has Cisco Secure Policy Manager (CSPM) installed on it. The installer for Security Monitor attempts to install the Cisco IDS PostOffice software in a second location on the host, causing it to function incorrectly.

Client Requirements

Your users access Security Monitor via a browser on their system. These systems, however, should also meet certain minimum requirements to ensure successful system operation. Your client systems should meet the following requirements:

- IBM PC-compatible or Solaris SPARCstation or Sun Ultra 10
- 300-MHz or faster processor
- Minimum 256 MB RAM
- 400 MB virtual memory (free space on hard drive)

Along with these requirements, your clients need to run one of the following operating systems:

- Windows 2000 Professional with Service Pack 3
- Windows 2000 Server with Service Pack 3
- Windows 2000 Advanced Server with Service Pack 3
- Windows XP Professional
- Solaris 2.8

NOTE Requirements for the client systems are frequently updated. For the latest client requirements, refer to the documentation on the Cisco website (such as the "Quick Start for VPN/Security Management Solution").

One final requirement is that your client systems need to use one of the following web browsers:

- Internet Explorer 6.0 (Service Pack 1) with Microsoft Virtual Machine
- Netscape Navigator 4.79

NOTE These are the only browsers that have been tested and are guaranteed to work. Other browsers might work as well, but their use is not supported by the Cisco Technical Assistance Center (TAC).

User Interface

Although the Security Monitor user interface is graphical and easy to use, it is helpful to understand how the interface is structured. The Security Monitor user interface is composed of the following major sections (see Figure 17-1):

- Configuration tabs
- Options bar
- TOC
- Path bar
- Instructions box
- Content area
- Tools bar

Figure 17-1 *Security User Interface*

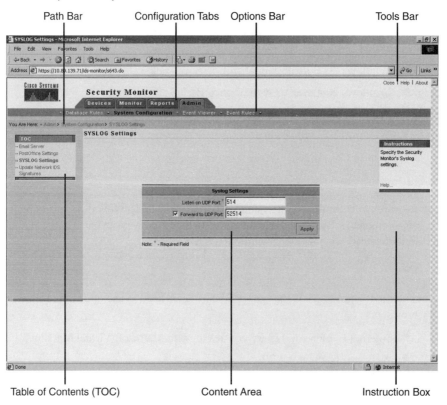

Path Bar   Configuration Tabs   Options Bar   Tools Bar

Table of Contents (TOC)   Content Area   Instruction Box

Configuration Tabs

The configuration tabs are broken down into the following four major categories:

- **Devices**—Enables you to perform initial setup of devices to be monitored by Security Monitor
- **Monitor**—Enables you to monitor information about your devices and launch the Event Viewer
- **Reports**—Enables you to generate reports, view scheduled reports, and view reports
- **Admin**—Enables you to administer system and database settings

To access one of the categories, you click the tab labeled with the appropriate name. These tabs are located across the top of the Security Monitor display.

Options Bar

After clicking one of the major configuration tabs, the options for that selection display in a list that is located on the screen just below the configuration tabs. Figure 17-1 shows a screen in which the user clicked the Admin tab. The options associated with the Admin tab are as follows:

- Database Rules
- System Configuration
- Event Viewer
- Event Rules

Clicking any of these options causes a menu of available choices to display on the left side of the Security Monitor interface (known as the TOC).

Table of Contents (TOC)

The table of contents (TOC) is a menu of choices that displays down the left side of the Security Monitor interface. It represents the list of suboptions that you can select (based on the option chosen). Figure 17-1 shows the Admin>System Configuration option, which has the following selections:

- Email Server
- PostOffice Settings
- Syslog Settings
- Update Network IDS Signatures

NOTE In Figure 17-1, the Syslog Settings option has been selected. So it displays in bold, and the syslog settings are shown in the content area.

Path Bar

The path bar provides a visual road map indicating where you are with respect to the Security Monitor interface. It is located above the TOC and under the options bar, and it begins with the text "You Are Here."

Figure 17-1 shows a situation in which the path bar's value is Admin>System Configuration>Syslog Settings. This indicates that you performed the following steps to reach the current screen:

Step 1 Clicked the Admin tab

Step 2 Selected the System Configuration option from the options bar

Step 3 Selected the Syslog Settings option from the TOC

Instructions Box

Some pages provide you with an instructions box on the right side of the Security Monitor display. This box (when displayed) provides you with a brief overview of the page that you selected. This information is a quick summary of information provided through the Help option on the tools bar.

Content Area

The content area displays the information associated with the selection that you clicked on the TOC menu. Sometimes the option selected from the options bar has no TOC options. In this situation, clicking the option from the options bar directly displays information in the content area. An example of this is Admin>Database Rules (see the "Database Maintenance" section later in this chapter).

Tools Bar

Located at the upper-right portion of the Security Monitor interface is the tools bar. From the tools bar, you can access the following items:

- Close
- Help
- About

Close enables you to close the Security Monitor program. The Help option displays Security Monitor's help information in a separate browser window. Finally, the About option displays the Security Monitor software version.

Security Monitor Configuration

Before you can use Security Monitor to analyze the events from your IDS devices, you must add or import them to Security Monitor. You can configure the rules that Security Monitor uses to access alerts from the different devices being monitored. For Remote Data Exchange Protocol (RDEP) devices, you can also monitor connection and statistical information. This section focuses on the following Security Monitor configuration operations:

- Adding devices
- Monitoring devices
- Event notification

Adding Devices

Security Monitor enables you to view alerts from various Cisco IDS devices deployed throughout your network. Before you can monitor these devices, however, you must add them to Security Monitor. The Devices window (see Figure 17-2) shows you the devices that you have already added to Security Monitor and enables you to add or import new devices as well as perform the following operations on existing devices:

- Edit
- Delete
- View

Security Monitor monitors the following types of devices.

- RDEP IDS
- PostOffice IDS
- IOS IDS
- PIX

NOTE   The Cisco host solution uses the Cisco Security Agent (CSA) technology. The Event Monitor that is part of the Management Center for Cisco Security Agents 4.0 (CSA MC) handles alerts from these agents. Refer the Chapter 14, "Host Intrusion Prevention," for more information on CSA MC.

Figure 17-2   *The Devices Window in Security Monitor*

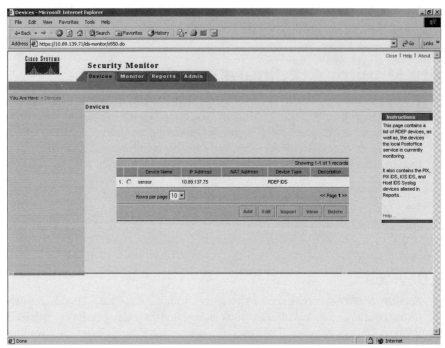

Adding Remote Data Exchange Protocol (RDEP) Devices

Security Monitor uses RDEP to communicate with your Cisco IDS version 4.0 and later sensors. When adding an RDEP device to Security Monitor, you must to specify the following information about the device:

- IP address
- Device name
- Web server port
- Username
- Password
- Minimum event level

The IP Address, Device Name, and Web Server Port fields identify the device so that Security Monitor can communicate with it. The Username and Password fields provide the login credentials necessary to access the RDEP device. Finally, the Minimum Event Level field sets the minimum alert level for the events that Security Monitor will retrieve from the device. By default, only medium-severity events and higher are retrieved.

To add an RDEP device to Security Monitor, follow these steps:

Step 1   Click the Devices tab on the main Security Monitor screen. The Devices window appears in the content area.

Step 2   Click the Add button. The Select Device Type window appears in the content area (see Figure 17-3).

Figure 17-3   *The Select Device Type Window*

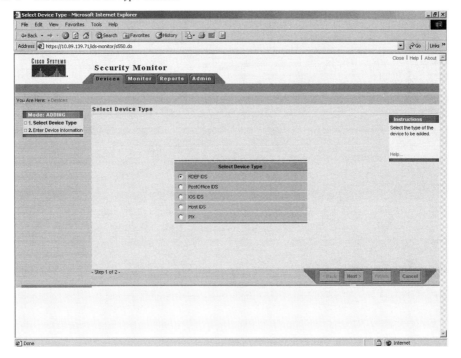

Step 3   Click the radio button next to type of device being added. In this situation, you want to click the radio button next to RDEP IDS.

Step 4   Click the Next button to continue. The Enter Device Information window appears in the content area (see Figure 17-4).

Step 5   Enter the information required for Security Monitor to access the new device.

Step 6   Click the Finish button to add the new device to Security Monitor.

Figure 17-4   *The Identification Window for RDEP Devices*

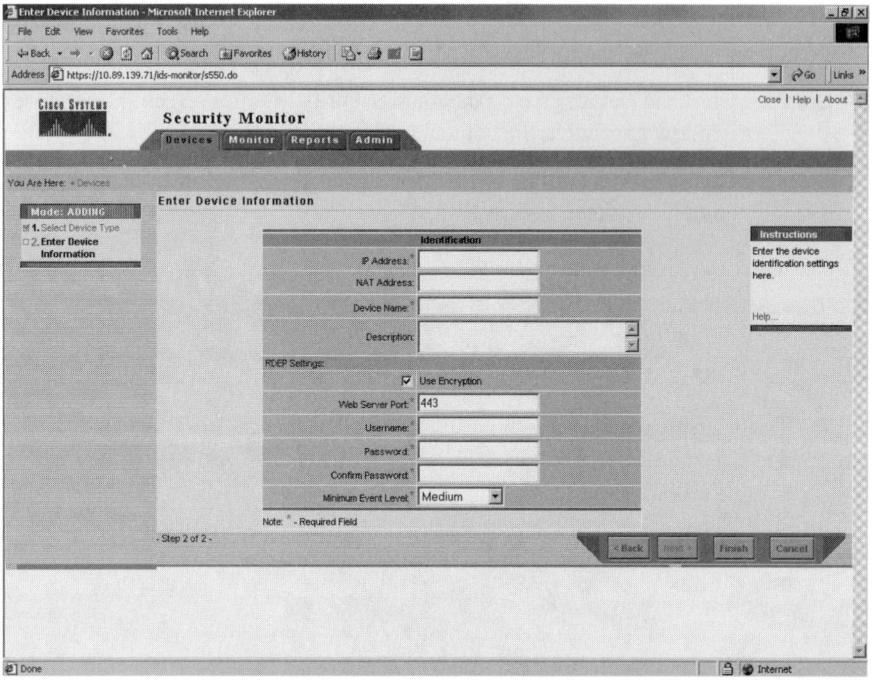

Adding PostOffice Devices

Security Monitor can receive events from Cisco IDS version 3.x sensors. You can add these devices selecting the PostOffice IDS radio button when adding a new device. When adding a version 3.x sensor, you must specify the following fields (see Figure 17-5):

- IP Address
- Device Name
- Host ID
- OrgName
- Org ID
- Port
- Heartbeat

Figure 17-5 *The Enter Device Information Window for PostOffice Devices*

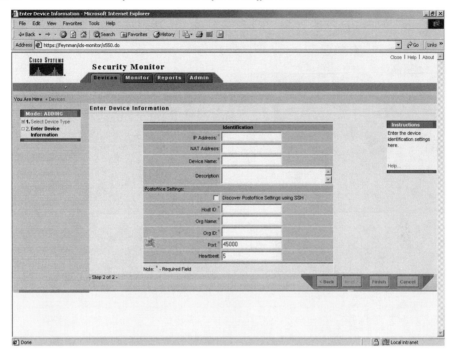

NOTE	Instead of specifying the PostOffice parameters (Host ID, OrgName, and Org ID), you can have Security Monitor retrieve these values from the sensor using Secure Shell (SSH) by checking the Discover PostOffice Settings Using SSH check box. To retrieve this information, you must supply a valid username and password on the sensor (see Figure 17-6).

Figure 17-6 *Discover PostOffice Settings Using SSH*

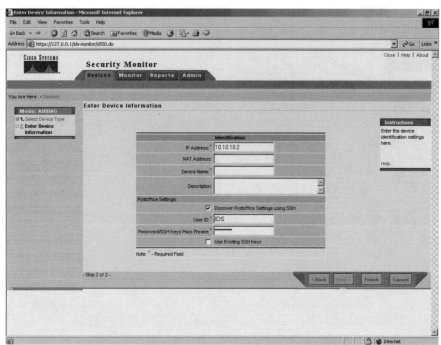

Adding Internetworking Operating System (IOS) Devices

Besides receiving events from Cisco IDS sensors, Security Monitor can also receive events from other Cisco IDS devices. You can add IOS devices by selecting the IOS IDS radio button when adding a new device. When adding an IOS IDS device, you must specify the fields (see Figure 17-7):

- IP Address
- Device Name

Some IOS devices can run the PostOffice protocol. If you want Security Monitor to communicate with the IOS device using PostOffice, you need to check the Use PostOffice check box. This enables you to enter the following PostOffice parameters (see Figure 17-8):

- Host ID
- OrgName
- Org ID
- Port
- Heartbeat

Figure 17-7 *The Enter Device Information Window for IOS IDS Devices*

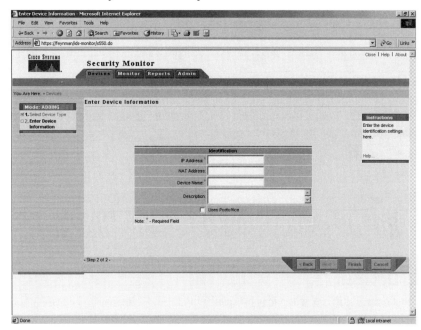

Figure 17-8 *Adding an IOS IDS Device Running PostOffice*

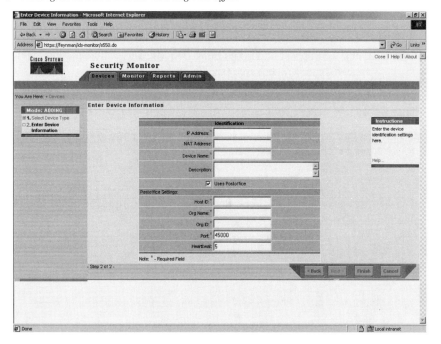

NOTE	If the IOS device does not support the PostOffice protocol, it will communicate with Security Monitor using syslog messages.

Adding PIX Devices

Similar to IOS IDS devices, you can have Security Monitor receive events from PIX firewalls. The information required to add these devices is identical to IOS IDS devices in that you must specify the following fields:

- IP Address
- Device Name

Because the PIX firewalls can't communicate via the PostOffice protocol, you do not have this option available for PIX devices like it is for IOS devices. Instead, the PIX devices communicate with the Security Monitor using syslog messages.

Importing Devices

Instead of adding new devices by specifying all the information necessary for Security Monitor to communicate with it, you can also import devices from an instance of IDS MC that is already monitoring the devices you want to add. To import a device from IDS MC into Security Monitor, follow these steps:

Step 1 Click the Devices tab on the main Security Monitor screen. The Devices window appears in the content area.

Step 2 Click the Import button. The Enter IDS MC Server Information window appears in the content area (see Figure 17-9).

Step 3 Enter the IP address (or host name) of the IDS MC server from which you want to import devices.

Step 4 Enter the web server port associated with the corresponding IDS MC server. The default value is 443.

NOTE	The IDS MC server that you import the device from can either be the local IDS MC server or a remote IDS MC server.

Figure 17-9 *The Enter IDS MC Server Information Window*

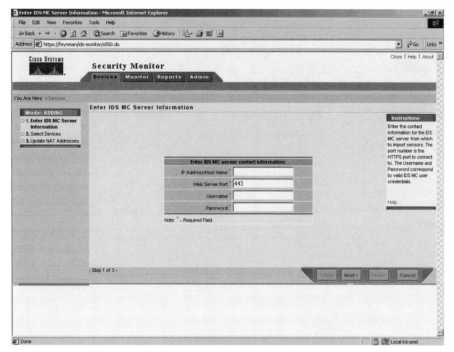

Step 5 Enter the username and password required to log in to the IDS MC server. The user account specified must have administrative privileges for the specified IDS MC server.

Step 6 Click the Next button to continue. The Select Devices window appears in the content area showing the devices that the IDS MC server manages (see Figure 17-10).

Step 7 Check the check box next to each sensor that you want to import.

Step 8 Click the Finish button to import the selected sensors. A Summary window displays in the content area indicating the sensors that you imported.

Figure 17-10 *The Select Devices Window*

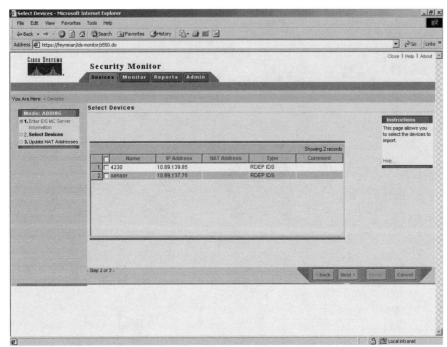

Event Notification

When multiple security devices are deployed throughout your network, they can generate a large number of events. Analyzing every one of these events using the Event Viewer can be a very time-consuming task. Furthermore, it might be impossible to monitor the Event Viewer 24 hours a day. Therefore, you can define event rules that perform specific actions when the Security Monitor receives traffic matching specific properties. You could use this functionality, for instance, to cause Security Monitor to email you when certain traffic is detected on your network.

When defining an event rule, you can identify traffic based on the alert characteristics shown in Table 17-1.

Table 17-1 *Event Rule Characteristics*

Characteristic	Description
Originating device	Enables you to specify a specific monitor device
Originating device address	Enables you to specify the originating address of the device
Attacker address	Enables you to filter based on the IP address of the attacker

Table 17-1 *Event Rule Characteristics (Continued)*

Characteristic	Description
Victim address	Enables you to filter based on the IP address of the victim or system being attacked
Signature name	Enables you to filter based on the name of a signature
Signature ID	Enables you to filter based on the ID of a signature
Severity	Enables you to filter based on the severity of the alarm received (informational, low, medium, and high)

For each characteristic, you specify a value and one of the following operators to equate the characteristic to the value:

- < (Less than)
- <= (Less than or equal)
- = (Equal)
- != (Not equal)
- >= (Greater than or equal)
- > (Greater than)

NOTE   Not all these operators are valid for each characteristic. For some of the characteristics (such as originating device), only equal and not equal are valid.

Each characteristic plus a value is known as a *clause*. You combine multiple clauses for a single rule by specifying one of the following logical operations:

- And
- Or
- Not

After entering the clauses that define which traffic the event rule applies to, you need to define the action that you want Security Monitor to perform for traffic that actually matches the rule. Each rule can perform one or more of the following actions:

- Notification via email
- Log a console notification event
- Execute a script

NOTE Each event rule that you define can have up to five clauses. Furthermore, you can define up to 10 event rules that you can have active at one time.

Using the email notification action, for instance, you can easily create a custom email message that is generated in response to a specific signature firing. You can also execute one of the default scripts to easily manipulate events in the Security Monitor database (see the "Database Maintenance" section later in this chapter).

Adding Event Rules

Event rules specify the criteria that an event must match to cause a specific action. When adding event rules, you need to perform the following four tasks:

- Assign a name to the event rule.
- Define the event filter criteria.
- Assign the event rule action.
- Define the event rule threshold and interval.

To add an event rule, follow these steps:

Step 1 Click the Admin tab on the main Security Monitor screen.

Step 2 Select Event Rules from the options bar (or from the content area). The Event Rules window appears in the content area (see Figure 17-11).

Figure 17-11 *The Event Rules Window*

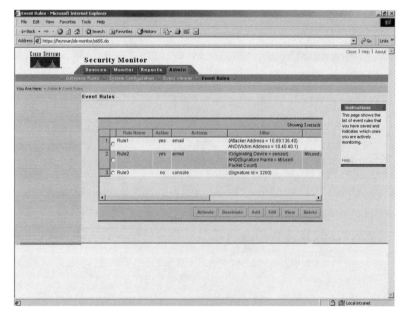

Step 3 Click the Add button. The Rule Identification window appears in the content area (see Figure 17-12).

NOTE You can also select existing event rules and either edit, view, or delete them by clicking the Edit, View, or Delete buttons.

Figure 17-12 *Rule Identification Window*

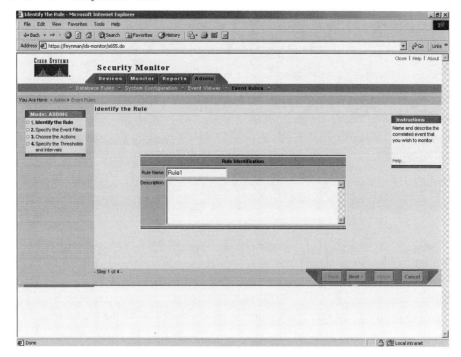

Step 4 Enter a name for the rule in the Rule Name field.

Step 5 Enter a textual description for the rule.

Step 6 Click the Next button. The Event Field Filtering window appears in the content area (see Figure 17-13).

Figure 17-13 *The Event Field Filtering Window*

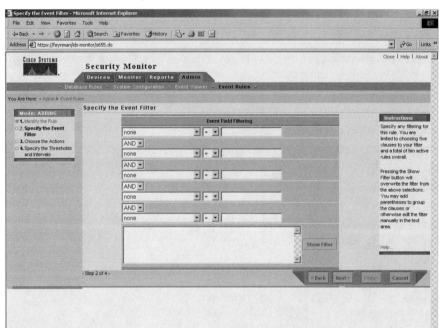

Step 7 Define the clauses that make up the event rule and the associations between clauses.

NOTE Clicking the Show Filter button displays the current filter in the textual window at the bottom of the window. This enables you to see the filter as a mathematical expression. In addition, you can manually edit this expression in the text box to customize your filter.

Step 8 Click the Next button to continue. The Rule Actions window appears in the content area (see Figure 17-14).

Figure 17-14   *The Rule Actions Window*

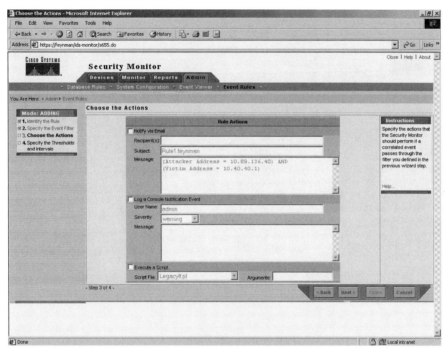

Step 9   Check the check box next to the actions that you want assigned to this event rule. Specify any rule-specific parameters (such as an email address for the Notify via Email option). You can assign one or more actions to each event rule.

NOTE   Using the email notification action assumes that you have already configured Security Monitor to use a valid mail server.

Step 10   Click the Next button to continue. The Thresholds and Intervals window appears in the content area (see Figure 17-15).

Figure 17-15 *The Thresholds and Intervals Window*

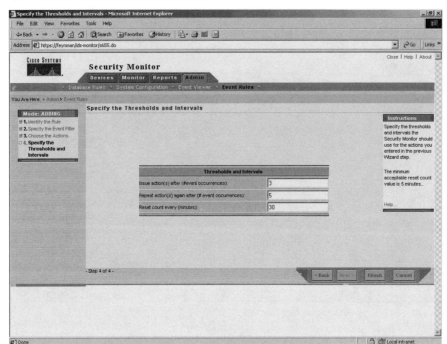

Step 11 Enter a value for how many event occurrences are needed to trigger the rule's actions by entering a number in to the Issue action(s) After (#Event Occurrences) field.

Step 12 Enter a value indicating how many more events (after the initial triggering of the rule) are needed before the actions are triggered again by entering a number in the Repeat Action(S) After (#Event Occurrences) field.

Step 13 Define how many minutes must elapse before the count value is reset by entering a value in the Reset Count Every (Minutes) field. The minimum reset value is 5 minutes.

Step 14 Click the Finish button to complete the definition of the event rule.

Activating Event Rules

After defining an event rule, you must activate the rule for it to become active. These event rules can be quickly deployed, and you can also easily disable (or deactivate) an event rule if it fails to produce the desired result. To activate a rule, follow these steps:

Step 1 Click the Admin tab on the main Security Monitor screen.

Step 2 Select Event Rules from the options bar (or from the content area). The Event Rules window appears in the content area (see Figure 17-11).

Step 3 Click the radio button next to the rule that you want to activate.

NOTE You can tell which event rules are active by examining the Active field. If a rule is active, this field has a value of Yes. Rules that have not been activated have a value of No in this field.

Step 4 Click the Activate button.

NOTE You can deactivate event rules by following this same procedure, but clicking the Deactivate button rather than the Activate button.

Monitoring Devices

You can monitor information about the devices that you have added to Security Monitor. This information falls into the following three categories:

- Connections
- Statistics
- Events

Monitoring Connections

Security Monitor needs to communicate with all the devices from which it receives information. With RDEP devices, Security Monitor connects to the sensor and retrieves the alerts. PostOffice devices send the information directly to Security Monitor. For RDEP and PostOffice devices, you can check the status of these connections using Monitor>Connections (see Figure 17-16).

Figure 17-16 *The Monitor Connections Window*

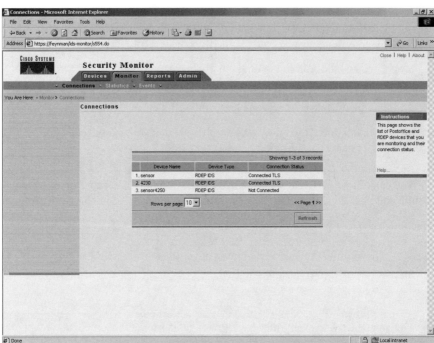

NOTE	IOS IDS devices (those not using PostOffice) and PIX firewalls do not show up in the connection list because they send information to the Security Monitor in a connectionless fashion using syslog messages.

If the status is either Connected or Connected TLS (Connected TLS only applies to RDEP devices), Security Monitor receives events from the device correctly. A status of Not Connected represents a problem and can indicate one of the following conditions:

- The device has been added to Security Monitor, but it is not yet configured to send event data. This situation commonly arises if you add devices to Security Monitor before you have actually deployed them on your network.

- The device is configured incorrectly. For PostOffice devices, verify that the device is sending events to the correct IP address (for Security Monitor) on the correct port.

- Security Monitor is configured incorrectly. Verify the settings for the device in Security Monitor to make sure that the PostOffice communication parameters match the actual device parameters or that the RDEP login credentials and IP address are valid.

- Network connectivity between Security Monitor and the device has been lost. Try to ping the device from the underlying operating system software on the Security Monitor server.

Monitoring Statistics

For your RDEP devices, you can view a wealth of statistical information about each device. Using the Monitor>Statistics window, you can view information about the following items (see Figure 17-17):

- **Analysis engine statistics**—MAC, virtual sensor, TCP stream reassembly, and signature database statistics

- **Authentication statistics**—Successful and failed login attempts to the RDEP device

- **Event server statistics**—General and specific subscription information about the devices with connections to the server

- **Event Store statistics**—General and number of specific events that have occurred

- **Host statistics**—Network statistics, memory usage, and swap file usage

- **Logger statistics**—Number of events and log messages written by the logger process

- **Network access control statistics**—Information about the sensor's current shunning (blocking) configuration

- **Transaction server statistics**—Counts indicating the failed and total number of control transactions for the server

- **Transaction source statistics**—Counts indicating the failed and total number of source control transactions

- **Web server statistics**—Configuration information for the device web server and statistics for connections to the web server

Figure 17-17 *The Monitor Statistics Window*

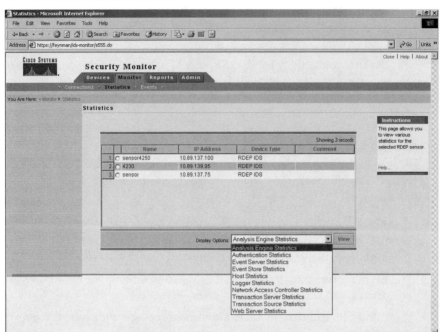

To view any of these statistics, following these steps:

Step 1   Click the Monitor tab on the main Security Monitor screen.

Step 2   Select Statistics from the options bar (or the content area). This displays the Statistics window in the content area (see Figure 17-17).

Step 3   Select the statistical information you want to view using the Display Options pull-down menu.

Step 4   Select the RDEP device for which you want to view the information by clicking the radio button next to the name of the sensor.

Step 5   Click the View button to view the selected information. The information displays in a separate browser window (see Figure 17-18).

Figure 17-18 *Analysis Engine Statistics for Device Sensor*

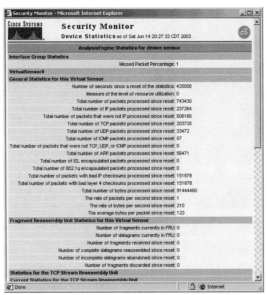

NOTE   You can view multiple statistical reports at a time because each of the reports displays in a new browser window. These reports are a snapshot of the information from the device and are not updated. To get updated information, you must generate another report.

Monitoring Events

Finally, you can monitor the events that Security Monitor receives from all the monitored devices. This is probably the most important feature of Security Monitor because it enables you to identify attacks against your network. You view the events that Security Monitor has collected through the Security Monitor Event Viewer, which is accessed from Monitor>Events. Before the Event Viewer is launched, you need to specify the criteria on which alerts should be included in the display (see Figure 17-19).

Figure 17-19   *The Launch Event Viewer Window*

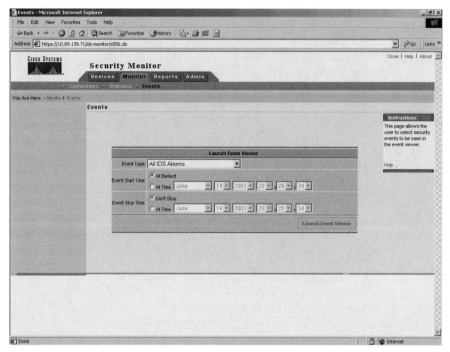

You basically specify a time window and event type for the information that you want included in the Event Viewer display by configuring the following three parameters:

- Event type
- Event start time
- Event end time

You can specify numerous options for the Event Type field using the Event Type pull-down menu. Some of the options that you can choose from are as follows:

- All IDS Alarms
- IDS PostOffice
- PIX IDS
- IOS IDS Syslog
- IDS IDIOM
- Audit Log
- PIX Deny Inbound

Any events in the Security Monitor database that match the specified criteria will display in the Event Viewer display. By default, the Event Type field is set to All IDS Alarms, the Event Start Time field is set to At Earliest, and the Event End Time field is set to Don't Stop. These values cause all the available IDS alarm events to display.

Security Monitor Event Viewer

The Event Viewer combines the functionality of a spreadsheet with that of a hierarchical, drill-down directory to create a collection of event records called a *drillsheet* (drill-down spreadsheet). The drillsheet displays groups of similar event records on a single row of the grid, enabling you to detect patterns in the data.

The Event Viewer contains a grid plane that organizes and displays event records. The Event Viewer can read and display both real-time and historical events from the Security Monitor database. You can configure the grid plane to display information about alerts detected by the monitored devices in a variety of ways, thereby customizing the interface to your requirements.

Configuring the Event Viewer involves understanding the following options:

- Moving columns
- Deleting rows and columns
- Collapsing columns
- Setting the event expansion boundary
- Expanding columns
- Suspending and resuming new events
- Changing display preferences
- Creating graphs
- View

Moving Columns

The default order of fields within an alarm entry might not suit your operational environment. You can change the order in which the columns are displayed in the Event Viewer. To move a column, click-and-drag the column header of the column that you want to move to the new position where you want it to be.

NOTE   Prior to version 1.2, moving columns was not a persistent change, meaning that closing the Event Viewer and re-opening it brought back the default column ordering.

Deleting Rows and Columns

When an alarm has been acknowledged, dealt with, or both, you might want to remove it from the Event Viewer grid or from the actual Security Monitor database. At other times, you want to remove certain columns from the Event Viewer display to make the display easier to work with. You can delete both rows and columns from the Event Viewer display. You access the delete options by clicking Delete in the TOC (see Figure 17-20).

Figure 17-20   *Event Viewer Delete Options*

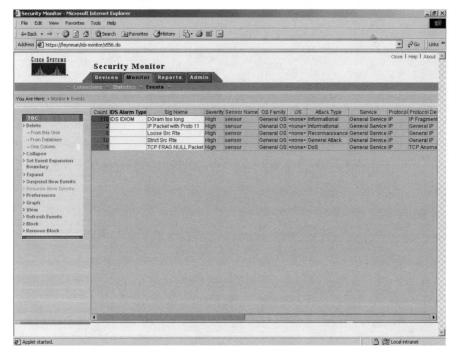

You have three deletion options from which to choose:

- From This Grid
- From Database
- One Column

NOTE   Before executing any of the delete options, you first need to select the row or column that you want to perform the operation on. Selecting the first column of the first row causes all the events to be selected, so take care when selecting the first row, especially when performing delete operations.

Delete>From This Grid

To remove a row from the Event Viewer display, select a specific row by clicking a field in the row to be deleted. Then click the From This Grid TOC option to delete the alarms from the Event Viewer where the action is being performed. It will not delete alarms from other Event Viewer instances or the Security Monitor database.

NOTE   This change is not persistent. If you open up another instance of the Event Viewer, the original rows are restored.

Delete>From Database

To remove a row from the Security Monitor database, you select the specific row by clicking a field in the row to be deleted. Then click the From Database TOC option to delete the selected alarm events from all the open Event Viewers as well as the Security Monitor database. If you use this option, the alarm is completely gone and you may not display it in the Event Viewer again, even if you open another Event Viewer instance.

Delete>One Column

To remove columns from the Event Viewer display, select a specific column by clicking a field in that column. Then click the One Column TOC option to remove the selected column from the Event Viewer display.

NOTE   This change is not persistent. If you open up another instance of the Event Viewer, the original columns are restored.

Collapsing Columns

To reduce the number of lines displayed on the Event Viewer grid, multiple alarms are collapsed into a single row based on a specific number of fields (known as the *expansion boundary*). By default, the expansion boundary is only the first field. All alarm entries with the same value for the first field are consolidated into a single row on the Event Viewer display.

To examine specific alarms, you can expand the display so that only a few alarms are consolidated on each row in the Event Viewer display. Although this is helpful when analyzing a specific attack, the Event Viewer grid can quickly become cluttered with more alarms than you can manage. When your Event Viewer display is too cluttered, you can collapse the display so that multiple alarms are consolidated onto a single line. You have the following three options to collapse rows in the Event Viewer (see Figure 17-21):

- One Column
- First Group
- All Columns

Figure 17-21 *Event Viewer Collapse Options*

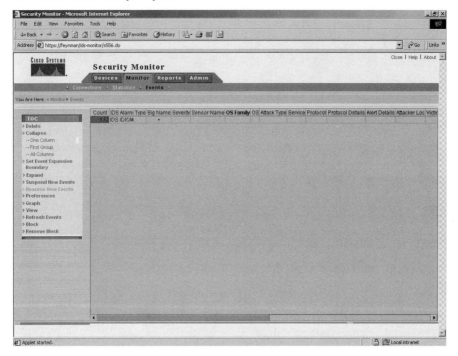

NOTE   These options are not persistent changes. This means that closing the Event Viewer and re-opening it will bring back the default settings and expansion boundary.

Collapse>One Column

To consolidate alarm details, you must collapse the columns until only the fields that you are interested in are expanded. When you collapse columns, however, the process begins with the column (that is not already collapsed) farthest to the right on the Event Viewer display. You cannot collapse specific columns only.

To collapse one column, select the row that you want to consolidate and then select Collapse>One Column from the TOC.

NOTE	When collapsing columns in your Event Viewer, you will eventually decrease the number of row entries being displayed. The Count field shows you how many entries are consolidated into a single row in the Event Viewer. This consolidation is based on the columns currently collapsed. As you collapse fields, more of the alarm entries will have the same values for all the collapsed columns. When you collapse all the columns, all alarm entries will eventually be represented by one alarm entry on a single row.

Collapse>First Group

The Event Viewer display contains numerous columns. If you have expanded all columns (so that each row in the display represents a single alarm entry), you can use the Collapse>One Column TOC option many times without any visual effect (because you are collapsing columns on the far right end of the Event Viewer display). Using the Collapse>First Group TOC option, you can quickly collapse a selected row to the first row that causes some consolidation to occur (a reduction in the number of lines displayed in the Event Viewer).

Collapse>All Columns

The Collapse>All Columns TOC option enables you to quickly consolidate all the alarm entries based on the first column in the Event Viewer display.

Setting the Event Expansion Boundary

By default, the Event Viewer expands the first column of the grid. If you want to automatically expand more fields than this, you need to change the expansion boundary. To change the expansion boundary for the current instance of the Event Viewer, click a field in the column where you want the expansion boundary to end. Then click Set Event Expansion Boundary from the TOC. The new expansion boundary is indicated by the column name becoming bold.

Expansion Boundary

The expansion boundary represents the block of columns that will be automatically expanded when a new alarm entry comes into the table. The block of columns is contiguous and starts at the first column in the Event Viewer. By default, the expansion boundary expands the first field of an alarm entry. When setting a new expansion boundary, you only have to specify the last column to be expanded. All columns from the first column to the column that you specify will now be expanded for new alarm entries.

Expanding Columns

Besides collapsing the entries on the display, you frequently need to expand the amount of alarm detail shown on the Event Viewer grid. Expanding columns provides more information and causes more rows to display in the Event Viewer. When expanding columns, you have the following three options (see Figure 17-22).

- One Column
- First Group
- All Columns

Figure 17-22 *Event Viewer Expand Options*

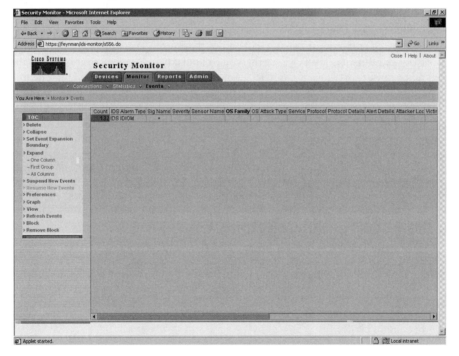

NOTE   These options are not persistent changes. This means that closing the Event Viewer and reopening it will bring back the default settings and expansion boundary. To make persistent changes to your display preferences, see the"Defining Event Viewer Preferences" section later in this chapter.

Expand>One Column

By default, the Event Viewer consolidates or "collapses" alarms based on the first column. The rest of the fields in the alarm entry have a gray background to indicate that they have been collapsed. (The collapsed fields can indicate actual field values or a plus sign [+].) To view these collapsed fields, you must expand the collapsed columns until the fields that you are interested in are shown. To expand fields one column at a time, select the row that you want to expand, and then click Expand>One Column from the TOC.

NOTE   When expanding columns in your Event Viewer, you will eventually increase the number of row entries being displayed. The Count field shows you how many entries are consolidated into a single row in the Event Viewer. This consolidation is based on the columns currently expanded. As you expand fields, fewer of the alarm entries will have the same values for all the expanded columns. When you expand all the columns, each row will probably only represent one alarm entry (count equal to one), because it is unlikely that two separate alarm entries will have the exact same values for every column.

Expand>First Group

Instead of expanding columns one at a time, you can click Expand>First Group from the TOC. This option expands the fields until the first field causes more rows to be displayed. This is much easier than expanding columns one at a time.

Expand>All Columns

Expanding an alarm entry one row at a time can be tedious, especially if the column that you are interested in is many fields away. In one click, you can expand all the fields for the currently selected row. To expand all the columns for the current alarm entry, click Expand>All Columns from the TOC.

NOTE   This is not a persistent change. This means that closing the Event Viewer and re-opening it will bring back the default settings and expansion boundary. To make persistent changes to your display preferences, see the "Defining Event Viewer Preferences" section later in this chapter.

Suspending and Resuming New Events

Sometimes you might want to freeze the Event Viewer display and temporarily not display any more alarms. This might happen during a flood of alarms. If alarms continually updating the Event Viewer, you might have difficulty analyzing what is happening. At this point, it is nice to freeze your Event Viewer window so that you can research the alarms that you already have in the window.

Security Monitor provides you the capability to suspend the Event Viewer from displaying new alarms. To suspend the Event Viewer, choose Suspend New Events from the TOC. To resume alarms, choose Resume New Events from the TOC. Only one of the options is available at a time. When you have suspended alarms, for instance, the Resume option becomes available. (It is no longer grayed out.) Furthermore, suspending alarms does not prevent new alarms from being added to the Security Monitor database. It only prevents them from being displayed in your current Event Viewer.

Changing Display Preferences

This section describes the different preference settings that you can use to customize the Event Viewer. To access the Preferences window, click Preferences from the TOC. This displays the Preferences pop-up window (see Figure 17-23).

Figure 17-23 *The Event Viewer Preferences Window*

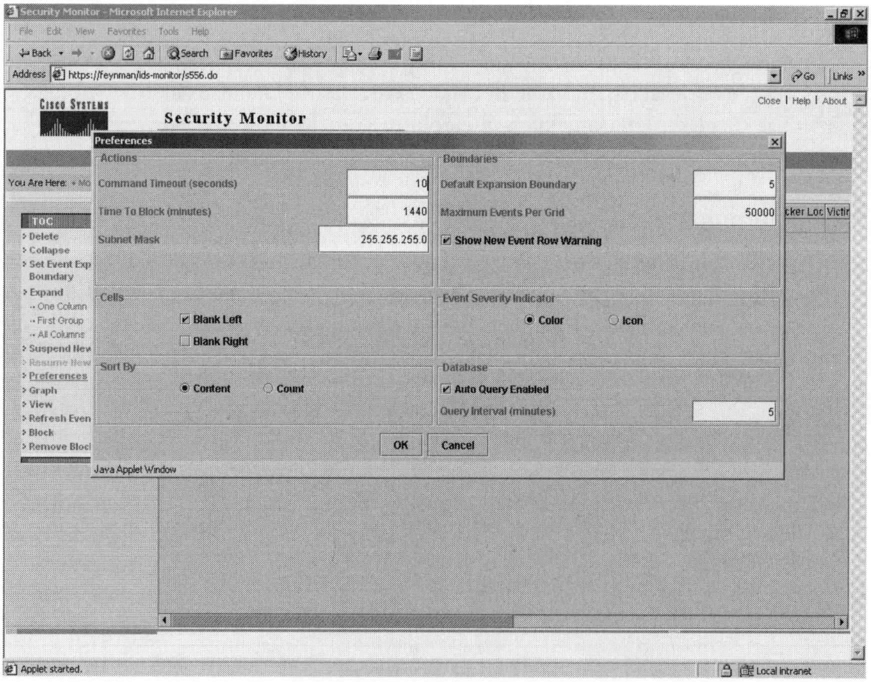

These settings fall into six basic categories:

- Actions
- Cells
- Sort By
- Boundaries
- Event Severity Indicator
- Database

NOTE   The display preferences specified using this option are not persistent. They are lost when you close the Event Viewer. To make persistent changes to your display preferences, see the "Defining Event Viewer Preferences" section later in this chapter.

Actions

The Actions group box in the Preferences window (see Figure 17-23) enables you to set the following values:

- Command Timeout
- Time to Block
- Subnet Mask

The Command Timeout value applies to all functions that require communication through the PostOffice infrastructure. For example, functions such as retrieving sensor statistics, viewing sensor block lists, and requesting that the sensor blocks a particular IP address all must be completed within the Command Timeout value. This timeout value is not used for non-PostOffice functions, such as DNS queries. The default value is 10 seconds, with an allowable range between 1 and 3600 seconds (1 hour).

The Command Timeout value determines how long, in seconds, the Event Viewer will wait for a response from the sensor before it concludes that it has lost communication with the sensor. In most cases, you will not need to modify this value. If you get frequent Command Timeout errors, you might consider increasing the Command Timeout value, or diagnose the reason that your Event Viewer experiences such a slow response time.

The Time to Block value specifies how long (in minutes) the sensor blocks traffic from the specified source when you issue a block command from the Event Viewer. The block duration value that can be specified applies only to blocks generated automatically by that sensor. The Time to Block value in the Preferences dialog box applies only to manually generated blocks from the Event Viewer. The default value is 1440 minutes (1 day). The allowable range is from 1 to 525,600 minutes (1 year).

NOTE	In software versions prior to 1.3, the manual blocking functionality was not available for sensors communicating with Security Monitor using RDEP.

The Subnet Mask value is used to define the network portion of the IP address that will be used to block a range of addresses. Your sensors use this information when they publish a blocking rule to the blocking devices on your network. The Subnet Mask value is only applied to the to the Block>Network and Remove Block>Network options from the Event Viewer. The default value is 255.255.255.0, which represents a Class C address range.

Cells

The Blank Left and Blank Right check boxes in the Cells section of the Preference window enable you to specify whether certain cells will be blank or filled in (see Figure 17-23):

- Blank Left
- Blank Right

Choosing the Blank Left check box controls whether values that are suggested by a cell above a row are filled in on following rows in the Event Viewer. For example, consider the following alarms triggered by the same source IP address of 172.30.4.150: WWW perl interpreter attack, WWW IIS view source attack, and WWW IIS newdsn attack. If the Blank Left box is selected, the grid appears as follows:

172.30.4.150	WWW perl interpreter attack
<blank>	WWW IIS view source attack
<blank>	WWW IIS newdsn attack

If the Blank Left box is not selected, the grid appears as follows:

172.30.4.150	WWW perl interpreter attack
172.30.4.150	WWW IIS view source attack
172.30.4.150	WWW IIS newdsn attack

Choosing Blank Right affects how the collapsed cells display in the Event Viewer. When cells are collapsed, their background color is gray; and if the collapsed values are different, a plus sign (+) displays. When Blank Right is selected, a plus sign displays in a collapsed cell regardless of whether the cell values differ.

The default setting is for Blank Right not to be selected. In this state, a plus sign displays only in collapsed cells if the values in the cells differ. If the values in the collapsed cell are the same, the actual value displays in the Event Viewer.

Sort By

The Sort By group box in the Preferences (see Figure 17-23) enables you to specify how the events are sorted in the Event Viewer. You can choose from the following two options:

- Count
- Content

When sorting by Count, the entries in the Event Viewer are sorted by the count of alarms listed in the first column of each row. If you sort by Content, the entries in the Event Viewer are sorted alphabetically by the first field that is unique (starting with the first field and moving to the right until a differing field value is found).

Boundaries

The Boundaries group box in the Preferences window (see Figure 17-23) enables you to set the following values:

- Default Expansion Boundary
- Maximum Events per Grid
- Event Batching Timeout

The Default Expansion Boundary specifies the default number of columns in which the cells of a new event are expanded. By default, only the first field of an event is expanded.

The Maximum Events per Grid defines the maximum number of alarms that can be displayed in a single Event Viewer. When the maximum value is reached, an error message displays. The default value is 50,000 alarms.

Event Severity Indicator

There are two Even Severity Indicator options from which you can select (see Figure 17-23):

- Color
- Icon

The default setting is for the severity to be indicated in the Event Viewer with colors. The color affects the background of the Count field. The following colors are used to indicate alarm severity:

- Red
- Yellow
- Green

High-severity alarms are shown in red. Yellow is used for medium-severity alarms, and low-severity alarms display in green.

Besides the default color severity indicator, you can also choose to display the severity of your alarms using icons. The icons used to display alarm severity are as follows:

- Red exclamation point
- Yellow flag

High-severity alarms display a red exclamation point icon. A yellow flag icon indicates medium-severity alarms, and low-severity alarms do not use any icon.

Database

The Database group box in the Preferences window (see Figure 17-23) enables you to configure whether the Event Viewer automatically retrieves new events from the Security Monitor database. If you check the Auto Query Enabled check box, you can configure how often the Event Viewer automatically retrieves events from the Security Monitor database.

NOTE   You can manually retrieve new events from the Security Monitor database by clicking Refresh Events from the TOC.

Creating Graphs

You can create a graph of the data, or a subset of the data, shown in Event Viewer. The graphs represent a static snapshot of the information and are not updated dynamically. You can choose from the following two types of graphs (see figure 17-24):

- By Child
- By Time

Figure 17-24 *Event Viewer Graph Options*

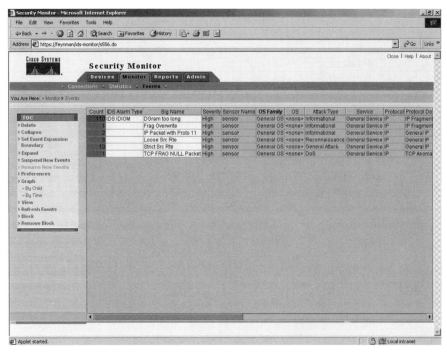

By Child

To see the distribution of events by some field value in the display, select Graph>By Child from the TOC on the Event Viewer window. The graph displays the children events (the events in the column to the right of the selected field) across the X-axis of the graph and the number of occurrences along the Y-axis. Event severity is indicated by the color of the bar.

Suppose, for instance, that you want to graph all the Intrusion Detection Interaction and Operations Messages (IDIOM) events by attack type. First you need to move the IDS Alarm Type column to the right of the Count column. Next, move the Attack Type column to the right of the IDS Alarm Type column. Finally, select the cell in the IDS Alarm Type column (containing IDIOM) and click Graph>Child. The bars on the resulting graph represent the different attack types.

By Time

To see how the selected events were distributed over time, select Graph>By Time from the TOC on the Event Viewer window. The graph displays along the x-axis the range of time over which the event occurred; along the y-axis, the number of occurrences. Event severity is indicated by the color of the bar.

View

Clicking View in the TOC enables you to access the following options:

- Context Buffer
- Host Names
- Network Security Database
- Statistics

Context Buffer

For TCP-based signatures that trigger on patterns in the TCP data stream, the sensor captures up to 256 characters of the TCP stream, which may be examined from the Event Viewer. These capture characters are called the *context buffer*, and it contains keystrokes, data, or both in the connection stream around the string of characters that triggered the signature. You can use this feature to determine whether the triggered alarm was from a deliberate attack or whether it is an accidental set of keystrokes. To view the context information for an alarm, follow these steps:

Step 1   Select an alarm entry clicking one of its fields in the Event Viewer.

Step 2   Click View>Context Buffer from the Event Viewer TOC. The context information (if available for the selected alarm entries) displays in a pop-up window (see Figure 17-25).

Figure 17-25   *Context Buffer Window*

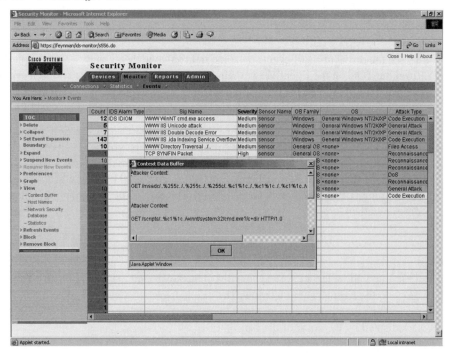

NOTE	Beginning with Cisco IDS version 4.0, the context buffer actually includes the information that caused the signature to trigger.

Host Names

By default, the alerts stored by the Event Viewer indicate the IP addresses of the systems involved in the alert. Using the View>Host Names option from the TOC, you can cause the Event Viewer to attempt to resolve the host names for the IP addresses in the selected alerts. The Event Viewer will attempt to resolve both the source and destination addresses. This information displays in a pop-up window in the content area (see Figure 17-26).

Figure 17-26 *Resolving Host Names*

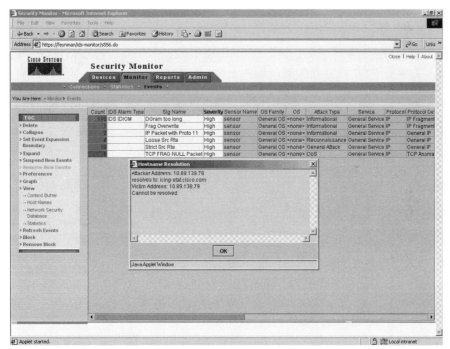

NOTE	Because a single row can represent multiple alarms, it can take the Event Viewer a significant amount of time to resolve all the IP addresses. If you attempt to resolve a large number of alerts, a pop-up warning will appear in the content area indicating that your request could take a couple of minutes to complete. Furthermore, you must have your Security Monitor server configured to communicate with a DNS server capable of providing the host name resolution.

Network Security Database

The Network Security Database (NSDB) is the Cisco HTML-based encyclopedia of network vulnerability information. You can examine the NSDB for information on a specific alarm. The Cisco Secure Encyclopedia (CSEC) is the online equivalent of the NSDB. (For more information on the NSDB, see Chapter 9, "Cisco IDS Device Manager and Event Viewer.")

CSEC has been developed as a central warehouse of security knowledge to provide Cisco security professionals with an interactive database of security vulnerability information. CSEC contains detailed information about security vulnerabilities such as countermeasures, affected systems and software, and Cisco Secure products that can help you test for vulnerabilities or detect when malicious users attempt to exploit your systems. The CSEC can be found at www.cisco.com/go/csec.

Statistics

You can view event statistics for a row in Event Viewer. The statistics include the following information:

- The severity level for the row
- The number of child nodes for the row
- The number of events represented by the row
- The percentage of the total events (based on the events currently displayed by the Event Viewer) that the selected row represents.

To access the statistics for a specific row, select the row by clicking a field in the row. Then you click View>Statistics from the TOC. A pop-up window appears in the content area indicating the statistics (see Figure 17-27).

Figure 17-27   *Event Statistics Pop-up Window*

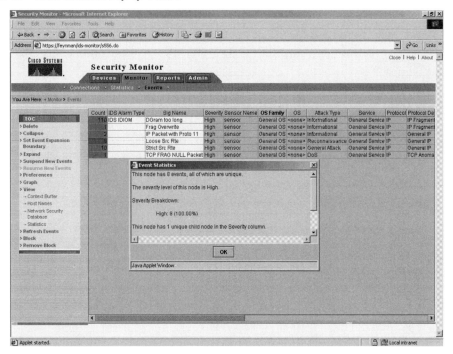

Security Monitor Administration

Although a large percentage of your time will be spent using the Event Viewer functionality of Security Monitor, you might also need to perform various tasks to administer and maintain your Security Monitor software. Security Monitor server administration and maintenance falls into the following categories:

- Database maintenance
- System configuration
- Defining Event Viewer preferences

Database Maintenance

When the Security Monitor database becomes large, system performance can begin to degrade. How large the database can become depends upon many factors, including system specifications and the number and types of applications running on the system. Using database rules, you can automatically manage the size of your database, send email notifications, log a console notification event, or execute a script when specific thresholds or intervals are met. Examples of database thresholds include whether the database exceeds a certain size or whether the database receives more than a defined number of events.

Executing a script enables you to easily prune your Security Monitor events database. Some of the default scripts provided to prune events in your Security Monitor database are the following:

- PruneByAge.pl
- PruneByDate.pl
- PruneBySeverity.pl

These scripts reduce the number of events in your Security Monitor database based on specific criteria. The PruneByAge.pl script removes events that are older than a specified number of days. Similarly, PruneByDate.pl removes events that are older than a specified date. Finally, PruneBySeverity.pl removes events that match a specified severity level.

By defining your own custom database rules, you can keep you Security Monitor database working at its peak efficiency. To add your own custom database rule, follow these steps:

Step 1   Click the Admin tab on the main Security Monitor screen.

Step 2   Select Database Rules from the options bar (or the content area). This displays the Database Rules window in the content area (see Figure 17-28).

Figure 17-28   *The Database Rules Window*

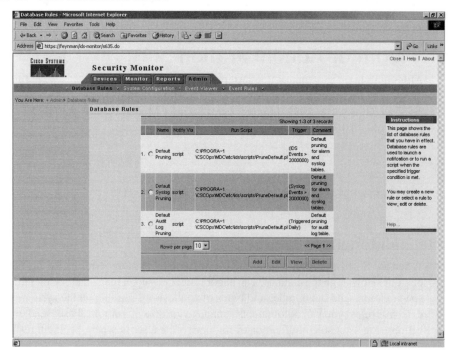

Step 3 Click the Add button. The Specify the Trigger Conditions window appears in the content area (see Figure 17-29).

Figure 17-29 *The Specify the Trigger Conditions Window*

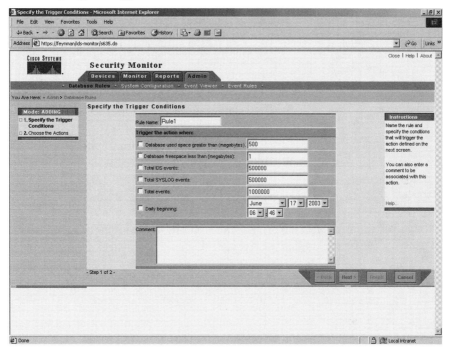

Step 4 Enter a name for the rule being created.

Step 5 Select any of the parameters shown in Table 17-2 that you want to use in the database rule by clicking the radio button next to the parameter and adjusting the value for the parameter.

Table 17-2 *Database Rule Parameters*

Parameter	Description
Database Used Space Greater Than (Megabytes)	If selected, this parameter triggers the database rule when the database reaches a size greater than the value specified. The default is 500 MB.
Database Freespace Less Than (Megabytes)	If selected, this parameter triggers the database rule when the free space on the drive (where the database is installed) falls below the specified size. The default is 1.

continues

Table 17-2 *Database Rule Parameters (Continued)*

Parameter	Description
Total IDS Events	If selected, this parameter triggers the database rule when the total number of IDS events is more than the specified value. The default is 500,000.
Total Syslog Events	If selected, this parameter triggers the database rule when the total number of syslog events is more than the specified value. The default is 500,000.
Total Events	If selected, this parameter triggers the database rule when the total number of IDS and syslog events is more than the specified value. The default is 1,000,000.
Daily Beginning	If selected, this parameter allows the database rule to be triggered daily beginning at the specified date and time. The default is set to 24 hours from the current clock value on the Security Monitor.

Step 6 Click the Next button. The Rule Actions window appears in the content area.

Step 7 Select the actions to be performed when the database rules triggers. These actions are the same as those that you specify for event rules (see the section "Event Notification" earlier in this chapter).

Step 8 Click the Finish button to complete the addition of the new database rule.

System Configuration Settings

Selecting Admin>System Configuration enables you to configure the following communication properties:

- Email server
- PostOfice settings
- Syslog settings
- Update network IDS signatures

Selecting Email Server enables you to specify the email server that Security Monitor uses for event notifications and configure the email server's properties (such as IP address and host name). The PostOffice Settings option enables you to specify the settings used to establish the communication infrastructure between Security Monitor and Cisco IDS version 3.x IDS devices. The Syslog Settings option enables you to specify the port that Security Monitor uses to monitor syslog messages.

Attackers continually develop new attacks to launch against your network. Therefore, it is important that you keep your signature definitions as current as possible. Chapter 15, "Cisco IDS Maintenance and Troubleshooting," explains how you can update your sensor's software using IDS MC. You can also perform this same update using the Update Network IDS Signatures option in Security Monitor.

NOTE   Although the option is titled Update Network IDS Signatures, you can use it to apply signature updates as well as service packs on your sensors.

Defining Event Viewer Preferences

When working in the Event Viewer, you can configure your Event Viewer preferences (see the section "Changing Display Preferences" earlier in this chapter). These changes, however, are not persistent and are lost whenever you close the Event Viewer. If you want to change your preferences so that they are applied every time that you open the Event Viewer, you need to change the Event Viewer preferences using the administration options. Administratively, you can configure your Event Viewer preferences using the following two options:

- Your Preferences
- Default Preferences

When choosing Your Preferences, you can configure your own personal display preferences. These changes apply only to the user with whom you are currently logged in to Security Monitor. These options enable you to customize the Event Viewer to your own personal preferences.

Default Preferences, on the other hand, change the default display settings for all users. You can use this option to establish display preferences that all users will benefit from (such as Blank Right and the Default Expansion Boundary).

Security Monitor Reports

Security Monitor enables you to generate reports based on the audit and alarm information collected by Security Monitor. To reduce the quantity of information in the reports, you can filter the report output using the content of various alarm fields, such as Event Level and Source IP Address. These reports can be generated immediately, or you can schedule them to be generated at a later time. Security Monitor provides the following report templates:

- **Security Alarm Source Report**—Summarizes alarms received on the syslog port by the source of the events. If Security Monitor receives alarms from a PIX firewall, for example, use this report to view the alarm information. Filterable by event level, source IP address, and time/date.

- **Security Alarm Detailed Report**—Provides detailed information for each security alarm received. Filterable by event level, source IP address, and time/date.

- **IDS Top Sources Report**—Reports the specified number of source IP addresses that have generated the most events during a specified time period. Filterable by date/time, top *n* (where *n* is the number of sources), destination direction, destination IP address, signature or signature category, sensor, and event level.

- **IDS Top Source/Destination Pairs Report**—Reports the specified number of source/destination pairs (that is, connections or sessions) that have generated the most alarms during a specified time period. Filterable by date/time, top *n* (where *n* is the number of source/destination pairs), signature or signature category, sensor, event level, source direction, destination direction, source address, and destination address.

- **IDS Top Destinations Report**—Reports the specified number of destination IP addresses that have been targeted for attack during a specified time period. Filterable by date/time, top *n* (where *n* is the number of destinations), source direction, source address, signature or signature category, sensor, and event level.

- **IDS Top Alarms Report**—Reports the specified number of top alarms, by signature name, that have been generated during a specified time period. Filterable by date/time, top *n* (where *n* is the number of alarms), source direction, destination direction, source address, destination address, signature or signature category, sensor, event level, and signature or signature category.

- **IDS Summary Report**—Provides a summary of event information for an organization during a specified time period. Filterable by date/time, organization, source direction, destination direction, signature or signature category, and event level.

- **IDS Alarms by Sensor Report**—Reports logged alarms based on the sensor (host ID) that detected the event. Filterable by date/time, source direction, destination direction, source address, destination address, signature or signature category, sensor, event level, and event count.

- **IDS Alarms by Hour Report**—Reports alarms in 1-hour intervals over the time specified by the user. Filterable by date/time, source direction, destination direction, source address, destination address, signature or signature category, sensor, event level, and event count.

- **IDS Alarms by Day Report**—Reports alarms in 1-day intervals over the time specified by the user. Filterable by date/time, source direction, destination direction, source address, destination address, signature or signature category, sensor, event level, and event count.

- **IDS Alarm Source/Destination Pair Report**—Reports logged alarms based on source/destination IP address pairs (that is, connections or sessions). Filterable by date/time, signature or signature category, sensor, event level, alarm count, source direction, destination direction, source address, and destination address.

- **IDS Alarm Source Report**—Reports alarms based on the source IP address that generated the alarm. Filterable by date/time, destination direction, destination address, signature or signature category, sensor, event level, alarm count, source direction, and source address.

- **IDS Alarm Report**—Reports logged alarms based on signature names. Filterable by date/time, source direction, destination direction, source address, destination address, sensor, event level, event count, and signature or signature category.

- **IDS Alarm Destination Report**—Reports alarms based on the destination IP address that generated the alarm. Filterable by date/time, source direction, source address, signature or signature category, sensor, event level, event count, destination direction, and destination address.

- **Daily Metrics Report**—Reports event traffic totals, by day, from the selected date until the current date. Reporting occurs in 24-hour intervals, starting at midnight. The report shows events by platform (PIX, IOS, sensor, or RDEP) and event type (IDS or security).

- **24-Hour Metrics Report**—Reports all alarm traffic from the most recent 24 hours in 15-minute intervals. This report has no filters.

Creating a report using Security Monitor involves the following tasks:

- Defining the report type and filtering parameters
- Scheduling the report
- Viewing the report

Defining the Report

When creating an IDS report using Security Monitor, you can filter the output based on the following parameters (see Figure 17-30):

- Event level
- Event count
- Source direction
- Source IP address
- Destination direction
- Destination IP address
- IDS devices
- IDS signatures
- IDS signature categories

Figure 17-30 *The Report Filtering Window*

Scheduling the Report

When scheduling an IDS report to run using Security Monitor, you need to specify the following parameters (see Figure 17-31):

- Report name
- Scheduling information
- Notification information

Figure 17-31 *The Schedule Report Window*

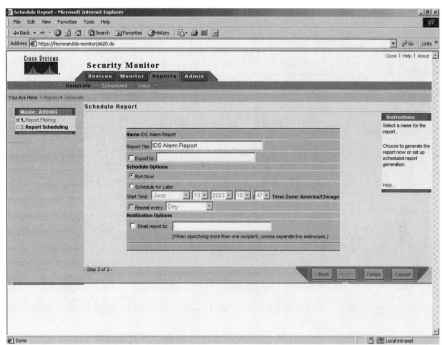

You can also save the HTML report to a file by entering the exact filename in the Export To text field. When scheduling reports, you might want to be notified via email when the report actually runs. You can do this by entering a valid email address in the Email Report To Text field.

Viewing the Report

After generating your reports, you can view them by accessing Reports>View. This displays the Choose Completed Report window in the content area (see Figure 17-32).

Figure 17-32 *The Choose Completed Report Window*

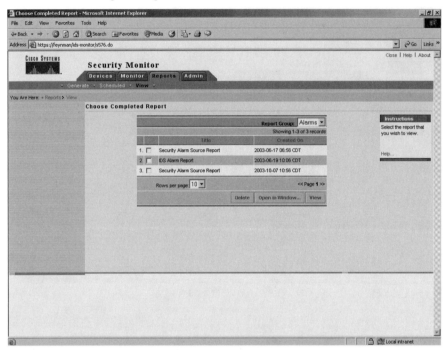

To view a report that you have generated, you first need to click the radio button next to the report. Then you have to choose one of the following two methods to view your reports:

- View

- Open in Window

The difference between these options is that the Open in Window option causes the report to display in a new browser window, as shown in Figure 17-33.

Figure 17-33 *Security Alarm Source Report*

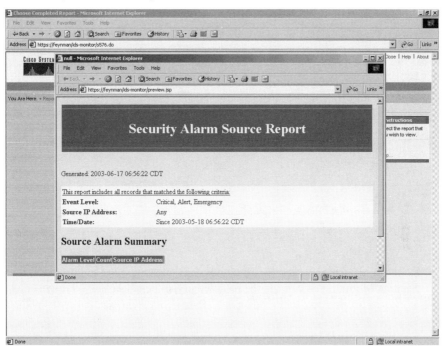

Summary

When deploying a large number of Cisco IDS sensors on your network, you need a way in which to collect and correlate the alerts from all these IDS devices. Security Monitor enables you to monitor up to 300 IDS devices across your network.

The Monitoring Center for Security (Security Monitor) is a component of the CiscoWorks Virtual Private Network (VPN)/Security Management Solution (VMS) product. This VMS product integrates numerous security applications into a single solution.

Using Security Monitor, you can receive IDS from numerous Cisco IDS–capable devices such as the following:

- Appliance sensors
- IDS modules
- Router modules
- IOS routers
- PIX firewalls

Security Monitor runs on Windows 2000 Professional, Server, Advanced Server, and Solaris 2.8 and enables you to access it via the client browser on your computer. Security Monitor supports the following browser types:

- Internet Explorer
- Netscape Navigator

The user interface for Security Monitor is divided into the following major sections to enable you to effectively use the program:

- Configuration tabs
- Options bar
- TOC
- Path bar
- Instructions box
- Content area
- Tools bar

Before you can monitor events from an IDS device, you must add or import the device to Security Monitor. You can add the following types of devices to Security Monitor:

- RDEP devices
- PostOffice devices
- IOS routers
- PIX firewalls

To efficiently monitor the events from multiple devices on your network, you can configure event rules for Security Monitor. An event rule takes action based on one or more of the following traffic characteristics:

- Originating device
- Originating device address
- Attacker address
- Victim address
- Signature name
- Signature ID
- Severity

One of the major benefits of event rules is that they enable you to perform one of the following actions when Security Monitor receives certain events:

- Send an email notification
- Generate an audit (console) message
- Execute a script

One of the major features of Security Monitor is the Event Viewer. The Event Viewer enables you to view the alerts received by your monitored devices in a graphical interface. When you launch the Event Viewer, you need to specify the type of events that you want to view along with the starting and ending time and date window of which events to include in the display.

Some of the tasks that you can use to customize the Event Viewer to your personal tastes include the following:

- Moving columns
- Deleting rows and columns
- Collapsing columns
- Setting the event expansion boundary
- Expanding columns
- Suspending and resuming new events
- Changing the display preferences
- Creating event graphs

Using Security Monitor you can also generate reports based on the information stored in the Security Monitor database. These reports are based on one of many reports templates supplied with Security Monitor.

When producing a report, you need to perform the following tasks:

- Defining the report type and filtering parameters
- Scheduling the report
- Viewing the report

Review Questions

The following questions test your retention of the material presented in this chapter. The answers to the review questions are in Appendix B, "Answers to Chapter Review Questions."

1 How many devices can Security Monitor manage?

2 What two types of web browsers does Security Monitor support?

3 Before Security Monitor can monitor a device, what must you do?

4 When you import devices, where do the devices come from?

5 What three actions can you specify for an event rule?

6 How many clauses can you specify in an event rule?

7 How many event rules can you have active at one time?

8 For what type of devices can you monitor the statistics of various processes on the device?

9 For which two types of devices can you monitor the status of their connection with Security Monitor?

10 What are your two options with respect to deleting rows from the Event Viewer?

11 What is the expansion boundary?

12 What are your two options when sorting the rows in the Event Viewer display using display preferences?

13 What is a database rule?

14 When launching the Event Viewer, what three parameters do you need to specify?

15 What are the fields that you can use to filter the information that is included in generate reports?

Upon completion of this chapter, you will be able to perform the following tasks:

- Understand the benefits of Cisco Threat Response (CTR)
- Identify the CTR predefined policy types
- Understand the CTR user interface
- Identify the CTR investigation levels
- Identify the IDS devices supported by CTR
- Understand the CTR terminology

CHAPTER 18

Cisco Threat Response

The increasingly complex security threats that your network faces make it critical that you maintain a high level of intrusion protection on your network. Wasting resources investigating false alarms can detract from legitimate threats against your network. Cisco Threat Response is another component in the overall Cisco intrusion protection solution. It works in concert with other IDS components to virtually eliminate false alarms, escalate real attacks, and aid in the remediation of costly intrusions.

Overview

Cisco Threat Response (CTR) works with your existing IDS sensors to provide an efficient intrusion protection solution. Unlike other intrusion management solutions, CTR performs a just-in-time analysis of each targeted system to determine whether an attack has succeeded. By examining the actual targeted systems, CTR separates real intrusions from false alarms so that you can concentrate your security resources on quickly addressing the real threats to your network.

Benefits

CTR is a great asset to your existing network security solution. It increases your efficiency and helps you reduce your costs by providing the following:

- Elimination of false alarms
- Escalation of real attacks
- Fast, consistent, and automated processes
- Easy deployment

By examining the target system, CTR can determine whether an IDS alarm represents an actual threat to your network. It provides this functionality 24 hours a day to provide robust analysis of the attack traffic launched against your network. Furthermore, because CTR investigates your hosts without the need for software agents, this translates to rapid deployment and ease of maintenance.

When investigating IDS alarms, CTR uses the following three-phased approach:

- Basic investigation
- Advanced investigation
- Forensic data capture

Basic Investigation

The first phase of analysis involves a noninvasive examination of the target system. This analysis is done in real time with the goal being to determine the following items:

- Operating system
- Operating system patch levels
- Operating system services

This information is used to determine whether the attack launched against the system could have succeeded. At this level, the main goal is to determine whether the attack would obviously fail because it was launched against the incorrect operating system (such as a Windows attack launched against a Linux system). Attacks that would obviously fail are downgraded, whereas other alarms are marked as potentially successful attacks until they can be investigated further by the more detailed analysis phases.

CTR has an extensive database of known vulnerabilities that indicates which operating system versions are susceptible to which vulnerabilities and which ones are not. This information is used during the basic investigation to identify whether an operating system is vulnerable to the attack detected by the IDS. The CTR vulnerability information is continually being enhanced to include new vulnerability information.

Advanced Investigation

The second analysis phase is a detailed system-level investigation that includes the capture of the following types of information:

- Web logs
- System logs
- Other relevant information

This information is used to determine whether the attack succeeded or failed after an attack has been launched against a system and the attack passes the basic investigation phase (meaning that the system is vulnerable to the attack detected). Failed attacks are again downgraded to enable your security resources to focus their valuable time on real intrusions.

NOTE	Advanced investigation is only available as part of the CiscoWorks VPN Security Management Solutions (VMS) technology bundle.

Forensic Data Capture

The final phase of analysis involves collecting forensic evidence that provides you with the information necessary to make informed decisions in response to the intrusion. The following types of information are immediately copied to preserve them:

- Audit trails
- Log files
- Intrusion traces

By safely and quickly retrieving these files, you prevent the intruder from being able to cover his or her tracks by altering the information on the system.

NOTE	Forensic data capture is only available as part of the CiscoWorks VMS technology bundle.

Terms and Definitions

To help you understand CTR, it is helpful to review the following terms that are used in describing this technology:

- **Action**—Action that CTR takes to tackle a given alarm.

NOTE	Before CTR was incorporated into VMS, these actions were known as *agents* (not to be confused with an actual software agent, such as Cisco Security Agent). They are software processes that reside on the CTR server and do not need to be installed or maintained remotely on network nodes or target systems.

- **Alarm**—A specific occurrence of intrusive activity.
- **Event**—A type of an alarm.
- **Security zone**—A pairing of possible attack sources with target IP addresses to which you assign a policy.
- **Protected system**—The collection of protected hosts and protected domains that you define for CTR to protect.

- **Protected host**—A specific system or collection of systems that you define by IP address (or IP address ranges) that you want CTR to protect.
- **Protected domains**—Any domain that you define as needing to be protected by CTR.

NOTE Domains are convenient groupings of network systems that are organized along functional guidelines.

Investigation Levels

CTR uses the following three investigation levels when examining alarms detected on your network:

- Level 0 investigation
- Level 1 investigation
- Level 2 investigation

Level 0 Investigation

Level 0 investigations are rule-based and carried out by Level 0 actions. These actions do not conduct an analysis of the target system. Instead, they just upgrade or downgrade alarms based on the rule that the action is configured to follow.

Level 1 Investigation

Basic investigation actions perform Level 1 investigation and do not require password access to the target system. Usually these actions cannot confirm that an attack was successful. Their goal is to determine whether the target system might be vulnerable to the attack being launched.

An example of a basic investigation action is an action that performs operating system (OS) detection, known as the OS detection action. It is responsible for determining the OS type of the target system and comparing this to the necessary OS type for a specific alarm.

Level 2 Investigation

Advanced investigation actions perform Level 2 investigations. This investigation requires password access to the target system. These actions can actually determine whether an intrusion attempt was successful. These actions provide you with the most accurate analysis to separate false alarms from real alarms.

Predefined Policy Types

Policies map an action or actions to specific event types. CTR comes configured with the following six built-in policies:

- Default policy
- Downgrade all
- Downgrade and clear all
- Upgrade all
- Ignore DNS activity
- Ignore threat response activity

You can also add new policies or modify these existing policies to tailor them to your network environment.

Default Policy

The default policy enables CTR to investigate the target system to the fullest extent possible. This policy includes Level 2 investigation, but this analysis can only be performed if you specify a username and password for the target system using the Config>Protected Systems tab. Level 0 and Level 1 investigation can be performed whether or not you have configured a valid username and password for the target system. This policy is recommended for your systems that require the highest degree of protection.

Downgrade All

The downgrade all policy does not perform an investigation of the target system. Instead, it automatically downgrades all attacks in a security zone. You can use this policy in situations where you might not have adequate access to the target systems (such as on the Internet) but you still want to maintain a log or record of what has occurred.

Downgrade and Clear All

Like the downgrade all policy, the downgrade and clear all policy does not perform an investigation of the target system. Instead, it automatically downgrades and clears all attacks in a security zone. This policy proves useful for lab environments where you do not want to see the alarms.

Upgrade All

The upgrade all policy does not perform an investigation of the target system. Instead, it automatically upgrades all of the alarms in a security zone. You can use this policy in situations where you want all attacks upgraded to critical for your review (without any CTR investigation).

Ignore DNS Activity

The ignore DNS activity policy is like a filtered default policy. Actions related to the Domain Name System (DNS) activity are configured to downgrade and clear so that normal DNS activity is eliminated from analysis. Nevertheless, it still allows CTR to investigate suspicious activity stemming from the DNS server. You can use this policy for a security zone in which you have configured the DNS server as both the source and target IP address (combined with port 53).

Ignore Threat Response Activity

If your security zone contains the CTR system as a source address, you probably do not want the investigation performed by CTR to generate alarms. The ignore threat response activity policy handles this situation. It operates similarly to the default policy, except that the actions that handle event types related to CTR investigations are configured to downgrade and clear the alarms. Therefore, the investigation by CTR does not generate alarms based on its own investigation activity. This rule, however, does not prevent the generation of other alarms that originate from the CTR system.

Cisco Threat Response (CTR) Requirements

When deploying CTR, your installation must consider several requirements. Each of these requirements can impact the operation of CTR. You must consider the following when installing CTR on your network:

- System requirements
- IDS requirements
- Firewall settings

System Requirements

CTR is comprised of two following two components:

- Threat response server
- Threat response client

Server Requirements

The threat response server is the system on which the alarm data is managed as well as the system that conducts the investigation. To operate efficiently, your CTR server should meet the following requirements:

- **Operating system**—Windows 2000 Professional, Service Pack 3
- **Browser**—Internet Explorer 6.0 (or later)

- **Processor**—1 GHz or higher recommended
- **Memory**—512 MB minimum
- **Disk drive**—10 GB minimum (40 GB recommended)

NOTE   You must install the CTR software on an NT File System (NTFS) partition.

The system on which you install your CTR server should be dedicated to CTR. This application requires extensive system resources. To ensure efficient operation, do not install any other applications in conjunction with the CTR software.

NOTE   CTR is being incorporated into the CiscoWorks VPN/Security Management Solution (VMS) software. During this merging process, some of the CTR functionality will be incorporated into existing VMS components, such as the Security Monitor. (See the section "Migration to CiscoWorks VPN/Security Management Solution" later in this chapter for more information.) Furthermore, the server and client requirements can also change during this migration. Refer to the Cisco documentation for the latest server requirements.

NOTE   Although you can access the CTR graphical user interface (GUI) from the server itself, this is not recommended due to performance considerations. Using a separate client machine to access the GUI provides the best performance.

Client Requirements

The threat response client is the system that you use to connect to the CTR server so that you can view the alarm data and configure the CTR server. The connection is made using a web browser interface over HTTPS. Even though your client machine accesses the CTR server using a web browser, it still has the following requirements for optimal performance:

- **Web browser**—Internet Explorer 6.0 (or later)
- **CPU**—1 GHz or higher recommended
- **Memory**—128 MB minimum
- **Hard disk**—10 GB minimum

When accessing the CTR GUI, you should set your system's screen resolution to at least 1024×768 for the most efficient operation. Viewing the alarm information effectively requires this level of resolution or better. You will probably also want to have large monitor.

NOTE   CTR does not support any version of Netscape Navigator. Furthermore, only the English version of Internet Explorer is supported. Because CTR is incorporated into VMS, however, the client requirements can change. Refer to the Cisco documentation for the most current client requirements.

IDS Requirements

CTR investigates security alarms to determine their validity. These security alarms need to be generated by an intrusion detection system. CTR can accept alarm information from Cisco IDS sensors version 3.0 or higher.

Firewall Settings

If your CTR server is separated from your IDS sensors by a firewall, you need to open certain ports on your firewall to provide access to the CTR server. Table 18-1 lists the ports that need to be open to allow communication between your CTR server and your network monitoring devices.

Table 18-1   *Firewall Port Settings*

Device	Port
Cisco IDS sensors (version 3.x)	UDP 45000 (PostOffice)
Cisco IDS sensors (version 4.x)	TCP (443 or 80)

Your CTR server must also have the capability to access the target systems to perform its alarm investigation. For Level 1 investigation, the CTR server must have access to all ports (on the target system) to effectively perform its analysis. To enable Level 2 investigation, your CTR server must be able to log on to the target system.

Migration to CiscoWorks VPN/Security Management Solution

CTR is being migrated into the CiscoWorks VPN/Security Monitoring System software bundle. As this integration happens, some of the functionality available in the initial CTR release will be migrated into existing CiscoWorks VMS software applications, such as the Monitoring Center for Security (Security Monitor).

Some of the changes include the following:

- The auto update will become part of Security Monitor.
- User authentication will be through CiscoWorks.
- The CTR Alarm Display screen will be incorporated into Security Monitor.
- The CTR reporting will be incorporated into Security Monitor.

NOTE   As this migration occurs, some of the functionality explained in this chapter will obviously change. Refer to the Cisco documentation for the most current information on the CTR functionality.

Software Installation

To install the CTR server software, you need to log on to your server with a Window 2000 account that has local Administrator privileges. The installation process uses standard Windows installation screens. During the installation process, you must provide the username and password for an account on the system that has administrative privileges. At the end of the installation process, you need to reboot the system to complete the installation process.

The initial version of CTR maintains its own username and password information (separate from the underlying operating system). This user account information will be replaced by CiscoWorks user roles as CTR is incorporated into the CiscoWorks VPN/Security Management Solution product.

NOTE   If the installation process does not accept the username and password that you enter, examine the "Cisco Threat Response User Guide" for information on a workaround. Furthermore, during the installation process, a default account of cisco (with a password of cisco) is created. You can use this account to initially access the CTR software.

Accessing the CTR Graphical User Interface (GUI)

Although your CTR software runs on a specific server, you can access the CTR GUI from other systems on your network using the Internet Explorer web browser. Communication with the CTR software uses HTTPS to protect the traffic across the network from unauthorized access.

To access the CTR GUI, follow these steps:

Step 1 Launch your Internet Explorer web browser.

Step 2 Enter **https://<IP address>** in the address field (where *<IP address>* is the IP address of your CTR server).

Step 3 Click the OK button when the Security Alert pop-up window appears.

Step 4 Click the OK button in response to the second Security Alert pop-up to accept the certificate from the CTR server. The CTR login screen appears in your browser (see Figure 18-1).

Figure 18-1 *Cisco Threat Response Login Screen*

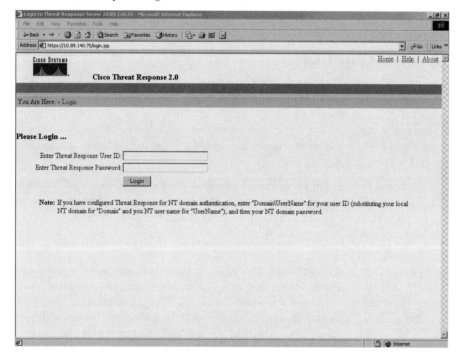

Step 5 Enter a valid username. The default account is cisco.

Step 6 Enter the password for the username specified. The password for the default cisco account is cisco.

Step 7 Click the Login button to log in to the CTR software. If this is first time that you are accessing CTR, you will receive the Quick Start screen. Otherwise, you will see the CTR Home page.

Quick Start

To use CTR, you must initially configure a minimal set of parameters that enable Level 0 and Level 1 action investigation. To quickly and efficiently enter these parameters, you can use the Quick Start Wizard. The first time that you access CTR, you automatically launch the Quick Start Wizard (see Figure 18-2). The Quick Start Wizard enables you to configure the following:

- Server pass phrase
- Automatic update information
- Security zones
- IDS sensors and event collectors

Figure 18-2   *Cisco Threat Response Quick Start Screen*

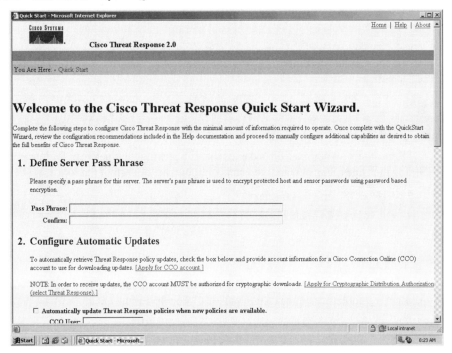

Server Pass Phrase

CTR needs to have passwords to access both sensors and protected hosts. Storing these credentials could represent a potential security risk. To minimize this risk, you can specify a pass phrase that is used to encrypt these important credentials.

Automatic Update Information

To maintain the effectiveness of your CTR software, you can automatically update your policies from the Cisco website. To enable automatic updates, you need to specify a valid CCO Cisco.com registered user account. This account will be used to retrieve the updates from the Cisco website.

Security Zones

A security zone consists of the following two characteristics:

- IP address or address range
- CTR policy

Through the Quick Start Wizard, you can specify an IP address or address range. These addresses will automatically have the default policy applied to them.

NOTE   Using the regular CTR interface, you can create other security zones and apply any of the CTR policies.

IDS Sensors

CTR must receive alarms from a device that is watching your network for intrusive activity. Using the Quick Start Wizard, you can configure one of each of the following device types:

- Cisco IDS version 4.0 sensor
- Cisco IDS version 3.x sensor

Initial Configuration

You cannot bypass the Quick Start Wizard. You must at least enter a security zone and a sensor to complete the Quick Start Wizard. To complete the Quick Start configuration Wizard, follow these steps:

Step 1   Enter a pass phrase in the Pass Phrase field. To verify your pass phrase, you need to re-enter the value in the Confirm field.

Step 2   If you want to enable automatic updates, enter a valid CCO Cisco.com registered user account using the CCO User and CCO Password fields and check the Automatically Update Threat Response Policies When New Policies Are Available option.

NOTE   To automatically update the CTR policies, your system will need access to the Internet.

Step 3   Enter the range of addresses that you want CTR to protect in the Protected IP Address Range field.

Step 4   Define the sensors that you want to process alarms from. You need to specify the fields listed in Table 18-2 for Cisco IDS version 4.x sensors. For information on the PostOffice fields required for Cisco IDS version 3.x sensors, refer to the "Cisco Threat Response User Guide" or help documentation.

Table 18-2   *Basic Cisco IDS Version 4.x Sensor Fields*

Field	Description
IP Address	The IP address that CTR will use to communicate with the sensor
Device Name	The configured name of the sensor
Web Port	The TCP port that CTR will use to communicate with the sensor's management interface
Username	A valid username on the sensor
Password	The password for the specified user account

Step 5   Click the Configure Threat Response with These Values button to complete the Quick Start Wizard.

NOTE   Although you perform the basic configuration tasks using the Quick Start Wizard, it is still recommended that you refine your configuration using the tasks explained in both the "Basic Configuration" and "Advanced Configuration" sections later in this chapter.

Using Cisco Threat Response

After you perform the minimal configuration using the Quick Start Wizard, you can access the normal CTR interface. This interface is comprised of the following four main pages:

- Home page
- Alarms page
- Reports page
- Config page

Each of these pages provides you with different information or capabilities with respect to using CTR.

Home Page

The Home page is the initial page that you see when you log in to the CTR software (see Figure 18-3).

Figure 18-3 *Cisco Threat Response Welcome Screen*

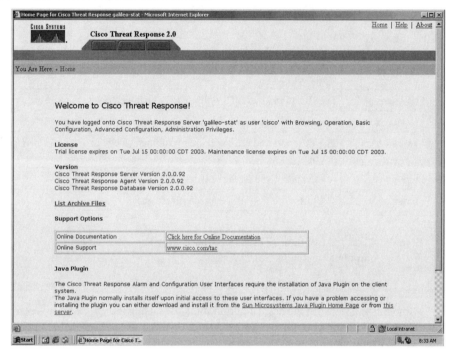

The Home page enables you to view the following information:

- License file currently in use
- CTR server version
- CTR action version
- CTR database version

From this screen, you can access all the CTR functionality. You can even access your archived alarms files, view online documentation, and access online Technical Assistance Center (TAC) support. Most of the CTR functionality is accessed through the following three configuration tabs:

- Alarms
- Reports
- Config

NOTE	When you select one of the three configuration tabs, a Java applet is used to display the information on the page. Depending on the capabilities of your client system, this can take a couple of minutes to initially load the page, especially if your client system does not meet the minimum requirements.

Alarms Page

You can access the Alarms page by clicking the Alarm tab on the top of the Home page. It enables you to view the alarms as they occur from your active alarm feeds (see Figure 18-4). Along with seeing information on ongoing alarm investigations, you can view the alarm information based on one of the criteria shown in Table 18-3.

Table 18-3   *Alarm Display Criteria*

Criteria	Description
Sources	The Sources tab enables you to view the alarm information based on the systems that generate alarms.
Targets	The Targets tab enables you to view the alarm information based on the systems that are attacked.
Events	The Events tab enables you to view the alarm information categorized by the events.
Details	The Details tab enables you to view the alarm detail information for a single alarm that you have highlighted.

Figure 18-4   *Cisco Threat Response Alarms Page*

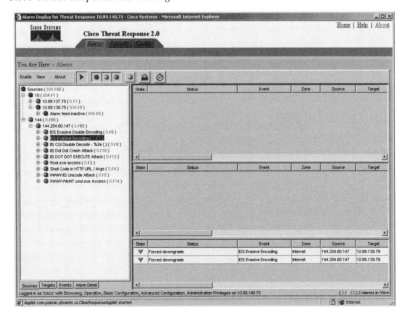

Reports Page

You can access the Reports page by clicking the Reports tab on the top of the Home page. It enables you to generate the following two types of reports (see Figure 18-5):

- Alarm reports
- Configuration reports

Figure 18-5 *Cisco Threat Response Reports Page*

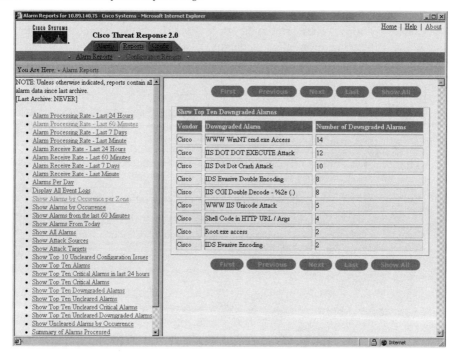

Config Page

You can access the Config page by clicking the Config tab on the top of the Home page. It enables you to configure the characteristics of the CTR software to match your network environment. From the Config page, you can access the following configuration options (see Figure 18-6):

- Alarm Source
- Security Zones
- Protected Systems
- Users and Passwords
- Advanced Configuration Options

Figure 18-6 *Cisco Threat Response Config Page*

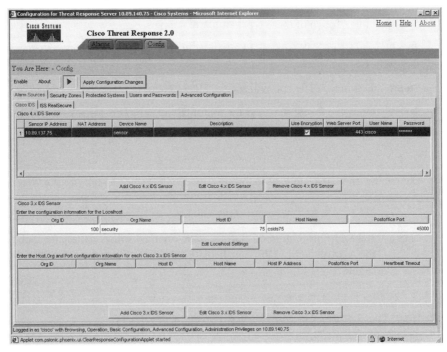

Basic Configuration

Even though the Quick Start Wizard enables you to perform a very simple configuration of your CTR server, you probably still need to perform other configuration tasks to effectively use CTR to protect your entire enterprise. Other tasks that you might need to perform include the following:

- Defining more alarm sources
- Configuring multiple security zones
- Defining protected systems

Defining Alarm Sources

CTR analyzes alarms and determines their validity. Using this information, it can then either upgrade or downgrade the alarm to more accurately reflect the threat to your network. The alarms can come from the following two types of sources:

- Cisco IDS version 4.x sensors (Remote Data Exchange Protocol [RDEP])
- Cisco IDS version 3.x sensors (PostOffice)

You must configure each alarm source that you want CTR to analyze the alarm feed from. During the initial configuration using the Quick Start Wizard, you were only able to configure one of each of these types of alarm sources.

To add more Cisco IDS version 4.x alarm sources (or edit existing alarm sources), follow these steps:

Step 1 Log in to CTR. You will see the Home page.

Step 2 Click the Config tab near the top of the screen. This causes the Config page to display.

NOTE Depending on your system's capabilities, the Config page can take a little while to display.

Step 3 If the current configured alarm sources do not display on the screen, click the Alarm Sources tab. This displays the Alarm Sources screen (see Figure 18-7).

Figure 18-7 *Cisco Threat Response Alarm Sources Screen*

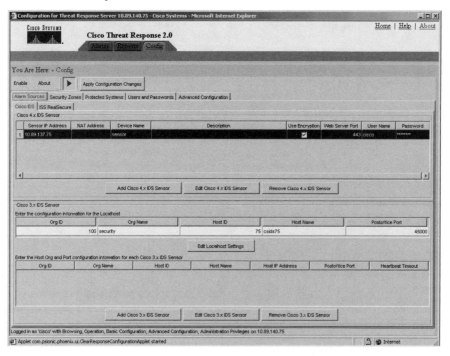

Step 4   Click the Add Cisco 4.x IDS Sensor button. The Cisco 4.x IDS Sensor
Configuration pop-up window displays (see Figure 18-8).

Figure 18-8   *Cisco 4.x IDS Sensor Configuration Pop-up Window*

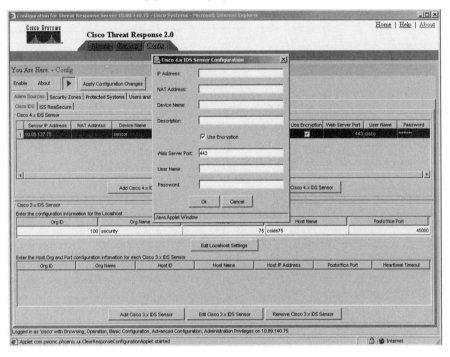

Step 5   Define the parameters for the new sensor by configuring the fields shown
in Table 18-4.

Table 18-4   *Cisco 4.x IDS Sensor Parameters*

Parameter	Description
IP Address	(Required) The IP address indicates the actual IP address of the sensor that CTR will retrieve alarms from.
NAT Address	If a NAT device is located between CTR and the sensor, this address specifies the address that CTR uses to communicate with the sensor across the network.
Device Name	(Required) The host name of the sensor.
Description	The description enables you to enter an informative description about the sensor being added.
Web Server Port	By default, this field already contains port 443 (for HTTPS). If you change this to a regular HTTP port, you need to also uncheck the Use Encryption check box.

continues

Table 18-4 *Cisco 4.x IDS Sensor Parameters (Continued)*

Parameter	Description
User Name	(Required) The username of a valid account on the sensor with administrative privileges.
Password	(Required) The password for the account specified by the User Name field.

Step 6 Click OK to add the sensor. The new sensor now displays on the screen.

Step 7 To complete the process, click the Apply Configuration Changes button. This button is highlighted to indicate that you have configuration changes that need to be applied to CTR (see Figure 18-9).

Figure 18-9 *Applying Configuration Changes*

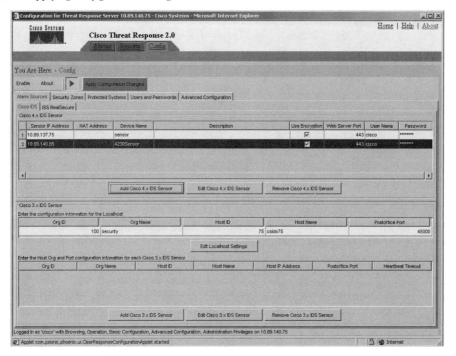

NOTE For information on how to add Cisco IDS version 3.x, refer to the "Cisco Threat Response User Guide" or help documentation.

The procedure to edit the characteristics of an existing sensor is similar to adding a new sensor, except that you highlight the sensor to be modified (by clicking it) and then click Edit Cisco 4.x IDS Sensor. You can also delete a sensor by highlighting the sensor and clicking Remove Cisco 4.x IDS Sensor.

Configuring Security Zones

A security zone is defined by the following parameters:

- Source IP addresses
- Source ports
- Destination IP addresses
- Destination ports
- Security policy

Basically, the security zone defines a specific CTR policy that will be applied to any alarms that match the address and port criteria specified. The CTR policy indicates the level of investigation that CTR will perform on the alarms that match the zone characteristics.

When you used the Quick Start Wizard, you specified a range of protected IP addresses. Assume that you specified the following values:

- Protected addresses (10.89.138.0–10.89.138.255)
- Threat response server (10.89.140.75)

Using these protected addresses and the address of the CTR server, the Quick Start Wizard automatically creates the security zones shown in Table 18-5.

Table 18-5   *Security Zones from Quick Start*

Zone Name	Source Address	Source Port	Destination Address	Destination Port	Policy
Threat Response	10.89.140.75	*	*	*	Ignore threat response activity
LAN	*	*	10.89.138.0–10.89.138.255	*	Default
Ignore Broadcast	*	*	0.0.0.0, 255.255.255.255	*	Default downgrade and clear all
Internet	*	*	!10.89.138.0–10.89.138.255		Default downgrade all

The LAN security zone causes CTR to perform a full investigation of alarms that are targeted against your protected systems. The Internet security zone causes CTR to ignore any alarms against systems that are not one of your protected systems. The Threat Response security zone prevents the investigation performed by your CTR server from generating any alarms.

Defining a Security Zone

Using security zones, you can regulate the way that CTR treats different types of attacks to different segments of your network. The initial zones created by the Quick Start Wizard will probably need to be enhanced by security zones of your own. To create a security zone, follow these steps:

Step 1 From the CTR Home page, click Config to bring up the configuration page.

Step 2 Click Security Zones. This brings up the Security Zones screen (see Figure 18-10).

Figure 18-10 *Security Zones Screen*

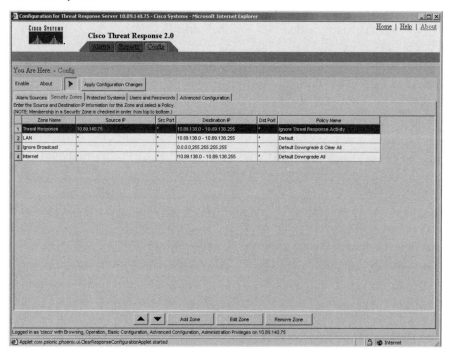

Step 3   Click Add Zone. This displays the Security Zone Configuration pop-up
(see Figure 18-11).

Figure 18-11   *Security Zone Configuration Pop-up*

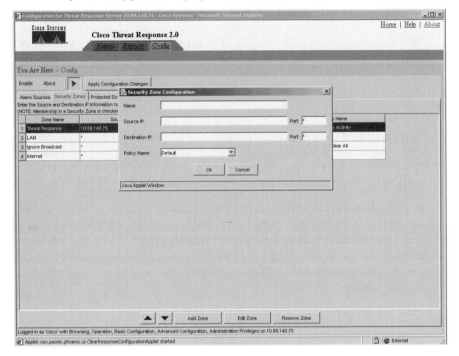

Step 4   Define your new security zone using the fields shown in Table 18-6.

Table 18-6   *Security Zone Parameters*

Parameter	Description
Name	Name of the security zone being created.
Source IP	Source IP address or addresses that the security zone will apply to. (Use * to indicate all IP addresses.)
Port	Source ports to apply to the security zone. (Use * to indicate all ports.)
Destination IP	Destination IP address or addresses that the security zone will apply to. (Use * to indicate all IP addresses.)
Port	Destination ports to apply to the security zone. (Use * to indicate all ports.)
Policy Name drop-down menu	Name of the security policy that will be applied to the security zone. The policy dictates the level of investigation performed by CTR for the alarms that match the zone criteria.

Step 5   Click OK to save the new security zone.

Step 6   Click Apply Configuration Changes to commit the changes to the CTR configuration.

NOTE   You can also edit or delete existing security zones by first selecting a zone by clicking it and then using the Edit Zone and Remove Zone buttons.

Policy Order

When you add a security zone, each new zone is added at the top of the list of security zones. When alarms are processed, CTR begins at the top of the list of zones and works it way to the bottom of the list. Therefore, the first zone that applies to the alarm can override the investigation that would be performed by zones listed later in the list.

Suppose that you created the security zones listed in Table 18-7. The *New Zone* and *LAN* security zones overlap. Currently, the investigation for the LAN security zone takes precedence over the New Zone investigation because it comes first in the list. This means that the DNS events (for 10.89.138.10 and 10.89.138.11) will be investigated by the Default security policy (instead of being downgraded and cleared by the Ignore DNS Activity security policy).

Table 18-7   *Sample Security Zones List*

Zone Name	Source Address	Source Port	Destination Address	Destination Port	Security Policy
Threat Response	10.89.140.75	*	*	*	Ignore threat response activity
LAN	*	*	10.89.138.0–10.89.138.255	*	Default
New Zone	*	*	10.89.138.10, 10.89.138.11	*	Ignore DNS activity
Ignore Broadcast	*	*	0.0.0.0, 255.255.255.255	*	Default downgrade and clear all
Internet	*	*	!10.89.138.0–10.89.138.255		Default downgrade all

To remedy this situation, you need to change the order of the security zones using the following steps:

Step 1 From the CTR Home page, click Config to bring up the Configuration page.

Step 2 Click Security Zones. This brings up the Security Zones screen.

Step 3 Highlight the New Zone by clicking it (see Figure 18-12).

Figure 18-12 *Moving a Security Zone*

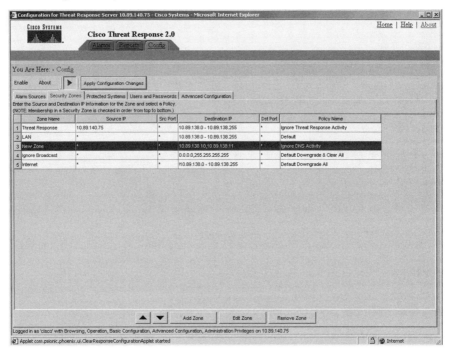

Step 4 Click the Up Arrow button at the bottom of the screen. This causes the New Zone security zone to move up in the list of zones so that it is now ahead of the LAN security zone (see Figure 18-13).

Figure 18-13   *Altered Security Zones Order*

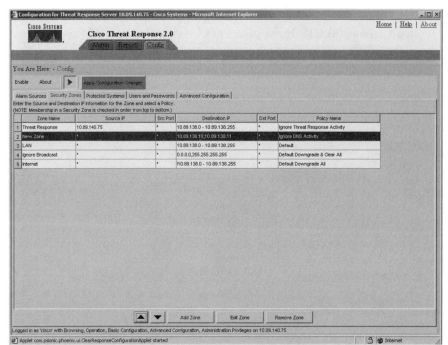

Step 5   Click Apply Configuration Changes to commit the changes to the CTR configuration.

Defining Protected Systems

CTR maximizes your security resources by eliminating false alarms. Similarly, you need to maximize CTR's resources by defining the systems that CTR needs to protect. These protected systems fall into the following two categories:

- Protected hosts
- Protected domains

Protected Domains

Protected domains are convenient groupings of network systems that you can create based on functional guidelines in which CTR uses a common username and password for system access.

When determining the validity of an alarm, the first thing that CTR needs to determine is the operating system on the target system. CTR can determine this information in the following ways:

- Dynamically determine OS
- Remember dynamically determined OS
- Statically mapped OS

When CTR dynamically determines the OS for a specific IP address or group of addresses, you can configure CTR to cache this information for a specific number of seconds. This frees CTR from continually having to use resources to calculate the OS repeatedly for the same system during a configured period of time.

To perform Level 2 analysis, CTR needs to actually access the target system. You enable CTR to access the target systems by supplying a username and password to access the protected systems. You can either specify these credentials based on individual IP addresses or by specifying the credentials for an entire domain.

Defining Protected Hosts

When you create a protected host entry, you can apply it to a single IP address, multiple IP addresses, or a range of IP addresses. You specify multiple IP addresses by separating them with commas. To specify a range of IP addresses, you define the address range separated by a dash.

To add a protected host to CTR, follow these steps:

Step 1 From the CTR Home page, click Config to bring up the Configuration page.

Step 2 Click Protected Systems. This brings up the Protected Systems screen (see Figure 18-14).

Figure 18-14 *Protected Systems Screen*

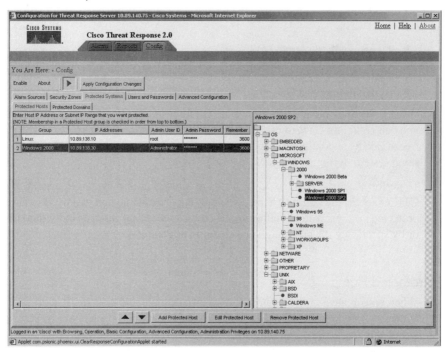

Step 3 If the Protected Hosts screen is not visible, click the Protected Hosts tab.

Step 4 Click Add Protected Host. This brings up the Protected Host Configuration pop-up (see Figure 18-15).

Step 5 Define the protected host by entering the fields shown in Table 18-8.

Table 18-8 *Protected Host Parameters*

Parameter	Description
Group	The name of the group that the protected host belongs to
IP Address(es)	Single address, multiple addresses, or range of addresses for the protected hosts entry
Admin User ID	Administrative user account that CTR will use to check the system
Password	Administrative password
Remember	Period of time that CTR remembers the OS that CTR determined was running on the protected host

Step 6 If you want to permanently map an OS to the protected host entry, you need to select the OS from the OS tree on the left side of the screen.

Figure 18-15 *Protected Host Configuration Pop-up*

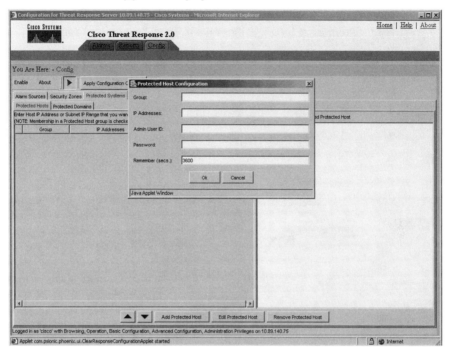

NOTE	You will usually permanently map operating systems to systems where only the operating systems will not change (with respect to their IP address). This usually includes core systems (such as web servers) that have static IP addresses.

Step 7	Click Apply Configuration Changes. This commits the changes to the CTR configuration.

NOTE	You will probably want to create an account specifically for CTR access to your systems. This enables you to tailor the access privileges of the account to match the needs of CTR. By using a separate account, it also enables you to more closely monitor the access on your systems.

Defining Protected Domains

Besides defining the administrative account using a protected host entry, you can also specify this information for a specific domain. To add a protected domain, follow these steps:

Step 1   From the CTR Home page, click Config to bring up the Configuration page.

Step 2   Click Protected Systems. This brings up the Protected Systems screen.

Step 3   Click Protected Domains. This displays the Protected Domains screen (see Figure 18-16).

Figure 18-16   *Protected Domains Screen*

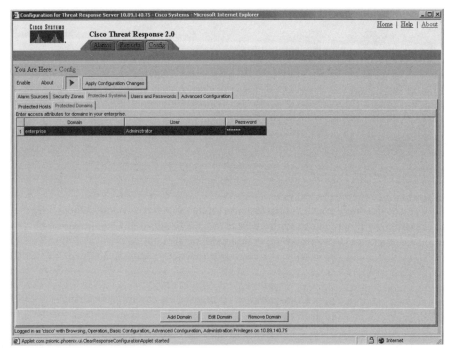

Step 4   Click Add Domain. This brings up the Domain Access Configuration pop-up (see Figure 18-17).

Figure 18-17   *Domain Access Configuration Pop-up*

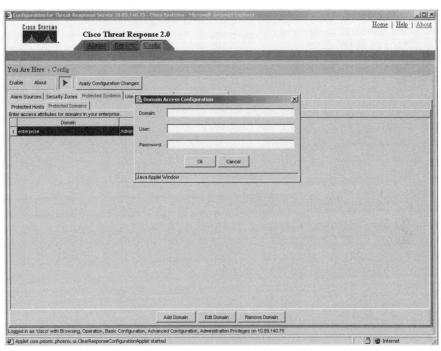

Step 5   Define the protected domain using the fields shown in Table 18-9.

Table 18-9   *Protected Domain Parameters*

Parameter	Description
Domain	The name assigned to the hosts grouped as a CTR domain
User	The administrative user ID for the domain
Password	Administrative password

Step 6   Click OK to save the new protected domain.

Step 7   Click Apply Configuration Changes to commit the changes to the CTR configuration.

NOTE   You can edit and delete existing CTR protected domains by selecting the CTR protected domain and clicking either the Edit Domain or Remove Domain buttons.

Advanced Configuration

After installation, CTR already has the following items:

- A set of alarm types for Cisco IDS
- Specific CTR policies for the supplied alarm types
- Information on which operating systems are susceptible to each alarm type

During alarm investigation, CTR determines the OS on the target system and uses this information to help determine the validity of the alarm. For many network environments, these settings are sufficient. However, you can also enhance the operation of CTR if needed by performing the following advanced tasks:

- Defining events
- Defining additional policies
- Mapping events to operating systems
- Scheduling actions
- Defining an enterprise console

You can perform all these tasks by selecting the Advanced Configuration tab. Because these operations are not required for normal operation of CTR, they will not be covered in detail in this book. For more information on performing these tasks, refer to the "Cisco Threat Response User Guide" or help documentation.

NOTE   To perform the advanced configuration tasks, you need to log in to CTR with an account that has Advanced Configuration rights.

Alarms and Reports

After configuring CTR, you will spend most of your time analyzing the alarms that CTR investigates. You can view this information by using the Alarms display screen or by generating reports.

Displaying Alarms

You access the Alarms display screen in CTR by selecting the Alarms tab on the Home page. To use the alarms display effectively, however, you need to understand how the page is structured. This display is broken down into the following components (see Figure 18-18):

- Icon bar
- Alarm view buttons
- Display button

- Time button
- Alarm Filter pane
- Alarm Filter tabs
- Critical Alarm pane
- Under-Investigation Alarm pane
- Downgraded Alarm pane

Figure 18-18   *Alarms Display Screen*

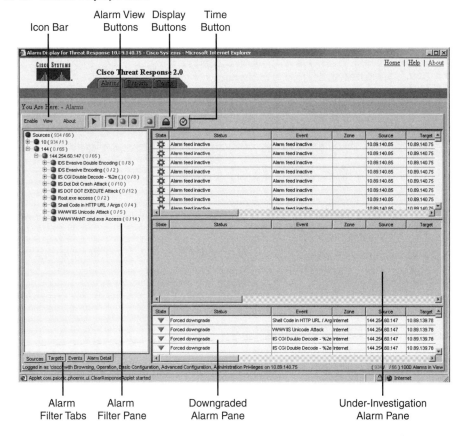

Icon Bar

The icon bar provides you with the following three options:

- Enable
- View
- About

Enable provides you with a mechanism with which to start and stop your CTR server. Clicking View displays a drop-down menu that includes the following options:

- Critical Alarms (Check indicates displayed.)
- Verifying Alarms (Check indicates displayed.)
- Downgraded Alarms (Check indicates displayed.)
- Cleared Alarms
- Lock the Display
- Display Time in GMT

The first four options provide a textual representation of the alarm status buttons. If the alarms are enabled (and displayed on the screen), the option has an initial check mark. The last two options (Lock the Display and Display Time in GMT) are textual representations of the Display button and the Time button.

Alarm Status Buttons

You can view the following types of alarms via the Alarms Display screen:

- Critical alarms
- Alarms being verified
- Downgraded alarms
- Cleared alarms

You can regulate which of these alarms display on the screen by clicking the Alarm Status buttons. These buttons (which operate as toggle switches) are colored balls and coded as follows:

- **Red ball**—Critical alarms
- **Yellow ball**—Alarms being verified
- **Green ball**—Downgraded alarms
- **Gray ball**—Cleared alarms

NOTE   You can also enable or disable the different alarm types using the View pull-down menu.

Display Button

The Display button looks like a padlock. It enables you to temporarily suspend the update of new alarms to the screen display. You can use this while you investigate the alarms that are currently displayed. Meanwhile, CTR still processes alarms in the background and will update the display when you unlock it.

Time Button

The Time button looks a little like a clock. You use this button to toggle the time between GMT and local time.

Alarm Filter Pane

The Alarm Filter pane provides you with a hierarchical display of the alarms that CTR processes. You can choose one of the following categories to group your alarms in the hierarchical display:

- Source address
- Target address
- Event type

The Alarm Filter pane shows information for groups of alarms.

NOTE   When you display the alarm detail information for a single alarm, this information displays in the Alarm Filter pane. In this situation, the information shown is for a single alarm as opposed to a group of alarms.

Alarm Filter Tabs

The Alarm Filter tabs change what information displays in the Alarm Filter pane. You can choose from the following tabs:

- **Source**—Groups alarms based on the source address that originated the attack
- **Targets**—Groups alarms based on the destination address of the host being attacked
- **Events**—Groups the alarms based on the type of attack
- **Alarm Details**—Displays all the alarm information available for the individual alarm selected on the right side of the screen

Critical Alarm Pane

The Critical Alarm pane shows the alarms that are rated critical. Each alarm has a State field that indicates its current status. The possible status icons are shown in Figure 18-19.

Figure 18-19 *Critical Alarm States*

State	Description
 ⊕	Threat Response's investigation indicates a confirmed attack, which requires immediate attention
 ⊙	Threat Response's investigation indicates that the attack is against the correct target, but it could not determine if the attack was successful.
▲	Your policy automatically upgraded this alarm. Threat Response does not perform analysis on forced upgrades so you should analyze this alarm.
 ✇	A configuration problem prevents Threat Response from completing it analysis. The Alarm Details might reveal the source of the problem.
❗	Something is preventing an agent from completing its processing on the target host. Refer to the Alarm Details for more information.

Under-Investigation Alarm Pane

The Under-Investigation Alarm pane shows the alarms that CTR is currently investigating. These alarms only have a single state that is represented by a hollow yellow circle.

Downgraded Alarm Pane

The Downgraded Alarm panel displays the alarm that CTR has downgraded. Alarms can be downgraded for the following two reasons:

- Attack failed
- Forced downgrade

The possible State icons for downgraded alarms are shown in Figure 18-20.

Figure 18-20 *Downgraded Alarm States*

State	Description
 ⊖	Threat Response's investigation indicates that the attack failed and was downgraded.
 ▼	Your policy automatically caused the alarm to be downgraded.

Filtering Alarms

CTR investigates alarms to verify their validity, thus reducing or eliminating false alarms. Therefore, viewing information about the alarms that CTR has processed is crucial to successfully using the CTR system. The CTR Alarm Display screen provides you with the following mechanisms in which to view information:

- Alarm Status panes
- Alarm Filter pane

The Alarm Status panes enable you to view individual alarms organized by the following categories:

- Critical alarms
- Alarms under investigation
- Downgraded alarms

Although viewing the individual alarms is helpful in many situations, it is also helpful to view groups of alarms to obtain a higher-level view of the events that are occurring on your network. The Alarm Filter pane enables you to view alarm groups by the following characteristics:

- Source addresses
- Target addresses
- Event types

Filtering Alarms by Source Addresses

When you select the Sources Alarm Filter tab, the alarms displayed in the Alarm Filter pane are organized based on the source addresses from where the attacks originate. This view enables you to quickly determine specific hosts that launch multiple attacks against your network.

This information displays in a hierarchical tree structure similar to Figure 18-21. The root of this tree indicates that there are six critical and 31 downgraded alarms. You can expand the tree to view the details of the attacks. In this example, the display is filtered by source address, so you can see that the HTTP_DotDot attack was launched against 10.89.140.40 a total of 13 times. The nine times from 200.20.13.10 were unsuccessful and downgraded, whereas the four times from 10.20.13.10 were successful and are marked as critical.

Figure 18-21 *Hierarchical Source Alarm Tree*

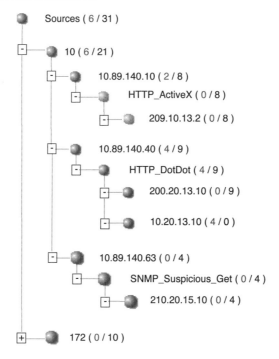

Sources (6 / 31)

- 10 (6 / 21)
  - 10.89.140.10 (2 / 8)
    - HTTP_ActiveX (0 / 8)
      - 209.10.13.2 (0 / 8)
  - 10.89.140.40 (4 / 9)
    - HTTP_DotDot (4 / 9)
      - 200.20.13.10 (0 / 9)
      - 10.20.13.10 (4 / 0)
  - 10.89.140.63 (0 / 4)
    - SNMP_Suspicious_Get (0 / 4)
      - 210.20.15.10 (0 / 4)
- 172 (0 / 10)

Filtering Alarms by Target Addresses

Using the Targets Alarm Filter tab, you can view the alarms grouped by the target addresses to which the attacks are being launched. This view enables you quickly see whether multiple attacks are being launched at a specific target address or network.

Filtering Alarms by Events

Instead of grouping alarms by source or destination, the Events Alarm Filter tab groups the alarms based on the attack or event type. Using this view, you can get a quick indication of how often a specific attack is being launched against your network. Figure 18-22 shows a sample of the type of information that you can observe in the Alarm Filter pane when viewing the alarms by events.

Figure 18-22   *Hierarchical Event Alarm Tree*

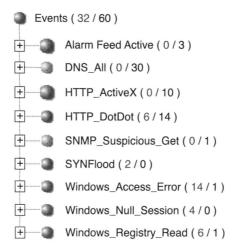

Events (32 / 60)

[+] Alarm Feed Active (0 / 3)

[+] DNS_All (0 / 30)

[+] HTTP_ActiveX (0 / 10)

[+] HTTP_DotDot (6 / 14)

[+] SNMP_Suspicious_Get (0 / 1)

[+] SYNFlood (2 / 0)

[+] Windows_Access_Error (14 / 1)

[+] Windows_Null_Session (4 / 0)

[+] Windows_Registry_Read (6 / 1)

Generating Reports

Besides viewing the alarms using the Alarm display screen, you can also generate reports based on the events that CTR analyzes. These reports fall into the following two categories:

- Alarm reports
- Configuration reports

Alarm Reports

The alarm reports provide you with different views of the alarm information based on numerous different templates. These reports usually include all the events since the last archive operation. Some of the templates supplied with CTR include the following:

- Alarms per Day
- Show Alarms by Occurrence
- Show Alarms by Occurrence per Zone
- Show Top 10 Critical Alarms
- Show Alarms from Today
- Summary of Alarms Processed

NOTE   For a complete list of the alarm report templates and a description of each report, refer to the help documentation provided with CTR.

To access the alarm reports, follow these steps:

Step 1 Click the Reports tab on the CTR Home page.

Step 2 Click Alarm Reports. This displays the list of alarm templates in the left window on the screen (see Figure 18-23).

Figure 18-23 *Alarm Reports Screen*

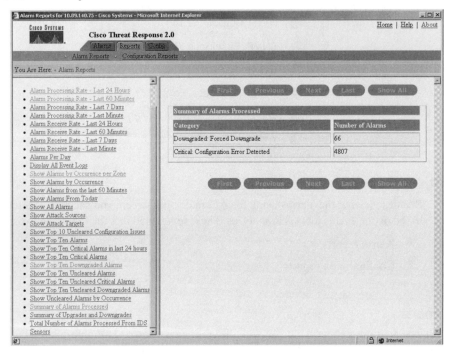

Step 3 Click the name of the report that you are interested in. This causes the report to display in the window pane on the right.

Configuration Reports

The configuration reports provide you with different views of the CTR configuration information based on numerous different templates. Some of the templates supplied with CTR include the following:

- Describe Actions
- Show Actions for Each Event Type by Security Zone
- Show Event Types for Each Action by Policy Name

- Show Event Types for Each Action by Security Zone
- Show Events by OS Application
- Show Policy Names

NOTE   For a complete list of the configuration report templates and their descriptions, refer to the help documentation provided with CTR.

To access the configuration reports, follow these steps:

Step 1   Click the Reports tab on the CTR Home page.

Step 2   Click Configuration Reports. This displays the list of configuration templates in the left window on the screen (see Figure 18-24).

Figure 18-24   *Configuration Reports Screen*

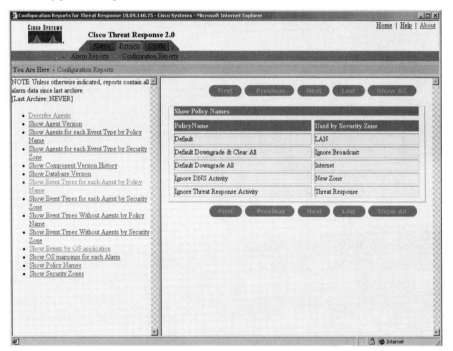

Step 3   Click the name of the report that you are interested in. This causes the report to be displayed in the window pane on the right.

Maintenance

While using CTR, you will also need to perform certain maintenance operations. Some of these, such as configuring the auto update functionality, you will normally do only once and then not change them very often if at all. Other operations, such as adding users, you will probably perform more often.

Auto Update

If you have a valid CCO Cisco.com registered user accountt, you can automatically receive notifications when CTR policy and software updates are available. You can also configure CTR to automatically download and deploy the policy updates on your CTR server.

NOTE   To retrieve the policy and software updates from the Cisco website, you must have a valid CCO Cisco.com registered user account that has cryptographic access.

To configure the automatic update functionality in CTR, follow these steps:

Step 1   Click the Config tab on the main CTR screen.

Step 2   Click the Advanced Configuration tab.

Step 3   Click the Auto Update Advanced Configuration tab. The Auto Update screen displays (see Figure 18-25).

Step 4   Check the Automatically update policies as soon as available check box.

Step 5   Click the Set CCO Login button to enter your CCO Cisco.com registered user account information. The CCO Login Account Configuration pop-up window displays (see Figure 18-26).

Figure 18-25   *Auto Update Screen*

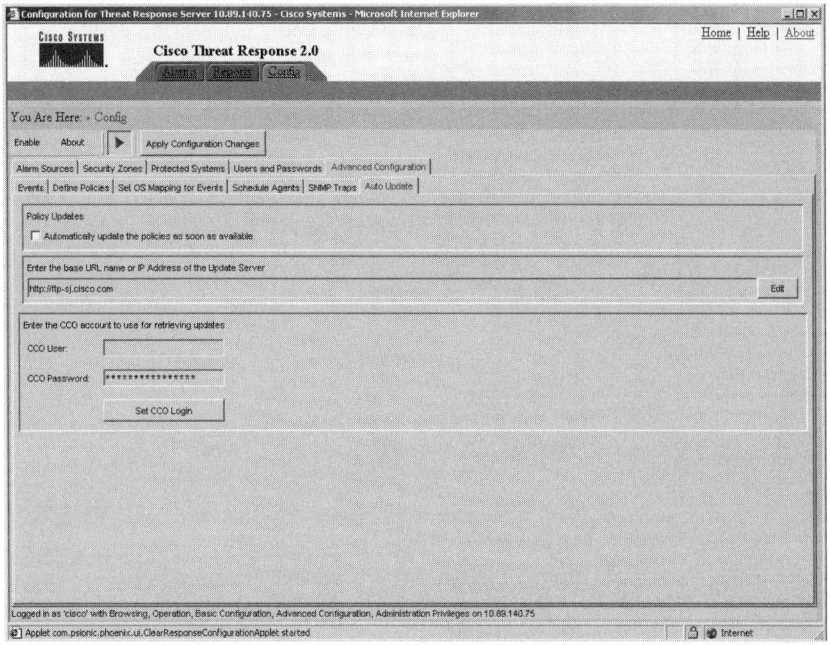

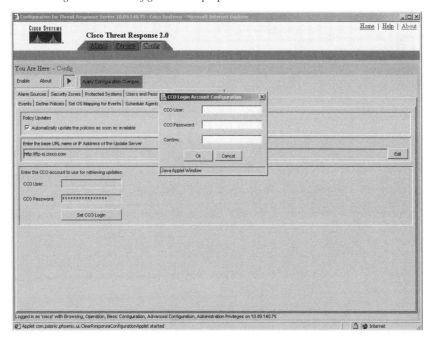

Figure 18-26   *CCO Login Account Configuration Pop-up Window*

Step 6   Enter your CCO Cisco.com registered user account and password.

Step 7   Click OK to save your CCO Cisco.com registered user account information.

NOTE   You can also configure CTR to use a local server instead of downloading updates directly from cisco.com. In this situation, you enter the URL for your local server in the Enter the Base URL Name or IP Address of the Update Server field. Then the CCO Cisco.com registered user account credentials become the credentials for your local server.

Users

To access the CTR software, you need a valid CTR account. When adding accounts to CTR, you can assign one or more of the privilege levels shown in Table 18-10.

Table 18-10   *User Privileges*

Privilege	Description
Browsing	This privilege is automatically assigned to all accounts. It enables the user to view the Alarms screen, the Reports screen, and the help document.
Operation	This privilege enables the user to manage alarms and run actions on a targeted host (through the Alarm Context menu) in the Alarm Display screen and enable or disable the processing of alarms.
Basic Configuration	This privilege enables the user to perform the basic-level configuration tasks.
Advanced Configuration	This privilege enables the user to perform the advanced configuration tasks.
Administration	This privilege enables the user to add and remove users and change their privileges.

To add a user to CTR, follow these steps:

Step 1   Click the Config tab on the main CTR screen.

Step 2   Click Users and Passwords. The Users and Passwords screen displays on the screen (see Figure 18-27).

Figure 18-27   *Users and Passwords Screen*

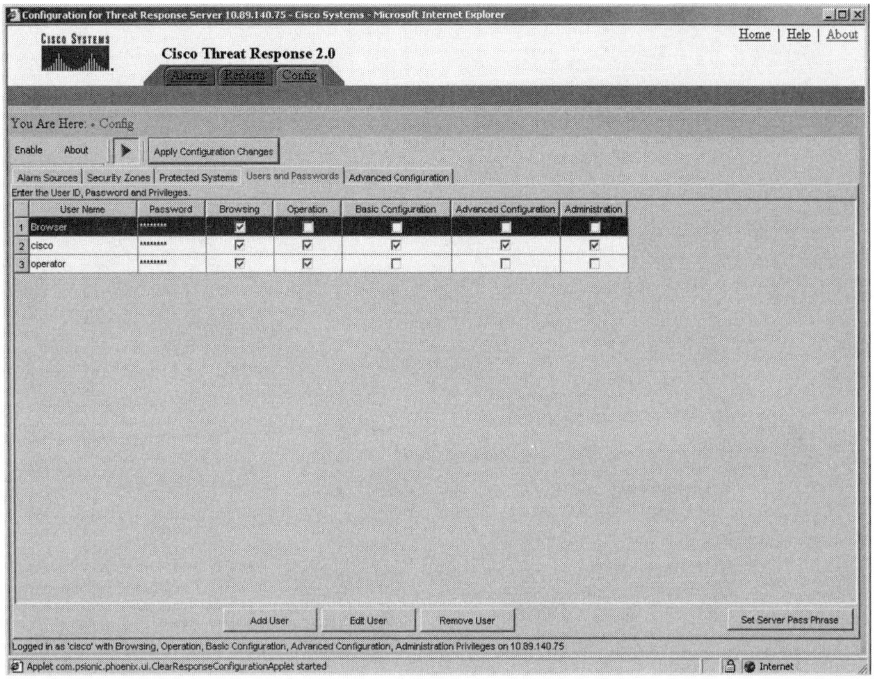

Step 3   Click Add User. This displays the User pop-up window (see Figure 18-28).

Step 4   Enter the username.

Step 5   Enter the password.

Step 6   Assign the privileges that you want to assign to the user by checking the appropriate check boxes.

Step 7   Click OK to save the user.

Step 8   Click Apply Configuration Changes to commit the changes to the CTR.

Figure 18-28   *Users Pop-up Window*

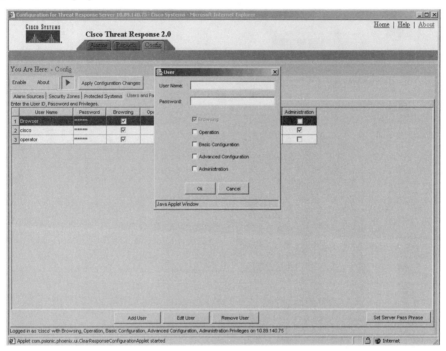

Summary

Processing the multitude of alarms generated by your IDS devices is a very complex task. Many of these alarms are valid attacks that are launched against systems that are not vulnerable to the attack. Analyzing these alarms wastes your valuable security resources. Cisco Threat Response (CTR) enables you to maximize your security resources by virtually eliminating the false alarms on your network.

Benefits provided by CTR include the following:

- Elimination of false alarms

- Escalation of real attacks

- Fast, consistent, automated investigation process

- Easy deployment

CTR works in conjunction with your IDS to further analyze the alarms detected on your network. CTR works with the following types of IDS devices:

- Cisco IDS version 4.x sensors

- Cisco IDS version 3.x sensors

When investigating alarms, your CTR uses the following three-phased approach:

- Basic investigation
- Advanced investigation
- Forensic data capture

When setting up CTR, you need to perform the following tasks:

- Defining alarm sources
- Configuring your security zones
- Defining protected systems

CTR divides your network into different security zones to which you apply specific policies that CTR uses to investigate the alarms in each zone. Each security zone defines which alarms (based on the source and destination addresses and ports) that CTR will examine.

CTR comes with the following built-in policies:

- Default policy
- Downgrade all
- Downgrade and clear all
- Upgrade all
- Ignore DNS activity
- Ignore threat response activity

Besides the built-in policies, you can also create your own custom policies to enhance CTR's protection of your network.

When viewing alarms using the Alarm display screen, you can filter alarms based on the following options:

- Source addresses
- Target addresses
- Event types

You can also display individual alarms based on the following alarm types:

- Critical alarms
- Alarms under investigation
- Downgraded alarms

Besides viewing alarms, you can also generate the following two types of reports:

- Alarm reports
- Configuration reports

Review Questions

The following questions test your retention of the material presented in this chapter. The answers to the review questions are in Appendix B, "Answers to Chapter Review Questions."

1 What are some of the benefits of Cisco Threat Response?

2 What is advanced investigation?

3 What is basic investigation?

4 What is a CTR action?

5 What is a security zone?

6 What is a protected host?

7 What does a Level 0 investigation entail?

8 What investigation does CTR perform when the default policy is applied to a security zone?

9 Why is the policy order important?

10 How can CTR determine the OS information for a host?

11 What fields do you need to define to configure a security zone?

12 What are the two reasons that CTR downgrades alarms?

CHAPTER 19

Cisco Intrusion Protection System Upcoming Functionality

Cisco is continually enhancing its intrusion protection system to make it easier for you to protect every facet of your network. To accomplish this task, Cisco is constantly evolving its protection capability by improving existing products and developing new products. This chapter explains some of the new features planned for the overall Cisco intrusion protection strategy in the immediate future as well as highlights existing functionality that has recently been incorporated. (Refer to the information on the Cisco website for a current list of functionality.)

Cisco Intrusion Protection System Overview

To understand how the new features fit into the Cisco solution, it is helpful to understand the elements necessary to deliver an efficient intrusion protection system. Cisco is constantly focusing on the following four critical factors:

- Accurate threat detection
- Intelligent threat investigation
- Ease of management
- Flexible deployment options

Accurate Threat Detection

The security landscape is continually changing with new exploits being released daily. Accurate threat detection involves consistently detecting the widest range of potential threats against your network. Supporting numerous code bases for various sensor models consumes engineering resources that could be used to improve existing signature functionality. To minimize this potential problem, Cisco IDS version 4.0 uses the same software base on multiple sensor platforms (thus requiring engineers to modify only a single code base). In version 4.0, the following platforms take advantage of a single code base:

- 4200 series sensors
- Second-generation IDS Module (IDSM-2)
- Router Network Module

Intelligent Threat Investigation

Any intrusion system receives many alarms that need to be investigated. Analyzing these alarms as efficiently as possible is vital to successfully protecting your network from various attacks. Processing *false alarms* wastes valuable resources. To eliminate false alarms, Cisco has incorporated Cisco Threat Response into its suite of protection products.

False Alarm

A *false alarm* is a situation in which an attacker launches a real attack against a target that is not vulnerable to the exploit. This could be launching a Windows exploit against a UNIX system, for instance. It can also include launching a Windows exploit against a Windows system that has already been patched. Although an attack can represent a severe threat to your network, launching it against a target system that is not vulnerable does not necessarily represent a severe threat (because the exploit will fail).

Ease of Management

Cisco management platforms provide powerful browser-based tools. The browser access simplifies user interaction. This combined with powerful analytical tools enables you to respond rapidly and efficiently to threats against your network.

The current Cisco management options include the following:

- Sensor command-line interface (CLI)
- IDS Device Manager (IDM)
- Management Center for IDS sensors (IDS MC)
- CiscoWorks Security Information Management Solution (SIMS)

Besides the Cisco-supplied management interfaces, various other partners have developed monitoring options using the Remote Data Exchange Protocol (RDEP). Because RDEP uses XML, it is easy to develop third-party applications that interact with the sensor.

Between Cisco management applications and third-party monitoring solutions, you have a wide range of management options to fit your unique operating environment.

Flexible Deployment Options

An intrusion protection system is only effective if it can easily protect every facet of the network. Cisco is expanding its intrusion protection capability into different components of your infrastructure to make it easier for you to monitor every segment of your network.

New Hardware Platforms

To provide more flexibility at low-bandwidth monitoring locations throughout your network, Cisco has added the following two sensor platforms:

- 4215 appliance sensor
- Router Network Module

These platforms expand the options available in the low-bandwidth areas of your network and complement the existing platforms, such as the 4200 series appliances and the IDSM2.

NOTE   Both the 4215 appliance sensor and the Router Network Module are currently available.

4215 Appliance Sensor

The Cisco IDS 4215 is an appliance sensor that delivers 80 Mbps of performance and is suitable for monitoring multiple T1 subnets. The Cisco 4215 IDS sensor supports up to five sniffing interfaces in a single one-rack unit form factor. The major features of this sensor are as follows:

- **Performance**—80 Mbps
- **Monitoring interface**—10/100BASE-T
- **Command and control interface**—10/100BASE-T
- **Optional interface**—Four 10/100BASE-TX (4FE) sniffing interfaces (a single quad card) to give a total of five sniffing interfaces
- **Performance upgrade**—No

Performance ratings can be misleading because the results depend on many factors. Some performance ratings can be artificially high by using specific traffic that is not necessarily representative of regular network traffic (or your network's traffic). Therefore, besides providing the performance rating, Cisco is also providing the criteria used when achieving that rating. The 80-Mbps performance rating for the Cisco IDS 4215 sensor is based on the following conditions. (For information on the other sensor platforms, refer to the documentation on the Cisco website.)

- 800 new TCP connections per second
- 800 HTTP transactions per second
- Average packet size of 445 bytes
- Running Cisco IDS 4.1 sensor software

Router Network Module

The Cisco IDS Network Module for access routers (also known as the Router Network Module) integrates the Cisco comprehensive signature-based intrusion detection functionality directly into your access routers. This is similar to the introduction of the IDS Module for the Catalyst 6500 switches. Because of the variety of IDS solutions available, you can deploy IDS sensors wherever they are needed in your network.

The Router Network Module is designed to incorporate a fully functional intrusion detection sensor into the following Cisco routers:

- Cisco 2600XM
- Cisco 3660
- Cisco 3700 series

Through collaboration with IPSec virtual private network (VPN) and Generic Routing Encapsulation (GRE) traffic, this solution can perform decryption, tunnel termination, and traffic inspection at the first point of entry into the network.

The major features of Router Network Module are as follows:

- **Performance (2600XM)**—10 Mbps
- **Performance**—45 Mbps
- **Monitoring interface**—Router internal bus
- **Command and control interface**—10/10 10/100BASE-T
- **Optional interface**—Four 10/100BASE-TX (4FE) sniffing interfaces (a single quad card) to give a total of five sniffing interfaces
- **Performance upgrade**—No

The performance rating for the Router Network Module is based on the following conditions:

- 500 new TCP connections per second
- 500 HTTP transactions per second
- Average packet size of 445 bytes
- Running Cisco IDS 4.1 sensor software

New Software Functionality

Cisco is constantly adding new functionality into its intrusion protection solution. Some of the new features and capabilities in Cisco IDS version 4.1 (which is already available) that merit mention are the following:

- Multiple interface support
- Capture packet

Multiple Interface Support

Previous sensors, such as the 4250XL, have already had multiple sniffing interfaces on the sensor. With Cisco IDS version 4.1, your sensor software can actually distinguish between multiple sniffing interfaces. This means that, initially, the alarm detail fields will indicate on which interface the alarm was generated. Then, eventually, this will become another column in the regular alarm information.

The first sensor that will support this capability will be the IDS 4215. You will be able to add four 10/100 Fast Ethernet interface quad cards to this sensor (giving it a total of five sniffing interfaces). Gradually, this capability will be included on other sensors, too.

The importance of having multiple sniffing interfaces is that you can easily support environments that have multiple, segregated data streams. It can also help in environments that are currently using Switch Port Analyzer (SPAN) ports to capture traffic, because the number of SPAN sessions is limited and varies depending on the switch that you use. Multiple interfaces can also provide better visibility for redundant and asymmetric network deployments.

Capture Packet

With Cisco IDS version 4.0, you can observe the actual trigger packet for an alarm if you use IP session logs. It is impractical, however, to use IP session logs for all of your signatures. Therefore, beginning in Cisco IDS version 4.1, the actual trigger packet will be included in the alarm. You can then easily examine this information in the form of a fully decoded packet.

In-Line IDS Processing

Because the initial deployment of a base set of signatures in the Cisco IOS firewall, Cisco has provided some in-line IDS support. Unlike the traditional passive IDS monitoring, in-line IDS functionality enables the normal blocking capability to actually stop attacks before they are allowed to reach the target system.

Currently, Cisco is enhancing its in-line support to make this functionality available in a variety of sensor platforms. Some of the factors that are required for this migration include the following:

- Reduction of false positives to prevent dropping legitimate traffic
- Improved performance to ensure inspection in high-bandwidth environments
- System-wide event correlation to identify attacks and coordinated threats

Cisco has been addressing each of these areas to enable the effective migration to in-line IDS functionality (such as the release of the Cisco-patented Threat Response technology that dynamically validates suspected threats).

New Signatures

Signatures are essential to the operation of your Cisco IDS sensors. Cisco continually updates the signatures by adding new signatures as well as tuning existing signatures to improve their operation. The following two signature updates have some interesting new signature types that enhance the functionality of your sensors:

- S44 signature update
- S46 signature update

S44 Signature Update

The S44 signature update includes several signatures to detect peer-to-peer (P2P) software applications. Besides consuming bandwidth on your network, these P2P file-sharing programs are frequently associated with the sharing of copyrighted material (such as music CDs, movies, and software). The use of these applications on your network can therefore represent legal liabilities. The S44 signature update includes the signatures listed in table 19-1 to detect P2P programs on your network.

Table 19-1   *S44 P2P Signatures*

Signature ID	Signature Name
11001	Gnutella Client Request
11002	Gnutella Server Reply
11003	Qtella File Request
11004	Bearshare File Request
11005	KaZaA GET Request
11006	Gnucleus File Request
11007	Limewire File Request
11008	Morpheus File Request
11009	Phex File Request
11010	Swapper File Request
11011	XoloX File Request
11012	GTK-Gnutella File Request
11013	Mutella File Request

P2P Software Applications

P2P software applications operate in an environment in which each system has the same capabilities and can initiate connections with other systems in the network. These applications are commonly used to share files across the Internet between any two systems, without requiring another system such as a server. This is different from the normal client/server model in which only the clients initiate connections to a limited number of servers.

S46 Signature Update

The S46 signature update includes various new signatures, including some signatures to detect the use of instant messenger software. Instant messenger software enables people to communicate with each other in real time, similar to a textual phone call. These programs can consume bandwidth on your network as well as reduce your employee's productivity. Using the new signatures listed in Table 19-2, you can monitor the activity of some common instant messenger software programs on your network.

Table 19-2   *S46 Instant Messenger Signatures*

Signature ID	Signature Name
11200	Yahoo Messenger Activity
11201	MSN Messenger Activity
11202	AIM / ICQ Messenger Activity

The S46 signature update also contains signatures to detect the use of the Hotline software on your network. This program is a combined chat and file-sharing application. The signatures related to Hotline are listed in Table 19-3.

Table 19-3   *S46 Hotline Signatures*

Signature ID	Signature Name
11014	Hotline Client Login
11015	Hotline File Transfer
11016	Hotline Tracker Login

Management

Management of alarms across multiple sensors is always a challenging task. To facilitate the development of third-party management applications, Cisco IDS version 4.0 incorporated open protocols such as RDEP and Intrusion Detection Interaction and Operations Messages (IDIOM). Using open protocols enables you, as well as third-party vendors, to develop management applications that can easily retrieve alarm information from your sensors.

Besides IDS Event Viewer (IEV) and Security Monitor, other management solutions are beginning to appear that enable you to more efficiently correlate and visualize security alerts from a variety of security devices deployed throughout your network. One of these solutions is CiscoWorks Security Information Management Solution (CiscoWorks SIMS).

CiscoWorks SIMS is based on technology from netForensics v3.1 and incorporates powerful features for gathering and analyzing the overwhelming amount of security event data that companies experience. Companies can manage their growing security infrastructure and effectively monitor millions of event messages, without additional staff. Using CiscoWorks SIMS, you have a security solution that provides the following:

- Complete event monitoring for Cisco SAFE and all multivendor security environments (For more information on Cisco SAFE, refer to http://www.cisco.com/go;/safe.)
- Real-time event correlation
- Advanced visualization for fast and intuitive security monitoring
- Integrated risk assessment to understand the overall vulnerability of different assets within your network
- Comprehensive reporting and forensics for levels of security operations
- Productivity gains and cost reduction

Host Intrusion Prevention (HIP)

Protecting your entire network is the goal of the Cisco intrusion protection solution. A key component of this solution is to provide a solid layer of protection at the host level. To address the protection of the hosts on your network, Cisco has incorporated the Cisco Security Agent (CSA) in its overall solution.

CSA is based on the Okena StormWatch software (see Chapter 14, "Host Intrusion Prevention"). As development on CSA continues, more host platforms will gradually be added based on customer requirements.

Summary

The security landscape is continually changing. New exploits are discovered daily. To maintain a comprehensive security solution, Cisco must also constantly evolve. To continue to provide a comprehensive intrusion protection solution, Cisco must continually improve the following critical factors:

- Accurate threat detection
- Intelligent threat investigation
- Ease of management
- Flexible deployment options

The 4200 series sensors provide a range of IDS protection from 80 Mbps all the way up to 1 Gbps and IDS load-balancing capabilities using Etherchannel on the Catalyst 6500 that allows load balancing up to 8 Gbps using eight 4250XL sensors. In conjunction with these appliance sensors, Cisco developed the IDS Module to integrate the IDS functionality into your Catalyst 6500 switch.

This wide range of deployment options is being enhanced again by integrating the IDS functionality into your access routers with the Router Network Module. By being part of you edge routers, this sensor can actually examine traffic for which the router is the termination point for encrypted tunnels.

Enhanced functionality (such as in-line IDS) is being migrated to more sensor platforms to provide stronger protection against attacks launched at you network. In conjunction, new signature updates are continually being released to enhance the effectiveness of your IDS sensors. Some of the recent signature updates have included signatures to address items such as the following:

- P2P software applications
- Instant messenger programs

In the host space, Cisco enhanced its host-based protection by incorporating the Okena StormWatch agent software.

Finally, new management solutions enable you to correlate security alerts on your network from all of your security devices, even if you deploy solutions from multiple vendors.

Cisco Intrusion Protection Solution Tuning: Case Studies

The Cisco intrusion protection solution incorporates numerous devices, products, and features. Understanding all of these components can be a very challenging task. Therefore, this appendix includes various case studies to help illustrate some of the key concepts that you need to understand to effectively use the Cisco IPS to provide a strong security foundation to protect your network. The following case studies are examined in this appendix:

- Deploying sensors on your network scenario
- Blocking and TCP reset using IDSM-2 scenario (CatIOS)
- Multi-IDSM-2 scenario (CatOS)
- Custom signature scenario
- Signature tuning scenario

Sensor Deployment: Network Scenario

Increasingly, computer networks are being used to support more functionality, from IP telephony to electronic commerce. These multifaceted environments are prime targets for attack. Furthermore, the increased dependence on these computer networks increases the severity of any attacks that disrupt the operation of the network.

The diagram shown in Figure A-1 represents a typical computer network. Besides protecting the hosts themselves, the following six network locations need to be protected:

- Network perimeter (1)
- Dialup access (2)
- VPN with business partner (3)
- Intranet boundary (4)
- Telecommuter access (5)
- DMZ (6)

Figure A-1   *Sample Network Layout*

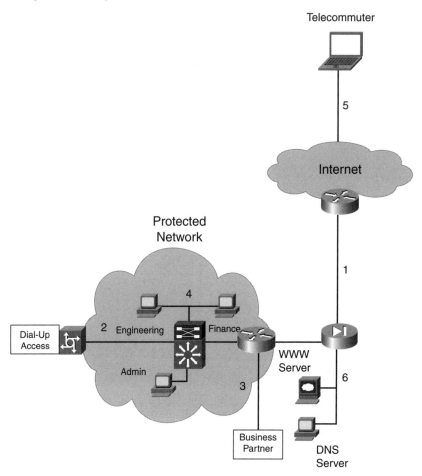

Each of these areas represents potential points at which an attacker can attempt to gain access to your network. One of the first steps that you can take is to at least protect your server systems (if not all of your systems) at the host level using Cisco Security Agent (CSA). By deploying agent software on your individual systems, you provide the following protection for your network:

- Zero-day protection
- Data protection
- Simplified server and desktop maintenance

Next you need to begin to analyze how you can secure the other areas of your network.

Network Perimeter

Your network perimeter is a prime target for attack. Therefore, you definitely need to monitor the traffic at this location. You have various options available to you. First, you can place an IDS appliance sensor either outside your PIX firewall or inside your firewall (see Figure A-2). The model of sensor will depend on the traffic volume coming into your network. Another option that you have at your disposal is to place a router module in your perimeter router (assuming you are using an access router).

Figure A-2 *Network Perimeter*

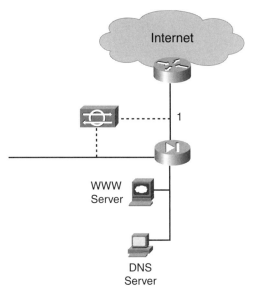

Placing your IDS device on the outside of your perimeter firewall enables you to detect all the attacks launched against your network, even though many of these attacks can be stopped by the firewall. On the other hand, placing the IDS device inside the firewall enables you to concentrate on the intrusive activity that has made it through your perimeter firewall.

NOTE   You can also configure your PIX (or your perimeter router) to watch for a limited number of IDS signatures.

Dialup Access

Because your dialup access comes directly into your core backbone switch, you have two options to monitor the traffic entering your network from the dialup users (see Figure A-3). First you can use an appliance sensor to monitor traffic on the dialup VLAN. You can also deploy a second-generation IDS Module (IDSM-2) in your Catalyst 6500 switch. By deploying an IDSM-2, you can use it to monitor several segments on your network, including your intranet boundaries (such as between Engineering and Finance).

Figure A-3   *Dialup Access*

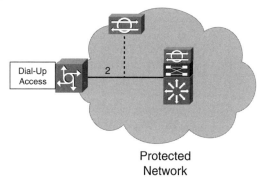

Protected
Network

Extranet Connection

Your business partner has a direct connection into your protected network. Therefore, you probably need to deploy a sensor on this segment (see Figure A-4). Again, you have a couple of options. The simplest option is to install an appliance sensor (or use the IDS network module in the router connected to the extranet connection) to monitor the link with the business partner. This link is important to monitor because if someone attacks your business partner through your network, there could be legal, liability issues.

NOTE   If you do not consider your business partner's network to be a significant threat (or your network as a significant threat to your business partner), you can also use the IDS features of the Cisco IOS firewall on your internal router to protect the link between your network and your business partner's network because it currently supports a limited signature set (compared to the appliance sensor).

Intranet Boundary

The intranet boundary between the Engineering and Finance segments can be protected using the same options available for the dialup access segment (see Figure A-5). The easiest solution is to use an existing IDSM-2 blade that monitors traffic directly from the switch. If the traffic volume is high enough, this boundary might warrant its own sensor.

Figure A-4   *Extranet Connection*

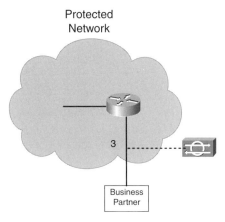

Protected
Network

3

Business
Partner

Figure A-5   *Intranet Connection*

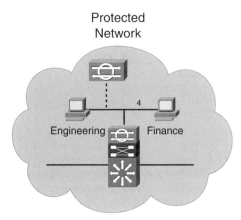

Protected
Network

4

Engineering   Finance

Telecommuter Access

Your telecommuters and business travelers come into your network via a virtual private network (VPN) connection (see Figure A-6) or dialup connection. The VPN traffic is encrypted coming into your network, so to monitor this traffic, you need to place your IDS sensor at a network segment after which the traffic has been decrypted. Usually this location is past the VPN tunnel termination point. For end-to-end encryption, the traffic is not decrypted until it reaches the target system, requiring software on the target system (such as CSA) to examine the traffic in decrypted form. CSA on your systems also provides continuous protection on the end systems (even when they are not connected to your network). This protection is critical. Otherwise, it is easy for an employee's computer (telecommuters or not) to become a risk to the corporate network. For instance, an employee may take the laptop home. While connected to a local Internet connection, the system can become infected with a virus. Then when the employee brings the computer back to work and connects it to the corporate network, it can possibly spread this virus to other systems.

Figure A-6   *Intranet Connection*

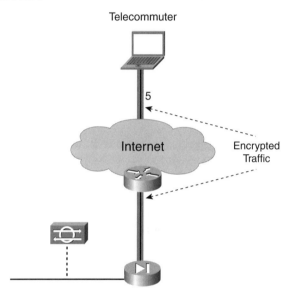

Telecommuter

5

Internet

Encrypted
Traffic

NOTE   In conjunction with CSA, you also need to use antivirus software to provide a solid defense-in-depth security foundation on your end systems.

Demilitarized Zone (DMZ)

To protect the hosts on the DMZ, you need to decide whether they warrant a fully functional IDS sensor (see Figure A-7). Using an appliance sensor provides you with the greatest degree of protection because it supports the largest signature database. You may decide, however, to use just CSA to monitor the traffic to these systems because they are already partially protected by the firewall. Furthermore, you can use the IDS functionality on the firewall itself as another basic protection mechanism (establishing defense-in-depth securitty). The signature set is much smaller than what is offered on an appliance sensor, but it might be adequate in this circumstance if you determine that the risk to the servers on the DMZ is low.

Figure A-7   *Demilitarized Zone*

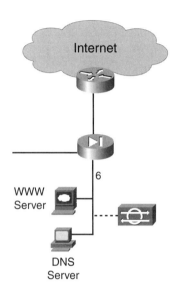

Blocking and TCP Reset Using IDSM-2 Scenario

The original IDSM did not support the TCP reset functionality. This deficiency was eliminated in IDSM-2, but correctly using this functionality can be a little tricky. Instead of sending the TCP resets out the sniffing interface, the TCP resets are sent out an interface specifically added for the TCP reset traffic.

NOTE   This is similar to configuring the IDS 4250XL. Both the 4250XL and the IDSM-2 use the same IDS Accelerator (XL) card, and these cards are not capable of transmitting the TCP resets. With the 4250XL, you need to send the TCP resets out the regular built-in sniffing interface.

Because the TCP resets are not sent out the sniffing interface, you need to make sure that you configure both ports (TCP reset and monitoring) correctly to ensure that the TCP resets can reach the systems that they are destined for.

For this scenario, assume that that the following characteristics apply:

- IDSM-2 is in slot 5.
- VLANs to monitor are 10, 11, 12, and 15.

Table A-1 shows the internal ports for the IDSM-2.

Table A-1   *IDSM-2 Internal Ports*

Port	Description
1	TCP reset port
2	Command and control port
7	Monitoring port
8	Monitoring port

NOTE   Although the IDSM-2 has two sniffing or monitoring ports, it can only successfully capture 600 Mbps. Therefore, you must be careful not to exceed this limit. Furthermore, you will probably use only one of these interfaces.

Your first step in configuring the IDSM-2 is to configure your switch to send the traffic to be analyzed to the IDSM-2. You can choose various ways in which to direct this traffic to the IDSM-2. The following scenario uses VACLs on a Catalyst 6500 switch that runs CatIOS. To configure VACLs using CatIOS, you need to perform the following tasks:

Step 1   Configure an ACL

Step 2   Create a VLAN access map

Step 3   Match the ACL to the access map

Step 4   Define the action for the access map

Step 5   Apply the access map to VLANs

Step 6   Configure capture ports

You also need to configure the TCP reset port to complete the configuration. This is not part of configuring your VACL, but it is necessary to ensure that the TCP reset traffic can reach the hosts for which it is destined.

Configure an Access Control List (ACL)

With CatIOS, specify the interesting traffic that you want to monitor using an ACL. Therefore, the first step in setting up a VACL is to create your ACL. Suppose for this example that you are using the IDSM-2 to protect a web server farm, and the subnet for the web servers is 172.12.31.0. You can create an ACL similar to the following to allow any hosts to make connections to port 80 on any system on the server farm subnet:

```
Router(Config)# access-list 110 permit tcp any 172.12.31.0 0.0.0.255 eq 80
```

NOTE	In many situations, you might be able to use ACLs that you have already constructed to restrict traffic into your network.

Create a Virtual Local Area Network (VLAN) Access Map

You begin to configure the VACL by establishing a VLAN access map using the **vlan access-map** command. After creating a VLAN access map, you must match it to an ACL and define its actions using the following two subcommands:

- match
- action

The **vlan access-map** command basically creates the access map and enables you to assign a name to it. The following command creates an access map named my_map:

```
Router(config)# vlan access-map my_map
```

Match the ACL to the Access Map

To specify which traffic the VLAN access map applies to, you need to associate it with an ACL on the router. You do this via the **match** subcommand. In this example, the ACL is 110, so the commands are as follows:

```
Router(config)# vlan access-map my_map
Router(config-access-map)# match ip address 110
```

Define the Action for the Access Map

Besides specifying the interesting traffic by associating an ACL to the VLAN access map, you must also specify an action to be performed on the traffic that the ACL matches. You accomplish this using the **action** subcommand. For this example, the action is to forward and capture the traffic, so the commands are as follows:

```
Router(config)# vlan access-map my_map
Router(config-access-map)# action forward capture
```

NOTE	Although you are interested in capturing the traffic, you must also specify the *forward* action. Otherwise, the traffic matched by the VLAN access map will not be sent by the switch functionality to its destination (similar to denying the traffic with an ACL **deny** statement).

Apply the Access Map to VLANs

Now you need to decide to which VLANs on your router that you are going to apply your VLAN access map. You accomplish this with the **vlan filter** command. For this example, you use the following command:

```
Router(config)# vlan filter my_map 10-12,15
```

Configure Capture Ports

Finally, you need to configure which port on your router will receive the captured traffic. You accomplish this with the **switchport capture** command. For this example the commands are as follows:

```
Router(config)# interface fa 5/7
Router(config-if) switchport capture allowed vlan 10-12,15
```

The **allowed** keyword enables you to limit the traffic sent to the capture port. Any VLANs that are not included in the allowed list will not be sent to the capture port. This option enables you to segregate captured traffic between multiple capture ports (such as if you have multiple IDSM-2 blades in the same chassis). The VACL captures all the interesting traffic. Then you limit which traffic is actually sent to each capture port.

Configure the TCP Reset Port

To enable the TCP reset traffic to reach its correct destination, the TCP reset port on the IDSM-2 must trunk all the VLANs for which the IDSM-2 monitoring port is analyzing traffic. In this example, the IDSM-2 is analyzing traffic for VLANs 10, 11, 12, and 15, so you need to configure the TCP reset port to trunk these VLANs. You can accomplish this using the following commands:

```
Router(config)# interface fa 5/1
Router(config-if) switchport trunk allowed vlan 10-12,15
```

Then when the IDSM-2 generates reset traffic, the switch port (associated with the TCP reset port on the IDSM-2) will accept this traffic and place it on the correct VLAN so that it can reach its destination.

Multiple IDSM-2 Blades Scenario

You can deploy multiple IDSM-2 blades in a single Catalyst 6500 chassis. This enables you to increase the traffic bandwidth that you can monitor, because each IDSM-2 is capable of monitoring 600 Mbps. By segregating the traffic correctly between the different blades, you can ensure that a single IDSM-2 will not be overloaded with more traffic than it can handle.

Assume that you have deployed two IDSM-2s in your Catalyst 6500 switch in slots 4 and 5. Furthermore, assume that Table A-2 outlines your network configuration and your approximate traffic loads.

Table A-2   *Traffic Load per Subnet*

VLAN	Approximate Traffic Load	Description
10	80	Engineering production subnet
15	80	Engineering lab subnet 1
20	60	Engineering lab subnet 2
25	75	Research production subnet
30	60	Research lab subnet 1
35	50	Research lab subnet 2
40	80	DevTest production subnet
45	85	DevTest lab subnet 1
50	85	Marketing production subnet
55	80	HR production subnet
60	75	Training subnet
65	50	Management subnet
70	70	Infrastructure servers
75	90	Web server farm

Because you have two blades, you can successfully monitor 1200 Mbps, but you must divide this traffic between the two IDSM-2s. Examining the network configuration in Table A-2, you can see that the total amount of traffic that you want to monitor is 1020 Mbps. The two blades can definitely handle this traffic volume, but you need to divide it into two blocks (each of which is less than 600 Mbps).

Assume that you decide to divide the traffic as shown in Table A-3.

Table A-3   *Traffic Load per IDSM-2*

VLAN	Approximate Traffic Load	IDSM-2 Slot
10	80	Slot 4
15	80	Slot 4
20	60	Slot 4
25	75	Slot 4
30	60	Slot 4
35	50	Slot 4

continues

Table A-3   *Traffic Load per IDSM-2 (Continued)*

VLAN	Approximate Traffic Load	IDSM-2 Slot
40	80	Slot 4
45	85	Slot 4
50	85	Slot 5
55	80	Slot 5
60	75	Slot 5
65	50	Slot 5
70	70	Slot 5
75	90	Slot 5

This places 570 Mbps going to the IDSM-2 in slot 4 and 450 Mbps going to the IDSM-2 in slot 5.

With the monitored VLANs specified, it is time to begin configuring the switch to pass the monitored traffic to the appropriate IDSM-2. Using VACLs on CatOS, you will need to perform the following tasks:

Step 1   Define a security ACL

Step 2   Commit the VACL to memory

Step 3   Map the VACL to the VLAN(s)

Step 4   Assign the capture port

Step 5   Modify trunking on the capture ports

Defining a Security ACL

You define a security ACL with the **set security acl** switch command. The **capture** option of this command enables you to determine which traffic the security ACL will pass to your capture ports. The following command captures the traffic needed for this scenario:

```
Cat6 (enable) set security acl ip IPACL1 permit ip any any capture

IPACL1 editbuffer modified. Use 'commit' to apply changes

Cat6k (enable)
```

NOTE	In this example, you are monitoring all the traffic on the switch. Therefore instead of specifying specific traffic with multiple security ACL commands, it is easier just to create a single command that captures all the IP traffic on the switch.

Commit the VACL to Memory

After using the **set security acl ip** command to define the interesting traffic to be captured, you need to commit the VACL to hardware. You use the **commit security acl** command to accomplish this. For this example, the following command commits the IPACL1 to hardware:

```
Cat6 (enable) commit security acl IPACL1

Hardware programming in progress...

ACL IPACL1 is committed to hardware

Cat6 (enable)
```

Map the VACL to the VLAN(s)

Next you need to map your security ACLs to specific VLANs on your switch through the **set security acl map** command. For this scenario, use the following commands:

```
Cat6 (enable) set security acl map IPACL1 10

ACL IPACL1 mapped to vlan 10

Cat6 (enable) set security acl map IPACL1 15

ACL IPACL1 mapped to vlan 15

Cat6 (enable) set security acl map IPACL1 20

ACL IPACL1 mapped to vlan 20

Cat6 (enable) set security acl map IPACL1 25

ACL IPACL1 mapped to vlan 25

Cat6 (enable) set security acl map IPACL1 30

ACL IPACL1 mapped to vlan 30

Cat6 (enable) set security acl map IPACL1 35

ACL IPACL1 mapped to vlan 35

Cat6 (enable) set security acl map IPACL1 40

ACL IPACL1 mapped to vlan 40

Cat6 (enable) set security acl map IPACL1 45

ACL IPACL1 mapped to vlan 45

Cat6 (enable) set security acl map IPACL1 50

ACL IPACL1 mapped to vlan 50

Cat6 (enable) set security acl map IPACL1 55

ACL IPACL1 mapped to vlan 55
```

```
Cat6 (enable) set security acl map IPACL1 60

ACL IPACL1 mapped to vlan 60

Cat6 (enable) set security acl map IPACL1 65

ACL IPACL1 mapped to vlan 65

Cat6 (enable) set security acl map IPACL1 70

ACL IPACL1 mapped to vlan 70

Cat6 (enable) set security acl map IPACL1 75

ACL IPACL1 mapped to vlan 75

Cat6 (enable)
```

These commands map all the VLANs that we are interested in to the security ACL. This step is necessary because the security ACL is defined using IP characteristics. The switch does not know on which VLANs to look for this IP traffic. Therefore, you tell the switch on which VLANs to apply the security ACL through the **set security acl map** command.

Assign the Capture Ports

You need to use the **set security acl capture-ports** command to define the ports on your switch that will receive the traffic captured by your security ACL. In this example, you use the following command:

```
Cat6 (enable) set security acl capture-ports 4/7,5/7

Successfully set 4/7,5/7 to capture ACL traffic.

Cat6 (enable)
```

You want to send the captured traffic to a monitoring port on each of the IDSM-2 blades. Then you will need to modify the trunking characteristics of the monitoring ports so that each IDSM-2 only analyzes a subset of the traffic captured.

NOTE   The second monitoring interface is not used on either IDSM-2 because the IDSM-2 can only analyze 600 Mbps and each monitoring interface is actually a Gigabit interface.

Modifying Trunking on Capture Ports

Finally, you need to change the trunk configuration on the capture ports. By default, the monitoring ports on IDSM-2 are configured to trunk traffic from all the VLANs configured on the switch. In this example, you need to segregate the traffic received by each IDSM-2 capture port. You accomplish this by configuring the monitoring port to trunk only the traffic that you want passed to the IDSM-2 for analysis.

NOTE	Your security ACL sends captured traffic to a capture port only if the port is configured to trunk the VLAN from which the traffic originated.

To change and view the trunk characteristics on a port, you use the following three commands:

- **show trunk**
- **clear trunk**
- **set trunk**

First you need to clear the existing trunks and then add the trunks that you want. In this example (because the monitoring ports are trunking all VLANS), it is easier to just remove all the VLANs with the **clear trunk** command. Before you can remove the unwanted VLANs, you need to know which VLANs are already being trunked. This information is available via the following command:

```
Cat6k (enable) show trunk 4/7 detail

Port    Vlans allowed on trunk
------- --------------------------------------------------
4/7     1-1005,1025-4094

Cat6k (enable) show trunk 5/7 detail

Port    Vlans allowed on trunk
------- --------------------------------------------------
5/7     1-1005,1025-4094

Cat6k (enable)
```

For this example, you want the VLANs to be as follows:

- **IDSM-2 in slot 4**   10,15,20,25,30,35,40,45
- **IDSM-2 in slot 5**   50,55,60,65,70,75

Using the **clear trunk** command, you can remove all the VLANs on the two monitoring ports using the following commands:

```
Cat6k (enable) clear trunk 4/7 2-1005,1025-4094

Cat6k (enable) clear trunk 5/7 2-1005,1025-4094
```

NOTE	On some Catalyst software versions, you cannot remove the default VLAN from a trunk port. On the Catalyst 6500, the default VLAN is 1.

Finally, you can add the appropriate VLANs to each monitored port using the following **set trunk** commands:

```
Cat6k (enable) set trunk 4/7 10,15,20,25,30,35,40,45

Adding vlans 10,15,20,25,30,35,40,45 to allowed list
Port(s) 4/7 allowed vlans modified to 10,15,20,25,30,35,40,45
Cat6k (enable) set trunk 5/7 50,55,60,65,70,75

Adding vlans 50,55,60,65,70,75 to allowed list
Port(s) 5/7 allowed vlans modified to 50,55,60,65,70,75
Cat6k (enable)
```

Custom Signature Scenario

Recently a distributed network malware scanning tool (called Stumbler) started appearing on numerous networks. At first the tool appeared to be a Trojan horse. However, further analysis proved that to be incorrect. Nevertheless, the tool attempted to scan for open services on different systems and report this information to a common system (refer to http://searchsecurity.techtarget.com/originalContent/0,289142,sid14_gci911816,00.html).

Because the tool generates random source and destination addresses, the replies are not guaranteed to return to a specific instance of the tool. However, each of the packets does match the following two characteristics:

- TCP SYN flag set
- TCP window size of 55,808

On each system where this tool runs, the tool promiscuously watches for replies on the network (which may have been initiated by itself or other instances of the tool). The information collected is then sent to port 22 on 12.108.65.76.

Currently, you can't create a Cisco IDS signature that checks for a TCP packet with a specific window size (the easiest way to detect this traffic). Nevertheless, you can still create a signature that detects the Stumbler tool by watching for the traffic sent to the fixed address of 12.108.65.76. To create a custom signature to detect this traffic, you need to perform the following tasks:

Step 1   Create a custom ATOMIC.TCP signature

Step 2   Create an exclude filter

Step 3   Create an include filter

Create a Custom ATOMIC.TCP Signature

The custom ATOMIC.TCP signature needs to have the following parameters specified:

- DstPort of 22
- Mask of SYN I FIN I URG I PSH I ACK I RST
- TcpFlags of SYN

This custom signature will alarm on all traffic to port 22 with only the SYN bit set. Obviously this signature by itself will generate many false positives (an alarm every time someone initiates a Secure Shell [SSH] session to a host on your network). Therefore, you need to use filters to narrow the range of IP addresses that can trigger the custom signature.

Create an Exclude Filter

First you need to create an exclude filter that prevents any addresses from triggering your new custom signature. This filter will prevent any host from triggering your new custom signature. Therefore, you will specify a wildcard for all addresses as the destination address, and supply the signature ID of the custom signature (see Figure A-8). After applying this filter to your new custom signature (signature ID 20001 in this example), no hosts will cause the signature to trigger.

Figure A-8 *Exclude Filter in IDM*

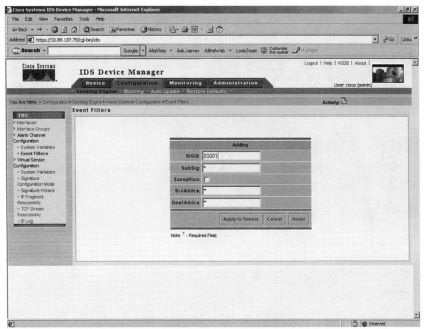

Create an Include Filter

Next you need to create an include filter that specifies the destination address of 12.108.65.76 (see Figure A-9). An include filter removes an address from your existing exclude filter. Therefore, after applying this filter, the new custom signature will only trigger if the destination of the packet is 12.108.65.76 (because all other addresses have been excluded).

Figure A-9 *Include Filter in IDM*

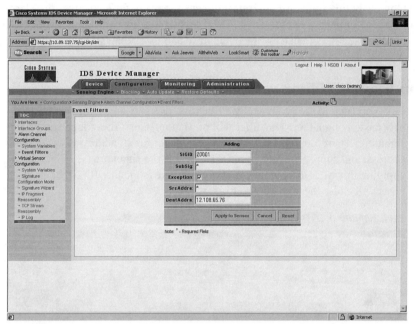

Signature Tuning Scenario

After deploying Cisco IDS on your network, you observe BO2K alarms being generated. These alarms appear to be originating from traffic going to a couple of machines on your network.

The first machine that you investigate turns out to be one of your perimeter routers. Immediately you conclude that the router is not running BO2K, but you are curious as to why the signature triggered on traffic to the router. So you examine the Network Security Database (NSDB) page for the BO2K signature, 3992-BackOrifice BO2K TCP Stealth-2 (see Figure A-10).

Examining the Benign Trigger(s) field, you see that a possible false positive is BGP routing traffic. After further investigation, you determine that your router is running BGP. This is probably the reason that the signature triggered incorrectly.

You do not want the signature to continually generate false positives on your BGP routing traffic in the future, so you decide to create an exclude filter. For this filter, you specify traffic to and from your routers that are running BGP. By applying this filter to the BO2K signature, you prevent the normal routing update traffic from potentially triggering the BO2K alarm accidentally. But you still monitor for BO2K activity from other systems on your network.

Figure A-10 *NSDB Exploit Page for Signature 3992*

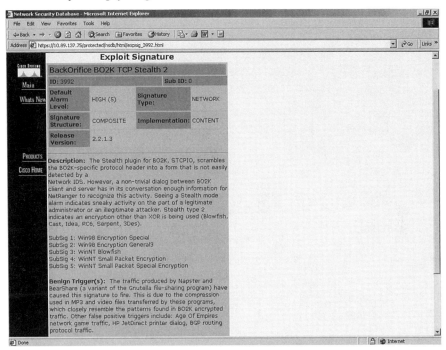

Next you observe the TCP Port Sweep (signature ID 3001) firing regularly on normal user traffic. After examination, you discover that a custom application on your network routinely resets TCP connections, causing the signature to fire incorrectly. Further analysis reveals that the number of reset connections varies between 6 to 8 during a 30-second interval. By default, the TCP Port Sweep signature is configured with the following options:

- **ThrottleInterval**—30 seconds
- **Unique**—5

To overcome the false positives that you have been experiencing, you can change the Unique parameter to 10. This will prevent the custom application on your network from triggering the TCP Port Sweep signature. You can also reduce the ThrottleInterval parameter to require the number of unique connections to occur more quickly.

Answers to Chapter Review Questions

Chapter 1

1 What are the four types of network security threats?

Answer: The four types of network security threats are unstructured threats, structured threats, external threats, and internal threats.

2 What are the three main attack types?

Answer: The three main attack types are reconnaissance, access, and denial-of-service.

3 What is the first line of defense against external attacks?

Answer: The perimeter defenses on your network provide the first line of defense against external attacks.

4 Why is network security needed?

Answer: The global connectivity of the Internet has enabled hackers to attack your network from anywhere in the world.

5 Attacks against network resources fall into what categories?

Answer: Attacks against network resources fall into data manipulation, account access, privilege escalation, and the exploitation of trust relationships.

6 What is a script kiddie?

Answer: A script kiddie is an inexperienced attacker who frequently runs scripts against computer networks, many times with blind disregard for the consequences.

7 What is reconnaissance?

Answer: Reconnaissance or information gathering is the unauthorized mapping of systems, services, or vulnerabilities on a network.

8 What are some common motivations behind computer attacks?

Answer: Some of the common motivations behind computer attacks are financial gain, political activism, and revenge.

9 What is a denial-of-service (DoS) attack?

Answer: A denial-of-service attack is designed to disrupt the operation of a specific system or network by denying access to that network resource.

10 What are the six security principles that define the security on your network?

Answer: The six security concepts are authentication, authorization, confidentiality, integrity, auditing, and availability.

11 What is the first step in a network attack?

Answer: To attack a network, your first step is to define the goals that you want your attack to accomplish. These goals then drive the remaining phases of your attack.

12 What are the two common mechanisms that an attacker uses to collect information about your network?

Answer: An attacker uses public data sources along with scanning and probing to collect information about your network and its topology.

13 What are some of the weak areas on your network that attackers frequently attack?

Answer: Some of the weak areas on your network that attackers exploit are weak authentication, common services configured poorly, protocol weaknesses, compromised trust relationships, back doors, and physical assets that are not secured.

14 What are some of the attack approaches commonly used by attackers?

Answer: The common attack approaches are ad hoc, methodical, surgical strike, and patient (slow).

15 What are some of common protocols with known vulnerabilities?

Answer: Some of the common protocols with known vulnerabilities are TCP, UDP, ICMP, IP, and ARP.

16 What are common network attack points?

Answer: The common network attack points are network resources and network protocols.

17 When collecting information about your network what are some of things that an attacker is looking for?

Answer: When collecting information on your network, an attacker looks for things such as operating systems with known vulnerabilities, protocols being used that have known weaknesses, which services and applications are being used on your network, and the overall network topology.

Chapter 2

1 What are the four steps in the Cisco Security Wheel?

Answer: The four steps in the Cisco Security Wheel are secure the network, monitor the network, test network security, and improve network security.

2 What is a security policy?

Answer: A security policy is a security framework that outlines the acceptable or required security procedures allowed on your network.

3 What two types of monitoring are commonly used to detect violations in your security policy?

Answer: The two types of monitoring that are commonly used are manual monitoring and automatic monitoring.

4 What are some of the procedures that your security policy should cover?

Answer: Your security policy should address at least the following procedures on your network: login procedures, user accounts and group procedures, directory and file procedures, data protection procedures, secure transmission procedures, remote and mobile user procedures, virus control procedures, and e-mail procedures.

5 What software tool do you use to test the security of your network?

Answer: Network scanners are used to test the security of your network.

6 How can IDS sensors be used to assist with implementing the Security Wheel?

Answer: By placing IDS sensors at strategic locations throughout your network, you can use them to help verify or test that your security policy is being enforced, as well as to monitor your network for traffic that violates your security policy.

7 What is an untrusted link?

Answer: An untrusted link is a network segment that is accessible by people you do not trust and who may attempt to sniff traffic on the network.

8 What are the endpoints commonly used for the encryption boundaries on VPNs?

Answer: The encryption on VPNs is either from host-to-host or site-to-site. With site-to-site encryption, the traffic is unencrypted until it reaches the VPN endpoint, whereas with host-to-host encryption the traffic is never transported unencrypted.

9 What are four areas that you need to examine to secure your network?

Answer: Four areas that need to be considered when securing your network security are tightening authentication, establishing security boundaries (installing firewalls), establishing VPNs, and vulnerability patching.

10   What is a firewall?

Answer: A firewall is a security component that limits traffic flow to a protected network based on a predefined security policy.

11   What basic security principle does a VPN provide?

Answer: A VPN provides confidentiality and prevents unauthorized people from viewing traffic being transmitted across the VPN connection.

12   What are the steps that you can take to tighten authentication on your network?

Answer: To tighten authentication on your network, you can define privilege groups, limit administrative access, eliminate default passwords, reduce anonymous access, minimize trust relationships, and use one-time passwords.

13   What is Cisco AVVID?

Answer: Cisco Architecture for Voice, Video, and Integrated Data is a framework that enables you to easily integrate emerging technologies into your network to increase your productivity through various Internet business solutions.

14   Where are two places that you can monitor security news on the Web?

Answer: Security news can be obtained from security mailing lists and security websites.

15   What is the difference between inclusive and exclusive security stances?

Answer: The inclusive security stance allows everything by default and only disallows known bad traffic, whereas an exclusive security stance denies everything by default and only allows known good traffic.

16   What are the two steps to establishing security boundaries on your network?

Answer: To establish security boundaries on your network you need to determine necessary traffic patterns and define logical security zones.

17   What is Cisco SAFE?

Answer: Cisco SAFE builds on Cisco AVVID by providing you with a flexible framework that will empower your company to securely and reliably take advantage of the Internet economy. More specifically, Cisco SAFE is a collection of white papers and design guides that provide you with concrete examples of how to effectively incorporate security into your unique network environment.

Chapter 3

1 What are the two major IDS monitoring locations?

Answer: The major IDS monitoring locations are host-based and network-based.

2 What are the three types of IDS triggering mechanisms?

Answer: The three types of IDS triggering mechanisms are anomaly (profile based), misuse detection (pattern matching), and protocol analysis.

3 What is the purpose of an IDS?

Answer: An IDS detects attacks against your network and misuse of your network resources.

4 What is anomaly detection?

Answer: Anomaly detection is the detection of alarms by observing actions that deviate from normal user activity.

5 What is the major drawback to host-based IDS monitoring?

Answer: The biggest drawback to host-based IDS monitoring is supporting multiple OSs. Limited network visibility can be minimized through the use of a network IDS in conjunction with your host-based solution.

6 What is misuse detection?

Answer: Misuse detection is the generation of alarms by matching data with signatures of known intrusive activity that are stored in a database.

7 What is a major benefit of anomaly detection?

Answer: Anomaly detection can detect previously unknown attacks.

8 What is protocol analysis?

Answer: Protocol analysis is an alarm-triggering mechanism in which the IDS decodes the packets based on a specific protocol to verify that the traffic is valid as well as look for patterns of intrusive activity.

9 What are two major limitations of network-based IDSs?

Answer: Two major limitations of network-based IDSs are bandwidth and encryption.

10 What is obfuscation?

Answer: Obfuscation is the disguising of network traffic so that it does not appear to be attack traffic, thus preventing the IDS device from detecting the attack.

11   What is a hybrid IDS?

Answer: A hybrid IDS combines multiple IDS technologies into a single IDS to produce enhanced functionality.

12   What are some common obfuscation techniques?

Answer: Some common obfuscation techniques are to use control characters, use hexadecimal representations for characters, and use Unicode representations for characters in the attack traffic.

13   What are some benefits to misuse-based IDSs?

Answer: Misuse-based IDSs have a signature database based on actual attack data, the attacks detected are well defined, the system is easy to understand, and it detects attacks immediately upon installation.

14   What are the drawbacks to pattern-matching detection?

Answer: Pattern-matching detection cannot detect unknown attacks, signature databases need to be updated with new attack signatures, and the system must maintain state information.

15   What are some common IDS response techniques?

Answer: The common IDS response capabilities are TCP resets, IP blocking, logging actual attack traffic, and restricting access to protected resources.

16   What are some drawbacks to anomaly detection?

Answer: Anomaly detection is complicated and difficult to understand, requires an initial training period, does not protect the network during training, must keep user profiles current, is hard to define normal activity, and there is not a one-to-one correspondence between alarms and attack type.

17   What is the difference between a true positive and a true negative?

Answer: A true positive is an alarm generated due to the offending traffic (that the signature is designed to detect), whereas a true negative represents the IDS correctly failing to generate an alarm for normal user traffic.

18   What are the common techniques used to evade detection by your IDS?

Answer: The common techniques used in an attempt to evade your IDS are flooding, fragmentation, encryption, obfuscation, and TTL manipulation.

19   What is the difference between a false positive and a false negative?

Answer: A false positive is an alarm generated due to normal user traffic, whereas a false negative represents the IDS failing to generate an alarm for a known attack (that it is designed to detect).

Chapter 4

1   What are the two monitoring and reporting options available with Cisco IDS version 4.0?

Answer: Cisco IDS version 4.0 supports IDS Event Viewer and IDS Security Monitor to analyze and report alarm traffic.

2   What are the two programs that you can use to configure and manage your sensors with Cisco IDS version 4.0?

Answer: Cisco IDS version 4.0 supports IDS Device Manager (IDM) and IDS Management Center (IDS MC) to configure and manage your deployed sensors.

3   How many different types of sensor platforms are supported by Cisco IDS?

Answer: Cisco IDS supports five types of sensors: 4200 series (PC appliances), switch sensors (the Catalyst 6000 IDS Module), router sensors (Cisco IOS based and Network Module), firewall sensors, and host-based agents.

4   Which 4200 series sensors can process the most traffic?

Answer: The IDS 4250XL is rated at gigabit speeds and can process more traffic than any other 4200 series sensor.

5   What are the three types of responses that a sensor can perform in reply to an attack?

Answer: The three sensor responses to an attack are TCP reset, blocking, and IP logging.

6   What is IDSM?

Answer: The IDS Module (IDSM) is a sensor blade that runs in your Catalyst 6500 series switch chassis.

7   What is Cisco Threat Response?

Answer: Cisco Threat Response is a product that enables you to identify false alarms, thus reducing the amount of time that you spend analyzing attacks directed at systems that are not vulnerable to the attack.

8   What is a false alarm?

Answer: A false alarm occurs when valid attack traffic is launched toward a device that is not vulnerable to the attack being used.

9   Where are the common network boundaries at which you need to deploy Cisco IDS sensors?

Answer: You commonly deploy Cisco IDS sensors at the following boundaries on your network: Internet boundaries, extranet boundaries, intranet boundaries, remote-access boundaries, and individual hosts (servers and desktops).

10   How many sensors can be managed by IDS MC?

Answer: A single IDS MC system can manage up to 300 sensors.

11   You can use IEV to view the alarms from how many sensors?

Answer: IEV can consolidate the alarms from up to five individual sensors.

12   If you are going to deploy 100 Cisco IDS sensors on your network, what management solution would you probably use?

Answer: To support 100 Cisco IDS sensors, you would probably use IDS MC because it enables you to manage all the sensors from a single system.

13   If your Cisco IDS solution consists of two sensors, what monitoring and reporting tool would you probably use?

Answer: To support two sensors, you would probably use IDS Event Viewer (IEV) to monitor the alarms generated by your sensors.

14   Cisco IDS provides an active defense for your network that focuses on what three factors?

Answer: Cisco IDS provides an active defense that focuses on detection, prevention, and reaction.

15   What is IP logging?

Answer: IP logging is a signature response option that causes the actual traffic from an attacking system to be captured on your sensor.

16   How does the TCP reset response work?

Answer: When a signature configured to perform a TCP reset response fires, your sensor generates TCP packets with the RST flag set and sends them to both hosts involved in the TCP connection to close the connection.

Chapter 5

1   How many different privilege roles can be assigned to a user account on your sensor?

Answer: You can assign four different privilege roles to the account on your sensor: Administrator, Operator, Viewer, and Service.

2   What protocol is used between your sensor and other Cisco IDS devices?

Answer: To communicate with other Cisco IDS devices, your sensor uses the Remote Data Exchange Protocol (RDEP). This protocol replaced the PostOffice protocol.

3 What three major processing steps does your sensor use to analyze your network traffic?

Answer: Your sensor performs the following three major processing steps when analyzing network traffic: packet capture and decoding, virtual sensor processing, and virtual alarm processing.

4 Instead of using the tokens found in previous versions of Cisco IDS, in what format does Cisco IDS version 4.0 store its configuration data?

Answer: Configuration files in version 4.0 are stored in XML format with a schema that is based on the IDIOM specification.

5 What is the most privileged role (that uses the sensor CLI) that you can assign to a user account?

Answer: The Administrator role is the most privileged CLI role, and it enables the user to perform all operations.

6 What is the least privileged role that you can assign to a user account?

Answer: The Viewer role is the least privileged user role, and it only enables a user to view information on the sensor without being able to change the sensor's configuration.

7 Is external sensor communication traffic via RDEP encrypted?

Answer: External sensor communication using RDEP uses HTTP over TLS/SSL. Yes, this traffic is encrypted.

8 How large is the circular buffer where your sensor stores event information?

Answer: Your sensor stores event information in a 4-GB circular queue (fixed-length file).

9 What are the three types of request messages supported by RDEP?

Answer: RDEP supports the following three request message types: event messages, IP log messages, and transaction messages.

10 What are two types of RDEP event requests?

Answer: RDEP supports two types of event requests: queries and subscriptions.

11 Can you assign the Service role to multiple accounts on your sensor?

Answer: No, you can only assign the Service role to one account on your sensor.

12 What is the purpose of the service account?

Answer: The purpose of the Service account is to enable TAC to troubleshoot the operation of your sensor.

13 Which protocol controls intraprocess communication?

Answer: The Intrusion Detection Application Program Interface (IDAPI) handles intraprocess communication on your sensor.

Chapter 6

1 What are the three main mechanisms to capture traffic for network analysis on your Cisco infrastructure switches?

Answer: To capture network traffic for analysis on your Cisco switches, you can you Switch Port Analyzer (SPAN), Remote SPAN (RSPAN), and VLAN access control lists (VACLs).

2 What are the three types of infrastructure devices that you use to capture network traffic for intrusion detection analysis?

Answer: You can capture traffic for intrusion detection analysis using hubs, network taps, and switches.

3 When using SPAN to capture network traffic on a Catalyst 6500 switch, what traffic keyword do you use to capture only traffic leaving the switch from the specified ports?

Answer: To capture only traffic that is leaving the switch (from your configured ports) on a Catalyst 6500, use the tx traffic option keyword.

4 What is local SPAN?

Answer: Local SPAN refers to a situation in which all of the ports that you are monitoring are located on the same switch.

5 What traffic capture commands are available on the 2900XL/3500XL Cisco switches?

Answer: With 2900XL/3500XL Cisco switches, you have two traffic capture commands that configure your SPAN capability: port monitor and monitor session.

6 If you plan to use the TCP reset signature action in conjunction with SPAN, what functionality must the switch support?

Answer: To use the TCP reset action, when you are capturing your network traffic via SPAN, your switch must support the capability for the SPAN destination port to receive incoming traffic.

7 What traffic capture options are available on the Catalyst 6500 switches?

Answer: The Catalyst 6500 switches support SPAN, RSPAN, and VACLs to capture network traffic for intrusion detection analysis.

8 What is RSPAN?

Answer: Remote SPAN (RSPAN) refers to the situation in which the ports that you want to monitor (for intrusion detection analysis) are not all located on the same switch, but instead are distributed across one or more switches.

9 What is the first step in defining a VACL (when using CatOS)?

Answer: The first step in defining a VACL (when using CatOS) is to define the interesting traffic by using the set security acl ip switch command.

10 What keyword do you need to use when defining your security ACL to enable you to make a copy of the traffic for intrusion detection analysis?

Answer: When defining your security ACL, you need to use the capture keyword to enable a copy of the traffic to be directed to your sensor.

11 What are some of the major ways that you can limit the traffic that your security ACL will capture?

Answer: When creating your security ACL, you can limit the traffic capture by specifying an IP protocol, a source or destination IP address, a source or destination port, or a combination of these three items.

12 Why does your sensor use random Ethernet MAC addresses when generating TCP reset packets?

Answer: The sensor uses random Ethernet MAC addresses so that the switch does not learn the Ethernet MAC address of the sensor, which could potentially enable an attacker to locate and attack the sensor.

13 What three traffic direction keywords can you use when defining a SPAN port on a Catalyst 6500 switch?

Answer: When defining a SPAN port on a Catalyst 6500 switch, you can specify rx (received traffic), tx (transmitted traffic), or both (traffic received and transmitted).

14 What command do you use to enable trunking on a specified port of a Catalyst 6500 switch?

Answer: You enable trunking on a switch port by using the set trunk switch command.

15 What switch command do you use to remove VLANs from a trunk port?

Answer: You use the clear trunk switch command to remove VLANs from the allowed list of VLANs for a trunk port.

16 What switch command do you use to add VLANs to a trunk port?

Answer: You use the set trunk switch command to add VLANs to the allowed list of VLANs for a trunk port.

17 What Cisco IOS firewall command can interfere with your ability to use security ACLs?

Answer: If you use the ip inspect router command on your MSFC, it will interfere with you security ACLs.

18 What is the main difference between a switch and a hub?

Answer: A hub floods all received traffic out of its ports. A switch maintains a content addressable memory (CAM) table and attempts to send received traffic only out the port belonging to the destination host.

Chapter 7

1 When you upgrade an IDS 4220 or IDS 4230-FE appliance, what must you do to ensure that you can monitor traffic correctly?

Answer: When you upgrade an IDS 4220 or IDS 4230-FE sensor, you need to switch the cables on the command and control interface and the monitoring interface.

2 Which configuration mode enables you to define trusted hosts that are able to establish TCP connections with the sensor?

Answer: The networkParams fourth-level configuration mode (accessible from the service host configuration mode) enables you to define trusted hosts that can connect to the sensor.

3 What character do you use to obtain help via the appliance CLI?

Answer: To get help when using the appliance CLI, use the question mark (?) character.

4 How can you recall a previous command that you entered when using the CLI?

Answer: You can cycle through the commands that you have entered using the Up Arrow key (or Ctrl+P) and the Down Arrow key (or the Ctrl+N).

5 What command enables you to allow a host or network to connect to the sensor?

Answer: The accessList command enables you to allow a host or network to access the sensor.

6 What keyword do you use to reverse the effect of a CLI command?

Answer: To reverse the effect of a CLI command, you precede the command with the no keyword (such as no shutdown).

7 How many different user roles are available to assign to accounts on your sensor?

Answer: The sensor software provides four different user roles (Administrator, Operator, Viewer, and Service).

8 What is the most privileged user role that you can assign to a user who uses the CLI?

Answer: The Administrator role is the most privileged user role that uses the CLI. It has access to all CLI operations.

9 Which user role enables only the user to examine the sensor's events and configuration but does not allow the user to change the configuration?

Answer: The Viewer role enables the user to look at the configuration of the sensor and monitor events, but not to change the configuration.

10 What parameters do you configure using the **setup** CLI command?

Answer: When you run the setup command, it enables you to configure the basic sensor characteristics, including the host name, IP address, and network mask, the default gateway (whether Telnet is enabled), and the web server port.

11 What is the purpose of the Service user role?

Answer: The Service user role enables you to configure an account that bypasses the CLI. This account is for support and to assist the TAC in trouble-shooting problems with your sensor.

12 What command do you enter on the CLI to enter global configuration mode?

Answer: Similar to what you enter with Cisco IOS, you use the command con-figure terminal to enter global configuration mode.

13 What command enables you to manually set the time via the CLI?

Answer: To manually set the time on the CLI, use the clock set command.

14 How many Service accounts can you have you have on your sensor?

Answer: You can only assign the Service role to a single account on your sensor.

15 What user role would you usually assign to the account that you use to enable monitoring applications to retrieve information from your sensor?

Answer: You would normally assign the Viewer role to your monitoring appli-cation, because it only needs to retrieve information from the sensor and not change the configuration.

16 What character do you use on the CLI to cause your sensor to automatically expand the rest of a command for you?

Answer: If you press the Tab key while entering a command at the CLI, the sys-tem will automatically expand the command if only one command matches the partial command that you entered.

17   What extra step might you need to perform before upgrading the software on an IDS 4235 appliance to version 4.0?

> **Answer: Before you install the version 4.0 software, you need to verify the BIOS version, and upgrade if necessary on both the IDS 4235 and IDS 4250 appliances.**

18   What character do you enter to abort the current CLI command line and start over with an empty command line?

> **Answer: To abort the current command line, use the Ctrl+Q or Ctrl+C characters.**

19   When a CLI command's output extends beyond a single screen, what character do you use to scroll the output up by a single line?

> **Answer: When the output of a CLI command extends beyond a single screen, the output stops at one screen's worth and displays the –more- prompt. To scroll the output by a single line, press the Enter key.**

20   When a CLI command's output extends beyond a single screen, what character do you use to show the next screen of information?

> **Answer: When the output of a CLI command extends beyond a single screen, the output stops at one screen's worth and displays the –more- prompt. To show the next screen of information, use the Space key.**

Chapter 8

1   What ports on the IDSM-2 are used to monitor network traffic?

> **Answer: Ports 7 and 8 on the IDSM-2 are used to monitor network traffic.**

2   Which Catalyst switch command do you use to configure the correct VLAN on the command and control port when using CatOS?

> **Answer: To configure the VLAN for the command and control port (when using CatOS), you need to use the set vlan command to place the command and control port on the correct VLAN so that other devices can communicate with it.**

3   What is the purpose of the TCP reset port on the IDSM-2?

> **Answer: The TCP reset port on the IDSM-2 is a port that was specifically created to enable the IDSM-2 to generate TCP resets (because this cannot be done through the monitoring ports).**

4 Through which port do other devices (such as management and monitoring applications) communicate with the IDSM-2?

Answer: The command and control port is port 2 on the IDSM-2 line card. Devices, such as management and monitoring applications, use this port to communicate with the IDSM-2.

5 Which port on the IDSM-2 is used to send out the TCP reset packets for signatures configured for TCP resets?

Answer: Port 1 on the IDSM-2 is the TCP reset port and is used to transmit all TCP reset packets in response to signatures configured for the TCP reset response.

6 What options do you have to capture traffic for IDSM-2 monitoring ports?

Answer: You can use the following three features to capture traffic for the IDSM-2 monitoring ports: RSPAN feature, SPAN feature, and VACL capture feature.

7 What command do you execute from the IDSM-2 CLI to reboot or power down the IDSM-2 line card?

Answer: To reboot the IDSM-2 line card, use the reset IDSM-2 CLI command. Adding the powerdown option to the reset command causes the IDSM-2 to be shut down instead of being rebooted.

8 What is the color of the IDSM-2 status LED when the module is operational?

Answer: When the IDSM-2 status LED is green, the module is operational.

9 What initial configuration command do you run from the IDSM-2 CLI to configure the basic IDSM-2 properties, such as host name and default gateway?

Answer: To initially configure the basic IDSM-2 properties, run the setup command from the IDSM-2 CLI.

10 What switch command can you execute to verify that the Catalyst 6500 switch has recognized the IDSM-2 line card?

Answer: From the switch console, execute the show module command to check the status of the line cards installed on the switch.

11 To support VACLs to capture network traffic, your switch must have what type of hardware?

Answer: To support VACLs, your Catalyst switch must have a Policy Feature Card (PFC).

12 What switch commands do you use to limit the traffic from different VLANs that is actually sent to a monitoring port on your IDSM-2?

Answer: To limit the traffic sent to your IDSM-2 monitoring port, use the set trunk and clear trunk commands to restrict which VLANs the monitoring port is trunking, which limits the traffic sent to the monitoring port on the IDSM-2.

13 What switch command can you use to verify which VLANs the monitoring port on your IDSM-2 is currently trunking?

Answer: You use the show trunk command to see which VLANs a specific switch port is currently trunking.

14 What three types of devices can your IDSM-2 perform device management on?

Answer: The IDSM-2 (like the appliance sensor) can perform device management on Cisco IOS routers, Catalyst 6500 switches, and PIX firewalls.

15 How many internal ports does the IDSM-2 have?

Answer: The IDSM-2 has the following four internal ports: command and control (port 2), TCP resets (port 1), and monitoring (ports 7 & 8).

16 Which port on your IDSM-2 has an actual IP address?

Answer: The command and control port on the IDSM-2 has an IP address because your external applications need to connect to this port when communicating with the module.

Chapter 9

1 How many sensors can you manage with Cisco IDS Event Viewer?

Answer: Cisco IDS Event Viewer can manage up to five IDS devices.

2 What is Cisco IDS Event Viewer based on?

Answer: Cisco IDS Event Viewer is a Java-based application that stores alarm information in a MySQL database that enables you to monitor alarms from up to five sensors.

3 Where does IEV store the events it retrieves from your sensors?

Answer: IEV stores retrieved information in a MySQL database.

4 After installing IEV, what do you need to add to the configuration to enable IEV to monitor a sensor on your network?

Answer: To monitor a sensor with IEV, you need to add an IDS device to IEV that identifies the sensor's information (such as IP address and account to use when connecting to the sensor).

5 What are the functions that you can filter traffic on when using IEV?

Answer: IEV can filter traffic on the following functions: By severity, by source address, by destination address, by signature name, by sensor name, by UTC time, and by status.

6 What are the two ways that you can specify IP addresses when defining either a source or destination address filter?

Answer: You can specify either single addresses or a range of addresses when specifying either a source or destination address filter.

7 What are the default views included with IEV?

Answer: IEV includes the following default views: Destination Address Group, Source Address Group, Severity Level Group, Sig Name Group, and Sensor Name Group.

8 How can you view the events coming from your sensor in real time?

Answer: To monitor the events coming from your sensor in real time, you can use the Realtime Dashboard.

9 What alarm statuses can you assign to alarm events?

Answer: IEV supports the following alarm status values: New, Acknowledged, Assigned, Closed, and Deleted.

10 How can you assign note information to a specific alarm?

Answer: You can assign information to a specific alarm event by entering information into the Notes field of the alarm entry via the Alarm Information Dialog window.

11 What does the context buffer display?

Answer: The context buffer displays up to 256 bytes of TCP data from the TCP stream that triggered the signature.

12 How large is the context buffer?

Answer: The context buffer contains a maximum of 256 bytes (characters).

13 What is the NSDB?

Answer: The Network Security Database (NSDB) is the Cisco HTML-based encyclopedia of network IDS and related vulnerability information.

14 What determines how often IEV retrieves information from your sensor to update the database tables?

Answer: IEV retrieves information from your sensors based on the refresh cycle settings (default once a minute).

15 When using IEV what are the database administration functions that you will likely perform?

Answer: When using IEV, the database administration functions are importing log files, exporting database tables, and deleting alarms.

16 What is the default rate at which IEV retrieves information from your sensors?

Answer: By default, IEV retrieves information from your sensors once every minute.

17 What is the default alarm status?

Answer: When alarms are initially received, their status is automatically set to New.

18 What are the main types of NSDB pages?

Answer: The NSDB is comprised of three main types of pages: signature exploit pages, vulnerability pages, and user notes pages.

19 When filtering on IP addresses, what are the two possible qualifiers that you can apply to the addresses to determine how they are used in the filter?

Answer: When specifying IP address filters, you can specify two address qualifiers: Excluded and Included.

20 What authentication does IEV use to retrieve information from your sensor?

Answer: When defining an IDS device, you need to specify a valid username and password for the sensor that IEV can use when retrieving information from the sensor.

21 What are the three checks performed by your browser on a TLS certificate?

Answer: When verifying a TLS certificate, your browser checks the issuer of the certificate, whether the certificate has expired, and whether the name in the certificate matches the host being connected to.

22 Which browser certificate check will the Cisco IDS sensor fail?

Answer: The certificate on you sensor is self-signed, so it will fail the check of the issuer because the certificate authority (CA) will be unknown to your browser.

Chapter 10

1 When adding a sensor to IDS MC, what is the minimum amount of information that you must provide?

Answer: To add a sensor to IDS MC, you must provide an IP address and a valid user account and password that enables IDS MC to log in to the sensor.

2 What is an advantage of placing sensors into a sensor group in IDS MC?

Answer: Placing sensors in a sensor group enables you to perform certain configuration options on the entire group.

3 By default, what network addresses are allowed to connect to the sensor?

Answer: By default, the sensor is only configured to allow IP addresses from the 10.1.9.0 Class C subnet.

4 What must you do on your sensor to enable it to communicate with an SSH server?

Answer: Before your sensor can connect to another SSH server, you must add the SSH server's host key to the sensor's list of known SSH host keys.

5 What are the four roles that you can assign a user account on your sensor?

Answer: The four roles that you can assign a user account on the sensor are Administrator, Operator, Viewer, and Service.

6 What determines the privileges that an account on your sensor has?

Answer: The user role assigned to a sensor account determines the user's privileges.

7 What information is included in the show tech-support command?

Answer: The show tech-support command provides the following information: current configuration, show version information, and system information (CidDump output).

8 What are the two ways to configure when daylight savings time starts and stops?

Answer: When configuring when daylight savings time starts and stops, you can specify specific dates or you can specify recurring relative dates (such as the first Sunday in April).

9 When making a significant time change on your sensor, what problem must you watch out for?

Answer: Before you change the time on your sensor significantly, you need to clear out any existing events in the Event Store. Otherwise, these old events can appear to have occurred after new events (due to the time change).

10 What are the two ways that you can configure time on the sensor?

Answer: You can specify the time manually on the sensor or you can configure the sensor to obtain the current time automatically from an NTP server.

11 What two methods of interactive access do you have to communicate with your sensor?

Answer: You can use either Telnet or SSH to gain interactive access to your sensor.

12 What is a common situation in which you need to add a known SSH host key?

Answer: To enable a sensor to communicate with a managed device via SSH, you need to add the managed device's SSH key to the sensor's list of known SSH hosts.

13 What is a situation in which you would need to add a trusted host certificate to your sensor?

Answer: To enable your sensor to perform upgrades using a SSL/TLS web server, you need to add the web server's certificate to the sensor's list of trusted host certificates.

14 What are the two ways that IDS MC can authenticate to a sensor?

Answer: You can configure IDS MC to authenticate with a sensor via a username and password and by using a username and a passphrase (with SSH keys).

Chapter 11

1 What are the two major global sensing parameters that impact the way that your sensor actually captures and analyzes traffic?

Answer: The two major global sensing parameters that impact the way your sensor actually captures and analyzes traffic are internal networks and reassembly options.

2 What are the two types of reassembly options that you can configure on your sensor?

Answer: You can configure both IP fragment reassembly and TCP stream reassembly options on your sensor.

3 What is the purpose of defining internal networks?

Answer: Defining internal networks enables you to use the keyword IN when defining your signature filters instead of using actual IP addresses. This can also provide a quick visual aid when distinguishing the source and destination of an attack.

4 What are the two main TCP stream reassembly modes?

Answer: The two TCP stream reassembly modes are strict and loose.

5 What are the main categories by which your can view the various signature groups?

Answer: The main categories by which you can view the various signature groups are Signature ID, Attack Type, L2/L3/L4 protocol, Operating System, and Service.

6 How does *strict* TCP stream reassembly work?

Answer: When you configure *strict* TCP stream reassembly, if a gap in a session is detected (a missing packet in the sequence), the sensor stops processing data for that TCP stream; otherwise, all packets are processed in their correct TCP sequence.

7 What is the main benefit of creating signature filters?

Answer: The main benefit of creating signature filters is to reduce the number of false positives that you must analyze.

8 How does *loose* TCP stream reassembly differ from *strict* TCP stream reassembly?

Answer: When using *loose* TCP stream reassembly, your sensor attempts to process the TCP packets in the correct TCP sequence, but if the session is missing packets, the sensor will process the packets that it has received.

9 What are the two types of signature filters that you can define?

Answer: You can define the following two filter types (or filter actions): include or exclude filters. (Include filters are also known as exceptions.)

10 What does an include (or exception) filter do?

Answer: An include filter causes attack traffic for an IP address (previously excluded by an exclude filter) to generate an alarm.

11 What are the two major tasks involved with respect to signature configuration?

Answer: The two major tasks involved in signature configuration are tuning existing signatures and creating custom signatures.

12 When tuning signatures, what are the three tasks that are considered basic signature configuration?

Answer: Basic signature configuration tasks involve enabling/disabling a signature, assigning a new severity, and assigning signature actions.

13 What are some of the factors that impact the selection of a signature engine for a custom signature?

Answer: When choosing a signature engine, it depends on the following characteristics of the attack traffic: network protocol, target address(es), target port(s), attack type, and inspection criteria.

14 What are the steps involved in creating a custom signature?

Answer: The steps involved in creating a custom signature are as follows: choose a signature engine, verify existing functionality, determine engine parameters, and test the effectiveness and efficiency of the new signature.

15 What is the difference between the TCP embryonic timeout and the TCP open establish timeout?

Answer: The TCP embryonic timeout regulates how long SYN connections that have not completed the three-way handshake are stored (before deletion), whereas the TCP open establish timeout regulates how long connections that have completed the three-way handshake are stored after not seeing traffic from the systems involved in the connection.

16 What are the major categories by which you can view the Cisco IDS built-in signatures?

Answer: You can view the Cisco IDS built-in signatures by the following major categories: Signature ID, Attack Type, L2/L3/L4 Protocol, Operating System, and Service.

17 What does the IP fragment reassemble timeout parameter control?

Answer: The IP fragment reassemble timeout parameter controls how long the sensor waits for the fragments of an IP datagram to arrive (before deleting them from the buffer or queue).

18 When viewing the Cisco IDS signatures using the Service category, what are most of the major signature groups based on?

Answer: Most of the groups in the Service signature category are groups that are based on specific network protocols (such as SSH, TFTP, and FTP).

19 What are the major fields you need to configure to define a signature filter?

Answer: To define a signature filter, you need to define the signatures that the filter is applied to, the source and destination IP addresses that the filter will operate on, and the filter type (inclusive or exclusive). For IDM, all filters are exclusive and you define exceptions to the filter.

20 Why is it important to test your custom signatures?

Answer: Testing your custom signatures ensures that they alarm on the correct traffic, and enables you to verify that they do not impact the performance of your sensor or network.

Chapter 12

1 What are the three signature responses supported by the Cisco IDS network appliance software (besides alarming)?

Answer: The Cisco IDS network appliance software supports the following three signature responses (besides alarming): IP blocking, TCP resets, and IP logging.

2 What are the two ways that you can shun traffic in response to a signature firing?

Answer: The two ways that you can shun traffic are by configuring a signature to automatically initiate a shun and by manually initiating a shun.

3 What are the two types of shuns that you can configure for a signature?

Answer: When a signature fires, it can shun all traffic from the attacking system (shunHost) or it can shun traffic from the attacking system that is destined for the specific destination port that caused the signature to trigger (shunConnection).

4 What is a blocking sensor?

Answer: A blocking sensor is a sensor that is configured to initiate blocking on one or more managed devices.

5 What are the three types of managed devices supported by Cisco IDS?

Answer: Cisco IDS supports using the following three types of blocking devices: Cisco routers, Catalyst 6000 switches, and PIX firewalls (and Firewall Switch Modules).

6 How does you blocking sensor perform blocking on a PIX-managed device?

Answer: To implement blocking on a PIX-managed device, your blocking sensor uses the PIX's shun command to block the network traffic.

7 Which type of managed device uses VACLs to block the traffic?

Answer: When you use a Catalyst 6000-managed device, your sensor uses VACLs to perform the blocking of the network traffic.

8 What is the managed interface?

Answer: The managed interface is the interface on the managed device to which the blocking sensor applies the blocking ACL.

9 What are the two ways that your blocking sensor communicates with your managed devices?

Answer: The blocking sensor communicates with its managed devices via Telnet or SSH.

10 Can you specify a traffic direction when blocking traffic using a VACL?

Answer: You can specify a traffic direction only when defining ACLs. VACLs are directionless.

11 Why is it advantageous to place your ACLs on your external router interface?

Answer: Placing your ACL on the external router interface enables you to stop the traffic before it is processed by your router.

12 What is the PreShun ACL?

Answer: The PreShun ACL is an ACL on your blocking device that specifies entries that the blocking sensor places at the beginning of the blocking ACL (before the dynamically created blocking entries).

13 What is the PostShun ACL?

Answer: The PreShun ACL is an ACL on your blocking device that specifies entries that the blocking sensor places at the end of the blocking ACL (after the dynamically created blocking entries).

14 What is a master blocking sensor?

Answer: A master blocking sensor performs blocking requests from other sensors for managed devices that it controls.

15 How many interfaces can a single sensor manage for IP blocking?

Answer: A single sensor can manage up to 10 different interfaces across 1 or more managed devices.

16 If you use SSH to communicate with your managed devices, what do you need to configure from the sensor's command line to enable this communication to take place successfully?

Answer: Before your sensor can successfully communicate with a managed device using SSH, you need to add the managed device's SSH key using the ssh host-key CLI command.

17 How can you limit the amount of traffic captured when you initiate manual IP logging?

Answer: When initiating manual IP logging, you can limit the amount of traffic captured by specifying one or more of the following parameters: duration (minutes), number of packets, and number of bytes.

18 When initiating manual blocking through IDM, what are the two options?

Answer: Using IDM, you can initiate manual blocks on single hosts as well as networks.

19 What is device management?

Answer: Deice management refers to the capability of a sensor to interact with certain Cisco devices and dynamically reconfigure them to block the source of an attack using an ACL, VACL, or shun command on the PIX (and FWSM).

20 On which signatures can you effectively configure the reset response?

Answer: The reset response is only applicable to TCP-based connections because it uses TCP resets to terminate an existing TCP connection.

Chapter 13

1 What are the four basic alarming modes?

Answer: Cisco IDS supports the following four basic alarming modes: FireAll, FireOnce, Summarize, and GlobalSummarize.

2 How does the FireOnce alarm mode work?

Answer: The FireOnce alarm mode causes an alarm to be generated when the first instance of the intrusive activity is detected. Then it does not alarm again (on duplicate alarms) until the time specified by the ThrottleInterval has expired. Duplicate alarms are dictated by the value of the SummaryKey parameter.

3 What is the difference between the Summarize and GlobalSummarize alarming modes?

Answer: The Summarize alarm mode generates one summary alarm for the ThrottleInterval that indicates how many alarms occurred (usually based on a pair of hosts), whereas GlobalSummarize provides a summary alarm for the ThrottleInterval based on all address combinations.

4 What is variable alarm summarization?

Answer: Variable alarm summarization is when an alarm is configured for one alarm mode (such as FireAll), but can automatically switch to a summarization mode when it detects multiple instances of the same traffic.

5 Which master parameter do you need to configure to enable variable alarm summarization?

Answer: To enable variable alarm summarization, you must configure the ChokeThreshold master engine parameter.

6 What are master engine parameters?

Answer: Master engine parameters are parameters common to all signatures.

7 What master engine parameter do you use to configure the signature's alarm mode?

Answer: You use the AlarmThrottle master engine parameter to configure the alarm mode for a signature.

8 What is an Atomic signature?

Answer: An Atomic signature is a signature that triggers on the contents of a single packet.

9 Which Atomic signature engine examines Layer 2 traffic?

Answer: The ATOMIC.ARP signature engine examines Layer 2 traffic.

10 What do the Flood signature engines detect?

Answer: The Flood signature engines detect attacks in which the attacker directs a flood of traffic against either a single host or the entire network in an attempt to cause a denial-of-service (DoS).

11 How do you enable the diagnostic mode for a signature based on the FLOOD.NET signature engine?

Answer: To enable the diagnostic mode, you configure the Rate parameter to zero.

12 Which type of signature engine provides protocol decode capability for various network protocols?

Answer: The Service signature engine provides protocol decode capability for numerous network protocols (such as DNS, FTP, and HTTP).

13 What is a host sweep?

Answer: A host sweep is when a single attacking system attempts to connect to more than a configured number of target systems.

14 What is a port sweep?

Answer: A port sweep is when a single attacking system attempts to connect to more than a configured number of ports on a single target system.

15 What are the two Host Sweep engines?

Answer: Cisco IDS supports the following two Host Sweep engines: SWEEP.HOST.ICMP and SWEEP.HOST.TCP.

16 Which master engine parameter do you configure to cause the sweep signature to reset the counter of unique connections seen (after an idle time between the host[s] involved)?

Answer: Configuring the ResetAfterIdle master engine parameter enables you to specify the idle time after which the counter of unique connections seen is reset to zero.

17 What is the SummaryKey (master engine parameter)?

Answer: The SummaryKey specifies what constitutes multiple instances of the same alarm based on the IP addresses and ports and is used for alarm summarization.

18 Which SummaryKey value uses only the source IP address to determine multiple instances of the same alarm?

Answer: Setting the SummaryKey to Axxx for a signature causes it to determine multiple alarm instances (for the same alarm) based solely on the source IP address.

19 What functionality do signatures based on the String signature engines provide?

> **Answer: Signatures based on the String signature engines enable you to alarm on pattern matches in the traffic being analyzed.**

20 Which signature engine specifically supports detecting scans from the SATAN scanning tools?

> **Answer: The SWEEP.MULTI signature is specifically designed to detect scans from the SATAN scanning tool.**

21 Which engine enables you to generate an alarm based on a specific IP protocol number that should not be present on your network?

> **Answer: The ATOMIC.L3.IP signature engine enables you to specify a specific IP protocol number using the ProtoNum parameter.**

22 What is the sampling rate used by the flood signatures?

> **Answer: The flood signatures measure their rate by sampling packets per second every second.**

Chapter 14

1 What are some of the problems faced when securing your endpoints?

> **Answer: When securing your endpoints, you need to handle zero-day protection, data protection, and server and desktop maintenance.**

2 What three levels of application protection does CSA provide?

> **Answer: CSA provides the following three levels of application protection: known malicious behavior, policy violations, and application profiling.**

3 What are the factors used by the agents when using rule-based policies to categorize traffic?

> **Answer: The agent software uses the following factors to categorize traffic based on rule-based policies: resource being accessed, operation being invoked, and the application initiating the action.**

4 Which three Windows operating systems are supported agent platforms?

> **Answer: The agent software is supported on Windows NT, Windows 2000, and Windows XP.**

5 Which UNIX operating system is a currently supported agent platform?

> **Answer: Solaris is the currently supported UNIX agent platform.**

6 Which CiscoWorks user role can manage hosts and groups, attach policies, and only has partial write access to the CSA MC database?

Answer: A user assigned the CiscoWorks Network Operations privilege role can manage hosts and groups and attach policies, but has only partial write access to the CSA MC database.

7 What are the three configuration tasks associated with CSA MC that require different privileges?

Answer: The three configuration tasks associated with CSA MC are as follows: configure, deploy, and monitor.

8 What are some of the criteria that you can use to group systems?

Answer: Some of the criteria that you can use to group systems include the following: system function, business group, geographical location, topological location, and importance to your organization.

9 What is major difference between the event log and the Event Monitor?

Answer: The information displayed by the Event Monitor is regularly updated to reflect new events.

10 What actions (alerts) can CSA MC take in response to events?

Answer: CSA MC can generate the following alerts in response to events: send an email message, generate a pager message, send SNMP notification, log information to a file, and run a custom script.

11 What is test mode?

Answer: Test mode enables you to verify the operation of your new policies by logging events but not actually performing the configured action operations.

12 Which rules can you use file sets with?

Answer: You can use file sets when you configure file access control rules and file monitor rules.

13 Which network service are data sets associated with?

Answer: Data sets contain a list of data strings that represent patterns that will be compared against the URI portion of HTTP requests.

14 What two types of application classes can you configure?

Answer: When using application classes, you can configure static and dynamic application classes.

15 List some rules that enable global event correlation?

Answer: Three rules that enable you to correlate events across agent systems are as follows: network shield rule, network worm rule, and Trojan detection rule.

16 What is the Profiler program?

Answer: The Profiler software monitors the actions of designated applications to determine the resources that they access during their normal operation so that you can use this information to develop a custom policy for the application.

Chapter 15

1 What two types of software updates do you regularly apply to your sensors?

Answer: You regularly apply signature updates and service packs to your sensor.

2 What is the difference between the two types of software updates?

Answer: Signature updates add new signatures to your sensor, whereas service packs enhance the functionality of your sensor's software.

3 Which command do you use on the sensor's CLI to update the sensor's software?

Answer: The upgrade command enables you to update the software on your sensor.

4 When using the sensor CLI, which server types can you use to retrieve the sensor software from?

Answer: When using the sensor CLI, you can update your sensor software by retrieving the new software from one of the following types of servers: FTP, HTTP, HTTPS, and SCP.

5 What command do you use to revert to the previous software version on your sensor?

Answer: Using the downgrade CLI command, you can revert to the previous software version (the one before the last software version applied by the upgrade command).

6 What CLI command can you use to re-image your sensor?

Answer: The recover CLI command enables you to re-image you sensor.

7 What CLI command enables you to see the status of the IDS processes running on your sensor?

Answer: The show version command enables you to see the status of the IDS processes on your sensor.

8 What CLI command can you use to view the statistics for only the command and control interface on your sensor?

Answer: The show interfaces command-control CLI command shows you the statistics for only the command and control interface.

9   What is the default interface group on the sensor?

Answer: The default interface group on the sensor is 0.

10   Which CLI command displays the statistics for all the interfaces on your sensor?

Answer: The show interfaces command shows statistics for the interfaces on your sensor.

11   Which user roles are allowed to run most of the show CLI commands on the sensor?

Answer: Because the show commands only display information, all three user roles (Administrator, Operator, and User) can execute these commands.

12   Which show CLI command requires administrator privileges to be run?

Answer: The show tech-support CLI command requires administrator privileges because it can potentially display passwords and other sensitive information.

13   The TAC typically uses the output from which command to debug operational problems with your sensor?

Answer: When debugging operational problems with your sensor, the TAC typically uses the output from the show tech-support CLI command.

14   Which CLI command enables you to view the alerts that are generated by your sensor?

Answer: Using the show events alerts CLI command, you can specifically display the alerts to the sensor's CLI as they happen. The show events command will display all events that are happening on the sensor.

15   Which CLI command would you use to show the information about your sensor's web server (such as persistent connections)?

Answer: The show statistics WebServer command shows the information about the web server on your sensor.

Chapter 16

1   How many sensors can you manage from one IDS MC server?

Answer: With one IDS MC server, you can manage up to 300 individual sensors.

2   What is the foundation that IDS MC is built on?

Answer: IDS MC is built upon CiscoWorks and therefore requires the VMS Common Services.

3 What authorization roles can you assign to users who use IDS MC?

Answer: The following authorization roles are relevant for IDS MC users: Help Desk, Approver, Network Operator, Network Administrator, and System Administrator.

4 What two operating systems do IDS MC servers run on?

Answer: You can run your IDS MC server on Windows 2000 and Solaris.

5 What features does the VMS Common Services provide?

Answer: The VMS Common Services feature set provides the following features: data storage and management, web interface, session management, user authentication/authorization management, and common environment for IDS MC.

6 What two browsers can you use to access IDS MC?

Answer: You can connect to IDS MC using the following two browsers: Internet Explorer version 6.0 (Service Pack 1) and Netscape Navigator 4.79 or later.

7 What privileges does a user receive from the Network Operator role?

Answer: The Network Operator authorization role provides read-only access for the entire system, report generation, and the capability to deploy configurations.

8 Which software handles user authentication and authorization for IDS MC?

Answer: The underlying CiscoWorks software handles user authentication and authorization for IDS MC users.

9 Which authorization role enables a user to perform all operations within IDS MC?

Answer: The System Administrator role enables a user to perform all operations within IDS MC.

10 How do client systems access your IDS MC server?

Answer: Client systems connect to IDS MC using a web browser.

11 How much RAM is recommended on your IDS MC server (for both Windows and Solaris deployments)?

Answer: The recommended amount of RAM for your IDS MC server is a minimum of 1 GB.

12 Can you install IDS MC and Security Monitor on a machine that already has CSPM installed on it?

Answer: No, you can not install Security Monitor on a machine that already has CSPM on it, because it will attempt to install PostOffice in a second location on that system.

13 What is the path bar on the IDS MC interface?

Answer: The path bar (You Are Here) on the IDS MC interface provides a quick indication or road map of where you are in the IDS MC user interface as well as how you arrived at the spot by showing the selections that you have chosen (for example, Configuration>Settings>Signatures).

14 What three steps are required to deploy updated configuration files when using IDS MC?

Answer: The deployment of updated configuration files (after the changes have been saved to the IDS MC database) involves the following three steps: Generate the updated configurations, approve the changes (default is automatic approval), and deploy the new configurations.

15 Which step in the deployment of an updated sensor configuration happens automatically by default?

Answer: By default, the approval of updated sensor configurations occurs automatically.

Chapter 17

1 How many devices can Security Monitor manage?

Answer: Security Monitor can manage up to 300 devices.

2 What two types of web browsers does Security Monitor support?

Answer: Security Monitor supports the following two types of web browsers: Internet Explorer and Netscape Navigator.

3 Before Security Monitor can monitor a device, what must you do?

Answer: For Security Monitor to process events from a device, you must add or import the device to Security Monitor.

4 When you import devices, where do the devices come from?

Answer: Importing devices enables you to add devices into Security Monitor that are currently being managed by IDS MC.

5 What three actions can you specify for an event rule?

Answer: An event rule can perform one or more of the following actions: notification via email, generating a console notification event, or executing a script.

6 How many clauses can you specify in an event rule?

Answer: You can specify up to five clauses in a single event rule.

7 How many event rules can you have active at one time?

Answer: You can have up to 10 event rules active at one time.

8 For what type of devices can you monitor the statistics of various processes on the device?

Answer: For RDEP devices, you can monitor the statistics for different processes on the device using Security Monitor.

9 For which two types of devices can you monitor the status of their connection with Security Monitor?

Answer: For both RDEP and PostOffice devices, you can monitor the status of their connection with Security Monitor. Syslog uses UDP and is connectionless; therefore, it is not monitored.

10 What are your two options with respect to deleting rows from the Event Viewer?

Answer: When deleting rows from the Event Viewer, you can delete the rows from the current Event Viewer instance or from the Security Monitor database.

11 What is the expansion boundary?

Answer: The expansion boundary represents the block of columns that are automatically expanded when a new alarm is added to the Event Viewer.

12 What are your two options when sorting the rows in the Event Viewer display using display preferences?

Answer: You can sort the rows in the Event Viewer display by either count or content.

13 What is a database rule?

Answer: A database rule enables you to trigger specific actions based on properties of the Security Monitor database (such as size and free space).

14 When launching the Event Viewer, what three parameters do you need to specify?

Answer: When launching the Event Viewer, you need to specify the event type, event start time, and the event end time.

15 What are the fields that you can use to filter the information that is included in generate reports?

Answer: To reduce the amount of information in generated reports, you can filter on event level, event count, source direction, source IP address, destination direction, destination IP address, signature, signature category, IDS devices, and date/time.

Chapter 18

1   What are some of the benefits of Cisco Threat Response?

Answer: Benefits of CTR include the following: elimination of false alarms; escalation of real attacks; fast, consistent automated investigation process; and easy deployment.

2   What is advanced investigation?

Answer: Advanced investigation is a detailed, system-level investigation that includes the capture of the following types of information: web logs, system logs, and other relevant information.

3   What is basic investigation?

Answer: Basic investigation is a noninvasive examination of the target system that is mainly trying to identify the OS type.

4   What is a CTR action?

Answer: A CTR action (originally called an agent) is an action that CTR takes to tackle or investigate a given alarm.

5   What is a security zone?

Answer: A security zone is a pairing of possible attack sources with target IP addresses to which you assign a policy.

6   What is a protected host?

Answer: A protected host is a system or collection of systems that you have configured CTR to protect.

7   What does a Level 0 investigation entail?

Answer: Level 0 investigations are system rule-based actions that either upgrade or downgrade alarms. No analysis is conducted.

8   What investigation does CTR perform when the default policy is applied to a security zone?

Answer: When the default policy is assigned to a security zone, CTR investigates the alarms to the fullest extent possible.

9   Why is the policy order important?

Answer: The policy order is important because CTR processes the policies in the order listed. Therefore, the order can impact whether certain alarms are investigated because they can be downgraded by an earlier policy.

10 How can CTR determine the OS information for a host?

Answer: CTR can determine the OS for a host using one of the following three methods: dynamic examination, cached value from previous determination, and statically mapped value.

11 What fields do you need to define to configure a security zone?

Answer: To create a security zone, you need to supply a name, the source addresses and ports, the destination addresses and ports, and a CTR policy.

12 What are the two reasons that CTR downgrades alarms?

Answer: CTR downgrades alarms automatically based on policy rules and when it determines that an attack was not successful.

GLOSSARY

A

Access Control Entry (ACE)   An ACE is one of the lines in an ACL. These lines specify the requirements for which type of network traffic the ACL will apply to.

Access Control List (ACL)   An ACL is a filter that you can apply to either packets coming into or leaving a physical interface on a Cisco router.

Anomaly Detection   Anomaly detection refers to an IDS triggering mechanism that uses user profiles as the basis for detecting attacks and policy violations. Anomaly detection is also sometimes referred to as profile-based detection. With anomaly detection, you must build profiles for each user group on the system. This profile incorporates a typical user's habits, the services he normally uses, and so on. This profile defines an established baseline for the activities that a normal user routinely does to perform his job.

Atomic Signature   Cisco IDS signatures that detect attacks that can be identified by analyzing a single network packet. Cisco IDS divides its signatures into two categories: atomic and composite.

Attack Signature   A Cisco IOS IDS signature that detects attacks attempted into the protected network, such as denial-of-service attempts or the execution of illegal commands during an FTP session. Cisco IOS IDS divides its signatures into two categories: information and attack.

B

Blocking Device   The Cisco device that blocks the traffic from a system that has triggered a signature that is configured for IP blocking (also known as the managed device).

Blocking Duration   The length of time that an IP block will be applied to your managed (blocking) device.

Blocking Interface   The interface on the managed (blocking) device where the sensor applies the dynamically created ACL (also known as the managed interface).

Blocking Sensor   A sensor that has been configured to control a managed device.

C–D

Composite Signature Cisco IDS signatures that detect attacks that require analyzing multiple network packets (which requires the storage of state information between the multiple packets). Cisco IDS divides its signatures into two categories: atomic and composite.

Context Buffer A 256-byte buffer of data collected (for TCP attacks) beginning with the traffic that triggered the alarm.

Cracker Someone who breaks into protected resources for profit, for altruistic purposes, or because of the challenge, usually with malicious intent.

Device Management The capability of a sensor to interact with a Cisco device and dynamically reconfigure the Cisco device to block the source of an attack.

distributed denial-of-service (DDoS) A DDoS attack is a form of a DoS attack where the attack launched against a victim host or network is launched from multiple attacking hosts.

Domain Name System (DNS) This is the Internet-wide host name-to-IP address mapping. DNS enables you to convert human-readable names into the IP addresses needed for network packets.

DoS A denial-of-service (DoS) attack is one whose goal is just to disrupt the operation of a specific system or network.

E–F

Electrostatic Discharge (ESD) The release of static electricity when two objects come into contact, such as walking across a carpet and touching a metal doorknob.

Event Horizon The maximum amount of time over which an attack signature can be successfully detected (from initial data to complete attack signature).

Expansion Boundary Represents the block of columns that will be automatically expanded when a new alarm entry comes into the Security Monitor Event Viewer display.

False Alarm An alarm generated in response to an attack that was unsuccessful (for instance, an attack that was launched against a system that is not susceptible to the attack).

False Negative When an IDS fails to generate an alarm for actual intrusive traffic that it is designed to detect.

False Positive   When an IDS triggers an alarm on normal user traffic as opposed to actual attack traffic.

Firewall   A security device that protects the perimeter of a network by restricting the flow of specific traffic types.

Fragmentation   IP fragmentation involves breaking a single IP packet into multiple segments that are all below the maximum transmission unit (MTU) for the network.

G–H

Graphical User Interface (GUI)   An easy-to-use graphical display that enables you to configure and use a specific application.

Hacker   Someone who gains unauthorized accessed to protected resources for personal amusement or gratification, usually without malicious intent. It can also refer to an expert or enthusiast who enjoys overcoming intellectual challenges and solving problems in creative ways.

Hypertext Transport Protocol Secure (HTTPS)   HTTPS is an extension to the standard HTTP protocol that provides confidentiality by encrypting the traffic from the web site using TLS/SSL. By default, this protocol uses TCP port 443.

Hypertext Transfer Protocol (HTTP)   The HTTP protocol is the standard protocol used by websites to convey information to web users. By default this protocol uses TCP port 80 (refer to RFC 2616, "Hypertext Transfer Protocol – HTTP/1.1").

I

Ident   The Identification (Ident) protocol provides a mechanism to prevent host name and address spoofing, as well as to identify false usernames (refer to RFC 1413).

IDS Sensor   The component in your IDS that actually monitors the network traffic, looking for intrusion attempts.

IDSM-2   The second-generation Cisco Catalyst 6500 Intrusion Detection System Module (IDSM-2) is a blade that provides IDS functionality by monitoring traffic directly off of the backplane of your Cisco Catalyst 6500 family switch.

Information Signature   A Cisco IOS IDS signature that detects information-gathering activities attempted against the protected network, such as port sweeps. Cisco IOS IDS divides its signatures into two categories: information and attack.

Intrusion Detection   The ongoing monitoring of network traffic for potential misuse or policy violations.

Intrusion Detection Interaction and Operations Messages (IDIOM) Specification on which the structure of XML documents that are communicated between Cisco IDS devices using the RDEP protocol are based.

Intrusion Detection System (IDS)   A system that monitors your network for intrusive activity and generates alarms when intrusive activity is detected (usually comprised of various components such as sensors, agents, and a management system).

Intrusion Protection System (IPS)   A system that monitors your network for intrusive activity and prevents certain intrusive activity from impacting your network.

M

Managed Device   *See* Blocking Device.

Managed Interface   *See* Blocking Interface.

Master Blocking Sensor   A sensor that performs blocking operations on a managed device on behalf of other sensors.

Maximum Transmission Unit (MTU)   The maximum transmission unit (MTU) represents the maximum packet size that a network segment can handle. If a packet is larger than the MTU, the sending host breaks it up into multiple frames and then transmits the multiple frames across the network for reassembly at the destination host.

Message Digest   A cryptographic hash of a message that is used to verify that the contents on the message have not been changed. Two common hash algorithms are MD5 and SHA1.

Misuse Detection   An IDS triggering mechanism (also known as signature-based detection) that looks for intrusive activity by matching patterns of traffic against specific signatures.

Multilayer Switch Feature Card (MSFC)   Card that delivers high-performance multilayer switching and intelligent network services for your Catalyst 6500 switch.

N

Network Access Controller (NAC)   A process that runs on a Cisco version 4.x sensor that controls blocking operations on a managed device.

Network Scanner   Tools that examine hosts on a network to locate security vulnerabilities (also known as vulnerability scanners).

Network Security Database (NSDB)   A database of security information that explains the signatures used by your Cisco IDS along with the vulnerabilities that these signatures are based on.

Network Time Protocol (NTP)   A protocol (TCP port 123) that is used to synchronize the time used by systems on a network (refer to RFC 1305, "Network Time Protocol [Version 3] Specification Implementation").

NTFS   Short for NT File System, this represents one of the file systems developed for Windows systems.

P–R

Policy Feature Card (PFC)   Card that provides quality of service (QoS) and advanced security features (such as VACL support) on your Catalyst 6500 switch.

PostOffice   The proprietary protocol used by Cisco IDS version 3.x sensors (and earlier) to communicate with other devices.

Protected Host   A system or systems that Threat Response is configured to protect and investigate attacks launched against it.

Regular Expression   A mechanism by which you can define how to search for a specified sequence of characters in a data stream or file. Many different programs use regular expressions (also known as regex) to enable you to create custom string searches. In the UNIX world, the **grep** command is probably the most common program that uses regular expressions to search for text.

Remote Data Exchange Protocol (RDEP)   Communication protocol, used by Cisco IDS version 4.x sensors to communicate with external systems, that uses a schema for XML documents that is based on the Intrusion Detection Interaction and Operations Messages (IDIOM) specification.

Remote Procedure Call (RPC)   A protocol that enables one program to request a service from another computer on a network. This protocol does not require the requesting computer to understand the layout of the network.

S

Secure Sockets Layer (SSL) A protocol that is designed to manage the transmission of messages across an untrusted network. It operates between the application layer (such as HTTP) and the transport layer (TCP).

Security Analysis Tool for Auditing Networks (SATAN) SATAN is one of the original network scanners that was created to enable system administrators to proactively check the security of their networks.

Security Policy A security policy is a set of policies or rules that define allowable practices and services on your network. By minimizing acceptable services and procedures, you can control the security of your overall network by reducing weak links.

Security Zone In Threat Response, this is a pairing of possible attack sources with target addresses to which you apply a specified investigation policy.

Signature A signature detects patterns of misuse in network traffic. In Cisco IDS, signatures are categorized into two implementation categories: atomic and composite (as opposed to Cisco IOS IDS, which uses attack and informational).

Signature Engine A component of the Cisco IDS analysis engine that analyzes network traffic for specific intrusive activity on the network.

Switch Port Analyzer (SPAN) SPAN ports enable you to direct traffic from various ports and VLANs on your switch to a specific destination port for analysis by your IDS.

T–Z

Transport Layer Security (TLS) A protocol that is designed to manage the transmission of messages across an untrusted network. It operates between the application layer (such as HTTP) and the transport layer (TCP). For more information on the TLS protocol, refer to RFC 2246.

True Negative Represents a situation in which your IDS signature does not alarm when the traffic that it examines is not malicious.

True Positive Generating an alarm correctly in response to detecting the real attack traffic that a signature is designed to detect.

VACL   VLAN ACL (VACL) is a security feature that enables access controls for all packets on a Catalyst 6000 switch via a Policy Feature Card (PFC). You can use VACLs to redirect a copy of network traffic from multiple VLANs to your IDSM for analysis.

Virtual Private Networks (VPN)   VPN provides confidentiality, integrity, and authentication for network traffic between hosts or networks using encryption (usually over an untrusted network).

D

E

I

J-K

L

M

N

V

W

X-Y-Z